The Heroes

of

John Buchan

Richard Hanny
in
The Thirty-Nine Steps

Edward Leithen
in
Sick Heart River

Sandy Arbuthnot
in
The Courts in the Morning

British Library Cataloguing-in-Publication Data
A catalogue record for this book is available from the
British Library

John Buchan

John Buchan, first Baron Tweedsmuir of Elsfield, was born in Perth, Scotland in 1875. In his youth, his father immersed him in the history, legends and myths of Scotland, and he was an avid reader, stating some years later that John Bunyan's *The Pilgrim's Progress* was a "constant companion" to him. Buchan's education was uneven, but at the age of seventeen he obtained a scholarship to study classics at Glasgow University, where he began to write poetry. His first work, *The Essays and Apothegms of Francis Lord Bacon*, was published in 1894, and a year later he enrolled at Oxford University to study law.

In 1900, Buchan moved to London, and two years later accepted a civil service post in South Africa. In the years leading up to World War I, he worked at a publishers, and also wrote *Prester John* (1910) – which later became a school reader, translated into many languages – as well as a number of biographies. In 1915, Buchan become a war correspondent for *The Times*, and published his most well-known book, the thriller *The Thirty-Nine Steps*. After the war he became a director of the news agency Reuters.

Over the course of his life, Buchan would eventually publish some one hundred books, forty or so of which were novels, mostly wartime thrillers. In the latter part of his life he worked in politics, serving as Conservative MP for the Scottish universities and Lord High Commissioner of the Church of Scotland (1933-34). In 1935, Buchan moved to Canada, where he became the thirty-fifth Governor General of Canada. He died in 1940, aged 64.

Contents

THE THIRTY-NINE STEPS

By

JOHN BUCHAN

TO
THOMAS ARTHUR NELSON
(LOTHIAN AND BORDER HORSE)

My Dear Tommy,

You and I have long cherished an affection for that elemental type of tale which Americans call the 'dime novel' and which we know as the 'shocker'—the romance where the incidents defy the probabilities, and march just inside the borders of the possible. During an illness last winter I exhausted my store of those aids to cheerfulness, and was driven to write one for myself. This little volume is the result, and I should like to put your name on it in memory of our long friendship, in the days when the wildest fictions are so much less improbable than the facts.

J.B.

CHAPTER ONE

The Man Who Died

I returned from the City about three o'clock on that May afternoon pretty well disgusted with life. I had been three months in the Old Country, and was fed up with it. If anyone had told me a year ago that I would have been feeling like that I should have laughed at him; but there was the fact. The weather made me liverish, the talk of the ordinary Englishman made me sick, I couldn't get enough exercise, and the amusements of London seemed as flat as soda-water that has been standing in the sun. 'Richard Hannay,' I kept telling myself, 'you have got into the wrong ditch, my friend, and you had better climb out.'

It made me bite my lips to think of the plans I had been building up those last years in Bulawayo. I had got my pile—not one of the big ones, but good enough for me; and I had figured out all kinds of ways of enjoying myself. My father had brought me out from Scotland at the age of six, and I had never been home since; so England was a sort of Arabian Nights to me, and I counted on stopping there for the rest of my days.

But from the first I was disappointed with it. In about a week I was tired of seeing sights, and in less than a month I had had enough of restaurants and theatres and race-meetings. I had no real pal to go about with, which probably explains things. Plenty of people invited me to their houses, but they didn't seem much interested in me. They would fling me a question or two about South Africa, and then get on their own affairs. A lot of Imperialist ladies asked me to tea to meet schoolmasters from New Zealand and editors from Vancouver, and that was the dismalest business of all. Here was I, thirty-seven years old, sound in wind and limb, with enough money to have a good time, yawning my head off all day. I had just about settled to clear out and get back to the veld, for I was the best bored man in the United Kingdom.

That afternoon I had been worrying my brokers about investments to give my mind something to work on, and on my way home I turned into my club—rather a pot-house, which took in Colonial members. I had a long drink, and read the evening papers. They were full of the row in the Near East, and there was an article about Karolides, the Greek Premier. I rather fancied the chap. From all accounts he seemed the one big man in the show; and he played a straight game too, which was more than could be said for most of them. I gathered that they hated him pretty blackly in Berlin and Vienna, but that we were going to stick by him, and one paper said that he was the only barrier between Europe and Armageddon. I remember wondering if I could get a job in those parts. It struck me that Albania was the sort of place that might keep a man from yawning.

About six o'clock I went home, dressed, dined at the Cafe Royal, and turned into a music-hall. It was a silly show, all capering women and monkey-faced men, and I did not stay long. The night was fine and clear as I walked back to the flat I had hired near Portland Place. The crowd surged past me on the pavements, busy and chattering, and I envied the people for having something to do. These shop-girls and clerks and dandies and policemen had some interest in life that kept them going. I gave half-a-crown to a beggar because I saw him yawn; he was a fellow-sufferer. At Oxford Circus I looked up into the spring sky and I made a vow. I would give the Old Country another day to fit me into something; if nothing happened, I would take the next boat for the Cape.

My flat was the first floor in a new block behind Langham Place. There was a common staircase, with a porter and a liftman at the entrance, but there was no restaurant or anything of that sort, and each flat was quite shut off from the others. I hate servants on the premises, so I had a fellow to look after me who came in by the day. He arrived before eight o'clock every morning and used to depart at seven, for I never dined at home.

I was just fitting my key into the door when I noticed a man at my elbow. I had not seen him approach, and the sudden appearance made me start. He was a slim man, with a short brown beard and small, gimlety blue eyes. I recognized him as the occupant of a flat on the top floor, with whom I had passed the time of day on the stairs.

'Can I speak to you?' he said. 'May I come in for a minute?' He was steadying his voice with an effort, and his hand was pawing my arm.

I got my door open and motioned him in. No sooner was he over the threshold than he made a dash for my back room, where I used to smoke and write my letters. Then he bolted back.

'Is the door locked?' he asked feverishly, and he fastened the chain with his own hand.

'I'm very sorry,' he said humbly. 'It's a mighty liberty, but you looked the kind of man who would understand. I've had you in my mind all this week when things got troublesome. Say, will you do me a good turn?'

'I'll listen to you,' I said. 'That's all I'll promise.' I was getting worried by the antics of this nervous little chap.

There was a tray of drinks on a table beside him, from which he filled himself a stiff whisky-and-soda. He drank it off in three gulps, and cracked the glass as he set it down.

'Pardon,' he said, 'I'm a bit rattled tonight. You see, I happen at this moment to be dead.'

I sat down in an armchair and lit my pipe.

'What does it feel like?' I asked. I was pretty certain that I had to deal with a madman.

A smile flickered over his drawn face. 'I'm not mad—yet. Say, Sir, I've been watching you, and I reckon you're a cool customer. I reckon, too, you're an honest man, and not afraid of playing a bold hand. I'm going to confide in you. I need help worse than any man ever needed it, and I want to know if I can count you in.'

'Get on with your yarn,' I said, 'and I'll tell you.'

He seemed to brace himself for a great effort, and then started on the queerest rigmarole. I didn't get hold of it at first, and I had to stop and ask him questions. But here is the gist of it:

He was an American, from Kentucky, and after college, being pretty well off, he had started out to see the world. He wrote a bit, and acted as war correspondent for a Chicago paper, and spent a year or two in South-Eastern Europe. I gathered that he was a fine linguist, and had got to know pretty well the society in those parts. He spoke familiarly of many names that I remembered to have seen in the newspapers.

He had played about with politics, he told me, at first for the interest of them, and then because he couldn't help himself. I read him as a sharp, restless fellow, who always wanted to get down to the roots of things. He got a little further down than he wanted.

I am giving you what he told me as well as I could make it out. Away behind all the Governments and the armies there was a big subterranean movement going on, engineered by very dangerous people. He had come on it by accident; it fascinated him; he went further, and then he got caught. I gathered that most of the people in it were the sort of educated anarchists that make revolutions, but that beside them there were financiers who were playing for money. A clever man can make big profits on a falling market, and it suited the book of both classes to set Europe by the ears.

He told me some queer things that explained a lot that had puzzled me—things that happened in the Balkan War, how one state suddenly came out on top, why alliances were made and broken, why certain men disappeared, and where the sinews of war came from. The aim of the whole conspiracy was to get Russia and Germany at loggerheads.

When I asked why, he said that the anarchist lot thought it would give them their chance. Everything would be in the melting-pot, and they looked to see a new world emerge. The capitalists would rake in the shekels, and make fortunes by buying up wreckage. Capital, he said, had no conscience and no fatherland. Besides, the Jew was behind it, and the Jew hated Russia worse than hell.

'Do you wonder?' he cried. 'For three hundred years they have been persecuted, and this is the return match for the pogroms. The Jew is everywhere, but you have to go far down the backstairs to find him. Take any big Teutonic business concern. If you have dealings with it the first man you meet is Prince von und Zu Something, an elegant young man who talks Eton-and-Harrow English. But he cuts no ice. If your business is big, you get behind him and find a prognathous Westphalian with a retreating brow and the manners of a hog. He is the German business man that gives your English papers the shakes. But if you're on the biggest kind of job and are bound to get to the real boss, ten to one you are brought up against a little white-faced Jew in a bath-chair with an eye like a rattlesnake. Yes, Sir, he is the man who is ruling the world just now, and he has his knife in the Empire of the Tzar, because his aunt was outraged and his father flogged in some one-horse location on the Volga.'

I could not help saying that his Jew-anarchists seemed to have got left behind a little.

'Yes and no,' he said. 'They won up to a point, but they struck a bigger thing than money, a thing that couldn't be bought, the old elemental fighting instincts of man. If you're going to be killed you invent some kind of flag and country to fight for, and if you survive you get to love the thing. Those foolish devils of soldiers have found something they care for, and that has upset the pretty plan laid in Berlin and Vienna. But my friends haven't played their last card by a long sight. They've gotten the ace up their sleeves, and unless I can keep alive for a month they are going to play it and win.'

'But I thought you were dead,' I put in.

'MORS JANUA VITAE,' he smiled. (I recognized the quotation: it was about all the Latin I knew.) 'I'm coming to that, but I've got to put you wise about a lot of things first. If you read your newspaper, I guess you know the name of Constantine Karolides?'

I sat up at that, for I had been reading about him that very afternoon.

'He is the man that has wrecked all their games. He is the one big brain in the whole show, and he happens also to be an honest man. Therefore he has been marked down these twelve months past. I found that out—not that it was difficult, for any fool could guess as much. But I found out the way they were going to get him, and that knowledge was deadly. That's why I have had to decease.'

He had another drink, and I mixed it for him myself, for I was getting interested in the beggar.

'They can't get him in his own land, for he has a bodyguard of Epirotes that would skin their grandmothers. But on the 15th day of June he is coming to this city. The British Foreign Office has taken to having International tea-parties, and the biggest of them is due on that date. Now Karolides is reckoned the principal guest, and if my friends have their way he will never return to his admiring countrymen.'

'That's simple enough, anyhow,' I said. 'You can warn him and keep him at home.'

'And play their game?' he asked sharply. 'If he does not come they win, for he's the only man that can straighten out the tangle. And if his Government are warned he won't come, for he does not know how big the stakes will be on June the 15th.'

'What about the British Government?' I said. 'They're not going to let their guests be murdered. Tip them the wink, and they'll take extra precautions.'

'No good. They might stuff your city with plain-clothes detectives and double the police and Constantine would still be a doomed man. My friends are not playing this game for candy. They want a big occasion for the taking off, with the eyes of all Europe on it. He'll be murdered by an Austrian, and there'll be plenty of evidence to show the connivance of the big folk in Vienna and Berlin. It will all be an infernal lie, of course, but the case will look black enough to the world. I'm not talking hot air, my friend. I happen to know every detail of the hellish contrivance, and I can tell you it will be the most finished piece of blackguardism since the Borgias. But it's not going to come off if there's a certain man who knows the wheels of the business alive right here in

London on the 15th day of June. And that man is going to be your servant, Franklin P. Scudder.'

I was getting to like the little chap. His jaw had shut like a rat-trap, and there was the fire of battle in his gimlety eyes. If he was spinning me a yarn he could act up to it.

'Where did you find out this story?' I asked.

'I got the first hint in an inn on the Achensee in Tyrol. That set me inquiring, and I collected my other clues in a fur-shop in the Galician quarter of Buda, in a Strangers' Club in Vienna, and in a little bookshop off the Racknitzstrasse in Leipsic. I completed my evidence ten days ago in Paris. I can't tell you the details now, for it's something of a history. When I was quite sure in my own mind I judged it my business to disappear, and I reached this city by a mighty queer circuit. I left Paris a dandified young French-American, and I sailed from Hamburg a Jew diamond merchant. In Norway I was an English student of Ibsen collecting materials for lectures, but when I left Bergen I was a cinema-man with special ski films. And I came here from Leith with a lot of pulp-wood propositions in my pocket to put before the London newspapers. Till yesterday I thought I had muddied my trail some, and was feeling pretty happy. Then ...'

The recollection seemed to upset him, and he gulped down some more whisky.

'Then I saw a man standing in the street outside this block. I used to stay close in my room all day, and only slip out after dark for an hour or two. I watched him for a bit from my window, and I thought I recognized him ... He came in and spoke to the porter ... When I came back from my walk last night I found a card in my letter-box. It bore the name of the man I want least to meet on God's earth.'

I think that the look in my companion's eyes, the sheer naked scare on his face, completed my conviction of his honesty. My own voice sharpened a bit as I asked him what he did next.

'I realized that I was bottled as sure as a pickled herring, and that there was only one way out. I had to die. If my pursuers knew I was dead they would go to sleep again.'

'How did you manage it?'

'I told the man that valets me that I was feeling pretty bad, and I got myself up to look like death. That wasn't difficult, for I'm no slouch at disguises. Then I got a corpse—you can always get a body in London if you know where to go for it. I fetched it back in a trunk on the top of a four-wheeler, and I had to be assisted upstairs to my room. You see I had to pile up some evidence for the inquest. I went to bed and got my man to mix me a sleeping-draught, and then told him to clear out. He wanted to fetch a doctor, but I swore some and said I couldn't abide leeches. When I was left alone I started in to fake up that corpse. He was my size, and I judged had perished from too much alcohol, so I put some spirits handy about the place. The jaw was the weak point in the likeness, so I blew it away with a revolver. I daresay there will be somebody tomorrow to swear to having heard a shot, but there are no neighbours on my floor, and I guessed I could risk it. So I left the body in bed dressed up in my pyjamas, with a revolver lying on the bed-clothes and a considerable mess around. Then I got into a suit of clothes I had kept waiting for emergencies. I didn't dare to shave for fear of leaving tracks, and besides, it wasn't any kind of use my trying to get into the streets. I had had you in my mind all day, and there seemed nothing to do but to make an appeal to you. I watched from my window till I saw you come home, and then slipped down the stair to meet you ... There, Sir, I guess you know about as much as me of this business.'

He sat blinking like an owl, fluttering with nerves and yet desperately determined. By this time I was pretty well convinced that he was going straight with me. It was the wildest sort of narrative, but I had heard in my time many steep tales which had turned out to be true, and I had made a practice of judging the man rather than the story. If he had wanted to get a location in my flat, and then cut my throat, he would have pitched a milder yarn.

'Hand me your key,' I said, 'and I'll take a look at the corpse. Excuse my caution, but I'm bound to verify a bit if I can.'

He shook his head mournfully. 'I reckoned you'd ask for that, but I haven't got it. It's on my chain on the dressing-table. I had to leave it behind, for I couldn't leave any clues to breed suspicions. The gentry who are after me are pretty bright-eyed citizens. You'll have to take me on trust for the night, and tomorrow you'll get proof of the corpse business right enough.'

I thought for an instant or two. 'Right. I'll trust you for the night. I'll lock you into this room and keep the key. Just one word, Mr Scudder. I believe you're straight, but if so be you are not I should warn you that I'm a handy man with a gun.'

'Sure,' he said, jumping up with some briskness. 'I haven't the privilege of your name, Sir, but let me tell you that you're a white man. I'll thank you to lend me a razor.'

I took him into my bedroom and turned him loose. In half an hour's time a figure came out that I scarcely recognized. Only his gimlety, hungry eyes were the same. He was shaved clean, his hair was parted in the middle, and he had cut his eyebrows. Further, he carried himself as if he had been drilled, and was the very model, even to the brown complexion, of some British officer who had had a long spell in India. He had a monocle, too, which he stuck in his eye, and every trace of the American had gone out of his speech.

'My hat! Mr Scudder—' I stammered.

'Not Mr Scudder,' he corrected; 'Captain Theophilus Digby, of the 40th Gurkhas, presently home on leave. I'll thank you to remember that, Sir.'

I made him up a bed in my smoking-room and sought my own couch, more cheerful than I had been for the past month. Things did happen occasionally, even in this God-forgotten metropolis.

I woke next morning to hear my man, Paddock, making the deuce of a row at the smoking-room door. Paddock was a fellow I had done a good turn to out on the Selakwe, and I had inspanned him as my servant as soon as I got to England. He had about as much gift of the gab as a hippopotamus, and was not a great hand at valeting, but I knew I could count on his loyalty.

'Stop that row, Paddock,' I said. 'There's a friend of mine, Captain—Captain' (I couldn't remember the name) 'dossing down in there. Get breakfast for two and then come and speak to me.'

I told Paddock a fine story about how my friend was a great swell, with his nerves pretty bad from overwork, who wanted absolute rest and stillness. Nobody had got to know he was here, or he would be besieged by communications from the India Office and the Prime Minister and his cure would be ruined. I am bound to say Scudder played up splendidly when he came to breakfast. He fixed Paddock with his eyeglass, just like a British officer, asked him about the Boer War, and slung out at me a lot of stuff about imaginary pals. Paddock couldn't learn to call me 'Sir', but he 'sirred' Scudder as if his life depended on it.

I left him with the newspaper and a box of cigars, and went down to the City till luncheon. When I got back the lift-man had an important face.

'Nawsty business 'ere this morning, Sir. Gent in No. 15 been and shot 'isself. They've just took 'im to the mortiary. The police are up there now.'

I ascended to No. 15, and found a couple of bobbies and an inspector busy making an examination. I asked a few idiotic questions, and they soon kicked me out. Then I found the man that had valeted Scudder, and pumped him, but I could see he suspected nothing. He was a whining fellow with a churchyard face, and half-a-crown went far to console him.

I attended the inquest next day. A partner of some publishing firm gave evidence that the deceased had brought him wood-pulp propositions, and had been, he believed, an agent of an American business. The jury found it a case of suicide while of unsound mind, and the few effects were handed over to the American Consul to deal with. I gave Scudder a full account of the affair, and it interested him greatly. He said he wished he could have attended the inquest, for he reckoned it would be about as spicy as to read one's own obituary notice.

The first two days he stayed with me in that back room he was very peaceful. He read and smoked a bit, and made a heap of jottings in a note-book, and every night we had a game of chess, at which he beat me hollow. I think he was nursing his nerves back to health, for he had had a pretty trying time. But on the third day I could see he was beginning to get restless. He fixed up a list of the days till June 15th, and ticked each off with a red pencil, making remarks in shorthand against them. I would find him sunk in a brown study, with his sharp eyes abstracted, and after those spells of meditation he was apt to be very despondent.

Then I could see that he began to get edgy again. He listened for little noises, and was always asking me if Paddock could be trusted. Once or twice he got very peevish, and apologized for it. I didn't blame him. I made every allowance, for he had taken on a fairly stiff job.

It was not the safety of his own skin that troubled him, but the success of the scheme he had planned. That little man was clean grit all through, without a soft spot in him. One night he was very solemn.

'Say, Hannay,' he said, 'I judge I should let you a bit deeper into this business. I should hate to go out without leaving somebody else to put up a fight.' And he began to tell me in detail what I had only heard from him vaguely.

I did not give him very close attention. The fact is, I was more interested in his own adventures than in his high politics. I reckoned that Karolides and his affairs were not my business, leaving all that to him. So a lot that he said slipped clean out of my memory. I remember that he was very clear that the danger to Karolides would not begin till he had got to London, and would come from the very highest quarters, where there would be no thought of suspicion. He mentioned the name of a woman—Julia Czechenyi—as having something to do with the danger. She would be the decoy, I gathered, to get Karolides out of the care of his guards. He talked, too, about a Black Stone and a man that lisped in his speech, and he described very particularly somebody that he never referred to without a shudder—an old man with a young voice who could hood his eyes like a hawk.

He spoke a good deal about death, too. He was mortally anxious about winning through with his job, but he didn't care a rush for his life.

'I reckon it's like going to sleep when you are pretty well tired out, and waking to find a summer day with the scent of hay coming in at the window. I used to thank God for such mornings way back in the Blue-Grass country, and I guess I'll thank Him when I wake up on the other side of Jordan.'

Next day he was much more cheerful, and read the life of Stonewall Jackson much of the time. I went out to dinner with a mining engineer I had got to see on business, and came back about half-past ten in time for our game of chess before turning in.

I had a cigar in my mouth, I remember, as I pushed open the smoking-room door. The lights were not lit, which struck me as odd. I wondered if Scudder had turned in already.

I snapped the switch, but there was nobody there. Then I saw something in the far corner which made me drop my cigar and fall into a cold sweat.

My guest was lying sprawled on his back. There was a long knife through his heart which skewered him to the floor.

CHAPTER TWO

The Milkman Sets Out on his Travels

I sat down in an armchair and felt very sick. That lasted for maybe five minutes, and was succeeded by a fit of the horrors. The poor staring white face on the floor was more than I could bear, and I managed to get a table-cloth and cover it. Then I staggered to a cupboard, found the brandy and swallowed several mouthfuls. I had seen men die violently before; indeed I had killed a few myself in the Matabele War; but this cold-blooded indoor business was different. Still I managed to pull myself together. I looked at my watch, and saw that it was half-past ten.

An idea seized me, and I went over the flat with a small-tooth comb. There was nobody there, nor any trace of anybody, but I shuttered and bolted all the windows and put the chain on the door. By this time my wits were coming back to me, and I could think again. It took me about an hour to figure the thing out, and I did not hurry, for, unless the murderer came back, I had till about six o'clock in the morning for my cogitations.

I was in the soup—that was pretty clear. Any shadow of a doubt I might have had about the truth of Scudder's tale was now gone. The proof of it was lying under the table-cloth. The men who knew that he knew what he knew had found him, and had taken the best way to make certain of his silence. Yes; but he had been in my rooms four days, and his enemies must have reckoned that he had confided in me. So I would be the next to go. It might be that very night, or next day, or the day after, but my number was up all right.

Then suddenly I thought of another probability. Supposing I went out now and called in the police, or went to bed and let Paddock find the body and call them in the morning. What kind of a story was I to tell about Scudder? I had lied to Paddock about him, and the whole thing looked desperately fishy. If I made a clean breast of it and told the police everything he had told me, they would simply laugh at me. The odds were a thousand to one that I would be charged with the murder, and the circumstantial evidence was strong enough to hang me. Few people knew me in England; I had no real pal who could come forward and swear to my character. Perhaps that was what those secret enemies were playing for. They were clever enough for anything, and an English prison was as good a way of getting rid of me till after June 15th as a knife in my chest.

Besides, if I told the whole story, and by any miracle was believed, I would be playing their game. Karolides would stay at home, which was what they wanted. Somehow or other the sight of Scudder's dead face had made me a passionate believer in his scheme. He was gone, but he had taken me into his confidence, and I was pretty well bound to carry on his work.

You may think this ridiculous for a man in danger of his life, but that was the way I looked at it. I am an ordinary sort of fellow, not braver than other people, but I hate to see a good man downed, and that long knife would not be the end of Scudder if I could play the game in his place.

It took me an hour or two to think this out, and by that time I had come to a decision. I must vanish somehow, and keep vanished till the end of the second week in June. Then I must somehow find a way to get in touch with the Government people and tell them what Scudder had told me. I wished to Heaven he had told me more, and that I had listened more carefully to the little he had told me. I knew nothing but the barest facts. There was a big risk that, even if I weathered the other dangers, I would not be believed in the end. I must take my chance of that, and hope that something might happen which would confirm my tale in the eyes of the Government.

My first job was to keep going for the next three weeks. It was now the 24th day of May, and that meant twenty days of hiding before I could venture to approach the powers that be. I reckoned that two sets of people would be looking for me—Scudder's enemies to put me out of existence, and the police, who would want me for Scudder's murder. It was going to be a giddy hunt, and it was queer how the prospect comforted me. I had been slack so long that almost any chance of activity was welcome. When I had to sit alone with that corpse and wait on Fortune I was no better than a crushed worm, but if my neck's safety was to hang on my own wits I was prepared to be cheerful about it.

My next thought was whether Scudder had any papers about him to give me a better clue to the business. I drew back the table-cloth and searched his pockets, for I had no longer any shrinking from the body. The face was wonderfully calm for a man who had been struck down in a moment. There was nothing in the breast-pocket, and only a few loose coins and a cigar-holder in the waistcoat. The trousers held a little penknife and some silver, and the side pocket of his jacket contained an old crocodile-skin cigar-case. There was no sign of the little black book in which I had seen him making notes. That had no doubt been taken by his murderer.

But as I looked up from my task I saw that some drawers had been pulled out in the writing-table. Scudder would never have left them in that state, for he was the tidiest of mortals. Someone must have been searching for something—perhaps for the pocket-book.

I went round the flat and found that everything had been ransacked—the inside of books, drawers, cupboards, boxes, even the pockets of the clothes in my wardrobe, and the sideboard in the dining-room. There was no trace of the book. Most likely the enemy had found it, but they had not found it on Scudder's body.

Then I got out an atlas and looked at a big map of the British Isles. My notion was to get off to some wild district, where my veldcraft would be of some use to me, for I would be like a trapped rat in a city. I considered that Scotland would be best, for my people were Scotch and I could pass anywhere as an ordinary Scotsman. I had half an idea at first to be a German tourist, for my father had had German partners, and I had been brought up to speak the tongue pretty fluently, not to mention having put in three years prospecting for copper in German Damaraland. But I calculated that it would be less conspicuous to be a Scot, and less in a line with what the police might know of my past. I fixed on Galloway as the best place to go. It was the nearest wild part of Scotland, so far as I could figure it out, and from the look of the map was not over thick with population.

A search in Bradshaw informed me that a train left St Pancras at 7.10, which would land me at any Galloway station in the late afternoon. That was well enough, but a more important matter was how I was to make my way to St Pancras, for I was pretty certain that Scudder's friends would be watching outside. This puzzled me for a bit; then I had an inspiration, on which I went to bed and slept for two troubled hours.

I got up at four and opened my bedroom shutters. The faint light of a fine summer morning was flooding the skies, and the sparrows had begun to chatter. I had a great revulsion of feeling, and felt a God-forgotten fool. My inclination was to let things slide, and trust to the

British police taking a reasonable view of my case. But as I reviewed the situation I could find no arguments to bring against my decision of the previous night, so with a wry mouth I resolved to go on with my plan. I was not feeling in any particular funk; only disinclined to go looking for trouble, if you understand me.

I hunted out a well-used tweed suit, a pair of strong nailed boots, and a flannel shirt with a collar. Into my pockets I stuffed a spare shirt, a cloth cap, some handkerchiefs, and a tooth-brush. I had drawn a good sum in gold from the bank two days before, in case Scudder should want money, and I took fifty pounds of it in sovereigns in a belt which I had brought back from Rhodesia. That was about all I wanted. Then I had a bath, and cut my moustache, which was long and drooping, into a short stubbly fringe.

Now came the next step. Paddock used to arrive punctually at 7.30 and let himself in with a latch-key. But about twenty minutes to seven, as I knew from bitter experience, the milkman turned up with a great clatter of cans, and deposited my share outside my door. I had seen that milkman sometimes when I had gone out for an early ride. He was a young man about my own height, with an ill-nourished moustache, and he wore a white overall. On him I staked all my chances.

I went into the darkened smoking-room where the rays of morning light were beginning to creep through the shutters. There I breakfasted off a whisky-and-soda and some biscuits from the cupboard. By this time it was getting on for six o'clock. I put a pipe in My Pocket and filled my pouch from the tobacco jar on the table by the fireplace.

As I poked into the tobacco my fingers touched something hard, and I drew out Scudder's little black pocket-book ...

That seemed to me a good omen. I lifted the cloth from the body and was amazed at the peace and dignity of the dead face. 'Goodbye, old chap,' I said; 'I am going to do my best for you. Wish me well, wherever you are.'

Then I hung about in the hall waiting for the milkman. That was the worst part of the business, for I was fairly choking to get out of doors. Six-thirty passed, then six-forty, but still he did not come. The fool had chosen this day of all days to be late.

At one minute after the quarter to seven I heard the rattle of the cans outside. I opened the front door, and there was my man, singling out my cans from a bunch he carried and whistling through his teeth. He jumped a bit at the sight of me.

'Come in here a moment,' I said. 'I want a word with you.' And I led him into the dining-room.

'I reckon you're a bit of a sportsman,' I said, 'and I want you to do me a service. Lend me your cap and overall for ten minutes, and here's a sovereign for you.'

His eyes opened at the sight of the gold, and he grinned broadly. 'Wot's the gyme?'he asked.

'A bet,' I said. 'I haven't time to explain, but to win it I've got to be a milkman for the next ten minutes. All you've got to do is to stay here till I come back. You'll be a bit late, but nobody will complain, and you'll have that quid for yourself.'

'Right-o!' he said cheerily. 'I ain't the man to spoil a bit of sport. 'Ere's the rig, guv'nor.'

I stuck on his flat blue hat and his white overall, picked up the cans, banged my door, and went whistling downstairs. The porter at the foot told me to shut my jaw, which sounded as if my make-up was adequate.

At first I thought there was nobody in the street. Then I caught sight of a policeman a hundred yards down, and a loafer shuffling past on the other side. Some impulse made me raise my eyes to the house opposite, and there at a first-floor window was a face. As the loafer passed he looked up, and I fancied a signal was exchanged.

I crossed the street, whistling gaily and imitating the jaunty swing of the milkman. Then I took the first side street, and went up a left-hand turning which led past a bit of vacant ground. There was no one in the little street, so I dropped the milk-cans inside the hoarding and sent the cap and overall after them. I had only just put on my cloth cap when a postman came round the corner. I gave him good morning and he answered me unsuspiciously. At the moment the clock of a neighbouring church struck the hour of seven.

There was not a second to spare. As soon as I got to Euston Road I took to my heels and ran. The clock at Euston Station showed five minutes past the hour. At St Pancras I had no time to take a ticket, let alone that I had not settled upon my destination. A porter told me the platform, and as I entered it I saw the train already in motion. Two station officials blocked the way, but I dodged them and clambered into the last carriage.

Three minutes later, as we were roaring through the northern tunnels, an irate guard interviewed me. He wrote out for me a ticket to Newton-Stewart, a name which had suddenly come back to my memory, and he conducted me from the first-class compartment where I had ensconced myself to a third-class smoker, occupied by a sailor and a stout woman with a child. He went off grumbling, and as I mopped my brow I observed to my companions in my broadest Scots that it was a sore job catching trains. I had already entered upon my part.

'The impidence o' that gyaird!' said the lady bitterly. 'He needit a Scotch tongue to pit him in his place. He was complainin' o' this wean no haein' a ticket and her no fower till August twalmonth, and he was objectin' to this gentleman spittin'.'

The sailor morosely agreed, and I started my new life in an atmosphere of protest against authority. I reminded myself that a week ago I had been finding the world dull.

CHAPTER THREE

The Adventure of the Literary Innkeeper

I had a solemn time travelling north that day. It was fine May weather, with the hawthorn flowering on every hedge, and I asked myself why, when I was still a free man, I had stayed on in London and not got the good of this heavenly country. I didn't dare face the restaurant car, but I got a luncheon-basket at Leeds and shared it with the fat woman. Also I got the morning's papers, with news about starters for the Derby and the beginning of the cricket season, and some paragraphs about how Balkan affairs were settling down and a British squadron was going to Kiel.

When I had done with them I got out Scudder's little black pocket-book and studied it. It was pretty well filled with jottings, chiefly figures, though now and then a name was printed in. For example, I found the words 'Hofgaard', 'Luneville', and 'Avocado' pretty often, and especially the word 'Pavia'.

Now I was certain that Scudder never did anything without a reason, and I was pretty sure that there was a cypher in all this. That is a subject which has always interested me, and I did a bit at it myself once as intelligence officer at Delagoa Bay during the Boer War. I have a head for things like chess and puzzles, and I used to reckon myself pretty good at finding out cyphers. This one looked like the numerical kind where sets of figures correspond to the letters of the alphabet, but any fairly shrewd man can find the clue to that sort after an hour or two's work, and I didn't think Scudder would have been content with anything so easy. So I fastened on the printed words, for you can make a pretty good numerical cypher if you have a key word which gives you the sequence of the letters.

I tried for hours, but none of the words answered. Then I fell asleep and woke at Dumfries just in time to bundle out and get into the slow Galloway train. There was a man on the platform whose looks I didn't like, but he never glanced at me, and when I caught sight of myself in the mirror of an automatic machine I didn't wonder. With my brown face, my old tweeds, and my slouch, I was the very model of one of the hill farmers who were crowding into the third-class carriages.

I travelled with half a dozen in an atmosphere of shag and clay pipes. They had come from the weekly market, and their mouths were full of prices. I heard accounts of how the lambing had gone up the Cairn and the Deuch and a dozen other mysterious waters. Above half the men had lunched heavily and were highly flavoured with whisky, but they took no notice of me. We rumbled slowly into a land of little wooded glens and then to a great wide moorland place, gleaming with lochs, with high blue hills showing northwards.

About five o'clock the carriage had emptied, and I was left alone as I had hoped. I got out at the next station, a little place whose name I scarcely noted, set right in the heart of a bog. It reminded me of one of those forgotten little stations in the Karroo. An old station-master was digging in his garden, and with his spade over his shoulder sauntered to the train, took charge of a parcel, and went back to his potatoes. A child of ten received my ticket, and I emerged on a white road that straggled over the brown moor.

It was a gorgeous spring evening, with every hill showing as clear as a cut amethyst. The air had the queer, rooty smell of bogs, but it was as fresh as mid-ocean, and it had the strangest effect on my spirits. I actually felt light-hearted. I might have been a boy out for a spring holiday tramp, instead of a man of thirty-seven very much wanted by the police. I felt just as I used to feel when I was starting for a big trek on a frosty morning on the high veld. If you believe me, I swung along that road whistling. There was no plan of campaign in my head, only just to go on and on in this blessed, honest-smelling hill country, for every mile put me in better humour with myself.

In a roadside planting I cut a walking-stick of hazel, and presently struck off the highway up a bypath which followed the glen of a brawling stream. I reckoned that I was still far ahead of any pursuit, and for that night might please myself. It was some hours since I had tasted food, and I was getting very hungry when I came to a herd's cottage set in a nook beside a waterfall. A brown-faced woman was standing by the door, and greeted me with the kindly shyness of moorland places. When I asked for a night's lodging she said I was welcome to the 'bed in the loft', and very soon she set before me a hearty meal of ham and eggs, scones, and thick sweet milk.

At the darkening her man came in from the hills, a lean giant, who in one step covered as much ground as three paces of ordinary mortals. They asked me no questions, for they had the perfect breeding of all dwellers in the wilds, but I could see they set me down as a kind of dealer, and I took some trouble to confirm their view. I spoke a lot about cattle, of which my host knew little, and I picked up from him a good deal about the local Galloway markets, which I tucked away in my memory for future use. At ten I was nodding in my chair, and the 'bed in the loft' received a weary man who never opened his eyes till five o'clock set the little homestead a-going once more.

They refused any payment, and by six I had breakfasted and was striding southwards again. My notion was to return to the railway line a station or two farther on than the place where I had alighted yesterday and to double back. I reckoned that that was the safest way, for the police would naturally assume that I was always making farther from London in the direction of some western port. I thought I had still a good bit of a start, for, as I reasoned, it would take some hours to fix the blame on me, and several more to identify the fellow who got on board the train at St Pancras.

It was the same jolly, clear spring weather, and I simply could not contrive to feel careworn. Indeed I was in better spirits than I had been for months. Over a long ridge of moorland I took my road, skirting the side of a high hill which the herd had called Cairnsmore of Fleet. Nesting curlews and plovers were crying everywhere, and the links of green pasture by the streams were dotted with young lambs. All the slackness of the past months was slipping from my bones, and I stepped out like a four-year-old. By-and-by I came to a swell of moorland which dipped to the vale of a little river, and a mile away in the heather I saw the smoke of a train.

The station, when I reached it, proved to be ideal for my purpose. The moor surged up around it and left room only for the single line, the slender siding, a waiting-room, an office, the station-master's cottage, and a tiny yard of gooseberries and sweet-william. There seemed no road to it from anywhere, and to increase the desolation the waves of a tarn lapped on their grey granite beach half a mile away. I waited in the deep heather till I saw the smoke of an east-going train on the horizon. Then I approached the tiny booking-office and took a ticket for Dumfries.

The only occupants of the carriage were an old shepherd and his dog—a wall-eyed brute that I mistrusted. The man was asleep, and on the cushions beside him was that morning's SCOTSMAN. Eagerly I seized on it, for I fancied it would tell me something.

There were two columns about the Portland Place Murder, as it was called. My man Paddock had given the alarm and had the milkman arrested. Poor devil, it looked as if the latter had earned his sovereign hardly; but for me he had been cheap at the price, for he seemed to have occupied the police for the better part of the day. In the latest news I found a further instalment of the story. The milkman had been released, I read, and the true criminal, about whose identity the police were reticent, was believed to have got away from London by one of the northern lines. There was a short note about me as the owner of the flat. I guessed the police had stuck that in, as a clumsy contrivance to persuade me that I was unsuspected.

There was nothing else in the paper, nothing about foreign politics or Karolides, or the things that had interested Scudder. I laid it down, and found that we were approaching the station at which I had got out yesterday. The potato-digging station-master had been gingered up into some activity, for the west-going train was waiting to let us pass, and from it had descended three men who were asking him questions. I supposed that they were the local police, who had been stirred up by Scotland Yard, and had traced me as far as this one-horse siding. Sitting well back in the shadow I watched them carefully. One of them had a book, and took down notes. The old potato-digger seemed to have turned peevish, but the child who had collected my ticket was talking volubly. All the party looked out across the moor where the white road departed. I hoped they were going to take up my tracks there.

As we moved away from that station my companion woke up. He fixed me with a wandering glance, kicked his dog viciously, and inquired where he was. Clearly he was very drunk.

'That's what comes o' bein' a teetotaller,' he observed in bitter regret.

I expressed my surprise that in him I should have met a blue-ribbon stalwart.

'Ay, but I'm a strong teetotaller,' he said pugnaciously. 'I took the pledge last Martinmas, and I havena touched a drop o' whisky sinsyne. Not even at Hogmanay, though I was sair temptit.'

He swung his heels up on the seat, and burrowed a frowsy head into the cushions.

'And that's a' I get,' he moaned. 'A heid better than hell fire, and twae een lookin' different ways for the Sabbath.'

'What did it?' I asked.

'A drink they ca' brandy. Bein' a teetotaller I keepit off the whisky, but I was nip-nippin' a' day at this brandy, and I doubt I'll no be weel for a fortnicht.' His voice died away into a splutter, and sleep once more laid its heavy hand on him.

My plan had been to get out at some station down the line, but the train suddenly gave me a better chance, for it came to a standstill at the end of a culvert which spanned a brawling porter-coloured river. I looked out and saw that every carriage window was closed and no human figure appeared in the landscape. So I opened the door, and dropped quickly into the tangle of hazels which edged the line.

it would have been all right but for that infernal dog. Under the impression that I was decamping with its master's belongings, it started to bark, and all but got me by the trousers. This woke up the herd, who stood bawling at the carriage door in the belief that I had committed suicide. I crawled through the thicket, reached the edge of the stream, and in cover of the bushes put a hundred yards or so behind me. Then from my shelter I peered back, and saw the guard and several passengers gathered round the open carriage door and staring in my direction. I could not have made a more public departure if I had left with a bugler and a brass band.

Happily the drunken herd provided a diversion. He and his dog, which was attached by a rope to his waist, suddenly cascaded out of the carriage, landed on their heads on the track, and rolled some way down the bank towards the water. In the rescue which followed the dog bit somebody, for I could hear the sound of hard swearing. Presently they had forgotten me, and when after a quarter of a mile's crawl I ventured to look back, the train had started again and was vanishing in the cutting.

I was in a wide semicircle of moorland, with the brown river as radius, and the high hills forming the northern circumference. There was not a sign or sound of a human being, only the plashing water and the interminable crying of curlews. Yet, oddly enough, for the first time I felt the terror of the hunted on me. It was not the police that I thought of, but the other folk, who knew that I knew Scudder's secret and dared not let me live. I was certain that they would pursue me with a keenness and vigilance unknown to the British law, and that once their grip closed on me I should find no mercy.

I looked back, but there was nothing in the landscape. The sun glinted on the metals of the line and the wet stones in the stream, and you could not have found a more peaceful sight in the world. Nevertheless I started to run. Crouching low in the runnels of the bog, I ran till the sweat blinded my eyes. The mood did not leave me till I had reached the rim of mountain and flung myself panting on a ridge high above the young waters of the brown river.

From my vantage-ground I could scan the whole moor right away to the railway line and to the south of it where green fields took the place of heather. I have eyes like a hawk, but I could see nothing moving in the whole countryside. Then I looked east beyond the ridge and saw a new kind of landscape—shallow green valleys with plentiful fir plantations and the faint lines of dust which spoke of highroads. Last of all I looked into the blue May sky, and there I saw that which set my pulses racing ...

Low down in the south a monoplane was climbing into the heavens. I was as certain as if I had been told that that aeroplane was looking for me, and that it did not belong to the police. For an hour or two I watched it from a pit of heather. It flew low along the hill-tops, and then in narrow circles over the valley up which I had come' Then it seemed to change its mind, rose to a great height, and flew away back to the south.

I did not like this espionage from the air, and I began to think less well of the countryside I had chosen for a refuge. These heather hills were no sort of cover if my enemies were in the sky, and I must find a different kind of sanctuary. I looked with more satisfaction to the green country beyond the ridge, for there I should find woods and stone houses.

About six in the evening I came out of the moorland to a white ribbon of road which wound up the narrow vale of a lowland stream. As I followed it, fields gave place to bent, the glen became a plateau, and presently I had reached a kind of pass where a solitary house smoked in the twilight. The road swung over a bridge, and leaning on the parapet was a young man.

He was smoking a long clay pipe and studying the water with spectacled eyes. In his left hand was a small book with a finger marking the place. Slowly he repeated—

As when a Gryphon through the wilderness
With winged step, o'er hill and moory dale
Pursues the Arimaspian.

He jumped round as my step rung on the keystone, and I saw a pleasant sunburnt boyish face.

'Good evening to you,' he said gravely. 'It's a fine night for the road.'

The smell of peat smoke and of some savoury roast floated to me from the house.

'Is that place an inn?' I asked.

'At your service,' he said politely. 'I am the landlord, Sir, and I hope you will stay the night, for to tell you the truth I have had no company for a week.'

I pulled myself up on the parapet of the bridge and filled my pipe. I began to detect an ally.

'You're young to be an innkeeper,' I said.

'My father died a year ago and left me the business. I live there with my grandmother. It's a slow job for a young man, and it wasn't my choice of profession.'

'Which was?'

He actually blushed. 'I want to write books,' he said.

'And what better chance could you ask?' I cried. 'Man, I've often thought that an innkeeper would make the best story-teller in the world.'

'Not now,' he said eagerly. 'Maybe in the old days when you had pilgrims and ballad-makers and highwaymen and mail-coaches on the road. But not now. Nothing comes here but motor-cars full of fat women, who stop for lunch, and a fisherman or two in the spring, and the shooting tenants in August. There is not much material to be got out of that. I want to see life, to travel the world, and write things like Kipling and Conrad. But the most I've done yet is to get some verses printed in CHAMBERS'S JOURNAL.' I looked at the inn standing golden in the sunset against the brown hills.

'I've knocked a bit about the world, and I wouldn't despise such a hermitage. D'you think that adventure is found only in the tropics or among gentry in red shirts? Maybe you're rubbing shoulders with it at this moment.'

'That's what Kipling says,' he said, his eyes brightening, and he quoted some verse about 'Romance bringing up the 9.15'.

'Here's a true tale for you then,' I cried, 'and a month from now you can make a novel out of it.'

Sitting on the bridge in the soft May gloaming I pitched him a lovely yarn. It was true in essentials, too, though I altered the minor details. I made out that I was a mining magnate from Kimberley, who had had a lot of trouble with I.D.B. and had shown up a gang. They had pursued me across the ocean, and had killed my best friend, and were now on my tracks.

I told the story well, though I say it who shouldn't. I pictured a flight across the Kalahari to German Africa, the crackling, parching days, the wonderful blue-velvet nights. I described an attack on my life on the voyage home, and I made a really horrid affair of the Portland Place murder. 'You're looking for adventure,' I cried; 'well, you've found it here. The devils are after me, and the police are after them. It's a race that I mean to win.'

'By God!' he whispered, drawing his breath in sharply, 'it is all pure Rider Haggard and Conan Doyle.'

'You believe me,' I said gratefully.

'Of course I do,' and he held out his hand. 'I believe everything out of the common. The only thing to distrust is the normal.'

He was very young, but he was the man for my money.

'I think they're off my track for the moment, but I must lie close for a couple of days. Can you take me in?'

He caught my elbow in his eagerness and drew me towards the house. 'You can lie as snug here as if you were in a moss-hole. I'll see that nobody blabs, either. And you'll give me some more material about your adventures?'

As I entered the inn porch I heard from far off the beat of an engine. There silhouetted against the dusky West was my friend, the monoplane.

He gave me a room at the back of the house, with a fine outlook over the plateau, and he made me free of his own study, which was stacked with cheap editions of his favourite authors. I never saw the grandmother, so I guessed she was bedridden. An old woman called Margit brought me my meals, and the innkeeper was around me at all hours. I wanted some time to myself, so I invented a job for him. He had a motor-bicycle, and I sent him off next morning for the daily paper, which usually arrived with the post in the late afternoon. I told him to keep his eyes skinned, and make note of any strange figures he saw, keeping a special sharp look-out for motors and aeroplanes. Then I sat down in real earnest to Scudder's note-book.

He came back at midday with the SCOTSMAN. There was nothing in it, except some further evidence of Paddock and the milkman, and a repetition of yesterday's statement that the murderer had gone North. But there was a long article, reprinted from THE TIMES, about Karolides and the state of affairs in the Balkans, though there was no mention of any visit to England. I got rid of the innkeeper for the afternoon, for I was getting very warm in my search for the cypher.

As I told you, it was a numerical cypher, and by an elaborate system of experiments I had pretty well discovered what were the nulls and stops. The trouble was the key word, and when I thought of the odd million words he might have used I felt pretty hopeless. But about three o'clock I had a sudden inspiration.

The name Julia Czechenyi flashed across my memory. Scudder had said it was the key to the Karolides business, and it occurred to me to try it on his cypher.

It worked. The five letters of 'Julia' gave me the position of the vowels. A was J, the tenth letter of the alphabet, and so represented by X in the cypher. E was XXI, and so on. 'Czechenyi' gave me the numerals for the principal consonants. I scribbled that scheme on a bit of paper and sat down to read Scudder's pages.

In half an hour I was reading with a whitish face and fingers that drummed on the table.

I glanced out of the window and saw a big touring-car coming up the glen towards the inn. It drew up at the door, and there was the sound of people alighting. There seemed to be two of them, men in aquascutums and tweed caps.

Ten minutes later the innkeeper slipped into the room, his eyes bright with excitement.

'There's two chaps below looking for you,' he whispered. 'They're in the dining-room having whiskies-and-sodas. They asked about you and said they had hoped to meet you here. Oh! and they described you jolly well, down to your boots and shirt. I told them you had been here last night and had gone off on a motor bicycle this morning, and one of the chaps swore like a navvy.'

I made him tell me what they looked like. One was a dark-eyed thin fellow with bushy eyebrows, the other was always smiling and lisped in his talk. Neither was any kind of foreigner; on this my young friend was positive.

I took a bit of paper and wrote these words in German as if they were part of a letter—

... 'Black Stone. Scudder had got on to this, but he could not act for a fortnight. I doubt if I can do any good now, especially as Karolides is uncertain about his plans. But if Mr T. advises I will do the best I ...'

I manufactured it rather neatly, so that it looked like a loose page of a private letter.

'Take this down and say it was found in my bedroom, and ask them to return it to me if they overtake me.'

Three minutes later I heard the car begin to move, and peeping from behind the curtain caught sight of the two figures. One was slim, the other was sleek; that was the most I could make of my reconnaissance.

The innkeeper appeared in great excitement. 'Your paper woke them up,' he said gleefully. 'The dark fellow went as white as death and cursed like blazes, and the fat one whistled and looked ugly. They paid for their drinks with half-a-sovereign and wouldn't wait for change.'

'Now I'll tell you what I want you to do,' I said. 'Get on your bicycle and go off to Newton-Stewart to the Chief Constable. Describe the two men, and say you suspect them of having had something to do with the London murder. You can invent reasons. The two will come back, never fear. Not tonight, for they'll follow me forty miles along the road, but first thing tomorrow morning. Tell the police to be here bright and early.'

He set off like a docile child, while I worked at Scudder's notes. When he came back we dined together, and in common decency I had to let him pump me. I gave him a lot of stuff about lion hunts and the Matabele War, thinking all the while what tame businesses these were compared to this I was now engaged in! When he went to bed I sat up and finished Scudder. I smoked in a chair till daylight, for I could not sleep.

About eight next morning I witnessed the arrival of two constables and a sergeant. They put their car in a coach-house under the innkeeper's instructions, and entered the house. Twenty minutes later I saw from my window a second car come across the plateau from the opposite direction. It did not come up to the inn, but stopped two hundred yards off in the shelter of a patch of wood. I noticed that its occupants carefully reversed it before leaving it. A minute or two later I heard their steps on the gravel outside the window.

My plan had been to lie hid in my bedroom, and see what happened. I had a notion that, if I could bring the police and my other more dangerous pursuers together, something might work out of it to my advantage. But now I had a better idea. I scribbled a line of thanks to my host, opened the window, and dropped quietly into a gooseberry bush. Unobserved I crossed the dyke, crawled down the side of a tributary burn, and won the highroad on the far side of the patch of trees. There stood the car, very spick and span in the morning sunlight, but with the dust on her which told of a long journey. I started her, jumped into the chauffeur's seat, and stole gently out on to the plateau.

Almost at once the road dipped so that I lost sight of the inn, but the wind seemed to bring me the sound of angry voices.

CHAPTER FOUR

The Adventure of the Radical Candidate

You may picture me driving that 40 h.p. car for all she was worth over the crisp moor roads on that shining May morning; glancing back at first over my shoulder, and looking anxiously to the next turning; then driving with a vague eye, just wide enough awake to keep on the highway. For I was thinking desperately of what I had found in Scudder's pocket-book.

The little man had told me a pack of lies. All his yarns about the Balkans and the Jew-Anarchists and the Foreign Office Conference were eyewash, and so was Karolides. And yet not quite, as you shall hear. I had staked everything on my belief in his story, and had been let down; here was his book telling me a different tale, and instead of being once-bitten-twice-shy, I believed it absolutely.

Why, I don't know. It rang desperately true, and the first yarn, if you understand me, had been in a queer way true also in spirit. The fifteenth day of June was going to be a day of destiny, a bigger destiny than the killing of a Dago. It was so big that I didn't blame Scudder for keeping me out of the game and wanting to play a lone hand. That, I was pretty clear, was his intention. He had told me something which sounded big enough, but the real thing was so immortally big that he, the man who had found it out, wanted it all for himself. I didn't blame him. It was risks after all that he was chiefly greedy about.

The whole story was in the notes—with gaps, you understand, which he would have filled up from his memory. He stuck down his authorities, too, and had an odd trick of giving them all a numerical value and then striking a balance, which stood for the reliability of each stage in the yarn. The four names he had printed were authorities, and there was a man, Ducrosne, who got five out of a possible five; and another fellow, Ammersfoort, who got three. The bare bones of the tale were all that was in the book—these, and one queer phrase which occurred half a dozen times inside brackets. '(Thirty-nine steps)' was the phrase; and at its last time of use it ran—'(Thirty-nine steps, I counted them—high tide 10.17 p.m.)'. I could make nothing of that.

The first thing I learned was that it was no question of preventing a war. That was coming, as sure as Christmas: had been arranged, said Scudder, ever since February 1912. Karolides was going to be the occasion. He was booked all right, and was to hand in his checks on June 14th, two weeks and four days from that May morning. I gathered from Scudder's notes that nothing on earth could prevent that. His talk of Epirote guards that would skin their own grandmothers was all billy-o.

The second thing was that this war was going to come as a mighty surprise to Britain. Karolides' death would set the Balkans by the ears, and then Vienna would chip in with an ultimatum. Russia wouldn't like that, and there would be high words. But Berlin would play the peacemaker, and pour oil on the waters, till suddenly she would find a good cause for a quarrel, pick it up, and in five hours let fly at us. That was the idea, and a pretty good one too. Honey and fair speeches, and then a stroke in the dark. While we were talking about the goodwill and good intentions of Germany our coast would be silently ringed with mines, and submarines would be waiting for every battleship.

But all this depended upon the third thing, which was due to happen on June 15th. I would never have grasped this if I hadn't once happened to meet a French staff officer, coming back from West Africa, who had told me a lot of things. One was that, in spite of all the nonsense talked in Parliament, there was a real working alliance between France and Britain, and that the two General Staffs met every now and then, and made plans for joint action in case of war. Well, in June a very great swell was coming over from Paris, and he was going to get nothing less than a statement of the disposition of the British Home Fleet on mobilization. At least I gathered it was something like that; anyhow, it was something uncommonly important.

But on the 15th day of June there were to be others in London—others, at whom I could only guess. Scudder was content to call them collectively the 'Black Stone'. They represented not our Allies, but our deadly foes; and the information, destined for France, was to be diverted to their pockets. And it was to be used, remember—used a week or two later, with great guns and swift torpedoes, suddenly in the darkness of a summer night.

This was the story I had been deciphering in a back room of a country inn, overlooking a cabbage garden. This was the story that hummed in my brain as I swung in the big touring-car from glen to glen.

My first impulse had been to write a letter to the Prime Minister, but a little reflection convinced me that that would be useless. Who would believe my tale? I must show a sign, some token in proof, and Heaven knew what that could be. Above all, I must keep going myself, ready to act when things got riper, and that was going to be no light job with the police of the British Isles in full cry after me and the watchers of the Black Stone running silently and swiftly on my trail.

I had no very clear purpose in my journey, but I steered east by the sun, for I remembered from the map that if I went north I would come into a region of coalpits and industrial towns. Presently I was down from the moorlands and traversing the broad haugh of a river. For miles I ran alongside a park wall, and in a break of the trees I saw a great castle. I swung through little old thatched villages, and over peaceful lowland streams, and past gardens blazing with hawthorn and yellow laburnum. The land was so deep in peace that I could scarcely believe that somewhere behind me were those who sought my life; ay, and that in a month's time, unless I had the almightiest of luck, these round country faces would be pinched and staring, and men would be lying dead in English fields.

About mid-day I entered a long straggling village, and had a mind to stop and eat. Half-way down was the Post Office, and on the steps of it stood the postmistress and a policeman hard at work conning a telegram. When they saw me they wakened up, and the policeman advanced with raised hand, and cried on me to stop.

I nearly was fool enough to obey. Then it flashed upon me that the wire had to do with me; that my friends at the inn had come to an understanding, and were united in desiring to see more of me, and that it had been easy enough for them to wire the description of me and the car to thirty villages through which I might pass. I released the brakes just in time. As it was, the policeman made a claw at the hood, and only dropped off when he got my left in his eye.

I saw that main roads were no place for me, and turned into the byways. It wasn't an easy job without a map, for there was the risk of getting on to a farm road and ending in a duck-pond or a stable-yard, and I couldn't afford that kind of delay. I began to see what an ass I had been to steal the car. The big green brute would be the safest kind of clue to me over the breadth of Scotland. If I left it and took to my feet, it would be discovered in an hour or two and I would get no start in the race.

The immediate thing to do was to get to the loneliest roads. These I soon found when I struck up a tributary of the big river, and got into a glen with steep hills all about me, and a corkscrew road at the end which climbed over a pass. Here I met nobody, but it was taking me too far north, so I slewed east along a bad track and finally struck a big double-line railway. Away below me I saw another broadish valley, and it occurred to me that if I crossed it I might find some remote inn to pass the night. The evening was now drawing in, and I was furiously hungry, for I had eaten nothing since breakfast except a couple of buns I had bought from a baker's cart. Just then I heard a noise in the sky, and lo and behold there was that infernal aeroplane, flying low, about a dozen miles to the south and rapidly coming towards me.

I had the sense to remember that on a bare moor I was at the aeroplane's mercy, and that my only chance was to get to the leafy cover of the valley. Down the hill I went like blue lightning, screwing my head round, whenever I dared, to watch that damned flying machine. Soon I was on a road between hedges, and dipping to the deep-cut glen of a stream. Then came a bit of thick wood where I slackened speed.

Suddenly on my left I heard the hoot of another car, and realized to my horror that I was almost up on a couple of gate-posts through which a private road debouched on the highway. My horn gave an agonized roar, but it was too late. I clapped on my brakes, but my impetus was too great, and there before me a car was sliding athwart my course. In a second there would have been the deuce of a wreck. I did the only thing possible, and ran slap into the hedge on the right, trusting to find something soft beyond.

But there I was mistaken. My car slithered through the hedge like butter, and then gave a sickening plunge forward. I saw what was coming, leapt on the seat and would have jumped out. But a branch of hawthorn got me in the chest, lifted me up and held me, while a ton or two of expensive metal slipped below me, bucked and pitched, and then dropped with an almighty smash fifty feet to the bed of the stream.

Slowly that thorn let me go. I subsided first on the hedge, and then very gently on a bower of nettles. As I scrambled to my feet a hand took me by the arm, and a sympathetic and badly scared voice asked me if I were hurt.

I found myself looking at a tall young man in goggles and a leather ulster, who kept on blessing his soul and whinnying apologies. For myself, once I got my wind back, I was rather glad than otherwise. This was one way of getting rid of the car.

'My blame, Sir,' I answered him. 'It's lucky that I did not add homicide to my follies. That's the end of my Scotch motor tour, but it might have been the end of my life.'

He plucked out a watch and studied it. 'You're the right sort of fellow,' he said. 'I can spare a quarter of an hour, and my house is two minutes off. I'll see you clothed and fed and snug in bed. Where's your kit, by the way? Is it in the burn along with the car?'

'It's in my pocket,' I said, brandishing a toothbrush. 'I'm a Colonial and travel light.'

'A Colonial,' he cried. 'By Gad, you're the very man I've been praying for. Are you by any blessed chance a Free Trader?'

'I am,' said I, without the foggiest notion of what he meant.

He patted my shoulder and hurried me into his car. Three minutes later we drew up before a comfortable-looking shooting box set among pine-trees, and he ushered me indoors. He took me first to a bedroom and flung half a dozen of his suits before me, for my own had been pretty well reduced to rags. I selected a loose blue serge, which differed most conspicuously from my former garments, and borrowed a linen collar. Then he haled me to the dining-room, where the remnants of a meal stood on the table, and announced that I had just five minutes to feed. 'You can take a snack in your pocket, and we'll have supper when we get back. I've got to be at the Masonic Hall at eight o'clock, or my agent will comb my hair.'

I had a cup of coffee and some cold ham, while he yarned away on the hearth-rug.

'You find me in the deuce of a mess, Mr—by-the-by, you haven't told me your name. Twisdon? Any relation of old Tommy Twisdon of the Sixtieth? No? Well, you see I'm Liberal Candidate for this part of the world, and I had a meeting on tonight at Brattleburn—that's my chief town, and an infernal Tory stronghold. I had got the Colonial ex-Premier fellow, Crumpleton, coming to speak for me tonight, and had the thing tremendously billed and the whole place ground-baited. This afternoon I had a wire from the ruffian saying he had got influenza at Blackpool, and here am I left to do the whole thing myself. I had meant to speak for ten minutes and must now go on for forty, and, though I've been racking my brains for three hours to think of something, I simply cannot last the course. Now you've got to be a good chap and help me. You're a Free Trader and can tell our people what a wash-out Protection is in the Colonies. All you fellows have the gift of the gab—I wish to Heaven I had it. I'll be for evermore in your debt.'

I had very few notions about Free Trade one way or the other, but I saw no other chance to get what I wanted. My young gentleman was far too absorbed in his own difficulties to think how odd it was to ask a stranger who had just missed death by an ace and had lost a 1,000-guinea car to address a meeting for him on the spur of the moment. But my necessities did not allow me to contemplate oddnesses or to pick and choose my supports.

'All right,' I said. 'I'm not much good as a speaker, but I'll tell them a bit about Australia.'

At my words the cares of the ages slipped from his shoulders, and he was rapturous in his thanks. He lent me a big driving coat—and never troubled to ask why I had started on a motor tour without possessing an ulster—and, as we slipped down the dusty roads, poured into my ears the simple facts of his history. He was an orphan, and his uncle had brought him up—I've forgotten the uncle's name, but he was in the Cabinet, and you can read his speeches in the papers. He had gone round the world after leaving Cambridge, and then, being short of a job, his uncle had advised politics. I gathered that he had no preference in parties. 'Good chaps in both,' he said cheerfully, 'and plenty of blighters, too. I'm Liberal, because my family have always been Whigs.' But if he was lukewarm politically he had strong views on other things. He found out I knew a bit about horses, and jawed away about the Derby entries; and he was full of plans for improving his shooting. Altogether, a very clean, decent, callow young man.

As we passed through a little town two policemen signalled us to stop, and flashed their lanterns on us.

'Beg pardon, Sir Harry,' said one. 'We've got instructions to look out for a car, and the description's no unlike yours.'

'Right-o,' said my host, while I thanked Providence for the devious ways I had been brought to safety. After that he spoke no more, for his mind began to labour heavily with his coming speech. His lips kept muttering, his eye wandered, and I began to prepare myself for a second catastrophe. I tried to think of something to say myself, but my mind was dry as a stone. The next thing I knew we had drawn up outside a door in a street, and were being welcomed by some noisy gentlemen with rosettes. The hall had about five hundred in it, women mostly, a lot of bald heads, and a dozen or two young men. The chairman, a weaselly minister with a reddish nose, lamented Crumpleton's absence, soliloquized on his influenza, and gave me a certificate as a 'trusted leader of Australian thought'. There were two policemen at the door, and I hoped they took note of that testimonial. Then Sir Harry started.

I never heard anything like it. He didn't begin to know how to talk. He had about a bushel of notes from which he read, and when he let go of them he fell into one prolonged stutter. Every now and then he remembered a phrase he had learned by heart, straightened his back, and gave it off like Henry Irving, and the next moment he was bent double and crooning over his papers. It was the most appalling rot, too. He talked about the 'German menace', and said it was all a Tory invention to cheat the poor of their rights and keep back the great flood of social reform, but that 'organized labour' realized this and laughed the Tories to scorn. He was all for reducing our Navy as a proof of our good faith, and then sending Germany an ultimatum telling her to do the same or we would knock her into a cocked hat. He said that, but for the Tories, Germany and Britain would be fellow-workers in peace and reform. I thought of the little black book in my pocket! A giddy lot Scudder's friends cared for peace and reform.

Yet in a queer way I liked the speech. You could see the niceness of the chap shining out behind the muck with which he had been spoon-fed. Also it took a load off my mind. I mightn't be much of an orator, but I was a thousand per cent better than Sir Harry.

I didn't get on so badly when it came to my turn. I simply told them all I could remember about Australia, praying there should be no Australian there—all about its labour party and emigration and universal service. I doubt if I remembered to mention Free Trade, but I said there were no Tories in Australia, only Labour and Liberals. That fetched a cheer, and I woke them up a bit when I started in to tell them the kind of glorious business I thought could be made out of the Empire if we really put our backs into it.

Altogether I fancy I was rather a success. The minister didn't like me, though, and when he proposed a vote of thanks, spoke of Sir Harry's speech as 'statesmanlike' and mine as having 'the eloquence of an emigration agent'.

When we were in the car again my host was in wild spirits at having got his job over. 'A ripping speech, Twisdon,' he said. 'Now, you're coming home with me. I'm all alone, and if you'll stop a day or two I'll show you some very decent fishing.'

We had a hot supper—and I wanted it pretty badly—and then drank grog in a big cheery smoking-room with a crackling wood fire. I thought the time had come for me to put my cards on the table. I saw by this man's eye that he was the kind you can trust.

'Listen, Sir Harry,' I said. 'I've something pretty important to say to you. You're a good fellow, and I'm going to be frank. Where on earth did you get that poisonous rubbish you talked tonight?'

His face fell. 'Was it as bad as that?' he asked ruefully. 'It did sound rather thin. I got most of it out of the PROGRESSIVE MAGAZINE and pamphlets that agent chap of mine keeps sending me. But you surely don't think Germany would ever go to war with us?'

'Ask that question in six weeks and it won't need an answer,' I said. 'If you'll give me your attention for half an hour I am going to tell you a story.'

I can see yet that bright room with the deers' heads and the old prints on the walls, Sir Harry standing restlessly on the stone curb of the hearth, and myself lying back in an armchair, speaking. I seemed to be another person, standing aside and listening to my own voice, and judging carefully the reliability of my tale. It was the first time I had ever told anyone the exact truth, so far as I understood it, and it did me no end of good, for it straightened out the thing in my own mind. I blinked no detail. He heard all about Scudder, and the milkman, and the note-book, and my doings in Galloway. Presently he got very excited and walked up and down the hearth-rug.

'So you see,' I concluded, 'you have got here in your house the man that is wanted for the Portland Place murder. Your duty is to send your car for the police and give me up. I don't think I'll get very far. There'll be an accident, and I'll have a knife in my ribs an hour or so after arrest. Nevertheless, it's your duty, as a law-abiding citizen. Perhaps in a month's time you'll be sorry, but you have no cause to think of that.'

He was looking at me with bright steady eyes. 'What was your job in Rhodesia, Mr Hannay?' he asked.

'Mining engineer,' I said. 'I've made my pile cleanly and I've had a good time in the making of it.'

'Not a profession that weakens the nerves, is it?'

I laughed. 'Oh, as to that, my nerves are good enough.' I took down a hunting-knife from a stand on the wall, and did the old Mashona trick of tossing it and catching it in my lips. That wants a pretty steady heart.

He watched me with a smile. 'I don't want proof. I may be an ass on the platform, but I can size up a man. You're no murderer and you're no fool, and I believe you are speaking the truth. I'm going to back you up. Now, what can I do?'

'First, I want you to write a letter to your uncle. I've got to get in touch with the Government people sometime before the 15th of June.'

He pulled his moustache. 'That won't help you. This is Foreign Office business, and my uncle would have nothing to do with it. Besides, you'd never convince him. No, I'll go one better. I'll write to the Permanent Secretary at the Foreign Office. He's my godfather, and one of the best going. What do you want?'

He sat down at a table and wrote to my dictation. The gist of it was that if a man called Twisdon (I thought I had better stick to that name) turned up before June 15th he was to entreat him kindly. He said Twisdon would prove his bona fides by passing the word 'Black Stone' and whistling 'Annie Laurie'.

'Good,' said Sir Harry. 'That's the proper style. By the way, you'll find my godfather—his name's Sir Walter Bullivant—down at his country cottage for Whitsuntide. It's close to Artinswell on the Kenner. That's done. Now, what's the next thing?'

'You're about my height. Lend me the oldest tweed suit you've got. Anything will do, so long as the colour is the opposite of the clothes I destroyed this afternoon. Then show me a map of the neighbourhood and explain to me the lie of the land. Lastly, if the police come seeking me, just show them the car in the glen. If the other lot turn up, tell them I caught the south express after your meeting.'

He did, or promised to do, all these things. I shaved off the remnants of my moustache, and got inside an ancient suit of what I believe is called heather mixture. The map gave me some notion of my whereabouts, and told me the two things I wanted to know—where the main railway to the south could be joined and what were the wildest districts near at hand. At two o'clock he wakened me from my slumbers in the smoking-room armchair, and led me blinking into the dark starry night. An old bicycle was found in a tool-shed and handed over to me.

'First turn to the right up by the long fir-wood,' he enjoined. 'By daybreak you'll be well into the hills. Then I should pitch the machine into a bog and take to the moors on foot. You can put in a week among the shepherds, and be as safe as if you were in New Guinea.'

I pedalled diligently up steep roads of hill gravel till the skies grew pale with morning. As the mists cleared before the sun, I found myself in a wide green world with glens falling on every side and a far-away blue horizon. Here, at any rate, I could get early news of my enemies.

CHAPTER FIVE

The Adventure of the Spectacled Roadman

I sat down on the very crest of the pass and took stock of my position.

Behind me was the road climbing through a long cleft in the hills, which was the upper glen of some notable river. In front was a flat space of maybe a mile, all pitted with bog-holes and rough with tussocks, and then beyond it the road fell steeply down another glen to a plain whose blue dimness melted into the distance. To left and right were round-shouldered green hills as smooth as pancakes, but to the south—that is, the left hand—there was a glimpse of high heathery mountains, which I remembered from the map as the big knot of hill which I had chosen for my sanctuary. I was on the central boss of a huge upland country, and could see everything moving for miles. In the meadows below the road half a mile back a cottage smoked, but it was the only sign of human life. Otherwise there was only the calling of plovers and the tinkling of little streams.

It was now about seven o'clock, and as I waited I heard once again that ominous beat in the air. Then I realized that my vantage-ground might be in reality a trap. There was no cover for a tomtit in those bald green places.

I sat quite still and hopeless while the beat grew louder. Then I saw an aeroplane coming up from the east. It was flying high, but as I looked it dropped several hundred feet and began to circle round the knot of hill in narrowing circles, just as a hawk wheels before it pounces. Now it was flying very low, and now the observer on board caught sight of me. I could see one of the two occupants examining me through glasses.

Suddenly it began to rise in swift whorls, and the next I knew it was speeding eastward again till it became a speck in the blue morning.

That made me do some savage thinking. My enemies had located me, and the next thing would be a cordon round me. I didn't know what force they could command, but I was certain it would be sufficient. The aeroplane had seen my bicycle, and would conclude that I would try to escape by the road. In that case there might be a chance on the moors to the right or left. I wheeled the machine a hundred yards from the highway, and plunged it into a moss-hole, where it sank among pond-weed and water-buttercups. Then I climbed to a knoll which gave me a view of the two valleys. Nothing was stirring on the long white ribbon that threaded them.

I have said there was not cover in the whole place to hide a rat. As the day advanced it was flooded with soft fresh light till it had the fragrant sunniness of the South African veld. At other times I would have liked the place, but now it seemed to suffocate me. The free moorlands were prison walls, and the keen hill air was the breath of a dungeon.

I tossed a coin—heads right, tails left—and it fell heads, so I turned to the north. In a little I came to the brow of the ridge which was the containing wall of the pass. I saw the highroad for maybe ten miles, and far down it something that was moving, and that I took to be a motor-car. Beyond the ridge I looked on a rolling green moor, which fell away into wooded glens.

Now my life on the veld has given me the eyes of a kite, and I can see things for which most men need a telescope ... Away down the slope, a couple of miles away, several men were advancing, like a row of beaters at a shoot ...

I dropped out of sight behind the sky-line. That way was shut to me, and I must try the bigger hills to the south beyond the highway. The car I had noticed was getting nearer, but it was still a long way off with some very steep gradients before it. I ran hard, crouching low except in the hollows, and as I ran I kept scanning the brow of the hill before me. Was it imagination, or did I see figures—one, two, perhaps more—moving in a glen beyond the stream?

If you are hemmed in on all sides in a patch of land there is only one chance of escape. You must stay in the patch, and let your enemies search it and not find you.

That was good sense, but how on earth was I to escape notice in that table-cloth of a place? I would have buried myself to the neck in mud or lain below water or climbed the tallest tree. But there was not a stick of wood, the bog-holes were little puddles, the stream was a slender trickle. There was nothing but short heather, and bare hill bent, and the white highway.

Then in a tiny bight of road, beside a heap of stones, I found the roadman.

He had just arrived, and was wearily flinging down his hammer. He looked at me with a fishy eye and yawned.

'Confoond the day I ever left the herdin'!' he said, as if to the world at large. 'There I was my ain maister. Now I'm a slave to the Goavernment, tethered to the roadside, wi' sair een, and a back like a suckle.'

He took up the hammer, struck a stone, dropped the implement with an oath, and put both hands to his ears. 'Mercy on me! My heid's burstin'!' he cried.

He was a wild figure, about my own size but much bent, with a week's beard on his chin, and a pair of big horn spectacles.

'I canna dae't,' he cried again. 'The Surveyor maun just report me. I'm for my bed.'

I asked him what was the trouble, though indeed that was clear enough.

'The trouble is that I'm no sober. Last nicht my dochter Merran was waddit, and they danced till fower in the byre. Me and some ither chiels sat down to the drinkin', and here I am. Peety that I ever lookit on the wine when it was red!'

I agreed with him about bed. 'It's easy speakin',' he moaned. 'But I got a postcard yestreen sayin' that the new Road Surveyor would be round the day. He'll come and he'll no find me, or else he'll find me fou, and either way I'm a done man. I'll awa' back to my bed and say I'm no weel, but I doot that'll no help me, for they ken my kind o' no-weel-ness.'

Then I had an inspiration. 'Does the new Surveyor know you?' I asked.

'No him. He's just been a week at the job. He rins about in a wee motor-cawr, and wad speir the inside oot o' a whelk.'

'Where's your house?' I asked, and was directed by a wavering finger to the cottage by the stream.

'Well, back to your bed,' I said, 'and sleep in peace. I'll take on your job for a bit and see the Surveyor.'

He stared at me blankly; then, as the notion dawned on his fuddled brain, his face broke into the vacant drunkard's smile.

'You're the billy,' he cried. 'It'll be easy eneuch managed. I've finished that bing o' stanes, so you needna chap ony mair this forenoon. Just take the barry, and wheel eneuch metal frae yon quarry doon the road to mak anither bing the morn. My name's Alexander Turnbull, and I've been seeven year at the trade, and twenty afore that herdin' on Leithen Water. My freens ca' me Ecky, and whiles Specky, for I wear glesses, being waik i' the sicht. Just you speak the Surveyor fair, and ca' him Sir, and he'll be fell pleased. I'll be back or mid-day.'

I borrowed his spectacles and filthy old hat; stripped off coat, waistcoat, and collar, and gave him them to carry home; borrowed, too, the foul stump of a clay pipe as an extra property. He indicated my simple tasks, and without more ado set off at an amble bedwards. Bed may have been his chief object, but I think there was also something left in the foot of a bottle. I prayed that he might be safe under cover before my friends arrived on the scene.

Then I set to work to dress for the part. I opened the collar of my shirt—it was a vulgar blue-and-white check such as ploughmen wear—and revealed a neck as brown as any tinker's. I rolled up my sleeves, and there was a forearm which might have been a blacksmith's, sunburnt and rough with old scars. I got my boots and trouser-legs all white from the dust of the road, and hitched up my trousers, tying them with string below the knee. Then I set to work on my face. With a handful of dust I made a water-mark round my neck, the place where Mr Turnbull's Sunday ablutions might be expected to stop. I rubbed a good deal of dirt also into the sunburn of my cheeks. A roadman's eyes would no doubt be a little inflamed, so I contrived to get some dust in both of mine, and by dint of vigorous rubbing produced a bleary effect.

The sandwiches Sir Harry had given me had gone off with my coat, but the roadman's lunch, tied up in a red handkerchief, was at my disposal. I ate with great relish several of the thick slabs of scone and cheese and drank a little of the cold tea. In the handkerchief was a local paper tied with string and addressed to Mr Turnbull—obviously meant to solace his mid-day leisure. I did up the bundle again, and put the paper conspicuously beside it.

My boots did not satisfy me, but by dint of kicking among the stones I reduced them to the granite-like surface which marks a roadman's foot-gear. Then I bit and scraped my finger-nails till the edges were all cracked and uneven. The men I was matched against would miss no detail. I broke one of the bootlaces and retied it in a clumsy knot, and loosed the other so that my thick grey socks bulged over the uppers. Still no sign of anything on the road. The motor I had observed half an hour ago must have gone home.

My toilet complete, I took up the barrow and began my journeys to and from the quarry a hundred yards off.

I remember an old scout in Rhodesia, who had done many queer things in his day, once telling me that the secret of playing a part was to think yourself into it. You could never keep it up, he said, unless you could manage to convince yourself that you were it. So I shut off all other thoughts and switched them on to the road-mending. I thought of the little white cottage as my home, I recalled the years I had spent herding on Leithen Water, I made my mind dwell lovingly on sleep in a box-bed and a bottle of cheap whisky. Still nothing appeared on that long white road.

Now and then a sheep wandered off the heather to stare at me. A heron flopped down to a pool in the stream and started to fish, taking no more notice of me than if I had been a milestone. On I went, trundling my loads of stone, with the heavy step of the professional. Soon I grew warm, and the dust on my face changed into solid and abiding grit. I was already counting the hours till evening should put a limit to Mr Turnbull's monotonous toil. Suddenly a crisp voice spoke from the road, and looking up I saw a little Ford two-seater, and a round-faced young man in a bowler hat.

'Are you Alexander Turnbull?' he asked. 'I am the new County Road Surveyor. You live at Blackhopefoot, and have charge of the section from Laidlawbyres to the Riggs? Good! A fair bit of road, Turnbull, and not badly engineered. A little soft about a mile off, and the edges want cleaning. See you look after that. Good morning. You'll know me the next time you see me.'

Clearly my get-up was good enough for the dreaded Surveyor. I went on with my work, and as the morning grew towards noon I was cheered by a little traffic. A baker's van breasted the hill, and sold me a bag of ginger biscuits which I stowed in my trouser-pockets against emergencies. Then a herd passed with sheep, and disturbed me somewhat by asking loudly, 'What had become o' Specky?'

'In bed wi' the colic,' I replied, and the herd passed on ... just about mid-day a big car stole down the hill, glided past and drew up a hundred yards beyond. Its three occupants descended as if to stretch their legs, and sauntered towards me.

Two of the men I had seen before from the window of the Galloway inn—one lean, sharp, and dark, the other comfortable and smiling. The third had the look of a countryman—a vet, perhaps, or a small farmer. He was dressed in ill-cut knickerbockers, and the eye in his head was as bright and wary as a hen's.

'Morning,' said the last. 'That's a fine easy job o' yours.'

I had not looked up on their approach, and now, when accosted, I slowly and painfully straightened my back, after the manner of roadmen; spat vigorously, after the manner of the low Scot; and regarded them steadily before replying. I confronted three pairs of eyes that missed nothing.

'There's waur jobs and there's better,' I said sententiously. 'I wad rather hae yours, sittin' a' day on your hinderlands on thae cushions. It's you and your muckle cawrs that wreck my roads! If we a' had oor richts, ye sud be made to mend what ye break.'

The bright-eyed man was looking at the newspaper lying beside Turnbull's bundle.

'I see you get your papers in good time,' he said.

I glanced at it casually. 'Aye, in gude time. Seein' that that paper cam' out last Setterday I'm just Sax days late.'

He picked it up, glanced at the superscription, and laid it down again. One of the others had been looking at my boots, and a word in German called the speaker's attention to them.

'You've a fine taste in boots,' he said. 'These were never made by a country shoemaker.'

'They were not,' I said readily. 'They were made in London. I got them frae the gentleman that was here last year for the shootin'. What was his name now?' And I scratched a forgetful head. Again the sleek one spoke in German. 'Let us get on,' he said. 'This fellow is all right.'

They asked one last question.

'Did you see anyone pass early this morning? He might be on a bicycle or he might be on foot.'

I very nearly fell into the trap and told a story of a bicyclist hurrying past in the grey dawn. But I had the sense to see my danger. I pretended to consider very deeply.

'I wasna up very early,' I said. 'Ye see, my dochter was merrit last nicht, and we keepit it up late. I opened the house door about seeven and there was naebody on the road then. Since I cam' up here there has just been the baker and the Ruchill herd, besides you gentlemen.'

One of them gave me a cigar, which I smelt gingerly and stuck in Turnbull's bundle. They got into their car and were out of sight in three minutes.

My heart leaped with an enormous relief, but I went on wheeling my stones. It was as well, for ten minutes later the car returned, one of the occupants waving a hand to me. Those gentry left nothing to chance.

I finished Turnbull's bread and cheese, and pretty soon I had finished the stones. The next step was what puzzled me. I could not keep up this roadmaking business for long. A merciful Providence had kept Mr Turnbull indoors, but if he appeared on the scene there would be trouble. I had a notion that the cordon was still tight round the glen, and that if I walked in any direction I should meet with questioners. But get out I must. No man's nerve could stand more than a day of being spied on.

I stayed at my post till five o'clock. By that time I had resolved to go down to Turnbull's cottage at nightfall and take my chance of getting over the hills in the darkness. But suddenly a new car came up the road, and slowed down a yard or two from me. A fresh wind had risen, and the occupant wanted to light a cigarette. It was a touring car, with the tonneau full of an assortment of baggage. One man sat in it, and by an amazing chance I knew him. His name was Marmaduke Jopley, and he was an offence to creation. He was a sort of blood stockbroker, who did his business by toadying eldest sons and rich young peers and foolish old ladies. 'Marmie' was a familiar figure, I understood, at balls and polo-weeks and country houses. He was an adroit scandal-monger, and would crawl a mile on his belly to anything that had a title or a million. I had a business introduction to his firm when I came to London, and he was good enough to ask me to dinner at his club. There he showed off at a great rate, and pattered about his duchesses till the snobbery of the creature turned me sick. I asked a man afterwards why nobody kicked him, and was told that Englishmen reverenced the weaker sex.

Anyhow there he was now, nattily dressed, in a fine new car, obviously on his way to visit some of his smart friends. A sudden daftness took me, and in a second I had jumped into the tonneau and had him by the shoulder.

'Hullo, Jopley,' I sang out. 'Well met, my lad!' He got a horrid fright. His chin dropped as he stared at me. 'Who the devil are YOU?' he gasped.

'My name's Hannay,' I said. 'From Rhodesia, you remember.'

'Good God, the murderer!' he choked.

'Just so. And there'll be a second murder, my dear, if you don't do as I tell you. Give me that coat of yours. That cap, too.'

He did as bid, for he was blind with terror. Over my dirty trousers and vulgar shirt I put on his smart driving-coat, which buttoned high at the top and thereby hid the deficiencies of my collar. I stuck the cap on my head, and added his gloves to my get-up. The dusty roadman in a minute was transformed into one of the neatest motorists in Scotland. On Mr Jopley's head I clapped Turnbull's unspeakable hat, and told him to keep it there.

Then with some difficulty I turned the car. My plan was to go back the road he had come, for the watchers, having seen it before, would probably let it pass unremarked, and Marmie's figure was in no way like mine.

'Now, my child,' I said, 'sit quite still and be a good boy. I mean you no harm. I'm only borrowing your car for an hour or two. But if you play me any tricks, and above all if you open your mouth, as sure as there's a God above me I'll wring your neck. SAVEZ?'

I enjoyed that evening's ride. We ran eight miles down the valley, through a village or two, and I could not help noticing several strange-looking folk lounging by the roadside. These were the watchers who would have had much to say to me if I had come in other garb or company. As it was, they looked incuriously on. One touched his cap in salute, and I responded graciously.

As the dark fell I turned up a side glen which, as I remember from the map, led into an unfrequented corner of the hills. Soon the villages were left behind, then the farms, and then even the wayside cottage. Presently we came to a lonely moor where the night was blackening the sunset gleam in the bog pools. Here we stopped, and I obligingly reversed the car and restored to Mr Jopley his belongings.

'A thousand thanks,' I said. 'There's more use in you than I thought. Now be off and find the police.'

As I sat on the hillside, watching the tail-light dwindle, I reflected on the various kinds of crime I had now sampled. Contrary to general belief, I was not a murderer, but I had become an unholy liar, a shameless impostor, and a highwayman with a marked taste for expensive motor-cars.

CHAPTER SIX

The Adventure of the Bald Archaeologist

I spent the night on a shelf of the hillside, in the lee of a boulder where the heather grew long and soft. It was a cold business, for I had neither coat nor waistcoat. These were in Mr Turnbull's keeping, as was Scudder's little book, my watch and—worst of all—my pipe and tobacco pouch. Only my money accompanied me in my belt, and about half a pound of ginger biscuits in my trousers pocket.

I supped off half those biscuits, and by worming myself deep into the heather got some kind of warmth. My spirits had risen, and I was beginning to enjoy this crazy game of hide-and-seek. So far I had been miraculously lucky. The milkman, the literary innkeeper, Sir Harry, the roadman, and the idiotic Marmie, were all pieces of undeserved good fortune. Somehow the first success gave me a feeling that I was going to pull the thing through.

My chief trouble was that I was desperately hungry. When a Jew shoots himself in the City and there is an inquest, the newspapers usually report that the deceased was 'well-nourished'. I remember thinking that they would not call me well-nourished if I broke my neck in a bog-hole. I lay and tortured myself—for the ginger biscuits merely emphasized the aching void—with the memory of all the good food I had thought so little of in

London. There were Paddock's crisp sausages and fragrant shavings of bacon, and shapely poached eggs—how often I had turned up my nose at them! There were the cutlets they did at the club, and a particular ham that stood on the cold table, for which my soul lusted. My thoughts hovered over all varieties of mortal edible, and finally settled on a porterhouse steak and a quart of bitter with a welsh rabbit to follow. In longing hopelessly for these dainties I fell asleep.

I woke very cold and stiff about an hour after dawn. It took me a little while to remember where I was, for I had been very weary and had slept heavily. I saw first the pale blue sky through a net of heather, then a big shoulder of hill, and then my own boots placed neatly in a blaeberry bush. I raised myself on my arms and looked down into the valley, and that one look set me lacing up my boots in mad haste.

For there were men below, not more than a quarter of a mile off, spaced out on the hillside like a fan, and beating the heather. Marmie had not been slow in looking for his revenge.

I crawled out of my shelf into the cover of a boulder, and from it gained a shallow trench which slanted up the mountain face. This led me presently into the narrow gully of a burn, by way of which I scrambled to the top of the ridge. From there I looked back, and saw that I was still undiscovered. My pursuers were patiently quartering the hillside and moving upwards.

Keeping behind the skyline I ran for maybe half a mile, till I judged I was above the uppermost end of the glen. Then I showed myself, and was instantly noted by one of the flankers, who passed the word to the others. I heard cries coming up from below, and saw that the line of search had changed its direction. I pretended to retreat over the skyline, but instead went back the way I had come, and in twenty minutes was behind the ridge overlooking my sleeping place. From that viewpoint I had the satisfaction of seeing the pursuit streaming up the hill at the top of the glen on a hopelessly false scent.

I had before me a choice of routes, and I chose a ridge which made an angle with the one I was on, and so would soon put a deep glen between me and my enemies. The exercise had warmed my blood, and I was beginning to enjoy myself amazingly. As I went I breakfasted on the dusty remnants of the ginger biscuits.

I knew very little about the country, and I hadn't a notion what I was going to do. I trusted to the strength of my legs, but I was well aware that those behind me would be familiar with the lie of the land, and that my ignorance would be a heavy handicap. I saw in front of me a sea of hills, rising very high towards the south, but northwards breaking down into broad ridges which separated wide and shallow dales. The ridge I had chosen seemed to sink after a mile or two to a moor which lay like a pocket in the uplands. That seemed as good a direction to take as any other.

My stratagem had given me a fair start—call it twenty minutes—and I had the width of a glen behind me before I saw the first heads of the pursuers. The police had evidently called in local talent to their aid, and the men I could see had the appearance of herds or gamekeepers. They hallooed at the sight of me, and I waved my hand. Two dived into the glen and began to climb my ridge, while the others kept their own side of the hill. I felt as if I were taking part in a schoolboy game of hare and hounds.

But very soon it began to seem less of a game. Those fellows behind were hefty men on their native heath. Looking back I saw that only three were following direct, and I guessed that the others had fetched a circuit to cut me off. My lack of local knowledge might very well be my undoing, and I resolved to get out of this tangle of glens to the pocket of moor I had seen from the tops. I must so increase my distance as to get clear away from them, and I believed I could do this if I could find the right ground for it. If there had been cover I would have tried a bit of stalking, but on these bare slopes you could see a fly a mile off. My hope must be in the length of my legs and the soundness of my wind, but I needed easier ground for that, for I was not bred a mountaineer. How I longed for a good Afrikander pony!

I put on a great spurt and got off my ridge and down into the moor before any figures appeared on the skyline behind me. I crossed a burn, and came out on a highroad which made a pass between two glens. All in front of me was a big field of heather sloping up to a crest which was crowned with an odd feather of trees. In the dyke by the roadside was a gate, from which a grass-grown track led over the first wave of the moor.

I jumped the dyke and followed it, and after a few hundred yards—as soon as it was out of sight of the highway—the grass stopped and it became a very respectable road, which was evidently kept with some care. Clearly it ran to a house, and I began to think of doing the same. Hitherto my luck had held, and it might be that my best chance would be found in this remote dwelling. Anyhow there were trees there, and that meant cover.

I did not follow the road, but the burnside which flanked it on the right, where the bracken grew deep and the high banks made a tolerable screen. It was well I did so, for no sooner had I gained the hollow than, looking back, I saw the pursuit topping the ridge from which I had descended.

After that I did not look back; I had no time. I ran up the burnside, crawling over the open places, and for a large part wading in the shallow stream. I found a deserted cottage with a row of phantom peat-stacks and an overgrown garden. Then I was among young hay, and very soon had come to the edge of a plantation of wind-blown firs. From there I saw the chimneys of the house smoking a few hundred yards to my left. I forsook the burnside, crossed another dyke, and almost before I knew was on a rough lawn. A glance back told me that I was well out of sight of the pursuit, which had not yet passed the first lift of the moor.

The lawn was a very rough place, cut with a scythe instead of a mower, and planted with beds of scrubby rhododendrons. A brace of black-game, which are not usually garden birds, rose at my approach. The house before me was the ordinary moorland farm, with a more pretentious whitewashed wing added. Attached to this wing was a glass veranda, and through the glass I saw the face of an elderly gentleman meekly watching me.

I stalked over the border of coarse hill gravel and entered the open veranda door. Within was a pleasant room, glass on one side, and on the other a mass of books. More books showed in an inner room. On the floor, instead of tables, stood cases such as you see in a museum, filled with coins and queer stone implements.

There was a knee-hole desk in the middle, and seated at it, with some papers and open volumes before him, was the benevolent old gentleman. His face was round and shiny, like Mr Pickwick's, big glasses were stuck on the end of his nose, and the top of his head was as bright and bare as a glass bottle. He never moved when I entered, but raised his placid eyebrows and waited on me to speak.

It was not an easy job, with about five minutes to spare, to tell a stranger who I was and what I wanted, and to win his aid. I did not attempt it. There was something about the eye of the man before me, something so keen and knowledgeable, that I could not find a word. I simply stared at him and stuttered.

'You seem in a hurry, my friend,'he said slowly.

I nodded towards the window. It gave a prospect across the moor through a gap in the plantation, and revealed certain figures half a mile off straggling through the heather.

'Ah, I see,' he said, and took up a pair of field-glasses through which he patiently scrutinized the figures.

'A fugitive from justice, eh? Well, we'll go into the matter at our leisure. Meantime I object to my privacy being broken in upon by the clumsy rural policeman. Go into my study, and you will see two doors facing you. Take the one on the left and close it behind you. You will be perfectly safe.'

And this extraordinary man took up his pen again.

I did as I was bid, and found myself in a little dark chamber which smelt of chemicals, and was lit only by a tiny window high up in the wall. The door had swung behind me with a click like the door of a safe. Once again I had found an unexpected sanctuary.

All the same I was not comfortable. There was something about the old gentleman which puzzled and rather terrified me. He had been too easy and ready, almost as if he had expected me. And his eyes had been horribly intelligent.

No sound came to me in that dark place. For all I knew the police might be searching the house, and if they did they would want to know what was behind this door. I tried to possess my soul in patience, and to forget how hungry I was.

Then I took a more cheerful view. The old gentleman could scarcely refuse me a meal, and I fell to reconstructing my breakfast. Bacon and eggs would content me, but I wanted the better part of a flitch of bacon and half a hundred eggs. And then, while my mouth was watering in anticipation, there was a click and the door stood open.

I emerged into the sunlight to find the master of the house sitting in a deep armchair in the room he called his study, and regarding me with curious eyes.

'Have they gone?' I asked.

'They have gone. I convinced them that you had crossed the hill. I do not choose that the police should come between me and one whom I am delighted to honour. This is a lucky morning for you, Mr Richard Hannay.'

As he spoke his eyelids seemed to tremble and to fall a little over his keen grey eyes. In a flash the phrase of Scudder's came back to me, when he had described the man he most dreaded in the world. He had said that he 'could hood his eyes like a hawk'. Then I saw that I had walked straight into the enemy's headquarters.

My first impulse was to throttle the old ruffian and make for the open air. He seemed to anticipate my intention, for he smiled gently, and nodded to the door behind me.

I turned, and saw two men-servants who had me covered with pistols.

He knew my name, but he had never seen me before. And as the reflection darted across my mind I saw a slender chance.

'I don't know what you mean,' I said roughly. 'And who are you calling Richard Hannay? My name's Ainslie.'

'So?' he said, still smiling. 'But of course you have others. We won't quarrel about a name.'

I was pulling myself together now, and I reflected that my garb, lacking coat and waistcoat and collar, would at any rate not betray me. I put on my surliest face and shrugged my shoulders.

'I suppose you're going to give me up after all, and I call it a damned dirty trick. My God, I wish I had never seen that cursed motor-car! Here's the money and be damned to you,' and I flung four sovereigns on the table.

He opened his eyes a little. 'Oh no, I shall not give you up. My friends and I will have a little private settlement with you, that is all. You know a little too much, Mr Hannay. You are a clever actor, but not quite clever enough.'

He spoke with assurance, but I could see the dawning of a doubt in his mind.

'Oh, for God's sake stop jawing,' I cried. 'Everything's against me. I haven't had a bit of luck since I came on shore at Leith. What's the harm in a poor devil with an empty stomach picking up some money he finds in a bust-up motor-car? That's all I done, and for that I've been chivvied for two days by those blasted bobbies over those blasted hills. I tell you I'm fair sick of it. You can do what you like, old boy! Ned Ainslie's got no fight left in him.'

I could see that the doubt was gaining.

'Will you oblige me with the story of your recent doings?'he asked. 'I can't, guv'nor,' I said in a real beggar's whine. 'I've not had a bite to eat for two days. Give me a mouthful of food, and then you'll hear God's truth.'

I must have showed my hunger in my face, for he signalled to one of the men in the doorway. A bit of cold pie was brought and a glass of beer, and I wolfed them down like a pig—or rather, like Ned Ainslie, for I was keeping up my character. In the middle of my meal he spoke suddenly to me in German, but I turned on him a face as blank as a stone wall.

Then I told him my story—how I had come off an Archangel ship at Leith a week ago, and was making my way overland to my brother at Wigtown. I had run short of cash—I hinted vaguely at a spree—and I was pretty well on my uppers when I had come on a hole in a hedge, and, looking through, had seen a big motor-car lying in the burn. I had poked about to see what had happened, and had found three sovereigns lying on the seat and one on the floor. There was nobody there or any sign of an owner, so I had pocketed the cash. But somehow the law had got after me. When I had tried to change a sovereign in a baker's shop, the woman had cried on the police, and a little later, when I was washing my face in a burn, I had been nearly gripped, and had only got away by leaving my coat and waistcoat behind me.

'They can have the money back,' I cried, 'for a fat lot of good it's done me. Those perishers are all down on a poor man. Now, if it had been you, guv'nor, that had found the quids, nobody would have troubled you.'

'You're a good liar, Hannay,' he said.

I flew into a rage. 'Stop fooling, damn you! I tell you my name's Ainslie, and I never heard of anyone called Hannay in my born days. I'd sooner have the police than you with your Hannays and your monkey-faced pistol tricks ... No, guv'nor, I beg pardon, I don't mean that. I'm much obliged to you for the grub, and I'll thank you to let me go now the coast's clear.'

It was obvious that he was badly puzzled. You see he had never seen me, and my appearance must have altered considerably from my photographs, if he had got one of them. I was pretty smart and well dressed in London, and now I was a regular tramp.

'I do not propose to let you go. If you are what you say you are, you will soon have a chance of clearing yourself. If you are what I believe you are, I do not think you will see the light much longer.'

He rang a bell, and a third servant appeared from the veranda.

'I want the Lanchester in five minutes,' he said. 'There will be three to luncheon.'

Then he looked steadily at me, and that was the hardest ordeal of all.

There was something weird and devilish in those eyes, cold, malignant, unearthly, and most hellishly clever. They fascinated me like the bright eyes of a snake.

I had a strong impulse to throw myself on his mercy and offer to join his side, and if you consider the way I felt about the whole thing you will see that that impulse must have been purely physical, the weakness of a brain mesmerized and mastered by a stronger spirit. But I managed to stick it out and even to grin.

'You'll know me next time, guv'nor,' I said.

'Karl,' he spoke in German to one of the men in the doorway, 'you will put this fellow in the storeroom till I return, and you will be answerable to me for his keeping.'

I was marched out of the room with a pistol at each ear.

The storeroom was a damp chamber in what had been the old farmhouse. There was no carpet on the uneven floor, and nothing to sit down on but a school form. It was black as pitch, for the windows were heavily shuttered. I made out by groping that the walls were lined with boxes and barrels and sacks of some heavy stuff. The whole place smelt of mould and disuse. My gaolers turned the key in the door, and I could hear them shifting their feet as they stood on guard outside.

I sat down in that chilly darkness in a very miserable frame of mind. The old boy had gone off in a motor to collect the two ruffians who had interviewed me yesterday. Now, they had seen me as the roadman, and they would remember me, for I was in the same rig. What was a roadman doing twenty miles from his beat, pursued by the police? A question or two would put them on the track. Probably they had seen Mr Turnbull, probably Marmie too; most likely they could link me up with Sir Harry, and then the whole thing would be crystal clear. What chance had I in this moorland house with three desperadoes and their armed servants?

I began to think wistfully of the police, now plodding over the hills after my wraith. They at any rate were fellow-countrymen and honest men, and their tender mercies would be kinder than these ghoulish aliens. But they wouldn't have listened to me. That old devil with the eyelids had not taken long to get rid of them. I thought he probably had some kind of graft with the constabulary. Most likely he had letters from Cabinet Ministers saying he was to be given every facility for plotting against Britain. That's the sort of owlish way we run our politics in the Old Country.

The three would be back for lunch, so I hadn't more than a couple of hours to wait. It was simply waiting on destruction, for I could see no way out of this mess. I wished that I had Scudder's courage, for I am free to confess I didn't feel any great fortitude. The only thing that kept me going was that I was pretty furious. It made me boil with rage to think of those three spies getting the pull on me like this. I hoped that at any rate I might be able to twist one of their necks before they downed me.

The more I thought of it the angrier I grew, and I had to get up and move about the room. I tried the shutters, but they were the kind that lock with a key, and I couldn't move them. From the outside came the faint clucking of hens in the warm sun. Then I groped among the sacks and boxes. I couldn't open the latter, and the sacks seemed to be full of things like dog-biscuits that smelt of cinnamon. But, as I circumnavigated the room, I found a handle in the wall which seemed worth investigating.

It was the door of a wall cupboard—what they call a 'press' in Scotland—and it was locked. I shook it, and it seemed rather flimsy. For want of something better to do I put out my strength on that door, getting some purchase on the handle by looping my braces round it. Presently the thing gave with a crash which I thought would bring in my warders to inquire. I waited for a bit, and then started to explore the cupboard shelves.

There was a multitude of queer things there. I found an odd vesta or two in my trouser pockets and struck a light. It was out in a second, but it showed me one thing. There was a little stock of electric torches on one shelf. I picked up one, and found it was in working order.

With the torch to help me I investigated further. There were bottles and cases of queer-smelling stuffs, chemicals no doubt for experiments, and there were coils of fine copper wire and yanks and yanks of thin oiled silk. There was a box of detonators, and a lot of cord for fuses. Then away at the back of the shelf I found a stout brown cardboard box, and inside it a wooden case. I managed to wrench it open, and within lay half a dozen little grey bricks, each a couple of inches square.

I took up one, and found that it crumbled easily in my hand. Then I smelt it and put my tongue to it. After that I sat down to think. I hadn't been a mining engineer for nothing, and I knew lentonite when I saw it.

With one of these bricks I could blow the house to smithereens. I had used the stuff in Rhodesia and knew its power. But the trouble was that my knowledge wasn't exact. I had forgotten the proper charge and the right way of preparing it, and I wasn't sure about the timing. I had only a vague notion, too, as to its power, for though I had used it I had not handled it with my own fingers.

But it was a chance, the only possible chance. It was a mighty risk, but against it was an absolute black certainty. If I used it the odds were, as I reckoned, about five to one in favour of my blowing myself into the tree-tops; but if I didn't I should very likely be occupying a six-foot hole in the garden by the evening. That was the way I had to look at it. The prospect was pretty dark either way, but anyhow there was a chance, both for myself and for my country.

The remembrance of little Scudder decided me. It was about the beastliest moment of my life, for I'm no good at these cold-blooded resolutions. Still I managed to rake up the pluck to set my teeth and choke back the horrid doubts that flooded in on me. I simply shut off my mind and pretended I was doing an experiment as simple as Guy Fawkes fireworks.

I got a detonator, and fixed it to a couple of feet of fuse. Then I took a quarter of a lentonite brick, and buried it near the door below one of the sacks in a crack of the floor, fixing the detonator in it. For all I knew half those boxes might be dynamite. If the cupboard held such deadly explosives, why not the boxes? In that case there would be a glorious skyward journey for me and the German servants and about an acre of surrounding country. There was also the risk that the detonation might set off the other bricks in the cupboard, for I had forgotten most that I knew about lentonite. But it didn't do to begin thinking about the possibilities. The odds were horrible, but I had to take them.

I ensconced myself just below the sill of the window, and lit the fuse. Then I waited for a moment or two. There was dead silence—only a shuffle of heavy boots in the passage, and the peaceful cluck of hens from the warm out-of-doors. I commended my soul to my Maker, and wondered where I would be in five seconds ...

A great wave of heat seemed to surge upwards from the floor, and hang for a blistering instant in the air. Then the wall opposite me flashed into a golden yellow and dissolved with a rending thunder that hammered my brain into a pulp. Something dropped on me, catching the point of my left shoulder.

And then I think I became unconscious.

My stupor can scarcely have lasted beyond a few seconds. I felt myself being choked by thick yellow fumes, and struggled out of the debris to my feet. Somewhere behind me I felt fresh air. The jambs of the window had fallen, and through the ragged rent the smoke was pouring out to the summer noon. I stepped over the broken lintel, and found myself standing in a yard in a dense and acrid fog. I felt very sick and ill, but I could move my limbs, and I staggered blindly forward away from the house.

A small mill-lade ran in a wooden aqueduct at the other side of the yard, and into this I fell. The cool water revived me, and I had just enough wits left to think of escape. I squirmed up the lade among the slippery green slime till I reached the mill-wheel. Then I wriggled through the axle hole into the old mill and tumbled on to a bed of chaff. A nail caught the seat of my trousers, and I left a wisp of heather-mixture behind me.

The mill had been long out of use. The ladders were rotten with age, and in the loft the rats had gnawed great holes in the floor. Nausea shook me, and a wheel in my head kept turning, while my left shoulder and arm seemed to be stricken with the palsy. I looked out of the window and saw a fog still hanging over the house and smoke escaping from an upper window. Please God I had set the place on fire, for I could hear confused cries coming from the other side.

But I had no time to linger, since this mill was obviously a bad hiding-place. Anyone looking for me would naturally follow the lade, and I made certain the search would begin as soon as they found that my body was not in the storeroom. From another window I saw that on the far side of the mill stood an old stone dovecot. If I could get there without leaving tracks I might find a hiding-place, for I argued that my enemies, if they thought I could move, would conclude I had made for open country, and would go seeking me on the moor.

I crawled down the broken ladder, scattering chaff behind me to cover my footsteps. I did the same on the mill floor, and on the threshold where the door hung on broken hinges. Peeping out, I saw that between me and the dovecot was a piece of bare cobbled ground, where no footmarks would show. Also it was mercifully hid by the mill buildings from any view from the house. I slipped across the space, got to the back of the dovecot and prospected a way of ascent.

That was one of the hardest jobs I ever took on. My shoulder and arm ached like hell, and I was so sick and giddy that I was always on the verge of falling. But I managed it somehow. By the use of out-jutting stones and gaps in the masonry and a tough ivy root I got to the top in the end. There was a little parapet behind which I found space to lie down. Then I proceeded to go off into an old-fashioned swoon.

I woke with a burning head and the sun glaring in my face. For a long time I lay motionless, for those horrible fumes seemed to have loosened my joints and dulled my brain. Sounds came to me from the house—men speaking throatily and the throbbing of a stationary car. There was a little gap in the parapet to which I wriggled, and from which I had some sort of prospect of the yard. I saw figures come out—a servant with his head bound up, and then a younger man in knickerbockers. They were looking for something, and moved towards the mill. Then one of them caught sight of the wisp of cloth on the nail, and cried out to the other. They both went back to the house, and brought two more to look at it. I saw the rotund figure of my late captor, and I thought I made out the man with the lisp. I noticed that all had pistols.

For half an hour they ransacked the mill. I could hear them kicking over the barrels and pulling up the rotten planking. Then they came outside, and stood just below the dovecot arguing fiercely. The servant with the bandage was being soundly rated. I heard them fiddling with the door of the dovecote and for one horrid moment I fancied they were coming up. Then they thought better of it, and went back to the house.

All that long blistering afternoon I lay baking on the rooftop. Thirst was my chief torment. My tongue was like a stick, and to make it worse I could hear the cool drip of water from the mill-lade. I watched the course of the little stream as it came in from the moor, and my fancy followed it to the top of the glen, where it must issue from an icy fountain fringed with cool ferns and mosses. I would have given a thousand pounds to plunge my face into that.

I had a fine prospect of the whole ring of moorland. I saw the car speed away with two occupants, and a man on a hill pony riding east. I judged they were looking for me, and I wished them joy of their quest.

But I saw something else more interesting. The house stood almost on the summit of a swell of moorland which crowned a sort of plateau, and there was no higher point nearer than the big hills six miles off. The actual summit, as I have mentioned, was a biggish clump of trees—firs mostly, with a few ashes and beeches. On the dovecot I was almost on a level with the tree-tops, and could see what lay beyond. The wood was not solid, but only a ring, and inside was an oval of green turf, for all the world like a big cricket-field.

I didn't take long to guess what it was. It was an aerodrome, and a secret one. The place had been most cunningly chosen. For suppose anyone were watching an aeroplane descending here, he would think it had gone over the hill beyond the trees. As the place was on the top of a rise in the midst of a big amphitheatre, any observer from any direction would conclude it had passed out of view behind the hill. Only a man very close at hand would realize that the aeroplane had not gone over but had descended in the midst of the wood. An observer with a telescope on one of the higher hills might have discovered the truth, but only herds went there, and herds do not carry spy-glasses. When I looked from the dovecot I could see far away a blue line which I knew was the sea, and I grew furious to think that our enemies had this secret conning-tower to rake our waterways.

Then I reflected that if that aeroplane came back the chances were ten to one that I would be discovered. So through the afternoon I lay and prayed for the coming of darkness, and glad I was when the sun went down over the big western hills and the twilight haze crept over the moor. The aeroplane was late. The gloaming was far advanced when I heard the beat of wings and saw it volplaning downward to its home in the wood. Lights twinkled for a bit and there was much coming and going from the house. Then the dark fell, and silence.

Thank God it was a black night. The moon was well on its last quarter and would not rise till late. My thirst was too great to allow me to tarry, so about nine o'clock, so far as I could judge, I started to descend. It wasn't easy, and half-way down I heard the back door of the house open, and saw the gleam of a lantern against the mill wall. For some agonizing minutes I hung by the ivy and prayed that whoever it was would not come round by the dovecot. Then the light disappeared, and I dropped as softly as I could on to the hard soil of the yard.

I crawled on my belly in the lee of a stone dyke till I reached the fringe of trees which surrounded the house. If I had known how to do it I would have tried to put that aeroplane out of action, but I realized that any attempt would probably be futile. I was pretty certain that there would be some kind of defence round the house, so I went through the wood on hands and knees, feeling carefully every inch before me. It was as well, for presently I came on a wire about two feet from the ground. If I had tripped over that, it would doubtless have rung some bell in the house and I would have been captured.

A hundred yards farther on I found another wire cunningly placed on the edge of a small stream. Beyond that lay the moor, and in five minutes I was deep in bracken and heather. Soon I was round the shoulder of the rise, in the little glen from which the mill-lade flowed. Ten minutes later my face was in the spring, and I was soaking down pints of the blessed water.

But I did not stop till I had put half a dozen miles between me and that accursed dwelling.

CHAPTER SEVEN

The Dry-Fly Fisherman

I sat down on a hill-top and took stock of my position. I wasn't feeling very happy, for my natural thankfulness at my escape was clouded by my severe bodily discomfort. Those lentonite fumes had fairly poisoned me, and the baking hours on the dovecot hadn't helped matters. I had a crushing headache, and felt as sick as a cat. Also my shoulder was in a bad way. At first I thought it was only a bruise, but it seemed to be swelling, and I had no use of my left arm.

My plan was to seek Mr Turnbull's cottage, recover my garments, and especially Scudder's note-book, and then make for the main line and get back to the south. It seemed to me that the sooner I got in touch with the Foreign Office man, Sir Walter Bullivant, the better. I didn't see how I could get more proof than I had got already. He must just take or leave my story, and anyway, with him I would be in better hands than those devilish Germans. I had begun to feel quite kindly towards the British police.

It was a wonderful starry night, and I had not much difficulty about the road. Sir Harry's map had given me the lie of the land, and all I had to do was to steer a point or two west of south-west to come to the stream where I had met the roadman. In all these travels I never knew the names of the places, but I believe this stream was no less than the upper waters of the river Tweed. I calculated I must be about eighteen miles distant, and that meant I could not get there before morning. So I must lie up a day somewhere, for I was too outrageous a figure to be seen in the sunlight. I had neither coat, waistcoat, collar, nor hat, my trousers were badly torn, and my face and hands were black with the explosion. I daresay I had other beauties, for my eyes felt as if they were furiously bloodshot. Altogether I was no spectacle for God-fearing citizens to see on a highroad.

Very soon after daybreak I made an attempt to clean myself in a hill burn, and then approached a herd's cottage, for I was feeling the need of food. The herd was away from home, and his wife was alone, with no neighbour for five miles. She was a decent old body, and a plucky one, for though she got a fright when she saw me, she had an axe handy, and would have used it on any evil-doer. I told her that I had had a fall—I didn't say how—and she saw by my looks that I was pretty sick. Like a true Samaritan she asked no questions, but gave me a bowl of milk with a dash of whisky in it, and let me sit for a little by her kitchen fire. She would have bathed my shoulder, but it ached so badly that I would not let her touch it.

I don't know what she took me for—a repentant burglar, perhaps; for when I wanted to pay her for the milk and tendered a sovereign which was the smallest coin I had, she shook her head and said something about 'giving it to them that had a right to it'. At this I protested so strongly that I think she believed me honest, for she took the money and gave me a warm new plaid for it, and an old hat of her man's. She showed me how to wrap the plaid around my shoulders, and when I left that cottage I was the living image of the kind of Scotsman you see in the illustrations to Burns's poems. But at any rate I was more or less clad.

It was as well, for the weather changed before midday to a thick drizzle of rain. I found shelter below an overhanging rock in the crook of a burn, where a drift of dead brackens made a tolerable bed. There I managed to sleep till nightfall, waking very cramped and wretched, with my shoulder gnawing like a toothache. I ate the oatcake and cheese the old wife had given me and set out again just before the darkening.

I pass over the miseries of that night among the wet hills. There were no stars to steer by, and I had to do the best I could from my memory of the map. Twice I lost my way, and I had some nasty falls into peat-bogs. I had only about ten miles to go as the crow flies, but my mistakes made it nearer twenty. The last bit was completed with set teeth and a very light and dizzy head. But I managed it, and in the early dawn I was knocking at Mr Turnbull's door. The mist lay close and thick, and from the cottage I could not see the highroad.

Mr Turnbull himself opened to me—sober and something more than sober. He was primly dressed in an ancient but well-tended suit of black; he had been shaved not later than the night before; he wore a linen collar; and in his left hand he carried a pocket Bible. At first he did not recognize me.

'Whae are ye that comes stravaigin' here on the Sabbath mornin'?' he asked.

I had lost all count of the days. So the Sabbath was the reason for this strange decorum.

My head was swimming so wildly that I could not frame a coherent answer. But he recognized me, and he saw that I was ill.

'Hae ye got my specs?' he asked.

I fetched them out of my trouser pocket and gave him them.

'Ye'll hae come for your jaicket and westcoat,' he said. 'Come in-bye. Losh, man, ye're terrible dune i' the legs. Haud up till I get ye to a chair.'

I perceived I was in for a bout of malaria. I had a good deal of fever in my bones, and the wet night had brought it out, while my shoulder and the effects of the fumes combined to make me feel pretty bad. Before I knew, Mr Turnbull was helping me off with my clothes, and putting me to bed in one of the two cupboards that lined the kitchen walls.

He was a true friend in need, that old roadman. His wife was dead years ago, and since his daughter's marriage he lived alone.

For the better part of ten days he did all the rough nursing I needed. I simply wanted to be left in peace while the fever took its course, and when my skin was cool again I found that the bout had more or less cured my shoulder. But it was a baddish go, and though I was out of bed in five days, it took me some time to get my legs again.

He went out each morning, leaving me milk for the day, and locking the door behind him; and came in in the evening to sit silent in the chimney corner. Not a soul came near the place. When I was getting better, he never bothered me with a question. Several times he fetched me a two days' old SCOTSMAN, and I noticed that the interest in the Portland Place murder seemed to have died down. There was no mention of it, and I could find very little about anything except a thing called the General Assembly—some ecclesiastical spree, I gathered.

One day he produced my belt from a lockfast drawer. 'There's a terrible heap o' siller in't,' he said. 'Ye'd better coont it to see it's a' there.'

He never even sought my name. I asked him if anybody had been around making inquiries subsequent to my spell at the road-making.

'Ay, there was a man in a motor-cawr. He speired whae had ta'en my place that day, and I let on I thocht him daft. But he keepit on at me, and syne I said he maun be thinkin' o' my gude-brither frae the Cleuch that whiles lent me a haun'. He was a wersh-lookin' sowl, and I couldna understand the half o' his English tongue.'

I was getting restless those last days, and as soon as I felt myself fit I decided to be off. That was not till the twelfth day of June, and as luck would have it a drover went past that morning taking some cattle to Moffat. He was a man named Hislop, a friend of Turnbull's, and he came in to his breakfast with us and offered to take me with him.

I made Turnbull accept five pounds for my lodging, and a hard job I had of it. There never was a more independent being. He grew positively rude when I pressed him, and shy and red, and took the money at last without a thank you. When I told him how much I owed him, he grunted something about 'ae guid turn deservin' anither'. You would have thought from our leave-taking that we had parted in disgust.

Hislop was a cheery soul, who chattered all the way over the pass and down the sunny vale of Annan. I talked of Galloway markets and sheep prices, and he made up his mind I was a 'pack-shepherd' from those parts—whatever that may be. My plaid and my old hat, as I have said, gave me a fine theatrical Scots look. But driving cattle is a mortally slow job, and we took the better part of the day to cover a dozen miles.

If I had not had such an anxious heart I would have enjoyed that time. It was shining blue weather, with a constantly changing prospect of brown hills and far green meadows, and a continual sound of larks and curlews and falling streams. But I had no mind for the summer, and little for Hislop's conversation, for as the fateful fifteenth of June drew near I was overweighed with the hopeless difficulties of my enterprise.

I got some dinner in a humble Moffat public-house, and walked the two miles to the junction on the main line. The night express for the south was not due till near midnight, and to fill up the time I went up on the hillside and fell asleep, for the walk had tired me. I all but slept too long, and had to run to the station and catch the train with two minutes to spare. The feel of the hard third-class cushions and the smell of stale tobacco cheered me up wonderfully. At any rate, I felt now that I was getting to grips with my job.

I was decanted at Crewe in the small hours and had to wait till six to get a train for Birmingham. In the afternoon I got to Reading, and changed into a local train which journeyed into the deeps of Berkshire. Presently I was in a land of lush water-meadows and slow reedy streams. About eight o'clock in the evening, a weary and travel-stained being—a cross between a farm-labourer and a vet—with a checked black-and-white plaid over his arm (for I did not dare to wear it south of the Border), descended at the little station of Artinswell. There were several people on the platform, and I thought I had better wait to ask my way till I was clear of the place.

The road led through a wood of great beeches and then into a shallow valley, with the green backs of downs peeping over the distant trees. After Scotland the air smelt heavy and flat, but infinitely sweet, for the limes and chestnuts and lilac bushes were domes of blossom. Presently I came to a bridge, below which a clear slow stream flowed between snowy beds of water-buttercups. A little above it was a mill; and the lasher made a pleasant cool sound in the scented dusk. Somehow the place soothed me and put me at my ease. I fell to whistling as I looked into the green depths, and the tune which came to my lips was 'Annie Laurie'.

A fisherman came up from the waterside, and as he neared me he too began to whistle. The tune was infectious, for he followed my suit. He was a huge man in untidy old flannels and a wide-brimmed hat, with a canvas bag slung on his shoulder. He nodded to me, and I thought I had never seen a shrewder or better-tempered face. He leaned his delicate ten-foot split-cane rod against the bridge, and looked with me at the water.

'Clear, isn't it?' he said pleasantly. 'I back our Kenner any day against the Test. Look at that big fellow. Four pounds if he's an ounce. But the evening rise is over and you can't tempt 'em.'

'I don't see him,' said I.

'Look! There! A yard from the reeds just above that stickle.'

'I've got him now. You might swear he was a black stone.'

'So,' he said, and whistled another bar of 'Annie Laurie'.

'Twisdon's the name, isn't it?' he said over his shoulder, his eyes still fixed on the stream.

'No,' I said. 'I mean to say, Yes.' I had forgotten all about my alias.

'It's a wise conspirator that knows his own name,' he observed, grinning broadly at a moor-hen that emerged from the bridge's shadow.

I stood up and looked at him, at the square, cleft jaw and broad, lined brow and the firm folds of cheek, and began to think that here at last was an ally worth having. His whimsical blue eyes seemed to go very deep.

Suddenly he frowned. 'I call it disgraceful,' he said, raising his voice. 'Disgraceful that an able-bodied man like you should dare to beg. You can get a meal from my kitchen, but you'll get no money from me.'

A dog-cart was passing, driven by a young man who raised his whip to salute the fisherman. When he had gone, he picked up his rod.

'That's my house,' he said, pointing to a white gate a hundred yards on. 'Wait five minutes and then go round to the back door.' And with that he left me.

I did as I was bidden. I found a pretty cottage with a lawn running down to the stream, and a perfect jungle of guelder-rose and lilac flanking the path. The back door stood open, and a grave butler was awaiting me.

'Come this way, Sir,' he said, and he led me along a passage and up a back staircase to a pleasant bedroom looking towards the river. There I found a complete outfit laid out for me—dress clothes with all the fixings, a brown flannel suit, shirts, collars, ties, shaving things and hair-brushes, even a pair of patent shoes. 'Sir Walter thought as how Mr Reggie's things would fit you, Sir,' said the butler. 'He keeps some clothes 'ere, for he comes regular on the week-ends. There's a bathroom next door, and I've prepared a 'ot bath. Dinner in 'alf an hour, Sir. You'll 'ear the gong.'

The grave being withdrew, and I sat down in a chintz-covered easy-chair and gaped. It was like a pantomime, to come suddenly out of beggardom into this orderly comfort. Obviously Sir Walter believed in me, though why he did I could not guess. I looked at myself in the mirror and saw a wild, haggard brown fellow, with a fortnight's ragged beard, and dust in ears and eyes, collarless, vulgarly shirted, with shapeless old tweed clothes and boots that had not been cleaned for the better part of a month. I made a fine tramp and a fair drover; and here I was ushered by a prim butler into this temple of gracious ease. And the best of it was that they did not even know my name.

I resolved not to puzzle my head but to take the gifts the gods had provided. I shaved and bathed luxuriously, and got into the dress clothes and clean crackling shirt, which fitted me not so badly. By the time I had finished the looking-glass showed a not unpersonable young man.

Sir Walter awaited me in a dusky dining-room where a little round table was lit with silver candles. The sight of him—so respectable and established and secure, the embodiment of law and government and all the conventions—took me aback and made me feel an interloper. He couldn't know the truth about me, or he wouldn't treat me like this. I simply could not accept his hospitality on false pretences.

'I'm more obliged to you than I can say, but I'm bound to make things clear,' I said. 'I'm an innocent man, but I'm wanted by the police. I've got to tell you this, and I won't be surprised if you kick me out.'

He smiled. 'That's all right. Don't let that interfere with your appetite. We can talk about these things after dinner.' I never ate a meal with greater relish, for I had had nothing all day but railway sandwiches. Sir Walter did me proud, for we drank a good champagne and had some uncommon fine port afterwards. It made me almost hysterical to be sitting there, waited on by a footman and a sleek butler, and remember that I had been living for three weeks like a brigand, with every man's hand against me. I told Sir Walter about tiger-fish in the Zambesi that bite off your fingers if you give them a chance, and we discussed sport up and down the globe, for he had hunted a bit in his day.

We went to his study for coffee, a jolly room full of books and trophies and untidiness and comfort. I made up my mind that if ever I got rid of this business and had a house of my own, I would create just such a room. Then when the coffee-cups were cleared away, and we had got our cigars alight, my host swung his long legs over the side of his chair and bade me get started with my yarn.

'I've obeyed Harry's instructions,' he said, 'and the bribe he offered me was that you would tell me something to wake me up. I'm ready, Mr Hannay.'

I noticed with a start that he called me by my proper name.

I began at the very beginning. I told of my boredom in London, and the night I had come back to find Scudder gibbering on my doorstep. I told him all Scudder had told me about Karolides and the Foreign Office conference, and that made him purse his lips and grin.

Then I got to the murder, and he grew solemn again. He heard all about the milkman and my time in Galloway, and my deciphering Scudder's notes at the inn.

'You've got them here?' he asked sharply, and drew a long breath when I whipped the little book from my pocket.

I said nothing of the contents. Then I described my meeting with Sir Harry, and the speeches at the hall. At that he laughed uproariously.

'Harry talked dashed nonsense, did he? I quite believe it. He's as good a chap as ever breathed, but his idiot of an uncle has stuffed his head with maggots. Go on, Mr Hannay.'

My day as roadman excited him a bit. He made me describe the two fellows in the car very closely, and seemed to be raking back in his memory. He grew merry again when he heard of the fate of that ass Jopley.

But the old man in the moorland house solemnized him. Again I had to describe every detail of his appearance.

'Bland and bald-headed and hooded his eyes like a bird ... He sounds a sinister wild-fowl! And you dynamited his hermitage, after he had saved you from the police. Spirited piece of work, that!' Presently I reached the end of my wanderings. He got up slowly, and looked down at me from the hearth-rug.

'You may dismiss the police from your mind,' he said. 'You're in no danger from the law of this land.'

'Great Scot!' I cried. 'Have they got the murderer?'

'No. But for the last fortnight they have dropped you from the list of possibles.'

'Why?' I asked in amazement.

'Principally because I received a letter from Scudder. I knew something of the man, and he did several jobs for me. He was half crank, half genius, but he was wholly honest. The trouble about him was his partiality for playing a lone hand. That made him pretty well useless in any Secret Service—a pity, for he had uncommon gifts. I think he was the bravest man in the world, for he was always shivering with fright, and yet nothing would choke him off. I had a letter from him on the 31st of May.'

'But he had been dead a week by then.'

'The letter was written and posted on the 23rd. He evidently did not anticipate an immediate decease. His communications usually took a week to reach me, for they were sent under cover to Spain and then to Newcastle. He had a mania, you know, for concealing his tracks.'

'What did he say?' I stammered.

'Nothing. Merely that he was in danger, but had found shelter with a good friend, and that I would hear from him before the 15th of June. He gave me no address, but said he was living near Portland Place. I think his object was to clear you if anything happened. When I got it I went to Scotland Yard, went over the details of the inquest, and concluded that you were the friend. We made inquiries about you, Mr Hannay, and found you were respectable. I thought I knew the motives for your disappearance—not only the police, the other one too—and when I got Harry's scrawl I guessed at the rest. I have been expecting you any time this past week.' You can imagine what a load this took off my mind. I felt a free man once more, for I was now up against my country's enemies only, and not my country's law.

'Now let us have the little note-book,' said Sir Walter.

It took us a good hour to work through it. I explained the cypher, and he was jolly quick at picking it up. He emended my reading of it on several points, but I had been fairly correct, on the whole. His face was very grave before he had finished, and he sat silent for a while.

'I don't know what to make of it,' he said at last. 'He is right about one thing—what is going to happen the day after tomorrow. How the devil can it have got known? That is ugly enough in itself. But all this about war and the Black Stone—it reads like some wild melodrama. If only I had more confidence in Scudder's judgement. The trouble about him was that he was too romantic. He had the artistic temperament, and wanted a story to be better than God meant it to be. He had a lot of odd biases, too. Jews, for example, made him see red. Jews and the high finance.

'The Black Stone,' he repeated. 'DER SCHWARZE STEIN. It's like a penny novelette. And all this stuff about Karolides. That is the weak part of the tale, for I happen to know that the virtuous Karolides is likely to outlast us both. There is no State in Europe that wants him gone. Besides, he has just been playing up to Berlin and Vienna and giving my Chief some uneasy moments. No! Scudder has gone off the track there. Frankly, Hannay, I don't believe that part of his story. There's some nasty business afoot, and he found out too much and lost his life over it. But I am ready to take my oath that it is ordinary spy work. A certain great European Power makes a hobby of her spy system, and her methods are not too particular. Since she pays by piecework her blackguards are not likely to stick at a murder or two. They want our naval dispositions for their collection at the Marineamt; but they will be pigeon-holed—nothing more.'

Just then the butler entered the room.

'There's a trunk-call from London, Sir Walter. It's Mr 'Eath, and he wants to speak to you personally.'

My host went off to the telephone.

He returned in five minutes with a whitish face. 'I apologize to the shade of Scudder,' he said. 'Karolides was shot dead this evening at a few minutes after seven.'

CHAPTER EIGHT

The Coming of the Black Stone

I came down to breakfast next morning, after eight hours of blessed dreamless sleep, to find Sir Walter decoding a telegram in the midst of muffins and marmalade. His fresh rosiness of yesterday seemed a thought tarnished.

'I had a busy hour on the telephone after you went to bed,' he said. 'I got my Chief to speak to the First Lord and the Secretary for War, and they are bringing Royer over a day sooner. This wire clinches it. He will be in London at five. Odd that the code word for a SOUS-CHEF D/ETAT MAJOR-GENERAL should be "Porker".'

He directed me to the hot dishes and went on.

'Not that I think it will do much good. If your friends were clever enough to find out the first arrangement they are clever enough to discover the change. I would give my head to know where the leak is. We believed there were only five men in England who knew about Royer's visit, and you may be certain there were fewer in France, for they manage these things better there.'

While I ate he continued to talk, making me to my surprise a present of his full confidence.

'Can the dispositions not be changed?' I asked.

'They could,' he said. 'But we want to avoid that if possible. They are the result of immense thought, and no alteration would be as good. Besides, on one or two points change is simply impossible. Still, something could be done, I suppose, if it were absolutely necessary. But you see the difficulty, Hannay. Our enemies are not going to be such fools as to pick Royer's pocket or any childish game like that. They know that would mean a row and put us on our guard. Their aim is to get the details without any one of us knowing, so that Royer will go back to Paris in the belief that the whole business is still deadly secret. If they can't do that they fail, for, once we suspect, they know that the whole thing must be altered.'

'Then we must stick by the Frenchman's side till he is home again,' I said. 'If they thought they could get the information in Paris they would try there. It means that they have some deep scheme on foot in London which they reckon is going to win out.'

'Royer dines with my Chief, and then comes to my house where four people will see him—Whittaker from the Admiralty, myself, Sir Arthur Drew, and General Winstanley. The First Lord is ill, and has gone to Sheringham. At my house he will get a certain document from Whittaker, and after that he will be motored to Portsmouth where a destroyer will take him to Havre. His journey is too important for the ordinary boat-train.

He will never be left unattended for a moment till he is safe on French soil. The same with Whittaker till he meets Royer. That is the best we can do, and it's hard to see how there can be any miscarriage. But I don't mind admitting that I'm horribly nervous. This murder of Karolides will play the deuce in the chancelleries of Europe.'

After breakfast he asked me if I could drive a car. 'Well, you'll be my chauffeur today and wear Hudson's rig. You're about his size. You have a hand in this business and we are taking no risks. There are desperate men against us, who will not respect the country retreat of an overworked official.'

When I first came to London I had bought a car and amused myself with running about the south of England, so I knew something of the geography. I took Sir Walter to town by the Bath Road and made good going. It was a soft breathless June morning, with a promise of sultriness later, but it was delicious enough swinging through the little towns with their freshly watered streets, and past the summer gardens of the Thames valley. I landed Sir Walter at his house in Queen Anne's Gate punctually by half-past eleven. The butler was coming up by train with the luggage.

The first thing he did was to take me round to Scotland Yard. There we saw a prim gentleman, with a clean-shaven, lawyer's face.

'I've brought you the Portland Place murderer,' was Sir Walter's introduction.

The reply was a wry smile. 'It would have been a welcome present, Bullivant. This, I presume, is Mr Richard Hannay, who for some days greatly interested my department.'

'Mr Hannay will interest it again. He has much to tell you, but not today. For certain grave reasons his tale must wait for four hours. Then, I can promise you, you will be entertained and possibly edified. I want you to assure Mr Hannay that he will suffer no further inconvenience.'

This assurance was promptly given. 'You can take up your life where you left off,' I was told. 'Your flat, which probably you no longer wish to occupy, is waiting for you, and your man is still there. As you were never publicly accused, we considered that there was no need of a public exculpation. But on that, of course, you must please yourself.'

'We may want your assistance later on, MacGillivray,' Sir Walter said as we left.

Then he turned me loose.

'Come and see me tomorrow, Hannay. I needn't tell you to keep deadly quiet. If I were you I would go to bed, for you must have considerable arrears of sleep to overtake. You had better lie low, for if one of your Black Stone friends saw you there might be trouble.'

I felt curiously at a loose end. At first it was very pleasant to be a free man, able to go where I wanted without fearing anything. I had only been a month under the ban of the law, and it was quite enough for me. I went to the Savoy and ordered very carefully a very good luncheon, and then smoked the best cigar the house could provide. But I was still feeling nervous. When I saw anybody look at me in the lounge, I grew shy, and wondered if they were thinking about the murder.

After that I took a taxi and drove miles away up into North London. I walked back through fields and lines of villas and terraces and then slums and mean streets, and it took me pretty nearly two hours. All the while my restlessness was growing worse. I felt that great things, tremendous things, were happening or about to happen, and I, who was the cog-wheel of the whole business, was out of it. Royer would be landing at Dover, Sir Walter would be making plans with the few people in England who were in the secret, and somewhere in the darkness the Black Stone would be working. I felt the sense of danger and impending calamity, and I had the curious feeling, too, that I alone could avert it, alone could grapple with it. But I was out of the game now. How could it be otherwise? It was not likely that Cabinet Ministers and Admiralty Lords and Generals would admit me to their councils.

I actually began to wish that I could run up against one of my three enemies. That would lead to developments. I felt that I wanted enormously to have a vulgar scrap with those gentry, where I could hit out and flatten something. I was rapidly getting into a very bad temper.

I didn't feel like going back to my flat. That had to be faced some time, but as I still had sufficient money I thought I would put it off till next morning, and go to a hotel for the night.

My irritation lasted through dinner, which I had at a restaurant in Jermyn Street. I was no longer hungry, and let several courses pass untasted. I drank the best part of a bottle of Burgundy, but it did nothing to cheer me. An abominable restlessness had taken possession of me. Here was I, a very ordinary fellow, with no particular brains, and yet I was convinced that somehow I was needed to help this business through—that without me it would all go to blazes. I told myself it was sheer silly conceit, that four or five of the cleverest people living, with all the might of the British Empire at their back, had the job in hand. Yet I couldn't be convinced. It seemed as if a voice kept speaking in my ear, telling me to be up and doing, or I would never sleep again.

The upshot was that about half-past nine I made up my mind to go to Queen Anne's Gate. Very likely I would not be admitted, but it would ease my conscience to try.

I walked down Jermyn Street, and at the corner of Duke Street passed a group of young men. They were in evening dress, had been dining somewhere, and were going on to a music-hall. One of them was Mr Marmaduke Jopley.

He saw me and stopped short.

'By God, the murderer!' he cried. 'Here, you fellows, hold him! That's Hannay, the man who did the Portland Place murder!' He gripped me by the arm, and the others crowded round. I wasn't looking for any trouble, but my ill-temper made me play the fool. A policeman came up, and I should have told him the truth, and, if he didn't believe it, demanded to be taken to Scotland Yard, or for that matter to the nearest police station. But a delay at that moment seemed to me unendurable, and the sight of Marmie's imbecile face was more than I could bear. I let out with my left, and had the satisfaction of seeing him measure his length in the gutter.

Then began an unholy row. They were all on me at once, and the policeman took me in the rear. I got in one or two good blows, for I think, with fair play, I could have licked the lot of them, but the policeman pinned me behind, and one of them got his fingers on my throat.

Through a black cloud of rage I heard the officer of the law asking what was the matter, and Marmie, between his broken teeth, declaring that I was Hannay the murderer.

'Oh, damn it all,' I cried, 'make the fellow shut up. I advise you to leave me alone, constable. Scotland Yard knows all about me, and you'll get a proper wigging if you interfere with me.'

'You've got to come along of me, young man,' said the policeman. 'I saw you strike that gentleman crool 'ard. You began it too, for he wasn't doing nothing. I seen you. Best go quietly or I'll have to fix you up.'

Exasperation and an overwhelming sense that at no cost must I delay gave me the strength of a bull elephant. I fairly wrenched the constable off his feet, floored the man who was gripping my collar, and set off at my best pace down Duke Street. I heard a whistle being blown, and the rush of men behind me.

I have a very fair turn of speed, and that night I had wings. In a jiffy I was in Pall Mall and had turned down towards St James's Park. I dodged the policeman at the Palace gates, dived through a press of carriages at the entrance to the Mall, and was making for the bridge before my pursuers had crossed the roadway. In the open ways of the Park I put on a spurt. Happily there were few people about and no one tried to stop me. I was staking all on getting to Queen Anne's Gate.

When I entered that quiet thoroughfare it seemed deserted. Sir Walter's house was in the narrow part, and outside it three or four motor-cars were drawn up. I slackened speed some yards off and walked briskly up to the door. If the butler refused me admission, or if he even delayed to open the door, I was done.

He didn't delay. I had scarcely rung before the door opened.

'I must see Sir Walter,' I panted. 'My business is desperately important.'

That butler was a great man. Without moving a muscle he held the door open, and then shut it behind me. 'Sir Walter is engaged, Sir, and I have orders to admit no one. Perhaps you will wait.'

The house was of the old-fashioned kind, with a wide hall and rooms on both sides of it. At the far end was an alcove with a telephone and a couple of chairs, and there the butler offered me a seat.

'See here,' I whispered. 'There's trouble about and I'm in it. But Sir Walter knows, and I'm working for him. If anyone comes and asks if I am here, tell him a lie.'

He nodded, and presently there was a noise of voices in the street, and a furious ringing at the bell. I never admired a man more than that butler. He opened the door, and with a face like a graven image waited to be questioned. Then he gave them it. He told them whose house it was, and what his orders were, and simply froze them off the doorstep. I could see it all from my alcove, and it was better than any play.

I hadn't waited long till there came another ring at the bell. The butler made no bones about admitting this new visitor.

While he was taking off his coat I saw who it was. You couldn't open a newspaper or a magazine without seeing that face—the grey beard cut like a spade, the firm fighting mouth, the blunt square nose, and the keen blue eyes. I recognized the First Sea Lord, the man, they say, that made the new British Navy.

He passed my alcove and was ushered into a room at the back of the hall. As the door opened I could hear the sound of low voices. It shut, and I was left alone again.

For twenty minutes I sat there, wondering what I was to do next. I was still perfectly convinced that I was wanted, but when or how I had no notion. I kept looking at my watch, and as the time crept on to half-past ten I began to think that the conference must soon end. In a quarter of an hour Royer should be speeding along the road to Portsmouth ...

Then I heard a bell ring, and the butler appeared. The door of the back room opened, and the First Sea

Lord came out. He walked past me, and in passing he glanced in my direction, and for a second we looked each other in the face.

Only for a second, but it was enough to make my heart jump. I had never seen the great man before, and he had never seen me. But in that fraction of time something sprang into his eyes, and that something was recognition. You can't mistake it. It is a flicker, a spark of light, a minute shade of difference which means one thing and one thing only. It came involuntarily, for in a moment it died, and he passed on. In a maze of wild fancies I heard the street door close behind him.

I picked up the telephone book and looked up the number of his house. We were connected at once, and I heard a servant's voice.

'Is his Lordship at home?' I asked.

'His Lordship returned half an hour ago,' said the voice, 'and has gone to bed. He is not very well tonight. Will you leave a message, Sir?'

I rang off and almost tumbled into a chair. My part in this business was not yet ended. It had been a close shave, but I had been in time.

Not a moment could be lost, so I marched boldly to the door of that back room and entered without knocking.

Five surprised faces looked up from a round table. There was Sir Walter, and Drew the War Minister, whom I knew from his photographs. There was a slim elderly man, who was probably Whittaker, the Admiralty official, and there was General Winstanley, conspicuous from the long scar on his forehead. Lastly, there was a short stout man with an iron-grey moustache and bushy eyebrows, who had been arrested in the middle of a sentence.

Sir Walter's face showed surprise and annoyance.

'This is Mr Hannay, of whom I have spoken to you,' he said apologetically to the company. 'I'm afraid, Hannay, this visit is ill-timed.'

I was getting back my coolness. 'That remains to be seen, Sir,' I said; 'but I think it may be in the nick of time. For God's sake, gentlemen, tell me who went out a minute ago?'

'Lord Alloa,' Sir Walter said, reddening with anger. 'It was not,' I cried; 'it was his living image, but it was not Lord Alloa. It was someone who recognized me, someone I have seen in the last month. He had scarcely left the doorstep when I rang up Lord Alloa's house and was told he had come in half an hour before and had gone to bed.'

'Who—who—' someone stammered.

'The Black Stone,' I cried, and I sat down in the chair so recently vacated and looked round at five badly scared gentlemen.

CHAPTER NINE

The Thirty-Nine Steps

'Nonsense!' said the official from the Admiralty.

Sir Walter got up and left the room while we looked blankly at the table. He came back in ten minutes with a long face. 'I have spoken to Alloa,' he said. 'Had him out of bed—very grumpy. He went straight home after Mulross's dinner.'

'But it's madness,' broke in General Winstanley. 'Do you mean to tell me that that man came here and sat beside me for the best part of half an hour and that I didn't detect the imposture? Alloa must be out of his mind.'

'Don't you see the cleverness of it?' I said. 'You were too interested in other things to have any eyes. You took Lord Alloa for granted. If it had been anybody else you might have looked more closely, but it was natural for him to be here, and that put you all to sleep.'

Then the Frenchman spoke, very slowly and in good English.

'The young man is right. His psychology is good. Our enemies have not been foolish!'

He bent his wise brows on the assembly.

'I will tell you a tale,' he said. 'It happened many years ago in Senegal. I was quartered in a remote station, and to pass the time used to go fishing for big barbel in the river. A little Arab mare used to carry my luncheon basket—one of the salted dun breed you got at Timbuctoo in the old days. Well, one morning I had good sport, and the mare was unaccountably restless. I could hear her whinnying and squealing and stamping her feet, and I kept soothing her with my voice while my mind was intent on fish. I could see her all the time, as I thought, out of a corner of my eye, tethered to a tree twenty yards away. After a couple of hours I began to think of food. I collected my fish in a tarpaulin bag, and moved down the stream towards the mare, trolling my line. When I got up to her I flung the tarpaulin on her back—'

He paused and looked round.

'It was the smell that gave me warning. I turned my head and found myself looking at a lion three feet off ... An old man-eater, that was the terror of the village ... What was left of the mare, a mass of blood and bones and hide, was behind him.'

'What happened?' I asked. I was enough of a hunter to know a true yarn when I heard it.

'I stuffed my fishing-rod into his jaws, and I had a pistol. Also my servants came presently with rifles. But he left his mark on me.' He held up a hand which lacked three fingers.

'Consider,' he said. 'The mare had been dead more than an hour, and the brute had been patiently watching me ever since. I never saw the kill, for I was accustomed to the mare's fretting, and I never marked her absence, for my consciousness of her was only of something tawny, and the lion filled that part. If I could blunder thus, gentlemen, in a land where men's senses are keen, why should we busy preoccupied urban folk not err also?'

Sir Walter nodded. No one was ready to gainsay him.

'But I don't see,' went on Winstanley. 'Their object was to get these dispositions without our knowing it. Now it only required one of us to mention to Alloa our meeting tonight for the whole fraud to be exposed.'

Sir Walter laughed dryly. 'The selection of Alloa shows their acumen. Which of us was likely to speak to him about tonight? Or was he likely to open the subject?'

I remembered the First Sea Lord's reputation for taciturnity and shortness of temper.

'The one thing that puzzles me,' said the General, 'is what good his visit here would do that spy fellow? He could not carry away several pages of figures and strange names in his head.'

'That is not difficult,' the Frenchman replied. 'A good spy is trained to have a photographic memory. Like your own Macaulay. You noticed he said nothing, but went through these papers again and again. I think we may assume that he has every detail stamped on his mind. When I was younger I could do the same trick.'

'Well, I suppose there is nothing for it but to change the plans,' said Sir Walter ruefully.

Whittaker was looking very glum. 'Did you tell Lord Alloa what has happened?' he asked. 'No? Well, I can't speak with absolute assurance, but I'm nearly certain we can't make any serious change unless we alter the geography of England.'

'Another thing must be said,' it was Royer who spoke. 'I talked freely when that man was here. I told something of the military plans of my Government. I was permitted to say so much. But that information would be worth many millions to our enemies. No, my friends, I see no other way. The man who came here and his confederates must be taken, and taken at once.'

'Good God,' I cried, 'and we have not a rag of a clue.'

'Besides,' said Whittaker, 'there is the post. By this time the news will be on its way.'

'No,' said the Frenchman. 'You do not understand the habits of the spy. He receives personally his reward, and he delivers personally his intelligence. We in France know something of the breed. There is still a chance, MES AMIS. These men must cross the sea, and there are ships to be searched and ports to be watched. Believe me, the need is desperate for both France and Britain.'

Royer's grave good sense seemed to pull us together. He was the man of action among fumblers. But I saw no hope in any face, and I felt none. Where among the fifty millions of these islands and within a dozen hours were we to lay hands on the three cleverest rogues in Europe?

Then suddenly I had an inspiration.

'Where is Scudder's book?' I cried to Sir Walter. 'Quick, man, I remember something in it.'

He unlocked the door of a bureau and gave it to me.

I found the place. THIRTY-NINE STEPS, I read, and again, THIRTY-NINE STEPS—I COUNTED THEM—HIGH TIDE 10.17 P.M.

The Admiralty man was looking at me as if he thought I had gone mad.

'Don't you see it's a clue,' I shouted. 'Scudder knew where these fellows laired—he knew where they were going to leave the country, though he kept the name to himself. Tomorrow was the day, and it was some place where high tide was at 10.17.'

'They may have gone tonight,' someone said.

'Not they. They have their own snug secret way, and they won't be hurried. I know Germans, and they are mad about working to a plan. Where the devil can I get a book of Tide Tables?'

Whittaker brightened up. 'It's a chance,' he said. 'Let's go over to the Admiralty.'

We got into two of the waiting motor-cars—all but Sir Walter, who went off to Scotland Yard—to 'mobilize MacGillivray', so he said. We marched through empty corridors and big bare chambers where the charwomen were busy, till we reached a little room lined with books and maps. A resident clerk was unearthed, who presently fetched from the library the Admiralty Tide Tables. I sat at the desk and the others stood round, for somehow or other I had got charge of this expedition.

It was no good. There were hundreds of entries, and so far as I could see 10.17 might cover fifty places. We had to find some way of narrowing the possibilities.

I took my head in my hands and thought. There must be some way of reading this riddle. What did Scudder mean by steps? I thought of dock steps, but if he had meant that I didn't think he would have mentioned the number. It must be some place where there were several staircases, and one marked out from the others by having thirty-nine steps.

Then I had a sudden thought, and hunted up all the steamer sailings. There was no boat which left for the Continent at 10.17 p.m.

Why was high tide so important? If it was a harbour it must be some little place where the tide mattered, or else it was a heavy-draught boat. But there was no regular steamer sailing at that hour, and somehow I didn't think they would travel by a big boat from a regular harbour. So it must be some little harbour where the tide was important, or perhaps no harbour at all.

But if it was a little port I couldn't see what the steps signified. There were no sets of staircases on any harbour that I had ever seen. It must be some place which a particular staircase identified, and where the tide was full at 10.17. On the whole it seemed to me that the place must be a bit of open coast. But the staircases kept puzzling me.

Then I went back to wider considerations. Whereabouts would a man be likely to leave for Germany, a man in a hurry, who wanted a speedy and a secret passage? Not from any of the big harbours. And not from the Channel or the West Coast or Scotland, for, remember, he was starting from London. I measured the distance on the map, and tried to put myself in the enemy's shoes. I should try for Ostend or Antwerp or Rotterdam, and I should sail from somewhere on the East Coast between Cromer and Dover.

All this was very loose guessing, and I don't pretend it was ingenious or scientific. I wasn't any kind of Sherlock Holmes. But I have always fancied I had a kind of instinct about questions like this. I don't know if I can explain myself, but I used to use my brains as far as they went, and after they came to a blank wall I guessed, and I usually found my guesses pretty right.

So I set out all my conclusions on a bit of Admiralty paper. They ran like this:

FAIRLY CERTAIN

(1) Place where there are several sets of stairs; one that matters distinguished by having thirty-nine steps.

(2) Full tide at 10.17 p.m. Leaving shore only possible at full tide.

(3) Steps not dock steps, and so place probably not harbour.

(4) No regular night steamer at 10.17. Means of transport must be tramp (unlikely), yacht, or fishing-boat.

There my reasoning stopped. I made another list, which I headed 'Guessed', but I was just as sure of the one as the other.

GUESSED

(1) Place not harbour but open coast.

(2) Boat small—trawler, yacht, or launch.

(3) Place somewhere on East Coast between Cromer and Dover.

It struck me as odd that I should be sitting at that desk with a Cabinet Minister, a Field-Marshal, two high Government officials, and a French General watching me, while from the scribble of a dead man I was trying to drag a secret which meant life or death for us.

Sir Walter had joined us, and presently MacGillivray arrived. He had sent out instructions to watch the ports and railway stations for the three men whom I had described to Sir Walter. Not that he or anybody else thought that that would do much good.

'Here's the most I can make of it,' I said. 'We have got to find a place where there are several staircases down to the beach, one of which has thirty-nine steps. I think it's a piece of open coast with biggish cliffs, somewhere between the Wash and the Channel. Also it's a place where full tide is at 10.17 tomorrow night.'

Then an idea struck me. 'Is there no Inspector of Coastguards or some fellow like that who knows the East Coast?'

Whittaker said there was, and that he lived in Clapham. He went off in a car to fetch him, and the rest of us sat about the little room and talked of anything that came into our heads. I lit a pipe and went over the whole thing again till my brain grew weary.

About one in the morning the coastguard man arrived. He was a fine old fellow, with the look of a naval officer, and was desperately respectful to the company. I left the War Minister to cross-examine him, for I felt he would think it cheek in me to talk.

'We want you to tell us the places you know on the East Coast where there are cliffs, and where several sets of steps run down to the beach.'

He thought for a bit. 'What kind of steps do you mean, Sir? There are plenty of places with roads cut down through the cliffs, and most roads have a step or two in them. Or do you mean regular staircases—all steps, so to speak?'

Sir Arthur looked towards me. 'We mean regular staircases,' I said.

He reflected a minute or two. 'I don't know that I can think of any. Wait a second. There's a place in Norfolk—Brattlesham—beside a golf-course, where there are a couple of staircases, to let the gentlemen get a lost ball.'

'That's not it,' I said.

'Then there are plenty of Marine Parades, if that's what you mean. Every seaside resort has them.'

I shook my head. 'It's got to be more retired than that,' I said.

'Well, gentlemen, I can't think of anywhere else. Of course, there's the Ruff—'

'What's that?' I asked.

'The big chalk headland in Kent, close to Bradgate. It's got a lot of villas on the top, and some of the houses have staircases down to a private beach. It's a very high-toned sort of place, and the residents there like to keep by themselves.'

I tore open the Tide Tables and found Bradgate. High tide there was at 10.17 P.m. on the 15th of June.

'We're on the scent at last,' I cried excitedly. 'How can I find out what is the tide at the Ruff?'

'I can tell you that, Sir,' said the coastguard man. 'I once was lent a house there in this very month, and I used to go out at night to the deep-sea fishing. The tide's ten minutes before Bradgate.'

I closed the book and looked round at the company.

'If one of those staircases has thirty-nine steps we have solved the mystery, gentlemen,' I said. 'I want the loan of your car, Sir Walter, and a map of the roads. If Mr MacGillivray will spare me ten minutes, I think we can prepare something for tomorrow.'

It was ridiculous in me to take charge of the business like this, but they didn't seem to mind, and after all I had been in the show from the start. Besides, I was used to rough jobs, and these eminent gentlemen were too clever not to see it. It was General Royer who gave me my commission. 'I for one,' he said, 'am content to leave the matter in Mr Hannay's hands.'

By half-past three I was tearing past the moonlit hedgerows of Kent, with MacGillivray's best man on the seat beside me.

CHAPTER TEN

Various Parties Converging on the Sea

A pink and blue June morning found me at Bradgate looking from the Griffin Hotel over a smooth sea to the lightship on the Cock sands which seemed the size of a bell-buoy. A couple of miles farther south and much nearer the shore a small destroyer was anchored. Scaife, MacGillivray's man, who had been in the Navy, knew the boat, and told me her name and her commander's, so I sent off a wire to Sir Walter.

After breakfast Scaife got from a house-agent a key for the gates of the staircases on the Ruff. I walked with him along the sands, and sat down in a nook of the cliffs while he investigated the half-dozen of them. I didn't want to be seen, but the place at this hour was quite deserted, and all the time I was on that beach I saw nothing but the sea-gulls.

It took him more than an hour to do the job, and when I saw him coming towards me, conning a bit of paper, I can tell you my heart was in my mouth. Everything depended, you see, on my guess proving right.

He read aloud the number of steps in the different stairs. 'Thirty-four, thirty-five, thirty-nine, forty-two, forty-seven,' and 'twenty-one' where the cliffs grew lower. I almost got up and shouted.

We hurried back to the town and sent a wire to MacGillivray. I wanted half a dozen men, and I directed them to divide themselves among different specified hotels. Then Scaife set out to prospect the house at the head of the thirty-nine steps.

He came back with news that both puzzled and reassured me. The house was called Trafalgar Lodge, and belonged to an old gentleman called Appleton—a retired stockbroker, the house-agent said. Mr Appleton was there a good deal in the summer time, and was in residence now—had been for the better part of a week. Scaife could pick up very little information about him, except that he was a decent old fellow, who paid his bills regularly, and was always good for a fiver for a local charity. Then Scaife seemed to have penetrated to the back door of the house, pretending he was an agent for sewing-machines. Only three servants were kept, a cook, a parlour-maid, and a housemaid, and they were just the sort that you would find in a respectable middle-class household. The cook was not the gossiping kind, and had pretty soon shut the door in his face, but Scaife said he was positive she knew nothing. Next door there was a new house building which would give good cover for observation, and the villa on the other side was to let, and its garden was rough and shrubby.

I borrowed Scaife's telescope, and before lunch went for a walk along the Ruff. I kept well behind the rows of villas, and found a good observation point on the edge of the golf-course. There I had a view of the line of turf along the cliff top, with seats placed at intervals, and the little square plots, railed in and planted with bushes, whence the staircases descended to the beach. I saw Trafalgar Lodge very plainly, a red-brick villa with a veranda, a tennis lawn behind, and in front the ordinary seaside flower-garden full of marguerites and scraggy geraniums. There was a flagstaff from which an enormous Union Jack hung limply in the still air.

Presently I observed someone leave the house and saunter along the cliff. When I got my glasses on him I saw it was an old man, wearing white flannel trousers, a blue serge jacket, and a straw hat. He carried field-glasses and a newspaper, and sat down on one of the iron seats and began to read. Sometimes he would lay down the paper and turn his glasses on the sea. He looked for a long time at the destroyer. I watched him for half an hour, till he got up and went back to the house for his luncheon, when I returned to the hotel for mine.

I wasn't feeling very confident. This decent common-place dwelling was not what I had expected. The man might be the bald archaeologist of that horrible moorland farm, or he might not. He was exactly the kind of satisfied old bird you will find in every suburb and every holiday place. If you wanted a type of the perfectly harmless person you would probably pitch on that.

But after lunch, as I sat in the hotel porch, I perked up, for I saw the thing I had hoped for and had dreaded to miss. A yacht came up from the south and dropped anchor pretty well opposite the Ruff. She seemed about a hundred and fifty tons, and I saw she belonged to the Squadron from the white ensign. So Scaife and I went down to the harbour and hired a boatman for an afternoon's fishing.

I spent a warm and peaceful afternoon. We caught between us about twenty pounds of cod and lythe, and out in that dancing blue sea I took a cheerier view of things. Above the white cliffs of the Ruff I saw the green and red of the villas, and especially the great flagstaff of Trafalgar Lodge. About four o'clock, when we had fished enough, I made the boatman row us round the yacht, which lay like a delicate white bird, ready at a moment to flee. Scaife said she must be a fast boat for her build, and that she was pretty heavily engined.

Her name was the ARIADNE, as I discovered from the cap of one of the men who was polishing brasswork. I spoke to him, and got an answer in the soft dialect of Essex. Another hand that came along passed me the time of day in an unmistakable English tongue. Our boatman had an argument with one of them about the weather, and for a few minutes we lay on our oars close to the starboard bow.

Then the men suddenly disregarded us and bent their heads to their work as an officer came along the deck. He was a pleasant, clean-looking young fellow, and he put a question to us about our fishing in very good English. But there could be no doubt about him. His close-cropped head and the cut of his collar and tie never came out of England.

That did something to reassure me, but as we rowed back to Bradgate my obstinate doubts would not be dismissed. The thing that worried me was the reflection that my enemies knew that I had got my knowledge from Scudder, and it was Scudder who had given me the clue to this place. If they knew that Scudder had this clue, would they not be certain to change their plans? Too much depended on their success for them to take any risks. The whole question was how much they understood about Scudder's knowledge. I had talked confidently last night about Germans always sticking to a scheme, but if they had any suspicions that I was on their track they would be fools not to cover it. I wondered if the man last night had seen that I recognized him. Somehow I did not think he had, and to that I had clung. But the whole business had never seemed so difficult as that afternoon when by all calculations I should have been rejoicing in assured success.

In the hotel I met the commander of the destroyer, to whom Scaife introduced me, and with whom I had a few words. Then I thought I would put in an hour or two watching Trafalgar Lodge.

I found a place farther up the hill, in the garden of an empty house. From there I had a full view of the court, on which two figures were having a game of tennis. One was the old man, whom I had already seen;

the other was a younger fellow, wearing some club colours in the scarf round his middle. They played with tremendous zest, like two city gents who wanted hard exercise to open their pores. You couldn't conceive a more innocent spectacle. They shouted and laughed and stopped for drinks, when a maid brought out two tankards on a salver. I rubbed my eyes and asked myself if I was not the most immortal fool on earth. Mystery and darkness had hung about the men who hunted me over the Scotch moor in aeroplane and motor-car, and notably about that infernal antiquarian. It was easy enough to connect those folk with the knife that pinned Scudder to the floor, and with fell designs on the world's peace. But here were two guileless citizens taking their innocuous exercise, and soon about to go indoors to a humdrum dinner, where they would talk of market prices and the last cricket scores and the gossip of their native Surbiton. I had been making a net to catch vultures and falcons, and lo and behold! two plump thrushes had blundered into it.

Presently a third figure arrived, a young man on a bicycle, with a bag of golf-clubs slung on his back. He strolled round to the tennis lawn and was welcomed riotously by the players. Evidently they were chaffing him, and their chaff sounded horribly English. Then the plump man, mopping his brow with a silk handkerchief, announced that he must have a tub. I heard his very words—'I've got into a proper lather,' he said. 'This will bring down my weight and my handicap, Bob. I'll take you on tomorrow and give you a stroke a hole.' You couldn't find anything much more English than that.

They all went into the house, and left me feeling a precious idiot. I had been barking up the wrong tree this time. These men might be acting; but if they were, where was their audience? They didn't know I was sitting thirty yards off in a rhododendron. It was simply impossible to believe that these three hearty fellows were anything but what they seemed—three ordinary, game-playing, suburban Englishmen, wearisome, if you like, but sordidly innocent.

And yet there were three of them; and one was old, and one was plump, and one was lean and dark; and their house chimed in with Scudder's notes; and half a mile off was lying a steam yacht with at least one German officer. I thought of Karolides lying dead and all Europe trembling on the edge of earthquake, and the men I had left behind me in London who were waiting anxiously for the events of the next hours. There was no doubt that hell was afoot somewhere. The Black Stone had won, and if it survived this June night would bank its winnings.

There seemed only one thing to do—go forward as if I had no doubts, and if I was going to make a fool of myself to do it handsomely. Never in my life have I faced a job with greater disinclination. I would rather in my then mind have walked into a den of anarchists, each with his Browning handy, or faced a charging lion with a popgun, than enter that happy home of three cheerful Englishmen and tell them that their game was up. How they would laugh at me!

But suddenly I remembered a thing I once heard in Rhodesia from old Peter Pienaar. I have quoted Peter already in this narrative. He was the best scout I ever knew, and before he had turned respectable he had been pretty often on the windy side of the law, when he had been wanted badly by the authorities. Peter once discussed with me the question of disguises, and he had a theory which struck me at the time. He said, barring absolute certainties like fingerprints, mere physical traits were very little use for identification if the fugitive really knew his business. He laughed at things like dyed hair and false beards and such childish follies. The only thing that mattered was what Peter called 'atmosphere'.

If a man could get into perfectly different surroundings from those in which he had been first observed, and—this is the important part—really play up to these surroundings and behave as if he had never been out of them, he would puzzle the cleverest detectives on earth. And he used to tell a story of how he once borrowed a black coat and went to church and shared the same hymn-book with the man that was looking for him. If that man had seen him in decent company before he would have recognized him; but he had only seen him snuffing the lights in a public-house with a revolver.

The recollection of Peter's talk gave me the first real comfort that I had had that day. Peter had been a wise old bird, and these fellows I was after were about the pick of the aviary. What if they were playing Peter's game? A fool tries to look different: a clever man looks the same and is different.

Again, there was that other maxim of Peter's which had helped me when I had been a roadman. 'If you are playing a part, you will never keep it up unless you convince yourself that you are it.' That would explain the game of tennis. Those chaps didn't need to act, they just turned a handle and passed into another life, which came as naturally to them as the first. It sounds a platitude, but Peter used to say that it was the big secret of all the famous criminals.

It was now getting on for eight o'clock, and I went back and saw Scaife to give him his instructions. I arranged with him how to place his men, and then I went for a walk, for I didn't feel up to any dinner. I went round the deserted golf-course, and then to a point on the cliffs farther north beyond the line of the villas.

On the little trim newly-made roads I met people in flannels coming back from tennis and the beach, and a coastguard from the wireless station, and donkeys and pierrots padding homewards. Out at sea in the blue dusk I saw lights appear on the ARIADNE and on the destroyer away to the south, and beyond the Cock sands the bigger lights of steamers making for the Thames. The whole scene was so peaceful and ordinary that I got more dashed in spirits every second. It took all my resolution to stroll towards Trafalgar Lodge about half-past nine.

On the way I got a piece of solid comfort from the sight of a greyhound that was swinging along at a nursemaid's heels. He reminded me of a dog I used to have in Rhodesia, and of the time when I took him hunting with me in the Pali hills. We were after rhebok, the dun kind, and I recollected how we had followed one beast, and both he and I had clean lost it. A greyhound works by sight, and my eyes are good enough, but that buck simply leaked out of the landscape. Afterwards I found out how it managed it. Against the grey rock of the kopjes it showed no more than a crow against a thundercloud. It didn't need to run away; all it had to do was to stand still and melt into the background.

Suddenly as these memories chased across my brain I thought of my present case and applied the moral. The Black Stone didn't need to bolt. They were quietly absorbed into the landscape. I was on the right track, and I jammed that down in my mind and vowed never to forget it. The last word was with Peter Pienaar.

Scaife's men would be posted now, but there was no sign of a soul. The house stood as open as a market-place for anybody to observe. A three-foot railing separated it from the cliff road; the windows on the ground-floor were all open, and shaded lights and the low sound of voices revealed where the occupants were finishing dinner. Everything was as public and above-board as a charity bazaar. Feeling the greatest fool on earth, I opened the gate and rang the bell.

A man of my sort, who has travelled about the world in rough places, gets on perfectly well with two classes, what you may call the upper and the lower. He understands them and they understand him. I was at home with herds and tramps and roadmen, and I was sufficiently at my ease with people like Sir Walter and the men I had met the night before. I can't explain why, but it is a fact. But what fellows like me don't understand is the great comfortable, satisfied middle-class world, the folk that live in villas and suburbs. He doesn't know how they look at things, he doesn't understand their conventions, and he is as shy of them as of a black mamba. When a trim parlour-maid opened the door, I could hardly find my voice.

I asked for Mr Appleton, and was ushered in. My plan had been to walk straight into the dining-room, and by a sudden appearance wake in the men that start of recognition which would confirm my theory. But when I found myself in that neat hall the place mastered me. There were the golf-clubs and tennis-rackets, the straw hats and caps, the rows of gloves, the sheaf of walking-sticks, which you will find in ten thousand British homes. A stack of neatly folded coats and waterproofs covered the top of an old oak chest; there was a grandfather clock ticking; and some polished brass warming-pans on the walls, and a barometer, and a print of Chiltern winning the St Leger. The place was as orthodox as an Anglican church. When the maid asked me for my name I gave it automatically, and was shown into the smoking-room, on the right side of the hall.

That room was even worse. I hadn't time to examine it, but I could see some framed group photographs above the mantelpiece, and I could have sworn they were English public school or college. I had only one glance, for I managed to pull myself together and go after the maid. But I was too late. She had already entered the dining-room and given my name to her master, and I had missed the chance of seeing how the three took it.

When I walked into the room the old man at the head of the table had risen and turned round to meet me. He was in evening dress—a short coat and black tie, as was the other, whom I called in my own mind the plump one. The third, the dark fellow, wore a blue serge suit and a soft white collar, and the colours of some club or school.

The old man's manner was perfect. 'Mr Hannay?' he said hesitatingly. 'Did you wish to see me? One moment, you fellows, and I'll rejoin you. We had better go to the smoking-room.'

Though I hadn't an ounce of confidence in me, I forced myself to play the game. I pulled up a chair and sat down on it.

'I think we have met before,' I said, 'and I guess you know my business.'

The light in the room was dim, but so far as I could see their faces, they played the part of mystification very well.

'Maybe, maybe,' said the old man. 'I haven't a very good memory, but I'm afraid you must tell me your errand, Sir, for I really don't know it.'

'Well, then,' I said, and all the time I seemed to myself to be talking pure foolishness—'I have come to tell you that the game's up. I have a warrant for the arrest of you three gentlemen.'

'Arrest,' said the old man, and he looked really shocked. 'Arrest! Good God, what for?'

'For the murder of Franklin Scudder in London on the 23rd day of last month.'

'I never heard the name before,' said the old man in a dazed voice.

One of the others spoke up. 'That was the Portland Place murder. I read about it. Good heavens, you must be mad, Sir! Where do you come from?'

'Scotland Yard,' I said.

After that for a minute there was utter silence. The old man was staring at his plate and fumbling with a nut, the very model of innocent bewilderment.

Then the plump one spoke up. He stammered a little, like a man picking his words.

'Don't get flustered, uncle,' he said. 'It is all a ridiculous mistake; but these things happen sometimes, and we can easily set it right. It won't be hard to prove our innocence. I can show that I was out of the country on the 23rd of May, and Bob was in a nursing home. You were in London, but you can explain what you were doing.'

'Right, Percy! Of course that's easy enough. The 23rd! That was the day after Agatha's wedding. Let me see. What was I doing? I came up in the morning from Woking, and lunched at the club with Charlie Symons. Then—oh yes, I dined with the Fishmongers. I remember, for the punch didn't agree with me, and I was seedy next morning. Hang it all, there's the cigar-box I brought back from the dinner.' He pointed to an object on the table, and laughed nervously.

'I think, Sir,' said the young man, addressing me respectfully, 'you will see you are mistaken. We want to assist the law like all Englishmen, and we don't want Scotland Yard to be making fools of themselves. That's so, uncle?'

'Certainly, Bob.' The old fellow seemed to be recovering his voice. 'Certainly, we'll do anything in our power to assist the authorities. But—but this is a bit too much. I can't get over it.'

'How Nellie will chuckle,' said the plump man. 'She always said that you would die of boredom because nothing ever happened to you. And now you've got it thick and strong,' and he began to laugh very pleasantly.

'By Jove, yes. Just think of it! What a story to tell at the club. Really, Mr Hannay, I suppose I should be angry, to show my innocence, but it's too funny! I almost forgive you the fright you gave me! You looked so glum, I thought I might have been walking in my sleep and killing people.'

It couldn't be acting, it was too confoundedly genuine. My heart went into my boots, and my first impulse was to apologize and clear out. But I told myself I must see it through, even though I was to be the laughing-stock of Britain. The light from the dinner-table candlesticks was not very good, and to cover my confusion I got up, walked to the door and switched on the electric light. The sudden glare made them blink, and I stood scanning the three faces.

Well, I made nothing of it. One was old and bald, one was stout, one was dark and thin. There was nothing in their appearance to prevent them being the three who had hunted me in Scotland, but there was nothing to identify them. I simply can't explain why I who, as a roadman, had looked into two pairs of eyes, and as Ned Ainslie into another pair, why I, who have a good memory and reasonable powers of observation, could find no satisfaction. They seemed exactly what they professed to be, and I could not have sworn to one of them.

There in that pleasant dining-room, with etchings on the walls, and a picture of an old lady in a bib above the mantelpiece, I could see nothing to connect them with the moorland desperadoes. There was a silver cigarette-box beside me, and I saw that it had been won by Percival Appleton, Esq., of the St Bede's Club, in a golf tournament. I had to keep a firm hold of Peter Pienaar to prevent myself bolting out of that house.

'Well,' said the old man politely, 'are you reassured by your scrutiny, Sir?'

I couldn't find a word.

'I hope you'll find it consistent with your duty to drop this ridiculous business. I make no complaint, but you'll see how annoying it must be to respectable people.'

I shook my head.

'O Lord,' said the young man. 'This is a bit too thick!'

'Do you propose to march us off to the police station?' asked the plump one. 'That might be the best way out of it, but I suppose you won't be content with the local branch. I have the right to ask to see your warrant, but I don't wish to cast any aspersions upon you. You are only doing your duty. But you'll admit it's horribly awkward. What do you propose to do?'

There was nothing to do except to call in my men and have them arrested, or to confess my blunder and clear out. I felt mesmerized by the whole place, by the air of obvious innocence—not innocence merely, but frank honest bewilderment and concern in the three faces.

'Oh, Peter Pienaar,' I groaned inwardly, and for a moment I was very near damning myself for a fool and asking their pardon.

'Meantime I vote we have a game of bridge,' said the plump one. 'It will give Mr Hannay time to think over things, and you know we have been wanting a fourth player. Do you play, Sir?'

I accepted as if it had been an ordinary invitation at the club. The whole business had mesmerized me. We went into the smoking-room where a card-table was set out, and I was offered things to smoke and drink. I took my place at the table in a kind of dream. The window was open and the moon was flooding the cliffs and sea with a great tide of yellow light. There was moonshine, too, in my head. The three had recovered their composure, and were talking easily—just the kind of slangy talk you will hear in any golf club-house. I must have cut a rum figure, sitting there knitting my brows with my eyes wandering.

My partner was the young dark one. I play a fair hand at bridge, but I must have been rank bad that night. They saw that they had got me puzzled, and that put them more than ever at their ease. I kept looking at their faces, but they conveyed nothing to me. It was not that they looked different; they were different. I clung desperately to the words of Peter Pienaar.

Then something awoke me.

The old man laid down his hand to light a cigar. He didn't pick it up at once, but sat back for a moment in his chair, with his fingers tapping on his knees.

It was the movement I remembered when I had stood before him in the moorland farm, with the pistols of his servants behind me.

A little thing, lasting only a second, and the odds were a thousand to one that I might have had my eyes on my cards at the time and missed it. But I didn't, and, in a flash, the air seemed to clear. Some shadow lifted from my brain, and I was looking at the three men with full and absolute recognition.

The clock on the mantelpiece struck ten o'clock.

The three faces seemed to change before my eyes and reveal their secrets. The young one was the murderer. Now I saw cruelty and ruthlessness, where before I had only seen good-humour. His knife, I made certain, had skewered Scudder to the floor. His kind had put the bullet in Karolides.

The plump man's features seemed to dislimn, and form again, as I looked at them. He hadn't a face, only a hundred masks that he could assume when he pleased. That chap must have been a superb actor. Perhaps he had been Lord Alloa of the night before; perhaps not; it didn't matter. I wondered if he was the fellow who had first tracked Scudder, and left his card on him. Scudder had said he lisped, and I could imagine how the adoption of a lisp might add terror.

But the old man was the pick of the lot. He was sheer brain, icy, cool, calculating, as ruthless as a steam hammer. Now that my eyes were opened I wondered where I had seen the benevolence. His jaw was like chilled steel, and his eyes had the inhuman luminosity of a bird's. I went on playing, and every second a greater hate welled up in my heart. It almost choked me, and I couldn't answer when my partner spoke. Only a little longer could I endure their company.

'Whew! Bob! Look at the time,' said the old man. 'You'd better think about catching your train. Bob's got to go to town tonight,' he added, turning to me. The voice rang now as false as hell. I looked at the clock, and it was nearly half-past ten.

'I am afraid he must put off his journey,' I said.

'Oh, damn,' said the young man. 'I thought you had dropped that rot. I've simply got to go. You can have my address, and I'll give any security you like.'

'No,' I said, 'you must stay.'

At that I think they must have realized that the game was desperate. Their only chance had been to convince me that I was playing the fool, and that had failed. But the old man spoke again.

'I'll go bail for my nephew. That ought to content you, Mr Hannay.' Was it fancy, or did I detect some halt in the smoothness of that voice?

There must have been, for as I glanced at him, his eyelids fell in that hawk-like hood which fear had stamped on my memory.

I blew my whistle.

In an instant the lights were out. A pair of strong arms gripped me round the waist, covering the pockets in which a man might be expected to carry a pistol.

'SCHNELL, FRANZ,' cried a voice, 'DAS BOOT, DAS BOOT!' As it spoke I saw two of my fellows emerge on the moonlit lawn.

The young dark man leapt for the window, was through it, and over the low fence before a hand could touch him. I grappled the old chap, and the room seemed to fill with figures. I saw the plump one collared, but my eyes were all for the out-of-doors, where Franz sped on over the road towards the railed entrance to the beach stairs. One man followed him, but he had no chance. The gate of the stairs locked behind the fugitive, and I stood staring, with my hands on the old boy's throat, for such a time as a man might take to descend those steps to the sea.

Suddenly my prisoner broke from me and flung himself on the wall. There was a click as if a lever had been pulled. Then came a low rumbling far, far below the ground, and through the window I saw a cloud of chalky dust pouring out of the shaft of the stairway.

Someone switched on the light.

The old man was looking at me with blazing eyes.

'He is safe,' he cried. 'You cannot follow in time ... He is gone ... He has triumphed ... DER SCHWARZE STEIN IST IN DER SIEGESKRONE.'

There was more in those eyes than any common triumph. They had been hooded like a bird of prey, and now they flamed with a hawk's pride. A white fanatic heat burned in them, and I realized for the first time the terrible thing I had been up against. This man was more than a spy; in his foul way he had been a patriot.

As the handcuffs clinked on his wrists I said my last word to him.

'I hope Franz will bear his triumph well. I ought to tell you that the ARIADNE for the last hour has been in our hands.'

Three weeks later, as all the world knows, we went to war. I joined the New Army the first week, and owing to my Matabele experience got a captain's commission straight off. But I had done my best service, I think, before I put on khaki.

Sick Heart River

By

John Buchan

PART I

"Thus said Alfred:
If thou hast a woe, tell it not to the weakling,
Tell it to thy saddle-bow, and ride singing forth."
—*Proverbs of Alfred.*

1

Leithen had been too busy all day to concern himself with the thoughts which hung heavily at the back of his mind. In the morning he had visited his bankers to look into his money affairs. These were satisfactory enough: for years he had been earning a large income and spending little of it; his investments were mostly in trustee stocks; he found that he possessed, at a safe computation, a considerable fortune, while his Cotswold estate would find a ready sale. Next came his solicitors, for he was too wise a man to make the mistake of many barristers and tinker with his own will. He gave instructions for bringing the old one up to date. There were a few legacies by way of mementoes to old friends, a considerable gift to his college, donations to certain charities, and the residue to his nephew Charles, his only near relation.

He forced himself to lunch at one of his clubs, in a corner where no one came near him, though Archie Roylance waved a greeting across the dining-room. Then he spent a couple of hours with his clerk in his Temple chambers, looking through the last of his briefs. There were not a great many, since, for some months, he had been steadily refusing work. The batch of cases for opinion he could soon clear off, and one big case in the Lords he must argue next week, for it involved a point of law in which he had always taken a special interest. The briefs for the following term would be returned. The clerk, who had been with him for thirty years, was getting on in life and would be glad to retire on an ample pension. Still, it was a painful parting.

"It's a big loss to the Bar, Sir Edward, sir," old Mellon said, "and it's pretty well the end of things for me. You have been a kind master to me, sir, and I'm proud to have served you. I hope you are going to have many happy years yet."

But there had been a look of pain in the old man's eyes which told Leithen that he had guessed what he dared not hint at.

He had tea at the House of Commons with the Chief Whip, a youngish man named Ritson, who in the War had been a subaltern in his own battalion. Ritson listened to him with a wrinkled brow and troubled eyes.

"Have you told your local people?" he asked.

"I'll write to them tomorrow. I thought I ought to tell you first. There's no fear of losing the seat. My majority has never been less than six thousand, and there's an excellent candidate ready in young Walmer."

"We shall miss you terribly, you know. There's no one to take your place."

Leithen smiled. "I haven't been pulling my weight lately."

"Perhaps not. But I'm thinking of what's coming. If there's an election, we're going to win all right, and we'll want you badly in the new Government. It needn't be a law office. You can have your pick of half a dozen jobs. Only yesterday the Chief was speaking to me about you." And he repeated a conversation he had had with the man who would be the next Prime Minister.

"You're all very kind. But I don't think I want anything. I've done enough, as Napoleon said, 'pour chauffer la gloire.'"

"Is it your health?" Ritson asked.

"Well, I need a rest. I've been pretty busy all my days and I'm tired."

The Chief Whip hesitated.

"Things are pretty insecure in the world just now. There may be a crisis any day. Don't you think you ought--"

Leithen smiled.

"I've thought of that. But if I stayed on I could do nothing to help. That isn't a pleasant conclusion to come to, but it's the truth."

Ritson stood at the door of his room and watched his departing guest going down the corridor to the

Central Lobby. He turned to a junior colleague who had joined him--

"I wonder what the devil's the matter! There's been a change in him in the last few months. But he doesn't look a sick man. He was always a bad colour, of course, but Lamancha says he is the hardest fellow he ever knew on the hill."

The other shook a wise head. "You never can tell. He had a roughish time in the War and the damage often takes years to come out. I think he's right to slack off, for he must have a gruelling life at the Bar. My father tried to get him the other day as leader in a big case, and he wasn't to be had for love or money. Simply snowed under with work!"

Leithen walked from the House towards his rooms in Down Street. He was still keeping his thoughts shut down, but in spite of himself the familiar streets awakened memories. How often he had tramped them in the far-off days when he was a pupil in chambers and the world was an oyster waiting to be opened. It was a different London then, quieter, cosier, dirtier perhaps, but sweeter smelling. On a summer evening such as this the scents would have been a compound of wood paving, horse-dung, flowers, and fresh paint, not the deadly monotony of petrol. The old land-marks, too, were disappearing. In St. James's Street only Mr. Lock's modest shop-window and the eighteenth-century façade of Boodle's recalled the London of his youth. He remembered posting up this street with a high heart after he had won his first important case in court . . . and the Saturday afternoon's strolls in it when he had changed his black regimentals for tweeds or flannels . . . and the snowy winter day when a tiny coffin on a gun-carriage marked the end of Victoria's reign . . . and the shiny August morning in 1914 when he had been on his way to enlist with a mind half-anxious and half- exulting. He had travelled a good deal in his time, but most of his life had been spent in this square mile of west London. He did not regret the changes; he only noted them. His inner world was crumbling so fast that he had lost any craving for permanence in the externals of life.

In Piccadilly he felt his knees trembling and called a taxi. In Down Street he took the lift to his rooms, though for thirty years he had made a ritual of climbing the stairs.

The flat was full of powdery sunlight. He sank into a chair at the window to get his breath, and regarded the comfortable, shabby sitting-room. Now that he seemed to be looking at it with new eyes he noted details which familiarity had long obscured. The pictures were school and college groups, one or two mountain photographs, and, over the mantelpiece, Raeburn's portrait of his grandfather. He was very little of a connoisseur, though at Borrowby he had three Vandykes which suited its Jacobean solemnity. There were books everywhere; they overflowed into the dining-room and his bedroom and the little hall. He reflected that what with these, and the law library in his chambers and his considerable collection at Borrowby, he must have at least twenty thousand volumes. He had been happy here, happy and busy, and for a moment--for a moment only--he felt a bitter pang of regret.

But he was still keeping his thoughts at a distance, for the time had not come to face them. Memories took the vacant place. He remembered how often he had left these rooms with a holiday zest, and how he had always returned to them with delight, for this, and not Borrowby, was his true home. How many snug winter nights had he known here, cheerful with books and firelight; and autumn twilights when he was beginning to get into the stride of his work after the long vacation; and spring mornings when the horns of elfland were blowing even in Down Street. He lay back in his chair, shut his eyes and let his memory wander. There was no harm in that, for the grim self-communion he had still to face would have no room for memories. He almost dozed.

The entry of his man, Cruddock, aroused him.

"Lord Clanroyden called you up, sir. He is in Town for the night and suggests that you might dine with him. He said the Turf Club at eight. I was to let him know, sir."

"Tell him to come here instead. You can produce some kind of a dinner?" Leithen rather welcomed the prospect. Sandy Clanroyden would absorb his attention for an hour or two and postpone for a little the settlement with himself which his soul dreaded.

He had a bath and changed. He had been feeling listless and depressed, but not ill, and the cold shower gave him a momentary sense of vigour and almost an appetite for food. He caught a glimpse of himself naked in the long mirror, and was shocked anew by his leanness. He had given up weighing himself, but it looked as if he had lost pounds in the past month.

Sandy arrived on the stroke of eight. Leithen, as he greeted him, reflected that he was the only one of his closer friends whom he could have borne to meet. Archie Roylance's high spirits would have been intolerable, and Lamancha's air of mastery over life, and Dick Hannay's serene contentment.

He did not miss the sharp glance of his guest when he entered the room. Could some rumours have got abroad? It was clear that Sandy was setting himself to play a part, for his manner had not its usual ease. He was not talking at random, but picking his topics.

A proof was that he did not ask Leithen about his holiday plans, which, near the close of the law term, would have been a natural subject. He seemed to feel that his host's affairs might be delicate ground, and that it was his business to distract his mind from some unhappy preoccupation. So he talked about himself and his recent doings. He had just been to Cambridge to talk to the Explorers' Club, and had come back with strong views about modern youth.

"I'm not happy about the young entry. Oh! I don't mean all of it. There's plenty of lads that remind me of my own old lot. But some of the best seem to have become a bit too much introverted--isn't that the filthy word? What's to be done about the Owlish Young, Ned?"

"I don't see much of youth nowadays," said Leithen. "I seem to live among fogies. I'm one myself."

"Rot! You are far and away the youngest of us."

Again Leithen caught a swift glance at his face, as if Sandy would have liked to ask him something, but forbore.

"Those boys make me anxious. It's right that they should be serious with the world slipping into chaos, but they need not be owlish. They are so darned solemn about their new little creeds in religion and politics, forgetting that they are as old as the hills. There isn't a ha'porth of humour in the bunch, which means, of course, that there isn't any perspective. If it comes to a show-down I'm afraid they will be pretty feeble folk. People with half their brains and a little sense of humour will make rings round them."

Leithen must have shown his unconcern about the future of the world by his expression, for Sandy searched for other topics. Spring at Laverlaw had been diviner than ever. Had Leithen heard the curlews this year? No? Didn't he usually make a pilgrimage somewhere to hear them? For northerners they, and not the cuckoo, were the heralds of spring. . . . His wife was at Laverlaw, but was coming to London next day. Yes, she was well, but--

Again Leithen saw in the other's face a look of interrogation. He wanted to ask him something, tell him something, but did not feel the moment propitious.

"Her uncle has just turned up here. Apparently there's a bit of family trouble to be settled. You know him, don't you? Blenkiron-- John Scantlebury Blenkiron?"

Leithen nodded. "A little. I was his counsel in the Continental Nickel case some years ago. He's an old friend of yours and Hannay's, isn't he?"

"About the best Dick and I have in the world. Would you like to see him again? I rather think he would like to see you."

Leithen yawned and said his plans for the immediate future were uncertain.

Just before ten Sandy took his leave, warned by his host's obvious fatigue. He left the impression that he had come to dinner to say something which he had thought had better be left unsaid, and Leithen, when he looked at his face in his dressing-table mirror, knew the reason. It was the face of a very sick man.

That night he had meant, before going to sleep, to have it out with himself. But he found that a weary body had made his brain incapable of coherent thought, so he tumbled into bed.

2

The reckoning came six hours later, when his bedroom was brightening with the fore-glow of a June dawn. He awoke, as he usually did nowadays, sweating and short of breath. He got up and laved his face with cold water. When he lay down again he knew that the moment had arrived.

Recent events had been confused in a cloud of misery, and he had to disengage the details. . . . There was no one moment to which he could point when his health had begun to fail. Two years before he had had a very hard summer at the Bar, complicated by the chairmanship of a Royal Commission, and a trip to Norway for the August sea trout had been disastrous. He had returned still a little fatigued. He no longer got up in the morning with a certain uplift of spirit, work seemed duller and more laborious, food less appetising, sleep more imperative but less refreshing.

During that winter he had had a bout of influenza for the first time in his life. After it he had dragged his wing for a month or two, but had seemed to pick up in the spring when he had had a trip to Provence with the Clanroydens. But the hot summer had given him a set-back, and when he went shooting with Lamancha in the autumn he found to his dismay that he had become short of breath and that the hills were too steep for him. Also he was clearly losing weight. So on his return to

London he sought out Acton Croke and had himself examined. The great doctor had been ominously grave. Our fathers, he said, had talked unscientifically about the "grand climacteric," which came in the early sixties, but there was such a thing as a climacteric which might come any time in middle life, when the physical powers adjusted themselves to the approach of age. That crisis Leithen was now enduring, and he must go very carefully and remember that the dose of gas he got in the War had probably not exhausted its effect. Croke put him on a diet, prescribed a certain routine of rest and exercise, and made him drastically cut down his engagements. He insisted also on seeing him once a fortnight.

A winter followed for Leithen of steadily declining health. His breath troubled him and a painful sinking in the chest. He rose languidly, struggled through the day, and went to bed exhausted. Every moment he was conscious of his body and its increasing frailty. Croke sent him to a nursing home during the Christmas vacation, and for a few weeks he seemed to be better. But the coming of spring, instead of giving him new vigour, drained his strength. He began to suffer from night sweats which left him very feeble in the morning. His meals became a farce. He drove himself to take exercise, but now a walk round the Park exhausted one who only a few years back could walk down any Highland gillie. Croke's face looked graver with each visit.

Then the day before yesterday had come the crisis. He went by appointment to Croke--and demanded a final verdict. The great doctor gave it: gravely, anxiously, tenderly, as to an old friend, but without equivocation. He was dying, slowly dying.

Leithen's mind refused to bite on the details of his own case with its usual professional precision. He was not interested in these details. He simply accepted the judgment of the expert. He was suffering from advanced tuberculosis, a retarded consequence of his gas poisoning. Croke, knowing his patient's habit of mind, had given him a full diagnosis, but Leithen had scarcely listened to his exposition of the chronic fibrous affection and broncho- pulmonary lesions. The fact was enough for him.

"How long have I to live?" he asked, and was told a year, perhaps a little longer.

"Shall I go off suddenly, or what?" The answer was that there would be a progressive loss of strength until the heart failed.

"You can give me no hope?"

Croke shook his head.

"I dare not. The lesions MIGHT heal, the fibrous patch MIGHT disappear, but it would be a miracle according to present knowledge. I must add, of course, that our present knowledge may not be final truth."

"But I must take it as such, I agree. Miracles don't happen."

Leithen left Harley Street almost cheerfully. There was a grim satisfaction in knowing the worst. He was so utterly weary that after coffee and a sandwich in his rooms he went straight to bed.

Soon he must think things out, but not at once. He must first make some necessary arrangements about his affairs which would keep him from brooding. That should be the task of the morrow. It all reminded him of his habit as a company commander in the trenches when an attack was imminent: he had busied himself with getting every detail exact, so that his mind had no time for foreboding. . . .

As he lay watching his window brighten with the morning he wondered why he was taking things so calmly. It was not courage--he did not consider himself a brave man, though he had never greatly feared death. At the best he had achieved in life a thin stoicism, a shallow fortitude. Insensibility, perhaps, was the best word. He remembered Dr. Johnson's reply to Boswell's "That, sir, was great fortitude of mind."--"No, sir, stark insensibility."

At any rate he would not sink to self-pity. He had been brought up in a Calvinistic household and the atmosphere still clung to him, though in the ordinary way he was not a religious man. For example, he had always had an acute sense of sin, which had made him something of a Puritan in his way of life. He had believed firmly in God, a Being of ineffable purity and power, and consequently had had no undue reverence for man. He had always felt his own insignificance and imperfections and was not inclined to cavil at fate. On the contrary, he considered that fortune had been ludicrously kind to him. He had had fifty-eight years of health and wealth. He had survived the War, when the best of his contemporaries had fallen in swathes. He had been amazingly successful in his profession and had enjoyed every moment of his work. Honours had fallen to him out of all proportion to his merits. He had had a thousand pleasures--books, travel, the best of sport, the best of friends.

His friends--that had been his chief blessing. As he thought of their warm companionship he could not check a sudden wave of regret. THAT would be hard to leave. He had sworn Acton Croke to secrecy, and he meant to keep his condition hidden even from his closest intimates--from Hannay and Clanroyden and Lamancha and Palliser-Yeates and Archie Roylance. He could not endure to think of their anxious eyes. He would see less of them than before, of course, but he would continue to meet them on the old terms. Yes-- but how? He was giving up Parliament and the Bar--London, too. What story was he to tell? A craving for rest and leisure? Well, he must indulge that craving at a distance, or otherwise his friends would discover the reason.

But where? . . . Borrowby? Impossible, for it was associated too closely with his years of vigour. He had rejoiced in reshaping that ancient shell into a house for a green old age; he remembered with what care he had planned his library and his garden; Borrowby would be intolerable as a brief refuge for a dying man. . . . Scotland?--somewhere in the Lowland hills or on the sounding beaches of the west coast? But he had been too happy there. All the romance of childhood and forward-looking youth was bound up with those places and it would be agony to revisit them.

His memory sprawled over places he had seen in his much-travelled life. There was a certain Greek island where he had once lived dangerously; there were valleys on the Italian side of the Alps, and a saeter in the Jotunheim to which his fancy had often returned. But in his survey he found that the charm had gone from them; they were for the living, not the dying. Only one spot had still some appeal. In his early youth, when money had not been plentiful, he had had an autumn shooting trip in northern Quebec because it was cheap. He had come down on foot over the height of land, with a single Montagnais guide back-packing their kit, and one golden October afternoon he had stumbled on a place which he had never forgotten. It was a green saddle of land, a meadow of wild hay among the pines. South from it a stream ran to the St. Lawrence; from an adjacent well another trickle flowed north on the Arctic watershed. It had seemed a haven of pastoral peace in a shaggy land, and he recalled how loth he had been to leave it. He had often thought about it, often determined to go back and look for it. Now, as he pictured it in its green security, it seemed the kind of sanctuary in which to die. He remembered its name. The spring was called Clairefontaine, and it gave its name both to the south-flowing stream and to a little farm below in the valley.

Supposing he found the proper shelter, how was he to spend his closing months? As an invalid, slowly growing feebler, always expectant of death? That was starkly impossible. He wanted peace to make his soul, but not lethargy either of mind or body. The body!--that was the rub. It was failing him, that body which had once been a mettled horse quickly responding to bridle or spur. Now he must be aware every hour of its ignoble frailty. . . . He stretched out his arms, flexing the muscles as he used to do when he was well, and was conscious that there was no pith in them.

His thoughts clung to this physical shell of his. He had been proud of it, not like an athlete who guards a treasure, but like a master proud of an adequate servant. It had added much to the pleasures of life. . . . But he realised that in his career it had mattered very little to him, for his work had been done with his mind. Labouring men had their physical strength as their only asset, and when the body failed them their work was done. They knew from harsh experience the limits of their strength, what exhaustion meant, and strife against pain and disablement. They had to endure all their days what he had endured to a small degree in the trenches. . .

. Had he not missed something, and, missing it, had failed somehow in one of the duties of man?

This queer thought kept returning to him with the force of a revelation. His mood was the opposite of self-pity, a feeling that his life had been too cosseted and fur-lined. Only now that his body was failing did he realise how little he had used it. . . . Among the oddly assorted beliefs which made up his religious equipment, one was conditional immortality. The soul was only immortal if there was such a thing as a soul, and a further existence had to be earned in this one. He had used most of the talents God had given him, but not all. He had never, except in the War, staked his body in the struggle, and yet that was the stake of most of humanity. Was it still possible to meet that test of manhood with a failing body? . . . If only the War were still going on!

His mind, which had been dragging apathetically along, suddenly awoke into vigour. By God! there was one thing that would not happen. He would not sit down and twiddle his thumbs and await death. His ship, since it was doomed, should go down in action with every flag flying. Lately he had been re-reading Vanity Fair and he remembered the famous passage where Thackeray moralises on the trappings of the conventional death-bed, the soft-footed nurses, the hushed voices of the household, the alcove on the staircase in which to rest the coffin. The picture affected him with a physical nausea. That, by God! should never be his fate. He would die standing, as Vespasian said an emperor should. . . .

The day had broadened into full sunlight. The white paint and the flowered wallpaper of his bedroom glowed with the morning freshness, and from the street outside came pleasant morning sounds like the jingle of milk-cans and the whistling of errand-boys. His mind seemed to have been stabbed awake out of a flat stoicism into a dim but masterful purpose.

He got up and dressed, and his cold bath gave him a ghost of an appetite for breakfast.

3

His intention was to go down to his chambers later in the morning and get to work on the batch of cases for opinion. As always after a meal, he felt languid and weak, but his mind was no longer comatose. Already it was beginning to move steadily, though hopelessly, towards some kind of plan. As he sat huddled in a chair at the open window Cruddock announced that a Mr. Blenkiron was on the telephone and would like an appointment.

This was the American that Sandy Clanroyden had spoken of. Leithen remembered him clearly as his client in a big case. He remembered, too, much that he had heard about him from Sandy and Dick Hannay. One special thing, too--Blenkiron had been a sick man in the War and yet had put up a remarkable show. He had liked him, and, though he felt himself now cut off from human companionship, he could hardly refuse an interview, for Sandy's sake. The man had probably some lawsuit in hand, and if so it would not take long to refuse.

"If convenient, sir, the gentleman could come along now," said Cruddock.

Leithen nodded and took up the newspaper.

Blenkiron had aged. Eight years ago Leithen recalled him as a big man with a heavy shaven face, a clear skin, and calm ruminant grey eyes. A healthy creature in hard condition, he could have given a good account of himself with his hands as well as his head. Now he was leaner and more grizzled, and there were pouches under his eyes. Leithen remembered Sandy's doings in South America; Blenkiron had been in that show, and he had heard about his being a sort of industrial dictator in Olifa, or whatever the place was called.

The grey eyes were regarding him contemplatively but keenly. He wondered what they made of his shrunken body.

"It's mighty fine to see you again, Sir Edward. And all the boys, too. I've been stuck so tight in my job down south that I've gotten out of touch with my friends. I'm giving myself a holiday to look them up and to see my little niece. I think you know Babs."

"I know her well. A very great woman. I had forgotten she was your niece. How does the old gang strike you?"

"Lasting well, sir. A bit older and maybe a bit wiser and settling down into good citizens. They tell me that Sir Archibald Roylance is making quite a name for himself in your Parliament, and that Lord Clanroyden cuts a deal of ice with your Government. Dick Hannay, I judge, is getting hayseed into his hair. How about yourself?"

"Fair," Leithen said. "I'm going out of business now. I've worked hard enough to be entitled to climb out of the rut."

"That's fine!" Blenkiron's face showed a quickened interest. "I haven't forgotten what you did for me when I was up against the Delacroix bunch. There's no man on the globe I'd sooner have with me in a nasty place than you. You've a mighty quick brain and a mighty sound judgment and you're not afraid to take a chance."

"You're very kind," said Leithen a little wearily. "Well, that's all done with now. I am going out of harness."

"A man like you can't ever get out of harness. If you lay down one job you take up another."

Blenkiron's eyes, appraising now rather than meditative, scanned the other's face. He leaned forward in his chair and sank his voice.

"I came round this morning to say something to you, Sir Edward-- something very special. Babs has a sister, Felicity--I guess you don't know her, but she's something of a person on our side of the water. Two years younger than Babs, and married to a man you've maybe heard of, Francis Galliard, one of old Simon

Ravelston's partners. Young Galliard's gotten a great name in the city of New York, and Felicity and he looked like being a happy pair. But just lately things haven't been going too well with Felicity."

In common politeness Leithen forced a show of attention, but Blenkiron had noted his dull eyes.

"I won't trouble you with the story now," he went on, "for it's long and a bit ravelled, but the gist of it is that Francis Galliard has disappeared over the horizon. Just leaked out of the landscape without a word to Felicity or anybody else. No! There is no suggestion of kidnapping or any dirty work--the trouble is in Francis's own mind. He is a Canuck--a Frenchman from Quebec--and I expect his mind works different from yours and mine. Now, he has got to be found and brought back--first of all to Felicity, and second, to his business, and third, to the United States. He's too valuable a man to lose, and in our present state of precarious balance we just can't afford it."

Blenkiron stopped as if he expected some kind of reply. Leithen said nothing, but his thoughts had jumped suddenly to the upland meadow of Clairefontaine of which he had been thinking that morning. Odd that that remote memory should have been suddenly dug out of the lumber-room of the past!

"We want help in the job," Blenkiron continued, "and it's not going to be easy to find it. We want a man who can piece together the bits that make up the jigsaw puzzle, though we haven't got much in the way of evidence. We want a man who can read himself into Francis's mind and understand the thoughts he might have been thinking, and, most of all, we want a man who can put his conclusions into action. Finding Francis may mean a good deal of bodily wear and tear and taking some risks."

"I see." Leithen spoke at last. "You want a combination of detective, psychologist, and sportsman."

"Yep." Blenkiron beamed. "You've hit it. And there's just the one man I know that fills the bill. I've had a talk with Lord Clanroyden and he agrees. If you had been going on at the Bar we would have offered you the biggest fee that any brief ever carried, for there's money to burn in this business--though I don't reckon the fee would have weighed much with you. But you tell me you are shaking loose. Well, here's a job for your leisure and, if I judge you right, it's the sort of job you won't turn down without a thought or two."

Leithen raised his sick eyes to the eager face before him, a face whose abounding vitality sharpened the sense of his own weakness.

"You've come a little late," he said slowly. "I'm going to tell you something which Lord Clanroyden and the others don't know, and will never know--which nobody knows except myself and my doctor-- and I want you to promise to keep it secret. . . . I'm a dying man. I've only about a year to live."

He was not certain what he expected, but he was certain it would be something which would wind up this business for good. He had longed to have one confidant, only one, and Blenkiron was safe enough. The sound of his voice speaking these grim words somehow chilled him, and he awaited dismally the conventional sympathy. After that Blenkiron would depart and he would see him no more.

But Blenkiron did not behave conventionally. He flushed deeply and sprang to his feet, upsetting his chair.

"My God!" he cried. "If I ain't the blightedest, God-darned blundering fool! I might have guessed by your looks you were a sick man, and now I've hurt you in the raw with my cursed egotistical worries. . . . I'm off, Sir Edward. Forget you ever saw me. God forgive me, for I won't soon forgive myself."

"Don't go," said Leithen. "Sit down and talk to me. You may be the very man I want."

4

His hostess noticed his slow appraising look round the table, which took each of the guests in turn.

"You were here last in '29," she said. "Do you think we have changed?"

Leithen turned his eyes to the tall woman at his left hand. Mrs. Simon Ravelston had a beautiful figure, ill-chosen clothes, and the weather-beaten face of an English master of fox-hounds. She was magnificently in place on horseback, or sailing a boat, or running with her beagles, but no indoor setting could fit her. Sprung from ancient New England stock, she showed her breeding in a wonderful detachment from the hubbub of life. At her own table she would drift into moods of reverie and stare into vacancy, oblivious of the conversation, and then when she woke up would turn such kind eyes upon her puzzled interlocutor that all offences were forgiven. When her husband had been Ambassador at the Court of St. James's she had been widely popular, a magnet for the most sophisticated young men; but of this she had been wholly unconscious. She was deeply interested in life and very little interested in herself.

Leithen answered, "Yes, I think you all look a little more fine- drawn and harder trained. The men, that is. The women could never change."

Mrs. Ravelston laughed. "I hope that you're right. Before the depression we were getting rather gross. The old Uncle Sam that we took as our national figure was lean like a Red Indian, but in late years our ordinary type had become round-faced, and puffy, and pallid, like a Latin John Bull. Now we are recovering Uncle Sam, though we have shaved him and polished him up." Her eyes ran round the table and stopped at a youngish man with strong rugged features and shaggy eyebrows who was listening with a smile to the talk of a very pretty girl.

"George Lethaby, for example. Thank goodness he is a career diplomat and can show himself about the world. I should like people to take him as a typical American." She lowered her voice, for she was speaking now of her left-hand neighbour, "Or Bronson, here. You know him, don't you? Bronson Jane."

Leithen glanced beyond his hostess to where a man just passing into middle life was peering at an illegible menu card. This was the bright particular star of the younger America, and he regarded him with more than curiosity, for he counted upon him for help. On paper Bronson Jane was almost too good to be true. He had been a noted sportsman and was still a fine polo player; his name was a household word in Europe for his work in international finance; he was the Admirable Crichton of his day and it was rumoured that in the same week he had been offered the Secretaryship of State, the Presidency of an ancient University, and the control of a great industrial corporation. He had chosen the third, but seemed to have a foot also in every other world. He had a plain sagacious face, a friendly mouth, and deep-set eyes, luminous and masterful.

Leithen glanced round the table again. The dining-room of the Ravelston house was a homely place; it had no tapestries or panelling, and its pictures were family portraits of small artistic merit. In each corner there were marble busts of departed Ravelstons. It was like the rest of the house, and, like their country homes in the Catskills and on the Blue Ridge, a dwelling which bore the mark of successive generations who had all been acutely conscious of the past. Leithen felt that he might have been in a poor man's dwelling, but for the magnificence of the table flowers and silver and the gold soup plates which had once belonged to a King of France. He let his gaze rest on each of the men.

"Yes," he told his hostess, "you are getting the kind of face I like."

"But not the right colour perhaps," she laughed. "Is that worry or too much iced water, I wonder?" She broke off suddenly, remembering her neighbour's grey visage.

"Tell me who the people are," he said, to cover her embarrassment. "I have met Mr. Jane and Mr. Lethaby and Mr. Ravelston."

"I want you to know my Simon better," she said. "I know why you have come here--Mr. Blenkiron told me.

Nobody knows about it except in the family. The story is that Mr. Galliard has gone to Peru to look into some pitchblende propositions. Simon is terribly distressed and he feels so helpless. You see, we only came back to America from England four months ago, and we have kind of lost touch."

Simon Ravelston was a big man with a head like Jove, and a noble silvered beard. He was president of one of the chief private banking houses in the world, which under his great-grandfather had financed the first railways beyond the Appalachians, under his grandfather had salved the wreckage of the Civil War, and under his father had steadied America's wild gallop to wealth. He had a dozen partners, most of whom understood the technique of finance far better than himself, but on all major questions he spoke the last word, for he had the great general's gift of reducing complexities to a simple syllogism. In an over-worked world he seemed always to have ample leisure, for he insisted on making time to think. When others of his calling were spending twelve hectic hours daily in their offices, Simon would calmly go fishing. No man ever saw him rattled or hustled, and this Olympian detachment gave him a prestige in two continents against which he himself used to protest vigorously.

"They think I'm wise only because I don't talk when I've nothing to say," he used to tell his friends. "Any fool these days can get a reputation if he keeps his mouth shut."

He was happy because his mind was filled with happy interests; he had no itching ambitions, he did his jobs as they came along with a sincere delight in doing them well, and a no less sincere delight in seeing the end of them. He was the extreme opposite of the man whose nerves demand a constant busyness because, like a bicyclist, he will fall down if he stays still.

Leithen's gaze passed to a young man who had Simon's shape of head but was built on a smaller and more elegant scale. His hostess followed his eyes.

"That's our boy, Eric, and that's his wife, Delia, across the table. Pretty, isn't she? She has the southern complexion, the real thing, which isn't indigestion from too much hot bread at breakfast. What's he doing? He's on the John Hopkins staff and is making a big name for himself in lung surgery. Ever since a little boy he's been set on doctoring and nothing would change him. He had a pretty good training--Harvard--two years at Oxford--a year in Paris--a long spell in a Montreal hospital. That's a new thing about our boys, Sir Edward. They're not so set nowadays on big business. They want to do things and make things, and they consider that there are better tools than dollars. George Lethaby is an example. He's a poor man and always will be, for a diplomat can't be a money-maker. But he's a happier man than Harold Downes, though he doesn't look it."

Mr. Lethaby's rugged face happened at the moment to be twisted into an expression of pain out of sympathy with some tale of the woman to whom he was talking, while his vis-à-vis, Mr. Downes, was laughing merrily at a remark of his neighbour.

"Harold has a hard life," said Mrs. Ravelston. "He's head of the Fremont Banking Corporation and a St. Sebastian for everyone to shoot arrows at. Any more to be catalogued? Why, yes, there are the two biggest exhibits of all."

She directed Leithen's eyes to two men separated by a handsome old woman whose hair was dressed in the fashion of forty years ago.

"You see the man on the far side of Ella Purchass, the plump little man with the eagle beak who looks like he's enjoying his food. What would you set him down as?"

"Banker? Newspaper proprietor?"

"Wrong. That's Walter Derwent. You've heard of him? His father left him all kinds of wealth, but Walter wasted no time in getting out of oil into icebergs. He has flown and mushed and tramped over most of the Arctic, and there are heaps of mountains and wild beasts named after him. And you'd never think he'd moved farther than Long Island. Now place the man on this side of Ella."

Leithen saw a typical English hunting man--lean brown face with the skin stretched tight over the cheek-bones, pale, deep-set eyes, a small clipped moustache, shoulders a little stooped from being much on horse-back.

"Virginian squire," he hazarded. "Warrenton at a guess."

"Wrong," she laughed. "He wouldn't be happy at Warrenton, and I'm certain he wouldn't be happy on a horse. His line is deep learning. He's about our foremost pundit--professor at Yale--dug up cities in Asia Minor--edited Greek books. Writes very nice little stories, too. That's Clifford Savory."

Leithen looked with interest at the pleasant vital face. He knew all about Clifford Savory. There were few men alive who were his equals in classical scholarship, and he had published one or two novels, delicate historical reconstructions, which were masterpieces in their way.

His gaze circled round the table again, noting the friendliness of the men's eyes, the atmosphere of breeding and simplicity and stability. He turned to his hostess--

"You've got together a wonderful party for me," he said. "I feel what I always feel when I come here--that you are the friendliest people on earth. But I believe, too, that you are harder to get to know than our awkward, difficult, tongue-tied folk at home. To get to know really well, I mean--inside your plate-armour of general benevolence."

Mrs. Ravelston laughed. "There may be something in that. It's a new idea to me."

"I think you are sure of yourselves, too. There is no one at this table who hasn't steady nerves and a vast deal of common sense. You call it poise, don't you?"

"Maybe, but this is a picked party, remember."

"Because of its poise?"

"No. Because every man here is a friend of Francis Galliard."

"Friend? Do you mean acquaintance or intimate?"

The lady pursed her lips.

"I'm not sure. I think you are right and that we are not an easy people to be intimate with unless we have been brought up with the same background. Francis, too, is scarcely cut out for intimacy. Did you ever meet him?"

"No. I heard his name for the first time a few weeks ago. Which of you knows him best? Mr. Ravelston?"

"Certainly not Simon, though he's his business partner. Francis has a good many sides, and most people know only one of them. Bronson could tell you most about his work. He likes my Eric, but hasn't seen much of him in recent years. I know he used to go duck-shooting in Minnesota with George Lethaby, and he's a trustee of Walter Derwent's Polar Institute. I fancy Clifford Savory is nearer to him than most people. And yet . . . I don't know. Maybe nobody has got to know the real Francis. He has that frank, forthcoming manner which conceals a man, and he's mighty busy too, too busy for intimacies. I used to see him once or twice a week, but I couldn't tell you anything about him that everybody doesn't know. It won't be easy, Sir Edward, to get a proper notion of him from second-hand evidence. Felicity's your best chance. You haven't met Felicity yet?"

"I'm leaving her to the last. What's she like? I know her sister well."

"She's a whole lot different from Babs. I can tell you she's quite a person."

Leithen felt that if his hostess had belonged to a different social grade she would have called her a "lovely woman." Her meaning was clear. Mrs. Galliard was someone who mattered.

He was beginning to feel very weary, and, knowing that he must ration his strength, he made his excuses and did not join the women after dinner. But he spent a few minutes in the library, to which the men retired for coffee and cigars. He had one word with Clifford Savory.

"I heard you five years ago at the Bar Association," Savory said. "You spoke on John Marshall. I hope you're going to give me an evening on this visit."

Bronson Jane accompanied him to the door.

"You're taking it easy, I understand, Sir Edward, and going slow with dinners. What about the Florian tomorrow at half-past five? In these hot days that's a good time for a talk."

5

The library of the Florian Club looked out on the East River, where the bustle of traffic was now dying down and the turbid waters catching the mellow light of the summer evening. It might have been a room in an old English country house with its Chippendale chairs and bookcases, and the eighteenth-century mezzo-tints on the walls. The two men sat by the open window, and the wafts of cool evening air gave Leithen for the first time that day a little physical comfort.

"You want me to tell you about Francis Galliard?" Bronson Jane's wholesome face showed no signs of fatigue, though he had been having a gruelling day.

"I'll tell you all I can, but I warn you that it's not much. I suppose I'm as close to him as most people, but I can't say I knew him well. No one does--except perhaps his wife. But I can give you the general lay-out. First of all, he is a French-Canadian. Do you know anything about French Canada?"

"I once knew a little--a long time ago."

"Well, they are a remarkable race there. They ought to have made a rather bigger show in the world than they have. Here's a fine European stock planted out in a new country and toughened by two centuries of hardship and war. They keep their close family life and their religion intact and don't give a cent for what we call progress. Yet all the time they have a pretty serious fight with nature, so there is nothing soft in them. You would say that boys would come out of those farms of theirs with a real kick in them, for they have always been a race of pioneers. But so far Laurier is their only great man. You'd have thought that now and then they would have produced somebody big in the business line, like the Scots. You have young Highlanders, haven't you, coming out of the same primitive world, who become business magnates? We have had some of them in this country."

"Yes. That is not uncommon in Scotland."

"Well, Francis is the only specimen I've struck from French Canada. He came out of a farm in the Laurentians, somewhere back of the Glaubsteins' new pulp town at Chateau-Gaillard. I believe the Gaillards go right back to the Crusades. They came to Canada with Champlain, and were the seigneurs of Chateau-Gaillard, a tract of country as big as Rhode Island. By and by they came down in the world until now they only possess a little bit of a farm at the end of nowhere."

"What took him out of the farm? The French don't part easily from the land."

"God knows. Ambition? Poverty? He never told me. I don't just know how he was raised, for he never speaks of his early days. The village school, I suppose, and then some kind of college, for his first notion was to be a priest. He had a pretty good education of an old-fashioned kind. Then something stirred in him and he set off south like the fairy-tale Younger Son, with his pack on his back and his lunch in his pocket. He must have been about nineteen then."

Leithen's interest quickened. "Go on," he said, as Bronson paused. "How did he make good?"

"I'm darned if I know. There's a fine story there, but I can't get it out of him. He joined a French paper in Boston, and went on to another in Louisiana, and finished up in Chicago on a financial journal. I fancy that several times he must have pretty nearly starved. Then somehow he got into the bond Business and discovered that he had a genius for one kind of finance. He was with Connolly in Detroit for a time, and after that with the Pontiac Trust here, and then Ravelstons started out to discover new blood and got hold of him. At thirty-five he was a junior partner, and since then he has never looked back. To-day he's forty-three, and there aren't five men in the United States whose repute stands higher. Not bad for a farm boy, I'll say."

"Does he keep in touch with his people?"

"Not he. That door is closed and bolted. He has never been back to Canada. He's a naturalised American citizen. He won't speak French unless he's forced to, and then it's nothing to boast of. He writes his name

'Galliard,' not Gaillard. He has let himself become absorbed in our atmosphere."

"Really absorbed?"

"Well--that's just the point. He has adopted the externals of our life, but I don't know how much he's changed inside. When he married Felicity Dasent five years ago I thought we had got him for keeps. You don't know Mrs. Galliard?"

Leithen shook his head. He had been asked this question now a dozen times since he landed.

"No?" Well, I won't waste time trying to describe her, for you'll soon be able to judge for yourself; but I should call her a possessive personality, and she certainly annexed Francis. Oh, yes, he was desperately in love and only too willing to do what she told him. He's a good-looking fellow, but he hadn't bothered much about his appearance, so she groomed him up and made him the best- dressed man in New York. They've got a fine apartment in Park Avenue and her dinners have become social events. The Dasents are a horsey family and I doubt if Francis had ever mounted a horse until his marriage, but presently she had him out regularly with the Westbrook. He bought a country place in New Jersey and is going to start in to breed 'chasers. Altogether she gives him a pretty full life."

"Children?"

"No, not yet. A pity, for a child would have anchored Francis. I expect he has family in his blood like all his race."

"He never appeared to be restless, did he?" Leithen asked.

"Not that I noticed. He seemed perfectly content. He used to work too hard and wear himself out, and every now and then have to go off for a rest. That's the tom-fool habit we all have here. You see, he hadn't any special tastes outside his business to make him keen about leisure. Felicity changed all that. She isn't anything of the social climber, or ambitious for herself, but she's mighty ambitious for her man. She brought him into all kinds of new circles, and he shines in them, too, for he has excellent brains-- every kind of brains. All the gifts which made him a power in business she developed for other purposes. He was always a marvel in a business deal, for he could read other men's minds, and he would have made a swell diplomatist. Well, she turned that gift to social uses, with the result that every type mixes well at their parties. You'll hear as good talk at their table as you'll get anywhere on the civilised globe. He can do everything that a Frenchman can do, or an Englishman or an American. She has made him ten times more useful to Ravelstons than before, for she has made him a kind of national figure. The Administration has taken to consulting him, and he's one of the people that foreigners coming over here have got to see. I fancy she has politics at the back of her mind--last winter, I know, they were a good deal in Washington."

Bronson lit a fresh cigar.

"All set fair, you'd say, for the big success of our day. And then suddenly one fine morning he slips out of the world like the man in Browning's poem, and God knows what's become of him."

"You know him reasonably well? Is he happy?"

Bronson laughed. "That's a question I couldn't answer about my own brother. I doubt if I could answer it about myself. He is gay-- that is the French blood, maybe. I doubt if he has ever had time to consider whether he is happy or not, he lives such a bustling life. There can't be much of the introvert in Francis."

A man had entered the room and was engaged in turning over the magazines on one of the tables.

"Here's Savory," Bronson whispered. "Let's have him join us. He's a rather particular friend of Francis." He raised his voice. "Hullo, Clifford! Come and have a drink. Sir Edward wants to see you."

Clifford Savory, looking more like a country squire than ever in his well-cut grey flannels, deposited his long figure in an armchair and sipped the whisky-and-soda which the club servant brought him.

"We were talking about Galliard," Bronson said. "Sir Edward has heard a lot about him and is keen to meet him. It's just too bad that he should be out of town at present. It seems that Francis has got a reputation across the water. What was it you wanted to ask, Sir Edward? How much of his quality comes from his French blood?"

Savory joined his finger-tips and regarded them meditatively.

"That's hard to say. I don't know enough of the French in Canada, for they're different from the French in Europe. But I grant you that Galliard's power is exotic--not the ordinary gifts that God has given us Americans. He can argue a case brilliantly with the most close-textured reasoning; but there are others who can do that. His real strength lies in his flair, which can't be put down in black and white. He has an extra sense which makes him conscious of things which are still in the atmosphere--a sort of instinct of what people are going to think quite a bit ahead, not only in America, but in England and Europe. His mind is equipped with no end of sensitive antennæ. When he trusts that instinct he is never wrong, but now and then, of course, he is over-ridden by prosaic folk. If people had listened to him in '29 we should be better off now."

"That's probably due to his race," said Leithen. "Whenever you get a borderland where Latin and Northman meet, you get this uncanny sensitiveness."

"Yes," said Savory, "and yet in other things his race doesn't show up at all. Attachment to family and birthplace, for instance. Francis has forgotten all about his antecedents. He cares as little about his origin as Melchizedek. He is as rootless as the last-arrived Polish immigrant. He has pulled up his roots in Canada, and I do not think he is getting them down here--too restless for that."

"Restless?" Leithen queried.

"Well, I mean mobile--always on the move. He is restless in another way, too. I doubt if he is satisfied by what he does, or particularly happy. A man can scarcely be if he lives in a perpetual flux."

6

A figure was taking shape at the back of Leithen's mind, a figure without material mould, but an outline of character. He was beginning to realise something of the man he had come to seek. The following afternoon, when he stood in the hall of the Galliards' apartment in Park Avenue, he had the chance of filling in the physical details, for he was looking at a portrait of the man.

It was one of the young Van Rouyn's most celebrated achievements, painted two years earlier. It showed a man in riding breeches and a buff leather coat sitting on a low wall above a flower garden. His hair was a little ruffled by the wind, and one hand was repelling the advances of a terrier. Altogether an attractive detail of what should have been a "conversation piece." Leithen looked at the picture with the liveliest interest. Galliard was very different from the conception he had formed of him. He had thought of him as a Latin type, slim and very dark, and it appeared that he was more of a Norman, with well-developed shoulders like a football player. It was a pleasant face, the brown eyes were alight with life, and the mouth was both sensitive and firm. Perhaps the jaw was a little too fine drawn, and the air of bonhomie too elaborate to be quite natural. Still, it was a face a man would instinctively trust, the face of a good comrade, and there could be no question about its supreme competence. In every line there was energy and quick decision.

Leithen gazed at it for some time, trying to find what he had expected.

"Do you think it a good likeness?" he asked the woman at his side.

"It's Francis at his best and happiest," she answered.

Felicity Galliard was a fair edition of her sister Barbara. She was not quite so tall or quite so slim, and with all her grace she conveyed an impression, not only of physical health, but of physical power. There was a charming athleticism about her; she had none of Barbara's airy fragility. Her eyes were like her sister's, a cool grey with sudden lights in them which changed their colour. She was like a bird, always poised to fly, no easy swoop or flutter, but, if need be, a long stern flight against weather and wind.

She led Leithen into the drawing-room. Her house was very different from the Ravelstons', where a variety of oddments represented the tastes of many generations. It was a "period" piece, the walls panelled in a light, almost colourless wood, the scanty furniture carefully chosen, an Aubusson carpet, and hangings and chintzes of grey and old rose and silver. A Nattier over the fireplace made a centre for the exquisite harmony. It was a room without tradition or even individuality, as if its possessors had deliberately sought out something which should be non-committal, an environment which should neither reflect nor influence them.

"You never met Francis?" she asked as she made tea. "We have been twice to Europe since we married, but only once in England, and then only for a few days. They were business trips, and he didn't have a moment to himself."

Her manner was beautifully composed, with no hint of tragedy, but in her eyes Leithen read an anxiety so profound that it was beyond outward manifestation. This woman was living day and night with fear. The sight of her, and of the picture in the hall, moved him strangely. He felt that between the Galliards and the friendly eupeptic people he had been meeting there was a difference, not of degree, but of kind. There was a quality here, undependable, uncertain, dangerous perhaps, but rare and unmistakable. There had been no domestic jar--of that he was convinced. But something had happened to one of them to shatter a happy partnership. If he could discover that something he would have a clue for his quest.

"I have never met your husband," he said, "but I've heard a great deal about him, and I think I'm beginning to understand him. That picture in the hall helps, and you help. I know your sister and your uncle, and now that I'm an idle man I've promised to do what I can. If I'm to be of any use, Mrs. Galliard, I'm afraid I must ask you some questions. I know you'll answer them frankly. Tell me first what happened when he went away."

"It was the fourth day of May, a perfect spring day. I went down to Westchester to see an old friend. I said good-bye to Francis after breakfast, and he went to the office. I came back about five o'clock and found a note from him on my writing-table. Here it is."

She produced from an escritoire a half-sheet of paper. Leithen read--

Dearest, I am sick--very sick in mind. I am going away. When I am cured I will come back to you. All my love.

"He packed a bag himself--the butler knew nothing about it. He took money with him--at least there was a large sum drawn from his account. No, he didn't wind up things at the office. He left some big questions undecided, and his partners have had no end of trouble. He didn't say a word to any of them, or to anybody else that I know of. He left no clue as to where he was going. Oh, of course, we could have put on detectives and found out something, but we dare not do that. Every newspaper in the land would have started a hue and cry, and there would have been a storm of gossip. As it is, nobody knows about him except his partners, and one or two friends, and Uncle Blenkiron, and Babs and you. You see he may come back any day quite well again, and I would never forgive myself if I had been neurotic and let him down."

Leithen thought that neurotic was the last word he would have chosen to describe this wise and resolute woman.

"What was he like just before he left? Was there any change in his manner? Had he anything to worry him?"

"Nothing to worry him in business. Things were going rather specially well. And, anyhow, Francis never let himself be worried by affairs. He prided himself on taking things lightly--he was always what the old folk used to call debonair. But--yes, there were little changes in him, I think. All winter he had been almost too good and gentle and yielding. He did everything I asked him without questioning, and that was not always his way. . . . Oh! and he did one funny thing. We used to go down to Florida for a fortnight after Christmas--we had a regular foursome for golf, and he liked to bask in the sun. This year he didn't seem to care about it, and I didn't press him, for I'm rather bored with golf, so we stayed at home. There was a good deal of snow at Combermere-- that's our New Jersey home--and Francis got himself somewhere a pair of snow-shoes and used to go for long walks alone. When he came back he would sit by the hour in the library, not dozing, but thinking. I thought it was a good way of resting and never disturbed him."

"You never asked what he was thinking about?"

"No. He thought a good deal, you see. He always made leisure to think. My only worry was about his absurd modesty. He was sure of himself, but not nearly so sure as I was, and recently when people praised him and I repeated the praise he used to be almost cross. He wrote a memorandum for the Treasury about some tax scheme, and Mr. Beverley said that it was a work of genius. When I told him that, I remember he lay back in his chair and said quite bitterly, 'Quel chien de génie!' He never used a French phrase except when he was tired or upset. I remember the look on his face--it was as if I had really pained him. But I could find nothing to be seriously anxious about. He was perfectly fit and well."

"Did he see much of anybody in particular in the last weeks?"

"I don't think so. We always went about together, you know. He liked to talk to Mr. Jane and Mr. Savory, and they often dined with us. I think young Eric Ravelston came once or twice to the house-- Walter Derwent, too, I think. But he saw far more of me than of anybody else."

Her face suddenly stiffened with pain.

"Oh, Sir Edward, you don't think that he's dead--that he went away to die?"

"I don't. I haven't any fear of that. Any conclusion of mine would be worthless at the present stage, but my impression is that Mr. Galliard's trouble has nothing to do with his health. You and he have made a wonderful life together. Are you certain that he quite fitted into it?"

She opened her eyes.

"He was a huge success in it."

"I know. But did the success give him pleasure?"

"I'm sure it did. At least for most of the time."

"Yes, but remember that it was a strange world to him. He hadn't been brought up in it. He may have been homesick for something different."

"But he loved me!" she cried.

"He loved you. And therefore he will come back to you. But it may be to a different world."

7

New scenes, new faces, the interests of a new problem had given Leithen a few days of deceptive vitality. Then the reaction came, and for a long summer's day he sat on the veranda of his hotel bedroom in body a limp wreck, but with a very active mind. He tried to piece together what he had heard of Galliard, but could reach no conclusion. A highly strung, sensitive being, with Heaven knew what strains in his ancestry, had been absorbed into a new world in which he had been brilliantly successful. And then something had snapped, or some atavistic impulse had emerged from the deeps, something strong enough to break the tie of a happy marriage. The thing was sheer mystery. He had abandoned his old world and had never shown the slightest hankering after it. What had caused this sudden satiety with success?

Bronson Jane and Savory thought that the trouble was physical, a delicate machine overwrought and overloaded. The difficulty was that his health had always been perfect, and there was no medical adviser who could report on the condition of his nerves. His friends thought that he was probably lying hidden in some quiet sunny place, nursing himself back to vigour, with the secretiveness of a man to whom a physical breakdown was so unfamiliar that it seemed a portent, almost a crime.

But Savory had been enlightening. Scholarly, critical, fastidious, he had spoken of Galliard, the ordinary successful financier with no special cultural background, with an accent almost of worship.

"This country of ours," he told Leithen, "is up against the biggest problem in her history. It is not a single question like slavery or state rights, or the control of monopolies, or any of the straightforward things that have made a crisis before. It is a conglomeration of problems, most of which we cannot define. We have no geographical frontier left, but we've an eternal frontier in our minds. Our old American society is really in dissolution. All of us have got to find a new way of life. You're lucky in England, for you've been at the job for a long time and you make your revolutions so slowly and so quietly that you don't notice them--or anybody else. Here we have to make ours against time, while we keep shouting about them at the top of our voices. Everybody and everything here has to have a new deal, and the different deals have to be fitted together like a jig-saw puzzle, or there will be an infernal confusion. We're a great people, but we're only by fits and starts a nation. You're fortunate in your British Empire. You may have too few folk, and these few scattered over big spaces, but they're all organically connected, like the separate apples on a tree. Our huge population is more like a collection of pebbles in a box. It's only the containing walls of the box that keep them together."

So much for Savory's diagnosis.

"Francis is just the kind of fellow we need," he went on. "He sees what's coming. He's the most intellectually honest creature God ever made. He has a mind which not only cuts like a scalpel, but is rich and resourceful--both critical and creative. He hasn't any prejudices to speak of. He's a fascinating human being and rouses no antagonisms. It looks like he has dragged his anchor at present. But if we could get him properly moored again he's going to be a power for good in this country. We've got to get him back, Sir Edward--the old Francis."

The old Francis? Leithen had queried.

"Well, with the old genius. But with an extra anchor down. I've never been quite happy about the strength of his moorings."

8

Walter Derwent at first had nothing to tell him. Francis Galliard had not been interested in travel in far places. He was treasurer of his Polar Institute, but that was out of personal friendship. Francis had not much keenness in field sports either, though his wife had made him take up fox-hunting. He never went fishing, and in recent years he had not shot much, though he sometimes went after duck to Minnesota and the Virginia shore. He was not much of a bird-shot, but he was deadly with the rifle on the one occasion when Derwent had been with him after deer. . . .

Derwent screwed up his pleasant rosy face till, with his eagle beak, he looked like a benevolent vulture. And then suddenly he let drop a piece of information which made Leithen sit up.

"But he did ask me--I remember--if I could recommend him a really first-class guide, a fellow that understood woodcraft and knew the Northern woods. Maybe he was asking on behalf of someone else, for he couldn't have much use himself for a guide."

"When was that?" Leithen asked sharply.

"Some time after Christmas. Early February, I reckon. Yes, it was just after our Adventurers' Club dinner."

"Did you recommend one?"

"Yes. A fellow called Lew Frizel, a 'breed, but of a very special kind. His mother was a Cree Indian and his father one of the old- time Hudson's Bay factors. I've had Lew with me on half a dozen trips. I discovered him on a trap-line in northern Manitoba."

"Where is he now?"

"That's what I can't tell you. He seems to have gone over the horizon. I wanted him for a trip up the Liard this fall, but I can get no answer from any of his addresses. He has a brother Johnny who is about as good, but he's not available, for he has a job with the Canadian Government in one of its parks--Waskesieu, up Prince Albert way."

Leithen paid a visit to the Canadian Consulate, and after a talk with the Consul, who was an old friend, the telegraph was set in motion. Johnny Frizel, sure enough, had a job as a game warden at Waskesieu.

Another inquiry produced a slender clue. Leithen spent a morning at the Ravelston office and had a long talk with Galliard's private secretary, an intelligent young Yale man. From the office diary he investigated the subjects which had engaged Galliard's attention during his last weeks in New York. They were mostly the routine things on which the firm was then engaged, varied by a few special matters on which he was doing

Government work. But one point caught Leithen's eye. Galliard had called for the papers about the Glaubstein pulp mill at Chateau-Gaillard and had even taken them home with him.

"Was there anything urgent about them?" he asked.

The secretary said no. The matter was dead as far as Ravelstons were concerned. They had had a lot to do with financing the original proposition, but long ago they had had their profit and were quit of it.

9

Leithen's last talk was with young Eric Ravelston. During the days in New York he had felt at times his weakness acutely, but he had not been conscious of any actual loss of strength. He wanted to be assured that he had still a modest reservoir to draw upon. The specialist examined him carefully and then looked at him with the same solemn eyes as Acton Croke.

"You know your condition, of course?" he asked.

"I do. A few weeks ago I was told that I had about a year to live. Do you agree?"

"It's not possible to fix a time schedule. You may have a year--or a little less--or a little more. If you went to a sanatorium and lived very carefully you might have longer."

"I don't propose to lead a careful life. I've only a certain time and a certain amount of dwindling strength. I'm going to use them up on a hard job."

"Well, in that case you may fluff out very soon, or you may go on for a year or more, for the mind has something to say in these questions."

"There's no hope of recovery?"

"I'm afraid there's none--that is to say, in the light of our present knowledge. But, of course, we're not infallible."

"Not even if I turn myself into a complete invalid?"

"Not even then."

"Good. That's all I wanted to know. Now I've one other question. I'm going to look for Francis Galliard. You know him, but you never treated him, did you?"

Eric Ravelston shook his head.

"He didn't want any treatment. He was as healthy as a hound."

Something in the young man's tone struck Leithen.

"You mean in body. Had you any doubt about other things--his mind, for instance?"

The other did not at first reply.

"I have no right to say this," he spoke at last. "And, anyhow, it isn't my proper subject. But for some time I have been anxious about Francis. Little things, you know. Only a doctor would notice them. I thought that there was something pathological about his marvellous vitality. Once I had Garford, the neurologist, staying with me and the Galliards came to dinner. Garford could not keep his eyes off Francis. After they had gone he told me that he would bet a thousand dollars that he crumpled up within a year. . . . So if there's a time limit for you, Sir Edward, there's maybe a time limit also for Francis."

10

Leithen disembarked on a hot morning from the Quebec steamer which served the north shore of the St. Lawrence. Chateau-Gaillard was like any other pulp-town--a new pier with mighty derricks, the tall white cylinders of the pulp mill, a big brick office, and a cluster of clapboard shacks which badly needed painting. The place at the moment had a stagnant air, for the old cutting limits had been exhausted and the supply of pulp-wood from the new area was still being organised. A stream came in beyond the pier, and the background was steep scrub-clad hills cleft by a wedge-like valley beyond which there rose distant blue lines of mountain.

For the first mile or two the road up the valley was a hard, metalled highway. Leithen had not often felt feebler in body or more active in mind. Thoreau had been a favourite author of his youth, and he had picked up a copy in New York and had read it on the boat. Two passages stuck in his memory. One was from Walden--

"If you stand right fronting and face to face to a fact, you will see the sun glimmer on both its surfaces, as if it were a cimiter, and feel its sweet edge dividing you through the heart and marrow, and so you will happily conclude your mortal career. Be it life or death we crave only reality. If we are really dying, let us hear the rattle in our throat and feel the cold in the extremities; if we are alive, let us go about our business."

The other was only a sentence--

"The cost of a thing is the amount of what I will call life which is required to be exchanged for it."

How valuable was that thing for which he was bartering all that remained to him of life? At first Blenkiron's story had been no more than a peg on which to hang a private determination, an excuse, partly to himself and partly to the world, for a defiant finish to his career. The task fulfilled the conditions he wanted--activity for the mind and a final activity for the body. Francis Galliard was a disembodied ghost, a mere premise in an argument.

But now--Felicity had taken shape as a human being. There was an extraordinary appeal in her mute gallantry, her silent, self- contained fortitude. Barbara Clanroyden could not under any circumstances be pathetic; her airy grace was immune from the attacks of fate; she might bend, but she would never break. But her sister offered an exposed front to fortune. She was too hungry for life, too avid of experience, too venturesome, and more, she had set herself the task of moulding her husband to her ambitions. No woman, least of all his wife, would attempt to mould Sandy Clanroyden. . . . And the gods had given her tough material--not a docile piece of American manhood, but something exotic and unpredictable, something for which she had acquired a desperate affection, but of which she had only a dim understanding.

As for Francis, that shadow too was taking form. Leithen now had a picture of him in his mind, but it was not that of the portrait in the hall of the Park Avenue apartment. Oddly enough, it was of an older man, with a rough yellow beard. His eyes were different too, wilder, less assured, less benevolent. He told himself that he had reconstructed the physical appearance to match his conception of the character. For he had arrived at a provisional assessment of the man. . . . The chains of race and tradition are ill to undo, and Galliard, in his brilliant advance to success, had loosened, not broken them. Something had happened to tighten them again. The pull of an older world had jerked him out of his niche. But how? And whither?

11

The valley above the township was an ugly sight. The hillsides had been lumbered out and only scrub was left, and the shutes where the logs had been brought down were already tawny with young brushwood. In the bottom was a dam, which had stretched well up the slopes, for the lower scrub was bleached and muddied with water. But the sluices had been opened and the dam had shrunk to a few hundred yards in width, leaving the near hillsides a hideous waste of slime, the colour of a slag-heap. The place was like the environs of a town in the English Black Country.

Suddenly he was haunted by a recollection, a shadow at the back of his mind. The outline of the hills was familiar. Looking back, he realised that he had seen before the bluff which cut the view of the St. Lawrence into a wedge of blue water. He had forgotten the details of that journey thirty years ago when he had tramped down from the mountains; but it must have been in this neighbourhood. There was a navvy on some job by the roadside, and he stopped the car and spoke to him.

The man shook his head. "I'm a newcomer here. There's a guy up there--a Frenchie--maybe he'd tell you."

Johnny Frizel went up the track in the bush to where a countryman was cutting stakes. He came back and reported.

"He says that before the dam was made there was a fine little river down there. The Clairefontaine was the name of it."

Leithen's memory woke into vivid life. This valley had been his road down country long ago. He remembered its loveliness when Chateau-Gaillard had been innocent of pulp mills and no more than a hamlet of painted houses and a white church. There had been a strip of green meadow-land by the waterside grazed by old-fashioned French cattle, and the stream had swept through it in deep pools and glittering shallows, while above it pine and birch had climbed in virgin magnificence to the crests. Now all the loveliness had been butchered to enable some shoddy newspaper to debauch the public soul. He had only seen the place once long ago at the close of a blue autumn day, but the desecration beat on his mind like a blow. What had become of the little Clairefontaine farm at the river head, and that delicate place on the height of land which had of late been haunting him? . . . He felt a curious nervousness and it brought on a fit of coughing.

At the end of the dam the road climbed the left side of the valley through patches of spruce and a burnt-out area of blackened stumps. A ridge separated it from the stream, and when it turned again to the water's edge the character of the valley had changed. The Clairefontaine rumbled in a deep gorge, and as the aged Ford wheezed its way up the dusty roads Chateau-Gaillard and its ugliness were shut off and Leithen found himself in a sanctuary of the hills. He could not link up the place with his memory of thirty years ago when he had descended it on foot in the gold and scarlet of autumn. Then it had been a pathway to the outer world; now it was the entry into a secret and strange land. There was no colour in the scene, except the hard blue of the sky. The hot noon had closed down like a lid on an oppressive dull green waste which offered no welcome.

His mind was full of Francis Galliard. Once this had been the seigneur of his family, running back from the tide water some scores of miles into the wilderness. He felt the man here more vividly than ever before, but he could not affiliate him with the landscape, except that he also was a mystery. . . .

Why had his wife and his friends in New York been so oddly supine in looking for him? They had waited and left it for a stranger to take on the job. Fear of publicity, of course, in that over-public world. But was that the only reason? Was there not also fear of Galliard? He was not of their world, and they admired and loved him, but uncomprehendingly. Even Felicity. What did they fear? That they might wreck a subtle mechanism by a too heavy hand? They were all sensitive people and highly intelligent, and they would have not walked so delicately without a cause. Only now, when he was entering the cradle of Galliard's race, did he realise how intricate was the task to which he had set himself. And one to be performed against time. He remembered the young

Ravelston's words. There was a time limit for Francis Galliard, as there was one for Edward Leithen.

The valley mounted by steps, each one marked by the thunder of a cataract in the gorge. Presently they rose above the woods, and came out on a stretch of open upland where the stream flowed among patches of crops and meadows of hay. Now his memory was clearer, for he remembered this place in exact detail. There was the farm of Clairefontaine, with its shingled, penthouse roof, its white- painted front, its tall weather-beaten barn, its jumble of decrepit outhouses. There was the little church of the parish, the usual white box, with a tin-coated spire now shining like silver in the sun, and beside it a hump-backed presbytery. And there was something beyond of which the memory was even sharper. For the valley seemed to come to an end, the wooded ranges closed in on it, but there was a crack through which the stream must flow from some distant upland. He knew what lay beyond that nick which was like the back-sight of a rifle.

"We won't stop here," he told Johnny, who handled the Ford like an artist. "Go on as far as the road will take us."

It did not take them far. They bumped among stumps and roots over what was now a mere cart track, but at the beginning of the cleft the track died away into a woodland trail. They got out, and Leithen led the way up the Clairefontaine. There was something tonic in the air which gave him a temporary vigour, and he was surprised that he could climb the steep path without too great discomfort. When they rested on a mossy rock by the stream he found that he ate his sandwiches with some appetite. But after that it was heavy going, for there was the inevitable waterfall to surmount, and, weary and panting, he came out into the ultimate meadow of the Clairefontaine, which was fixed so clearly in his recollection.

It was a cup in the hills, floored not with wild hay, but with short, crisp pasture like an English down. From its sides descended the rivulets which made the Clairefontaine, and in the heart of it was a pool fringed with flags, so clear that through its six-foot depth the little stir in the sand could be seen where the water bubbled up from below. The place was so green and gracious that all sense of the wilds was lost, and it seemed like a garden in a long-settled land, a garden made centuries ago by the very good and the very wise.

But it was a watch-tower as well as a sanctuary. Looking south, the hills opened to show Le Fleuve, the great river of Canada, like a pool of colourless light. North were higher mountains, which seemed to draw together with a purpose, huddling to shepherd the streams towards a new goal. They were sending the waters, not to the familiar St. Lawrence, but to untrodden Arctic wastes. That was the magic of the place. It was a frontier between the desert and the sown. To Leithen it was something more. He felt again the spell which had captured him here in his distant youth.

It was the borderline between the prosaic world, where things went by rule and rote and were all fitted to the human scale, and the world as God first made it out of chaos, which had no care for humanity.

He stretched himself full length on the turf, his eyes feasting on the mystery of the northern hills. Almost he had a sense of physical well-being, for his breath was less troublesome. Then Johnny Frizel came into the picture, placidly smoking an old black pipe. He fitted in well, and Leithen began to reflect on his companion, who had docilely, at the order of his superiors, flown over half Canada to join him.

Johnny was a small man, about five feet six, with broad shoulders and sturdy, bandy legs. He wore an old pair of khaki breeches and a lumberman's laced boots, but the rest of his garb was conventional, for he had put on his best clothes, not knowing what his duties might be. He had a round bullet head covered with black hair cut very short, and his ears stuck out like the handles of a pitcher. His Indian mother showed in his even brown colouring, and his father in his mild, meditative blue eyes. So far Leithen had scarcely realised him, except to admire his speech, which was a wonderful blend of the dialect of the outlands, the slang of America, and literary idioms, for Johnny was a great reader--all spoken in the voice of a Scots shepherd, and with a broad Scots accent. When the War broke out Johnny had been in the Labrador and his brother Lew on the lower Mackenzie, and both, as soon as they got the news, had made a bee-line for France and the front. They had been notable snipers in the Canadian Corps, as the notches on the butts of their service rifles witnessed.

"You have been lent to me, Johnny," Leithen said. "Seconded for special service, as we used to say in the army. I had better tell you our job." Briefly he sketched the story of Francis Galliard.

"This is the place where he was brought up," he said. "My notion is that he's in Canada now. I think he is with your brother--at any rate, I know that he was making enquiries about him in the early spring. You haven't heard from your brother lately?"

"Not since Christmas. Lew never troubles to put me wise about his doings. He may be anywhere on God's earth."

"We want to find out if we can, from old Gaillard at the farm and the priest, if the young Galliard has been here. Or your brother. If my guess is right they won't be very willing to speak, but with luck they may give themselves away. If the young Galliard has been here it gives us a bit of a clue. They are a hospitable lot, so I propose that we quarter ourselves on them for the night to have the chance of a talk. You can put up at the farm, and I dare say I can get a shake-down at the presbytery."

Johnny nodded approval. His blue eyes dwelt searchingly on Leithen's thin face, from which the flush of bodily exercise had gone, leaving a grey pallor.

They retraced their steps when the sun had sunk behind the hills and the evening glow was beginning, soft as the bloom on a peach. The Ford was turned, and rumbled down the valley until it was parked in the presbytery yard. The priest, Father Paradis, came out to greet them, a tall, lean old man much bent in the shoulders, who, like all the Quebec clergy, wore the cassock. He had been gardening, and his lumberjack's boots were coated with soil.

To Leithen's relief Father Paradis spoke the French of France, for, though Canadian born, he had been trained in a seminary at Beauvais.

"But of a surety," he cried. "You shall sleep here, monsieur, and share my supper. I have a guest room, though it is as small as the Prophet's Chamber of the Scriptures."

He would have Johnny stay also.

"No doubt Augustin can lodge Monsieur Frizel, but I fear he will have rough quarters."

Leithen's kit was left at the presbytery and he and Johnny walked to the farm to pay their respects to the squire of Clairefontaine. He had ascertained that this

Augustin Gaillard, to whom the farm had descended, was an uncle of Francis. The priest had given him a rapid sketch of the family history. The mother had died in bearing Francis; the father a year after Francis had left for the States. There had been an elder brother, Paul, who two years ago had disappeared into the north, leaving his uncle from Chateau-Gaillard in his place. There were also two sisters who were Grey Nuns serving somewhere in the west--the priest did not know where.

Augustin Gaillard was a man of perhaps sixty years, with a wisp of grey beard and a moist, wandering eye. Everything about him bespoke the drunkard. His loud-patterned shirt had a ragged collar and sleeves, his waistcoat was discoloured with the dribbling of food, his trousers had holes at the knees, and his bare feet were shod with bottes-sauvages. There was nothing in his features to suggest the good breeding which Leithen had noted in the picture of Francis. The house, which was more spacious than the ordinary farm, was in a condition of extreme dirt and disorder. Somewhere in the background Leithen had a glimpse of an ancient crone, who was doubtless the housekeeper.

But Augustin had the fine manners of his race. He placed his dwelling and all that was in it at their disposal. He pressed Leithen to remove himself from the presbytery.

"The good father," he said, "has but a poor table. He will give you nothing to drink but cold water."

Leaving Johnny deep in converse in the habitant patois, Leithen went back in the dusk to the presbytery. He was feeling acutely the frailty of his body, as he was apt to do at nightfall. Had he chosen a different course he would be going back to delicate invalid food, to a soft chair and a cool bed; now he must make shift with coarse fare and the hard pallet of the guest room. He wondered for a moment if he had not been every kind of fool.

But no sick-nurse could have been more attentive than Father Paradis. He had killed and cooked a chicken with his own hands. For supper there was soup and the fowl, and coffee made by one who had learned the art in France. The little room was lit by a paraffin lamp, the smell of which brought back to Leithen far-away days in a Scots shooting box. The old man saw his guest's weakness, and after the meal he put a pillow in his chair and made him rest his legs on a stool.

"I see you are not in good health, monsieur," he said. "Do you travel to restore yourself? The air of these hills is well reputed."

"Partly. And partly in hope of finding a friend. I am an Englishman, as you see, and am a stranger in Canada, though I have visited it once before. On that occasion I came to hunt, but my hunting days are over."

Father Paradis screwed up his old eyes.

"At home you were perhaps a professor?"

"I have been a lawyer--and also a Member of our Parliament. But my working days are past, and I would make my soul."

"You are wise. You are then in retreat? You are not, I think, of the Faith?"

Leithen smiled. "I have my faith to find, and perhaps I have little time in which to find it."

"There is little time for any of us," said the old man. He looked at Leithen with eyes long experienced in life, and shook his head sadly.

"I spoke of a friend," said Leithen. "Have you had many visitors this summer?"

"Few come here nowadays. A pedlar or two, and a drover in the fall for the farm cattle. There is no logging, for our woods are bare. People used to come up from Chateau-Gaillard on holiday, but Chateau-Gaillard is for the moment stagnant. Except for you and Monsieur Frizel it is weeks since I have seen a stranger."

"Had you no visitor from New York--perhaps in May? A man of the name of Francis Galliard?"

Leithen, from long practice in cross-examination, was accustomed to read faces. He saw the priest's eyes suddenly go blank, as if a shutter had been drawn over them, and his mouth tighten.

"No man of that name has visited us," he said.

"Perhaps he did not give that name. The man I mean is still young," and he described the figure as he had seen it in the New York portrait. "He is a kinsman, I think, of the folk at the farm."

Father Paradis shook his head.

"No, there has been no Francis Galliard here."

But there was that in the old man's eyes which informed Leithen that he was not telling all he knew, and also that no cross- examination would elicit more. His face had the stony secrecy of the confessional.

"Well, I must look elsewhere," Leithen said cheerfully. "Tell me of the people at the farm. I understand they are one of the oldest families in Canada."

Father Paradis's face lightened.

"Most ancient, but now, alas! pitifully decayed. The father was a good man, and a true son of the Church, but his farm failed, for he had little worldly wisdom. As for Augustin, he is, as you see, a drunkard. The son Paul was a gallant young man, but he was not happy on this soil. He was a wanderer, as his race was in the old days."

"Wasn't there a second son?"

"Yes, but he left us long ago. He forsook his home and his faith. Let us not speak of him, for he is forgotten."

"Tell me about Paul."

"You must know, monsieur, that once the Gaillards were a stirring race. They fought with Frontenac against the Iroquois, and very fiercely against the English. Then, when peace came, they exercised their hardihood in distant ventures. Many of the house travelled far into the west and the north, and few of them returned. There was one, Aristide, who searched for the lost British sailor Frankolin--how do you call him?--and won fame. And only the other day there was Paul's uncle--also an Aristide--who found a new road to the Arctic shores and discovered a great river. Its name should be the Gaillard, but they tell me that the maps have the Indian word, the Ghost."

Leithen, who had a passion for studying maps, remembered the river which flowed from north of the Thelon in the least-known corner of Canada.

"Is that where Paul went?" he asked.

"That is what we think. He was restless ever after his father died. He would go off for months to guide parties of hunters--even down to the Labrador, and in his dreams he had always his uncle Aristide; he was assured he was still alive and that if he went to the Ghost River he would find him. So one day he summons the other uncle, the worthless one, and bids him take over the farm of Clairefontaine."

"You have heard nothing of him since?"

"Not a word has come. Why should it? He has no care for Clairefontaine. . . . Now, monsieur, it is imperative that you go to bed, for you are very weary. I will conduct you to the Prophet's Chamber."

Leithen was in the habit of falling asleep at once--it was now his one bodily comfort--but this night he lay long awake. He thought that he had read himself into the soul of Francis Galliard, a summary and provisional reading, but enough to give him a starting point. He was convinced beyond doubt that he had come to Clairefontaine in the spring. He could not mistake the slight hesitation in the speech of Father Paradis, the tremor of the eyelids, the twitch of the mouth before it set--he had seen these things too often in the courts to be wrong. The priest had not lied, but he had equivocated, and had he been pressed would have taken refuge in obstinate silence. Francis had been here and had enjoined secrecy on the priest and no doubt on old Augustin. He was on a private errand and wanted to shut out the world.

He could picture the sequence of events. The man, out of tune with his environment, had fallen into the clutches of the past. He had come to Chateau-Gaillard and seen the ravaged valley--ravaged by himself and his associates--and thereby a bitter penitence had been awakened. His purpose now was to make his peace with the past-- with his family, his birth-place and his religion. No doubt he had confessed himself to the priest. Perhaps he had gone, as Leithen had gone, to the secret meadow at the river head, and, looking to the north, had had boyish memories and ambitions awakened. It was his business--so Leithen read his thoughts--to make restitution, to appease his offended household gods. He must shake off the bonds of an alien civilisation, and, like his uncle and his brother and a hundred Gaillards of old, worship at the altars of the northern wilds.

Leithen fell asleep with so clear a picture in his mind that he might have been reading in black and white Francis's confession.

12

"We go back to Quebec," he told Johnny next morning. "But first I want to go up the stream again."

The mountain meadow haunted his imagination. There, the afternoon before, he had had the first hour of bodily comfort he had known for months. The place, too, inspired him. It seemed to stiffen his purpose and to quicken his fancy.

Once again he lay on the warm turf beside the spring looking beyond the near forested hills to the blue dimness of the far mountains. It was that halcyon moment of the late Canadian summer when there are no flies, and even the midday is cool and scented, and the first hints of bright colour are stealing into the woods.

"I didn't get a great deal out of the old man," said Johnny. "He kept me up till three in the morning listenin' to his stuff. He was soused when he began, and well pickled before he left off, but he was never lit up--the liquor isn't brewed that could light up that old carcase. I guess he's got a grouse against the whole world. But I found out one thing. Brother Lew has been here this year."

Leithen sat up. "How do you know?"

"Why, he asked me if I was any relation to another man of my name-- a fellow with half a thumb on his left hand and a scar above his right eyebrow. That's Lew to the life, for he got a bit chawed up at Vimy. When I asked more about the chap he felt he had said too much and shut up like a clam. But that means that Lew has been here all right, and that Augustin saw him, for to my certain knowledge Lew was never before east of Quebec, and yon old perisher has never stirred out of this valley. So I guess that Lew and your pal were here, for Lew wouldn't have come on his own."

Leithen reflected for a moment.

"Was Lew ever at the Ghost River?" he asked. "I mean the river half-way between Coronation Gulf and the top of Hudson's Bay."

"Never heard of it. Nope. I'm pretty sure brother Lew was never within a thousand miles of it. It ain't his bailliewick."

"Well, I fancy he's there now. . . . You and I are setting out for the Ghost River."

13

Leithen spent two weary days in Montreal, mostly at the telephone, a business which in London he had always left to Cruddock or his clerk. He knew that the Northland was one vast whispering gallery, and that it was easier to track a man there than in the settled countries, so he hoped to get news by setting the machine of the R.C.M.P. to work. There was telephoning and telegraphing far and wide, but no result. No such travellers as Galliard and Lew Frizel had as yet been reported north of the railways. One thing he did ascertain. The two men had not flown to the Ghost River. That was the evidence of the Air Force and the private aeroplane companies. Leithen decided that this was what he had expected. If Galliard was on a mission of penitence he would travel as his uncle Aristide and his brother Paul had travelled--by canoe and trail. If he had started early in May he should just about have reached the Arctic shores.

The next task was to get a machine for himself. He hired an aeroplane from Air-Canada, a Baird-Sverisk of a recent pattern, and was lucky enough to get one of the best of the northern flyers, Job Teviot, for his pilot, and one Murchison as his mechanic. The contract was for a month, but with provision for an indefinite extension. All this meant bringing in his bankers, and cabling home, and the influence of Ravelstons had to be sought to complete the business. The barometer at Montreal stood above 100 degrees, and there were times before he and Johnny took off when he thought that his next move would be to a hospital.

He felt stronger when they reached Winnipeg, and next day, flying over the network of the Manitoba lakes, he found that he drew breath more easily. He had flown little before, and the air at first made him feel very sleepy. This passed, and, since there was no demand for activity, his mind turned in on itself. He felt like some disembodied creature, for already he seemed to have shed all ordinary interests. Aforetime on his travels and his holidays he had been acutely interested in what he saw and heard, and part of his success at the Bar had been due to the wide range of knowledge thus acquired. But now he had no thoughts except for the job on hand. He had meant deliberately to concentrate on it, in order to shut out fruitless meditations on his own case; but he found that this concentration had come about automatically. He simply was not concerned about other things. In New York he had listened to well- informed talk about politics and business and books, and it had woke no response in his mind. Here in Canada he did not care a jot about the present or future of a great British Dominion. The Canadian papers he glanced at were full of the perilous situation in Europe--any week there might be war. The news meant nothing to him, though a little while ago it would have sent him home by the next boat. The world had narrowed itself to Francis Galliard and the frail human creature that was following him.

By and by it was the latter that crowded in on his thoughts. Since he had nothing to do except watch a slowly moving landscape and the cloud shadows on lake and forest, he began to reflect on the atom, Edward Leithen, now hurrying above the world. The memory of Felicity kept returning--the sudden anguish in her eyes, her cry "I love him! I love him!" and he realised how lonely his life had been. No woman had ever felt like that about him; he had never felt like that about any woman. Was it loss or gain? Gain, he told himself, for he implicated no one in his calamity. But had he not led a starved life? A misfit like Galliard had succeeded in gaining something which he, with all his social adaptability, had missed. He found himself in a mood almost of regret. He had made a niche for himself in the world, but it had been a chilly niche. With a start he awoke to the fact that he was very near the edge of self-pity, a thing forbidden.

In a blue windless twilight they descended for the night at a new mining centre on the Dog-Rib River. Johnny pitched a tent and cooked supper, while the pilot and the mechanic found quarters with other pilots who ran the daily air service to the south. There was a plague of black flies and mosquitoes, but Leithen was too tired to be troubled by them, and he had eight hours of heavy, unrefreshing sleep.

When he stood outside the tent next morning, looking over a shining lake and a turbulent river, he had a moment of sharp regret. How often he had stood like this on a lake shore--in Scotland, in Norway, in Canada long ago--and watched the world heave itself out of night into dawn! Like this--but how unlike! Then he had been exhilarated with the prospect of a day's sport, tingling from his cold plunge, ravenous as a hawk for breakfast, the blood brisk in his veins and every muscle in trim. Now he could face only a finger of bacon and a half-cup of tea, and he was weary before the day had begun.

"There's plenty here knows Lew," Johnny reported. "They haven't come this way. If they're at the Ghost River, my guess is that they've gone by the Planchette and The Old Man Falls."

They crossed Great Slave Lake and all morning flew over those plains miscalled the Barrens, which, seen from above, are a delicate lace-work of lakes and streams criss-crossed by ridges of bald rock and banks of gravel, and with now and then in a hollow a patch of forest. They made camp early at the bend of a river, which Johnny called the Little Fish, for Murchison had some work to do on the engine. While Leithen rested by the fire Job went fishing and brought back three brace of Arctic char. He announced that there was another camp round the next bend--a white man in a canoe with two Crees--a sight in that lonely place as unexpected as the great auk. Somewhat refreshed by his supper, Leithen in the long-lighted evening walked upstream to see his neighbour.

He found a middle-aged American cleaning a brace of ptarmigan which he had shot, and doing it most expertly. He was a tall man, in breeches, puttees, and a faded yellow shirt, and Leithen took him for an ordinary trapper or prospector until he heard him speak. "I saw you land," the stranger said. "I was coming round presently to pass the time of day. Apart from my own outfit you are the first man I've seen for a month."

He prepared a bed of hot ashes, and with the help of rifle rods set the birds to roast. Then he straightened himself, filled a pipe, and had a look at Leithen.

"I'm an American," he said. "New York."

Leithen nodded. He had already detected the unmistakable metropolitan pitch of the voice.

"You're English? Haven't I seen you before? I used to be a good deal in London. . . . Hold on a minute. I've got it. I've heard you speak in the British Parliament. That would be in--" And he mentioned a year.

"Very likely," said Leithen. "I was in Parliament then. I was Attorney-General."

"You don't say. Well, we're birds of the same flock. I'm a corporation lawyer. My name's Taverner. Yours--wait a minute--is Leven."

"Leithen," the other corrected.

"Odd we should meet here in about the wildest spot in North America. It's easy enough to come by air, like you, but Matthew and Mark and I have taken two blessed months canoeing and portaging from railhead, and it will take us about the same time to get back."

"Can corporation lawyers like you take four months' holiday?"

Mr. Taverner's serious face relaxed in a smile. "Not usually. But I had to quit or smash. No, I wasn't sick. I was just tired of the dam' racket. I had to get away from the noise. The United States is getting to be a mighty noisy country."

The cry of a loon broke the stillness, otherwise there was no sound but the gurgle of the river and the grunting of one of the Indians as he cleaned a gun.

"You get silence here," said Leithen.

"I don't mean physical noise so much. The bustle in New York doesn't worry me more than a little. I mean noise in our minds. You can't get peace to think nowadays." He broke off. "You here for the same cause?"

"Partly," said Leithen. "But principally to meet a friend."

"I hope you'll hit him off. It's a biggish country for an assignation. But you don't need an excuse for cutting loose and coming here. I pretend I come to fish and hunt, but I only fish and shoot for the pot. I'm no sort of sportsman. I'm just a poor devil that's been born in the wrong century. There's quite a lot of folk like me. You'd be surprised how many of us slip off here now and then to get a little quiet. I don't mean the hearty, husky sort of fellow who goes into the woods in a fancy mackinaw and spends his time there drinking whisky and playing poker. I mean quiet citizens like myself, who've simply got to breathe fresh air and get the din out of their ears. Canada is becoming to some of us like a mediæval monastery to which we can retreat when things get past bearing."

Taverner, having been without white society for so long, seemed to enjoy unburdening himself.

"I'm saying nothing against my country. I know it's the greatest on earth. But my God! I hate the mood it has fallen into. It seems to me there isn't one section of society that hasn't got some kind of jitters--big business, little business, politicians, the newspaper men, even the college professors. We can't talk except too loud. We're bitten by the exhibitionist bug. We're all boosters and high-powered salesmen and propagandists, and yet we don't know what we want to propagand, for we haven't got any kind of common creed. All we ask is that a thing should be colourful and confident and noisy. Our national industry is really the movies. We're one big movie show. And just as in the movies we worship languishing Wops and little blonde girls out of the gutter, so we pick the same bogus deities in other walks of life. You remember Emerson speaks about some nations as having guano in their destiny. Well, I sometimes think that we have got celluloid in ours."

There was that in Leithen's face which made Taverner pause and laugh.

"Forgive my rigmarole," he said. "It's a relief to get one's peeves off the chest, and I reckon I'm safe with you. You see, I come of New England stock, and I don't fit in too well with these times."

"Do you know a man called Galliard?" Leithen asked. "Francis Galliard--a partner in Ravelstons?"

"A little. He's a friend of Bronson Jane, and Bronson's my cousin. Funny you should mention him, for if I had to choose a fellow that fitted in perfectly to the modern machine, I should pick Galliard. He enjoys all that riles me. He's French, and that maybe explains it. I've too much of the Puritan in my blood. You came through New York, I suppose. Did you see Galliard? How is he? I've always had a liking for him."

"No. He was out of town."

Leithen got up to go. The long after-glow in the west was fading, and the heavens were taking on the shadowy violet which is all the northern summer darkness.

"When do you plan to end your trip?" Taverner asked as he shook hands.

"I don't know. I've no plans. I've been ill, as you see, and it will depend on my health."

"This will set you up, never fear. I was a sick man three years ago and I came back from Great Bear Lake champing like a prize- fighter. But take my advice and don't put off your return too late. It don't do to be trapped up here in winter. The North can be a darn cruel place."

14

Late next afternoon they reached the Ghost River delta, striking in upon it at an angle from the southwest. The clear skies had gone, and the "ceiling" was not more than a thousand feet. Low hills rimmed the eastern side, but they were cloaked in a light fog, and the delta seemed to have no limits, but to be an immeasurable abscess of decay. Leithen had never imagined such an abomination of desolation. It was utterly silent, and the only colours were sickly greens and drabs. At first sight he thought he was looking down on a bit of provincial Surrey, broad tarmac roads lined with asphalt footpaths, and behind the trim hedges smooth suburban lawns. It took a little time to realise that the highways were channels of thick mud, and the lawns bottomless quagmires. He was now well inside the Circle, and had expected from the Arctic something cold, hard, and bleak, but also clean and tonic. Instead he found a horrid lushness--an infinity of mire and coarse vegetation, and a superfluity of obscene insect life. The place was one huge muskeg. It was like the no-man's-land between the trenches in the War--a colossal no-man's-land created in some campaign of demons, pitted and pocked with shell-holes from some infernal artillery.

They skirted the delta and came down at its western horn on the edge of the sea. Here there was no mist, and he could look far into the North over still waters eerily lit by the thin evening sunlight. It was like no ocean he had ever seen, for it seemed to be without form or reason. The tide licked the shore without purpose. It was simply water filling a void, a treacherous, deathly waste, pale like a snake's belly, a thing beyond humanity and beyond time. Delta and sea looked as if here the Demiurge had let His creative vigour slacken and ebb into nothingness. He had wearied of the world which He had made and left this end of it to ancient Chaos.

Next morning the scene had changed, and to his surprise he felt a lightening of both mind and body. Sky and sea were colourless, mere bowls of light. There seemed to be no tides, only a gentle ripple on the grey sand. Very far out there were blue gleams which he took to be ice. The sun was warm, but the body of the air was cold, and it had in it a tonic quality which seemed to make his breathing easier. He remembered hearing that there were no germs in the Arctic, that the place was one great sanatorium, but that did not concern one whose trouble was organic decay. Still, he was grateful for a momentary comfort, and he found that he wanted to stretch his legs. He walked to the highest point of land at the end of a little promontory.

It was a place like a Hebridean cape. The peaty soil was matted with berries, though a foot or two beneath was eternal ice. The breeding season was over and the migration not begun, so there was no bird life on the shore; the wild fowl were all in the swamps of the delta. The dead-level of land and sea made the arc of sky seem immense, the "intense inane" of Shelley's poem. The slight recovery of bodily vigour quickened his imagination. This was a world not built on the human scale, a world made without thought of mankind, a world colourless and formless, but also timeless; a kind of eternity. It would be a good place to die in, he thought, for already the clinging ties of life were loosened and death would mean little since life had ceased.

To his surprise he saw a small schooner anchored at the edge of a sandbank, a startling thing in that empty place. Johnny had joined him, and they went down to inspect it. An Eskimo family was on board, merry, upstanding people from far-distant Gordans Land. The skipper was one Andersen, the son of a Danish whaling captain and an Eskimo mother, and he spoke good English. He had been to Herschell Island to lay in stores, and was now on his way home after a difficult passage through the ice of the Western Arctic. The schooner was as clean as a new pin, and the instruments as well kept as on a man-o'-war. It had come in for fresh water, and Job was able to get from it a few tins of gasolene, for it was a long hop to the next fuelling stage. The visit to the Andersens altered Leithen's mood. Here was a snug life being lived in what had seemed a place of death. It switched his interest back to his task.

Presently he found what he had come to seek. On the way to the tent they came on an Eskimo cemetery. Once there had been a settlement here which years ago had been abandoned. There were half a dozen Eskimo graves, with skulls and bones showing through chinks in the piles of stone, and in one there was a complete skeleton stretched as if on a pyre. There was something more. At a little distance in a sheltered hollow were two crosses of driftwood. One was bent and weathered, with the inscription, done with a hot iron, almost obliterated, but it was possible to read . . . . TID . GAIL . . . D. There was a date too blurred to decipher. The other cross was new and it had not suffered the storms of more than a couple of winters. On it one could read clearly PAUL LOUIS GAILLARD and a date eighteen months back.

To Leithen there was an intolerable pathos about the two crosses. They told so much, and yet they told nothing. How had Aristide died? Had Paul found him alive? How had Paul died? Who had put up the memorials? There was a grim drama here at which he could not even guess. But the one question that mattered to him was, had Francis seen these crosses?

Johnny, who had been peering at the later monument, answered that question.

"Brother Lew has been here," he said.

He pointed to a little St. Andrew's cross freshly carved with a knife just below Paul's name. Its ends were funnily splayed out.

"That's Lew's mark," he said. "You might say it's a family mark. Long ago, when Dad was working for the

Bay, there was a breed of Indians along the Liard, some sort of Slaveys, that had got into their heads that they were kind of Scots, and every St. Andrew's Day they would bring Dad a present of a big St. Andrew's Cross, very nicely carved, which he stuck above the door like a horse- shoe. So we all got into the way of using that cross as our trade mark, especially Lew, who's mighty particular. I've seen him carve it on a slab to stick above a dog's grave, and when he writes a letter he puts it in somewhere. So whenever you see it you can reckon Lew's ahead of you."

"They can't be long gone," said Leithen.

"I've been figuring that out, and I guess they might have gone a week ago--maybe ten days. Lew's pretty handy with a canoe. What puzzles me is where they've gone and how. There's no place hereaways to get supplies, and it's a good month's journey to the nearest post. Maybe they shot caribou and smoked 'em. I tell you what, if your pal's got money to burn, what about him hiring a plane to meet 'em here and pick 'em up? If that's their game it won't be easy to hit their trail. There's only one thing I'm pretty sure of, and that is they didn't go home. If we fossick about we'll maybe find out more."

Johnny's forecast was right, for that afternoon they heard a shot a mile off, and, going out to inquire, found an Eskimo hunter. At the sight of them the man fled, and Johnny had some trouble rounding him up. When halted he stood like a sullen child, a true son of the Elder Ice, for he had a tattooed face and a bone stuck through his upper lip. Probably he had never seen a white man before. He had been hunting caribou before they migrated south from the shore, and had a pile of skins and high-smelling meat to show for his labours. He stubbornly refused to accompany them back to the tent, so Leithen left him with Johnny, who could make some shape at the speech of the central Arctic.

When Johnny came back Andersen and the schooner had sailed, and Ghost River had returned to its ancient solitude.

"Lew's been here right enough," he said. "He and his boss and a couple of Indians came in two canoes eleven days back--at least I reckoned eleven days as well as I could from yon Eskimo's talk. Two days later a plane arrived for them. The Eskimo has never seen a horse or an automobile, but he knows all about aeroplanes. They handed over the canoes and what was left of the stores to the Indians and shaped a course pretty well due west. They've gotten the start of us by a week or maybe more."

That night after supper Johnny spoke for the first time at some length.

"I've been trying to figure this out," he said, "and here's what I make of it. Mr. Galliard comes here and sees the graves of his brother and uncle. So far so good. From what you tell me that's not going to content him.

He wants to do something of his own on the same line by way of squarin' his conscience. What's he likely to do? Now, let's see just where brother Lew comes in. I must put you wise about Lew."

Johnny removed his pipe from his mouth.

"He's a wee bit mad," he said solemnly. "He's a great man; the cutest hunter and trapper and guide between Alaska and Mexico, and the finest shot on this continent. But he's also mad--batty-- loony--anything you like that's out of the usual. It's a special kind of madness, for in most things you won't find a sounder guy. Him and me was buck privates in the War until they made a sharpshooter of him, and you wouldn't hit a better-behaved soldier than old Lew. I was a good deal in trouble, but Lew never. He has just the one crazy spot in him, and it reminds me of them Gaillards you talk about. It's a kind of craziness you're apt to find in us Northerners. There's a bit of country he wants to explore, and the thought of it comes between him and his sleep and his grub. Say, did you ever hear of the Sick Heart River?"

Leithen shook his head.

"You would if you'd been raised in the North. It's a fancy place that old-timers dream about. Where is it? Well, that's not easy to say. You've heard maybe of the South Nahanni that comes in the north bank of the Liard about a hundred miles west of Fort Simpson? Dad had a post up the Liard and I was born there, and when I was a kid there was a great talk about the South Nahanni. There's a mighty big waterfall on it, so you can't make it a canoe trip. Some said the valley was full of gold, and some said that it was as hot as hell owing to warm springs, and everybody acknowledged that there was more game there to the square mile than in the whole of America. It had a bad name, too, for at least a dozen folk went in and never came out. Some said that was because of bad Indians, but that was punk, for there ain't no Indians in the valley. Our Indians said it was the home of devils, which sounds more reasonable."

Johnny stopped to relight his pipe, and for a few minutes smoked meditatively.

"Do you get to Sick Heart by the South Nahanni?" Leithen asked.

"No, you don't. Lew's been all over the South Nahanni, and barring the biggest grizzlies on earth and no end of sheep and goat and elk and caribou, he found nothing. Except the Sick Heart. He saw it from the top of a mountain, and it sort of laid a charm on him. He said that first of all you had snow mountains bigger than any he had ever seen, and then ice-fields like prairies, and then forests of tall trees, the same as you get on the coast. And then in the valley bottom, grass meadows and an elegant river. A Hare Indian that was with him gave him the name--the Sick Heart, called after an old-time chief that got homesick for the place and pined away. Lew had a try at getting into it and found it no good--there was precipices thousands of feet that end. But he come away with the Sick Heart firm in his mind, and he ain't going to forget it."

"Which watershed is it on?" Leithen asked.

"That's what no man knows. Not on the South Nahanni's. And you can't get into it from the Yukon side, by the Pelly or the Peel or the Ross or Macmillan--Lew tried 'em all. So it looks as if it didn't flow that way. The last time I heard him talk about it he was kind of thinking that the best route was up from the Mackenzie, the way the Hare Indians go for their mountain hunting. There's a river there called the Big Hare. He thought that might be the road."

"Do you think he's gone there now?"

"I don't think, but I suspicion. See here, mister. Lew's a strong character and mighty set on what he wants. He's also a bit mad, and mad folks have persuasive ways with them. He finds this Galliard man keen to get into the wilds, and the natural thing is that he persuades him to go to his particular wilds, which he hasn't had out of his mind for ten years."

"I think you're probably right," said Leithen. "We will make a cast by way of the Sick Heart. What's the jumping-off ground?"

"Fort Bannerman on the Mackenzie," said Johnny. "Right, we'll start tomorrow morning. We can send back the planes from there and collect an outfit. We'll want canoes and a couple of Hares as guides."

And then he fell silent and stared into the fire. Now and then he took a covert glance at Leithen. At last he spoke a little shyly.

"You're a sick man, I reckon. I can't help noticin' it, though you don't make much fuss about it. If Lew's on the Sick Heart and we follow him there it'll be a rough passage, and likely we'll have to go into camp for the winter. I'm wondering can you stand it? There ain't no medical comforts in the Mackenzie mountains."

Leithen smiled. "It doesn't matter whether I stand it or not. You're right. I'm a sick man. Indeed, I'm a dying man. The doctors in England did not give me more than a year to live, and that was weeks ago. But I want to find Galliard and send him home, and after that it doesn't matter what happens to me."

"Is Galliard your best pal?"

"I scarcely know him. But I have taken on the job to please a friend, and I must make a success of it. I want to die on my feet, if you see what I mean."

Johnny nodded.

"I get you. I'm mighty sorry, but I get you. . . . Once I had a retriever bitch, the best hunting dog I ever knew, and her and me had some great times on the hills. She could track a beast all day, and minded a blizzard no more than a spring shower. Well, she got something mortally wrong with her innards, and was dying all right. One morning I missed her from her bed beside the stove, and an Indian told me he'd seen her dragging herself up through the woods in the snow. I followed her trail and found her dead just above the tree line, the place she'd been happiest in when she was well. She wanted to die on her feet. I reckon that's the best way for men and hounds."

15

For three days Leithen was in abject misery. They had no receiver in their plane and therefore no means of getting weather reports, and when they took off the next morning the only change was an increased chill in the air. By midday they had run into fog, and, since in that area Job was uncertain of his compass, they went north again to the Arctic coast, and followed it to the Coppermine. Here it began to blow from the north, and in a series of rainstorms they passed the Dismal Lakes and came to the shore of the Great Bear Lake. Job had intended to pass the night at the Mines, but there was no going further that evening in the mist and drizzle.

Next day they struggled to the Mines with just enough gasolene. Leithen looked so ill that the kindly manager would have put him to bed, but he insisted on restarting in the afternoon. They had a difficult take-off from the yeasty lake--Job insisted on their getting into their life-jackets, for he said the betting was that in three minutes they would be in the water. The lake was safely crossed, but Job failed to hit off the outlet of the Great Bear River, and with the low "ceiling" he feared to try a compass course to the Mackenzie because of the Franklin mountains. It was midnight before they struck the outlet and they had another wretched bivouac in the rain.

After that things went better. The weather returned to bright sun, clear skies, and a gentle wind from the north-east. Presently they were above the Mackenzie and far in the west they saw the jumble of dark ridges which were the foothills of the Mackenzie mountains. In the afternoon the hills came closer to the river, and on the left bank appeared a cluster of little white shacks with the red flag of the Hudson's Bay flying from a post.

"Fort Bannerman," said Johnny, as they circled down. "That's the Big Hare, and somewhere at the back of it is the Sick Heart. Mighty rough country."

The inhabitants of the fort were grouped at the mud bank where they went ashore--the Hudson's Bay postmaster, two Oblate Brothers, a fur trader, a trapper in for supplies, and several Indians. The trapper waved a hand to Johnny--

"Hullo, boy!" he said. "How goes it? Lew's been here. He lit out for the mountains ten days ago."

PART II

"There is a river, the streams whereof shall make glad the city of God."

Psalm xlvi.

1

It took three days to get the proper equipment together. Johnny was leaving little to chance.

"If we find Lew and his pal we may have to keep 'em company for months. It won't be easy to get to the Sick Heart, but it'll be a darn sight harder to get out. We've got to face the chance of a winter in the mountains. Lucky for us the Hares have a huntin' camp fifty miles up-river. We can dump some of our stuff there and call it our base."

The first question was that of transport. Water was the easiest until the river became a mountain torrent. The common Indian craft was of moose hides tanned like vellum and stretched on poplar ribs; but Johnny managed to hire from a free-trader a solid oak thirty-foot boat with an outboard motor; and, as subsidiaries, a couple of canoes brought years ago from the south, whose seams had been sewn up with strips of tamarack root and caulked with resin. Two Indians were engaged, little men compared with the big Plains folk, but stalwart for the small-boned Hares. They had the slanting Mongol eyes of the Mackenzie River tribes, and had picked up some English at the Catholic mission school. Something at the back of Leithen's brain christened them Big Klaus and Little Klaus, but Johnny, who spoke their tongue, had other names for them.

Then the Hudson's Bay store laid open its resources, and Johnny was no niggardly outfitter. Leithen gave him a free hand, for they had brought nothing with them. There were clothes to be bought for the winter--parkas and fur-lined jerkins, and leather breeches, and lined boots; gloves and flapped caps, blankets and duffel bags. There were dog packs, each meant to carry twenty-five pounds. There was a light tent--only one, for the Hares would fend for themselves at the up-river camp, and Lew and Galliard were no doubt already well provided. There were a couple of shotguns and a couple of rifles and ammunition, and there was a folding tin stove. Last came the provender: bacon and beans and flour, salt and sugar, tea and coffee, and a fancy assortment of tinned stuffs.

"Looks like we was goin' to start a store," said Johnny, "but we may need every ounce of it and a deal more. If it's a winter-long job we'll sure have to get busy with our guns. Don't look so scared, mister. We've not got to back-pack that junk. The boat'll carry it easy to the Hares' camp, and after that we'll cache the feck of it."

Leithen's quarters during these days were in the spare room of the Bay postmaster. Fort Bannerman was a small metropolis, for besides the Bay store it had a Mounted Police post, a hospital run by the Grey Nuns, and an Indian school in charge of the Oblate Brothers. With one of the latter he made friends, finding that he had served in a French battalion which had been on the right of the Guards at Loos. Father Duplessis was from Picardy. Leithen had once been billeted in the shabby flat-chested chateau near Montreuil where his family had dwelt since the days of Henri Quatre. The Fathers had had a medical training and could at need perform straightforward operations, such as that on an appendix, or the amputation of a maimed limb. Leithen sat in his little room at the hospital, which smelt of ether and carbolic, and they talked like two old soldiers.

Once they walked together to where the Big Hare strained to the Mackenzie through an archipelago of sandy islets.

"I have been here seven years," Father Duplessis told him. "Before that I was three years in the eastern Arctic. That, if you like, was isolation, for there was one ship a year, but here we are in a thoroughfare. All through the winter the planes from the northern mines call weekly, and in summer we have many planes as well as the Hudson's Bay boats."

Leithen looked round the wide circle of landscape--the huge drab Mackenzie two miles broad, to the east and south interminable wastes of scrub spruce, to the west a chain of tawny mountains, stained red in parts with iron, and fantastically sculptured.

"Do you never feel crushed by this vastness?" he asked. "This country is out-size."

"No," was the answer, "for I live in a little world. I am always busy among little things. I skin a moose, or build a boat, or hammer a house together, or treat a patient, or cobble my boots or patch my coat--all little things. And then I have the offices of the Church, in a blessedly small space, for our chapel is a midget."

"But outside all that?" said Leithen, "you have an empty world and an empty sky."

"Not empty," said Father Duplessis, smiling, "for it is filled with God. I cannot say, like Pascal, 'le silence éternel de ces espaces infinis m'effraie.' There is no silence here, for when I straighten my back and go out of doors the world is full of voices. When I was in my Picardy country there were little fields like a parterre, and crowded roads. There, indeed, I knew loneliness--but not here, where man is nothing and God is all."

2

They left Fort Bannerman on a clear fresh morning when the sky was a pale Arctic blue, so pale as to be almost colourless, and a small cold wind, so tiny as to be little more than a shudder, blew from the north. The boat chugged laboriously up the last feeble rapids of the Big Hare, and then made good progress through long canal- like stretches in a waste of loess and sand. Here the land was almost desert, for the scrub pines had ceased to clothe the banks. These rose in shelves and mantelpieces to the spurs of the mountains, and one chain of low cliffs made a kind of bib round the edge of the range. There was no sound except the gurgle of the water and an occasional sandpiper's whistle. A selvedge of dwarf willow made the only green in the landscape, though in distant hollows there were glimpses of poplar and birch. The river was split into a dozen channels, and the Hares kept the boat adroitly in deep water, for there was never a moment when it grounded. It was an ugly country, dull as a lunar landscape, tilted and eroded ridges which were the approach to the granite of the high mountains.

The three days at Fort Bannerman had done Leithen good, and though he found his breathing troublesome and his limbs weak, the hours passed in comparative comfort, since there was no need for exertion. On the Arctic shore and in the journey thence he had realised only that he was in a bleak infinity of space, a natural place in which to await death. But now he was conscious of the details of his environment. He watched the drifting duck and puzzled over their breed, he noted the art with which the Hares kept the boat in slack and deep water, and as the mountains came nearer he felt a feeble admiration for one peak which had the shape of Milan Cathedral. Especially he was aware of his companion. Hitherto there had been little conversation, but now Johnny came into the picture, sitting on the gunwale, one lean finger pressing down the tobacco in his pipe, his far-sighted eyes searching the shelves for game.

Johnny was very ready to talk. He had discovered that Leithen was Scots, and was eager to emphasise the Scottish side of his own ancestry. On the little finger of his left hand he wore a ring set with a small blood stone. He took it off and passed it to Leithen.

"Dad left me that," he said. "Lew has a bigger and better one. Dad was mighty proud of the rings and he told us to stick to them, for he said they showed we come of good stock."

Leithen examined it. The stone bore the three cinquefoils of Fraser. Then he remembered that Frizel had been the name for Fraser in the Border parish where he had spent his youth. He remembered Adam Fraser, the blacksmith, the clang of his smithy on summer mornings, the smell of sizzling hooves and hot iron on summer afternoons. The recollection gave Johnny a new meaning for him; he was no longer a shadowy figure in this fantastic world of weakness; he was linked to the vanished world of real things, and thereby acquired a personality.

As they chugged upstream in the crisp afternoon, hourly drawing nearer to the gate of the mountains, Leithen enjoyed something which was almost ease, while Johnny in his slow drawling voice dug into his memory. That night, too, when they made camp at the bottom of a stone-shoot, and, since the weather was mild, kept the driftwood fire alight more for show than for warmth, Johnny expanded further. Since in his experience all sickness was stomachic, he had included invalid foods among the stores, and was surprised when Leithen told him that he need not fuss about his diet. This made him take a more cheerful view of his companion's health, and he did not trouble to see him early to bed. In his sleeping-bag on a couch of Bay blankets Leithen listened to some chapters of Johnny's autobiography.

He heard of his childhood on Great Slave Lake and on the Liard, of his father (his mother had died at his birth), of his brother Lew-- especially of Lew.

"We was brothers," said Johnny, "but also we was buddies, which ain't always according to rule."

He spoke of his hunting, which had ranged from the Stikine to the Churchill, from the Clearwater to the Liard, and of his trapping, which had been done mostly about the upper waters of the Peace. Johnny as talker had one weak point--he was determined that his auditor should comprehend every detail, and he expounded in minutiæ. He seemed resolved that Leithen should grasp the difference in method between the taking of mink and marten, the pen on the river bank and the trap up in the hills. He elaborated also the technique of the spearing of muskrats, and he was copious on the intricate subject of fox. . . . In every third sentence there was a mention of Lew, his brother, until the picture that emerged for Leithen from the talk was not that of wild animals but of a man.

It was a picture which kept dislimning, so that he could not see it clearly; but it impressed him strangely. Lew came into every phase of Johnny's recollections. He had said this or that; he had done this or that; he seemed to be taken as the ultimate authority on everything in heaven and earth. But Johnny's attitude was something more than the admiration for an elder brother, or the respect of one expert for a greater. There was uneasiness in it. He seemed to bring in Lew's name in a kind of ritual, as if to convince himself that Lew was secure and happy. . . . What was it that he had said on the Arctic shore? He had called Lew mad, meaning that he was possessed by a dream. Now Lew was hot on the trail of that dream, and Johnny was anxious about him. Of that there was no doubt.

Leithen laughed. He looked at Johnny's bat ears and bullet head. Here was he, one who had seen men and cities and had had a hand in great affairs, with his thoughts concentrated on an unknown brother of an Indian half-breed! Galliard had almost gone out of the picture; to Johnny he was only Lew's "pal," the latest of a score or two of temporary employers. Even to Leithen himself the errant New Yorker, the husband of Blenkiron's niece, the pillar of Ravelstons, seemed a minor figure compared to the masterful guide who was on the quest for a mysterious river. Had Lew inspired Galliard with his fancies? Or was the inspiration perhaps Galliard's? What crazy obsession would he find if and when he overtook the pair somewhere in that wild world behind which the sun was setting?

That night they made camp at the very doorstep of the mountains, where the river, after a string of box-canyons, emerged from the foothills. It was an eerie place, for the Big Hare, after some miles of rapids, drowsed in a dark lagoon beneath sheer walls of rock. Leithen's mind, having been back all day in the normal world, now reacted to a mood of black depression. What had seemed impressive a few hours before was now merely grotesque and cruel. His errand was ridiculous--almost certainly futile, and trivial even if it succeeded. What had he to do with the aberrations of American financiers and the whims of half-breeds? Somewhere in those bleak hills he would die--a poor ending for a not undignified life! . . . But had his life been much of a thing after all? He had won a certain amount of repute and made a certain amount of money, but neither had meant much to him. He had had no wife, no child. Had his many friends been more, after all, than companions?

In the retrospect his career seemed lonely, self-centred, and barren, and what was this last venture? A piece of dull stoicism at the best--or, more likely, a cheap bravado.

3

All next morning they smelt their way through the box-canyons, sometimes with the engine shut off and the Hares poling madly. There were two dangerous rapids, but navigation was made simpler by the fact that there were no split channels and no shallows. They were going through the limestone foothills, and the cliffs on either side were at least seven hundred feet high, sheer as a wall where they did not overhang. Johnny had a tale about the place. Once the Hares had been hunted by the Crees--he thought it was the Crees, his own people, but it might have been the Dogribs. At that time the Big Hare River had come out of the mountains underground. The Hare boats were no match for the fleet Cree canoes, and the wretched tribe, fleeing upstream, looked for annihilation when they reached the end of the waterway. But to their amazement they found the mountains open before them and a passage through the canyons to the upper valley where was now the Hares' hunting camp. When they looked back there were no pursuing Crees, for the mountain wall had closed behind them. But some days later, when the disappointed enemy had gone back to their Athabaska swamps, the passage opened again, and the Hares could return when they pleased to the Mackenzie.

"Big magic," said Johnny. "I reckon them Hares got the story out of the Bible, when the missionaries had worked a bit on them, for it's mighty like the children of Israel and old Pharaoh."

Suddenly the boat shot into a lake, the containing walls fell back, and they were in a valley something less than a mile wide, with high mountains, whose tops were already powdered with snow, ringing it and blocking it to the north. The shores were green with scrub- willow, and the lower slopes were dark with spruce and pine.

At the upper end of the lake, on a half-moon of sward between the woods and the water, was the Hares' encampment. Big Klaus and Little Klaus set up a howl as they came in sight of it, and they were answered by a furious barking of dogs.

The place was different from Leithen's expectation. He remembered from old days the birch-bark lodges of eastern Canada; but in this country, where the birches were small, he had looked for something like the tall teepees of the Plains, with their smoke-holes and their covering of skins. Instead he found little oblong cabins thatched with rush-mats or brushwood. They had a new look as if they had recently been got ready for the winter, and a few caribou- skin tents showed what had been the summer quarters. On the highest point of ground stood what looked like a chapel, a building of logs surmounted at one end by a rough cross. Penned near it was an assortment of half-starved dogs who filled the heavens with their clamour.

The place stank foully, and when they landed Leithen felt nausea stealing over him. His legs had cramped with the journey and he had to lean on Johnny's shoulder. They passed through a circle of silent Indians, and were greeted by their chief, who wore a medal like a soup plate. Then a little old man hobbled up who introduced himself as Father Wentzel, the Oblate who spent the summer here. He was about to return to Fort Bannerman, he said, when his place would be taken for the winter by Father Duplessis. He had a little presbytery behind the chapel, where he invited Leithen to rest while Johnny did his business with the Hares.

The priest opened the door which communicated with the chapel, lit two tapers on the altar, and displayed with pride a riot of barbaric colours. The walls were hung with cloths painted in bedlamite scarlets and purples and oranges--not the rude figures of men and animals common on the teepees, but a geometrical nightmare of interwoven cubes and circles. The altar cloth had the same byzantine exuberance.

"That is the work of our poor people," said the priest. "Helped by Brother Onesime, who had the artist's soul. To you, monsieur, it may seem too gaudy, but to our Indians it is a foretaste of the New Jerusalem."

Leithen sat in the presbytery in a black depression. The smells of the encampment--unclean human flesh, half-dressed skins of animals, gobbets of putrefying food-

-were bad enough in that mild autumn noon. The stuffy little presbytery was not much better. But the real trouble was that suddenly everything seemed to have become little and common. The mountains were shapeless, mere unfinished bits of earth; the forest of pine and spruce had neither form nor colour; the river, choked with logs and jetsam, had none of the beauty of running water. In coming into the wilderness he had found not the majesty of Nature, but the trivial, the infinitely small--an illiterate half-breed, a rabble of degenerate Indians, a priest with the mind of a child. The pettiness culminated in the chapel, which was as garish as a Noah's Ark from a cheap toyshop. . . . He felt sick in mind and very sick in body.

Father Wentzel made him a cup of tea, which he could barely swallow. The little priest's eyes rested on him with commiseration in them, but he was too shy to ask questions. Presently Johnny arrived in a bustle. He would leave certain things, if he were permitted, in the presbytery cellar. He had arranged with the chief about dogs when they were wanted, but that was not yet, for it would be a fortnight at least before snow could be looked for, even in the high valleys, and, since they would travel light, they did not need dogs as pack animals. They would take the boat, for a stage or two was still possible by it; after that they would have the canoes, and he had kept the Hares as canoe-men--"for the portagin' business would be too much for you, mister."

He had news of Lew. The two men were not more than a week ahead, for a sudden flood in the Big Hare had delayed them. They had canoes, but no Indians, and had gone in the first instance to Lone Tree Lake. "That's our road," said Johnny. "Maybe they've made a base camp there. Anyhow, we'll hit their trail."

He had other news. It was the end of the seven years' cycle, and disease had fallen on the snow-shoe rabbit, upon which in the last resort all wild animals depend. Therefore the winter hunting and trapping of the Hares would be poor, and there might be a shortage of food in their camp. "You tell Father Duplessis that when you get back to Fort Bannerman," he told the priest. Their own camp, if they were compelled to make one, might run short. "Lucky we brought what we did," he told Leithen. "If we catch up with Lew we'll be all right, for he'd get something to eat off an iceberg."

They passed one night in the presbytery. While Johnny slept the deep, short sleep of the woodsman, Leithen had a word with Father Wentzel.

"The two men who have gone before?" he asked. "One is the brother of my guide, and the other is a friend of my friends. How did they impress you?"

The child-like face of the priest took on a sudden gravity.

"The gentleman, he was of the Faith. He heard mass daily and made confession. He was a strange man. He looked unhappy and hungry and he spoke little. But the other, the guide, he was stranger. He had not our religion, but I think he had a kind of madness. He was in a furious haste, as if vengeance followed him, and he did not sleep much. When I rose before dawn he was lying with staring eyes. For his companion, the gentleman, he seemed to have no care-- he was pursuing his own private errand. A strong man, but a difficult. When they left me I did not feel happy about the two messieurs."

4

Out of the encumbered river by way of easy rapids the boat ran into reaches which were like a Scottish salmon stream on a big scale, long pools each with a riffle at its head. The valley altered its character, becoming narrower and grassier, with the forest only in patches on infrequent promontories. The weather, too, changed. The nights were colder, and a chill crept into even the noontide sunshine. But it was immensely invigorating, so that Johnny sang snatches of Scots songs instead of sucking his pipe, and Leithen had moments of energy which he knew to be deceptive. The air had a quality which he was unable to describe, and the scents were not less baffling. They were tonic and yet oddly sedative, for they moved the blood rather to quiescence than to action. They were aromatic, but there was nothing lush or exotic in them. They had on the senses the effect of a high violin note on the ear, as of something at the extreme edge of mortal apprehension.

But the biggest change was in Leithen's outlook. The gloomy apathy of the Oblate's presbytery disappeared, and its place was taken by a mood which was almost peace. The mountains were no longer untidy rock heaps, but the world which he had loved long ago, that happy upper world of birds and clouds and the last magic of sunset. He picked out ways of ascent by their ridges and gullies, and found himself noting with interest the riot of colour in the woods: the grey splashes of caribou moss, the reds of partridge-berry, cranberry, blueberry, and Saskatoon; the dull green interspaces where an old forest fire had brought forth acres of young spruces; above all the miracle of the hardwood trees. The scrub by the river, red-dog-willow, wolfberry willow, had every shade of yellow, and poplar and birch carried on the pageant of gold and umber far up the mountain sides. Birds were getting infrequent; he saw duck and geese high up in the heavens, but he could not identify them. Sometimes he saw a deer, and on bare places on the hills he thought he detected sheep. Black bears were plentiful, revelling among the berries or wetting their new winter coats in the river's shallows, and he saw a big grizzly lumbering across a stone shoot.

Three long portages took them out of the Big Hare valley to Lone Tree Lake, which, in shape like a scimitar, lay tucked in a mat of forest under the wall of what seemed to be a divide. They reached it in the twilight, and, since the place was a poor camping-ground, they launched the canoes and paddled half-way up till they found a dry spit, which some ancient conflagration had cleared of timber. The lake was lit from end to end with the fires of sunset, and later in the night the aurora borealis cast its spears across the northern end. The mountains had withdrawn, and only one far snow peak was visible, so that the feeling of confinement, inevitable in the high valleys, was gone, and Leithen had a sense of infinite space around him. He seemed to breathe more freely, and the chill of the night air refreshed him, for frost crisped the lake's edges. He fell asleep as soon as he got under his blankets.

He awoke after midnight to see above him a wonderful sky of stars, still shot with the vagrant shafts of the aurora. Suddenly he felt acutely his weakness, but with no regret in his mind, and indeed almost with comfort. He had been right in doing as he had done, coming out to meet death in a world where death and life were colleagues and not foes. He felt that in this strange place he was passing, while still in time, inside the bounds of eternity. He was learning to know himself, and with that might come the knowledge of God. A sentence of St. Augustine came into his head as he turned over and went to sleep again: "Deum et animam scire cupio. Nihil ne plus? Nihil omnino."

5

He woke to find himself sweating under his blankets. The weather had changed to a stuffy mildness, for a warm chinook wind was blowing from the south-west. Johnny was standing beside him with a grave face.

"Lew's been here," he said. "He's left his mark all right. Eat your breakfast and I'll show you."

At the base of the promontory there was a stand of well-grown spruce. A dozen of the trees had been felled, stripped, cut into lengths, and notched at each end. An oblong had been traced on a flat piece of ground, and holes dug for end-posts. A hut had been prospected, begun--and relinquished.

"Lew's been on this job," said Johnny. "You can't mistake his axe- work."

He stood looking with unquiet eyes at the pile of cut logs.

"Him and his pal put in a day's work here. And then they quit. What puzzles me is why Lew quit. It ain't like him."

"Why shouldn't he change his mind?" Leithen asked. "He must have decided that this was not the best place for a base camp."

Johnny shook his head.

"It ain't like him. He never starts on a job until he has thought all round it and made sure that he's doin' right, and then hell fire wouldn't choke him off it. No, mister. There's something queer about this, and I don't like it. Something's happened to Lew."

The mild blue eyes were cloudy with anxiety.

"They've back-packed their stuff and gone on. They've cached their canoe," and he nodded to where a bulky object was lashed in the lower branches of a tall poplar. "We've got to do the same. We'll cache most of our stuff, for when we catch up with Lew we can send back for it. We'll take the Indians, for you ain't fit to carry a load. Their trail won't be hard to follow. I've been over the first bit of it. Lew pushed on ahead, and the other was about fifty yards back of him and limping. Looks like they've quarrelled."

6

The trail led away from the lake shore up a tributary stream towards what looked like the main wall of the divide. The berry- clad, ferny hillside made easy walking, and since the timber was small there were few troublesome windfalls. Johnny carried his .44 rifle, his axe, and a bag containing his own personal effects and most of Leithen's; the Hares, Big Klaus and Little Klaus, had the heavy stuff, tent, cooking utensils, portable stove, stores; while Leithen had no more than a light haversack about the weight which he had often carried in the Alps. The pattern of his day was now so familiar that he found it hard to fit into it the astounding novelties in his life--his quest for a man whom he had never seen, in the least-known corner of North America--the fact that presently somewhere in this wilderness he must die.

New also in his experience were the weather and his own weakness. The sun was getting low and the days were shortening; each night frost crisped the edges of the streams, and the first hour of the morning march was through crackling pools and frozen herbage. But by noon the sun was warm and it set daily over their left shoulders in a haze of opal and pearl. The morning and evening chills were keenly felt, but the tonic air seemed to soothe his coughing. It was the very quintessence of air, quickening every sense so that he smelt more keenly, heard more clearly, saw things in sharper outline. He had never used spectacles, and he found that his eyes were fully the equal of Johnny's when he knew what to look for.

He might have had an appetite, too, had it not been for his fatigue. He was so tired when they made camp for the night that he could scarcely eat, and Johnny had to turn his beans and bacon into a kind of soup before he could swallow them. He would lie in a half-stupor drawing his breath painfully for the better part of an hour, while Johnny and the Hares built the fire. Johnny was merciful, and accommodated his pace to his dragging feet, but the easiest gait was too much for him, and soon he had to have hourly rests. The trail went in and out of the glens, rising slowly to the higher benches, and, but for a few patches of swamp and one laborious passage over a rockfall, it was a road a child could have walked. But except for a very few minutes in the day it was for Leithen one long purgatory.

He started out in the morning with wobbling legs. After a mile or so, when his blood moved more briskly, he had a short spell of comfort. Then his breath began to trouble him, and long before midday he was plodding like a conscientious drunkard. He made it a point of honour to continue until Johnny called a halt, and, though Johnny did this often, he found himself always near the limits of his strength, and would drop like a log when the word was given. He returned unconsciously to an old habit of his mountaineering days, when he had had a long dull course to complete, counting his steps up to a thousand and walking to the rhythm of "Old Soldiers never Die. . . ."

At the head of a little pass Johnny halted, though the march had only been going for twenty minutes. The Hares, when they came up, set down their packs and broke into a dismal howling, which seemed to be meant for a chant. There was a big jack-pine with the lower branches lopped off, and some fifty feet from the ground a long bundle was lashed to the trunk, something wrapped in caribou skin tanned white.

Johnny removed his disreputable hat. "That's a chief up there. Good old scout he was--name of Billy Whitefish. . . . Passed out last fall."

7

One blue day succeeded another, and each was followed by a colder night. The earth was yawning before it turned to its winter sleep. Leithen, though the days tired him to desperation, yet found the nights tolerable, and could let his thoughts stray from his bodily discomfort. He listened to Johnny's talk.

Johnny talked much, for he had lost his shyness of Leithen, and this kind of trip was child's play to him.

"This is a pretty good land," he said, "to them that knows their way about. I guess a man could starve in the barrens, but not in the woods. Why, there's forty kinds of berries--and a whole lot of different sorts of mushrooms--and rock-tripe--and bark you can boil to make porridge. And there's all the animals that Noah had in the Ark. And there's nothing to hurt a body provided the body's got sense, and don't tackle a grizzly up-hill."

He had strong views on food. "B'ar's right enough in the fall when he's fat. A young un's as good as mutton, but an old un's plain shoe leather." He did not care for moose meat, preferring caribou or deer, and he liked best partridge or ptarmigan in half-plumage.

"What's here? Grizzly, black b'ar, brown b'ar, moose, caribou, three kinds of sheep--everything except goats. The Almighty left goats out when He stocked them mountains."

It was clearly his purpose to picture the land as an easy place even for a sick man to travel in. "Canadians," he said (he used the word as the equivalent of strangers, embracing everybody except the men of the North-west), "think we've got hell's own climate up here. They're wrong. We get milder winters than the Prairies. Besides, winter's a fine time to travel if you know the ways of it. You'll be snugger in a hole in the snow at forty below than in an apartment house in Winnipeg, and a darn lot healthier.

"But you've got to watch your step in the Northland," he would add. He would tell experiences of his own to show the cruelty of the wilds, though he was always careful to explain that his misfortunes were due to his own folly. He was a white-water man, though not of Lew's class, and above all things he hated towing a boat with a long trackline. "The thing's just waitin' to murder you," he said, "trip you over a cliff, or drown you, or get round your neck and saw your head off. . . ."

He had been near starvation. "I can go three days without food and not feel it, and I've done it pretty often. I reckon Lew could go five. But there's never been no reason for it except my own dam' folly. Once I lost all my kit in a river, including my knife which I had in my teeth, and I had to make shift with flint-flakes to kill and skin. I once lived for a week on berries and one porcupine."

He had had his accidents, too, as when a pine he was chopping down split with the cold and sent a sliver through his shoulder. He had once walked twenty miles to find a bottle of pain-killer which he had cached, his throat choking with laryngitis. But his worst adventure--he seemed shy in telling it--was when he was caught without snow-shoes in an early fall blizzard, and crossed unknowingly a bottomless half-frozen sphagnum swamp which heaved under his tread and made him vomit up his soul.

He would talk, too, about the secret lore of the woods. He could make the crows speak to him, and the squirrels, but not the whisky- jacks, because they were fools with only a cry and no speech. Lew could make anything talk.

It was always Lew, the mentor, the magician. But he never spoke his brother's name, or so it seemed to Leithen, without an accent of disquiet. He followed unerringly Lew's blazing of the trail, and often the blazes were so small that only a skilled woodman could have noticed them. He studied carefully every bivouac. Sometimes in marshy places he found the moccasin tracks still fresh, and then his anxiety seemed to increase.

"Lew's settin' a terrible pace," he said, "and the other's laggin'. They're still messin' together at night, but the other must be getting in pretty late, and he can't be having much sleep, for each morning they starts together. . . . I don't like it somehow. I wonder what brother Lew's aiming at?"

8

The trail wound intricately along the slopes of deep parallel glens, now and then crossing from one to another by a low pass. Johnny had been over it before, and was puzzled. "Them rivers run down to the Yukon," he told Leithen. "But Lew swears the Sick Heart don't do that, and we're over the divide from the Mackenzie. I reckon it can't have nothin' to do with the Peel, so it must disappear into the earth. That's my guess. Anyhow, this trail ain't going to get us nowhere except to the Yukon."

The celestial weather continued, wintry in the small hours of the night, but in the sun as balmy as June. Leithen had fallen into a state which was neither ease nor mal-ease, but something neutral like his bodily condition at the end of a hard term at the Bar, when he was scarcely ill but assuredly not well. He could struggle through the day and have a slender margin for the interests of the road.

There was one new thing--the wild animals were beginning to show themselves, as if they were stretching their legs for the last time before the snows came. One morning he saw the first moose--well up the hillside in a patch of dwarf spruce, showing against the background like elephants.

"Them beasts ain't happy here," Johnny said. "They want the hardwood country, for they ain't like caribou that feed on moss-- they likes the juicy underbrush. I guess they'll come down before the snow to the bottoms and stamp out a ravage so as to get to the shoots. I'll tell you a queer thing. The moose is pushin' further north. I mind the day when there wasn't one north of the Great Slave Lake, and now Lew has seen them on the Arctic shore east of the Mackenzie. I wonder what's bitin' them?"

The caribou had not yet appeared, being still on the tundras, but there were birds--ptarmigan and willow grouse--and big Arctic hares just getting into their winter coats. Also there were wolves, both the little grey wolves and the great timber wolves. They did not howl, but Johnny--and Leithen also--could hear them padding at night in the forest. Sometimes dim shapes slipped across a glade among the trees. One night, too, when Leithen could not sleep, he got up and watched the northern heavens where the aurora flickered like a curtain of delicate lace wrought in every tint of the rainbow. It lit up the foreground across which stalked a procession of black forms like some frieze on a Greek urn.

He found Johnny at his side. "That's the North," he said solemnly. "The wolves and the Aurory. God send us a kind winter."

9

One day the trail took an odd turn, for it left the parallel ridges and bore away to the east to higher ground. Johnny shook his head. "This is new country for me," he said. "Here's where Lew has taken the big chance."

Mountains prematurely snow-covered had been visible from the Hares' settlement, and Leithen at Lone Tree Camp had seen one sharp white peak in a gap very far off. Ever since then they had been moving among wooded ridges at the most two thousand feet high. But now they suddenly came out on a stony plateau, the trees fell away, and they looked on a new world.

The sedimentary rocks had given place to some kind of igneous formation. In front were cliffs and towers as fantastic as the Dolomites, black and sinister against a background of great snowfields, sweeping upward to ice arêtes and couloirs which reminded Leithen of Dauphiné. In the foreground the land dropped steeply into gorges which seemed to converge in a deep central trough, but they were very unlike the mild glens through which they had been ascending. These were rifts in the black rock, their edges feathered with dwarf pines, and from their inky darkness in the sunlight they must be deep. The rock towers were not white and shining like the gracious pinnacles above Cortina, but as black as if they had been hewn out of coal by a savage Creator.

But it was not the foreground that held the eye, but the immense airy sweep of the snow-fields and ice pinnacles up to a central point, where a tall peak soared into the blue. Leithen had seen many snow mountains in his time, but this was something new to him-- new to the world. The icefield was gigantic, the descending glaciers were on the grand scale, the central mountain must compete with the chief summits of the southern Rockies. But unlike the Rockies the scene was composed as if by a great artist--nothing untidy and shapeless, but everything harmonised into an exquisite unity of line and colour.

His eyes dropped from the skyline to the foreground and the middle distance. He shivered. Somewhere down in that labyrinth was Galliard. Somewhere down there he would leave his own bones.

Johnny was staring at the scene without speaking a word, without even an exclamation. At last he drew a long breath.

"God!" he said. "Them's the biggest mountains in the Northland and only you and me and Lew and his pal has seen 'em, and some Indians that don't count. But it's going to be a blasted country to travel. See that black gash? I reckon that's where the Sick Heart River flows, and it'll be hell's own job to get down to it."

"D'you think Lew and Galliard are there?" Leithen asked.

"Sure. I got their trail a piece back on the sand of that little pond we passed. We'll pick it up soon on them shale slides."

"Is the road possible?"

"Lew thinks it is. I told you he'd seen the Sick Heart once but couldn't get down the precipices. It couldn't have been this place or he wouldn't have gone on, for he don't try impossibilities. He sure knows there's a way down."

Leithen, sitting on the mountain gravel, had a sudden sharp pang of hopelessness, almost of fear. He realised that this spectacle of a new mountain-land would once have sent him wild with excitement, the excitement both of the geographer and the mountaineer. But now he could only look at it with despair. It might have been a Pisgah-sight of a promised land; but now it was only a cruel reminder of his frailty. He had still to find Galliard, but Galliard had gone into this perilous labyrinth. Could he follow? Could he reach him? . . . But did it matter after all? The finding of Galliard was a task he had set himself, thinking less of success than of the task. It was to tide away the time manfully before his end so that he could die standing. A comforting phrase of Walt Whitman's came back to him, "the delicious near-by assurance of death."

Sometimes lately he had been surprised at himself. He had not thought that he possessed this one-idea'd stoicism which enabled him to climb the bleak staircase of his duty with scarcely a look behind. . . . But perhaps this was the way in which most men faced death. Had his health lasted he would be doing the same thing a dozen or a score of years ahead. Soon his friends would be doing it--Hannay and Lamancha and Clanroyden--if they were fated to end in their beds. It was the lot of everyone sooner or later to reach the bleak bag's-end of life into which they must creep to die.

10

They soon picked up the tracks of their forerunners in the long spouts of gravel, and as they slowly zigzagged downhill to the tree line the weather changed. The cold blue sky beyond the mountains dulled to a colder grey and all light went out of the landscape. It was like the coming of the Polar Night of which he had read, the inexorable drawing down of a curtain upon the glory of the world. The snow began to fall in big flakes, not driven by any wind, but like the gentle emptying of a giant celestial bin. Soon there was nothing but white round them, except the tops of the little gnarled firs.

Luckily they had reached the tree line before the snow began, for otherwise they might have lost the trail. As it was, Johnny soon picked it up from the blazes on the diminutive trunks. It led them down a slope so steep that it was marvellous that any roots could cling to it. They had to ford many ice-cold streams, and before they reached flat ground in the evening Leithen was tottering on the very outside edge of his strength. He scarcely heard Johnny's mutter, "Looks like Lew has lost his pal. Here's where he camped and there's just the one set of tracks." He was repeating to himself Whitman's words like a prayer.

Johnny saw his weariness and mercifully said no more, contenting himself with making camp and cooking supper. Leithen fell asleep as soon as he had finished his meal, and did not wake until he heard the crackling of the breakfast fire. The air was mild and most of the snow had gone, for the wind had shifted to the south- west. Every limb ached after the long march of yesterday, but his chest was easier and there seemed more pith in his bones.

Johnny wore an anxious face. "We've made up on 'em," he said. "I reckon Lew's not two days ahead."

Leithen asked how he knew this, but Johnny said he knew but could not explain--it would take too long and a stranger to the wilds would not understand.

"He's gone on alone," he repeated. "This was his camping-ground three nights back, and the other wasn't here. They parted company some time that day, for we had the trail of both of 'em on the shale slides. What in God's name has happened? Lew has shook off his pal, and that pal is somewhere around here, and, being new to the job, he'll die. Maybe he's dead already."

"Has Lew gone on?"

"Lew's gone on. I've been over a bit of his trail. He's not wastin' time."

"But the other--my friend--won't he have followed Lew's blazes?"

"He wouldn't notice 'em, being raw. Lew's blazed a trail for his use on the way back, not for any pal to follow."

So this was journey's end for him--to have traced Galliard to the uttermost parts of the earth only to find him dead. Remembrance of his errand and his original purpose awoke exasperation, and exasperation stirred the dying embers of his vitality.

"Our job is to find Mr. Galliard," he said. "We stay here until we get him, dead or alive."

Johnny nodded. "I guess that's right, but I'm mighty anxious about brother Lew. Looks like he's gone haywire."

The snow was the trouble, Johnny said. It was disappearing fast under sun and wind, and its melting would obliterate all tracks on soft ground, almost as completely as if it still covered them. He thought that the Hares were better trackers than himself and they might find what he missed. He proposed that Leithen should lie up in camp while he and the Indians went back on yesterday's trail in the hope of finding the place where the two men had parted.

Johnny packed some food and in half an hour he and the Hares were climbing the steep side of the glen. Leithen carried his blankets out to a patch which the sun had already dried, and basked in the thin winter sunshine. Oddly enough, Johnny's news had not made him restless, though it threatened disaster to his journey. He had wanted that journey to succeed, but the mere finding of Galliard would not spell success, or the loss of him failure. Success lay in his own spirit. A slight increase of bodily comfort had given him also a certain spiritual ease. This sun was good, though soon for him it would not rise again.

The search-party did not return until the brief twilight. Johnny, as he entered the tent, shook his head dolefully.

"No good, mister. We've found where the other feller quit the trail--them Hares are demons at that game. Just what I expected-- up on the barrens where there ain't no trees to blaze and brother Lew had got out of sight. But after that we couldn't pick up no trail. He might have gone left or he might have gone right, but anyhow he must have gone down into the woods. So we started to beat out the woods, each of us takin' a line, but we've struck nothin'. Tomorrow we'll have another try. I reckon he can't have gone far, for he's dead lame. He must be lyin' up somewhere and starvin'."

Johnny counted on his fingers.

"Say, look! He's been three days quit of Lew--he's dead lame, and I reckon he wasn't carryin' more'n his own weight--if he didn't catch up with Lew at night he didn't have no food--maybe he wasn't able to make fire--

maybe he didn't carry more'n one blanket--if he's alive he's mighty cold and mighty hungry."

He was silent until he went to bed, a certain proof of anxiety.

"This sure is one hell of a business," he said as he turned in. "Lew kind of mad and streakin' off into space, and his pal aimin' to be a corpse. It's enough to put a man off his feed."

11

Johnny and the Hares were off at dawn next morning. The weather was mild, almost stuffy, and there had been little frost in the night. Leithen sat outside the tent, but there was no sun to warm him, only a grey misty sky which bent low on the hills. He was feeling his weakness again, and with it came a deep depression of spirit. The wilds were brutal, inhuman, the abode of horrid cruelty. They had driven one man mad and would be the death of another. Not much comfort for Felicity Galliard in his report-- "Discovered where your man had gone. Followed him and found him dead." That report would be carried by Johnny some time down into the civilised places, and cabled to New York, signed with the name of Leithen. But he would not see Felicity's grief, for long before then he would be out of the world.

In the afternoon the weather changed. The heavens darkened and suddenly burst into a lace-work of lightning. It was almost like the aurora, only it covered the whole expanse of sky. From far away there was a kind of muttering, but there were no loud thunder peals. After an hour it ceased and a little cold wind came out of the west. This was followed by a torrential rain, the heaviest Leithen had ever seen, which fell not in sheets but with the solid three dimensions of a cataract. In five minutes the hillside was running with water and the floor of the tent was a bog. In half an hour the brook below was a raving torrent. The downpour ceased and was followed by a burst of sunshine from a pale lemon sky, and a sudden sharpening of the air. Johnny had spoken of this; he had said that the winter would not properly be on them until they had the father and mother of a thunderstorm and the last rains.

Leithen pulled on his gum-boots and went out for a breath of air. The hill was melting under him, and only by walking in the thicker patches of fern and berries could he find decent foothold. Somehow his depression had lifted with the passing of the storm, and in the sharp air his breath came easier. It was arduous work walking in that tangle. "I had better not go far," he told himself, "or I'll never get home. Not much chance for Johnny and the Indians after such a downpour."

He turned to look back. . . . There seemed to be a lumbering body at the door of the tent trying to crawl inside. A bear, no doubt. If the brute got at the food there would be trouble. Leithen started to slither along the hillside, falling often, and feeling his breath run short.

The thing was inside. He had closed the door-flap before leaving, and now he tore it back to let in the light. The beast was there, crouching on its knees on the muddy floor. It was a sick beast, for it seemed to nuzzle the ground and emit feeble groans and gasps of pain. A bear! Its hinder parts were one clot of mud, but something like a ragged blanket seemed to be round its middle. The head! The head looked like black fur, and then he saw that this was a cap and that beneath it was shaggy human hair.

The thing moaned, and then from it came a sound which, though made by dry lips, was articulate speech.

"Frizelle!" it said. "Oh, Frizelle! . . . pour l'amour de Dieu!"

12

It took all Leithen's strength to move Galliard from the floor to his bed. He folded a blanket and put it under his head. Then he undid the muffler at his throat and unbuttoned the shirt. The man's lips were blue and sore, and his cheeks were shrunk with hunger and fatigue. He seemed to be in pain, for as he lay on his back he moaned and screwed up his eyes. His wits were dulled in a stupor, and, apart from his first muttered words, he seemed to be unconscious of his environment.

Leithen mixed a little brandy and tinned milk and forced it between his lips. It was swallowed and immediately vomited. So he lit the stove and put on the kettle to boil, fetching water from the nearby spring. The moaning continued as if the man were in pain, and he remembered that Johnny had guessed at a wounded foot. The sight of another mortal suffering seemed to give Leithen a certain access of strength. He found himself able to undo Galliard's boots, and it was no light task, for they were crusted thick with mud. The left one had been sliced open like a gouty man's shoe, to give ease to a wound in his shin, a raw, ragged gash which looked like an axe cut. Before the boot could be removed the moaning had several times changed to a gasp of pain. Leithen made an attempt to wash the wound, and bound it up with a handkerchief, which was all he had in the way of a bandage. That seemed to give Galliard relief, and the moaning ceased.

The kettle was boiling and he made tea. Galliard tried to take the pannikin, but his hands were shaking so that Leithen had to feed him like a child. He swallowed all that he did not spill and seemed to want more. So Leithen tried him again with brandy and milk, the milk this time thinned and heated. Now two brown eyes were staring at him, eyes in which consciousness was slowly dawning. The milk was drunk and Galliard lay for a little blinking at the tent wall. Then his eyes closed and he slept.

Leithen laid himself down on Johnny's mattress and looked at the shapeless heap which had been the object of his quest. There was the tawny beard which he had come to expect, but for the rest--it was unfamiliar wreckage. Little in common had it with the gracious portrait in the Park Avenue hall, or the Nattier, or the Aubusson carpet, or Felicity's rose-and-silver drawing-room. This man had chosen the wilderness, and now the wilderness had taken him and tossed him up like the jetsam of a flood.

There was no satisfaction for Leithen in the fact that he had been successful in his search. By an amazing piece of luck he had found Galliard and in so doing had achieved his purpose. But now the purpose seemed trivial. Was this derelict of so great importance after all? The unaccustomed bending in his handling of Galliard had given him a pain in his back, and the smell of the retched brandy and milk sickened him. He felt a desperate emptiness in his body, in his soul, and in the world.

It was almost dark when Johnny and the Hares returned. Leithen jerked his thumb towards the sleeping Galliard. Johnny nodded.

"I sort of suspicioned he'd be here. We got his tracks, but lost them in the mud. The whole darned hill is a mud-slide." He spoke slowly and flatly, as if he were very tired.

But his return set the little camp going, and Leithen realised what a blundering amateur he was compared with Johnny and the Indians. In a few minutes a fire was crackling before the tent door. Galliard, still in a coma, was lifted and partly unclothed, and his damaged leg was washed and rebandaged by Johnny with the neatness of a hospital nurse. The tent was tidied up and supper was set cooking--coffee on the stove and caribou steaks on the fire. Johnny concocted a dish of his own for the sick man, for he made a kind of chicken broth from a brace of willow grouse he had shot.

"You'd better eat," he said. "We'll feed the soup to that feller when he wakes. Best let him sleep a little longer. How you feelin' yourself? When I come in you looked mighty bad."

"I found Galliard more than I could manage; but never mind me. What about him?"

Johnny's bat's ears seemed to prick up as he bent over the sleeping figure. He was like a gnome in a fairy-tale; but he was human enough when he turned to Leithen, and the glow of the fire showed his troubled blue eyes.

"He'll come through a' right," he said. "He's been a healthy man and he ain't bottomed his strength yet. But he's plumb weary. He can't have fed proper for three days, and I reckon he can't have slept proper for a week."

"The wound?"

"Nasty cut he's got, and he'll have to watch his self if he don't want to go lame all his days. He can't move for a good spell."

"How long?"

"Ten days--a fortnight--maybe more."

Leithen had the appetite of a bird, but Johnny was ordinarily a good trencherman. Tonight, however, he ate little, though he emptied the coffee-pot. His mind was clearly on his brother, but Leithen asked no questions. At last, after half an hour's sucking at his pipe, he spoke.

"I figure that him"--and he nodded towards Galliard--"and brother Lew has been agreein' about as well as a carcajou and a sick b'ar. Lew'd gotten into a bad mood and this poor soul didn't know what the matter was, and got no answer when he asked questions. But he was bound to hang on to Lew or get lost and perish. Pretty nasty time he's been havin'. Lew's been actin' mighty mean, I'd say. But you can't just blame Lew, for, as I figure it, he don't know what he's doin'. He ain't seein' his pal, he ain't seein' nothin' except the trail he's blazin' and somethin' at the end of it."

"What's that?"

"The old Sick Heart River."

"Then he's gone mad?"

"You might say so. And yet Lew for ordinar' is as sane as you, mister, and a darn lot saner than me. He's gotten a vision and he's bound to go after it."

"What's to be done?"

"Our first job is to get this feller right. That was the reason you come down North, wasn't it? Every man's got to skin his own skunk. But I don't mind tellin' you I'm worried to death about brother Lew."

The attention of both was suddenly diverted to Galliard, who had woke up, turned on his side, and was looking at them with wide- awake eyes--pained eyes, too, as if he had awakened to suffering. Johnny took the pannikin of soup which had been heating on the stove, and began to feed the sick man, feeding him far more skilfully than Leithen had done, so that little was spilt. The food seemed to revive him and ease his discomfort. He lay back for a little, staring upward, and then he spoke.

His voice was hoarse, little above a croak. Johnny bent over him to catch his words. He shook his head.

"It's French, but Godamighty knows what he means. It don't sound sense to me."

Leithen dragged himself nearer. The man was repeating some form of words like a litany, repeating it again and again, so that the same phrase kept recurring. To his amazement he recognised it as a quotation from Chateaubriand, which had impressed him long ago and which had stuck to his fly-paper memory.

"S'il est parmi les anges," the voice said, "comme parmi des hommes, des campagnes habitées et des lieux déserts."

There was a pause. Certain phrases followed, "Solitudes de la terre"--"Solitudes célestes." Then the first sentence was repeated. Galliard spoke the words in the slurred patois of Quebec, sounding harshly the final consonants.

"He is quoting a French writer who lived a century ago," Leithen told Johnny. "It's nonsense. Something about the solitary places of heaven."

Galliard was speaking again. It was a torrent of habitant French and his voice rose to a pitch which was almost a scream. The man was under a sudden terror, and he held out imploring hands which Johnny grasped. The latter could follow the babble better than Leithen, but there was no need of an interpreter, for the pain and fear in the voice told their own tale. Then the fit passed, the eyes closed, and Galliard seemed to be asleep again.

Johnny shook his head. "Haywire," he said. "Daft--and I reckon I know the kind of daftness. He's mortal scared of them woods. You might say the North's gotten on his mind."

"But it was a craze for the North that dragged him here."

"Yep, but having gotten here he's scared of it. His mind's screwed right round. It's a queer thing, the North, and you need to watch your step for fear it does you down. This feller was crazy for it till he poked his head a wee bit inside, and now he's scared out of his life, and would give his soul to quit. I've known it happen before. Folks come down here thinking the North's a pretty lady, and find that she can be a cruel, bloody-minded old bitch, and they scurry away from her like jack-rabbits from a forest fire. I've seen them as had had a taste of her ugly side, and ever after the stink of smoke-dried Indian moccasins, and even the smell of burning logs, would turn out their insides. . . . I reckon this feller's had a pretty purifyin' taste of it. Ever been lost?"

"Never."

"Well, it ain't nice, and it tests a man's guts."

The air sharpened in the night and the little tent with its three occupants was not too stuffy. Galliard never stirred. Johnny had the short sound slumbers of a woodman, waking and rising before dawn; but Leithen slept badly. He had found his man, but he was a lunatic--for the time being. His task now was to piece together the broken wits. It seemed to him a formidable and unwelcome business. Could a dying man minister to a mind diseased? He would have preferred his old job--to go on spending his bodily strength till he had reached the end of it. That would, at any rate, have given him peace to make his soul.

Johnny set the camp stirring and was everywhere at once, like a good housewife. Galliard was washed and fed and his wound dressed. Leithen found that he had more power in his legs, and was able to make a short promenade of the shelf on which the camp stood, breathing air which was chilly as ice and scented with a thousand miles of pines. Johnny and the Hares were busy with measurements.

Leithen, huddled in the lee of the fire, watched the men at work. They were laying out the ground plan of a hut. It was to be built against the hillside, the gravel of which, when cut away, would make its back wall, and it seemed to be about twenty feet square. The Hares did the levelling of the shelf, and presently came the sound of Johnny's axe from the woods. In a couple of hours the four corner posts were cut, trimmed, and set up, and until the midday meal all three were busy felling well-grown spruce and pine.

Johnny's heavy preoccupation lightened a little as they ate.

"We need a hut whatever happens," he said. "The feller"--that was how he referred to Galliard--"will want something snugger than a tent when the cold sets in, for he ain't goin' to get well fast. Then there's you, a mighty sick man. And, please God, there'll be brother Lew."

"Is there no way of getting back to the Hares' camp?"

"For Lew and me--not for you and the feller. We got to plan to spend the winter here, or hereabouts. We can send the Indians back for stores and dog teams, and maybe we could get out in February when the good snows come. But we got to plan for the winter. I can fix up a tidy hut, and when we get the joints nicely chinked up with mud, and plenty of moss and sods on the roof, we'll be as snug as an old b'ar in its hole. I'm aimin' to fix a proper fireplace inside, for there's the right kind of clay in the creek for puddlin'."

"Let me help."

"You can't do nothin' yet, so long as we're on the heavy jobs, but I'll be glad of you when it comes to the inside fixin'. You get into the tent beside the feller and sleep a bit. I'm all right if I wasn't worried about Lew."

Johnny was attending to the bodily needs of the sick man like a hospital nurse, feeding him gruel and chicken broth and weak tea. Galliard slept most of the time, and even his waking hours were a sort of coma. He was asleep when Leithen entered the tent, and presently, to the accompaniment of Johnny's axe in the woods, Leithen himself drowsed off, for by this time of the day he was very weary. But sleep was for him the thinnest of films over the waking world and presently he was roused by Galliard's voice. This time it sounded familiar, something he had heard before, and not the animal croak of yesterday.

Two dull brown eyes were staring at him, eyes in which there was only the faintest spark of intelligence. They moved over his person, lingering some time at his boots, and then fastened on his face. There was bewilderment in them, but also curiosity. Their owner seemed to struggle for words, and he passed his tongue over his dry lips several times before he spoke.

"You are--what?"

He spoke in English, but his hold on the language seemed to slip away, for when Leithen replied in the same tongue the opaque eyes showed no comprehension.

"I am a friend of your friends," he said. "We have come to help you. I have the brother of Lew Frizel with me."

After a pause he repeated the last sentence in French. Some word in it caught Galliard's attention. His face suddenly became twisted with anxiety, and he tried to raise himself on his bed. Words poured from him, words tumbling over each other, the French of Quebec. He seemed to be imploring someone to wait for him--to let him rest a little and then he would go on--an appeal couched in queer childish language, much of which Leithen could not understand. And always, like the keynote of a threnody, came the word Rivière--and Rivière again--and once Rivière du Cœur Malade.

The partner of Ravelstons had suffered a strange transformation. Leithen realised that it would be idle to try to link this man's memory with his New York life. He had gone back into a very old world, the world of his childhood and his ancestors, and though it might terrify him, it was for the moment his only world.

The babbling continued. As Leithen listened to it the word that seemed to emerge from the confusion was Lew's name. It was on Lew that Galliard's world was now centred. If he was to be brought back to his normal self Lew must be the chief instrument. . . . And Lew was mad himself, raving mad, far away in the mountains on a crazy hunt for a mystic river! A sudden sense of the lunatic inconsequence of the whole business came over

Leithen and forced from him a bitter laugh. That laugh had an odd effect upon Galliard, for it seemed to frighten him into silence. It was as if he had got an answer to his appeals, an answer which slammed the door.

13

Next day the cold was again extreme, but the sun was out for six hours, and the shelf in the forest was not uncomfortable. Johnny, after sniffing the air, pronounced on the weather. The first snow had fallen; there would be three days of heavy frost; then for maybe ten days there would be a mild, bright spell; then a few weeks before Christmas would come the big snows and the fierce cold. The fine spell would enable him to finish the hut. A little drove of snow-buntings had passed yesterday; that meant, he said, since the birds were late in migrating, that winter would be late.

"You call it the Indian Summer?"

"The Hares call it the White Goose Summer. It ends when the last white goose has started south."

That day Leithen made an experiment. Galliard was mending well, the wound in the leg was healing, he could eat better, only his mind was still sick. It was important to find out whether the time had come to link his memory up with his recent past, to get him on the first stage on the road back to the sphere to which he belonged.

He chose the afternoon, when his own fatigue compelled him to rest, and Galliard was likely to be wakeful after the bustle of the midday meal. He had reached certain conclusions. Galliard had lost all touch with his recent life. He had reverted to the traditions of his family, and now worshipped at ancestral shrines, and he had been mortally scared by the sight of the goddess. These fears did not impel him to mere flight, for he did not know where to flee to. It drove him to seek a refuge, and that refuge was Lew. He was as much under the spell of Lew as Lew was under the spell of his crazy river. Could this spell be lifted?

So far Galliard had been a mere automaton. He had spoken like a waxwork managed by a ventriloquist. It was hardly possible to recognise a personality in that vacant face, muffled in a shaggy beard, and unlit by the expressionless eyes. Yet the man was regaining his health, his wound was healing fast, his cheeks had lost their famished leanness. As Leithen looked at him he found it hard to refrain from bitterness. He was giving the poor remnants of his strength to the service of a healthy animal with years of vigour before him.

He crushed the thought down and set himself to draw Galliard out of his cave. But the man's wits seemed to be still wandering. Leithen plied him with discreet questions but got an answer to neither French nor English. He refrained from speaking his wife's name, and the names of his American friends, even of Ravelstons itself, woke no response. He tried to link up with Chateau- Gaillard, and Clairefontaine--with Father Paradis--with Uncle Augustin--with the Gaillards, Aristide and Paul Louis, who had died on the Arctic shores. But he might have been shouting at a cenotaph, for the man never answered, nor did any gleam of recognition show in his face. It was only when Leithen spoke again of Lew that there was a flicker of interest; more than a flicker, indeed, for the name seemed to stir some secret fear; the pupils of the opaque eyes narrowed, the lean cheeks twitched, and Galliard whimpered like a lost dog.

Leithen felt wretchedly ill all that day, but after supper, according to the strange fashion of his disease, he had a sudden access of strength. He found that he could think clearly ahead and take stock of the position. Johnny, who was labouring hard all day, should have tumbled into bed after supper and slept the sleep of the just. But it was plain that there was too much on his mind for easy slumber. He sucked at his pipe, kept his eyes on the fire outside the open door, and spoke scarcely a word.

"How is he getting on?" Leithen asked.

"Him? The feller? Fine, I guess. He's a mighty tough body, for he ha'n't taken no scaith, barrin' the loss of weight. He'll be a' right."

"But his mind is gone. He remembers nothing but what happened in the last weeks. A shutter has come down between him and his past life. He's a child again."

"Aye. I've known it happen. You see he was scared out of his skin by something--it may have been Lew, or it may have been jest loneliness. He's got no sense in him and it's goin' to take quite a time to get it back. That's why I'm fixin' this hut. He wants nursin' and quiet, and a sort of feel that he's safe, and for that you need four walls, even though they're only raw lumber. If you was to take him out in the woods you'd have him plumb ravin' and maybe he'd never get better. I've seen the like before. It don't do to play tricks with them wild places."

"I don't understand," said Leithen. "Lew goes mad and terrifies Galliard and lets him lag behind so that he nearly perishes. Galliard has the horror of the wilds on him, but no horror of Lew. He seems to be crying for him like a child for his nurse."

"That's so. That's the way it works. The feller don't know that his troubles was all Lew's doin'. He's gotten scared of loneliness in this darned great wild country, and he claws on to anything human. The only human thing near at hand is brother Lew. But that ain't all. If it was all you and me might take Lew's place, for I guess we're human enough. But, as I figure it, Lew has let him in on his Sick Heart daftness, and kind of enthused him about it, and, the feller bein' sick anyhow, it has got possession of his mind. You told me back in Quebec that he'd a notion, which runs in his family, of pushing north, and we seen the two graves at Ghost River."

"Still I don't understand," said Leithen. "He's frightened of the wilds and yet he hankers to get deeper into them, right to a place where nobody's ever been."

Johnny shook out his pipe.

"He's not thinkin' of the Sick Heart as part of the woods. He's thinkin' of it the same as Lew, as a sort of Noo Jerusalem--the kind of place where everything'll be a' right. He and Lew ain't thinkin' of it with sane minds, and if Lew's there now he won't be lookin' at it with sane eyes. Sick Heart is a mighty good name for it."

"What sort of place do you think it is?"

"An ordinary creek, I guess. It's hard to get near, and that's maybe why Lew's crazy about it. My father used to have a sayin' that he got out of Scotland, 'Faraway hills is always shiny.'"

"Then how is Galliard to be cured of this madness?"

"We've got to get Lew back to him--and Lew in his right mind. At least, that's how I figure it. I mind once I was huntin' with the Caribou-Eaters in the Thelon, east of Great Slave Lake. There was an Indian boy--Two-sticks, his name was--and he come under the spell of my Chipewyan hunter, him they called White Partridge. Well, the trip came to an end and we all went home, but next year I heard that Two-sticks had been queer all winter. He wasn't cured until they fetched old White

Partridge to him. And that meant a three-hundred-mile trip from Nelson Forks to the Snowdrift River."

"How can we get Lew back?"

"Godamighty knows! If I was here on my own I'd be on his trail like a timber wolf. Maybe he's sick in body as well as in mind. Anyhow, he's alone, and it ain't good to be alone down North, and he's all that's left to me in the family line. But I can't leave here. I took on a job with you and I've got to go through with it. There's the feller, too, to nurse, and he'll want a tidy bit o' nursin'. And there's you, mister. You're a pretty sick man."

"Go after Lew and fetch him back and I'll stay here."

Johnny shook his head.

"Nothin' doin'. You can't finish this hut. The Hares are willin' enough, but they've got to be told what to do. And soon there'll be need of huntin' for fresh supplies, for so far we've been living mostly on what we back-packed in. And we've got to send out to the Hares' camp for some things. Besides, you ain't used to the woods, and what's easy for me would be one big trouble for you. But most of all you're sick--godawful sick--a whole lot sicker than the feller. So I say Nothin' doin', though I'm sure obliged to you. We've got to carry on with our job and trust to God to keep an eye on brother Lew."

Leithen did not reply. There was a stubborn sagacious dutifulness in that bullet head, that kindly Scots face, and those steadfast blue eyes which was beyond argument.

14

He spent a restless night, for he felt that the situation was slipping out of his control. He had come here to expend the last remnants of his bodily strength in a task on which his mind could dwell, and so escape the morbidity of passively awaiting death. He had fulfilled part of that task, but he was as yet a long way from success. Galliard's mind had still to be restored to its normal groove. This could only be done--at least so Johnny said--by fetching and restoring to sanity the man who was the key to its vagaries. Johnny could not be spared, so why should he not go himself on Lew's trail, with one of the Hares to help him? It was misery to hang about this camp, feeling his strength ebbing and getting no further on with his job. That would be dying like a rat in a hole. If it had to be, far better to have found a hole among the comforts of home. If he followed Lew, he would at any rate die in his boots, and whether he succeeded or failed, the end would come while he was fighting.

He told Johnny of his decision and at first was derided. He would not last two days; a Hare might be a good enough tracker, but he wanted a white man to guide him, one who was no novice. The road to the Sick Heart was admittedly difficult and could only be traversed, if at all, by a fit man; there might be storms and the mountains made impassable. Moreover, what would he say to Lew, to whom he was a stranger? If Lew was found he would for certain resent any intrusion in his lair. This was the point to which Johnny always returned.

"You've heard of mad trappers and the trouble they give the Mounties. If Lew's mad he'll shoot, and he don't miss."

"I know all that," said Leithen, "and I've made my book for it. You must understand that anyhow I am going to die pretty soon. If I hurry on my death a little in an honest way, I won't be the loser. That's how I look at it. If I never get to Lew, and perish on the road, why, that's that. If I find Lew and his gun finds me, well, that's that. There is just the odd chance that I may persuade him to be reasonable and bring him back here, and that is a chance I'm bound to take. Don't you worry about me, for I tell you I'm taking the easiest way. Since I've got to die, I want to die standing."

Johnny held out his hand. "You got me beat, mister. Lew and myself ain't reckoned timid folk, but for real sand there's not your like on this darned continent."

15

Leithen found the ascent of the first ridge from the valley bottom a stern business, for Lew had not zigzagged for ease, but had cut his blazes in the straight line of a crow's flight. But once at the top the road led westerly along a crest, the trees thinned out, and he had a prospect over an immense shining world.

The taller of the Hares, the one he called Big Klaus, was his companion. He himself travelled light, carrying little except a blanket and extra clothing, but the Indian had a monstrous pack which seemed in no way to incommode him. He had the light tent (the hut being now far enough advanced to move Galliard into it), a rifle and shot-gun, axes, billy-can, kamiks to replace moccasins, and two pairs of snow-shoes. The last were of a type new to Leithen--not the round "bear-paws" of eastern Canada made for the deep snow of the woods, but long, narrow things, very light, constructed of two separate rods joined by a toe-piece, and raised in front at a sharp angle. The centres were of coarse babiche with a large mesh, so as to pick up the least amount of snow, and since the meshing entered the frame by holes and was not whipped round it, the wooden surface was as smooth as skis. On such shoes, Johnny said, an active man could travel forty miles in a day.

Once the ridge had been gained, Leithen found that his breath came a little more easily. He seemed to have entered a world where the purity of the air was a positive thing, not the mere absence of impure matter, but the quintessence of all that was vital in Nature. The Indian Summer forecast by Johnny had begun. There was a shuddering undercurrent of cold, but the sun shone, and though it gave light rather than warmth, it took much of the bleakness out of the landscape. Also there was no wind. The huge amphitheatre, from the icy summit of the central peak to the gullies deep-cut in the black volcanic rock, was as quiet as a summer millpond. Yet there was nothing kindly in this peace; it seemed unnatural, as if the place were destined for strife. On the scarps the little spruces were bent and ragged with the winds, and the many bald patches were bleached by storms. This cold, raw hilltop world was not made for peace; its temporary gentleness was a trap to lure the unwary into its toils.

It was not difficult to follow Lew's blazes, and in a little swamp they found his tracks. He must be a bigger man than Johnny, Leithen thought, or else heavily laden, for the footprints went deep.

The Hare plodded steadily on with his queer in-toed stride. He could talk some English, and would answer questions, but he never opened a conversation. He was a merciful man, and kept turning in his tracks to look at Leithen, and when he thought he seemed weary, promptly dropped his pack and squatted on the ground. His methods of cooking and camping were not Johnny's, but in their way they were efficient. At the midday and evening meals he had a fire going at miraculous speed with his flint and steel and punk-box, and he could make a good bed even of comfortless spruce boughs. His weapon was a cheap breech-loader obtained from some trader, and with it he managed to shoot an occasional partridge or ptarmigan, so that Leithen had his bowl of soup. The second night out he made a kind of Dutch oven and roasted a porcupine, after parboiling it, and he cooked ash-cakes which were nearly as palatable as the pease-meal bannocks which Leithen had eaten in his youth.

That second night he talked. It had been a melancholy summer, for it had been foretold that many of the Hare people would presently die, and the whole tribe had fasted and prepared for their end. The manner of death had not been predicted--it might be famine, or disaster, or a stupendous storm. They had been scolded for this notion by Father Duplessis at Fort Bannerman and by Father Wentzel at the mountain camp, and before the end of the summer the spirits of the tribe had risen, and most believed that the danger had passed. But not all; some wise men thought that bad trouble was coming in the winter.

"It is not good to wait too long on death," said Big Klaus. "Better that it should come suddenly when it is not expected." He looked reflectively at Leithen as if he knew that here was one who was in the same case as the Hares.

For three days they followed the network of ridges according to Lew's blazing. They seemed rarely to lose elevation, for they passed gullies and glens by the scarps at their head waters. But nevertheless they had been steadily descending, for the great rift where the Sick Heart was believed to flow was no longer in the prospect, and the hanging glaciers, the ice couloirs and arêtes, and the poised avalanches of the central peak now overhung and dominated the landscape.

It was a strange world through which Leithen stumbled, conserving his strength greedily and doling it out like a miser. There was sun, light, no great cold, no wind; but with all these things there was no kindness. Something had gone out of the air and that something was hope. Night was closing down, a long night from which there would be a slow awakening. Scarcely a bird could be seen, and there were no small innocent frightened beasts to scurry into hiding. Everything that could move had gone to sanctuary against the coming wrath. The tattered pines, the bald, blanched pastures, were no more a home for life than the pinnacles of intense ice that glittered in mid-heaven. Dawn came punctually, and noon, and nightfall, and yet the feeling was of a perpetual twilight.

In these last weeks Leithen's memory seemed to have become a closed book. He never thought of his past, and no pictures from it came to cheer or torture him.

He might have been like the Hare, knowing no other world than this of laborious days and leaden nights. A new discomfort scarcely added to his misery, and food and fine weather did not lighten it. Every hour he was looking at marvels of natural beauty and magnificence, but they did not affect him. Life now awoke no response in him, and he remembered that some wise man had thus defined death. The thought gave him a queer comfort. He was already dead; there only remained the simple snapping of the physical cord.

16

They came on it suddenly in the afternoon of the third day. The scraggy forest of jack-pines, which seemed to stretch to the very edge of the snows, suddenly gave place to empty air, and Leithen found himself staring breathlessly not up, but down--down into a chasm nearly a mile wide and two thousand feet deep. From his feet the ground fell away in screes to a horizontal rib of dark rock, below which, in a blue mist very far down, were the links of a river. Beyond it were meadows and woods, and the woods were not of scrub pine, but of tall timber--from one or two trees in scattered clumps he judged them to be a hundred feet high. Beyond them again the opposite wall rose sheer to fantastic aiguilles of dark rock. He was looking at some mighty volcanic rift which made a moat to the impregnable castle of the snows.

The strength seemed to go from his limbs, and he collapsed among the crowberries and pine cones. He fumbled in a pocket to find his single Zeiss glass, but gave up the search when he realised the weakness of his hands. This sudden vision had drained the power from his body by its intense quickening of his senses and mind. It seemed to him that he was looking at the most marvellous spectacle ever vouchsafed to man. The elements were commonplace--stone and wood, water and earth--but so had been the pigments of a Raphael. The celestial Demiurge had combined them into a masterpiece.

He lay full in the pale sun and the air was mild and mellow. As his eyes thirstily drank in the detail he saw that there was little colour in the scene. Nearly all was subfusc, monochrome, and yet so exquisite was the modelling that there was nothing bleak in it; the impression rather was of a chaste, docile luxuriance. The valley bottom, so far as he could see it, seemed to be as orderly as a garden. The Sick Heart was like a Highland salmon river, looping itself among pools and streams with wide beaches of pebbles, beaches not black like the enclosing cliffs, but shining white. Along its course, and between the woods, were meadows of wild hay, now a pale russet against the ripple of the stream and the evergreen of the trees. . . . Something from his past awoke in Leithen. He was far up in the Arctic north; winter had begun, and even in this false summer the undercurrent of cold was stinging his fingers through his mitts. But it was not loneliness or savagery that was the keynote of this valley. Pastoral breathed from it; it was comforting and habitable. He could picture it in its summer pride, a symphony of mild airs and singing waters. Stripped and blanched as it was, it had a preposterous suggestion of green meadows and Herrick and sheep.

"We'll camp here," he told Big Klaus. "There's nothing to show us the road down. It'll take some finding."

He found the Zeiss glass at last and tried to make out further details. There must be hot springs, he thought, natural in a volcanic country; that would explain the richness of the herbage. The place, too, was cunningly sheltered from the prevailing winds, and probably most of the river that he could see never froze. That would mean wildfowl and fish, even in the depths of winter. . . . He pocketed his glass, for he did not want to learn more. He was content with what he saw. No wonder the valley had cast its spell on the old Indian chief and on Lew Frizel. It was one of those sacred places on which Nature had so lavished her art that it had the magic of a shrine.

Big Klaus made camp in a little half-moon of shingle on the verge of the cliffs, with trees to shelter it on north and east. He built an enormous fire on a basis of split wood, piled like a little wigwam, and felled two spruces so that they met in the centre of the heap, and as their ends burned away would slip further down and keep alight without tending until morning.

"It will be very cold," said the Hare, sniffing towards the north like a pointer dog.

Leithen ate little at supper, for his mind was in a fever. He had won a kind of success as he was nearing the brink of death, for he had found something which other men had longed to find and about which the world knew nothing. Some day there would be books of travel and guide-books, and inevitably it would be written that among the discoverers of the secret valley was one Edward Leithen, who had once been His Majesty's

Attorney-General in England, and who had died soon afterwards. . . . This unexpected feat obscured the fact that he had also found Galliard, for, setting out on one task he had incidentally accomplished a greater, like Saul the son of Kish who, seeking his father's asses, stumbled upon a kingdom.

The big fire roared and crackled at the mouth of the little tent, and beyond it was a blue immensity, sapphire in the mid-heaven, but of a milky turquoise above the mountains where the moon was rising.

He fell asleep early, and awoke after midnight to a changing world. The fire had sunk, but it was still fierce around the point where the spruce trunks intersected. The moon had set and the sky was hung with stars and planets--not inlaid, but hung, for the globes of sheer light were patently suspended in the heavens, and it seemed as if the eye could see behind them into aboriginal darkness. The air had suddenly become bitterly cold, cold almost beyond bearing. The shudder which had for some days lurked behind the sunlight had sharpened to an icy rigour. Frost like a black concrete was settling over everything, gumming the eyes and lips together. He buried his head under his blankets but could not get warm again. . . .

Some time towards dawn he fell into an uneasy sleep. When he awoke Big Klaus was tending the fire, white as an icicle and bent double against the fury of a northwest wind. Snow was drifting in flakes like pigeons' eggs. With a bound winter had come upon them.

Movement was impossible, and the two men lay all day in the tent, Leithen half in a stupor, for the sudden onrush of cold seemed to have drained the remnants of his strength. With the snow the first rigour abated, and presently the wind sank, and the smoke of the fire no longer choked the tent. The Hare split wood and rose every hour or so to tend the fire; for the rest he dozed, but he had a clock in his brain and he was never behindhand in his stoking. There was no fresh meat, so he cooked bacon and camp biscuit for luncheon, and for supper made a wonderful stew of tinned bully-beef and beans.

At twilight the snow ceased, and with the dark the cold deepened. The silence deepened, too, except for trees cracking in the fierce stricture of the frost. Leithen had regained some vitality during the day, enough to let him plan ahead. It was his business to get down into the valley where, beyond question, Lew had preceded him. It would be hard to find Lew's route, for there were no trees to blaze, and the weather of the past week would have obliterated his trail. To a mountaineer's eye it seemed an ugly place to descend, for the rock did not fissure well into foot-holds and handgrips. But the snow might solve the problem. The wind from the north-west had plastered it against the eastern side of the valley, the side on which they had made camp. It must have filled the couloirs and made it possible to get down by step-cutting or glissade. He had only two fears--whether his body was not too feeble, and whether the Hare was sufficient of a mountaineer for the attempt.

Morning brought no fresh snow, and the extreme cold seemed to slacken. Leithen thought that it could not be more than ten degrees below zero. Having an immediate practical task before him, he found himself possessed of a certain energy. He ate his meagre breakfast almost with relish, and immediately after was on his feet. There must be no delay in getting down into the valley.

With Big Klaus he explored the rim of the cliffs, following the valley downward, as he was certain Lew had done. Mercifully it was easy going, for with the trees withdrawn from the scarp there was no tangle of undergrowth, and what normally might have been loose screes was now firm snow.

For a little the cliffs overhung or fell sheer. Then came fissures by which, in open weather, a trained mountaineer might have descended, but which now were ice-choked and impossible. Leithen had walked more than a mile and come very near the limit of his strength before he found what he sought. The rocks fell back into a V-shaped bay, and down the bay to the valley floor swept a great wave of snow, narrow at the top and spreading out fanwise beneath. The angle was not more than thirty or thirty-five degrees. This must have been Lew's route, and no doubt he had had to face awkward rock falls and overhangs which now were obliterated in one great smooth white swirl. Leithen got out his glass and searched the lower slopes. No, there seemed to be no snags there; a good skier would tackle the descent without a thought.

"We must shift our stuff here," he told the Hare. "But first make a fire or I will freeze."

He cowered beside the blaze until Big Klaus had brought up the camp baggage. They cooked the midday meal, and then ransacked the stores. There was rope, but not enough of it. First they must pack their kit so that it would be kept together in the descent, for Leithen knew what a sepulchre snowdrifts could be for a man's belongings. Then he would have liked another hundred feet of rope for the Hare and himself. He meant to go down slowly and carefully, feeling his way and humouring his wretched body.

The baggage took up every inch of rope. Leithen had the gun and rifle lashed on his own back, and the rest made up a huge bundle which was attached to Big Klaus and himself by short lengths of cord. It was the best he could do, but it was an unwieldy contraption, and he prayed that there might be no boulders or pockets in the imperfectly seen lower reaches, for it would be impossible to steer a course. The Hare was sent into the wood to cut two long poles. He did not seem to realise the purpose until he returned and Leithen explained what must be done.

"The snow is firm enough," he said. "It will give good foot-holds. One step at a time, remember, and we must never move together. I stand still when you move. For God's sake keep your balance. If you slip, turn on your face and dig in your hands and feet. Don't let the kit pull you out of your steps. You understand?"

He repeated the instructions several times, but Big Klaus stared at him dully. When at last he realised that it was proposed to descend the shoot, he shook his head violently. He patted his stomach and made the motions of one about to be sick. Twice he went to the edge and peered down, and each time there was something like panic in his heavy eyes.

"Come on! There's no time to be lost. Even if we roll all the way it won't kill us."

Leithen took two steps down, leaning inward as he moved.

"Come on, you fool!"

The Hare put out a foot, like a timid bather in cold water. He was a brave man, for, though he was mortally afraid, he kept his eyes away from the void and imitated Leithen in hugging the slope.

At first all went well. The grade was steeper than had appeared above, but not much, and, though the baggage wobbled and swayed, they managed to keep their balance.

They had emerged from the throat of the couloir, and were out on the fan of the lower and easier slopes when disaster overtook them. The Hare miscalculated a foot-hold at a place where there was glazed ice on the snow, and shot downward on his back. He, and the weight of the baggage, plucked Leithen from his stance, and the next second the whole outfit had started a mad glissade. The rope round Leithen's middle choked the breath out of him. He cannoned into the baggage and ricochetted off; he cannoned into Big Klaus; his mouth and eyes were choked with snow; some rib of rock or ice caught his thigh and hurt him. . . . Once, climbing at Courmayeur alone, he had slipped on a snowfield and been whirled to what he believed to be his end in a bergschrund (which happened to be nearly full of snow into which he had dropped comfortably). Now once again, before his senses left him, he had the same certainty of death and the same apathy. . . .

17

He recovered consciousness to find the Hare attempting a kind of rough massage of his chest. For a minute or two he lay comatose, breathing heavily, but not suffering pain except for his bruised thigh. Slowly, with immense difficulty, he tested his body for damage. There seemed to be little--no concussion--the bruise--the breath knocked out of him but returning under the Hare's ministrations. It was not until he tried to get to his feet that he realised how much the glissade had taken toll of his strength.

The valley bottom was like a new creation, for the whole flavour of the landscape was changed. It was no longer the roof of the world where the mind and eye were inured to far horizons, but a place enclosed, muffled, defended by great rock bastions from the bleak upper air. Against the eastern wall the snow lay piled in big drifts, but there was no snow on the western side and very little in the intervening meadows. In these same meadows there was what looked like frozen pools, but the rigour of the frost had not touched the whole river, for below one of the patches of forest there was a gleam of running water. There was not a breath of wind, the slanting sunlight gilded the russet grasses and snow patches, the air was unbelievably mild. Here in this fantastic sanctuary was nothing of North America. Apart from the sheer containing walls, the scene might have been a Northumbrian pasture in an English December.

But all the pith had gone out of him. It seemed as if the strain of the descent had damaged some nerve control, for his weakness was worse than pain. He struggled to his feet and clutched at the Hare to keep himself from falling. The latter had got the baggage straightened out and was restrapping the guns. He nodded down the valley--

"He has gone that way," he said. But how he had guessed Lew's route he did not tell, nor did the other inquire.

For to Leithen it looked as if in this strange place he had got very near his journey's end. He toiled in the wake of the Hare for something less than a mile, counting each step, utterly oblivious of anything but the dun herbage under foot. He tried to step in the Indian's prints, but found them too long for his enfeebled legs. He who had once had the stride of a mountaineer now teetered like an affected woman. He made little bets with himself--how many steps until he fell?--would Big Klaus turn back, see his distress, and stop of his own accord? . . . The latter guess was right. The Indian, turning, saw a face like death, and promptly flung down his pack and announced that he would make camp.

There was a patch of gravel where the stream made a sharp bend, and there, in the lee of a tall coppice, a fire was lit. The Hare had to loosen the light pack from Leithen's shoulders, for he had lost all muscular power. His fingers seemed to bend back on him if he tried to lift a blanket. Also his breath was so troublesome that in that open place he panted like a man suffocating in a hole. The fit passed and by the time the tent was up and the beds laid his main trouble was his desperate weakness. Big Klaus fed him for supper with gruel and strong tea, but he was able to swallow little. His throat was as impotent as his hands and legs.

But his mind was no longer wholly apathetic, for he had stumbled on a queer corner of recollection. He had been conscious of the apathy of his memory, for, had he been able to choose, he would have been glad in those evil days to "count his mercies," to remember with a wry satisfaction the many pleasant things in his life. No present misery could kill his gratitude for past joys. But the past had remained a closed book to him, and he had had no thoughts except for the moment.

Now suddenly, with blinding clearness, he saw a picture. Outside his bedroom door in a passage on the upper floor of the old Scots country house of his boyhood, there had hung a print. It was a Munich photogravure called Die Toten-Insel, and showed an island of tall cliffs, and within their angle a grove of cypresses, while a barge full of bent and shrouded figures approached this home of the dead. The place was Sick Heart Valley--the same sheer cliffs, the same dark, evergreen trees; the Hare and he, bowed and muffled figures, were approaching the graveyard. . . . As a boy he had been puzzled by the thing, but had rather liked it. As he dashed out on a spring morning its sombreness had pleased him by its contrast with his own sunlit world. . . . Now, though he saw the picture of those April days, he could not recapture the faintest flavour of that spring rapture. He saw only the dark photogravure on the distempered passage wall, and his interest was faintly touched by its likeness to his present environment. . . . Surely he was already dead, for he had ceased to react to life!

Through the open tent door he could see the northern heavens ablaze with the aurora. The frost was closing down again, for the Dancers seemed to give out a crackling sound as if the sky were the back- cloth of a stage with the painted canvas strained to cracking- point. The spectacle did not stir his apathy. This blanched world was rioting in colour, but it was still blanched and bleached, the enemy of all life.

As he lay wakeful, scarcely conscious of the dull pain in his chest or of the spasms in his breathing, but desperately aware of his weakness, he felt the shadow of eternity deepening over him. Like Job, the last calamities had come on him. Thank Heaven he was free from loquacious friends. Like Job he bowed his head and had no impulse to rebel. The majesty of God filled his universe. He was coming face to face with his religion.

He had always been in his own way a religious man. Brought up under the Calvinistic shadow, he had accepted a simple evangel which, as he grew older, had mellowed and broadened. At Oxford he had rationalised it in his philosophical studies, but he had never troubled to make it a self-sufficing logical creed. Certain facts were the buttresses of his faith, and the chief of them was the omnipotence and omnipresence of God. He had always detested the glib little humanism of most of his contemporaries.

But his creed had remained something aloof from his life. He had no communion with the omnipotent God and no craving for it. It rarely impinged on his daily experience. When things went well he felt a dim gratitude to Omnipotence; when badly, it was a comfort to tell himself that it was God's will and to take misfortune cheerfully. In the War it had been different. Then he felt a relation so close as to be almost communion--that he was not only under God's ultimate command, but under His direct care. That was why his nerves had been so steady. It was foolish to worry about what was preordained.

Then had come long years of spiritual sloth. The world had been too much with him. But certain habits had continued. Still in his heart he had praised God for the pleasures of life, and had taken disappointments with meekness, as part of a divine plan. Always, when he reflected, he had been conscious of being a puppet in Almighty hands. So he had never been much cast down or much puffed up. He had passed as a modest man--a pose, some said; a congenital habit, said others. His friends had told him that if he had only pushed himself he might have been Prime Minister. Foolish! These things were ordained.

Now his castles had been tumbled down. Pleasant things they had been, even if made of paste-board; in his heart he had always known that they were pasteboard. Here was no continuing city. God had seen fit to change the sunlight for a very dark shadow. Well, under the shadow he must not quail but keep his head high, not in revolt or in defiance, but because He, who had made him in His image, expected such courage. "Though Thou slay me, yet will I trust in Thee."

There was no shade of grievance in Leithen's mind, still less self- pity. There was almost a grim kind of gratitude. He was now alone with God. In these bleak immensities the world of man had fallen away to an infinite distance, and the chill of eternity was already on him. He had no views about an after-life. That was for God's providence to decree. He was an atom in infinite space, the humblest of slaves waiting on the command of an august master.

He remembered a phrase of Cromwell's about putting his mouth in the dust. That was his mood now, for he felt above everything his abjectness. In his old bustling world there were the works of man's hands all around to give a false impression of man's power. But here the hand of God had blotted out life for millions of miles and made a great tract of the inconsiderable ball which was the earth, like the infinite interstellar spaces which had never heard of man.

18

He woke to a cold which seemed to sear that part of his face which the blanket left exposed. There was a great rosy light all about the tent which the frost particles turned into a sparkling mist.

The Hare stood above him.

"There is a man," he said, "beyond the river under the rocks. I have seen a smoke."

The news gave Leithen the extra incentive that made it possible for him to rise. He hung on to the Hare's shoulder, and it was in that posture that he drank some strong tea and swallowed a mouthful of biscuit. The smoke, he was told, was perhaps a mile distant in a nook of the cliffs. The long pool of the river was frozen hard, and beyond it was open ground.

Leithen's strength seemed suddenly to wax. A fever had taken him, a fever to be up and doing, to finish off his business once for all. His weakness was almost a physical anguish, and there was a horrid background of nausea. . . . But what did it all matter? He was very near his journey's end. One way or another in a few hours he would be quit of his misery.

The Hare guided him--indeed, half carried him--over the frozen hummocks of the pool. Beyond was a slight rise, and from that a thin spire of smoke could be seen in an angle of the cliffs. In the shelter of the rise Leithen halted.

"You must stay here," he told the Indian, "and see what happens to me. If I am killed you will go back to where we came from and tell my friend what has happened. He may want to come here, and in that case you will show him the road. If I do not die now you will make camp for yourself a little way off and at dawn tomorrow you will come where the smoke is. If I am alive you may help me. If I am dead you must return to my friend. Do you understand?"

The Hare shook his head. The orders seemed to be unacceptable, and Leithen had to repeat them again before he nodded in acquiescence.

"Good-bye," he said. "God bless you for an honest man."

The turf was frozen hard, but it was as level as a croquet lawn and made easy walking. All Leithen's attention was concentrated on his crazy legs. They wobbled and shambled and sprawled, and each step was a separate movement which had to be artfully engineered. He took to counting them--ten, twenty, thirty, one hundred. He seemed to have made no progress. Two hundred, three hundred--here he had to scramble in and out of a small watercourse--four hundred, five hundred.

A cry made him lift his eyes, and he saw a man perhaps two hundred yards distant.

The man was shouting, but he could not hear what he said. A horrid nausea was beginning to afflict him--the overpowering sickness which comes to men who reach the extreme limits of their strength. Then there was a sound which was not the human voice, and something sang not far from his left shoulder. He had taken perhaps six further steps when the same something passed somewhere on his right.

His dulled brain told him the meaning of it. "He must be bracketing," he said to himself. "The third shot will get me in the heart or the head, and then all will be over." He found himself longing for it as a sick man longs for the morning. But it did not come. Instead came the nausea and the extremity of weakness. The world swam in a black mist, and strength fled from his limbs, like air from a slit bladder.

19

When Leithen's weakness overpowered him he might lose consciousness, but when he regained it there was no half-way house of dim perception to return to. He alternated between a prospect of acid clarity and no prospect at all. . . . Now he took in every detail of the scene, though he was puzzled at first to interpret them.

At first he thought that it was night and that he was lying out of doors, for he seemed to be looking up to a dark sky. Then a splash of light on his left side caught his attention, and he saw that it outlined some kind of ceiling. But it was a ceiling which lacked at least one supporting wall, for there was a great blue vagueness pricked out with points of light, and ruddy in the centre with what looked like flames. It took him some time to piece together the puzzle. . . . He was in a cave, and towards the left he was looking to the open where a big fire was burning.

There was another light, another fire it seemed. This was directly in front of him, but he could not see the flames, only the glow on floor and roof, so that it must be burning beyond a projecting rib of rock. There must be a natural flue there, he thought, an opening in the roof, for there was no smoke to make his eyes smart.

He was lying on a pile of spruce boughs covered with a Hudson's Bay blanket. There was a bitter taste on his lips as he passed his tongue over them--brandy or whisky it seemed; anyhow some kind of spirit. Somebody, too, had been attending to him, for the collar of his dicky had been loosened, and he was wearing an extra sweater which was not his own. Also his moccasins had been removed and his feet rolled snugly in a fold of the blanket. . . .

Presently a man came into the light of the inner fire. The sight of him awoke Leithen to memory of the past days. This could only be Lew Frizel, whom he had come to find--a man who had gone mad, according to his brother's view, for he had left Galliard to perish; one who a few hours back had beyond doubt shot at himself. Then he had marched forward without a tremor, expecting a third bullet to find his heart, for it would have been a joyful release. Now, freed from the extreme misery of weakness, he found himself nervous about this brother of Johnny's--why, he did not know, for his own fate was beyond caring about. Lew's madness, whatever it was, could not be wholly malevolent, for he had taken some pains to make comfortable the man he had shot at. Besides, he was the key to Galliard's sanity, and Galliard was the purpose of his quest.

He was a far bigger man than Johnny, not less, it appeared, than six feet two; a lean man, and made leaner by his dress, which was deerskin breeches, a tanned caribou shirt worn above a jersey, and a lumberman's laced boots. His hair, as flaxen as a girl's, had been self-cut into a bunch and left a ridiculous fringe on his forehead. It was only the figure he saw, a figure apparently of immense power and activity, for every movement was like the releasing of a spring.

The man glanced towards him and saw that he was awake. He lit a lantern with a splinter from the fire, and came forward so that Leithen could see his face. Plainly he was Johnny's brother, for there was the same shape of head and the same bat's ears. But his eyes were a world apart. Johnny's were honest, featureless pools of that indistinct colour which is commonly called blue or grey, but Lew's were as brilliant as jewels, pale, but with the pallor of intense delicate colour, the hue of a turquoise, but clear as a sapphire, and with an adamantine brilliance. They were masterful, compelling eyes, wild, but to Leithen not mad--at least it was the madness of a poet and not of a maniac.

He bent his big shoulders and peered into Leithen's face. There was nothing of the Indian in him, except the round head and the bat's ears. The man was more Viking, with his great high-bridged nose, his straight, bushy eyebrows, his long upper lip, and his iron chin. He was clean-shaven, too, unlike his brother, who was as shaggy as a bear. The eyes devoured Leithen, puzzled, in a way contemptuous, but not hostile.

"Who are you? Where do you come from?"

The voice was the next surprise. It was of exceptional beauty, soft, rich, and musical, and the accent was not

Johnny's lingua franca of all North America. It was a gentle, soothing Scots, like the speech of a Border shepherd.

"I came with Johnny--your brother. He's in camp three days' journey back. We've found Galliard, the man who was with you. He was pretty sick and wanted nursing."

"Galliard!" The man rubbed his eyes. "I lost him--he lost himself. Come to think of it, he wasn't much of a pal. Too darned slow. I had to hurry on."

He lowered his blazing splinter and scanned Leithen's thin face and hollow eyes and temples. He looked at the almost transparent wrist. He lifted the blanket and put his head close to his chest so that he could hear his breathing.

"What brought you here?" he asked fiercely. "You haven't got no right here."

"I came to find you. Galliard needs you. And Johnny."

"You took a big risk."

"I'm a dying man, so risk doesn't matter."

"You're over Jordan now. The Sick Heart is where you come to when you're at the end of your road. . . . I had a notion it was the River of the Water of Life, same as in Revelation."

The man's eyes seemed to have lost their glitter and become pools of melancholy.

"Well, it ain't. It's the River of the Water of Death. The Indians know that and they only come here to die. Some, at least; but it isn't many that gets here, it being a damn rough road."

He took Leithen's hand in his gigantic paw.

"You're sick. Terrible sick. You've got what the Hares call tfitsiki and white folk T.B. We don't suffer from it anything to signify, but it's terrible bad among the Indians. It's poor feeding with them; but that's not what's hunting you. Where d'you come from? Edmonton way, or New York like the man Galliard?"

"I come from England. I'm Scots, same as you."

"That's mighty queer. You've come down north to look for Galliard? He's a sick man, too, sick in his mind, but he'll cure. You're another matter. You've a long hill to climb and I doubt if you'll win to the top of it."

"I know. I'm dying. I made my book for that before I left England."

"And you're facing up to it! There's guts left in the old land. What's your name? Leithen! That's south country. We Frizels come from the north."

"I've seen Johnny's ring with the Frazer arms."

"What's brother John thinking about me?"

"He's badly scared. He had to stay to attend to Galliard, and it's partly to ease his mind that I pushed on here."

"I guess his mind wanted some easing. Johnny's thinking about mad trappers. Well, maybe he's right. I was as mad as a loon until this morning. . . . I've been looking for the Sick Heart River since I was a halfling, and Galliard come along and gave me my chance at last. God knows what HE was looking for, but he fell in with me all right, and I treated him mighty selfish. I was mad and I don't mind telling you. That's the way the Sick Heart takes people. I thought when I found it I'd find a New Jerusalem with all my sins washed away, and the angels waiting for me. . . . Then you come along. I shot at you, not to kill, but to halt you--when I shoot to kill I reckon I don't miss. And you came on quite regardless, and that shook me. Here, I says, is someone set on the Sick Heart, and he's going to get there. And then you tumbled down in a heap, and I reckoned you were going to die anyway."

Lew was speaking more quietly and the light had gone from his eyes.

"Something sort of clicked inside my head," he went on, "and I began to look differently at things. The sight of you cleared my mind. One thing I know--this is the River of the Water of Death. You can't live in this valley. There's no life here. Not a bird or beast, not a squirrel in the woods, not a rabbit in the grass, let alone bear or deer."

"There are warm springs," Leithen said. "There must be duck there."

"Devil a duck! I looked to find the sedges full of them, geese and ducks that the Eskimos and Indians had hurt and that couldn't move south. Devil a feather! And devil a fish in the river! When God made this place He wasn't figuring on humans taking up lots in it. . . . I got a little provender, but if you and I don't shift we'll be dead in a week."

"What have you got?"

"A hindquarter of caribou--lean, stringy meat--a couple of bags of flour--maybe five pounds of tea."

"There's an Indian with me," said Leithen. "He's gone to earth a mile or so back. I told him to wait and see what happened to me. He'll be hanging about tomorrow morning, and he's got some food."

Lew rapped out a dozen questions, directed to identifying the Hare. Finally he settled who he was and gave him a name.

"What's he got?" he demanded.

"Flour and oatmeal and bacon and tea, and some stuff in tins. Enough for a week or so."

"That's no good," said Lew bitterly. "We' got to winter here or perish. Man, d'you not see we're in a trap? Nothing that hasn't wings could get out of this valley."

"How did you get in?"

Lew smiled grimly. "God knows! I was mad, as I told you. I found a kind of crack in the rocks and crawled down it like a squirrel, helping myself with tree roots and creepers. The snow hadn't come yet. I fell the last forty feet, but by God's mercy it was into a clump of scrub cedar. I lost nothing except half my kit and the skin of my face. But now the snow is here and that door is shut."

"The Hare and I came down by the snow, and it's the snow that's going to help us out again."

Lew looked at him with unbelief in his eyes.

"You're a sick man--sick in the head, too. Likewise you're tireder than a flightin' woodcock. You've got to sleep. I'm goin' to shift your bed further out. Frost won't be bad tonight, and you want the air round you. See, I'll give you another blanket."

Leithen saw that Lew was robbing his own bed, but he was too feeble to protest. He dropped straight away into the fathomless depths of exhausted sleep.

When he woke, with rime on his blankets and sunlight in his eyes, he saw that the Hare had been retrieved and was now attending to the breakfast fire. For a little he lay motionless, puzzling over what had happened to him. As always now at the start of a day, he felt wretchedly ill, and this morning had been no exception. But his eyes were seeing things differently. . . . Hitherto the world had seemed to him an etching without colour, a flat two-dimensioned thing which stirred no feeling in his mind of either repulsion or liking. He had ceased to respond to life. A landscape was a map to him which his mind grasped, but which left his interest untouched. . . .

Now he suddenly saw the valley of the Sick Heart as a marvellous thing. This gash in the earth, full of cold, pure sunlight, was a secret devised by the great Artificer and revealed to him and to him only. There was no place for life in it--there could not be-- but neither was there room for death. This peace was beyond living and dying. He had a sudden vision of it under a summer sun--green lawns, green forests, a blue singing stream, and cliffs of serrated darkness. A classic loveliness, Tempe, Phæacic.

But no bird wing or bird song, no ripple of fish, no beast in the thicket--a silence rather of the world as God first created it, before He permitted the coarse welter of life.

Lew boiled water, gave Leithen his breakfast, and helped him to wash and dress.

"You lie there in the sun," he said. "It's good for you. And listen to what I've got to say. How you feeling?"

"Pretty bad."

Lew shook his head. "But I've seen a sicker man get better."

"I've had the best advice in the world, so I don't delude myself. I haven't got the shadow of a chance."

Lew strode up and down before the cave like a sentry.

"You haven't a chance down here, living in a stuffy hole and eating the sweepings of a store. You want strong air, it don't matter how cold, and you want fresh-killed meat cooked rare. I've seen that work miracles with your complaint. But God help you! there's no hope for you here. You're in your grave already--and so are all of us. The Hare knows. He's squatting down by the water and starting on the dirges of his tribe."

Then he took himself off, apparently on some futile foraging errand, and Leithen, half in the sun, half in the glow of the fire, felt his weakness changing to an apathy which was almost ease. This was the place to die in--to slip quietly away with no last convulsive attempt to live. He had reacted for a moment to life, but only to the afterglow of it. The thought of further effort frightened him, for there could be no misery like the struggle against such weakness as his. It looked as if the fates which had given him so much, and had also robbed him so harshly, had relented and would permit a quiet end. Whitman's phrase was like a sweetmeat on his tongue: "the delicious nearby assurance of death."

Lew and the Indian spent a day of furious activity. They cut huge quantities of wood and kept both fires blazing. Fire-tending seemed to give Lew some comfort, as if it spelled life in a dead place. He wandered round the outer fire like a gigantic pixie, then, as the evening drew on, he carried Leithen into the cave, and, having arranged a couch for him, stood over him like an angry schoolmaster.

"D'you believe in God?" he demanded.

"I believe in God."

"I was brought up that way too. My father was bedrock Presbyterian, and I took after him--not like brother Johnny, who was always light-minded. There was times when my sins fair bowed me down, and I was like old

Christian in The Pilgrim's Progress--I'd have gone through fire and water to get quit of 'em. Then I got the notion of this Sick Heart as the kind of place where there was no more trouble, a bit of the Garden of Eden that God had kept private for them as could find it. I'd been thinking about it for years, and suddenly I saw a chance of gettin' to it and findin' peace for evermore. Not dying--I wasn't thinking of dying--but living happily ever after, as the story books say. That was my aim, fool that I was!"

His voice rose to a shout.

"I was mad! It was the temptation of the Devil and not a promise of God. The Sick Heart is not the Land-of-Beulah but the Byroad- to-Hell, same as in Bunyan. It don't rise like a proper river out of little springs--it comes full-born out of the rock and slinks back into it like a ghost. I tell you the place is no' canny. You'd say it had the best grazing in all America, and yet there's nothing can live here. There's a curse on this valley when I thought there was a blessing. So there's just the one thing to do if we're to save our souls, and that's to get out of it though we break our necks in the job."

The man's voice had become shrill with passion, and even in the shadow Leithen could see the fire in his eyes.

"You're maybe thinking different," he went on. "You think you're dying and that this is a nice quiet place to die in. But you'll be damned for it. There's a chance of salvation for you if you pass out up on the cold tops, but there's none if your end comes in this cursed hole."

Leithen turned wearily on his side to face the speaker.

"You'd better count me out. I'm finished. I'd only be a burden to you. A couple of days here should see me through, and then you can do what you like."

"By God I won't! I can't leave you--I'd never hold up my head again if I did. And I can't stay here with Hell waitin' to grab me. Me and the Hare will help you along, for our kit will be light. Besides, you could show us the road out. The Hare says you know how to get along on steep snow.

"Have you any rope?" Leithen asked.

Lew's wild face sobered. "It's about all I have. I've got two hundred feet of light rope. Brought it along with the notion it might come in handy and I can make some more out of caribou skin."

Leithen had asked the question involuntarily, for the thing did not interest him. The deep fatigue which commonly ended his day had dropped on him like a mountain of lead. Death was very near, and where could he meet it better than in this gentle place, remote alike from the turmoil of Nature and of man?

But after his meagre supper, as he watched Lew and the Indian repack their kit, the power of thought returned to him. This was the last lap in the race; was he to fail in it? Why had he come here when at home he might have had a cushioned death-bed among friends? Was it not to die standing, to go out in his boots? And that meant that he must have a purpose to fill his mind, and let that purpose exclude foolish meditations on death. Well, he had half-finished his job--he had found Galliard; but before he could get Galliard back to his old world he must bring to him the strange man who had obsessed his mind and who, having been mad, was now sane. Therefore he must get Lew out of the Sick Heart valley. He did not believe that Lew could find his way out alone. The long spout of snow was ice in parts, and Lew knew nothing of step- cutting. Leithen remembered the terror of the Hare in the descent. Mountaineering to men like Lew was a desperate venture. Could he guide them up the spout? It would have been child's play in the old days, but now! . . . He bent his knees and elbows. Great God! his limbs were as flaccid as indiarubber. What kind of a figure would he cut on an ice slope?

And yet what was the alternative? To lie here dying by inches--by feet and yards, perhaps, but still slowly--with Lew in a panic and restrained from leaving him only by the iron camaraderie of the North. His own utter weakness made him crave for immobility, but something at the back of his mind cried out against it. Why had he left England if he was to cower in a ditch and not stride on to the end? That had always been his philosophy. He remembered that long ago in his youth he had written bad verses on the subject, demanding that he meet death "with the wind in his teeth and the rain in his face." It was no false stoicism, but the creed of a lifetime.

By and by he fell asleep, and--a rare thing for one whose slumbers seemed drugged--woke in the small hours. Lew could be heard snoring, but he must have been recently awake, for he had stoked both fires. A queer impulse seized Leithen to get up. With some difficulty he crawled out of his sleeping-bag and stumbled to his feet, wrapping a blanket round him. . . .

It was a marvellous night, cold, but not bitterly cold, and the flames of the outer fire were crimson against a sky of burnished gold. Moonshine filled the valley and brimmed over the edge of the cliffs. Those cliffs caught no reflection of light, but were more dark and jagged than by day; except that on the eastern side, where lay the snowdrifts, there was a wave of misty saffron.

Moonlight is a soothing thing, softening the raw corners of the world, but suddenly to Leithen this moonlight seemed monstrous and unearthly. The valley was a great golden mausoleum with ebony walls, a mausoleum, not a kindly grave for a common mortal. Kings might die here and lie here, but not Edward Leithen. There was a tremor in his steady nerves, a fluttering in his sober brain. He knew now what Lew meant. . . . With difficulty he got back into his sleeping-bag and covered his head so that he could not see the moon. He must get out of this damned place though he used the last pennyweight of his strength.

20

Lew and the Indian had Leithen between them, steadying himself with a hand on each of their huge back-packs. The Hare's rope had gone to the cording of the dunnage, and Lew's was in a coil on Leithen's shoulder. The journey to the snow shoot was made in many short stages, across a frozen pool of the river, and then in the snow- sprinkled herbage below the eastern crags. The weather was changing, for a yellow film was creeping from the north over the sky.

"There'll be big snow on the tops," said Lew, "and maybe a god- awful wind."

It was midday before they reached the foot of the couloir. The lower slopes, down which Leithen and the Hare had rolled, were set at a gentle angle, and the firm snow made easy going; it was up in the narrows of the cleft that it changed to a ribbon of ice. The problem before him stirred some forgotten chord in Leithen's mind, and he found himself ready to take command. First he sent Lew and the Hare with the kit up to the edge of the ice, and bade them anchor the packs there to poles driven into the last soft snow. That done he made the two men virtually carry him up the easy slopes. He had a meagre remnant of bodily strength, and he would need it all for the task before him.

In an hour's time the three were at the foot of the sunless narrows where the snow was hard ice. There he gave Lew his orders.

"I will cut steps, deep ones with plenty of standing room. Keep looking before you, and not down. I'll rope, so that if I fall you can hold me. If I get to the top I'll try to make the rope fast, and the Hare must follow in the steps. He will haul up the kit after him; then he will drop the rope for you, and you must tie it on. If you slip he will be able to hold you."

Leithen chose the Hare to go second, for the Indian seemed less likely than Lew to suffer from vertigo. He had come up the lower slopes impassively while Lew had had the face of one in torment.

Lew's hatchet was a poor substitute for an ice axe. Leithen's old technique of step-cutting had to be abandoned, and the notches he hacked would have disgusted a Swiss guide. He had to make them deep and sloping inward for the sake of Lew's big moccasined feet. Also he had often to cut hand-holds for himself so that he could rest plastered flat against the ice when his knees shook and his wrists ached and his head swam with weariness.

It was a mortal slow business, and one long agony. Presently he was past the throat of the gully and in snow again, soft snow with a hard crust, but easier to work than the ice of the narrows. Here the wind, which Lew had foretold, swirled down from the summit, and he almost fell. The last stage was a black nightmare. Soon it would be all over, he told himself--soon, soon, there would be the blessed sleep of death.

He reached the top with a dozen feet of rope to spare, and straightway tumbled into deep snow. There he might have perished, drifting into a sleep from which there would be no awakening, had not tugs on the rope from Lew beneath forced him back into consciousness. With infinite labour he untied the rope from his middle. With frail, fumbling, chilled hands he made the end fast to a jack-pine which grew conveniently near the brink. He gave the rope the three jerks which was the agreed signal that he was at the summit and anchored. Then a red mist of giddiness overtook him, and he dropped limply into the snow at the tree roots.

21

When Leithen came to his senses he found it hard to link the present with the past. His last strong sensation had been that of extreme cold; now it was as warm as if he were in bed at home, and he found that his outer garments had been removed and that he was wearing only underclothes and a jersey. It was night, and he was looking up at a sky of dark velvet, hung with stars like great coloured lamps. By and by, as his eyes took in the foreground, he found that he was in a kind of pit scooped in deep snow with a high rampart of snow around it. The floor was spread with spruce boughs, but a space had been left in the middle for a fire, which had for its fuel the butt-ends of two trees which met in the middle and slipped down as they smouldered.

He did not stay long awake, but in those minutes he was aware of something new in his condition. The fit of utter apathy had passed. He was conscious of the strangeness of this cache in the snow, this mid-winter refuge in a world inimical to man. The bitter diamond air, like some harsh acid, had stung him back to a kind of life--at any rate to a feeble response to life.

Next day he started out in a state of abject decrepitude. Lew put snow-shoes on him, but he found that he had lost the trick of them, and kept on tangling up his feet and stumbling. The snow lay deep, and under the stricture of the frost was as dry and powdery as sand, so that his feet sank into it. Lew went first to break the trail, but all his efforts did not make a firm track, so that the stages had to be short, and by the midday meal Leithen was at the end of his tether. The glow of a fire and some ptarmigan broth slightly revived him, but his fatigue was such that Lew made camp an hour before nightfall.

That night, in his hole in the snow, Leithen's thoughts took a new turn. For long his mind had been sluggish, cognisant of walls but of no windows. Now suddenly it began to move and he saw things. . . .

Lew was taking shape in his thoughts as a man and not as a portent. At first he had been a mystery figure, an inexplicable Providence which dominated Johnny's mind, and which had loomed big on Leithen's own horizon. Then he had changed to a disturbing force which had mastered Galliard and seemed to be an incarnation of the secret madness of the North. And then in the Sick Heart valley he had become a Saul whose crazy fit was passing, a man who was seeking something that he had lost and had reached his desired goal only to find that it was not there. Lew and Galliard were in the same boat, sufferers from the same spell.

But Lew had returned by way of panic to normal life. For a moment this strong child of Nature had been pathetic, begging help and drawing courage from Leithen himself, a dying man. The splendid being had been a suppliant to one whose body was in decay. The irony of it induced in Leithen a flicker of affection. He seemed, too, to draw a transitory vigour from a creature so instinct with life. His numb stoicism was shot with a momentary warmth and colour. Lew on the trail, shouting oddments of Scots songs in his rich voice, and verses of the metrical Psalms of his youth, engaged in thunderous discourse with the Hare in his own tongue, seemed to dominate the snowdrifts and the blizzards and the spells of paralysing cold. Leithen found that he had won a faint warmth of spirit from the proximity of Lew's gusto. And the man was as gentle as a woman. His eyes were never off Leithen; he arranged the halts to suit his feebleness, and at each of them tended him like a mother. At night he made his bed and fed him with the care of a hospital nurse.

"This ain't the food for you," he declared. "You want fresh meat. It's time we were at Johnny's camp where I can get it for you."

Half a gale was blowing. He detected the scepticism in Leithen's eye and laughed.

"It don't look good for hunting weather, says you. Maybe not, but I'll get you what you need. We're not in the barrens to depend on wandering caribou. There's beasts in these mountains all the year round, and I reckon I know where to find 'em. There's caribou, the big woods kind, and there's more moose than anyone kens, except the Hares. They'll have stamped out their yards and we've got to look for 'em."

"What's that?"

"Stamping the snow to get at the shoots. Yards they call 'em down east. But the Hares call 'em ravages. Got the name from the French missionaries."

Next day the stages were short and difficult. There was a cruel north-east wind, and the snow was like kitchen salt and refused to pack. The Hare broke the trail, but Leithen, who followed, often sank to his knees in spite of his snow-shoes. ("We need bear-paws like they use down East," Lew proclaimed. "These northern kind are too narrow to spread the weight.") An hour's march brought him to utter exhaustion, and there were moments when he thought that that day would be his last.

At the midday meal he heard what stung his sense of irony into life. Lew had placed him in the lee of a low-growing spruce which broke the wind, and had forgotten his presence, for while he and the Indian collected wood for the fire they talked loudly, shouting against the blast. The Hare chose to speak English, in which he liked to practise himself.

"Him lung sick," he said. There could be no doubt about his reference.

"Yeah," Lew grunted.

"Him soon die, like my brother and my uncles."

The reply was an angry shout.

"No, by God, he won't! You chew on that, you bloody-minded heathen. He's going to cheat old man Death and get well."

Leithen smiled wryly. It was Uncle Toby's oath, but Uncle Toby's efforts had failed, and so would Lew's.

That night, since the day's journey had been short, his fatigue was a little less than usual, and after supper, instead of falling at once into a heavy sleep, he found himself watching Lew, who, wrapped in his blankets, was smoking his short pipe, and now and then stirring the logs with the spruce pole which he used as a poker. His eyes were half-closed, and he seemed to be in a not unpleasant reverie. Leithen--to his surprise, for he had resolved that his mind was dead to all mundane interests--found his curiosity roused. This was one of the most famous guides in the North. The country fitted him as a bearskin fitted the bear. Never, surely, was man better adapted to his environment. What had shaken him loose from his normal life and sent him on a crazy pilgrimage to a legendary river? It could not have been only a craving to explore, to find out what lay far away over the hills. There had been an almost mystical exaltation in the quest, for it had caused him to forget all his traditions, and desert Galliard, and this exaltation had ended in a panicky rebound. When he had met him he had found a strong man in terror, shrinking from something which he could not name. It must have been a strange dream which resulted in so cruel an awakening.

He asked Lew the question point-blank. The man came out of his absorption and turned his bright eyes on the questioner.

"I've been trying to figure that out myself," he said. "All my life since I was a callant I've been looking for things and never findin' 'em."

He stopped in some embarrassment.

"I don't know that I can rightly explain, for you see I'm not used to talking. When I was about eighteen I got kinda sick of my life, and wanted to get away south, to the cities. Johnny was never that way, nor Dad neither. But I reckon there were Frizels far back that had been restless too. Anyway, I was mighty restless. Then Dad died, and I had to take on some of his jobs, and before I knew I was deep in the business of guiding and feeling good about it. I wanted nothing except to know more about pelts than any trapper, and more about training than any Indian, and to keep my body as hard as whinstone, and my hearing like a timber wolf's, and my eyesight like a fishhawk's."

"That was before the War?"

Lew nodded. "Before the War. The War came and Johnny and me went overseas. We made a bit of a name as snipers, Johnny pretty useful and me a wee bit better. I enjoyed it right enough, and barring my feet, for I wasn't used to wearing army boots, I was never sick or sorry. But I was god-awful homesick, and when I smelt a muskeg again and saw the pointed sticks I could have grat with pleasure."

Lew shook out his pipe.

"But the man that came back wasn't the same as him that crossed the sea. I was daft about the North, and never wanted to leave it, but I got a notion that the North was full of things that I didn't know nothing about--and that it was up to me to find 'em. I took to talking a lot with Indians and listening to their stories. And then I heard about the Sick Heart and couldn't forget it."

Lew's embarrassment had returned. His words came slowly, and he kept his eyes on the hot ashes.

"It happened that I'd a lot of travelling to do by my lone--one trail took three months when I was looking for some lost gold- diggers. For two years I hadn't much guiding."

"You were with Mr. Walter Derwent, weren't you?"

"Yeah. Mr. Derwent's a fine little man and my very good friend. But mostly I was alone and I was thinkin' a lot. Dad brought us up well, for he was mighty religious, and I got to puzzling about my soul. I had always lived decent, but I reckoned decent living wasn't enough. Out in the bush you feel a pretty small thing in the hands of God. There was a book of Dad's I had a fancy for, The Pilgrim's Progress, and I got to thinking of myself as the Pilgrim, and looking for the same kind of thing to happen to me. I can see now it wasn't sense, but at the time it seemed to me I was looking at a map of my own road. At the end there was the River for the Pilgrim to cross, and I got to imagining that the River was the Sick Heart. I guess I was a bit loony, but I thought I was the only sensible man, for what did it matter what the other folks were doing, running about and making money, and marrying and breeding, when there was this big business of saving your soul?

"Then Mr. Galliard got hold of me. He was likewise a bit loony, but his daftness and mine was different, for he was looking for something in this world and, strictly speaking, I was looking for something outside the world. He didn't know what I wanted, and I didn't worry about him. But as it fell out he gave me the chance I'd been looking for, and we took the trail together. I behaved darned badly, for I wasn't sane, and by the mercy of God you and Johnny found the man I deserted. . . . I pushed on like a madman and found the Sick Heart, and then, praise God, my daftness left me.

"I don't know what I'd expected. A land flowing with milk and honey, and angels to pass the time of day! What opened my eyes was when I found there was no living thing in that valley. That was uncanny, and gave me the horrors. And then I considered that that great hole in the earth was a grave, a place to die in but not to live in, and not a place either for an honest man to die in. I'm like you, I'm sworn to die on my feet."

Lew checked himself with a glance of apology.

"I had to get out," he said, "and I had to get you out, for there's no road to Heaven from the Sick Heart. What did I call it?--a by- road to Hell!"

"You are cured?" Leithen asked.

"Sure I am. I'm like a man getting better of a fever. I see things in their proper shape and size now, and not big as mountains and dancing in the air. I've got to save my soul, and that's to be done by a sane man, and not by a loony, and in a man's job. I'm the opposite to King David, for God's goodness to me has been to get me away from yon green pastures and still waters, back among the rocks and the jack-pines."

22

In two days, said Lew, they should make Johnny's camp and Galliard. But he would not talk about Galliard. He left that problem to the Omnipotence who had solved his own.

The man was having a curious effect on Leithen, the same effect on his spirit that food had on his body, nourishing it and waking it to a faint semblance of life. The blizzard died away, and there followed days of sun, when a rosy haze lay on the hills, and the air sparkled with frost crystals. That night Leithen was aware that another thought had stabbed his dull mind into wakefulness.

When he left England he had reasoned himself into a grim resignation. Life had been very good to him, and, now that it was ending, he made no complaint. But he could only show his gratitude to life by maintaining a stout front to death. He was content to be a pawn in the hands of the Almighty, but he was also a man, and, as Lew put it, must die standing. So he had assumed a task which interested him not at all, but which would keep him on his feet. That task he must conscientiously pursue, but success in it mattered little, provided always he relaxed no effort.

Looking back over the past months, he realised that his interest in it, which at first had been a question of mere self-coercion, was now a real thing. He wanted to succeed, partly because of his liking for a completed job, and partly because the human element had asserted itself. Galliard was no longer a mathematical symbol, a cipher in a game, but a human being and Felicity's husband, and Lew was something more, a benefactor, a friend.

It was the remembrance of Lew that convinced Leithen that a change had come over his world of thought. He had welcomed the North because it matched his dull stoicism. Here in this iron and icy world man was a pigmy and God was all in all. Like Job, he was abashed by the divine majesty and could put his face in the dust. It was the temper in which he wished to pass out of life. He asked for nothing--"nut in the husk, nor dawn in the dusk, nor life beyond death." He had already much more than his deserts! and what Omnipotence proposed to do with him was the business of Omnipotence; he was too sick and weary to dream or hope. He lay passive in all-potent hands.

Now there suddenly broke in on him like a sunrise a sense of God's mercy--deeper than the fore-ordination of things, like a great mercifulness. . . . Out of the cruel North most of the birds had flown south from ancient instinct, and would return to keep the wheel of life moving. Merciful! But some remained, snatching safety by cunning ways from the winter of death. Merciful! Under the fetters of ice and snow there were little animals lying snug in holes, and fish under the frozen streams, and bears asleep in their lie-ups, and moose stamping out their yards, and caribou rooting for their grey moss. Merciful! And human beings, men, women, and children, fending off winter and sustaining life by an instinct old as that of the migrating birds. Lew nursing like a child one whom he had known less than a week--the Hares stolidly doing their jobs, as well fitted as Lew for this harsh world--Johnny tormented by anxiety for his brother, but uncomplainingly sticking to the main road of his duty. . . . Surely, surely, behind the reign of law and the coercion of power there was a deep purpose of mercy.

The thought induced in Leithen a tenderness to which he had been long a stranger. He had put life away from him, and it had come back to him in a final reconciliation. He had always hoped to die in April weather when the surge of returning life would be a kind of earnest of immortality. Now, when presently death came to him, it would be like dying in the spring.

23

That night he spoke of plans. The laborious days had brought his bodily strength very low, but some dregs of energy had been stirring in his mind. His breath troubled him sorely, and his voice had failed, so that Lew had to come close to hear him.

"I cannot live long," he said.

Lew received the news with a stony poker face.

"Something must be settled about Galliard," he went on. "You know I came here to find him. I know his wife and his friends, and I wanted a job to carry me on to the end. . . . We must get him back to his own people."

"And who might they be?" Lew asked.

"His wife. . . . His business associates. He has made a big place for himself in New York."

"He didn't talk like that. I never heard him mention 'em. He hasn't been thinkin' much of anythin' except his old-time French forbears, especially them as went North."

"You went to Clairefontaine with him?"

"Yeah. I wasn't supposed to tell, but you've been there and you've guessed it. It was like coming home for him, and yet not comin' home. We went to a nice place up the stream and he sat down and grat. Looked like it had once been his home, but that his home had shifted and he'd still to find it. After that he was in a kind of fever--all the way to the Arctic and then on here. He found that his brother and his uncle had died up there by the Ghost River."

"I know. I saw the graves."

Lew's eyes opened. "You and Johnny went there? You stuck mighty close to our trail. . . . Well, up to then Galliard had been the daft one. I could get no sense out of him, and most of the time he'd sit dreaming like an old squaw by the fire. After Fort Bannerman it was my turn. I don't rightly remember anything he said after that, for I wasn't worryin' about him, only about myself and that damned Sick Heart. . . . What was he like when you found him?"

"He was an ill man, but his body was mending. His mind--well, he'd been lost for three days and had the horrors on him. But I won't say he was cured. You can have the terror of the North on you and still be under its spell."

"That's so. It's the worst kind."

"He kept crying out for you. It looks as though you were the only one that could release him. Your madness mastered his, and now that you are sane again he might catch the infection of your sanity."

Lew pondered. "It might be," he said shortly.

"Well, I'm going out, and it's for you to finish the job. You must get him down country and back to his friends. I've written out the details and left them with Johnny. You must promise, so that I can die with an easy mind."

For a little Lew did not speak.

"You're not going to die," he said fiercely.

"The best authorities in the world have told me that I haven't the ghost of a chance."

"They're wrong, and by God we'll prove them wrong!" The blue eyes had a frosty sternness.

"Promise me, anyhow. Promise that you'll see Galliard back among his friends. You could get him out, even in winter?"

"Yeah. We can get a dog-team from the Hares' camp if he isn't fit for the trail. And once at Fort Bannerman we can send word to Edmonton for a plane. . . . If it's to do you any good I promise to plant the feller back where he belongs. But you've got to take count of one thing. He must be cured right here in the bush. If he isn't cured before he goes out he'll never be cured. It's only the North can mend what the North breaks."

24

Next day Leithen collapsed utterly, for the strength went from his legs, and his difficult breathing became almost suffocation. The business of filling the lungs with air, to a healthy man an unconscious function, had become for him a desperate enterprise where every moment brought the terror of failure. He felt every part of his decrepit frame involved, not lungs and larynx only, but every muscle and nerve from his brain to his feet. The combined effort of all that was left of him to feed the dying fires of life. A rough sledge was made and Lew and the Hare dragged him laboriously through the drifts. Fortunately they had reached the wind-swept ridges, where the going was easier. Twenty-four hours later there was delivered at Johnny's camp a man who looked to be in the very article of death.

PART III

"I had a singular feeling at being in his company. For I could hardly believe that I was present at the death of a friend, and therefore I did not pity him."

Plato, Phædo 58.

1

In the middle of January there was a pause in the sub-zero weather, and a mild wind from the west made the snow pack like cheese, and cleared the spruce boughs of their burden. In front of the hut some square yards of flat ground had been paved by Johnny with stones from the brook, and, since the melting snow drained fast from it, it was dry enough for Leithen to sit there. There was now a short spell of sun at midday, and though it had no warmth it had light, and that light gave him an access of comfort.

He reminded himself for the thousandth time that a miracle had happened, and that he was not in pain. His breath was short, but not difficult. He was still frail, but the utter overwhelming weakness had gone.

As yet he scarcely dared even to hint to himself that he might get well. His reason had been convinced that that was impossible. There had been no doubts in the minds of Acton Croke and young Ravelston. . . . Yet Croke had refused to be too dogmatic. He had said, "in the present position of our knowledge." He had admitted that medical science was only beginning to understand the type of tuberculosis induced by gas-poisoning. Technicalities had begun to recur to Leithen's memory: Croke's talk of "chronic fibrous infection," and "broncho-pulmonary lesions." Sinister-sounding phrases, but he remembered, too, reading or hearing somewhere that fibrous areas in the lungs could be walled off and rendered inert. That meant some sort of cure, at any rate a postponement of death.

Lew and the Hares had no doubt about it. "You're getting well," the former repeated several times a day. "Soon you'll be the huskiest of the lot of us." And the Indians had ceased to look at him furtively like something stricken. They ignored him, which was a good sign, for they knew better than most the signs of the disease which had decimated their people.

Lew's nursing had been drastic and tireless. Leithen's recollections of his arrival in camp from the Sick Heart River were vague, for he had been in a stupor of weakness. He remembered his first realisation that he was under a roof--the smoke from the fire which nearly choked him--alternate over-doses of heat and cold--food which he could not swallow--horrid hours of nausea. And then his memories were less of pain and weakness than of grim discomfort. Lew's tyrannical hand had been laid on him every hour. He was made to eat food when he was retching, or at any rate to absorb the juices of it. His tongue was like a stick, and he longed for cold water, but he was never allowed it. He was wrapped in blankets like a mummy, and kept in the open air when frost gummed his lips like glue, and every breath was like swallowing ice, and the air smote on his exposed face like a buffet.

He bore it dumbly, wretched but submissive. He might have been in a clinic, for he had surrendered his soul--not to a parcel of doctors and nurses, but to one fierce backwoodsman. Lew was life incarnate, and the living triumphed over what was half dead. The conscious effort involved in every hour of his past journey was at an end. He was not called on for decisions; these were made for him, and his mind sank into a stagnation which was almost painless.

Then strange things began to happen. He was stirred out of his apathy by little stabs of feeling which were remotely akin to pleasure. The half-raw meat seemed to acquire a flavour; he discovered the ghost of an appetite; he actually welcomed his morning cup of tea. He turned on his side to sleep without dismal forebodings about his condition when he woke. . . . His beard worried him, for in his old expeditions he had always shaved regularly, and one morning, to his immense surprise, he demanded his razor, and with Lew's approval shaved himself clean. He made a messy business of it, and took a long time over it, but the achievement pleased him. Surely the face that he looked at in the mirror was less cadaverous, the eyes less leaden, the lips less pallid, the texture of the skin more wholesome!

There was one memorable morning when, the intense cold having slackened, Lew stripped him to the buff, and he lay on a pile of skins before the fire while one of the Hares massaged his legs and arms. After that he took tottering walks about the hut, and one midday ventured out to the little platform. Presently Lew made him take daily exercise and in all weathers.

He was becoming conscious, too, of his surroundings. First came the hut. Assuredly Johnny was no slouch at hut-making. The earthen floor had been beaten flat and smooth by the Hares, whose quarters were a little annexe at one end. The building was some sixty feet square, but the floor space within was oblong, since four bunks had been built into one side. The walls were untrimmed spruce logs, and the roof was the same, but interwoven and overlaid with green boughs. Every chink in both walls and roof was filled with moss or mud. Johnny had constructed a fireplace of stones, with a bottle-shaped flue made of willow saplings puddled with clay. The fire was the special charge of the smaller Hare, and was kept going night and day to supplement the stove.

Warmth was a simple matter, but, though Leithen did not know it, food soon became a problem. Lew and Galliard had had scanty supplies, for they had set out on their journey with fevered brains. Johnny and the Hares had back-packed a fair amount, but the bulk of what they had brought from Fort Bannerman was cached at the Hares' camp or at Lone Tree Lake. It had been Johnny's intention to send the Hares back to bring up the reserves with a dog-team, and in the meantime to supplement the commissariat by hunting. He was a good shot, Lew was a famous shot, and the Indians were skilled trappers. That was well enough for the first weeks after Lew and Leithen joined them. There were ptarmigan and willow grouse to be got in the bush, and the woodland caribou, still plump from his autumn guzzling, whence came beef tea and under-done steaks for Leithen, and full meals of flesh for all.

But in the tail-end of December for ten days a blizzard blew. It came out of the north-east and found some alleyway into the mountains, for these gave no protection, so that it raged as fiercely as in the open barrens. The cold was not great, and it was therefore possible to keep the fire low and prevent the back smoke from choking the hut. But there was little fresh air for Leithen, though in the gaps of the storm Lew carried him out of doors and brought him back plastered like a snow man. There were three days when a heavy weight of snow fell, but for the rest it was rather a carnival of the winds, which blew sometimes out of a clear sky, swirling the fallen snow in a tourmente, and sometimes filled every aisle of the woods with thick twisting vapours.

Hunting was all but impossible--whether in the driving snow or in the Scots-mist type of weather the visibility was nil. Leithen was aware that the men were out, for often he was left alone, and in the few light hours there was never more than one at home, but his mind was still dull and he had no curiosity about what they were doing. It was as well, for he did not notice the glum faces and the anxious eyes of the others. But he did notice the change in his food.

He had come to like the fresh, bitter flavour of the half-raw caribou meat. That was his staple fare, that and his carefully measured daily dose of tomato juice; he rarely tasted Johnny's flap-jacks. Now there was little fresh meat, and instead he was given pemmican, which he swallowed with difficulty, or the contents of one of the few remaining tins.

Johnny was getting very grave about supplies. As soon as the weather cleared an attempt must be made to get up the reserves from the Hares' camp. They were out of sugar, almost out of tea and coffee, and their skins would give trouble unless they had fruit juice. But, above all, the hunting must be resumed. That was their main source of supply, and since Christmas the caribou had been harder to get, and February might bring savage weather.

Of these anxieties Leithen knew nothing. He was overwhelmed with the miracle of vigour creeping back into his moribund body. On the road from the Sick Heart River he had found himself responding again to life, and had welcomed the change as the proper mood in which to die. But this was different--it was not the recognition of life, but life itself, which had returned to him.

At night in the pit in the snow with Lew and the Hare he had become suddenly conscious of the mercifulness of things. There was a purpose of pity and tenderness in the iron compulsion of fate. Now this thought was always with him--the mercy as well as the omnipotence of God. His memory could range over the past and dwell lovingly and thankfully on its modest pleasures. A little while ago such memories, if he could have revived them, would have been a torment.

His mind ran up and down the panorama of his life, selecting capriciously. Oddly enough, it settled on none of the high lights. There had been moments of drama in his career--an adventure in the Ægean island of Plakos, for example, and more than one episode in the War. And there had been hours of special satisfaction--when he won the mile at school and college, his first big success at the Bar, his maiden speech in the House, his capture of the salmon when he and Lamancha and Palliser-Yeates poached in the Highlands. But though his memory passed these things in review, it did not dwell on them. Three scenes seemed to attract it especially, and he found that he could spend hours contentedly in reconstructing them and tasting their flavour.

The first belonged to his childhood. One morning in spring he had left his Border home determined to find what lay beyond the head of a certain glen. He had his rod with him, for he was an ardent fisherman, and lunch in his pocket--two jam sandwiches, a dainty known as a currant scone, two bread-and-butter sandwiches, a hard-boiled egg, and an apple--lovingly he remembered every detail. His short legs had crossed the head of the glen beyond the well-eye of the burn, and had climbed to the tableland of peat haggs and gravel, which was the watershed. Here he encountered an April hailstorm, and had to shelter in a hagg, where he ate his luncheon with intense relish. The hail passed, and a mild blue afternoon succeeded, with the Cheviots clear on the southern sky-line.

He had struggled across the peat bog, into the head of the glen beyond the watershed, where another burn fell in delectable pools among rowans and birches, and in these pools he had caught trout whose bellies were more golden and whose spots were brighter than the familiar fish in his own stream. Late in the evening he had made for home, and had crossed the hills in an April sunset of rose and saffron. He remembered the exultation in his small heart, the sense of being an explorer and an adventurer, which competed with a passionate desire for food.

Everything that day had gone exactly right. No one had upbraided him for being late. The trout had been justly admired. He had sat down to a comfortable supper, and had fallen asleep and rolled off his chair in the middle of it. Assuredly a day to be marked with a white stone. He could recall the sounds that accompanied it--the tinkle of the burn in its tiny pools, the perpetual wail of curlews, the sudden cackle of a nesting grouse. And the scents, too--peat, wood smoke, crushed mountain fern, miles of dry bent, the pure, clean odour of icy water.

This memory came chiefly in the mornings. In the afternoons, when he was not asleep, he was back at Oxford. The scene was always the same--supper in the college hall, a few lights burning, the twilight ebbing in the lancet windows, the old portraits dim as a tapestry. There was no dinner in hall in the summer term, only supper, when you could order what you pleased. The memory of the fare almost made him hungry--fried eggs, cold lamb and mint sauce and salad, stewed gooseberries and cream, cheese and wheaten bread, and great mugs of home-brewed beer. . . . He had been in the open air most of the day, riding over Shotover or the Cumnor hills, or canoeing on the upper Thames in the grassy meadows above Godstow, or adventuring on a bicycle to fish the dry-fly in the Cotswold streams. His body had been bathed in the sun and wind and fully exercised, so his appetite was immense. But it was not the mere physical comfort which made him dwell on the picture. It was the mood which he remembered, and could almost recapture, the mood which saw the world as a place of long sunlit avenues leading to marvellous horizons. That was his twentieth year, he told himself, which mankind is always longing to find again.

The third memory was the most freakish. It belonged to his early days at the Bar, when he lived in small ugly rooms in one of the Temple courts, and had very little money to spend. It was the first day of the Easter vacation, and he was going to Devonshire with Palliser-Yeates to fish the Exmoor hill streams. The cheapest way was to drive with his luggage direct to

Paddington, after the meagre breakfast which his landlady provided. But it seemed an occasion to celebrate, so he had broken his journey at his club in St. James's Street, a cheerful, undistinguished young man's establishment, and had breakfasted there with his friend. It had been a fresh April morning; gulls had been clamorous as he drove along the Embankment, and a west wind had been stirring the dust in Pall Mall. . . . He remembered the breakfast in the shabby old coffee room, and Palliser-Yeates' fly-book which he spilt all over the table. Above all he remembered his own boyish anticipations. In twenty-four hours he would be in a farmhouse which smelt of paraffin and beeswax and good cooking, looking out on a green valley with a shallow brown stream tumbling in riffles and drowsing in pools under banks of yellow bent. The larch plantations would be a pale mist on the hillsides, the hazel coverts would be budding, plovers would be everywhere, and water ouzels would be flashing their white breasts among the stones. . . . The picture was so dear and home-like that he found himself continually returning to it. It was like a fire at which he could warm his hands.

But there came a time when this pleasant picture-making ceased, and his mind turned back on itself. He had lost the hard stoical mood in which he had left London, but he was not clear as to what had replaced it. What was he doing here in a hut inside the Arctic Circle, among mountains which had never been explored and scarcely visited, in the company of Indians and half-breeds? . . . And then he slowly became conscious of Galliard.

All these weeks he had not noticed Galliard's presence or inquired what had happened to him. This man, the original purpose of his journey, had simply dropped out of his line of vision. He pondered on the queer tricks which the mind can play. The Frizels and the Indians were the human background to his life, but it was a background undifferentiated, for he never troubled to distinguish between the two Hares, and Lew, who was his daily ministrant, seemed to have absorbed the personality of Johnny. Galliard had sunk also into this background. One evening, when he saw what appeared to be three Frizels in the hut, he thought his mind wandering.

Moreover, the broken man, bedridden, half crazy, whom he had left behind when he set out for the Sick Heart River had disappeared. What he saw now was a big fellow, dressed in the same winter kit as Lew and Johnny, and busy apparently on the same jobs. He cut down young spruces and poplars for fuel, he looked after the big fire which burned outside and was used chiefly for melting snow and ice into water, and sometimes he hunted and brought back game. Slowly his figure disentangled itself from its background and was recognised. It had followed Leithen's example and shaved its beard, and the face was very much like that of the picture in the Park Avenue apartment.

Leithen's vitality had sunk so low that he had spoken little during his early recovery, and afterwards had been too much engaged with his own thoughts. This detachment had prevented him listening to the talk in the hut. His attention was only engaged when he was directly addressed, and that was done chiefly by Lew. But now, while he did not attempt to overhear, he was conscious of the drone of conversation after supper in the evening, and began to distinguish the different notes in it. There was no mistaking Lew's beautiful rich tones with their subtle Scots cadences, and Johnny's harsher and more drawling voice. Then he became aware of a third note, soft like Lew's, but more nasal, and one afternoon, at the tail-end of a blizzard, when Leithen lay abed in the firelight and the others were getting kindlings from the wind- felled trees, this voice addressed him.

"Can we talk now?" it said. "I've been waiting for this chance now that you're mending. I think we have much to say to each other."

Leithen was startled. This was what he had not heard for months, an educated voice, a voice from his own world. A stone had been thrown into the pool of his memory and the ripples stretched to the furthest shore. This was Galliard; he remembered everything about Galliard, reaching back to Blenkiron's first mention of him in his Down Street rooms.

"Tell me who you are," the voice continued.

Leithen did not answer. He was wondering how to begin an explanation of a purpose which must seem wholly fantastic. He, the shell of a creature, had set out to rescue this smiling frontiersman who seemed to fit perfectly into his environment.

"Johnny says that you know some of my friends. Do you mind telling me your name? I don't trust Johnny's ear, but I think he said 'Leven.'"

"Not quite. Leithen."

Galliard repeated the word, boggling, like all his countrymen, at the "th." "Scotch, aren't you?"

"Yes, but I live in England."

"You've been a pretty sick man, I gather, but you're mending fast. I wonder what brought a sick man to this outlandish place in midwinter? These mountains are not exactly a sanatorium. . . . You don't mind my asking questions? You see, we come out of the same world, and we're alone here--the only people of our kind for a thousand miles."

"I want you to ask questions. It's the easiest way for me to tell you my story. . . . I crossed the Atlantic last summer thinking that I was a dying man. The best English authority said so, and the best American authority confirmed his view. I'm unmarried, and I didn't want to die in a nursing-home. I've always been an active man, and I proposed to keep going until I dropped. So I came out here."

Galliard nodded. His brown eyes had a smiling, comprehending friendliness.

"That I understand--and admire. But why to America?--Why just here?--And on a trip like this?"

"I had to have a job. I must be working under orders, for it was the only way to keep going. And this was the job that offered itself."

"Yes, but please tell me. How did it happen that a sick Englishman was ordered to the Arctic Circle? What kind of job?"

Leithen smiled. "You will think it fantastic. The idea came from a kinsman of yours--a kinsman by marriage. His name is Blenkiron."

Galliard's face passed from an amused inquisitiveness to an extreme gravity.

"Our Uncle John! Tell me, what job did he give you?"

"To find out where you had gone, and join you, and, if possible, bring you back. No, not BRING you--for I expected to be dead before that--but to persuade you."

"You were in New York? You saw our Uncle John there?"

"No. In London. I know his other niece, Lady Clanroyden-- Clanroyden was at school and college with me--and I had some business once with Blenkiron. He came to my rooms one morning last summer, and told me about you."

Galliard's eyes were on the ground. He seemed to have been overcome by a sudden shyness, and for a moment he said nothing. Then he asked--

"You took on the job because you liked Blenkiron? Or perhaps Lady Clanroyden?"

"No. I happen to like Lady Clanroyden very much--and old Blenkiron, too. But my motive was purely selfish. I wasn't interested in you--I didn't want to do a kindness to anybody--I wanted something that would keep me on my feet until I died. It wouldn't have mattered if I had never heard the name of any of the people concerned. I was thinking only of myself, and the job suited me."

"You saved my life. If you and Johnny hadn't followed our trail I would long ago have been a heap of bones under the snow." Galliard spoke very softly, as if he were talking to himself.

Leithen felt acutely uncomfortable.

"Perhaps," he said. "But that was an accident, and there's no gratitude due, any more than to the policeman who calls an ambulance in a street accident."

Galliard raised his head.

"You were in New York? Whom did you meet there? My wife?"

"Yes. The Ravelstons, of course. And some of your friends like Bronson Jane, and Derwent, and Savory. But principally your wife."

"Can you"--the man stuttered--"can you tell me about her?"

"She is a brave woman, but I need not tell you that. Anxious and miserable, of course, but one would never guess it. She keeps a stiff face to the world. She tells people that you are in South America inquiring into a business proposition. She won't have any fuss made, for she thinks it might annoy you when you come back."

"Come back! She believes I will come back?"

"Implicitly. She thinks you had reached crossroads in your mind and had to go away and think it out and decide which one to take. When you have decided, she thinks you will come back."

"Then why did she want you to go to look for me?"

"Because there was always a chance you might be dead--or sick. I sent her a message from Fort Bannerman saying that I had ascertained you were alive and well up to a week before."

"How did you find me?"

"I guessed that you had gone first to Clairefontaine. I got no news of you there, but some little things convinced me that you had been there. Then I guessed you had gone North where your brother and your uncle had gone. So I followed. I saw their graves, and then Johnny told me about Lew's craze for the Sick Heart River, and I guessed again that he had taken you there. It was simply a series of lucky guesses. If you like, you can call them deductions from scanty evidence. I was lucky, but that was because I had made a guess at what was passing in your mind, and I think I guessed correctly."

"You didn't know me--never met me. What data had you?"

"Little things picked up in New York and at Clairefontaine. You see I am accustomed to weighing evidence."

"And what did you make of my psychology?"

"I thought you were a man who had got into a wrong groove and wanted to get out before it was too late. . . . No, that isn't the right way to put it. If it had been that way, there was no hope of getting you back. I thought you were a man who thought he had sold his birthright and was tortured by his conscience and wanted to buy it back."

"You think that a more hopeful state of affairs?"

"Yes. For it is possible to keep your birthright and live in a new world. Many men have done it."

Galliard got up and pulled on his parka and mitts. "I'm going out," he said, "for I want to think. You're a wizard, Mr. Leithen. You've discovered what was wrong with me; but you're not quite right about the cure I was aiming at. . . . I was like Lew, looking for a Sick Heart River. . . . I was seeking the waters of atonement."

For a moment Leithen was alarmed. Galliard had seemed the sanest of men, all the saner because he had divested himself of his urban trappings and had yet kept the accent of civilisation. But his last words seemed an echo of Lew--Lew before his cure. But a glance at the steady eyes and grave face reassured him.

"I mean what I say," Galliard continued. "I had been faithless to a trust and had to do penance for it. I had forgotten God and had to find Him. . . . We have each of us to travel to his own Sick Heart River."

2

In the days of short commons Lew was a tower of strength. He ran the camp in an orderly bustle, the Indians jumped to his orders, and Johnny worked with him like an extra right hand. His friendly gusto kept up everyone's spirits, and Leithen was never aware of the scarcity of rations.

It was a moment when he seemed to have reached the turning-point of his disease. Most of his worst discomforts had gone, and only weakness vexed him and an occasional scantiness of breath. The night sweats had ceased, and the nausea, and he could eat his meals with a certain relish. Above all, power was creeping back into his limbs. He could put on his clothes without having to stop and pant, and something of his old striding vigour was returning to his legs. He felt himself fit for longer walks than the weather and the narrow camp platform permitted.

Lew watched him with an approving eye. As he passed he would stop and pat him on his shoulder.

"You're doing fine," he would say. "Soon you'll be fit to go huntin'. You much of a shot?"

"Fair."

Lew laughed. "If an Old Countryman 'lows he's a fair shot, it means he's darned good."

One evening just before supper when the others were splitting firewood, Lew sat himself down before Leithen and tapped him on the knee.

"Mr. Galliard," he said--"I'd like to say something about Mr. Galliard. You know I acted mighty bad to him, but then I was out of my senses, and he wasn't too firm in his. Well, I'm all right now, but I'm not so sure that he is. His health's fine, and he can stand a long day in the bush. But he ain't happy--no happier than when he first hired me way back last spring. I mean he's got his wits back, and he's as sensible as you and me, but there's a lot worryin' him." Lew spoke as if he found it difficult to say what he wanted.

"I feel kindo' responsible for Mr. Galliard," he said, "seeing that he's my master and is paying me pretty high. And you must feel kindo' responsible for him or you wouldn't have come five thousand miles looking for him. . . . I see you've started talking to him. I'd feel easier in my mind if you had a good long pow-wow and got out of him what's biting him. You don't happen to know?"

Leithen shook his head.

"Only that he wasn't happy and thought he might feel better if he went North. But the plan doesn't seem to have come off."

The conversation, as it fell out, was delayed until early in February, when, in a spell of fine weather, Johnny and the smaller Indian had set off to the Hares' camp to bring back supplies by dog-team. It was about three o'clock in the afternoon, and the sun was beginning to go down in a sea of gold and crimson. Leithen sat at the hut door, facing the big fire on the platform which Galliard had been stoking. The latter pulled out a batch of skins and squatted on them opposite him.

"Can we talk?" he said. "I've kept away from you, for I've been trying to think out what to say. Maybe you could help me. I'd like to tell you just how I was feeling a year ago."

Then words seemed to fail him. He was overcome with extreme shyness, his face flushed, and he averted his eyes.

"I have no business to trouble you with my affairs," he stammered. "I apologise . . . I am a bore."

"Get on, man," said Leithen. "I have crossed half the world to hear about your affairs. They interest me more than anything on earth."

But Galliard's tongue still halted, and he seemed to find it impossible to start.

"Very well," said Leithen. . . . "I will begin by telling you what I know about you. You come from the Clairefontaine valley in Quebec, which Glaubsteins have now made hideous with a dam and a pulp mill. I believe your own firm had a share in that sacrilege. You belong to an ancient family, now impoverished, and your father farmed a little corner of the old seigneury. . . . When you were nineteen or so you got sick of your narrow prospects and went down to the States to try your luck. After a roughish time you found your feet, and are now a partner in Ravelstons, and one of the chief figures in American finance. . . . Meantime your father died, soon after you left him. Your brother Paul carried on the farm, and then he also got restless, and a year or two ago went off to the North, pretending he was going to look for your uncle Aristide, who disappeared there years before. Paul got to the river which Aristide discovered, and died there--the graves of both are there, and you saw them last summer. . . . At the other end something happened to YOU. You started out for Clairefontaine with Lew, and then you were at Ghost River, and then came on here. Is that sketch correct?"

Galliard nodded. His eyes were abstracted, as if he were in the throes of a new idea.

"Well, you must fill out the sketch. But let me tell you two other things. I went to Clairefontaine after you, and after you to the Ghost River, and I saw the crosses in the graveyard. Also, long ago, when I was a young man, I went hunting in Quebec, and I came out by way of

Clairefontaine. I found the little meadow at the head of the stream, and I have never forgotten it. When I knew I had to die, my first thought was to go there, for it seemed the place to find peace."

Galliard's face woke to a sudden animation.

"By God! that's a queer thing. I went to that meadow--the first thing I did after I left New York. There's a fate in this! . . . I think now I can get on with my story. . . ."

It was a tale which took long in the telling, and it filled several of the short winter twilights. There were times when the narrative lagged, and times when it came fast and confusedly. Galliard had curious tricks of speech; sometimes elaborate, the product of wide reading, and sometimes halting, amateurish, almost childlike, as if he were dragging his thoughts from a deep well.

From the village school of Chateau-Gaillard, he said, he had gone to the University of Laval. He was intended for the law, and his first courses were in classics and philosophy. He enjoyed them, and for a little even toyed with the notion of giving his life to those studies and looking for a university post. What switched his thoughts to another line was a slow revolt against the poverty- stricken life at Clairefontaine. He saw his father and brother bowed down with toil, for no purpose except to win a bare living. In the city he had occasional glimpses of comfort and luxury, and of a wide coloured world, and these put him wholly out of temper with his home. He did a good deal of solid thinking. If he succeeded as a lawyer he would exchange the narrow world of a country farm for the narrow world of a provincial city--more ease, certainly, but something far short of his dreams. He must make money, and money could only be made in big business. In Canada his own French people did little in business, having always left that to the English, and in Canada he might have to fight against prejudice. So he determined to go to the country where he believed there was no prejudice, where business was exalted above all callings, and where the only thing required of a man was to be good at his job.

He left Laval and went to a technical college, where he acquired the rudiments of accounting and a smattering of engineering science. The trouble came when his father discovered the change. The elder Gaillard had something of the seigneur left in him. There was a duty owed to gentle birth. A gentleman might be a farmer who laboured from dawn to dusk in the fields; he could be a priest; he could be a lawyer; but if he touched trade he forfeited his gentility. Moreover, the father hated the very word America. So when the son frankly announced his intention there was a violent family quarrel. Next day he left for Boston and he never saw his father again.

Galliard scarcely mentioned his early struggles. They had to be taken for granted like infantile ailments. He took up the tale when he had come to New York and had met Felicity Dasent.

To Leithen's surprise he spoke of Felicity without emotion. He seemed to be keeping his mind fixed on the need to make his story perfectly clear--an intellectual purpose which must exclude sentiment.

He had fallen deeply in love with her after a few meetings. To him she represented a new world very different from the tough world of buying and selling in which he had found his feet. It was a world which satisfied all the dreams of his boyhood and youth, a happy, gracious place with, as its centre, the most miraculous of beings. It was still more different from Clairefontaine with its poverty and monotony and back-breaking toil. Felicity seemed far further removed from Clairefontaine than from the grubbiest side of Wall Street. The old petty world of Mass and market was infinitely remote from her gracious and civilised life. It was a profanation to think of the two together. Only the meadow at the head of the stream seemed to harmonise with his thoughts about her.

Then came their marriage, and Galliard's entry into society, and his conspicuous social success. After that the trouble began in his soul. . . .

He was not very clear about its beginnings. He found things in which he had had an acute interest suddenly go stale for him. He found himself in revolt against what he had once joyfully accepted, and when he probed for the reason he discovered, to his surprise, that it was because it clashed with some memory which he thought he had buried. At first he believed that it was only regret for his departing youth. Boyish recollections came back to him gilded by time and distance. But presently he realised that the trouble was not nostalgia for his dead boyhood, but regret for a world which was still living and which he had forsaken. Not exactly regret, either; rather remorse, a sense that he had behaved badly, had been guilty in some sense of a betrayal.

He fought against the feeling. It was childish, with no basis of reason. He was a rich man, and, if he liked, could have a country house in Quebec, which would offer all the enchantments of his youth without its poverty. . . . But he realised miserably that this was no solution. It was not Quebec that he wanted, but a different world of thought, which was hopelessly antagonistic to that in which he now dwelt. To his consternation he discovered that distaste for his environment was growing fast. What had been the pleasures of his life became its boredoms; high matters of business were only a fuss about trifles; men whom he had once reverenced seemed now trivial and wearisome. A lost world kept crowding in on him; he could not recover it, but he felt that without it there was no peace for him in life. There was only one stable thing, Felicity, who moved in a happy sphere of her own, from which he daily felt more estranged.

Ridiculous little things tormented him--a tune which reminded him of a French chanson, the smell of a particular tobacco which suggested the coarse stuff grown at Clairefontaine. He dared not go shooting or fishing because of their associations; golf, which belonged wholly to his new world, he came to loathe.

"It was like a cancer," he said. "A doctor once told me that cancer was a growth of certain cells at a wild pace--the pace at which a child grows in the womb--a sort of crazy resurgence of youth. It begins by being quite innocent, but soon it starts pressing in on other cells and checking their growth, and the thing becomes pathological. That was what happened to me. The old world came to bulk so big in my life that it choked the rest of me like a cancer in the mind."

He had another trouble, the worst of all. He had been brought up a strict Catholic, but since he left home he had let his religion fall from him. He had never been to Mass. Felicity was an Episcopalian who took her creed lightly, and they had been married in a fashionable New York church. Now all the fears and repressions of his youth came back to him. He had forgotten something of desperate importance, his eternal welfare. He had never thought much about religion, but had simply taken it for granted till he began to neglect it, so he had no sceptical apparatus to support him. His conduct had not been the result of enlightenment, but flat treason.

"I came to realise that I had forgotten God," he said simply.

The breaking-point came because of his love for Felicity. The further he moved away from her and her world, the dearer she became. The one thing he was resolved should not happen was a slow decline in their affection. Either he would recover what he had lost and harmonise it with what he had gained, or a clean cut would be made, with no raw edges to fester. . . . So on a spring morning, with a breaking heart, he walked out of Felicity's life. . . .

"You have guessed most of this?" he asked.

"Most of it," said Leithen. "What I want to know is the sequel. You have been nearly a year looking for your youth. What luck?"

"None. But you don't put it quite right, for I was willing enough to grow old decently. What I had to recover was the proper touch with the world which I had grown out of and could no more reject than my own skin. Also I had to make restitution. I had betrayed something ancient and noble, and had to do penance for my sins."

"Well?" Leithen had to repeat the question, for words seemed to have failed Galliard.

"I did both," he said slowly. "To that extent I succeeded. I got into touch with my people's life, and I think I have done penance. But I found that more was needed. I belong to the North, and to go on living I had to master the North. . . . But it mastered me."

Leithen waited for Galliard to expound this saying, but he waited a long time. The other's face had darkened, and he seemed to be wrestling with difficult thoughts. At last he asked a question.

"I cannot explain," said Galliard, "for I don't quite know what happened. . . . I thought that if I found my brother, or at least found out what had become of him, that I should have done the right thing--done the kind of thing my family have always been doing-- defied the North, scored off it. It didn't work out like that. Up there on the Ghost River I was like a haunted man--something kept crushing me down. Yes, by God! I was afraid. Naked fear!--I had never known it before. . . . I had to go on or give up altogether. Then Lew started in about his Sick Heart River. He was pretty haywire, but I thought he was on the track of something wonderful. He said it was a kind of Paradise where a man left his sins behind him. It wasn't sense, if I'd stopped to think, but I was beyond thinking. Here was a place where one could be reconciled to the North--where the North ceased to be a master and became a comforter. I can tell you I got as mad about the thing as Lew.

"But Lew was no good to me," he went on. "He forgot all about me. Being mad, he was thinking only of himself. I hurt my foot and had a difficult time keeping up with him. Pretty bad days they were--I don't want to go through anything of the sort again. Then I lost him and would have perished if you hadn't found me. You know the rest. Johnny nursed me back to bodily health, and partly to sanity, for he is the sanest thing ever made. But not quite. Lew has come back cured, but not me, though I dare say I look all right."

He turned his weather-beaten, wholesome face to Leithen, and in his eyes there was an uncertainty which belied the strong lines of mouth and jaw.

"I will tell you the truth," he said. "I'm afraid, black afraid of this damned country. But I can't leave it until I've got on terms with it. And God knows how that is to be managed."

3

Leithen found that his slowly mending health was having a marked effect upon his mind. It was like a stream released from the bondage of frost. Before, he had been plodding along in a rut with no inclination to look aside; now he was looking about him and the rut was growing broad and shallow. Before, he had stopped thinking about his body, for it was enough to endure what came to it; now he took to watching his sensations closely, eager to find symptoms of returning strength. This must mean, he thought, a breakdown of his stoicism, and he dreaded that, for it might be followed by the timidity which he despised.

But this new mental elasticity enabled him to reflect on the problem of Galliard--on Galliard himself, who was ceasing to be a mere problem and becoming flesh and blood. For months Leithen had been insensitive to human relationships. Even his friends at home, who had warmed and lit his life, had sunk into the background, and the memory of them when it revived was scarcely an extra pang. His mind had assessed the people he met in New York, but they might have been ninepins for all he cared about them, though for Felicity he had felt a certain dim tenderness. But the return journey from Sick Heart River had wrought a change. His sudden realisation of the mercifulness behind the rigour of Nature had made him warm towards common humanity. He saw the quality of Lew and Johnny, and thanked God for it. Now he was discovering Galliard, and was both puzzled and attracted by him.

A man--beyond question. Leithen saw that in him which had won him an enchanting wife and a host of friends. There was warmth, humour, loyalty. Something more, that something which had made Clifford Savory insistent that he must be brought back for the country's sake. There was a compelling charm about him which would always win him followers, and there was intellect in his brow and eyes. Leithen, accustomed all his life to judge men, had no doubt about Galliard.

But he was broken. As broken by fear as Lew had been at Sick Heart River, and, being of a more complex make-up than Lew, the mending would be harder. A man of a stiff fibre had been confronted by fear and had been worsted by it. There could be no settlement for Galliard until he had overcome it.

Leithen brooded over that mysterious thing, the North. A part of the globe which had no care for human life, which was not built to man's scale, a remnant of that Ice Age which long ago had withered the earth. As a young man he had felt its spell when he looked from the Clairefontaine height of land towards the Arctic watershed. The Gaillard family for generations had felt it. Like brave men they had gone out to wrestle with it, and had not returned. Johnny, even the stolid Johnny, had confessed that he had had his bad moments. Lew--Heaven knows what aboriginal wildness was mingled with his Highland blood!--had gone hunting for a mystic river and had then got the horrors of the unknown and fled from it. But he was bred to the life of the North and could fall back upon its ritual and defy it by domesticating it. Yet at any moment the fire might kindle again in him. As for Galliard, he was bound to the North by race and creed and family tradition; it was not hard for the gods of the Elder Ice to stretch a long arm and pluck him from among the flesh-pots.

What puzzled him was why he himself had escaped. He had had an hour of revulsion at Sick Heart River, but it had passed like a brief nightmare. His mind had been preoccupied with prosaic things like cold and weariness, and his imagination had been asleep. The reason was plain. He had been facing death, waiting stoically on its coming. There was no space for lesser fears when the most ancient terror was close to him, no room for other mysteries when he was nearing the ultimate one.

What had happened to him? Had he come out of the Valley of the Shadow, or had the Shadow only shifted for a moment to settle later on, darker and deeper? He deliberately refused to decide. A sense of reverence, almost of awe, deterred him. He had committed himself to God's hands and would accept with a like docility mercy and harshness. But one thing he knew--he had found touch with life. He was reacting to the external world. His mind had feelers out again to its environment. Therefore Galliard had assumed a new meaning. He was not a task to be plodded through with, but a fellow-mortal to be helped, a companion, a friend.

4

Johnny and the Hares reached camp when a sudden flurry of snow ended the brief daylight. Lew and the other Indian ran to receive them, and presently Galliard joined the group.

"Queer folk in the North," Leithen thought. "They don't make much fuss over a reunion, though it's three weeks since they parted." Out of the corner of his eye he saw the team of dogs, great beasts, half wolf, half malamute, weighing a hundred pounds each, now sending up clouds of grey steam into the white snowfall. He had a glimpse, too, of Johnny, who looked tired and anxious.

The better part of an hour passed, while Leithen sat alone in the hut mending a pair of moccasins. Then Johnny appeared with a grave face, and handed him a letter.

"Things ain't goin' too well with them Hares," he said. "They've got a blight on 'em like Indians get. They're starvin', and they're goin' mad."

The letter, written on a dirty half-sheet of mission paper, and secured between two pieces of birch-bark, was from the priest, Father Duplessis, who had taken Father Wentzel's place for the winter. It was written with indelible pencil in a foreign pointed script.

"They tell me you are recovering health, my friend, and for your sake I rejoice. Also for my own, for I am enabled to make you an appeal. My poor people here are in great sorrow. They have little food, and they will not try to get more, for a disease has come upon them, a dreadful accidie which makes them impotent and without hope. Food must be found for them, and above all they must be roused out of their stupor and made to wish to live. I wrestle with them, and I have the might of the Church behind me, but I am alone and I am but a weak vessel. If you can come to my aid, with God's help we may prevail, but if not I fear this little people will be blotted out of the book of life."

5

That night after supper four men sat in council. Johnny made his report, much interrupted by Lew's questions, and once or twice the two Hares were summoned to give information. Johnny was a very weary man, for his bandy legs had broken the trail for the dogs through the snow-encumbered forest, and he had forced the pace for man and beast. His pale blue eyes, which had none of Lew's brilliance, had become small and troubled. One proof of his discomfort was that when he broke off to speak to his brother it was in the Cree tongue. Never before had Leithen heard him use his mother's speech.

Leithen found himself presiding over the council, for the others seemed to defer to him, after Lew had cross-examined his brother about what supplies he had brought.

"Father Duplessis says there's trouble in the Hares' camp," he said. "Let's hear more about it. Father Wentzel in the fall was afraid of something of the sort."

Johnny scratched the tip of one of his bat's ears.

"Sure there's trouble. Them gol-darned Hares has gone loony and it ain't the first time neither. They think they're Christians, but it's a funny kind of religion, for they're always hankerin' after old bits of magic. Comin' up in the fall I heard they'd been consultin' the caribou bone."

He explained a little shamefacedly.

"It's a caribou's shoulder-blade, and it's got to be an old buck with a special head of horns. They'd got one and there's a long crack down the middle, and their medicine men say that means famine."

Lew snorted. "They needn't have gone to an old bone for that. This year the hares and rabbits has gone sick and that means that every other beast is scarce. The Hares ain't much in the way of hunters--never have been--but they know all about rabbits. That's how they've gotten their name. Maybe you thought they was so- called because they hadn't no more guts than a hare. That ain't right. They're a brave enough tribe, though in old days the Crees and the Chipewyans had the upper hand of them. But the truth is that they haven't much sense and every now and then they go plumb crazy."

"You say they're starving," Leithen addressed Johnny. "Is that because they cannot get food or because they won't try to get it?"

"Both," was the answer. "I figured it out this way. As a general thing they fish all summer and dry their catch for the winter. That gives 'em both man's meat and dog's meat. But this year the white fish and pike was short in the lakes and the rivers. I heard that in the fall when we were comin' in. Well then, it was up to them to make an extra good show with the fall huntin'. But, as Lew says, the fall huntin' was a washout anyhow. Moose and caribou and deer were scarce, because the darned rabbits had gone sick. It happens that way every seven years or so. So them pitiful Hares started the winter with mighty poor prospects."

Johnny spat contemptuously.

"For you and me that would've meant a pretty hard winter's work. There's food to be got up in them mountains even after the freeze- up, if you know where to look for it. You can set bird traps, for there's more partridges here than in Quebec. You can have deadfalls for deer, and you can search out the moose's stamping grounds. I was tellin' you that the moose were shifting further north. The Hares ain't very spry hunters, as Lew says, for they've got rotten guns, but they're dandies at trappin'. Well, as I was sayin', if it'd been you and me we'd have got busy, and, though we'd have had to draw in our belts, somehow or other we'd have won through. But what does them crazy Hares do?"

Johnny spat again, and Lew joined him in the same gesture of scorn.

"They done nothin'! Jest nothin'. The caribou shoulder-blade had 'em scared into fits. It's a blight that comes on 'em every now and then, like the rabbit sickness. If a chief dies they mourn for him, sittin' on their rumps, till they're pretty well dead themselves. In the old fightin' days what they lost in a battle was nothin' to what they lost afterwards lamentin' it. So they're takin' their bad luck lyin' down and it jest ain't sense. It looks as if that tribe was fixed to be cleaned out before spring."

Jonnny's contemptuous eyes became suddenly gentle.

"It's a pitiful business as ever I seen. Their old chief--Zacharias they call him--he must be well on in the eighties, but he's the only one that ain't smit with paralysis. Him and Father Duplessis. But Zacharias is mighty bad with lumbago and can't get about enough, and the Father ain't up to the ways of them savages. He prays for 'em and he argues with 'em, but he might as well argue and pray with a skunk. A dog whip would be the thing if you'd the right man to handle it."

Johnny's melancholy eyes belied his words. They were not the eyes of a disciplinarian.

"And yet," he went on, "I don't know, but I somehow can't keep on bein' angry with the creatures. They sit in their shacks and but for the women they'd freeze, for they don't seem to have the strength to keep themselves warm. The children are bags of bones and crawl about like a lot of little starved owls. It's only the women that keep the place goin', and they won't be able to stick it much longer, for everythin's runnin' short--

food for the fire as well as food for the belly. The shacks are fallin' into bits and the tents are gettin' ragged, and the Hares sit like broody hens reflectin' on their sins and calculatin' how soon they'll die. You couldn't stir 'em if you put a charge of dynamite alongside of 'em-- you'd blow 'em to bits, but they'd die broody."

"Father Duplessis has the same story," Leithen said.

"Yep, and he wants your help. I guess he's asked for it. He says it's a soldier's job and you and him are two old soldiers, but that he's a private and you're the sergeant-major."

Galliard, who had been listening with bowed head, suddenly looked up.

"You fought in the War?" he asked.

Leithen nodded. His eyes were on Lew's face, for he saw something there for which he was not prepared. Lew had hitherto said little, and he had been as scornful as Johnny about the Hares. The brothers had never shown any pride in their Indian ancestry; their pride was reserved for the Scots side. They had treated the Hares with friendliness, but had been as aloof from them and their like as Leithen and Galliard. It was not any sense of kinship that had woke the compassion in Lew's face and the emotion in his voice.

"You can't be angry with the poor devils," he said. "It's an act of God, and as much a disease as T.B. I've seen it happen before, happen to tougher stocks than the Hares. Dad used to talk about the Nahannis that once ranged from the Peace to the Liard. Where are the Nahannis today? Blotted out by sickness of mind. Blotted out like the Snakeheads and the White Pouches and the Big Bellies. And the Hares are going the same way, and then it'll be the turn of the Chipewyans and the Yellow Knives and the Slaves. We white folk can treat the poor devils' bodies, but we don't seem able to do anything for their minds."

No, it was not race loyalty. Leithen saw in Lew and Johnny at that moment something finer than the duty of kinship. It was the brotherhood of all men, white and red and brown, who have to fight the savagery of the North.

His eyes turned to Galliard, who was looking puzzled. He wondered what thoughts this new situation had stirred in that subtle and distracted brain.

"We'd better sleep over this," he announced, for Johnny seemed dropping with fatigue. . . .

Yet Johnny was the last to go to bed. Leithen was in the habit of waking for a minute or two several times in the night. When his eyes opened shortly after midnight he saw Johnny before the fire, not mending it, but using its light to examine something. It was the shoulder-blade of a caribou, which he had dug out of the rubbish-heap behind the camp. The Hares were not the only dabblers in the old magic.

6

Leithen slept ill that night. He seemed to have been driven out of a sanctuary into the turmoil of the common earth. Problems were being thrust on him, and he was no longer left to that narrow world in which he was beginning to feel almost at ease.

Of course he could do nothing about the wretched Hares. Father Duplessis' appeal left him cold. He had more urgent things to think about than the future of a few hundred degenerate Indians who mattered not at all in his scheme of things. His business was with Galliard, who mattered a great deal. But he could not fix his mind on Galliard, and presently he realised something which made him wakeful indeed and a little ashamed. At the back of his head was the thought of his own health. The curtain which had shut down on his life was lifting a corner and revealing a prospect. He was conscious, miserably conscious, that the chief hope in his mind was that he might possibly recover. And that meant a blind panicky fear lest he should do anything to retard recovery.

He woke feeling a tightness in his chest and a difficulty in breathing, from which for some weeks he had been free. He woke, too, to an intense cold. The aurora had been brilliant the night before; and now in the pale sky there were sun-dogs, those mock suns which attend the extreme winter rigours of the North. Happily there was no wind, but the temperature outside the hut struck him like a blow, and he felt that his power of resistance had weakened. This was how he had felt on the road to the Sick Heart River.

He was compelled by his weakness to lie still much of the day and could watch the Frizels and Galliard. Something had happened to change the three--subtly, almost imperceptibly in Galliard's case, markedly in the other two. Johnny had a clouded face; he had seen the Hares' suffering and could not forget it. In Lew's face there were no clouds, but it had sharpened into a mask of intense vitality, in which his wonderful eyes blazed like planets. The sight made Leithen uneasy. Lew had shed the sobriety for which he had been conspicuous in recent weeks. He looked less responsible, less intelligent, almost a little mad. Leithen, intercepting his furtive looks, was unpleasantly reminded of the man who had met him at Sick Heart River. As for Galliard, he was neither dejected nor exalted, but he seemed to have much to think about. He was doing his jobs with a preoccupied face, and he, too, was constantly stealing a glance at Leithen. He seemed to be waiting for a lead.

It was this that Leithen feared. For some strange reason he, a sick man--till the other day, and perhaps still, a dying man--was being forced by a silent assent into the leadership of the little band. It was to him that Father Duplessis had appealed, but that was natural, for they had served together under arms. But why this mute reference to his decision of the personal problems of all the others? These men were following the urge of a very ancient loyalty. Perhaps even Galliard. Who was he to decide on a thing wholly outside his world?

His own case was first in his mind. All his life he had been mixed up in great affairs. He had had his share in "moulding a state's decrees" and "shaping the whisper of a throne." He had left England when Europe was a powder magazine and every patriot was bound to put himself at the disposal of his distracted land. Well, he had cast all that behind him--rightly, for he had to fight his own grim battle. In that battle he seemed to have won a truce, perhaps even a victory, and now he was being asked to stake all his winnings on a trivial cause--the malaise of human kites and crows roosting at the end of the earth.

It may have been partly due to the return of his malady, but suddenly a great nausea filled his mind. He had been facing death with a certain courage because an effort was demanded of him, something which could stir the imagination and steel the heart. But now he was back among trivialities. It was not a surrender to the celestial will that was required of him, but a decision on small mundane questions--how to return a batch of lunatics to sanity, what risks a convalescent might safely run? He felt a loathing for the world, a loathing for himself, so when Lew sat himself down beside him he found sick eyes and an ungracious face.

"We've got to leave," Lew said. "We're too high up here for the winter hunting, and it'll be worse when the big snows come in February. We should be getting down to the bird country and the moose country. I reckon we must take the Hares' camp on our road to see about our stuff. There's a lot of tea and coffee left cached in the priest's cellar."

Leithen turned a cold eye on him.

"You want to help the Hares?" he said.

"Why, yes. Johnny and me thought we might give the poor devils a hand. We could do a bit of hunting for them. We know the way to more than one moose ravage, and a few meals of fresh deer meat may put a little life into them."

"That sounds a big job. Am I fit to travel?"

"Sure you're fit to travel! We've got the huskies and we'll go canny. It's cold, but you'll be as snug in a hole in the snow as in this camp. When you're in good timber and know the way of it you can be mighty comfortable though it's fifty under. Man! it's what's wanted to set you up. By the time the thaw-out comes you'll be the toughest of the bunch."

"But what can I do? Hunt? I haven't the strength for it, and I would only be an encumbrance."

"You'll hunt right enough."

Lew's frosty eyes had a smile in their corners. He had clearly expected argument, perhaps contradiction, but Leithen had no impulse to argue. He was too weary in body and sick in soul.

It was different when Galliard came to him. Here was a man who had nothing to suggest, one who was himself puzzled. Confined for months to a small company, Leithen had become quick to detect changes of temper in his companions. Johnny never varied, but he could read Lew's mutations like a book. Now he saw something novel in Galliard, or rather an intensifying of what he had already observed. This man was afraid, more than afraid; there was something like panic in his face when he allowed it to relax from restraint. This tale of the Hares' madness had moved him strongly-- not apparently to pity, but to fear, personal fear. It was another proof of the North's malignity and power.

He was clinging to Leithen through fear, clinging like a drowning man to a log. Leithen could bring the forces of a different world to fight the dominance of that old world which had mastered him. He wanted to be reassured about Leithen, to know that this refuge could be trusted. So he asked him a plain question.

"Who are you? I know your name. You know my friends. But I know nothing more about you . . . except that you came out here to die-- and may live."

The appeal in Galliard's voice was so sincere that his question had no tinge of brusqueness. It switched Leithen's mind back to a forgotten world which had no longer any meaning. To reply was like recalling a dream.

"Yes, you are entitled to ask me that," he said. "Perhaps I should have been more candid with you. . . . My name is Edward Leithen-- Sir Edward Leithen--they knighted me long ago. I was a lawyer-- with a great practice. I was also for many years a Member of Parliament. I was for a time the British Attorney-General. I was in the British Cabinet, too--the one before the present."

Galliard repeated the name with mystified eyes which seemed straining after a recollection.

"Sir Edward Leithen! Of course I have heard of you. Many people have spoken of you. You were for my wife's uncle in the Continental Nickel case. You had a big reputation in the States. . . . You are a bachelor?"

"I have no wife or any near relations."

"Anything else?"

"I don't know. But I was once what I suppose you would call a sportsman. I used to have a kind of reputation as a mountaineer. I was never sick or sorry until this present disease got hold of me--except for a little damage in the War."

Galliard nodded. "You told me you were in the War. As what?"

"I was chief staff officer of a rather famous British division."

Galliard looked at him steadily and in his face there was something like hope.

"You have done a lot. You are a big man. To think of you roosting with us in this desert!--two half-breeds, two Indians, and a broken man like me. By God! Sir Edward, you've got to help me. You've got to get well, for I'm sunk without you."

He seized the other's right hand and held it in both his own. Leithen felt that if he had been a woman he would have kissed it.

7

Galliard's emotion gave the finishing touch to Leithen's depression. He ate no supper and fell early asleep, only to waken in the small hours when the fire was at its lowest and the cold was like the clutch of a dead hand. He managed to get a little warmth by burying his head in the flap of his sleeping-bag. Drowsiness had fled from him, and his brain was racing like a flywheel.

He had lost all his philosophy. The return of pain and discomfort after an apparent convalescence had played havoc with his stoicism. Miserably, penitently, he recalled the moods he had gone through since he had entered the North. At first there had been sullen, hopeless fortitude, a grim waiting upon death. There had been a sense of his littleness and the omnipotence of God, and a resignation like Job's to the divine purpose. And then there had come a nobler mood, when he had been conscious not only of the greatness but of the mercy of God, and had realised the vein of tenderness in the hard rock of fate. He had responded again to life, and after that response his body seemed to have laboured to reach the sanity of his mind. His health had miraculously improved. . . . And now he had lost all the ground he had made, and was down in the dust again.

His obsession was the fear that he would not recover and--at the heart of everything--lay the fear of that fear.

He knew that it meant that his whole journey to the North had failed of its true purpose, and that he might as well be dying among the pillows and comforts of home. The thought stung him so sharply that he shut his mind to it and fixed his attention resolutely on the immediate prospect.

Lew and Johnny wanted to go to the Hares' assistance. Lew said that in any case they must be getting down country. Once there they must hunt both for the Hares' sake and for their own. Lew had said that he, Leithen, would be able to hunt--arrant folly, for a few days of it in his present state would kill him.

Had he been a mere subaltern in the party he would have accepted this programme as inevitable. But he knew that whatever Lew might plan it would be for him to approve, and ultimately to carry out. The Frizels were old professionals at the business, and yet it would be he, the novice, who would have to direct it. His weakness made him strongly averse to any exertion of mind and body, especially of mind. He might endure physical torment like a Spartan, but he shrank with horror from any necessity to think and scheme. Let the Frizels carry him with them wherever they liked, inert and passive, until the time came when they could shovel his body into the earth.

But then there was Galliard. He was the real problem. It was to find him and save him that he had started out. He had found him, but he had yet to save him. . . . Now there seemed to be a way of salvation. The man was suffering from an ancient fear and there could be no escape except by facing that fear and beating it. This miserable business of the Hares had provided an opportunity. Here was a chance to meet one of the North's most deadly weapons, the madness with which it could affect the human mind, and by checking that madness defeat the North. He had seen this motive confusedly in Galliard's eyes.

He could not desert a man who belonged to his own world, and who mattered much to that world, a man, too, who had flung himself on his mercy. But to succeed in Galliard's business would involve more than hunting docilely in Lew's company with Lew to nurse him.

As he fell asleep to the sound of one of the Hares making up the morning fire he had the queer fancy that the Sick Heart River was dogging them. It had come out of its chasm and was flowing in their tracks, always mastering their course and their thoughts. Waters of Death!--or Waters of Healing?

8

They broke camp on a morning which, as Johnny declared in disgust, might have been April. In the night the wind had backed to the south-west and the air was moist and heavy, though piercingly cold. It was the usual thaw which, in early February, precedes the coming of the big snows.

The sledges were loaded with the baggage and the dogs harnessed. Johnny and one of the Hares were in charge of them, while Lew went ahead to break the trail. All of the men except Leithen had back- packs. He carried only a slung rifle, for Lew had vetoed his wish to take a share of the burden. The hut was tidied up, all rubbish was burnt, and, according to the good custom of the North, a frozen haunch of caribou and a pile of cut firewood were left behind for any belated wanderer.

Leithen looked back at the place which for weeks had been his home with a sentimental regret of which he was half-ashamed. There he had had a promise of returning health and some hours of what was almost ease. Now that promise seemed to have faded away. The mental perturbation of the last days had played the devil with his precarious strength. His breath was troubling him again, and his legs had a horrid propensity to buckle under him.

The first part of the road was uphill, out of the woods into the scattered spruces, and then to the knuckle of barrens which was the immediate height of land, and from which he had first had a view of the great mountain country where the Sick Heart flowed. That ascent of perhaps three miles was a heavy task for him. Lew mercifully set a slow pace, but every now and then the dogs would quicken and the rest of the party had to follow suit. Leithen found that after the first half-mile his feet were no longer part of his body, his moccasins clogged with the damp snow, and at each step he seemed to be dragging part of the hillside after him. His thighs, too, numbed, and he had a sickening ache in his back. He managed to struggle beyond the tree line into the barrens and then collapsed in a drift.

Galliard picked him up and set him on the end of one of the sledges. He promptly got off and again fell on his face. A whistle from Galliard brought Lew back and a glance showed the latter where the trouble lay.

"You got to ride," he told Leithen. "The dogs ain't too heavy loaded, and the ground's easy. If you don't you'll be a mighty sick man, and there's no camp for a sick man until we get over the divide into the big timber."

Leithen obeyed, and finished the rest of the ascent in a miserable half-doze, his arms slung through the baggage couplings to keep him from falling off. But at the divide, where a halt was called and tea made, he woke to find his body more comfortable. He was able to swallow some food, and when they started again he insisted on walking with Galliard. They were now descending, and Galliard's arm linked with his steadied his shambling footsteps.

"You're getting well," Galliard told him.

"I'm feeling like death!"

"All the same you're getting well. A month ago you couldn't have made that first mile. You are feeling worse than you did last week, but you've forgotten how much worse you were a month ago. You remember young Ravelston, the doctor man? I once heard him say that Nature's line of recovery was always wavy and up and down, and that if a man got steadily better without any relapse there was trouble waiting for him."

Leithen felt himself preposterously cheered by Galliard's words. They were now descending into the nest of shallow parallel glens which ultimately led to Lone Tree Lake. They followed the trail which Johnny had lately taken, and though it required to be broken afresh owing to recent snow, it was sufficiently well marked to make easy travelling. Before the light faded in the afternoon it was possible for Leithen and Galliard to lag well behind the sledges without any risk of losing themselves. The descent was never steep, and the worst Leithen had to face were occasional slopes of mushy snow where the foot-holds were bad. He had a stick to help him, and Galliard's right arm. There was no view, for the clouds hung low on the wooded ridges, and streamers of mist choked the aisles of the trees. Exertion had for Leithen taken the sting out of the cold, and his senses were alive again. There were no smells, only the bleak odour of sodden snow, but the woods had come out of their winter silence. The hillside was noisy with running water and the drip of thawing spruces.

Galliard had the in-toed walk which centuries ago his race learned from the Indians. He moved lightly and surely in difficult places where the other slipped and stumbled, and he could talk with no need to save his breath.

"You left England a month or two after I left New York. What was the situation in Europe in the summer? It was bad enough in the spring."

"I wasn't thinking about Europe then," Leithen answered. "You see, I did not see how it could greatly concern me. I didn't give much attention to the press. But my impression is that things were pretty bad."

"And in the United States?"

"There I think they took an even graver view. They did not talk about it, for they thought I would not live to see it. But again my impression is that they were looking for the worst. I heard Bronson Jane say something to Lethaby about zero hour being expected in September."

"Then Europe may have been at war for months. Perhaps the whole world. At this moment Canadian troops may be on the seas. American, too, maybe. And up here, on the same continent, we don't know one thing about it. You and I have dropped pretty completely out of the world, Sir Edward."

"Supposing there is war," he went on. "Some time or other Lew and Johnny will get the news. They won't say much, but just make a bee-line for the nearest end of steel, same as they did in '14. They won't worry what the war is about. There's a scrap, and Britain is in it, and, being what they are, they're bound to be in it too. It must be a wonderful thing to have an undivided mind."

He glanced curiously at his companion. "You have that mind," he said. "You've got a hard patch to hoe, but you've no doubts about it."

"If I live I shall have doubts in plenty," was the answer. "But YOU--you seem to fit into this life pretty well. You go hunting with Lew as if you were bred to it. You're as healthy as a hound. You have a body that can defy the elements. What on earth is there for you to fear? Look at me. I'd be an extra-special crock in a hospital for the sick and aged. You stride like a free man and I totter along like a sick camel. The cold invigorates you and it paralyses me. You face up to the brutishness of Nature, and I shrink and cower and creep under cover. You can defy the North, but my only defiance is that the infernal thing can't prevent my escape by death."

"You are wrong," said Galliard solemnly. "You have already beaten the North--you have never been in danger--because you know in your heart that you do not give a cent for it. I am beaten because it has closed in on me above and below, and I cannot draw breath without its permission. You say I stride like a free man. I tell you that whatever my legs do my heart crawls along on sufferance. I look at those hills and I am terrified at what may lie behind them. I look at the sky and think what horrid cruelty it is planning--freezing out the little weak sprouts of life. You would say that the air here is as pure as mid-ocean, but I tell you that it sickens me as if it came from a charnel house. . . . That's the right word. It's a waft of death. I feel death all around me. Not swift, clean annihilation, but death with torture and horror in it. I am in a world full of spectres, and they are worse than the Wendigo ghoul that the Montagnais Indians used to believe in at home. They said that you knew it was coming by the smell of corruption in the air. And I tell you I feel that corruption-- here--now."

Galliard's square, weather-beaten face was puckered like an old woman's. He had given Leithen his arm to support him, and now he pressed the other's elbow to his side as if the contact was his one security.

9

That night when Leithen stumbled into camp he found that even in the comfortless thaw Lew had achieved comfort. The camp was made in an open place away from the dripping trees. The big hollow which the men had dug with their snow-shoes was floored with several layers of spruce branches, and on a bare patch in the centre a great fire was blazing. The small tent had been set up for Leithen, but since there was no fall the others were sufficiently dry and warm on the fir boughs.

Movement and change had revived him and though his legs and back ached he was not too much exhausted by the day's journey. Also he found to his surprise that his appetite had come back. Lew had managed to knock down a couple of grouse, and Leithen with relish picked the bones of one of them. All soon went to sleep except Johnny, who was busy mending one of his snow-shoes by the light of the fire.

Leithen watched him through the opening of his tent, a humped, gnome-like figure that cast queer shadows. He marvelled at his energy. All day Johnny had been wrestling with refractory dogs, he had been the chief worker in pitching camp, and now he was doing odd jobs while the others slept. Not only was his industry admirable; more notable still were his skill and resourcefulness. There was no job to which he could not turn his hand. That morning Leithen had admired the knots and hitches with which he bound the baggage to the sledges--each exactly appropriate to its purpose, and of a wonderful simplicity. A few days earlier one of the camp kettles was found to be leaking. Johnny had shaved a bullet, melted the lead, and neatly soldered a patch to cover the hole. . . . He remembered, too, what Galliard had said about the summons to war. Lew and Johnny were supremely suited to the life which fate had cast for them. They had conquered the North by making an honourable deal with it.

And yet . . . As Leithen brooded in the flicker of the firelight before he fell asleep he came to have a different picture. He saw the Indians as tenuous growths, fungi which had no hold on the soil. They existed in sufferance; the North had only to tighten its grip and they would disappear. Lew and Johnny, too. They were not mushrooms, for they had roots and they had the power to yield under strain and spring back again, but were they any better than grassy filaments which swayed in the wind but might any day be pinched out of existence? Johnny was steadfast enough, but only because he had a formal and sluggish mind; the quicker, abler Lew could be unsettled by his dreams. They, too, lived on sufferance. . . . And Galliard? He had deeper roots, but they were not healthy enough to permit transplanting. Compared to his companions Leithen suddenly saw himself founded solidly like an oak. He was drawing life from deep sources. Death, if it came, was no blind trick of fate, but a thing accepted and therefore mastered. He fell asleep in a new mood of confidence.

10

In the night the wind changed, and the cold became so severe that it stirred the men out of sleep and set them building up the fire. Leithen awoke to an air which bit like a fever, and a world which seemed to be made of metal and glass.

The cold was more intense than anything he had ever imagined. Under its stress trees cracked with a sound like machine-guns. The big morning fire made only a narrow circle of heat. If for a second he turned his face from it the air stung his eyelids as if with an infinity of harsh particles. To draw breath rasped the throat. The sky was milk-pale, the sun a mere ghostly disc, and it seemed to Leithen as if everything--sun, trees, mountains--were red-rimmed. There was no shadow anywhere, no depth or softness. The world was hard, glassy, metallic; all of it except the fantasmal, cotton-wool skies.

The cold had cowed the dogs, and it was an easy task to load the sledges. Leithen asked Johnny what he thought the temperature might be.

"Sixty below," was the answer. "If there was any sort of wind I reckon we couldn't have broke camp. The dogs wouldn't have faced it. We'd have had to bury ourselves all day in a hole. Being as it is, we ought to make good time. Might make Lone Tree Lake by noon tomorrow."

Leithen asked if the cold spell would last long.

"A couple of days. Maybe three. Not more. A big freeze often comes between the thaw and the snows. The Indians call it the Bear's Dream. The cold pinches the old bear in his den and gives him bad dreams."

He sniffed the air.

"We're getting out of the caribou country, but it's like they'll be round today. They're not so skeery in a freeze. You keep a rifle handy, and you'll maybe get a shot."

Leithen annexed Johnny's Mannlicher and filled the magazine. To his surprise the violent weather, instead of numbing him, had put life into his veins. He walked stiffly, but he felt as if he could go on for hours, and his breath came with a novel freedom. Galliard, who also carried a rifle, remarked on his looks as they followed the sledges.

"Something has come over you," he said. "Your face is pasty with the cold, but you've gotten a clear eye, and you're using your legs different from yesterday. Feeling fine?"

"Fair," said Leithen. "I'm thankful for small mercies."

He was afraid to confess even to himself that his body was less of a burden than it had been for many months. And suddenly there woke in him an instinct to which he had long been strange, the instinct of the chase. Once he had been a keen stalker in Scottish deer forests, but of late he had almost wholly relinquished gun and rifle. He had lost the desire to kill any warm-blooded animal. But that was in the old settled lands, where shooting was a sport and not a necessity of life. Here in the wilds, where men lived by their marksmanship, it was a duty and not a game. He had heard Lew say that they must get all the caribou they could, since it was necessary to take a load of fresh meat into the Hares' camp. Johnny and the Indians were busy at the sledges, and Lew had the engrossing job of breaking the trail, so such hunting as was possible must fall to him and Galliard.

He felt a boyish keenness which amazed and amused him. He was almost nervous. He slung his Zeiss glass loose round his neck and kept his rifle at the carry. His eyes scanned every open space in the woods which might hold a caribou.

Galliard observed him and laughed.

"You take the right side and I'll take the left. It'll be snap shooting. Keep your sights at two hundred yards."

Galliard had the first chance. He swung round and fired standing at what looked to Leithen to be a grey rock far up on the hillside. The rock sprang forward and disappeared in the thicket.

"Over!" said a disgusted voice. The caravan had halted and even the dogs seemed to hold their breath.

Leithen's chance came half an hour later. The sledges were toiling up a hill where the snow lay thin over a maze of tree-roots, and the pace was consequently slow. His eyes looked down a long slope to a little lake; there had been a bush fire recently, so the ground was open except for one or two skeleton trunks and a mat of second-growth spruce. Something caught his eye in the tangle, something grey against the trees, something which ended in what he took to be withered boughs. He saw that they were antlers.

He tore off his right-hand mitt and dropped on one knee. He heard Galliard mutter "Three hundred," and pushed up his sights. The caribou had its head down and was rooting for moss in the snow. A whistle from Galliard halted the sledges. The animal raised its head and turned slightly round, giving the chance of a rather difficult neck shot.

A single bullet did the job. The caribou sank on the snow with a broken spine, and the Indians left the sledges and raced downhill to the gralloch.

"Good man!" said Galliard, who had taken Leithen's glass and was examining the kill.

"A bull--poorish head, but that doesn't matter--heavy carcase. Every inch of three-fifty yards, and a very prettily placed shot."

"At home," said Leithen, "I would have guessed one-twenty. What miraculous air!"

He was ashamed of the childish delight which he felt. He had proved that life was not dead in him by bringing off a shot of which he would have been proud in his twenties.

The caribou was cut up and loaded on one of the sledges, maddening the dogs with the smell of fresh meat. For the rest of the afternoon daylight Leithen moved happily in step with Galliard. The road was easy, the extreme cold was abating, he felt a glow of satisfaction which he had not known for many a day. He was primitive man again who had killed his dinner. Also there was a new vigour in his limbs--not merely the absence of discomfort and fatigue, but something positive, a "plus" quantity of well-being.

When they made camp he was given the job of attending to the dogs, whose feet were suffering. The malamutes, since their toes were close together, were all right, but with the huskies the snow had balled and frozen hard, and in biting their paws to release the congested toes they had broken the skin and left raw flesh. Johnny provided an antiseptic ointment which tasted evilly and so would not be licked off. The beasts were wonderfully tractable, as if they knew that the treatment was for their good. Leithen had always been handy with dogs, and he found a great pleasure in looking into their furry, wrinkled faces and sniffing their familiar smell. Here was something which belonged most intimately to the North and yet had been adapted to the homely needs of man.

That night he dined with relish off caribou steaks and turned early to bed. But he did not fall asleep at once. There was a pleasant ferment in his brain, for he was for the first time envisaging what life would be if he were restored to it. He allowed his thoughts to run forward and plan.

It was of his friends that he thought chiefly, of his friends and of one or two places linked with them. Their long absence from his memory had clarified his view of them, and against the large background of acquaintances a few stood out who, he realised, were his innermost and abiding comrades. None of his colleagues at the Bar were among them, and none of his fellow-politicians. With them he had worked happily, but they had remained on the outer rim of his life. The real intimates were few, and the bond had always been something linked with sport and country life. Charles Lamancha and John Palliser-Yeates had been at school and college with him, and they had been together on many hillsides and by many waters. Archie Roylance, much younger, had irrupted into the group by virtue of an identity of tastes and his own compelling charm. Sandy Clanroyden had been the central star, radiating heat and light, a wandering star who for long seasons disappeared from the firmament. And there was Dick Hannay, half Nestor, half Odysseus, deep in Oxfordshire mud, but with a surprising talent for extricating himself and adventuring in the ends of the earth.

As he thought of them he felt a glow of affection warm his being. He pictured the places to which they specially belonged: Lamancha on the long slopes of Cheviot; Archie Roylance on the wind-blown thymy moors of the west; Sandy in his Border fortress; and Dick Hannay by the clear streams and gentle pastures of Cotswold. He pictured his meeting with them--restored from the grave. They had never been told about his illness, but they must have guessed. Sandy at least, after that last dinner in London. They must have been talking about him, lamenting his absence, making futile inquiries. . . . He would suddenly appear among them, a little thinner and older perhaps, but the same man, and would be welcomed back to that great companionship.

How would he spend his days? He had finished with his professions, both law and politics. The State must now get on without him. He would be much at Borrowby--thank Heaven he had not sold it! He would go back to his Down Street rooms, for though he had surrendered the lease he would find a way of renewing it. He had done with travel; his last years would be spent at home among his friends. Somebody had once told him that a man who recovered from tuberculosis was pretty well exempt from other maladies. He might live to an old age, a careful, moderate old age filled with mild pleasures and innocent interests. . . . On the pillow of such thoughts he fell asleep.

11

The snow began just as they reached Lone Tree Lake. At first it came gently, making the air a dazzle of flakes, but not obscuring the near view. At the lake they retrieved the rest of their cached supplies, and tramped down its frozen surface until they reached its outlet, a feeder of the Big Hare, now under ten feet of ice and snow. Here the snow's softness made the going difficult, for the northern snow-shoes offered too narrow a surface. The air had become almost mild, and that night, when a rock shelf gave them a comparatively dry bivouac, Leithen deliberately laid his blankets well away from the fire.

Next day they halted to hunt, looking for fresh meat to take to the Hares' camp. Johnny and Lew found a small stamping-ground of moose, and since in the snow the big animals were at a disadvantage, they had no difficulty in getting two young bulls. Leithen helped to drag in the meat and found that the change in the weather had not weakened his new vigour. His mind was in a happy maze, planning aimlessly and making pictures which he did not try to complete.

Lew watched him with satisfaction.

"I've got to learn you things," he said. "You haven't got the tricks, and you're wasting your strength, but"--

and he repeated his old phrase--"you're going to be the huskiest of the lot of us. And I seen you shoot!"

They reached the Hares' camp late on an afternoon, when the snow had so thickened that it had the look of a coarse-textured cloth ceaselessly dropped from the skies. Huts, tents, the little church were for the moment buried under the pall. Lew chose a camping site about a quarter of a mile distant, for it was important to avoid too close a contact at first with the stricken settlement.

Johnny and the Indians went off to prospect. Half an hour later Johnny returned with startled eyes.

"I got news," he stammered. "The Father told me--seems there was a dog-team got down to the Fort, and come back. There's fightin' in Europe--been goin' on for months. Seems it's them darned Germans again. And Britain's in it. Likewise Canada."

12

The taller Indian spoke from behind Johnny.

"My father is dead," he said, and slipped back into the dusk.

"Yes," said Johnny, "there's been a lot of deaths among them Hares. Their camp's like a field hospital. Talkin' of field hospitals, what about this war?"

"We'll sleep on that," Leithen answered.

Lew did not open his mouth, nor Galliard. Supper was prepared and eaten in silence, and each man by tacit consent went immediately to his blankets. Leithen, before turning in, looked at the skies. The snowfall was thinning, and the air was sharpening again. There was an open patch in the west and a faint irradiation of moonshine. Tomorrow would be very cold.

His bodily well-being continued. The journey down from the mountains had left its mark, for his face was scarred by patches of frost-bite, his lips were inflamed, the snow-shoes had made the calves of his legs ache like a bad tooth, and under his moccasins his feet were blistered. Nevertheless he felt that vigour had come back to him. It reminded him of his mountaineering days, when he would return to London with blistered cheeks and aching shoulder muscles and bleared eyes, and yet know that he was far fitter than the smoothly sunburnt creature that emerged from a holiday at home.

But though his body craved for it his mind would not permit of sleep. He had been living with life, and now suddenly death seemed to have closed down on the world. The tall Indian's cry rang in his ears like a knell.

What had become of the bright pictures he had been painting?

The world was at war again and somewhere in Europe men were grappling with death. The horrors of campaigning had never been much in his mind, for as a soldier he had been too busy to brood over the macabre. But now a flood of dimly remembered terrors seemed to flow in upon him--men shot in the stomach and writhing in no-man's-land; scarecrows that once were human crucified on the barbed wire and bleached by wind and sun; the shambles of a casualty clearing station after a battle.

His thoughts had been dwelling on his reunion with friends. Those friends would all be scattered. Sandy Clanroyden would be off on some wild venture. Archie Roylance would be flying, game leg and all. Hannay, Palliser-Yeates, Lamancha, they would all be serving somehow and somewhere. He would be out of it, of course. A guarded flame, a semi-invalid, with nothing to do but to "make" his soul. . . . As he fell asleep he was ashamed of his childishness. He had promised himself a treat which was not going to come off, and he was whining about it.

He woke with a faint far-off tinkle in his ears. He had been dreaming of war and would not have been surprised if he had heard a bugle call. He puzzled over the sound until he hit on the explanation. Father Duplessis in his little church was ringing the morning Angelus.

That tinny bell had an explosive effect on Leithen's mind. This was a place of death, the whole world was full of death--and yet here was one man who stood stubbornly for life. He rang the bell which should have started his flock on their day's work. Sunk in weakness and despair they would remain torpid, but he had sounded the challenge. Here was one man at any rate who was the champion of life against death.

13

It was a silent little band that broke camp and set out in the late winter dawn. Johnny's face was sullen with some dismal preoccupation, and Lew's eyes had the wildness of the Sick Heart River, while Galliard's seemed to have once again the fear which had clouded them when he was recovering from his exhaustion.

To his surprise Leithen found that this did not depress him. The bell still tinkled in his ears. The world was at war again. It might be the twilight of the gods, the end of all things. The globe might swim in blood. Death might resume his ancient reign. But, by Heaven, he would strike his blow for life, even a pitiful flicker of it.

The valley opened before them. Frost had stiffened the snow to marble, and they were compelled to take off their snow-shoes, which gave them no foot-hold. The sky was a profound blue, and the amphitheatre of peaks stood out against it in a dazzling purity, matched below by the unbroken white sheet of the lake. The snow was deep, for the near woods were so muffled as to have lost all clean contours, and when they came to the flat where the camp lay the wretched huts had no outlines. They might have been mounds to mark where the dead lay in some hyperborean graveyard. Only the little church on the higher ground looked like the work of men's hands. From the adjoining presbytery rose a thin wisp of smoke, but elsewhere there was no sign of humanity.

Lew spoke at last.

"God! The Hares have gone to earth like chipmunks! Or maybe they're all dead."

"Not all," said one of the Indians, "but they are dying."

They soon had evidence. They passed a small grove of spruce and poplar, and in nearly every tree there was a thing like a big nest, something lashed to snowy boughs. Lew nodded towards them. "That's their burying-ground. It's new since we was here before." Leithen thought freakishly of Villon and "King Louis's orchard close." There were funny little humps, too, on the flat, with coverings of birch and spruce branches peeping from under the snow.

"Them's graves," said Johnny. "The big ones go up in the trees, the smaller ones are under them humps, and them of no account, like babies and old folk, just get chucked out in the drifts. There's been a power o' dyin' here."

Lew turned to Leithen for orders.

"Which comes first?" he asked, "Zacharias or the priest?"

"We will go to the presbytery," was the answer.

14

There was at first no sign of life in the irregular street of huts that made the ascent to the presbytery. The roofs of some of them were sagging with the weight of snow, and one or two had collapsed. But there were people in them, for, now that they were seen at closer quarters, wraiths of smoke came from the vents, which proved that there were fires within, though very meagre ones. Once a door opened and a woman looked out; she at once drew back with a scared look like an animal's; a whimper of a child seemed to come from indoors.

Then suddenly there rose a wild clamour from starving dogs picketed in the snow. Their own dogs answered it and the valley resounded with the din. After the deathly quiet the noise seemed a horrid impiety. There was nothing in it of friendly barking; it was like the howling of a starving wolf pack lost and forgotten at the world's end.

The sound brought Father Duplessis to the presbytery door. He was about Leithen's own age, but now he looked ten years older than at Fort Bannerman. Always lean, he was now emaciated, and his pallor had become almost cadaverous. He peered and blinked at the newcomers, and then his face lit up as he came forward with outstretched hands.

"God be praised!" he cried. "It is my English comrade-in-arms."

"Get hold of the chief," Leithen told Johnny. "Take the Indians with you and make a plan for distributing the meat. Then bring Zacharias up here."

He and Galliard and Lew followed the priest into the presbytery. In Father Wentzel's time the place had smelt stuffy, like a furniture store. Now it reeked of ether and carbolic, and in a corner stood a trestle table covered with a coarse linen cloth. He remembered that Father Duplessis was something of a doctor.

He was also most clearly a soldier, a soldier tired out by a long and weary campaign. There was nothing about him to tell of the priest except the chain which showed at his neck and which held a cross tucked under his shirt. He wore kamiks and a dicky of caribou skin and a parka edged with wolverine fur, and he needed all his clothing, for the presbytery was perishing cold. He might have been a trapper or a prospector but for his carriage, his squared shoulders and erect head, which showed the discipline of St. Cyr. His silky brown beard was carefully combed and trimmed. A fur skull-cap covered the head where the hair had been cut to the bone. He had the long, high-bridged nose of Picardy gentlefolk, and a fine forehead, round the edges of which the hair was greying. His blue eyes looked washed out and fatigued, but the straight lines of the brows gave an impression of power and reserve. The osseous structure of his face was as sharply defined as the features on a newly minted coin.

"Thank Heaven you have come," he said. "This campaign is too hard for one man. And perhaps I am not the man. In this task I am only a subaltern and I need a commanding officer."

He looked first at Galliard and then at Leithen, and his eyes remained on the latter.

"We are fighting a pestilence," he went on, "but a pestilence of the soul."

"One moment," Leithen broke in. "What about this war in Europe?"

"There is war," said the priest gravely. "The news came from the Fort when I sent a dog-team for supplies. But I know no more than that the nations are once again at each other's throats. Germany with certain allies against your country and mine. I do not think of it--Europe is very far away from my thoughts."

"Supplies? What did you get?"

"Not much. Some meal and flour, of which a balance remains. But that is not the diet for the poor folk here. Also a little coffee for myself. See, I will make you a cup."

He bustled for a minute or two at the stove, and the pleasant odour of coffee cut sharply into the frowst of the room.

"A pestilence of the mind?" Leithen asked. "You mean--?"

"In myself--and in you--it would be called accidie, a deadly sin. But not, I think, with this people. They are removed but a little way from the beasts that perish, and with them it is an animal sickness."

"They die of it?"

"But assuredly. Some have T.B. and their sickness of the mind speeds up that disease. Some are ageing and it makes them senile, so that they perish from old age. With some it unhinges the wits so that the brain softens. Up to now it is principally the men who suffer, for the women will still fight on, having urgent duties. But soon it will mean the children also, and the women will follow. Before the geese return in spring, I fear, I greatly fear, that my poor people will be no more in the land."

"What are you doing about it?"

Father Duplessis shrugged his shoulders and spread out his hands.

"There is little I can do. I perform the offices of the Church, and I strive to make them worship with me. I preach to them the way of salvation. But I cannot lift them out of the mire. What is needed is men--a man--who will force their life again into a discipline, so that they will not slip away into death. Someone who will give them hope."

"Have you no helpers?"

"There is the chief Zacharias, who has a stout heart. But he is old and crippled. One or two young men, perhaps, but I fear they are going the way of the rest."

15

Leithen had asked questions automatically and had scarcely listened to the replies, for in that dim, stuffy, frigid presbytery, where the only light came through the cracks in the door and a dirty window in the roof, he was conscious of something in the nature of a revelation. His mind had a bitter clarity, and his eyes seemed to regard, as from a high place, the kingdoms of the world and men's souls.

His will was rising to the same heights. At last, at long last, his own course was becoming crystal clear.

Memories of the war in which he had fought raced before him like a cinema show, all in order and all pointing the same truth. It had been waste, futile waste, and death, illimitable, futile death. Now the same devilment was unloosed again. He saw Europe as a carnage pit--shattered towns, desecrated homes, devastated cornlands, roads blocked with the instruments of war--the meadows of France and of Germany, and of his own kind England. Once again the free peoples were grappling with the slave peoples. The former would win, but how many free men would die before victory, and how many of the unhappy slaves!

The effluence of death seemed to be wafted to his nostrils over the many thousand miles of land and sea. He smelt the stench of incinerators and muddy trenches and bloody clothing. The odour of the little presbytery was like that of a hospital ward.

But it did not sicken him. Rather it braced him, as when a shore- dweller who has been long inland gets a whiff of the sea. It was the spark which fired within him an explosive train of resolution.

There was a plain task before him, to fight with Death. God for His own purpose had unloosed it in the world, ravening over places which had once been rich in innocent life. Here in the North life had always been on sufferance, its pale slender shoots fighting a hard battle against the Elder Ice. But it had maintained its brave defiance. And now one such pathetic slip was on the verge of extinction. This handful of Hares had for generations been a little enclave of life besieged by mortality. Now it was perishing, hurrying to share in the dissolution which was overtaking the world.

By God's help that should not happen--the God who was the God of the living. Through strange circuits he had come to that simple forthright duty for which he had always longed. In that duty he must make his soul.

There was a ring of happiness in his voice. "You have me as a helper," he said. "And Mr. Galliard. And Lew and Johnny. Between us we will save your Hares from themselves."

Lew's face set, as if he had heard something which he had long feared.

"You mean we've got to feed 'em?"

Leithen nodded. "Feed them--body and mind."

Lew's eyebrows fell.

"You coming out in the woods with us? I guess that's the right thing for you."

"No, that's your job, and Johnny's. I stay here."

Lew exploded. Even in the dimness his eyes were like points of blue fire.

"Hell!" he cried. "You can't do it. You jest can't do it. I was afeared you'd have that dam' foolish notion. Say, what d'you think life here would be like for you? You're on the road to be cured, but you ain't cured yet. Come out with me and Johnny and you'll be living healthy. We won't let you do too much. It's a mighty interesting job hunting moose in their ravages and you'll get some fine shooting. We'll feed you the kind of food that's good for you, and at night we'll make you as snug as a wintering bear. I'll engage by the spring you'll be a mighty strong man. That's good sense, ain't it?"

"Excellent good sense. Only it's not for me. My job is here."

"Man, I tell you it's suicide. Fair suicide. I've seen plenty cases like yours, and I've seen 'em get well and I've seen 'em die. There's one sure way to die and that's to live in a shack or among shacks, and breathe stinking air and be rubbing shoulders with sick folks, and wearing your soul out trying to put some pep into a herring-gutted bunch of Indians. You'll be sicker than ever before a week is out, and a corp in a month, and that'll be darned little use to anybody."

Lew's soft rich voice had become hoarse with passion. He got up from his seat and stood before Leithen like a suppliant, with his hands nervously intertwining.

"You may be right," Leithen said. "But all the same I must stay. It doesn't matter what happens to me."

"It matters like hell," said Lew, and there was that in his voice which made the presbytery a solemn place, for it was the cry of a deep affection.

"This is a war and I obey orders. I've got my orders. In a world where Death is king we're going to defy him and save life. The North has closed down on us and we're going to beat the North. That is to your address, Galliard."

Galliard was staring at him with bright comprehending eyes.

"In this fight we have each got his special job. I'm in command, and I hand them out. I've taken the one for myself that I believe I can do best. We're going to win, remember. What does my death matter if we defeat Death?"

Lew sat down again with his head in his hands. He raised it like a frightened animal at Leithen's next words.

"This is my Sick Heart River. Galliard's too, I think. Maybe yours, Lew. Each of us has got to find his river for himself, and it may flow where he least expects it."

Father Duplessis, back in the deep shadows, quoted from the Vulgate psalm, "Fluminis impetus laetificat civitatem Dei."

Leithen smiled. "Do you know the English of that, Lew? There is a river, the streams whereof shall make glad the city of God. That's what you've always been looking for."

16

The place was suddenly bright, for the door had opened. A wave of icy air swept out the frowst, and Leithen found himself looking into a radiant world, rimmed with peaks of bright snow and canopied by a sky so infinitely far away that it had no colour except that of essential light.

It was the old chief, conducted by Johnny. Zacharias was a very mountain of a man, and age had made him shapeless while lumbago had bent him nearly double. He walked with two sticks, and Johnny had to lower him delicately to a seat. The Hares were not treaty Indians, but nevertheless he wore one of the soup-plate Victorian silver medals, which had come to him through a Cree grandmother. His heavy face had a kind of placid good sense, and age and corpulence had not dimmed the vigour of his eye.

He greeted Leithen ceremonially, realising he was the leader of the newcomers. He had a few words of English, but Johnny did most of the interpreting. He sat with his hands on his knees, like a schoolboy interviewed by a headmaster, but though his attitude suggested nervousness his voice was calm.

"We are a ver' sick people," he repeated several times. It was his chief English phrase.

What he had to tell was much the same story that Johnny had brought to the mountain camp. But since then things had slipped further downhill. There had been more deaths of children and old people, and even of younger men. They did not die of actual starvation, but of low diet and low spirits. Less than half a dozen went hunting, and not many more brought in fuel, so there was little fresh meat and too little firewood. People sat huddled in icy shacks in all the clothes they could find, and dreamed themselves into decay. The heart had gone out of them. The women, too, had ceased to scold and upbraid, and would soon go the way of their menfolk.

"Then our people will be no more," said Zacharias grimly.

Leithen asked what help he could count on.

"There is myself," said the chief, "and this good Father. I have three sons who will do my bidding, and seven grandsons--no, five, for two are sick. There may be a few others. Say at the most a score."

"What would you advise?"

The old man shook his head.

"In our fathers' day the cure would have been a raid by Chipewyans or Dog-ribs! Then we would have been forced to be up and doing or perish. A flight of arrows is the best cure for brooding. Now--I do not know. Something harsh to get the sullenness out of their bones. You are a soldier?"

"The Father and I served in the same war."

"Good! Soldiers' ways are needed. But applied with judgment, for my people are weak and they are also children."

Leithen spoke to the company.

"There are a score of us for this job then. Mr. Galliard and I stay here. Lew and Johnny go hunting, and will take with them whom they choose. We shall need all the dog-teams we can get to bring back meat and cordwood. But first there are several jobs to be done. You've got to build a shack for Mr. Galliard and myself. You've got to get a mighty big store of logs, for a fire must be kept burning day and night."

He was addressing Lew, whose eyes questioned him.

"Why? Because these people must be kept in touch with life, and life is warmth and colour. A fire will remind them that there is warmth and colour in the world. . . . Tomorrow morning we will have a round-up and discover exactly what is the size of our job. . . . You've made camp, Johnny? Mr. Galliard and I will be there by supper-time. Now you and Lew go along and get busy. We've a lot to do in the next few days."

The door opened again and disclosed the same landscape of primitive forms and colours, its dazzle a little dimmed by the approach of evening.

This second glimpse had a strange effect on Leithen, for it seemed to be a revelation of a world which he had forgotten. His mind swooped back on it and for a little was immersed in memories. Zacharias was hoisted to his feet and escorted down the hill. Father Duplessis prepared a simple meal. There was a little talk about ways and means after Lew left, Galliard questioning Leithen and getting answers. Yet all the time the visualising part of Leithen's mind was many thousands of miles away in space and years back in time.

The stove had become too hot, so the door was allowed to remain half open, for the year had turned, and the afternoon sun was gaining strength. So his eyes were seeing a segment of a bright coloured world. The intense pure light brought a flood of pictures all linked with moments of exultant physical vigour. Also with friendships. He did not probe the cause, but these pictures seemed to imply companionship. In each Archie Roylance, or Clanroyden, or Lamancha was just round the corner waiting. . . . There was a July morning, very early, on the Nantillons glacier, on his way to make a traverse of the Charmoz which had once been famous. There was a moonlit night on an Ægean isle when he had been very near old mysteries. There were Highland dawns and twilights--one especially, when he sat on a half-submerged skerry watching for the wild geese--an evening when Tir-nan-og was manifestly re-created. There were spring days and summer days in English meadows, Border bent with the April curlews piping, London afternoons in May with the dear remembered smells fresh in his nostrils. . . . In each picture he felt the blood strong in his veins and a young power in his muscles. This was the man he once had been.

Once! He came out of his absorption to realise that these pictures had not come wholly through the Ivory Gate. He was no longer a dying man. He had been reprieved on the eve of execution, and by walking delicately the reprieve might be extended. His bodily strength was like a fragile glass vessel which one had to carry while walking on a rough road; with care it might survive, but a jolt would shatter it. . . . No, that was a false comparison. His health was like a small sum of money, all that was left of a big fortune. It might be kept intact by a stern economy, or it might be spent gallantly on a last venture.

Galliard and Father Duplessis were sitting side by side and talking earnestly. He caught a word of the priest's: "Dieu fait bien ce qu'il fait" and remembered the quotation. Was it La Fontaine? He laughed, for it fitted in with his own mood.

He had found the right word both for Galliard and himself. They were facing the challenge of the North, which a man must accept and repel or submit to servitude. Lew and Johnny and their kind did not face that challenge; they avoided it by walking humbly; they conciliated it by ingenious subterfuges; its blows were avoided and not squarely met, and they paid the price; for every now and then they fell under its terrors.

He was facing, too, the challenge of Death. Elsewhere in the world the ancient enemy was victorious. If here, against all odds, he could save the tiny germ of life from its maw he would have met that challenge, and done God's work.

Leithen's new-found mission for life gave him a happy retrospect over his own career. At first, when he left England, he had looked back with pain at the bright things now forbidden. In his first days in the North his old world had slipped from him wholly, leaving only a grey void which he must face with clenched teeth and with grim submission. He smiled as he remembered those days, with their dreary stoicism. He had thought of himself like Job, as one whose strength lay only in humbleness. He had been crushed and awed by God.

A barren creed! He saw that now, for its foundation had been pride of defiance, keeping a stiff neck under the blows of fate. He had been abject but without true humility. When had the change begun? At Sick Heart River, when he had a vision of the beauty which might be concealed in the desert? Then, that evening in the snow-pit had come the realisation of the tenderness behind the iron front of Nature, and after that had come thankfulness for plain human affection. The North had not frozen him, but had melted the ice in his heart. God was not only all-mighty but all-loving. His old happinesses seemed to link in with his new mood of thankfulness. The stream of life which had flowed so pleasantly had eternity in its waters. He felt himself safe in the hands of a power that was both God and friend.

Father Duplessis was speaking, and Galliard was listening earnestly. He seemed to be quoting the New Testament--"Heureux sont les morts qui meurent dans le Seigneur."

He had been inhuman, Leithen told himself, with the dreary fortitude of a sick animal. Now whatever befell him he was once again in love with his fellows. The cold infernal North magnified instead of dwarfing humanity. What a marvel was this clot of vivified dust! . . . The universe seemed to spread itself before him in immense distances lit and dominated by a divine spark which was man. An inconsiderable planet, a speck in the infinite stellar spaces; most of it salt water; the bulk of the land rock and desert and austral and boreal ice; interspersed mud, the detritus of æons, with a thin coverlet of grass and trees--that vegetable world on which every living thing was in the last resort a parasite! Man, precariously perched on this rotating scrap-heap, yet so much master of it that he could mould it to his transient uses and, while struggling to live, could entertain thoughts and dreams beyond the bounds of time and space! Man so weak and yet so great, the chief handiwork of the Power that had hung the stars in the firmament!

He was moved to a strange exaltation. Behind his new access of strength he felt the brittleness of his body. His stock of vigour was slender indeed, but he could spend it bravely in making his soul. Most men had their lives taken from them. It was his privilege to GIVE his, to offer it freely and joyfully in one last effort of manhood. The North had been his friend, for it had enabled him, like Jacob, to wrestle with the dark angel and extort a blessing.

The presbytery had warmed up, and Galliard had fallen asleep. He slept with his mouth shut, breathing through his nose, and the sleeping face had dignity and power in it. It would be no small thing to release this man from ancestral fears and gird him for his task in the world. In making his own soul he would also give back Galliard his. He would win the world too, for now the great, shining, mystic universe above him was no longer a foe but a friend, part with himself of an eternal plan.

Father Duplessis' voice broke in on his meditation and seemed to give the benediction words. He was reading his breviary, and broke off now and then to translate a sentence aloud in his own tongue-- "Car celui qui voudra sauver sa vie la perdra; et celui qui perdra sa vie pour l'amour de moi, la retrouvera."

17

From a report by Corporal S----, R.C.M.P., Fort Bannerman, to Inspector N----, R.C.M.P., Fort Macleod.

"Pursuant to instructions received, I left Fort Bannerman on the 21st day of April, accompanied by Constable F----, and after some trouble with my dog-team arrived at the Hares' winter camp on Big Hare Lake at 6.30 p.m. on the 22nd. The last part of the journey was in the dark, but we were guided by a great blaze coming apparently from the camp which was visible from the outlet of the lake. At first I thought the place was on fire, but on arrival found that this evening bonfire had become a regular custom.

"Rumours of distress among the Hares had reached Fort Bannerman during the winter. Father Wentzel, on his return to the Fort, had predicted a bad time, and Father Duplessis, who replaced him, had sent an urgent message asking not only for supplies of food but for someone to go up and advise. I duly reported this to you, and received your instructions to take an early opportunity of visiting the camp. This opportunity I was unable to find for several months, since the Force was short-handed, owing to the departure of men to the provost company in France, and, as you are aware, I was compelled to make two trips to Great Bear Lake in connection with the dispute at the Goose Bay Mine. So, as stated above, I could not leave Fort Bannerman until the 21st inst.

"Constable F---- and I were put up by Father Duplessis, and I received from him a satisfactory account of the condition of the Hare tribe. They are now in good health, and, what is more important, in good heart, for it seems that every now and then they get pessimism, like the measles, and die of it, since it prevents their looking for food. It appeared that they had had a very bad bout in the winter, of the risk of which Father Wentzel had warned us. Up to the beginning of February they were sitting in their huts doing nothing but expecting death, and very soon getting what they expected. A schedule attached to this report gives the number of deaths, and such details as could be ascertained.

"The Hares were saved by an incident which I think is the most remarkable I have ever heard of in my long experience of the Territory. In the early fall a party went into the Mackenzie mountains, travelling up the Big Hare River to a piece of country which has been very imperfectly explored. Or rather, two parties who ultimately joined hands. The party consisted of an American gentleman named Galliard, a New York business man, and an Englishman named Leithen. It had with it two Hare Indians, and as guides the brothers Frizel. The Frizels, Lew and Johnny, are men of high character and great experience. They both served with distinction in the ---- Battalion of the Canadian Expeditionary Force in the last war, and have long been favourably known to the Police. The younger, until recently, was a game warden at the National Park at Waskesieu.

"I received further information about the Englishman, Leithen. It appears that he was Sir Edward Leithen, a famous London lawyer and a British Member of Parliament. He was suffering from tuberculosis, and had undertaken the expedition with a view to a cure. The winter in the high mountains, where the weather has been mild for a Mackenzie River winter, had done him good, and he was believed to be on the way to recovery.

"The party, coming out early in February, reached the Hares' camp to find it in a deplorable condition. Sir E. Leithen at once took charge of the situation. He had been a distinguished soldier in the last war--in the Guards, I believe--and he knew how to handle men. With Mr. Galliard to help him, who had had large administrative experience in America, and with the assistance of Father Duplessis and the old chief Zacharias, they set to work at once.

"Their first job was to put some sense into the Hares. With the help of the Frizels, who knew the tribe well, a number of conferences were held, and there was a lot of straight talk. Father Duplessis said that it was wonderful how Sir E. Leithen managed to strike the note which most impressed the Indian mind.

"This, of course, was only the beginning. The next step was to organise the survivors into gangs, and assign to each a special duty. Food was the most urgent problem, for the Hares had been for a long time on very short commons, and were badly undernourished. As you are aware, the moose have been moving north in recent years. The two Frizels, with a selected band of Hares, made up a hunting party, and, knowing how to find the moose stamping-grounds, were able to send in a steady supply of fresh meat. They also organised a regular business of trapping hares and partridges, at which the Hares are very skilful, but which they had been too dispirited to attempt.

"The tribe had also got short of fuel, so wood-cutting parties were organised. Sir E. Leithen insisted on a big fire being kept going by night and day in the centre of the camp, in order to hearten the people.

"Transport was a serious problem. The dogs of the tribe had been allowed to become very weak from starvation, and many had died, for the fishing in the summer had been poor and the store of dried fish, which they use for dog feed, was nearly exhausted. Sir E. Leithen made them start again their winter fishing through the ice in the lake. Here they had a bit of luck, for it turned out very productive, and it was possible to get the dogs back into condition. This was important, since the dog-teams were in constant demand, to haul in firewood from the wood-cutters and fresh meat from the hunters.

"The Frizels did the field work, and Sir E. Leithen and Mr. Galliard managed the camp. I am informed by Father Duplessis that Leithen obtained almost at once an extraordinary influence over the Hares' minds. 'Far greater than mine,' the Father said, 'though I have been living for years among them.' This was partly due to his great ability and the confidence he inspired, but partly to the fact that he had been a very sick man, and was still regarded by the Hares as a sick man. The Indians have a superstitious respect for anyone whom they believe to be facing death.

"Sick man or not, in a month Sir E. Leithen had worked little short of a miracle. He had restored a degenerating tribe to something like health. He made them want to live instead of being resigned to die.

"And now, sir, I come to the event which kills all satisfaction in this achievement. It seems that the elder Frizel had repeatedly warned Sir E. Leithen that the work which he was undertaking would undo all the good of his sojourn in the high mountains, and would lead to certain death; but that Sir E. Leithen had declared that that work was his duty, and that he must take the risk. Frizel's prophecy proved only too true.

"I understand that his strength slowly declined. The trouble with his lungs revived, and, while he continued to be the directing mind, his power of locomotion gradually lessened. Lew Frizel, who came in frequently from the bush to inquire into his health, and implored him in vain to lessen his efforts, told me that by the end of March he had reached the conclusion that nothing could save him. The shack in which he lived was next door to the presbytery, and Father Duplessis, who has some knowledge of medicine, did his best to supply treatment. According to his account, the malady was such that only a careful life could have completed the cure begun in the mountains, and Sir E. Leithen's exertions by night and day were bound to bring it back in a violent form. The sick man, the Father told me, attended the Easter Mass, and after that was too weak to move. Myocarditis set in, and he died without pain during the night of April 19th.

"As I have already informed you, I arrived with Constable F---- on the evening of the 22nd. The camp was in mourning, and for a little there seemed a danger of the Hares slipping back to their former state of melancholy supineness. From this they were saved by the exhortations of Father Duplessis, and especially by Lew Frizel, who told them they could only show their love for Sir E. Leithen by continuing the course he had mapped out for them. Also, the tribe was now in a better mood, as spring was very near.

"Mr. Galliard was anxious that Sir E. Leithen should be buried at a spot in Quebec Province for which he had a special liking. On April 24th we started by dog-team with the body, the party being myself, Constable F----, Mr. Galliard, and the two Frizels. We had considerable difficulty with the ice in the Big Hare River, for the thaw-out promised to be early. We reached Fort Bannerman on the 25th, and were able, by radio, to engage a plane from Edmonton, Mr. Galliard being willing to pay any price for it.

"I have since heard by radio that the destination at Quebec was safely reached. The two Frizels were dropped at Ottawa, it being their intention, at all costs, to join the Canadian Forces in Europe. . . ."

18

An extract from the journal of Father Jean-Marie Duplessis, O.M.I., translated from the French.

"In this journal, which I have now kept for more than twenty years, I shall attempt to set down what I remember of my friend. I call him my friend, for though our intercourse was measured in time by a few weeks, it had the intimacy of comradeship in a difficult undertaking. Let me say by way of prologue that during our friendship I saw what is not often vouchsafed to mortal eyes, the rebirth of a soul.

"In the fall I had talked with L. at Fort Bannerman. He was clearly a man in bad health, to whom the details of living were a struggle. I was impressed by his gentleness and his power of self- control, but it was a painful impression, for I realised that it meant a continuous effort. I felt that no circumstances could break the iron armour of his fortitude. But my feeling for him had warmth in it as well as respect. We had been soldiers in the same campaign, and he knew my home in France.

"When things became bad early in the New Year I was in doubt whom to turn to. Father Wentzel at Fort Bannerman was old and feeble; and I could not expect the Police to spare me a man. Besides, I wanted something more than physical assistance. I wanted a man of education who could understand and cope with the Hares' malaise. So when one of L.'s guides reached the camp in early February I thought at once of him, and ventured to send him a message.

"It was a shot at a venture, and I was not prepared for his ready response. When he arrived with Monsieur Galliard I was surprised by the look of both. I had learned from Father Wentzel that Galliard was a man sick in the spirit, and I knew that L. was sick in body. Now both seemed to have suffered a transformation. Galliard had a look of robust health, though there was that in his manner which still disquieted me--a lack of confidence, an air of unhappy anticipation, a sense of leaning heavily upon L. As for L., he was very lean and somewhat short of breath, but from my medical experience I judged him to be a convalescent.

"The first day the party spent with me I had light on the situation. L. was all but cured--he might live for years with proper care. But proper care meant life in the open, no heavy duties, and not too much exertion. On this one of the hunters, Louis Frizelle, insisted passionately. Otherwise, he said, and M. Galliard bore him out, that in a little time he would be dead. This L. did not deny, but he was firm in his resolution to take up quarters in the camp and to devote all his powers to saving what was left of the Hare tribe. On this decision plans were made, with the successful result explained in the Police corporal's report, which I here incorporate. . . .

"At first I thought that L.'s conduct was that of a man of high humanitarian principles, who could not witness suffering without an attempt at relief. But presently I found that the motives were subtler, and if possible nobler, and that they involved his friend M. Galliard. L., not being of the Church, made no confession, and he did not readily speak of himself, but in the course of our work together I was able to gather something of his history.

"We talked first, I remember, about the war in Europe. I was deeply apprehensive about the fate of my beloved France, which once again in my lifetime would be bled white by war. L. seemed curiously apathetic about Europe. He had no doubts about the ultimate issue, and he repeated more than once that the world was witnessing again a contest between Death and Life, and that Life would triumph. He saw our trouble with the Hares as part of the same inscrutable purpose of the Almighty, and insisted that we were on one battlefront with the allies beyond the Atlantic. This he said often to M. Frizelle, whom it seemed to comfort.

"I observed that as the days passed he showed an increasing tenderness towards the Hares. At first I think he regarded their succour as a cold, abstract duty. But gradually he began to feel for them a protective and brotherly kindness. I suppose it was the gift of the trained lawyer, but he mastered every detail of their tribal customs and their confused habits of thought with a speed that seemed not less than miraculous. He might have lived most of his life among them. At first, when we sat at the conferences and went in and out of the huts, his lean, pallid face revealed no more than the intellectual interest which might belong to a scientific inquirer. But by degrees a kind of affection showed in his eyes. He smiled oftener, and his smile had an infinite kindliness. From the beginning he dominated them, and the domination became in the end, on their part, almost worship.

"What is the secret, I often ask myself, that gives one human being an almost mystical power over others? In the War I have known a corporal have it, when it was denied to a general of division. I have seen the gift manifest in a parish priest and lacking in an archbishop. It does not require a position of authority, for it makes its own authority. It demands a strong pre-eminence in brain and character, for it is based on understanding, but also, I think, on an effluence of sincere affection.

"I was puzzled at first by the attitude of Monsieur Galliard. He was a Catholic and had resumed--what he had for a time pretermitted-- the observances of the Church. He came regularly to Mass and confession. He was ultimately of my own race, though Les Canadiens differ widely from Les Français de France. He should have been easy for me to comprehend, but I confess that at first I was at a loss. He was like a man under the spell of a constant fear--not panic or terror, but a vague uneasiness. To L. he was like a faithful dog. He seemed to draw strength from his presence, as the mistletoe draws strength from the oak.

"What was notable was his steady advance in confidence till presently his mind was as healthy as his body. His eye cleared, his mouth no longer twitched when he spoke, and he carried his head like a soldier. The change was due partly to his absorption in his work, for to L. he was a right hand. I have rarely seen a man toil so devotedly. But it was largely due to his growing affection for L. When the party arrived from the mountains he was obviously under L.'s influence, but only in the way in which a strong nature masters a less strong. But as the days passed, I could see that his feeling was becoming a warmer thing than admiration. The sight of L.'s increasing weakness made his face often a tragic mask. He fussed as much as the elder Frizelle over L.'s health. He would come to me and implore my interference. 'He is winning,' he would repeat, 'but it will be at the cost of his life, and the price is too high.'

"Bit by bit I began to learn about Galliard, partly from L. and partly from the man himself. He had been brought up in the stiff tradition of Les Canadiens, had revolted against it, and had locked the door on his early life. But it was the old story. His ancestry had its revenge, a revenge bound to be especially harsh, I fancy, in the case of one of his breeding. He had fled from the glittering world in which he had won success and from a devoted wife, to the home of his childhood. And here came a tangle of motives. He had in his blood the pioneer craving to move ever further into the wilds; his family, indeed, had given more than one figure to the story of Arctic exploration. He conceived that he owed a duty to the family tradition which he had forsaken, and that he had to go into the North as an atonement. He also seems to have conceived it as part of the penance which he owed for the neglect of his family religion. He is a man, I think, of sentiment and imagination rather than of a high spirituality.

"But his penance turned out severer than he dreamed. He fell into a malaise which, it is my belief, was at bottom the same as the Hares' affliction, and which seems to be endemic in the North. It may be defined as fear of the North, or perhaps more accurately as fear of life. In the North, man to live, has to fight every hour against hostile forces; if his spirit fails and his effort slackens he perishes. But this dread was something more than a rational fear of a potent enemy. There was superstition in it, a horror of a supernatural and desperate malevolence. This set the Hares mooning in their shacks awaiting death, and it held Galliard, a man of education and high ability, in the same blind, unreasoning bondage. His recovered religion gave him no defence, for he read this fear as part of the price to be paid for his treason.

"Then L. came on the scene. He saved Galliard's life. He appeared when Frizelle, in a crazy fit, deserted him, and he had come from England in the last stage of a dire sickness to restore Galliard to his old world. In L.'s grim fortitude Galliard found something that steadied his nerves. More, he learned from L. the only remedy for his malaise. He must fight the North and not submit to it; once fought and beaten, he could win from it not a curse but a blessing.

"Therefore he eagerly accepted the task of grappling with the Hares' problem. Here was a test case. They were defying the North; they were resisting a madness akin to his own. If they won, the North had no more terrors for him--or life either. He would have conquered his ancestral fear.

"Then something was added to his armour. He had revered L., and soon he came to love him. He thought more of L.'s bodily well- being than of his own nerves. And in forgetting his own troubles he found they had disappeared. After a fortnight in the camp he was like the man in the Scriptures out of whom the devil spirit was cast--wholly sane and at peace, but walking delicately.

19

"But L. was my chief concern. I have said that in him I witnessed the rebirth of a soul, but that is not quite the truth. The soul, a fine soul, was always there. More, though not of the Church, I do not hesitate to say that he was of the Faith. Alids oves habeo quae non sunt ex hoc ovili. But he had been frozen by hard stoicism which sprang partly from his upbringing and partly from temperament. He was a strong man with an austere command of himself, and when he had to face death he divested himself of all that could palliate the suffering, and stood up to it with a stark resolution which was more Roman than Christian. What I witnessed was the thawing of the ice.

"He had always bowed himself before the awful majesty of God. Now his experience was that of the Church in the thirteenth century, when they found in the Blessed Virgin a gentle mediatrix between mortal and divine. Or perhaps I should put it thus: that he discovered that tenderness and compassion which Our Lord came into the world to preach, and, in sympathy with others, he lost all care for himself. His noble, frosty egoism was merged in something nobler. He had meant to die in the cold cathedral of the North, ceasing to live in a world which had no care for life. Now he welcomed the humblest human environment, for he had come to love his kind, indeed, to love everything that God had made. He once said (he told me he was quoting an

English poet) that he 'carried about his heart an awful warmth like a load of immortality.'

"When I first met him at Fort Bannerman he seemed to me the typical Englishman, courteous, aloof, the type I knew well in the War. But now there seemed to be a loosening of bonds. He talked very little, but he smiled often, and he seemed to radiate a gentle, compelling courtesy. But there was steel under the soft glove. He had always the air of command, and the Hares obeyed his lightest word as I am certain they never obeyed any orders before in their tribal history. As his strength declined he could speak only in a whisper, but his whispers had the authority of trumpets. For he succeeded in diffusing the impression of a man who had put all fear behind him and was already in communion with something beyond our mortality.

"He shared his confidences with no one. Monsieur Galliard, who had come to regard him with devotion, would never have dared to pierce his reserve. I tried and failed. With him I had not the authority of the Church, and, though I recognised that he was nearing death, I could not offer the consolations of religion unless he had asked for them. I should have felt it an impiety, for I recognised that in his own way he was making his soul. As the power of the sun waxed he liked to bask in it with his eyes shut, as if in prayer or a daydream. He borrowed my Latin Bible and read much in it, but the book would often lie on his knees while he watched with abstracted eyes the dazzle of light on the snow of the far mountains.

"It is a strange fact to chronicle, but I think his last days were his happiest. His strength was very low, but he had done his work and the Hares were out of the pit. Monsieur Galliard tended him like a mother or a sister, helped him to dress and undress, keeping the hut warm, cooking for him and feeding him. The hunters, the Frizelles and the Hares, came to visit him on every return journey. Old Zacharias would remain for hours near his door in case he might be summoned. But all respected his privacy, for they felt that he had gone into retreat before death. I saw him oftenest, and the miracle was that, as the spring crept back to the valley, there seemed to be a springtime in his spirit.

"He came often to Mass--the last occasion being the High Mass at Easter, which for the Hares was also a thanksgiving for recovery. The attendance was now exemplary. The little church with its gaudy colouring--the work of old Brother Onesime, and much admired by Father Wentzel--was crowded to the door. The Hares have an instinct for ritual, and my acolytes serve the altar well, but they have none for music, and I had found it impossible to train much of a choir. L. would sit in a corner following my Latin with his lips, and he seemed to draw comfort from it. I think the reason was that he was now sharing something with the Hares, and was not a director, but one of the directed. For he had come to love those poor childish folk. Hitherto a lonely man, he had found a clan and a family.

"After that Easter Sunday his body went fast downhill. I do not think he suffered much, except from weakness. His manner became gentler than ever, and his eyes used often to have the pleased look of a good child. He smiled, too, often, as if he saw the humours of life. The huskies--never a very good-tempered pack, though now they were well fed--became his friends, and one or two of the older beasts would accompany him out of doors with a ridiculous air of being a bodyguard. One cold night, I remember, one of them suddenly ensconced itself in an empty box outside the presbytery door. I can still hear L. talking to it. 'I know what you're saying, old fellow. "I'm a poor dog and my master's a poor man. I've never had a box like this to sleep in. Please don't turn me out."' So there it remained--the first time I have seen a husky with ambitions to become a house dog.

"He watched eagerly for the signs of spring. The first was the return of the snow buntings, shimmering grey flocks which had wintered in the south. These he would follow with his eyes as they fluttered over the pine woods or spread themselves like a pied shadow on the snow. Then the mountain we call Baldface suddenly shed most of its winter covering, the noise of avalanches punctuated the night, and the upper ribs were disclosed, black as ink in the daytime, but at evening flaming into the most amazing hues of rose and purple. I knew that he had been an alpinist of note, and in these moments I fancy he was recapturing some of the activities of his youth. But there was no regret in his eyes. He was giving thanks for another vision of the Glory of God.

"The last time he was able to go abroad Monsieur Galliard and I assisted him down to the edge of the lake. There was still a broad selvedge of ice--what the Canadian French call batture--but in the middle the ice was cracking, and there were lanes of water to reflect the pale blue sky. Also the streams were being loosed from their winter stricture. One could hear them talking under their bonds, and in one or two places the force of water had cleared the boulders and made pools and cascades. . . . A wonderful thing happened. A bull moose, very shaggy and lean, came out of the forest and stood in an open shallow at a stream's mouth. It drank its fill and then raised its ugly head, shook it and stared into the sunset. Crystal drops fell from its mouth, and the setting sun transfigured the beast into something magical, a beneficent dragon out of a fairy tale. I shall never forget L.'s delight. It was as if he had his last sight of the beauty of the earth, and found in it a pledge of the beauty of Paradise; though I doubt if there will be anything like a bull-moose in the Heavenly City. . . . Three days later he died in his sleep. There was no burial, for Monsieur Galliard wished the interment to be at his old home in Quebec. The arrival of two of the R.C.M.P. made it possible to convey the body to Fort Bannerman, whence it would be easy to complete the journey by air.

"Such is my story of the end of a true man-at-arms whose memory will always abide with me. He was not of the Church, but beyond doubt he died in grace. In his last hours he found not peace only, but beatitude. Dona aeternam quietem Domine et lux perpetua luceat ei."

20

The chief beauty of the Canadian spring is its air of fragility. The tints are all delicate; the sky is the palest blue, the green is faint and tender, with none of the riot of an English May. The airy distances seem infinite, for the mind compels the eye to build up other lands beyond the thin-pencilled horizons.

A man and a woman were sitting on the greening turf by the well of the Clairefontaine stream. The man wore a tweed suit of a city cut, but he had the colour and build of a countryman. The woman had taken off her hat, and a light wind was ruffling her hair. Beneath them was a flat pad of ground, and on it, commanding the source of both the north and south-flowing rivulets, was a wooden cross which seemed to mark a grave.

The eyes of both were turned northward where the wooded hills, rising sometimes to rocky scarps, shepherded the streams to the Arctic watershed.

Galliard slowly filled a pipe. His face had filled out, and his jaw was firmer. There were now no little lines of indecision about his mouth. Also his eyes were quiet and content.

For a little the two did not speak. Their eyes followed the slender north-flowing stream. It dropped almost at once into a narrow ravine, but it was possible to mark where that ravine joined a wider valley, and where that valley clove its way into the dark tangle of forested mountains.

"What happens away up there?" the woman asked. "I should like to follow the water."

"It becomes a river which breaks into the lowlands and wanders through muskegs and bush until it reaches the salt. Hudson's Bay, you know. Dull, shallow tides at first, and then the true Arctic, ice-bound for most of the year. Away beyond are the barrens, and rivers of no name, and then the Polar Sea, and the country where only the white bear and the musk ox live. And at the end a great solitude. Some day we will go there together."

"You don't fear it any more?"

"No. It has become part of me, as close to me as my skin. I love it. It is myself. You see, I have made my peace with the North, faced up to it, defied it, and so won its blessing. Consider, my dear. The most vital forces of the world are in the North, in the men of the North, but only when they have annexed it. It kills those who run away from it."

"I see," she said after a long pause. "I know what you mean. I think I feel it. . . . But the Sick Heart River! Wasn't that a queer fancy?"

Galliard laughed.

"It was the old habit of human nature to turn to magic. Lew Frizel wanted a short cut out of his perplexities. So did I, and I came under the spell of his madness. First I came here. Then I went to the Ghost River. Then I heard Lew's story. I was looking for magic, you see. We both had sick hearts. But it was no good. The North will always call your bluff."

"And Leithen? He went there, didn't he?"

"Yes, and brought Lew away. Leithen didn't have a sick heart. He was facing the North with clear eyes. He would always have won out."

"But he died!"

"That was victory--absolute victory. . . . But Leithen had a fleuve de rêve also. I suppose we all have. It was this little stream. That's why we brought his body here. It is mine, too--and yours--the place we'll always come back to when we want comforting."

"Which stream?" she asked. "There are two."

"Both. One is the gate of the North and the other's the gate of the world."

She faced round and looked down the green cup of the Clairefontaine. It was a pleasant, pastoral scene, with none of the wildness of the other--the white group of farm buildings in the middle distance and the patches of plough-land, and far beyond a blue shimmer which was the St. Lawrence.

The woman laughed happily.

"That is the way home," she said.

"Yes, it is the way home--to our home, Felicity, which please God will never again be broken. I've a lot of atoning to do. The rest of my life cannot be long enough to make up to you for what you have suffered."

She stroked his hair. "We'll forget all that. We're starting afresh, you know. This is a kind of honeymoon."

She stopped and gazed for a little at the glen, which suddenly overflowed with a burst of sunlight.

"It is also the way to the wars," she said gravely.

"Yes, I'm bound for the wars. I don't know where my battlefront will be. In Europe, perhaps, or maybe in New York or Washington. The North hasn't sent me back to malinger."

"No, of course not. But, anyhow, we're together--we'll always be together."

The two by a common impulse turned their eyes to the wooden cross on the lawn of turf. Galliard rose.

"We must hurry, my dear. The road back is none too good."

She seemed unwilling to go.

"I feel rather sad, don't you? You're leaving your captain behind."

Galliard turned to his wife, and she saw that in his eyes which made her smile.

"I can't feel sad," he said. "When I think of Leithen I feel triumphant. He fought a good fight, but he hasn't finished his course. I remember what Father Duplessis said--he knew that he would die; but he knew also that he would live."

THE END

The Courts of the Morning

By

John Buchan

PROLOGUE BY SIR RICHARD HANNAY

I

This story begins, so far as I am concerned, in the August of 192-, when I had for the second time a lease of the forest of Machray. Mary and Peter John and the household had gone north at the end of July, but I was detained for ten days in London over the business of a Rhodesian land company, of which I had recently become chairman. I was putting up at my club, and one morning I was rung up by Ellery Willis of the American Embassy, who had been wiring about me all over the country. He seemed to be in a hurry to see me, so I asked him to luncheon.

I had known Willis in the War, when he had had a field battery with the American 2nd Corps. After that he had been on the Headquarters Staff at Washington, and was now a military attache at the London Embassy. He seemed to have a good many duties besides the study of military affairs, and when I met him he was always discoursing about world politics and the need of England and America getting close to each other. I agreed with him about that, but used to tell him that the best way was not to talk too much, but to send Englishmen and Americans fishing together. He was an ardent, rather solemn young man, but with a quick sense of humour, and Mary said he was the best dancer in London.

He cut at once into business.

"You are a friend of Mr Blenkiron's--John S. Blenkiron," he said. "I want to know if you have heard from him lately?"

"Not for months," I said. "Blenkiron was never a regular correspondent, and the fount has dried up since last December."

He looked grave. "That's bad," he said.

"There's nothing wrong?" I asked anxiously.

"Only that nobody knows what has become of him."

"But that was always the old ruffian's way. He likes to cover his tracks, like Providence, and turn up suddenly when he is not expected. There's a lot of the child in him."

Willis shook his head. "I expect there's more to it this time than that. I'll tell you what we know. He made a dive back into Wall Street last fall, and did some big things in electrolytic zinc. Then he went to Santa Catalina, and returned to New York in the second week of January. On the 27th day of that month he sailed for Panama in a fruit-steamer, having previously shut up his office and wound up his affairs as if he were thinking of his decease. From that day no one has clapped eyes on him. He has nothing in the way of family life, but I needn't tell you that he has plenty of friends, and they are beginning to get anxious. All that we can find out is that last March a little Jew man turned up in New York with an order from Mr Blenkiron for a quarter of a million dollars. It was all right, and the money was handed over, and the shape it took was a draft on Valparaiso to be paid after countersignature by our consul there. We got in touch with the consul, and heard that the money had been collected on Mr Blenkiron's instructions by some fellow with a Spanish name."

"That sounds queer," I said.

"It certainly does. But there's something queerer still. In June Mr Neston of the Treasury got a letter--he had been a business associate of Mr Blenkiron's at one time and they used to go bass-fishing in Minnesota. It didn't come by mail, but was handed in one evening at Mr Neston's private residence. It bore no name, but there could be no doubt it was from Mr Blenkiron. I have seen a copy of it with Mr Neston's commentary, and I can tell you it was great stuff. The writer warned his old friend that there might be trouble brewing in certain parts of the world which he did not specify, and he begged him, as he was a good American, to keep his eyes skinned. He also said that he, the writer, might have to ask some day soon for help, and that he counted on getting it. The funny thing was that the letter was in a kind of cypher. I understand that Mr Blenkiron used to write to his friends in a high-coloured version of our national slang, and that he had a good many private expressions that were Choctaw to those that did not know him. That letter might have been read as the perfectly natural expression of a light-headed American, who had been having too many cocktails and was writing drivel about his health and his habits and the fine weather. But, knowing how to construe it, it made Mr Neston sit up and take notice...There was another thing.

"I have said that the letter had no name, but it was signed all the same. It seems that in any very important and intimate communication Mr Blenkiron used to make a hieroglyphic of his surname and stick J. S. after it in brackets. That was meant to be a kind of S.O.S. to his friends that the thing was mighty important. Well, this letter had the hieroglyphic in three places, scrawled in as if the writer had been playing absent-mindedly with his pen. Mr Neston's conclusion was that Mr Blenkiron had written it in some place where he was not allowed to communicate freely, and might be in considerable danger."

I admitted that it looked like it, and said that if Blenkiron had been captured by bandits and held up to ransom, I could vouch for it, from what I knew of him, that his captors had done the worst day's work of their lives. I asked what his Government was doing about it.

"Nothing official," said Willis, "for we are in this difficulty. We are afraid of spoiling Mr Blenkiron's game, whatever it may be. Washington has a very high respect for his talents, and we should hate to cross him by being officious. All the same, we are anxious, and that is why I have come to you."

He proceeded to give me one of his lectures on international affairs. America, by his way of it, was in a delicate position, in spite of being rich enough to buy up the globe. She was trying to set her house in order, and it was a large-sized job, owing to the melting-pot not properly melting but leaving chunks of undigested matter. That was the real reason why she could not take a big hand in world-affairs--the League of Nations and so forth; she had too much to do at home, and wanted all her energies for it.

That was the reason, too, why she was so set on prohibition of all kinds--drink, drugs, and aliens. But her hand might be forced, if anything went wrong in the American continent itself, because of her Monroe Doctrine. She didn't want any foreign complications at the moment. They would be very awkward for her, and possibly very dangerous, and she would resolutely keep out of them, unless they occurred, so to speak, opposite her front yard, in which case she would be bound to intervene. Therefore, if anyone wanted to do her the worst kind of turn, he would stir up trouble in some place like South America. Willis believed that Blenkiron had got on the track of something of the kind, and was trying to warn her.

That sounded reasonable enough, but what was not reasonable was Willis's straight request that I should put on my boots and go and look for him. "We can't do anything officially," he repeated. "An American would be suspected where an Englishman would get through. Besides, I believe you are his closest friend."

Of course I at once disabused him of that notion. I knew old Blenkiron too well to be nervous about him; he could no more be badly lost than Ulysses. I saw Willis's point about American politics, but they were no concern of mine. I told him in so many words that my travelling days were over, that I was a landowner and a married man and the father of a son, with all sorts of prior duties. But he was so downcast at my refusal, and so earnest that something should be done, that I promised to put the matter before Sandy Arbuthnot. I proposed in any case to go to Laverlaw for a couple of days on my way to Machray.

II

Laverlaw is a very good imitation of the end of the world. You alight at a wayside station in a Border valley, and drive for eight miles up a tributary glen between high green hills; then, when the stream has grown small and you think that the glen must stop, it suddenly opens into an upland paradise--an amphitheatre of turf and woodland which is the park and in the heart of it an old stone castle. The keep was once a peel-tower, famous in a hundred ballads, and the house which had grown round dated mostly from the sixteen century. I had never been there before, for the old Lord Clanroyden had lived sick and solitary for years, and Sandy had only succeeded in the previous February. When arrived in the early gloaming, with that green cup swimming in amber light and the bell-heather on the high ground smouldering in the sunset, I had to rub my eyes to make sure that the place was not a dream. I thought it the right kind of home for Sandy, a fairy-tale fortress lying secret in the hills from which he could descend to colour the prose of the world.

Sandy met me at the gates and made me get out of the car and walk the rest of the way with him. In his shocking old tweeds, with his lithe figure, his girlish colouring, and his steady, glowing eyes, he fitted well into the fantastic landscape. You could see that he was glad have me there, and he made me welcome with all his old warmth, but in the half-mile walk I felt a subtle change him. His talk didn't bubble over as it used to, and I had feeling that he was rather making conversation. I wonder if being a peer and a landowner and that sort of thing had sobered him, but I promptly dismissed the idea. I wasn't prepared to believe that external circumstances could have any effect on one who had about as much worldliness as fakir with his begging-bowl.

All the same there was a change, and I was conscious it during the evening. Archie Roylance and his young wife were staying there--like me, for the first time. I am prepared to rank Janet Roylance second only to Mary as the prettiest and most delightful thing in the world, and I knew that she and Sandy were close friends. In the daytime she was always, so to speak, booted and spurred, and seemed have the alertness and vigour of an active boy; in the evening she used to become the daintiest lit porcelain lady; and those who saw Janet as a Dresden shepherdess in a drawing-room would scarcely believe that it was the same person who that morning had been scampering over the heather. She was in tremendous spirits, and Archie is a cheerful soul, but they found it heavy going with Sandy.

We dined in what had been the hall of the thirteenth-century keep-stone walls, a fireplace like a cave, and Jacobean rafters and panelling. Sandy wore the green coat of some Border club, and sat like a solemn sprite in the great chair at the head of his table, while Janet tried to keep the talk going from the other end.

The ancient candelabra, which gave a dim religious light, and the long lines of mailed or periwigged Arbuthnots on the wall made the place too heavy a setting for one whom I had always known as a dweller in tents. I felt somehow as if the old Sandy were being shackled and stifled by this feudal magnificence.

The Roylances, having been married in the winter, had postponed their honeymoon, and Janet was full of plans for bringing it off that autumn. She rather fancied the East. Sandy was discouraging. The East, he said, was simply dusty bric-a-brac, for the spirit had gone out of it, and there were no mysteries left, only half-baked Occidentalism. "Go to Samarkand, and you will get the chatter of Bloomsbury intellectuals. I expect in Lhasa they are discussing Freud."

I suggested South Africa, or a trip up through the Lakes to the Nile. Janet vetoed this, because of Archie's stiff leg; she thought big-game hunting would be bad for him, and she considered with justice that if he were in the neighbourhood of wild beasts he would go after them.

Archie himself was inclined to South America. He said he had always had a romance about that part of the world, and he understood that it was the only place which still held some geographical secrets. Also it appeared that, though a poor linguist, he could talk a sort of Spanish, owing to having spent some time in the Madrid Embassy.

"I've never been there," said Sandy, "and I never want to go. It's too big and badly put together, like a child's mud castle. There's cannibal fish, and every kind of noxious insect, and it's the happy home of poisons, and the people of the future will be concerned with the New World. It might be rather useful to me in politics if I went and had a look round."

Sandy laughed. "Better go to the States. That's the power-house where you press the button."

This gave me the chance to talk about Blenkiron, and I told them what I had heard from Ellery Willis. Archie, who had only seen Blenkiron in the last year of the War, was rather excited; Sandy, who knew him intimately, was apathetic.

"He'll turn up all right. Trust John S. You can't mislay a battered warrior like that. You'd better tell Willis that he is doing a very poor service to Blenkiron by starting a hue-and-cry. The old man won't like it a bit."

"But, I assure you, Willis is very much in earnest. He wanted me to start out right away on a secret expedition, and to quiet him I promised to speak to you."

"Well, you've spoken," said Sandy, "and you can tell him I think it moonshine. Blenkiron will come back to his friends when his job is done, whatever it may be...Unless Archie likes to take the thing on?"

He seemed to want to drop the subject, but Janet broke in: "I always understood that Mr Blenkiron had no relations except the nephew who was killed in the War. But I met a girl last month who was a niece or a cousin of his. She told me she had been staying in the Borders and had been taken to see you at Laverlaw."

Sandy looked up, and I could have sworn that a shade of anxiety passed over his face.

"Her name was Dasent," Janet went on. "I can't remember her Christian name."

"Probably Irene--pronounced Ireen," said Sandy. "I remember her. She came over with the Manorwaters. She seemed to have got a little mixed about Scotland, for she wanted to know why I wasn't wearing a kilt, and I told her because I was neither a Highlander nor a Cockney stock-broker." He spoke sharply, as if the visit had left an unpleasant memory.

"I should like to meet a niece of Blenkiron's," I said "Tell me more about her."

In reply Sandy made a few comments on American young women which were not flattering. I could see what had happened--Sandy at a loose end and a little choked by his new life, and a brisk and ignorant lady who wanted to enthuse about it. They had met "head on," as Americans say.

"You didn't like her?" I asked.

"I didn't think enough about her to dislike her. Ask Janet."

"I only saw her for about an hour," said that lady. "She came to stay with Junius and Agatha at Strathlarrig just when I was leaving. I think I rather liked her. She was from South Carolina, and had a nice, soft, slurring voice. So far as I remember she talked very little. She looked delicious, too-tallish and slim and rather dark, with deep eyes that said all sorts of wonderful things. You must be as blind as a bat, Sandy, if you didn't see that."

"I am. I don't boast of it--indeed I'm rather ashamed of it--but I'm horribly unsusceptible. Once--long ago--when I was at Oxford, I was staying in the West Highlands, and in the evening we sat in a room which looked over the sea into the sunset, and a girl sang old songs. I don't remember whether she was pretty or not--I don't remember her name--but I remember that her singing made me want to fall in love...Since I grew up I've had no time."

Janet was shocked. "But, Sandy dear, you must marry."

He shook his head. "Never! I should make a rotten husband. Besides, Dick and Archie have carried off the only two women I love."

After that he seemed to cheer up. I remember that he took to telling stories of poisons--I suppose the mention of South America set him off on that. He showed us a box with three tiny pellets in it, things which looked like discoloured pearls, and which he said were the most mysterious narcotics in the world, and one of the deadliest poisons. They reminded me of pills I once got from an old Portugee prospector, which I carried about with me for years but never touched, pills to be used if you were lost in the bush, for one was said to put you into a forty-hours sleep and two gave a painless death. Sandy would explain nothing further about them, and locked them away.

What with one thing and another we had rather a jolly evening. But next morning, when the Roylances had gone, I had the same impression of some subtle change. This new Sandy was not the one I had known. We went for a long tramp on the hills, with sandwiches in our pockets, for neither of us seemed inclined to shoulder a gun. It was a crisp morning with a slight frost, and before midday it had become one of those blazing August days when there is not a breath of wind and the heather smells as hot as tamarisks.

We climbed the Lammer Law and did about twenty miles of a circuit along the hill-tops. It was excellent training for Machray, and I would have enjoyed myself had it not been for Sandy.

He talked a great deal and it was all in one strain, and--for a marvel--all about himself. The gist of it was that he was as one born out of due season, and mighty discontented with his lot.

"I can't grow old decently," he said. "Here am I--over forty--and I haven't matured one bit since I left Oxford. I don't want to do the things befitting my age and position. I suppose I ought to be ambitious--make speeches in the House of Lords--become an expert on some rotten subject--take the chair at public dinners--row my weight in the silly old boat--and end by governing some distant Dominion."

"Why not?" I asked.

"Because I don't want to. I'd rather eat cold mutton in a cabman's shelter, as Lamancha once observed about political banquets. Good Lord, Dick, I can't begin to tell you how I loathe the little squirrel's cage of the careerists. All that solemn twaddle about trifles! Oh, I daresay it's got to be done by somebody, but not by me. If I touched politics I'd join the Labour Party, not because I think then less futile than the others, but because as yet they haven't got such a larder of loaves and fishes."

"I want a job," he declared a little later. "I was meant by Providence to be in a service, and to do work under discipline--not for what it brought me, but because it has to be done. I'm a bad case of the inferiority complex. When I see one of my shepherds at work, or the hands coming out of a factory, I'm ashamed of myself. The all have their niche, and it is something that matters, whereas I am a cumberer of the ground. If I want to work I've got to make the job for myself, and the one motive is personal vanity. I tell you, I'm in very real danger of losing my self-respect."

It was no good arguing with Sandy in this mood, though there were a great many common-sense things I wanted the say. The danger with anyone so high-strung and imaginative as he is that every now and then come periods of self disgust and despondency.

"You're like Ulysses," I told him. "The fellow in Tennyson's poem, you know. Well, there's a widish world before you, and a pretty unsettled one. Ships sail every day to some part of it."

He shook his head.

"That's the rub. As I've told you, I can't grow up. There's a couple of lines by some poet that describes me accurately: 'He is crazed by the spell of far Arabia, It has stolen his mind away.' Far Arabia--that's my trouble. But the Ulysses business won't do for an ageing child of forty. Besides, what about the mariners? Where are the 'free hearts, free foreheads?' We used to have a rather nice little Round Table, Dick, but it is all broken up now and the wood turned into cigar-boxes for wedding present; Peter is dead, and you and Archie are married, and Leithe and Lamancha are happy parts of the machine."

"There's still Blenkiron."

"He doesn't count. He was a wandering star, that joined us and revolved cheerfully with us for a little, and then shot back to where it belonged...You can't alter it by talking, my dear chap. I'm the old buccaneer marooned on a rock, watching his ancient companions passing in ocean liners."

We had reached the top of the hill above Laverlaw and were looking down into the green cup filled with the afternoon sunlight, in which the house seemed as natural a thing is a stone from the hillside. I observed that it was a very pleasant rock to be marooned on. Sandy stared at the scene, and for a moment did not reply.

"I wish I had been born an Englishman," he said at last. "Then I could have lived for that place, and been quite content to grow old in it. But that has never been our way. Our homes were only a jumping-off ground. We loved them gainfully and were always home-sick for them, but we were very little in them. That is the blight on us--we never had my sense of a continuing city, and our families survived only by accident. It's a miracle that I'm the sixteenth Clanroyden...It's not likely that there will be a seventeenth."

III

Left Laverlaw rather anxious about Sandy, and during our time at Machray I thought a good deal about my friend. He was in an odd, jumpy, unpredictable state of mind, and didn't see what was to be the outcome of it. At Machray I had a piece of news which showed his restlessness. Martendale, the newspaper man, came to stay, and was talking about boats, for his chief hobby is yacht-racing.

"What's Arbuthnot up to now?" he asked. "I saw him it Cowes--at least I'm pretty sure it was he. In an odd get-up, even for him."

I said that I had been staying with Sandy in August and that he had never mentioned Cowes, so I thought he must be mistaken. But Martendale was positive. He had been on the Squadron lawn, looking down on the crowd passing below, and he had seen Sandy, and caught his eye. He knew him slightly, but apparently Sandy had not wanted to be recognised and had simply stared at him. Martendale noticed him later, lunching out of a paper bag with the other trippers on the front. He was dressed like a yacht's hand, rather a shabby yacht's hand, and Martendale said that he thought he had a glimpse of him later with some of the crew of the big Argentine steam yacht, the Santa Barbara, which had been at Cowes that year. "The dago does not make an ornamental sailor," said Martendale, "and if it was Arbuthnot, and I am pretty certain it was, he managed to assimilate himself very well to his background. I only picked him out of the bunch by his clean-cut face. Do you happen to know if he speaks Spanish? They were all jabbering that lingo."

"Probably," I said. "He's one of the best linguists alive. But, all the same, I think you were mistaken. I saw him a fortnight later, and, I can tell you, he isn't in the humour for escapades."

In November, when I ran up to London from Fosse for a few days, I got further news of Sandy which really disquieted me. It appeared that he had gone down to the grass countries to hunt--a fact which in itself surprised me, for, though a fine horseman, he had always professed to hate hunting society. But for some reason or other he kept a couple of horses at Birkham and spent a lot of time there. And he seemed to have got mixed up with a rather raffish lot, for since the War the company in the Shires has not been what you might call select. The story told to me was that at a dinner where much champagne was swallowed Sandy had had a drunken row with a young profiteering lout, which had just about come to blows. He seemed to have behaved rather badly at dinner and worse later, for after having made a scene he had bolted, shown the white feather, and refused to take responsibility for what he had done.

Of course I didn't believe a word of it. In the first place, Sandy was as abstemious as a Moslem; in the second place, he had the temper of a seraph and never quarrelled; and, in the third place, he didn't keep any white feathers in his collection. But the story was repeated everywhere and, I am sorry to say, was believed. You see, Sandy had a great reputation in a vague way, but he hadn't the kind of large devoted acquaintance which could be always trusted to give the lie to a slander. And I am bound to say that this story was abominably circumstantial. I had it from an eye-witness, quite a decent fellow whose word it was hard to disbelieve. He described a horrid scene--Sandy, rather drunk and deliberately insulting an ill-tempered oaf in the same condition, and then, when it almost came to fisticuffs, funking the consequences, and slipping off early next morning without a word of explanation.

I hotly denied the whole thing, but my denials did not carry very far. Sandy had disappeared again, and his absence gave gossip its chance. The ordinary story was that he had taken to drink or drugs--most people said drugs.

Even those who believed in him began to talk of a bad break-down, and explained that the kind of life he had led was bound some day to exact its penalty. I tried to get hold of him, but my telegrams to Laverlaw brought the answer that his lordship had gone abroad and left no address for letters.

Three days after Christmas I got the shock of my life. I opened The Times and found on the foreign page a short telegram from New York which reported the death of Mr John Scantlebury Blenkiron on board his yacht at Honolulu. The message said that he had once been well known as a mining engineer, and that at various times he had made coups in Wall Street.

I took the first train to London and interviewed Ellery Willis at the Embassy. He confirmed the news, for he had had a wire from Washington to the same effect.

"What did he die of?" I demanded. "And what was he doing at Honolulu? And in a yacht? He loathed the sea. He used to say that he would as soon take to yachting for pleasure as make his meals off emetics."

"He must have been ill some time," Willis suggested. "That would account for his disappearance. He wanted to be by himself, like a sick animal."

I simply wouldn't credit it, and I asked Willis to wire for details. But none came--only a recapitulation of the bare fact. When a week later I got the American papers my scepticism was a little shaken. For there were obituaries with photographs. The writers enlarged on his business career, but said nothing about his incursions into politics, nor did they give any further news of his illness. I was almost convinced, but not quite. The obituaries were full but not full enough, for Blenkiron had been a big figure and one would have expected the press to go large on his career and personality. But the notices all gave me the impression of having been written to order and deliberately keeping wide of the subject.

There was nothing in the way of personal reminiscences, no attempt to describe his character or assess his work. The articles were uncommonly like the colourless recitals you find in a biographic dictionary.

I wired about it to Sandy, and got a reply from his butler that he was still abroad, address unknown. I wished that I knew where to find the niece who had visited Laverlaw in the summer, but Janet Roylance, to whom I applied, could tell me nothing. She and Archie were setting off almost at once on their delayed honeymoon, and had chose South America.

I have one other incident to record before I bring the preliminaries to a close. Palliser-Yeates came to stay with us for a week-end in January, and one night, after Mary had gone to bed, we sat talking in the library. He had never known Blenkiron, but he was a friend of Sandy, and to him I unburdened my anxieties. I thought he listened to me with an odd look on his face.

"You don't believe the stories?" he asked.

"Not one blessed word," I said. "But the poor old chap has managed to get himself a pretty fly-blown reputation."

"Perhaps he wanted to," was the astounding answer.

I stared, and asked him what he meant.

"It's only a guess," he said. "But Sandy has for a long time had a unique reputation. Not with the world at large, but with the people who matter in two hemispheres. He was known to be one of the most formidable men in the world. Now, suppose that he was engaged, or about to be engaged, in some very delicate and dangerous business. He would be marked down from the start by certain, people who feared him. So he might wish to be counted out, to be regarded as no longer formidable, and what better way than of have it generally believed that his nerve had gone and that he was all to pieces? If I wanted to create that impression, I would lay the foundation of it in the Shires, where they make a speciality of scandal. If that was his purpose, he has certainly succeeded. By this time the rumour has gone all over Europe in the circles where his name was known."

I was digesting this startling hypothesis, when Palliser-Yeates told me the following story:

He had been in Paris just before Christmas on some business connected with Argentine banking, and one of his South American colleagues had taken him to dine at a restaurant much in vogue among the rastas. I think it was on the Rive Gauche, not a specially reputable place, but with amazingly good food. The proprietor was from the Argentine, and all the staff were South Americans. Palliser-Yeates noticed one of the waiters, not at his own table but a little way off, and he recognised the man's face. The hair and skin were darkened, but he was positive that it was Sandy--Sandy in a greasy dress suit and a made-up black tie. When the room filled up and got rather noisy, he made an errand to speak to the conductor of the orchestra, and managed to get a word with this waiter. He cannoned against him in one of the doors and said, "Sorry, Sandy."

The waiter knew him perfectly, and whispered from behind his pile of dishes, "Don't give me away, John. It's damnably serious. And never come here again." So Palliser-Yeates took himself off, and had scrupulously held his tongue except for telling me. He said that Sandy looked well enough, and seemed to have mastered his job, for you couldn't detect any difference between him and the rest of the outfit.

When I heard this, I decided to go to Paris myself and have a look at the restaurant, for anxiety about Sandy was coming between me and my sleep. There was something about Palliser-Yeates's story which took my memory back a dozen years to old Kuprasso's dancing-house in Constantinople and the man who had led the Company of the Rosy Hours. Sandy was on the war-path again, and I was bound to keep an eye on him.

But two days later I had a letter--from Blenkiron. It had a typed address and a Southampton postmark--which was no clue, for it had probably been brought over by passenger in a ship and posted at the port of arrival. The handwriting was Blenkiron's unmistakable scrawl. It ran as follows:

"The papers will say I have gotten across the River. Don't let that worry you. But the Golden Shore at present is important and I may have to stay there quite a time. Therefore keep up the requiems and dirges until further notice."

Also at last I got a reply from Sandy, in answer to my string of letters. It was a telegram from London, so he had left Paris, and it merely contained Abraham Lincoln's words: "You stop still and saw wood."

After that I stopped still. Both Blenkiron and Sand were up to some devilry, and I had an instinct that the were working together. I have set down here my slender personal knowledge of the beginning of the strange event now to be related. The rest comes from the actors themselves.

BOOK I - THE GRAN SECO

I

The open windows, protected by wire blinds as fine-meshed as gauze, allowed the cool airs from the sea to slip in from the dusk. The big restaurant was in a pleasant gloom broken by patches of candlelight from the few occupied tables. The Hotel de la Constitucion stands on a little promontory above the harbour of Olifa, so the noise of the streets comes to it only like the echo of waves from a breakwater. Archie Roylance, looking into the great square of velvet sky now beginning to be patterned by stars, felt as if he were still at sea.

The Vice-Consul interpreted his thoughts.

"You are surprised at the quiet," he said. "That is only because we dine early. In a little there will be many lights and a jigging band and young people dancing. Yet we have good taste in Olifa and are not garish. If you will be my guest on another occasion, I will take you to a club as well quipped as any in Pall Mall, or to a theatre where you will see better acting than in London, and I will give you a supper afterwards which Voisin's could not better. We have civilisation, you see--for what it is worth."

The Vice-Consul, whose name was Alejandro Gedd, was a small man with a neat, dark, clean-shaven face, and high cheek-bones from which his critics deduced Indian blood.

As a matter of fact they came from another ancestry. His grandfather, Alexander Geddes, had come out in his youth from Dundee as a clerk in a merchant's house, had prospered, married a pretty Olifera, begotten a son, and founded a bank which rose in the silver boom to fortune. That son had married a lady of pure Castilian descent, whose beauty was not equal to her lineage, so the grandson of old Geddes had missed both the vigour of the Scot and the suave comeliness of the Olifera. Don Alejandro was an insignificant little man, and he was growing fat. The father had sold his interest in the bank at a high figure, and had thereafter dabbled in politics and horse-breeding; the son, at his death, had promptly got rid of the stud and left the government of his country to get on without him. He had been sent to an English school, and later to the Sorbonne, and had emerged from his education a dilettante and a cosmopolitan. He professed a stout Olifa patriotism, but his private sentiment was for England, and in confidential moments he would speak of his life as exile. Already he had asked Archie a dozen questions about common friends, and had dwelt like an epicure on the recollections of his last visit--the Park on a May morning, an English garden in midsummer, the Solent in August, the October colouring of Scottish hills.

His dinner-jacket had been made in the vicinity of Hanover Square, and he hoped that his black stock and his black-ribboned eyeglass were, if not English, at any rate European.

Archie was looking at the windows. "Out there is the Pacific," he said, "nothing nearer you than China. What is it like the other way?"

"The coastal plain for a hundred miles. Then the foothills and the valleys where the wine is made. A very pretty light claret, I assure you. Then, for many hundreds of miles, the great mountains."

"Have you travelled there much?"

Don Alejandro shook his head. "I do not travel in this land. What is there to see? In the mountains there are nothing but Indians and wild animals and bleak forests and snow. I am content with this city, where, as I have said, there is civilisation."

"A man I met on the boat told me about a place called the Gran Seco. He said it was bound to be soon the greatest copper area in the world."

Don Alejandro laughed. "That ill-favoured spot becomes famous. Five years ago it was scarcely known. To-day many strangers ask me about it. The name is Indian-Spanish. You must understand that a hundred miles north of this city the coastal plain ends, and the Cordilleras swing round so that there is no room between them and the ocean.

"But at the curve the mountains, though high, are not the great peaks. These are far to the east, and you have for a big space a kind of tableland. That is what we call the Gran Seco--the Great Thirst--for it is mostly waterless and desert. But it is very rich in minerals. For long we have known that, and before the War there were many companies at work there. Now there is one great company, in which our Government has a share, and from which Olifa derives much of its wealth. The capital employed is mostly foreign--no, not American--European, but of what country I do not know. The labourers are the people of the hills, and the managers are Europeans of many nationalities. They pass through this city going and coming--through this hotel often--perhaps we may see some of them to-night. They are strange folk who do not mix freely with us of Olifa. I am told they are growing as wealthy as Rockefeller. There are no English among them, I think--Slavs mostly, with some Italians and now and Then a German, so I do not come across them in the way of business, and it would appear that they have no time for pleasure...May I ask, Sir Archibald, for what purpose especially you honour us with a visit? I want to know how best I can serve you."

Archie wrinkled his brow. "You are very kind, Don Alejandro. The fact is we're here mainly for the fun of it. This is a sort of belated honeymoon trip. Also, I'd like to know something about the politics of Olifa and South America generally. You see, I'm a Member of Parliament, and I've an idea that this part of the globe may soon become rather important. I have brought several introductions."

Don Alejandro waved his hand deprecatingly.

"That will be readily arranged. Your Minister is on leave, and the Embassy has left you in my hands. Without doubt you will be received by our President. I myself will take you to our Minister for External Affairs, who is my second cousin. Our Minister of Finance will expound to you our extravagant prosperity. But of politics in the old sense you will find little. We are too rich and too busy. When we were poor we talked government all the day. And we had revolutions--dictatorships tempered by revolutions. My father more than once saved his neck by the good blood of his racing stable. But now we are very tame and virtuous. Our Government is rich enough to be enlightened, and our people, being also rich, do not trouble their heads about theories. Even the peons on the estancias and the vaqueros in the hills are content. Olifa is--how do you say?--a plutocratic democracy--a liberal plutocracy. Once it was a battered little packet-boat, now it is a great liner careless of weather and tides. It has no problems, the fortunate country."

"Jolly place for a holiday," said Archie. "Well, we mean to have a good look round. What do you advise?"

Don Alejandro became lyrical. "You can go south for eight hundred miles in an ever-widening plain. There you will see such orange groves as the world cannot match, and nearer the mountains the savannahs which are the riche pasture on earth. I will write to my cousin at Veiro, and he will entertain you at the stud farm which was once my father's. It will not be like an English Sunday afternoon in the country, where a fat stud groom with a bunch of carrots takes the guests round the stables. It is a wild place between the knees of the hills, but there is some pretty horseflesh there."

"Can I get up into the mountains?" Archie put in, but Don Alejandro was not to be interrupted.

"You must visit our great cities, for Olifa, though the capital, is not the largest. Cardanio has now four to five hundred thousand souls. That is the port from which of fruits and hides and frozen beef are shipped. And there is Alcorta in the hinterland, which is our little Birmingham. But madame will weary of these commercial glories. She will be happier, I think, among the horses at Veiro, or some pretty hacienda..."

Janet Roylance had paid little heed to the conversation, being engaged in studying the slowly increasing number diners.

"I would like to go into the mountains," she said. "I saw them from far out at sea, and they looked like the battle-tents of Paradise."

"A very savage Paradise you would find it, Lady Roylance. None of your green Swiss valleys with snow-peaks arising from meadows. It is all dusty and bare and cruel. Take my advice and be content with our sunny estancias--"

"Look at these chaps, Janet," said Archie suddenly. "There's a queer class of lad for you!"

Don Alejandro fixed his eyeglass and regarded four men who had taken their seats at a table a little-way off. It was a curious quartet. There was a tall man with hair so pale that at first sight he looked like an albino; he had a stony face and skin like old parchment, but from his bearing it was clear that he was still young. Two were small and dark and Jewish, and the fourth was a short burly fellow, with the prognathous jaw of a negro but the luminous eyes of a Latin. All were dressed in well-cut evening clothes, and each wore in his buttonhole a yellow flower--to Archie it looked like a carnation. The notable things about them were their extreme pallor and their quiet. They sat almost motionless, speaking very little and showing that they were alive by only the tiniest gestures. A waiter brought them caviare, and poured champagne into their glasses, and as they moved their arms to eat and drink they had an odd suggestion of automata.

Don Alejandro dropped his eyeglass. "From the Gran Seco," he said. "That is the type Gran Seco. European, I think--the tall man might be a Swede--going from or returning to their place of work. No. I do not know any one of them. Olifa is full of these birds of passage, who linger only for a day. They do not mix with our society. They are civil and inoffensive, but they keep to themselves. Observe the chic of their clothes, and the yellow button-holes. That is the fashion of the copper magnates."

"They look to me like pretty sick men," said Archie.

"That, too, is their fashion. Those who go to that uncouth place speedily lose their complexions. It may be the copper fumes or some fever of the hills."

"I should rather like to go there," said Archie.

Don Alejandro laughed.

"Ah, you are intrigued. That is like an Englishman. He must be for ever hunting romance. No doubt a visit to the Gran Seco can be accomplished, but it must first be arranged. The railway beyond Santa Ana is not for the public. It is owned by the company, and their permission is necessary to travel on it. Also there must be a permit from the Gobernador of the province, who is also the Company's president, for the workers in the mines are a brutal race and the rule of the Gran Seco must be like the rule of the a country in war-time...If you wish, I will put the matter in train. But I do not think it is quite the place for a lady. Such cheeks as madame's are not for the withering airs of the hills."

"I will follow the Olifero custom," said Janet. "Your ladies, Don Alejandro, are very fond of pearl powder."

The restaurant was filling up. It appeared that many Oliferos were dining, for large lustrous women's eyes looked out of dead-white faces. At the far end of the room, close to the band, a noisy party took their seats at a table. They were all young, and, since they had not troubled to change, their clothes made a startling blotch of colour among the sober black and white of the other guests. All looked as if they had just left a golf-course, the men in knickerbockers of white flannel and both sexes in outrageous jumpers.

"Behold our protectors!" said Don Alejandro with a touch of acid in his tone. "Behold the flower of Yanqui youth! No. I do not know them--for that you must ask my colleague, Senor Wilbur. But I know where they come from. They are from the big Yanqui yacht now in the harbour. It is called the Corinna."

"Good lord! That was Mike Burminster's boat. I didn't know he had sold it." Archie regarded the party with disfavour.

"I do not know who is the present owner, except that he is a Yanqui. The guests I should judge from their appearance to have sprung from Hollywood."

"They were lunching here to-day," said Janet. "I saw them when Archie was inquiring about his lost kit-bag...There was a girl among them that I thought I must have seen before...I don't see her here to-night...I rather like the look of them, Don Alejandro. They are fresh, and jolly, and young."

"Believe me, they will not repay further acquaintance, Lady Roylance." Don Alejandro was unconsciously imitating his Castilian mother. "They come here in opulent yachts and behave as if Olifa were one of their vulgar joy-cities. That is what they call 'having a good time.' Yanqui youth, as I have observed it, is chronically alcoholic and amorous, and its manners are a brilliant copy of the parrot-house."

The three had their coffee in the spacious arcade which adjoined the restaurant. It was Don Alejandro's turn to ask questions, and he became for a little the English exile, seeking eagerly for news--who had married whom, what was thought in London of this and that--till Olifa dropped from him like a mantle and he felt himself once more a European. Presently their retreat was invaded by other diners, the band moved thither from the restaurant, and dancing began in a cleared space. The young Americans had not lingered over their meal, and had soon annexed the dancing-floor. Fragments of shrill badinage and endearments were heard in the pauses of the music.

Don Alejandro advised against liqueurs, and commended what he called the Olifa Tokay, which proved to be a light sweet wine of the colour of sloe-gin.

Holding his glass to the corona of light in the centre of the patio, he passed from reminiscence to philosophy.

"You are unfortunate pilgrims," he said. "You come seeking romance and I can only offer the prosaic. No doubt, Sir Archibald, you have been led to believe that we Latin Americans are all desperadoes, and our countries a volcanic territory sputtering with little fires of revolution. You find instead the typical bourgeois republic, as bourgeois as the United States. We do not worry about liberty, for we have learned that wealth is a better and less troublesome thing. In the old days we were always quarrelling with our neighbours, and because we conscripted our youth for our armies there was discontent and presently revolution. Now we are secure, and do not give occasion for discontent."

"Someone told me that you had a pretty effective army."

"We have a very effective police. As for our army, it is good, no doubt, but it is small. For what should we use our army? We have no ambition of conquest, and no enemy against whom we need defence."

"Still, you can't count on perpetual peace, you know. You are rich, and wealth means rivals."

"Have we not the League of Nations?" Don Alejandro cried merrily. "Is not Olifa even now a member of the Council? And is there not the Monroe

Doctrine, invented by the great-grandfathers of those depraved children who are dancing yonder?"

"Oh, well, if you like to put it that way--"

"I do not like to put it that way. I do not believe in the League of Nations, and I do not love the United States and I regard the Monroe Doctrine as an insult to my race. But what would you have, my dear Sir Archibald? W have chosen prosperity, and the price we pay for it is our pride. Olifa is a well-nourished body without a soul. Life and property are as safe here as in England, and what more can the heart of man desire? We have a stable Government because our people have lost interest in being governed. Therefore I say, do not propose to study our politics, for there is nothing to study. To you in England with a bankrupt Europe at your door and the poison of Communism trickling into your poverty, politics are life and death. To us, in our sheltered Hesperides, they are only a bad dream of the past. There is no mystery left in Olifa..."

As Don Alejandro spoke, the four men from the Gran Seco were moving through the arcade. They held then selves stiffly, but walked as lightly as cats, deftly steering their way among the tables and at the same time keeping close together. They looked neither to right nor left, but as they passed, Janet and Archie had a good view of their waxen faces. The eyes of all--the pale eyes of the tall man, the beady eyes of the Jews, and the fine eyes of the Latin--had the same look of unnatural composure, as if the exterior world did not exist for them and they were all the time looking inward in a profound absorption. They had something of the eerie detachment of sleepwalkers.

Don Alejandro was talking again.

"Be content, my friends, with what we can offer--our beauty and our civilisation. Think of us as a little enclave of colour between the glooms of the great sea and the clouds of the great mountains. Here man has made a paradise for himself, where during his short day of life he can live happily without questioning."

Archie had been looking at Janet.

"I think we both want to go to the Gran Seco," he said.

II

Archie left Janet writing letters and started oat next morning to explore the city. The first taste of a foreign town was always to him an intoxication, and, in the hot aromatic sunshine of that month which for Olifa is the sweet of the year, the place seemed a riot of coloured and exultant life. He descended the broad terraced road which by easy gradients led from the hotel to the twisted streets of the old city. Some of the calles were only narrow ravines of shade, where between high windowless walls country mule-carts struggled towards the market-place. Others were unhappily provided with screeching electric tramways, so that the passer-by on foot or on a horse had to mount high on the ill-paved side-walk to avoid destruction. Presently he came into a hot market-place, where around an old Spanish fountain were massed stalls laden with glowing flowers and fruit, and strange unwholesome fishes, and coarse pottery, and garish fabrics, and country-woven straw hats. Through his medley Archie limped happily, testing his Spanish on he vendors, or trying with most inadequate knowledge to disentangle the racial mixture. The town Oliferos were a small race, in which he thought there must be considerable negro blood, but the countryfolk were well-made and up-standing, often with a classic and melancholy dignity in their faces. There were lean, wild-looking people, too, whose speech was not any kind of Spanish, with an odd angle to their foreheads and the shyness of an animal in their small anxious eyes, who squatted in their dark ponchos beside their mules and spoke only to each other. An Indian breed, thought Archie--perhaps from the foothills.

A maze of calles took him to the main Plaza, where a great baroque cathedral raised its sculptured front above a medley of beggars and vendors of holy medals. The square was shamefully paved, the facades of the old Spanish houses were often in disrepair, but the crumbling plaster and the blotched paint blended into something beautiful and haunting. Here it was very quiet, as if the city hushed itself in the environs of the house of God. To Archie it seemed that he was looking upon that ancient Olifa, before the hustling modern world was born, Olifa as it had appeared to the eyes of Captain Cook's sailors when they landed, a city which kept the manners and faith of sixteenth-century Spain.

He entered the church, and found a vast, cavernous darkness like the inside of a mountain, candles twinkling like distant glow-worms, echoes of muttered prayers and the heavy sweetness of incense. After it the Plaza seemed as bright as a mountain-top.

Another labyrinth brought him into a different world. The great Avenida de la Paz is a creation of the last twenty years, and runs straight as a ruler from the villas of the most fashionable suburb to the old harbour of the city. In its making it has swallowed up much ancient derelict architecture, and many nests of squalid huts, but, since it was built with a clear purpose by a good architect, it is in itself a splendid thing, in which Olifa takes a fitting pride. Where Archie struck it, it was still residential, the home of the rank and fashion of the city, with the white mass of the Government buildings and the copper dome of the Parliament House rising beyond it. But as he walked westward it gradually changed. Soon it was all huge blocks of flats and shops, with here and there the arrogant palace of a bank or shipping company.

One of these caught Archie's attention. It was an immense square edifice built of the local marble, with a flight of steps running up to doors like those of the Baptistry in Florence. Two sentries with fixed bayonets were on guard, and at first he thought it a Government office. Then his eye caught a modest inscription above the entrance--Administracion de Gran Seco. The name had stuck in his memory from last night's talk--linked with the sight of the four copper magnates and Don Alejandro's aloofness.

The Gran Seco was a strange and comfortless place, and it was perched far up in the mountains. This gorgeous building was at variance with the atmosphere with which the name was invested for him, and he stared with lively curiosity at its magnificence.

Suddenly the great doors opened and a man came out, escorted by two bowing porters. The sentries saluted, a big limousine drew up, and he was borne away. Archie had a glimpse of a tall figure in dark grey clothes, and, what seemed out of keeping with the weather, a bowler hat.

The face was middle-aged and bearded--a trim black beard like a naval officer's. As he passed, the man had glanced at him, and, even in that short second of time, there was something in those eyes which startled him. They seemed so furiously alive. There was nothing inquisitive in them, but they were searching, all-embracing. Archie felt that this was one who missed nothing and forgot nothing; he had had an impression of supreme competence which was as vivid as an electric shock. No wonder the Gran Seco was a success, he thought, if it had men of that quality in its management.

The broad pavements, the double line of trams, the shop-windows as soberly rich as those of the Rue de la Paix, the high white buildings narrowing in the distance to enfold a blue gleam of the sea, made an impressive picture of wealth and enlightenment. There was a curious absence of colour, for the people he passed seemed all to be wearing dark clothes; they were a quiet people, too, who spoke without the southern vehemence. Emancipation had come to the ladies of Olifa, for there were many abroad, walking delicately on the pavement, or showing their powdered prettiness in motor-cars. Here was none of the riotous life of the old quarter, and Archie had an impression of the city as elaborately civilised and of its richer inhabitants as decorous to the point of inanity. There were no peasants to be seen nor a single beggar; the Avenida de la Paz seemed to be kept as a promenade for big business and cultivated leisure. Archie grinned when he remembered the picture he had formed of Olifa, as a decadent blend of ancient Spain and second-rate modern Europe, with a vast wild hinterland pressing in upon its streets. The reality was as polished and secure as Paris--a reticent Paris, with a dash of Wall Street.

One splash of colour caught his eye. It came from a big touring car, which had drawn up at the pavement's edge and had disgorged its occupants. The driver was a young man strangely clad in starched linen knickerbockers, a golf jumper designed in a willow-plate pattern of blue and white, pale blue stockings, and a wide-brimmed straw hat. He sat negligently at the wheel, and as Archie stared at him he tilted his hat over his brow. Presently there emerged from the shop two girls and a second youth--the youth in snow white flannels with a scarlet sash, and the girls in clothe the like of which Archie had never seen, but which in his own mind he classed as the kind of thing for a tropical garden party. He noticed, since the extreme shortness of their skirts made their legs their most notable feature, that they had black patent-leather shoes with silver buckles, and wonderful shot-silver stockings.

"You all right, honey?" one of them addressed the driver.

"Fine. Got the candy you want?"

Then an argument arose between the two girls and the other youth, an argument conducted in a dialect unintelligible to Archie, and in voices which forcibly reminded him of the converse of a basket of kittens. The four in that discreet monochrome place were indecently conspicuous, but they were without modesty, and among the stares and whispers of the crowded pavement conducted their private dispute with the freedom of children. The driver at last grew bored.

"Aw, come on, Baby," he cried. "Get off the side-walk and come aboard. We got to hustle."

They obeyed him, and the car presently slid into the traffic, the driver's hat still tilted over his brows. Archie believed that he recognised one of the young women as a member of the party from the American yacht who had been dining in the hotel restaurant the night before. He rather resented their presence in Olifa. These half-witted children of pleasure were out of the picture which he had made for himself; they even conflicted with Olifa's conception of herself. "The United States," he told himself, "won't be too popular in Latin America if it unlooses on the much goods of that type."

At last the Avenida passed from shops and offices into a broad belt of garden, flanked on one side by the Customs house and on the other by the building which housed the port authorities. Beyond them lay the green waters of the old harbour, and the very spot where the first Conquistadors had landed. The new harbour, where the copper from the Gran Seco was shipped, lay farther south, close of the railway-stations; the old one was now almost unused except for fishing-boats, and as a landing-place for the yachts which berthed in the outer basin behind the great breakwater. To the north was a little plaza, which was all that remained of the first port of Olifa. It was a picturesque half-moon of crumbling stone, and seemed to be mainly composed of cafes and cinema houses.

Archie sniffed the salt breeze from the west, and limped cheerfully along the water-front, for he loved to be near he sea. In the outer basin he saw the funnels and top-gear of the yacht Corinna, on which he had aforetime enjoyed he Duke of Burminster's hospitality. It annoyed him that his friend should have sold or chartered it to the kind of people he had seen in the motor-car.

A launch from the yacht was even then approaching the landing-stage. Archie could read the name on a sailor's jersey. Two men were landed, one who looked like a steward, and the other a thick-set fellow in an engineer's overalls. They separated at once, and the second of the two walked in Archie's direction. Archie had a bad memory for faces, but there was something in this figure which woke recollection. As they came abreast and their eyes met, both came half unconsciously to a halt. The man seemed to stiffen and his right hand to rise in a salute which he promptly checked. He had a rugged face which might have been hewn out of mahogany, and honest, sullen, blue eyes.

"Hullo," said Archie, "I've seen you before. Now, where on earth...?"

The man gave him no assistance, but stood regarding him in a sulky embarrassment. He sniffed, and in lieu of a handkerchief drew his hand across his nose, and the movement stirred some chord in Archie's memory.

"I've got it. You were with General Hannay. I remember you in that black time before Amiens. Hamilton's your name, isn't it? Corporal Hamilton?"

Like an automaton the figure stiffened. "Sirr, that's my name." Then it relaxed. It was as if Archie's words had recalled it for a moment to a military discipline which it hastened to repudiate.

"Do you remember me?"

"Ay. Ye're Captain Sir Erchibald Roylance." There was no 'sirr' this time.

"Well, this is a queer place to foregather. I think the occasion demands a drink. Let's try one of these cafes."

The man seemed unwilling. "I'm a wee bit pressed for time."

"Nonsense, Hamilton, you can spare five minutes. I want to hear how you've been getting on and what landed you here. Hang it, you and I and the General went through some pretty stiff times together. We can't part on this foreign strand with a how-d'ye-do."

Archie led the way to a cafe in the crescent of old houses which looked a little cleaner than the rest. "What'll you have, Hamilton?" he asked when they had found a table. "You probably don't fancy the native wine. Bottled beer? Or rum? Or can you face aguardiente, which is the local whisky?"

"I'm a teetotaller. I'll hae a glass o' syrup."

"Well, I'm dashed...Certainly--I never drink myself in the morning. Now, about yourself? You're a Glasgow man, aren't you? Pretty warm place, Glasgow. Are you and the other soldier-lads keeping the Bolshies in order?"

Hamilton's mahogany face moved convulsively, and his blue eyes wandered embarrassedly to the door.

"My opinions has underwent a change. I'm thinkin' of anither kind of war nowadays. I'm for the prolytawriat."

"The devil you are!" Archie gasped. "So am I, but my opinions are still the same. What exactly do you mean?"

The man's embarrassment increased. "I'm for the proly--prolytawriat. Us worrkers maun stick thegither and brek our chains. I've been fechtin' for the rights o' man."

"Fighting with what?"

"Wi' the pollis. That's the reason I'm out here. I made Govan a wee thing ower het for me."

Archie regarded him with a mystified face, which slowly broke into a smile. "I'm sorry to say that you're a liar, Hamilton."

"I'm tellin' ye God's truth," was the reply without heat.

Embarrassment had gone, and the man seemed to be speaking a part which he had already rehearsed.

"No. You're lying. Very likely you had trouble with the police, but I bet it wasn't over politics. More likely a public-house scrap, or a girl. Why on earth you should want to make yourself out a Bolshie...?"

"My opinions has underwent a change," the man chanted.

"Oh, drat your opinions! You got into some kind of row and cleared out. That's intelligible enough, though

I'm sorry to hear it. What's your present job? Are you in the Corinna?"

"Ay, I cam out in her. I'm in the engine-room."

"But you know nothing about ships?"

"I ken something aboot ship's engines. Afore the war I wrocht at Clydebank...And now, if ye'll excuse me I maun be off, for I've a heap o' jobs ashore. Thank ye for your kindness."

"I call this a perfectly rotten affair," said Archie. "You won't stay, you won't drink, and you keep on talking like a parrot about the proletariat. What am I to say to Genera Hannay when I meet him? That you have become a blithering foreign communist?"

"Na, na. Ye maunna say that." The man's sullenness had gone, and there was humour in his eye. "Say that Geordie Hamilton is still obeyin' orders, and daein' his duty up to his lights."

"Whose orders?" Archie asked, but the corporal was already making for the door.

The young man walked back to the hotel in a reflective mood, and at luncheon gave Janet a summary of the event of the morning. He had been storing up his impressions of Olifa for her, and had meant to descant upon the old city and the market and the Cathedral

Square, but he found these pictures obscured by his later experiences. "Most extraordinary thing. I ran up against a fellow who used to be Dick Hannay's batman--regular chunky Scots Fusilier and brave as a badger--Hamilton they call him. Well, he had the cheek to tell me that he had changed his views and become a Bolshie and had consequently had to clear out of Glasgow. I swear the chap was lying--could see it in his face--but I'm puzzled why he should want to lie to me...He says he has some kind of engineer's job on the Corinna...More by token, I saw a selection of the Corinna party in a motor-car in the Avenida. Dressed up like nothing on earth, and chattering like jays!"

"We had them here this morning," said Janet. "Pretty little savages with heads like mops. I've christened them the Moplahs."

"Was there a fellow in starched linen bags? He was the prize donkey."

Janet shook her head. "There was only one man with them and he wore white flannels. I can't quite make them at. They behave like demented trippers, and are always pawing and ragging each other, but I came on the young man suddenly when I went to the bureau to ask about postage, and when the clerk couldn't tell me he answered my question. His whole voice and manner seemed to change, and he became startlingly well-bred...I want to explore the Moplahs. And I would rather like to see again the tall girl I had a glimpse of yesterday. I can't get it out of my head that I've seen her before."

III

On the following evening Janet and Archie dined as Don Alejandro's guests at the Club de Residentes Extranjeros. The club, situated in one of the squares to the north of he Avenida, was a proof of Olifa's wealth and her cosmopolitanism. In the broad cool patio a fountain tinkled, and between it and the adjoining arcades tropical plants in green tubs made the air fragrant. The building was for the most part a copy of an old Spanish town house, but the billiard-room was panelled in oak with a Tudor ceiling, the card-room was Flemish, and the big dining-room Italian Renaissance. The night was freshly warm, with light airs stirring the oleanders, and, from the table which Don Alejandro had selected, the patio was a velvet dusk shot with gold and silver gleams like tiny searchlights.

The only other guest was the American Consul. Mr Roderick Wilbur was a heavy man, with the smooth pale face of eupeptic but sedentary middle-age. His years in Olifa had not mellowed his dry, high-pitched New England voice, or endowed him with a single Latin, grace. He looked upon the other diners with the disapproving air of a Scots elder of the kirk surveying a travelling theatrical company, and the humour which now and then entered his eye was like the frosty twinkle of a very distant star.

Don Alejandro was in a vivacious mood. He was the showman of his beloved city, but he was no less a representative of his beloved Europe; he wished the strangers to praise Olifa but to recognise him as a cosmopolitan. Archie and Janet satisfied his patriotism, for, having hired a car that afternoon and driven round the city, they over-flowed in admiration.

"You were right," Janet told him. "There is no mystery in Olifa. It is all as smooth and polished as a cabochon emerald, and, like a cabochon, you can't see far inside it. Your people have the satisfied look of London suburbanites on a Sunday up the river."

"Your police are too good," said Archie. "One doesn't see a single ragamuffin in the main streets. Janet and I prefer the old quarter. Some day, Don Alejandro, we want you to take us round it and tell us who the people are. They look like samples of every South American brand since the Aztecs."

"The Aztecs lived in Mexico," Janet corrected.

"Well, I mean the chaps that were downed by the Conquistadors."

Don Alejandro laughed. "Our old quarter is only a tourist spectacle, like the native city in Tangier. For the true country life you must go to the estancias and the savannahs. I have arranged by telegraph for your visit to my cousin at Veiro."

"And the Gran Seco?"

"That also is in train. But it is more difficult and will take time."

"I said there was no mystery in Olifa," Janet observed, "but I rather think I was wrong. There is the Gran Seco. It seems to be as difficult to get into it as into a munition factory. Have you been there, Mr. Wilbur?"

The American Consul had been devoting serious attention to his food, stopping now and then to regard Janet with benevolent attention.

"Why, yes, Lady Roylance," he said. "I've been up to the Gran Seco just the once since it blossomed out. I've no great call to go there, for Americans don't frequent it to any considerable extent."

"Wilbur hates the place," said Don Alejandro. "He thinks that every commercial undertaking on the globe should belong to his countrymen, and it vexes him that the Gran Seco capital should be European."

"Don't you pay any attention to Mr Gedd," said the big man placidly. "He's always picking on my poor little country. But I can't say I care for that salubrious plateau. I don't like being shepherded at every turn as if I was a crook, and I reckon the Montana sagebrush is more picturesque. Also they haven't much notion up there of laying out a township. They'd be the better of some honest-to-God Americans to look after the plumbing."

"See! He is all for standardising life. What a dull world the United States would make of it!"

"That's so. We prefer dullness to microbes. All the same, there's things about the Gran Seco which you can see with half an eye aren't right. I didn't like the look of the miners. You never in your days saw such a hang-dog, miserable bunch, just like some of our old Indian reservations where big chief Wet Blanket and his wives used to drink themselves silly on cheap bourbon. And how in thunder does Castor get his labour? He's got a mighty graft somewhere, but when I first came here the Gran Seco Indians were a difficult folk to drive. I've heard that in old times the Olifa Government had trouble with them over the conscription."

"They were savages," said Don Alejandro, "and they are savages still. Castor has doubtless the art of dealing with them, for he himself is on the grand scale a savage."

Archie pricked up his ears. "Castor? Who is he?"

"The Gobernador of the province. Also the President of the company."

"I saw a fellow coming out of the Gran Seco head office--a fellow with a black beard, who didn't look as if he missed much."

"That was Senor Castor. You are fortunate, Sir Archibald, for you, a new arrival, have already seen Olifa's great man, and that is a privilege but rarely granted to us Oliferos. He descends upon us and vanishes as suddenly as a river mist."

"Tell me about him," said Janet. "Where does he come from? What is his nationality?"

Don Alejandro shook his head. "I do not know. Mr Wilbur, who is a man of hasty judgments, will say that he is a Jew. He is certainly a European, but not a Spaniard, though he speaks our tongue. I can only say that he emerged out of nothing five years ago, and became at once a prince. He rules the Gran Seco, and its officials are altogether his creation. And since he rules the Gran Seco he rules Olifa. He has, as Mr Wilbur would say, this country of mine by the short hairs."

"He don't meddle with politics," said the American, and Janet noticed that as he spoke he cast a quick glance around him, as if he did not wish to be overheard. Don Alejandro, too, had lowered his voice.

"What nonsense!" said the latter. "He is money, and money is our politics to-day. Once we Latins of America were a great race. We were Europeans, with minds enlarged and spirits braced by a new continent. You are the soldier, Sir Archibald, and will remember that the bloodiest battles of last century were fought in La Plata and on the Uruguay. Our plains were the nursery of the liberties of Italy. But now we have but the one goddess. We are rich and nothing more. Soon we shall be richer, and then my dear Wilbur, we shall be the devotees of your great country, which is the high-priest of riches."

"I can't say that you're showing any special devotion just at present," said the other dryly. "My nationals--thank God there aren't many--are about the most unpopular in this State. But quit talking about politics. We're out to give you a good time, Lady Roylance, and we want to know just how you'd like us to set about it."

Janet was of a patient and philosophical temper, but Archie liked to take his sensations in gulps. So far Olifa, he admitted to himself, had been a little boring. The place, for all its beauty, had a deadly commonplaceness--it was the typical bourgeois State, as Don Alejandro had declared the first night. And yet he was conscious that this judgment did not exhaust the matter. There were moments when he felt that Olifa was a strange woman in a mask of cheap silk, a volcano overspread with suburban gardens. Behind even the decorousness of the Avenida he savoured a mystery. Into the pleasant monotony of the days had come wafts of air from some other sphere--a peasant's face in the market, the bearded Gobernador, the pallid men in the hotel, even the preposterous figure of Dick Hannay's former batman. These things had stirred in him an irrational interest...

Perhaps if he went into the hinterland he would find the clamour of Olifa, of whose existence he was convinced, but which had hitherto contrived to evade him.

The club dining-room was full, and when they left it for coffee on the terrace beside the patio they had difficulty in finding chairs. It was apparently the practice to dine elsewhere and come to the club to dance, for a band was pounding out ragtime, and a dozen couples were on the floor.

"The Moplahs," Janet sighed happily.

It was beyond doubt the American party from the yacht, and in that place they were as exotic as a tuberose in a bed of wallflowers. They had conformed to convention in their dress, for the four men wore dinner-jackets, and the four girls bright, short-skirted, silk-taffeta gowns and long pearl necklaces. Among the powdered Olifero ladies and the sallow Olifero cavaliers their fresh skins made a startling contrast, and not less startling were their shrill, toneless voices. They chattered incessantly, crying badinage to each other and to the band, as they danced the half-savage dances with an abandon which now suggested wild children and now the lunatic waltzing of hares in an April moonlight. Janet laughed aloud, the picture was so crazily fantastic. A Spanish girl, in a frock with wide flounces and with blue-black hair dressed high and surmounted by a gold comb, was suddenly cannoned into by a fluffy-headed minx, who apologised in a voice like a vindictive kitten's, and was rewarded by a stony stare. Just so, Janet remembered, she had seen a greyhound repel the impudence of a Skye terrier.

"I don't see my tall girl," she said.

"The fellow with the starched linen knickerbockers isn't here," said Archie. "I didn't see his face, but I think I would know him again. Who are they, Mr Wilbur?"

The American's eyes were hard with disapproval. "I can't tell you their names, but they're off the Corinna. They're in Burton Rawlinson's party. Mr Rawlinson isn't on board himself, and there can't be much of a restraining hand to shepherd the bunch. Some of them have been to my office, and I judge I'm going to hear of trouble with them before they quit these shores. They want this city to stop still and take notice of them."

Archie inquired concerning Mr Rawlinson.

"He's a fine man and a big man, one of the biggest on the Pacific coast. I've nothing against Burton. He's rich, and he's public-spirited, and he's gotten a mighty fine collection of pictures. I can't say I take to his offspring and their friends. There's more dollars than sense in that outfit."

"I like the Moplahs," said Janet. "I want to know them."

Archie, who was a connoisseur of dancing, observed that the men danced better than the women, a thing he had noticed before with Americans. "Did a fellow with starched linen bags ever come to your office?" he asked the Consul. "Slightly built fellow, a little shorter than me?"

Mr Wilbur shook his head. "Maybe, but I don't remember him. All their garments struck me as curious. Heaven knows what's going to become of our youth. Sir Archibald. They've quit behaving like ladies and gentlemen--running wild like bronchos, and their parents can't do the lassooing. They're hard cases at seventeen."

"There's an appalling innocence about them," said Janet and looked up smiling, for two of the dancers had left the floor and were approaching them.

The girl was small, and a little too plump, but very pretty, with a mop of golden curls like a mediaeval page's. The young man was thin and beaky, and his longish hair was parted in the middle.

"Say, what about dancing?" he said. "Won't you cut in?" He looked at Janet, while the girl smiled pleasantly on Archie.

"Most awfully sorry," said Archie. "I'd love to, but I've got a game leg."

"Pardon?"

"I mean I'm a bit lame."

Janet rose smiling and took the young man's arm.

"I don't know your name," said Mr Wilbur, who was a stickler for the conventions, "but I reckon you're with the Corinna party. This lady is Lady Roylance."

The youth regarded him solemnly. "You've said it, Grandpa," was his reply. "Come on, lady."

The girl was still partnerless, and Don Alejandro offered himself for the breach. He sprang to his feet and bowed deeply from the waist. "If I may have the honour," he said. Archie and the Consul were left alone to their cigars.

The dancing-place was soon crowded, and Janet and Don Alejandro seemed to have been completely absorbed into the whirl. Glimpses could be caught of Janet's porcelain elegance, and of an unwontedly energetic Don Alejandro in the grip of various corybantic maidens. The two men in the lounge-chairs presently ceased to be spectators and fell into talk.

Mr Wilbur, as if the absence of his colleague had unsealed his tongue, expanded and became almost confidential. He asked Archie for his impressions of

Olifa, and when he was told "tidy and contented and opulent," nodded an acquiescent head.

"You're about right, sir. That's Olifa first and last--the Olifa of to-day. Better policed than New York, and just about as clean as Philadelphia. Manicured, you might say. But it wasn't always like that. When I first came here Olifa was the ordinary South American republic, always on the edge of bankruptcy and revolution, and this city had one of the worst names on the coast. The water-front was a perfect rat-hole for every criminal in the Pacific--every brand of roughneck and dope-smuggler and crook--dagos with knives and niggers with razors and the scum of the United States with guns. To-day you could take your wife along it in perfect safety any hour of the night. The Treasury was empty, for politics were simply who could get their hands first and deepest into it. There was bad trouble up-country, and there was always a war going on in the mountains, which the little under-fed and never-paid soldiers couldn't win. Now we've got a big balance in the budget and the peace of God over the land. It's a kind of miracle. It's almost against nature, Sir Archibald."

"Why, it's principally the Gran Seco," he continued, in response to Archie's request for an explanation. "That, as you know, is the richest copper proposition on the globe, and the Government has a big share in it. There's money to burn for everybody nowadays. But there's more than money. Olifa's gotten a first-class brain to help her along."

"The President?"

Wilbur laughed.

"The Excelentisimo is a worthy gentleman, and he has gotten some respectable folks to help him, but it isn't the President of this republic that has made the desert blossom like the rose. There's a bigger brain behind him."

"You mean the Gran Seco fellow--what's his name?"

"I mean Mr Castor. At least I reckon it must be Mr Castor, for there isn't anybody else. You see, I can size up the members of the Government, because I know them, so it must be the man I don't know."

"I see. Well, it's clear that I must get alongside of this Castor if I'm to learn much about Olifa. What's the best way to work it?"

"Through the President, I reckon. I'd like to help you but I haven't much of a pull in Olifa just at the moment. You see, the United States is going through one of its periodical fits of unpopularity. Olifa has waxed fat, like the man in the Bible, and she's kicking, and when a South American nation kicks it's generally against the United States. Don Alejandro will fix an interview with the President for you, and he'll arrange your trip to the Gran Seco. He's a good little man, though he don't like my country."

Thereafter Mr Wilbur discoursed of his nation--its strength and its weakness, its active intelligence, imperfect manners, and great heart. He was a critic, but he was also an enthusiast. To this man, grown old in foreign lands in his country's service, America was still the America of his youth. Her recent developments he knew only from the newspapers, and he loyally strove to reconcile them with his old ideal. America only needed to be understood to be loved, but it was hard to get her true worth across the footlights. "You English," he said, "have got a neat, hard-shell national character, with a high gloss on it. Foreigners may not like it, but they can't mistake it. It hits them in the eye every time. But we're young and growing and have a lot of loose edges, and it's mighty hard to make people understand that often when we talk foolishness we mean wisdom, and that when we act high and mighty and rile our neighbours it's because we're that busy trying to get a deal through we haven't time to think of susceptibilities. You've got to forget our untidy fringes."

"Like the crowd from the yacht," said Archie. "They don't rile me a bit, I assure you...Just look at the way that lad dances. He might be David capering before the Lord."

"That's because you've seen a lot of the world, Sir Archibald. I reckon you've met enough Americans to know the real thing."

"No, I've met very few. You see, I've never crossed the Atlantic before. But I knew one American, and for his sake I'm ready to back your country against all corners. He was about the wisest and bravest and kindest old fellow ever came across."

Mr Wilbur asked his name.

"He's dead, poor chap. Died a few months ago. I daresay you've heard of him. His name was Blenkiron--John S. Blenkiron."

Archie had his eye on the Hebraic dancer or he might have noticed a sudden change in his companion's face. When Mr Wilbur spoke again--and that was after a considerable pause--it was in a voice from which all feeling had gone, the voice in which he conducted his consular duties.

"Yes. I've heard of Mr Blenkiron. Mighty fine man, they tell me. Just how well did you know him, Sir Archibald?"

"I only saw him for a week or two in the Amiens business of March '18. But they were pretty solemn weeks, and you get to know a man reasonably well if you're fighting for your life beside him. He was with a great pal of mine, General Hannay, and the two of them put up a famous show at Gavrelle. I can see old Blenkiron's face yet, getting cheerier the more things went to the devil, and fairly beaming when the ultimate hell was reached. I wouldn't ask for a better partner in a scrap. I'm most awfully sorry he died. I always hoped to see him again."

"Too bad," said Mr Wilbur, and he seemed to be absorbed in some calculation, for his brows were knitted.

A flushed Janet joined them, attended by two cavaliers who insisted on plundering the pot plants to give her flowers, Presently Don Alejandro also extricated himself from the dancers, with his black-corded eyeglass hanging over his left shoulder.

"These innocents are going to the Gran Seco," Janet announced. "They seem to think it is a sort of country club, but if your account is true, Mr Wilbur, they'll be like humming-birds in a dustbin."

"They surely will," said the Consul. "When do you expect your own permits, Lady Roylance?"

"They should be ready to-morrow," said Don Alejandro.

Archie and Janet left their caleche at the hotel gates, and walked up the steep avenue to enjoy the coolness of the night wind. At the esplanade on the top they halted to marvel at the view. Below them lay the old town with the cathedral towers white in the moonlight--a blur of shadows in which things like glow-worms twinkled at rare intervals, and from which came confused echoes of some secret nocturnal life. Beyond lay the shining belt of the Avenida, and the Ciudad Nueva mounting its little hills in concentric circles of light. On the other side the old harbour was starred with the riding lights of ships, and the lamps of the water-front made a double line, reflection and reality. To the south at the new harbour there was a glow of fires and the clamour of an industry which did not cease at sunset. To the west, beyond the great breakwater, sea and sky melted under the moon into a pale infinity.

Suddenly Archie's spirits awoke. He seemed to see Olifa as what he had hoped--not a decorous city of careerists, but a frontier post on the edge of mysteries. The unknown was there, crowding in upon the pert little pride of man. In the golden brume to the east were mountains--he could almost see them--running up to icefields and splintered pinnacles, and beyond them swamps and forests as little travelled as in the days of Cortes. Between the desert of the ocean and the desert of the hills lay this trivial slip of modernity, but a step would take him beyond it into an antique land. The whiff of a tropical blossom from the shrubberies and the faint odour of wood smoke unloosed a flood of memories--hot days in the African bush, long marches in scented Kashmir glens, shivering camps on Himalayan spurs. The War had overlaid that first youth of his, when he had gone east to see the world, but the rapture and magic were now returning. He felt curiously expectant and happy.

"I've a notion that we're going to have the time of our lives here," he told his wife.

But Janet did not reply. For three days she had been busy chasing a clue through her memory and now she had grasped it. She had suddenly remembered who was the tall girl she had seen with the party from the Corinna on the day of their arrival.

All night Archie dreamed of the Gran Seco. As he saw it, it was a desolate plateau culminating in a volcano. The volcano was erupting, and amid the smoke and fire a colossal human figure sat at its ease. Then the dream became a nightmare--for the figure revealed itself as having the face and beard of the man he had seen leaving the office in the Avenida, but the starched white linen knickerbockers of the preposterous young American.

IV

Archie set out on his exploration of Olifa with his nose in the air, like a dog looking for game. The spell of a new country had fallen on him, as had happened fifteen years before when he left school. The burden of the War and all it had brought, the cares of politics, the preoccupations of home had slipped from his shoulders, and he felt himself again an adventurer, as when he had first studied maps and listened hungrily to travellers' tales. But now he had one supreme advantage--he had a companion; and Janet, who had never before been out of Europe, was as eager as he was to squeeze the last drop out of new experience.

He left over his more important letters for the moment and used those introductions which had been given him by the friends he had made during his time at the Madrid Embassy. The result was that the pair were taken to the heart of a pleasant, rigid little society--as remote from interest in the Government of Olifa as an unreconstructed Southern planter is from a Republican White House, or a Royalist Breton from the Elysee. Archie was made a member of the Polo Club and played with agreeable young men, who had their clothes and saddlery from London and their manners from the eighteenth century. A ball was given in their honour, where the most popular dance, to Janet's amazement, was a form of Lancers. They met composed maidens who were still in bondage to their duennas, and young married women, languishing and voluble, of discreet and domesticated, among whose emphatic complexions Janet's delicate colouring was like a wood-anemone among gardenias: and witty grandmothers running terribly to fat: and ancient hidalgos with beaks like birds of prey. It was a comfortable society, with the secure good manners of a tiny aristocracy, but it knew of no world beyond its pale, and was profoundly uninterested in its neighbours.

They went a little, too, into business circles, both Olifero and alien, the representatives of shipping and trading companies and the big foreign banks. This, too, was a pleasant world, good-tempered and prosperous. Here they heard much of politics, but it was business politics. The existing Government was spoken of with respect, but not with intimate knowledge; it functioned well, kept the country solvent, and left trade in peace. Politicians were a class by themselves, a dubious class, though it was believed that the present lot were honest. But they met none of the Copper people. These seemed to form an oligarchy apart, and were mentioned respectfully but distantly. When Archie asked about the Gran Seco he was only given statistics of output and an encomium on its efficiency. Of its President the commercial world of Olifa spoke as an ordinary automobile-manufacturer might speak of Henry Ford, as one who was a law to himself, an object to admire, but not to emulate.

"This is a queer place," Archie told Janet. "It seems to have two Governors--the Castor fellow and the President--and the ordinary man don't seem to know or care much about either. It's about time we started out for the Gran Seco."

But when Don Alejandro was approached on the matter he had to explain with many apologies that their permits had not arrived. There was some inconceivably foolish hitch, which he had not yet tracked down.

"But the American troupe got through straight away," Archie complained. "They left a week ago."

"I know. That is a way Americans have. Perhaps in your case the difficulty is Mr Wilbur. Officiously and quite unnecessarily he interested himself in getting your passes, so he said--and he may have exhausted his purchase in franking his countrymen through and raised a prejudice. As I have told you, his nation is not loved by our Government."

Don Alejandro went on to explain that the delay could only be a matter of days. "Meantime, why not visit my cousin at Veiro? There you must go some time, and this hiatus gives you the chance."

So to Veiro they went--fifty miles by train and twenty by motor-car along a superb concrete highway, which suddenly gave out four miles from the house, so that the journey was completed by a sandy track over primeval prairie. They arrived just at sunset, when the place swam in a clear coppery gold. The house was low and white and seemed to cover acres, with its adobe outbuildings, its great corrals for the cattle, and its trim red-roofed stables built on the English model. The palms of the coast had been left behind, and at this elevation the tropics had faded from the landscape. The garden was ablaze with coverts of hibiscus and plots of scarlet zinnias among the rough lawns, and the wind-breaks which flanked it were of acacias and walnuts. A big irrigation dam to the right caught the last rays of the sun, and beyond it the tender green of the alfalfa fields seemed a continuation of its waters. Far to the east, above the lifting savannahs, was a saw-like edge of tenuous white mountains which seemed to hang in the central heavens. There was a succession of thin spires now picked out with gold and rose. Archie asked their name.

"Los Doce Apostolas--the Twelve Apostles," said the driver, and rattled off a list of uncouth syllables.

Don Mario Sanfuentes, the cousin of Don Alejandro, was small, spare, and blue-jowled, with the figure of a groom and the profound solemnity of the man who lives with horses. His wife was dead and his ranch and stables were to him both family and profession. He greeted his visitors with the grave courtesy of manner which needs no words to emphasise it. Their rooms were wide chambers with scrubbed wooden floors and windows looking across a broad verandah to a hundred miles of space, as bare and fresh as a convent dormitory. They had their meals in a dining-room which contained the remnants of the Sanfuentes heirlooms--cabinets of lacquer and tortoiseshell, a Murillo which had been an altar-piece in one of the forgotten churches of the Conquistadors, fantastic tapestries now faded into a mellow confusion, an Italian triptych of carved ivory, and a great galleon of tarnished silver. But they sat mostly in Don Mario's own room, where in the evenings a wood fire was lit in the wide fireplace--a room where every table was littered with books and papers and cigar-boxes and quirts and crops and spurs, and from the walls looked down the delicate heads of those descendants of the Darley Arab, the Byerley Turk, and the Godolphin Barb whose fame has gone abroad wherever men love horses.

By day Archie and Janet rode with their host about his state, examined his young stock, and tried out promising colts on the gallops, where by assiduous care a better turf lad been got than in the ordinary savannah. At every meal he talk was of horses, but at night, when the fire was lit, Don Mario from the depths of his well-rubbed armchair would speak at large of the land. In modern Olifa he had little interest, but he told of the diversions of his youth--his pack of foxhounds which had to be so constantly renewed from England that he gave up the game in despair, tiger hunting in the forest country, punitive expeditions against Indian horse-thieves from the hills. The time passed in a delicious calm: a combination, said Janet, of Newmarket and

Scotland. And then on the last day of their stay came another visitor.

"I cannot tell you about this country," Don Mario said, "for I am an old horse-breeder who lives apart. But I have bidden young Luis de Marzaniga to sleep the night. His mother was cousin to the husband of my great-aunt's niece. Luis has travelled abroad and seen the world, but specially he has travelled in Olifa. No. He is no politician, nor is he engaged in business. He is like me--what you call a country gentleman. But he has youth and inquisitiveness, both of which I have long since lost."

So, when the Roylances, having bathed and changed after a long ride in the sun, came down to dinner, they found a strange young man awaiting them. Don Mario's evening garb had been a little like that of a deaf-mute at a funeral, but this young man wore the trimmest of dinner-jackets and the neatest of patent-leather shoes. His hair was as fair as Archie's; but some colouring in his skin had made him sunburn not to Archie's brick-red but to a rich golden brown. His eyes were brown, and the large expanse of white in them was the only foreign thing in his appearance. Otherwise he looked like a young English cavalry subaltern, whose duties permitted him to hunt three days a week.

Dinner that evening was a cheerful meal. Don Luis chaffed his distant kinsman, with whom he was obviously in high favour, and Don Mario expanded in silent laughter. All spoke English--Don Mario very correct and stilted, Don Luis nobly ungrammatical but notably idiomatic. To Janet's questions he replied that his education had been chiefly in Olifa, but that he had visited Europe seven times, and during the last six months of the War had had a commission in the French Air Force. He had only just returned from Paris. The mention of flying woke up Archie, and for a little the room hummed with technicalities. Archie inquired concerning the Olifa Air Force, and was told that it was efficient but small--not more than five squadrons. The Olifero did not take readily to the air, and the pilots were mostly foreigners--Germans who had found their career cut short at home, and, Don Luis thought, one or two Russians. "It is like all our army," he said, "a little force of expert mercenaries. Olifa needs no army. In the future she will fight her battles with gold."

Don Luis was very ready to talk. He answered Archie's many questions on sport with enthusiasm, and drew sketch-maps to illustrate the lie of the land. As to politics, he had not Don Mario's apathy. He was ready with amusing portraits of Olifa's statesmen and with cogent summaries of policy. He was also a humorist, and had a repertoire of tales. But he was a discreet young man, and ventured no opinion of his own. He was neither reactionary nor progressive, only an interested spectator.

On the Gran Seco he was highly informing. He described the nature of the copper deposits, and the new processes which had reduced costs and made it the Golconda of Olifa. Castor he knew only by sight, "We of Olifa do not meet him, but we worship him from afar. He is the god who dwells in the sanctuary."

"The American Consul thought there might be trouble some day. The mine-labourers are rather a savage lot, aren't they?"

Don Luis laughed. "I think the wish may be--how you say?--mother to the thought. Senor Wilbur does not love the Gran Seco. No doubt it is a difficult place, but Senor Castor is beyond doubt a Napoleon and flourishes on difficulties. It will be all right."

"Why does he keep the place so tightly shut? We have been waiting a fortnight for a permit to enter."

"So! Then there must be some foolish mistake of clerks. Senor Castor is not likely to be uncivil--least of all to a charming lady and to a member of the English Parliament. He is a lover of Europe."

Don Luis had many questions to ask in turn, and it slowly dawned upon one of his hearers that this candid and friendly sung man was taking in more than he gave out. Archie was drawn to speak of his own past--his eastern travels, his experiences in the War, even of his friends, who could mean nothing to a South American who had only once been in England. He found himself quoting Sandy Arbuthnot by name, as if he had been in his club at home.

"I beg your pardon," he said confusedly. "You can't be interested in my yarning about people you never heard of."

"But I am deeply interested. Your friend is a wise man. How do you call him--Arbuttnot?"

"He was Sandy Arbuthnot, but his father is dead and he is Lord Clanroyden now."

"A lord! Clan--roy--den. Por dios! That is a strange name."

"Scotch," said Archie.

"Ah yes--Scotch. That is your Highlands? Your Gran Seco? This Lord Clay--roy--den, he is in Scotland?"

"I'm blessed if I know where he is at the moment. He's never long off the road."

Janet, too, to her surprise found herself talking to this stranger as if she had known him from childhood. She described vivaciously her encounter with the Moplahs.

"They are common as lentils in Olifa at certain seasons," said Don Luis, "those noisy, emancipated

American children. They have gone, you say, to the Gran Seco, where Americans are not loved. There may be work then for Senor Wilbur."

"They are really rather nice," said Janet. "I think I have met one of them before...Archie, I didn't tell you, but I believe the tall girl who was with the Moplahs the first day and whom we never saw again was the Miss Dasent who came to Strathlarrig. She was some sort of relation of Mr Blenkiron."

"Not really?" exclaimed the interested Archie. "That's curious. Did you ever hear of Blenkiron, Don Luis? He died the other day--American, rather a great man--he was the chap I was telling you about in the Shark-Gladas affair."

The other shook his head. "I do not think so. But American names are so difficult that it is hard to remember. They are worse than Clan--roy--den."

Don Mario made it his habit to retire to rest at ten o'clock, and Janet, being very sleepy, followed soon after. Archie and Don Luis lit a final cigar, and in the smoking of it strolled into the moonlit verandah. On this side of the house the view was not broken by outbuildings, and beyond a string of paddocks the eye passed to an endless sweep of yellow savannah which faded in the distance into a golden haze. The air was fresh, and, though the night was still, cool wafts seemed to drift soundlessly down from the hidden mountains.

"My countrymen and yours fought each other for three hundred years," said Don Luis, "but a Spaniard and an Englishman, when they meet, usually understand each other, I presume, with your permission, on that old sympathy, and I ask you boldly what are you doing here?"

The young man's manner had changed from the debonair ease which had marked it at dinner. It had become at once confidential and authoritative.

"Fact is, I don't know," was Archie's reply. "Principally, Janet and I are on a postponed honeymoon. I had a notion to pick up something about South American politics, which might be useful to me in Parliament."

"And you find Olifa rather barren ground?"

"I did at first...Now, I am not so sure."

"Will you let me advise you? We are both young men and have served in war. Stay a little in Olifa if you have not yet exhausted the charm of the capital, and then take our delightful lady on board the first ship and go straight home."

"Home? Why in the world?" Archie stared at the speaker.

"You can go to Valparaiso and Buenos Ayres if they amuse you. But get out of Olifa."

"But why?"

"I cannot tell you why. I am your friend, and a friend may venture to advise without reasons."

"But what's the trouble? Olifa is a great deal more peaceful than Europe. You don't mean to say that there's danger..."

"Olifa is a mask--you have not seen her face. Look in front of you. You see nothing but flat pastures. But beyond you know that there are wild mountains. So I tell you that behind the flatness of Olifa there are wild things."

"Well, I'm blessed! D'you know, Don Luis, you are making Olifa rather attractive. You are giving me a very good reason why I should stay."

"But madame..."

"I don't know. For heaven's sake, don't tell her what you're telling me, for if she gets a notion that there's mystery abroad she won't stop till she is up to the neck it. But of course I can't let her run any risks..."

"I do not think that you will be able to help yourself--if you stay. You may be caught up in a tide which will carry you to things very different from your respectable English politics...And these things will not be a honeymoon."

Archie stared at his companion's face. The moon was very bright and the face which it revealed was grave and set.

"You are talking in riddles," said Archie. "I wish you would be more explicit. You tell me to get out of the country, because if I stay I may have trouble. You can hardly leave it at that, you know. What kind of trouble? Perhaps it's the kind that Janet and I might rather fancy."

"That is why I warn you. You are a young man with a wife. It is easy to see that you are not the type who avoids danger. But a wife makes a difference--especially such a lady as yours. You would not wish to involve her and yet you may unwittingly, if you do not leave Olifa."

"Supposing I were a bachelor, what would you say?"

Don Luis laughed. "Ah, then, I should speak otherwise. I should make of you a confidant--perhaps an ally! You wish to visit the Gran Seco, but your passports are unaccountably delayed. I might offer to take you to the Gran Seco, but not by Santa Ana and the Company railway."

Archie pondered. "Everything in this country seems turn on the Gran Seco," he said, "and we don't seem to able to get there."

"It may be that that a blunder of officialdom is doing you a service," said Don Luis solemnly.

"Well, I've no desire to go there and get tangled up in a local shindy, which I take it is what you are hinting at. I remember Mr Wilbur said that the miners seemed to be ugly crowd. I'm very much obliged to you, Don Luis."

"You will not tell anyone that I have warned you."

"Certainly not...I'm rather inclined to take your advice, and tell Gedd to drop the passport business. I did come here looking for trouble--and, besides, there's my wife."

But in this Archie was not wholly candid. He told his self that what he called a "dago revolution" had no charms for him, especially with Janet to take care of. But realised that this phrase did not exhaust the mystery in Olifa, which had been slowly accumulating in his mind till the sense of it was like an atmosphere about him. And he had taken a strong liking to Don Luis. The young man had a curious appeal in his alternate gaiety and gravity. There was that in him which seemed to beckon to wild and delightful things; he was such a companion as Archie a dozen years ago would have welcomed to ride with over the edge of the world. But Archie--rangé, married, lame of one leg--decided with a half-sigh that such visions and such comrades were no longer for him.

V

On their return to the city they were met by an incensed Don Alejandro. Not only had the permits for the Gran Seco not arrived, they had been definitely refused. It was not the work of the Government--this he had ascertained from his second cousin, the Minister for External Affairs. The refusal came from the Company itself, and Don Alejandro was positive that it was due to the interference of the American Consul. No doubt Wilbur had meant well, but apparently he had pressed the request so that the Company had assumed that he was its principal sponsor, and had naturally refused, since they thought they had done enough for his unpopular country by permitting the entrance of the party from the Corinna. There was no doubt about it. Don Alejandro had heard from a friend who was deep in the Company's affairs that Wilbur was e cause of the refusal.

To Janet's surprise Archie seemed rather relieved than otherwise. "Just as well, perhaps," he said. "We should probably have got fever or something, and we didn't come six thousand miles to look at a mining district. We have plenty of them at home."

He had not told Janet of Don Luis's warning, but he had brooded over it, and with his separation from the giver good sense seemed to grow more convincing. Why on earth should Janet and he waste time in visiting a dusty plateau, even though it was the source of Olifa's prosperity and might have importance in Olifa's future politics? He would learn little in a hurried tour, and it wasn't his line to pick up gossip and go home and raise a racket in Parliament about Gran Seco atrocities...They would go the to Cardanio and Alcorta, and might make a short trip into the mountains. The Twelve Apostles would bear inspection from closer quarters...After that they would go home by Panama, and perhaps visit Jamaica. His mother's family had once owned big plantations there, established by an ancestor who had left the country hurriedly after Culloden.

So they fell back upon Olifa society, and Archie played polo daily at the club, and they gave a dinner at the hotel; and were just preparing to set out for Cardanio, when they were bidden to luncheon by no less a person than the President. A superb card of invitation, surmounted by the Olifa arms in gold, gave Archie the title of "Right Honourable," and designed Janet as the "Honourable Lady A. Roylance."

Archie consulted Don Alejandro as to his garments, and was informed that the manners of Olifa were English and that they might both wear what they pleased. So Janet and he appeared at the President's mansion in their ordinary clothes, to find most of the men in evening dress with ribands and stars, and all the women in Paris hats and what looked like wedding gowns. Janet promptly had a fit of giggles, and it was a flushed and embarrassed pair who made their bow to the heavy, sallow, bull-necked Excelentisimo.

The day was hot, the place where they sat was as heavily upholstered as a Victorian dining-room, and the conversation had the languor of a ceremonial banquet. Janet, as the guest of honour, sat on the President's right hand, while Archie at the other end was sandwiched between a voluminous elderly woman who was the President's wife and a sleepy Frenchwoman whose husband was Don Alejandro's kinsman. His head had been confused by many introductions, but he had made out that kinsman, a Sanfuentes of the younger branch, and a tall man with a forked beard who was Aribia, the Minister of Finance. There was a vacant chair on Janet's right side.

The meal seemed interminable. The food was pretentiously good, and the guests seemed to have been starved for days, for they refused none of the dishes. Sweet champagne was served, and the Olifa Tokay, but when Archie, greatly daring, asked for a whisky-and-soda, it was brought him and to his surprise was pre-War whisky. There seemed to be about twenty footmen, all in knee-breeches, mestizos who in their gaudy liveries had an air of comic opera. Archie tried his bad Spanish on his two ladies, and, having exhausted the beauties and greatness of Olifa, the distress of Europe, their families, and his visit to Veiro, was hard put to it for topics. Senora Sanfuentes received every mention of Don Alejandro with a shrug and a giggle, Madame la Presidente did not appear to have heard of him.

Suddenly there was a movement in the company. Someone had entered and taken the vacant chair by Janet's side.

The light in the room was very dim, and Archie saw only a tall figure, to greet whom the President and the other men rose and bowed. The man, whoever he was, was not in evening dress. Later, he saw Janet's fair head inclined towards him, and from the vivacity of her manner she seemed to be finding interest in the new guest.

At last, with a marvellous course of fruits and sweet-meats, the meal came to an end. The hostess rose heavily and led the ladies from the room, and the men moved up to a semi-circle round their host. Room was made for Archie next to the President, and beyond that impressive figure sat the late arrival. With a thrill he recognised the man he had seen the first day leaving the office in the Avenida, the great Senor Castor, the Gobernador of the province of the Gran Seco and the head of the Company.

Huge cigars had been provided, but the Gobernador had refused them, and, after asking his host's permission, had lit a short briar pipe. It was some minutes before the President formally introduced them, being himself engaged in a whispered conversation, so Archie had the opportunity to study the great man's features. Seen at close quarters they were not less impressive than in the fleeting view on the Avenida. The brow was broad and high, and had the heavy frontal development above the eyebrows which Archie had been told betokened mathematical genius. The complexion was pale, but clear and healthy; the nose short and finely formed, and springing from the forehead like the prow of a ship. The mouth was hidden by the beard, but it might be guessed that the lips were full. The eyes were the compelling feature. They were large and grey and set rather wide apart, and, though narrow-lidded, gave their possessor an air of steady, competent watchfulness. There was thought in them, and masterfulness, but no hint of passion, only a calm, all embracing intelligence. Among the beady opaque eyes around him, this man's were like pools of living light contrasted with scummed morasses. The face was grave and composed, but when Archie's name was spoken it broke into a curiously pleasant smile.

The Gobernador of the Gran Seco addressed him in flawless English. He inquired after his journey, spoke of the pleasure with which he had made Janet's acquaintance, and, on being informed by the President that Archie was a member of the British Legislature, asked one or two shrewd questions about current British politics. In five minutes' talk across the table he seemed to take soundings of Archie's mind, and elicited his special interest He even detected his love of birds, and had something say of the need for a sound ornithologist to investigate certain of the mountain areas. Archie had a feeling that this astonishing man, if he had been told that his hobby was marine zoology or Coptic antiquities, would have talked about it with the same intimate intelligence.

"You will visit us, I hope, in our little mountain kingdom. Perhaps you have heard of our Gran Seco?"

"I've heard about nothing else. But there's a hitch somewhere, and I've been told that we can't get passports for the present."

The Gobernador frowned. "What incomprehensible folly! That is a matter which shall at once be set right. I cannot think how the mistake has arisen. Your hotel? The Constitucion? Permits shall be sent round to you this afternoon, and you have only to fix the day of your journey and we shall make arrangements. What must you think of us, Sir Archibald! Believe me, we are not accustomed to treat distinguished strangers with impoliteness."

The manner of the Gobernador was so open and friendly that Archie's distaste for the Gran Seco and his memory of Don Luis's talk straightway vanished. The resident observed that in old days the Gran Seco had been a closed country, and that, as Sir Archibald would realise, it could not be thrown open in a day.

"I am positive Sir Archibald will understand," said the Gobernador. "We have established, as it were, a Sheffield and a Birmingham in a rude hill-country, and we must limit our administrative problems. The sixteenth century and the twentieth can co-exist only if the latter is given in small doses. Slowly they will harmonise--but slowly. You have the same problem in your India. I understand that you do not permit tourists, however well accredited, even to enter some of the hill-states."

"That's true," said Archie. "When I was there, they wouldn't let me put a foot across the Nepaul border."

"Also we are a big business, with our secrets, and we cannot have agents of our rivals prowling about the place, which is, so to speak, all one workshop. But--we welcome visitors who recognise our difficulties and submit to our modest rules."

"It is the Yanquis who give trouble," said the President darkly.

The Gobernador laughed. "Some Yanquis. I do not share his Excellency's distrust of the whole of that great nation. The bright special correspondent on the look-out for a 'scoop' is the most dangerous of created things. But we welcome the reasonable journalist. You may have read a series of articles on Olifa in the Saturday Evening Post. There you had the Gran Seco accurately portrayed with our full assent. Yet on the whole it is not the journalist who perplexes us most. It is the Yanqui tripper on a circular tour. We cannot have them making drunken fools of themselves in a place where the prestige of the white man is his only security."

"There was an American party at the hotel," said Archie. "Noisy young devils from a yacht. I think they went up to the Gran Seco a week ago."

The Gobernador shrugged his shoulders. "We do not antagonise the great, we who are business men. But those young people will not be given the privileges which await you, Sir Archibald."

Archie felt as if he were being treated with especial frankness and friendliness, and his susceptible soul was in a pleasant glow. Then the conversation became general and he had leisure to observe the company. The Gobernador said little, the Olifero statesmen much, but it seemed the Archie that they all talked under his eye and for his approbation. After an argument there came a hush, as if the deferred to him for the ultimate word. But he scarcely spoke. He sat silent, watchful, now and then smiling tolerantly. Once only he intervened. The Minister of Finance was discoursing on some aspect of the policy of the United States, and his comments were caustic. The Gobernador looked across at Archie and spoke in English.

"Yanquis are unpopular in England?" he asked.

"No. I shouldn't say that. Americans are popular with us, as they always have been. You see, we get the best of them. But the abstract thing, America, is unpopular. She always seems to have a rather left-handed Government."

A spark seemed to kindle in the other's eye.

"That is right. No section of humanity deserves blame. It is governments, not peoples, that offend."

Then the spark died out.

As Janet and Archie walked back to the hotel they spoke of the luncheon party. They had taken the road through the old town, and were in the market-place among stalls.

"That man Castor doesn't belong here," said Archie "He has nothing in common with those bland Oliferos. He's nearer to that lot," and he pointed to a group of Indians in shaggy ponchos squatted by the fountain.

"He is one of the most extraordinary people I ever met." said Janet. "Can you guess what he talked to me about? Ossian-Papa's bete noire, you know--Lord Balfour, and Marcel Proust! And I believe he could have talked just as well about clothes and Paris models."

"I never in my life got so strong an impression of all-round competence...I like him, too. I think he's a good fellow. Don't you?"

"I'm not so sure," said Janet. "I should like to see him clean-shaven. I've an idea that the mouth under that beard of his might be horribly cruel."

VI

The Gran Seco has not often appeared in the world's literature. Francisco de Toledo first entered it in the sixteenth century, but after that there is no mention of it till Calamity Brown wandered thither from the coast in the late years of the eighteenth. That luckless and probably mendacious mariner has little good to say of it; it was the abode of devilish insects and devilish men, and, if we are to believe him, he barely escaped with his life. In the nineteenth century it was partially explored by the Spanish naturalist, Mendoza, and a Smithsonian expedition investigated its peculiar geology. Its later history is written in the reports of its copper companies, but Sylvester Perry visited it in his celebrated journey round the globe, and it has a short and comminatory chapter in his Seeing Eyes. Mr Perry did not like the place, and in his characteristic way has likened it to a half-healed abscess, sloughed over with unwholesome skin.

Mr Perry was partially right. The Gran Seco is not built to the scale of man and it has no care for his comforts. But it has its own magnificence. Its gate is the town of Santa Ana, in whose market-place stands the colossal figure of the crucified Christ, first erected by Pizarro, many times destroyed by earthquakes, and always replaced, since it is the defiance of the plains to the mountains. But the gate is far from the citadel, for the avenue is a hundred miles long. The Gran Seco railway, now a double line most skilfully engineered, and wholly controlled by the Company, runs first up a long valley where only in mid-winter a river flows. Then it passes over tiers of high desert, sinks into hollows where sometimes there are waters and forests climbs again in tortuous gullies, till at length it emerges upon the great plateau; and always beside it can be traced the old highroad where once rode Toledo's men-at-arms, and only the other day the ore from the mines jolted down country on mule-back. But there are still many miles to go before the city of Gran Seco is reached, sunk in a shallow trough among its barren and blistered hills.

At first sight Sylvester Perry's phrase seems to have certain justice. Twenty years ago in the hollow there was only a wretched Indian puebla roosting among the ruins of an old city, for the copper from the distant mines was exported in its crude form. It was chiefly what is called virgin copper, with a certain amount of malachite and azurite ores. Ten years ago a new city began to rise, where the sulphuretted ores were first mined, and smelting was started. There was a furious rivalry among the companies till they were united in a great combine, and the whole mineral wealth gathered under a single direction. Process succeeded process, furnaces were multiplied till they coven many acres, wells were sunk and pumping-stations erected, great dams were built in the hills to catch the winter rail and street after street rose in the dust. The Castor method of calcination and electrolytic refining soon quadrupled in size. To one looking down from the surrounding ridges the place seems a hive of ugly activity: on one side a wilderness of furnaces and converters, with beyond them the compounds where the workmen are housed; on the other a modern city with high buildings and clanking electric trams. By day it is an inferno of noise and dust and vapours, with a dull metallic green the prevailing tint; by night a bivouac of devils warmed by angry fires. Mr Perry is right. The place has the look of a gangrening sore, with for the surrounding skin the pale shaly hills. And the climate is in itself a disease. In winter the hollow is scourged and frozen, and in summer the sun's heat, refracted from naked stone, strikes the face like a blow.

In the streets the first impression is of extreme orderliness. The traffic is methodically conducted by vigilant police in spruce uniforms--for the most part of the Indian or mestizo type, with European superintendents. They are a fine body of men; too good, the spectator decides, for such an environment. The main street, the Avenida Bolivar, is broad and paved with concrete, and along it rise structures which would not disgrace New York. The Regina Hotel is larger than the Ritz, and there are others; the offices of the Company's administration form a block scarcely smaller than Carlton House Terrace; there are clubs and many apartment houses, all built of the white local stone. But the shops are few and poor, and there are no villas in the environs, so that the impression grows that the Gran Seco is a camp, which its inhabitants regard as no continuing city. Hourly the sense of the bivouac expands in the traveller's mind. The place is one great caravanserai for pilgrims. These busy, preoccupied people are here for the day only and to-morrow will be gone.

Other things will soon strike him. There seem to be no peasants. No neighbouring countryside obtrudes itself into this monastic industry. Every man--there are few women--is regimented by the Company. If the traveller is escorted to the area of the smelting and refining plant (and his passports must be very high-powered to ensure this privilege), he will see the unskilled work done by Indians and mestizos--men with faces like mechanical automata--but the skilled foremen are all European. He will puzzle over these Europeans, for however wide his racial knowledge, he will find it hard to guess their nationality, since their occupation seems to have smoothed out all differences into one common type with a preoccupation so intense as to be almost furtive. In the streets, too, in the clubs and hotels, he will be struck by the waxwork look of some of the well-dressed employees. They are inhumanly pale, and so concentrated upon some single purpose that their faces are expressionless and their eyes unseeing.

He will be much shepherded and supervised, and, though his permission de sejour is for only a few days, he will be apt to find these days pass heavily. If he is a mining expert he will not be allowed to indulge his curiosity, for the Castor processes are jealously guarded. If he is the ordinary tourist, he will find no sights to repay him, and for the only amusement an occasional concert of austerely classical music given by the Administration staff. He will probably leave the place with relief, glad to have seen the marvel, but thankful that his lines are cast among ordinary humanity. At the station, on his departure, he will be presented with a wonderful booklet, containing an eloquent speech of the Gobernador, and extracts (with illustrations) from the recent articles on the Gran Seco in the Saturday Evening Post.

The young party from the Corinna did not appear to find the time hang heavy on their hands. There were ten them, five of each sex, with no older person to look aft them, though a very moderate chaperonage seemed to be exercised by a tall girl with fine eyes and a pleasant Southern voice. That their purchase was considerable was shown by their entertainment, for they were shown everything and went everywhere; that they were unwelcome visitors, unwillingly privileged, was proved by their close oversight. Indeed they were uncomfortable guests, for they made patch of garish colour in the drab of the Gran Seco and discord in its orderly rhythm. The mere sight of them the streets was enough to send the ordinary policeman the Commissary to ask for instructions.

They were patently harmless, but deplorably silly. The Regina was turned by them into a cabaret. They danced every night in the restaurant to the disquiet of the diners, and they chaffed mercilessly an unsmiling staff. Bedroom riots seemed to be their speciality, and it was an unlucky official of the Company who had his quarters in the corridor. When they were entertained to luncheon by Administration they asked questions so sublimely idiotic that the Vice-President, a heavy sallow man, called Rosas, of Mexican extraction, actually coloured, thinking that he was being made a fool of; and their visit to the smelting plant was attended by the same exasperating buffoonery.

Presently it appeared that their idiocy was congenital and not a pose. Their jazz chatter and jazz manners were the natural expression of jazz minds, and must be endured because of the prestige of Mr Burton Rawlinson. So "Baby" and "Bawby" and "Honey" and "Gerry" went their preposterous way, and the Gran Seco shrugged outraged shoulders and spat.

Nevertheless there were signs, had there been eyes to note them, that the yacht party was not quite what it seemed. In unguarded moments, as Janet had already observed, they could be betrayed into sanity and good breeding. At nights, too, when their ragging was over, there were odd discussions in the privacy of bedrooms. At least one of the young men would sit far into the dawn working at notes and plans.

Presently, as if they had had enough of the city, they extended their revels into the surrounding country. They procured two touring cars, and, after some trouble with the Commissary of Police, embarked on long excursions. The mines lie in three main groups--the San Tome, the

Alhuema, and the Universum--and they visited all three. There they seemed to find much to interest them, and the managers feverishly telephoned to headquarters for instructions. These children were imbeciles doubtless, they reported, but they were poking their noses into forbidden places. So on their return the troupe had to interview the Commissary of Police, who politely cautioned them against breaches of the regulations of the province.

Their next escapade was more serious. They packed luncheon-baskets and departed, as they said, for a visit to the caves of Marequito--a permitted excursion. Then for three days they disappeared, the police were furious and anxious, and a posse was sent out in motor-cars to discover their whereabouts. Six of the party--five girls and a man--and one of the cars were found two hundred miles off in a valley under the high peaks called the Spanish Ladies. They told a pitiful story; they had lost their road, exhausted their food, and had had to spend chilly nights on the ground. The other car had gone off the day before to find supplies, and had not returned.

The inspector of police wrung his hands. "Do you not know that in these parts the natives are dangerous? You have narrowly escaped throat-cutting." The party was sent back to the city in disgrace, but they did not seem to feel their position. They were inordinately cheerful and scarcely looked as if they had suffered a three days' fast.

In spite of the police activity no word came of the other car, till two days later it returned brazenly of its own accord The occupants told the same story--a lost road, a breakdown, semi-starvation, a lucky meeting in the end with an intelligent vaquero who put them on the way to the San Tome mine. This party did indeed show some signs of privation and one of the four men had his arm in a sling, the result he said, of a fall from a rock when he was trying to get a prospect.

There was a stern inquiry at the office of the Commissary and the four were closely cross-examined about their journey. But they proved to be bewildered and obtuse. Their accounts conflicted, and when maps were placed before them they were quite unable to point out their route. "Can't you realise that we were lost?" they repeated, "lost like a tick in a wood-pile? What d'you keep worrying about? It's no good quoting lists of your darned hills! We can't locate them."

After this episode the American party showed better behaviour. For the last days of their stay they confined themselves to the city, and got up a fancy-dress ball in the Regina, into which they dragged some of the unwilling residents. The young man with his arm in a sling did not appear at this function; indeed he did not leave his room, being a little fevered--so he told the hotel servants--by accident, though he refused to see a doctor. This was perhaps natural, for in the small hours after his return there had been some rough surgery in his bedroom. One of his companions had cut out a pistol bullet from above his left elbow, and the tall girl, who had once nursed in a hospital, had done the bandaging.

Archie and Janet were very different visitors. It almost appeared as if they were welcome ones. A special coach was attached for them to the Santa Ana train, and this was shunted on to the Gran Seco line. It contained two compartments, in one of which they were given excellent meals, while the other was on the lines of an observation car, so filled with bridal flowers that Archie looked anxiously about for rice and slippers. They were also given a guide, a well-mannered young Olifero who unobtrusively offered information. He pointed out the objects of interest on the way to Santa Ana, and during the hour of waiting there: conducted them over the cathedral, which has a famous altar-piece, and, under the great crucifix, told with pride the tale of the first Conquistadors. The long climb into the Gran Seco was enlivened by his anecdotes. He showed them the valley where Toledo's men had been ambushed by Indians, the corner where the copper convoy had once been destroyed by a landslide, the gully which had long defied the railway engineers. At the frontier station he had managed their passes for them, and as the train crawled on to the plateau had sketched for them vivaciously the history of the mining industry.

"We can't tip this fellow," Archie whispered to Janet. "He's a gentleman." And his wife had agreed.

He saw them to their hotel, where rooms had been secured or them by the Administration. On parting, Archie and Janet warmly thanked him, and asked him his name. The young man smiled pleasantly. "That is nice of you, for I think we shall meet again. They call me Carlos Rivero." He added, "I am a friend of Luis de Marzaniga," and it seemed to Archie that his eyes said something confidential which he could not fathom.

The Moplahs were in the hotel, but in a somewhat hastened mood. The tall girl, whom Janet believed she had recognised, did not appear, nor did the young man in the starched linen knickerbockers, though Archie looked for him longingly. But the corybants of the Club de Residentes Extranjeros were there and greeted them with boisterous friendliness, though, somewhat to Janet's surprise, they did not invite them to join their party.

In any case that would have been impossible, for the newcomers found a complex programme provided for their entertainment. They had no occasion to hire a car: the Administration provided one, a neat Daimler limousine which at all hours waited on their convenience. They were shown every phase of the great industry, and the day after their arrival they lunched with the Administration. The Gobernador himself appeared at the meal, an honour which, it was hinted, was almost unexampled. He apologised for the absence of the Vice-President, the same who had been made to blush by the Moplahs. "My colleague," he said, "sends his profound apologies, but at the moment he is suffering from a slight attack of jaundice. He deeply regrets that he cannot be here to welcome you, for he has many friends in your country and in Europe. He is of Mexico, and a Mexican is like a Russian--his country is so remote from the life of the world that he must needs adopt all countries. He is the true international."

The meal was a Spartan one compared, to the banquet at the President's mansion, but the food was perfectly cooked and, for a place in the heart of wild hills, extraordinarily varied. The company were all grave, pallid, perfectly mannered, with expressionless eyes and no gestures--what Don Alejandro had called the type Gran Seco. There was nothing of the hustling liveliness which Archie associate with a luncheon of commercial magnates. Also all seemed to be in awe of their President, and hung on his lips. Castor talked indeed, brilliantly and continuously, but it was a monologue, and he went through a series of subjects, adorning each and then dropping it. There was none of the give-and-take of good conversation. Yet the time passed pleasantly, and when they rose from table Castor offered to show them his office.

It was on the first floor of the main building, lit by four large windows, into which travellers on the top of the tram-cars could look and see the great man at his work.

Here there was no seclusion or mystery. The big bright chambers gave its occupant no more privacy than an aviary gives a bird, for not only could it be looked into from the street, but at one end was a glass partition separating it inadequately from a room full of busy secretaries. There were maps and plans of the Gran Seco on the walls, a complicated mechanism of desk telephones, a bookcase full of mining reports, an immense safe, a cigar cabinet--and that was all. It might have been the office of a real-estate agent in a provincial town in the United States or Canada.

The contrast between Castor's personality and his modest habitation was so startling that Janet laughed.

The Gobernador seemed to understand her feelings. "I have other lairs," he said, smiling. "One, much grander, is in Olifa, and I have my rooms too in Paris and London. But this is my true workshop."

He opened a door, which revealed a tiny bedroom and bathroom.

"Compact, is it not?" he said. "I need no more. I am a simple man."

That night Archie and Janet dined in the hotel with the Financial Secretary, and afterwards went to hear Beethoven performed by a string quartet in the music-room of the Gran Seco Club. When they returned to their apartments, Archie was loud in his praises of his hosts.

"Odd, isn't it? to find Castilian manners in business grandees! We didn't find them at Veiro, for old Sanfuentes was just like the ordinary country gentleman at home. But these fellows here are all hidalgos. I feel noisy and rather vulgar among them. And, good Lord! what must they think of the Moplahs?

"Castor too!" he went on. "What rot it was Gedd and Wilbur making him out a mystery man! He's an extraordinarily clever fellow, but as open as the day. A mystery man couldn't live in a place like a cricket pavilion!"

"Did you ever read a poem called 'How it strikes a Contemporary'? Browning, you know."

"No," said Archie.

"Well, the poem is all about a tremendous mystery man--the Corregidor, Browning calls him--and he lived in just such a way as Mr Castor. How does it go?--

"'Poor man, he lived another kind of life In that new stuccoed third house by the bridge, Fresh-painted, rather smart than otherwise! The whole street might o'erlook him as he sat Leg crossing leg--and--'

"I can't remember it all, but anyhow he played cribbage every night with his housekeeper and went to bed punctually at ten."

Their permit for the Gran Seco had specified no time-limit. For two days they explored the details of the industry, were conducted through vast laboratories, studied the latest types of furnace and converter, pored over blue prints in offices and gave themselves vile headaches. Archie declared that the smelting works were like the Ypres Salient after a gas attack. He tried to be intelligent, but found himself gravely handicapped by his lack of all scientific knowledge. "I have had the meaning of a reverberatory furnace explained to me a dozen times," he complained, "but I'm hanged if I can keep it in my head. And what Bessemerising is remains to me one of Allah's secrets. It's no good, Janet, this isn't my pidgin. Thank God, we're going to the Mines to-morrow. I think that should be more in my line."

They were taken to the Mines through a sad grey country a desert of shale and rock. "Calcined," Archie called it, having just acquired that word, and Janet said that she supposed it must be like the landscapes in the moon. Every stream-course was bone-dry, and the big dams they passed, with the green water very low in their beds, only accentuated the desiccation. Yet, where wells had been sunk, the soil was not without fertility, and the thin grasses seemed give a living to considerable flocks of sheep and goats. They passed many ruins--not only old mine workings, but the remains of Indian villages, which suggested that at of time the Gran Seco had been a more habitable country.

At the Mines they were shown little, for there was little time. Managers were ready with sheafs of statistics, and at the Universum they lunched luxuriously. But of the miners at work they saw nothing. They returned invigorated by the keen air of the steppes, and Archie, who had caught from a ridge a glimpse of the snowy peaks of the Spanish Ladies, had had his appetite whetted for further travel. But the Administration was not encouraging. That was all Indian country--policed, it was true, for it was the chief recruiting-ground of labour, but not open to ordinary travel. "We could send you there," said an urbane secretary, "but you would have to take an escort, and you would have to submit to be treated like a schoolboy. You will understand, Sir Archibald, that this Gran Seco of ours is in parts a delicate machine, and the presence of ever so little extraneous matter might do harm."

That evening after dinner Janet and Archie were in their sitting-room. The Regina was full of the preparations for departure of the Moplahs, who were going down-country by the night train, and their shrill cries could be heard in the corridor, since their rooms were on the same floor.

"We're extraneous matter here," said Archie. "What about it, Janet? They've given us a very good show, but I'm disillusioned about the Gran Seco. Wilbur must have been pulling my leg. The place is as humdrum as the Potteries, and just about as ugly. I should have liked to have had a shot at the high mountains, but I can see their reason for not encouraging visitors in their labour reserve. I rather like the crowd--they behave well and they must be the last word in efficiency...Confound those Moplahs! This is like living beside a hencoop!"

Janet looked serious, and, as was her way in such a mood, she sat with her hands idle in her lap. "Let's get away from this place," she said. "I hate it!"

"Why in the world...?"

"I hate it. Those soft-spoken, solemn men have got on my nerves. I think there's something inhuman about them. Most of the faces of the people at the smelting works and at the Mines were like masks...And at that awful luncheon!...I believe that sometimes I saw the devil grinning out from behind them...And in the streets. I saw one or two villainous ruffians, who should have been in rags, but were as spruce as bagmen. I felt as if I were in an orderly and well-policed Hell...Why did they shepherd us away from the Mines, for remember we saw nothing there? Why won't they let us go into the back country? I believe it is because they are concealing something, something so bad that the world must never know of it."

Archie stared.

"I must say you've got a lively imagination," he began, but Janet was not listening.

"Let us go away--at once--to-morrow morning. I should like to be going to-night...Ring up the Administration and say we must get home in a hurry...I think there's something infernal about this big, noiseless machine. I want to be back at Veiro, where there are human beings. I want to be with the honest silly little Moplahs. I want something more peaceful..."

"I should have thought that the Gran Seco was more peaceful than the Moplahs."

"No, it isn't, for there is death here, and death is unsettling."

"Well, we'll go off to-morrow, if you wish it. We're not likely to want for peace in the next few weeks. The thing is how to avoid boredom...By the way, oughtn't we to go downstairs and say good-bye to the Americans? They're friendly souls."

But Janet was in a strange mood. "You go. I don't think I'll come." She still sat with her hands in her lap, looking straight before her.

But the Americans were already packed into the station omnibus, and Archie could only shout to them from the doorway, and receive in return blown kisses from the ladies and hand-waves from the men. They seemed to be waiting for a member of their party, and as Archie turned into the hall he met the laggard charging through the crowd of waiters and porters. It was the one who had not yet shown himself, and Archie realised that it must be the driver of the car in the Avenida de la Paz, the youth in the linen knickerbockers. What his present clothes were could not be guessed, since he wore a tweed ulster, but he had the same preposterous, broad-brimmed hat on his head.

To his surprise the young man, whom he had never met, made straight for him, and gave him his hand. Something passed from it, and Archie's fist held a crumpled paper.

The next second he was gone, but not before Archie had had another shock. For this was not the youth of the Avenida de la Paz. It was Don Luis de Marzaniga, and in their moment of contact his eyes had looked into his and they had commanded silence.

Deeply mystified, Archie went upstairs with the paper held tight in his fingers. When his door closed behind him, opened it. The scrap contained a scrawl in pencil in a large, irregular hand. It read: "Please be both in your sitting-room at eleven o'clock."

He showed it to Janet.

"I said there was no mystery in the Gran Seco, but it seems I spoke too soon. I'm hanged if I can make it out. It was Luis that gave me this paper, but it was Luis pretending to be that American lad in the linen knickerbockers. You remember he was the one of the Moplahs we never saw."

"We never saw the tall girl either. I am positive that she was Miss Dasent." Janet looked at her wrist-watch. "Eleven, the note said. A quarter of an hour to wait."

That quarter of an hour was spent by Janet in the same contemplative immobility, while Archie tried to read, smoked two cigarettes feverishly, and occupied a few minutes in washing his hands. The bedroom opened from the sitting-room, and beyond it was the bathroom which he used as a dressing-room. He was just about to begin a third cigarette when he saw that the hands of the sham ormolu clock on the mantelpiece pointed to eleven. After that he kept his eyes on the door which led to the corridor.

But that door did not open. It was an exclamation from Janet that made him turn his head.

A waiter had appeared suddenly, entering from the bedroom. He carried a tray with three cups of mate, which he placed on the table at Janet's elbow.

"Look here, you've made a mistake," Archie said in his halting Spanish. "We gave no orders."

The man replied in English. "Didn't you? All the same, you'd be the better for cup. I'm going to have one myself. You might lock the door, Archie, and give me a cigarette."

While Archie stared thunderstruck, Janet laughed--a laugh which began as a low gurgle and ended in riotous merriment. She rose from her chair and stood before the waiter, her shoulders shaking, while she dabbed her small handkerchief on her eyes. Then, suddenly, she became grave. "You have been having a rough time. Sandy," she said, and she laid a hand on his shoulder. He winced, and drew back.

"So--so," he said. "That arm is still tender...What malign fate brought the pair of you here?"

The waiter was to all appearance an ordinary mestizo, sallow-skinned, with shaggy dark hair, handsome after a fashion because of his pleasant eyes. He wore ill-fitting dress trousers, a shirt not too clean, a short alpaca jacket and slippers rather down at heel. He smiled on Janet as he poured out the mate, and then from Archie's case took a cigarette.

"Yes. I want to know just how you managed it," continued. "Wilbur did his best to prevent you, and Luis told me he thought he had dissuaded you, and in spite of everything you bubble up. You're an incorrigible pair!"

"But why shouldn't we come here if we want?" Janet asked.

"Because it's deadly danger--for yourselves and for others. You go to lunch with the Administration, and the Vice-President hears of it just in time to have a touch of jaundice. You blunder into this hotel, and I can only save myself by making this assignation. You two innocents have been complicating my life."

Enlightenment broke in on Archie. "You were the bounder in the linen bags--the fellow that drove the car."

"I was. You were within an ace of recognising me, if I hadn't tilted my hat."

"Then what was Luis doing, got up in your rig?"

"He took my passport. This is a country of passports, you know, much more efficient than anything we had in the war zone in France. He came into the Gran Seco by a back door, and so didn't require one. But it was essential that mine should be used and that I should be believed to be out of the place. It was equally essential that I should remain here."

"How did you manage your present camouflage?"

The waiter looked down with pride at his spotty shirt.

"Rather successful, isn't it? I have a bit of a graft in this line. My weeks in the Cafe de l'Enfer were not altogether wasted."

He finished his mate and lit a cigarette. He looked at the two before him, Janet with her girlish wind-blown grace, Archie with his puzzled honesty, and he suddenly ceased to be a waiter. His brows bent, and his voice from friendly banter became the voice of authority.

"You must clear out at once," he said. "Tomorrow morning. Do you know that you are walking gaily on a road which is mined in every yard?"

"I knew it," said Janet. "I felt in my bones that this place was accursed."

"You don't know it. You cannot know just how accursed it is, and I have no time to explain. What I have to tell you is that you must go down to Olifa to-morrow morning. You will be encouraged to stay longer, but you must refuse."

"But look here, Sandy "--it was Archie who spoke--"they have nothing against us. Janet and I can't be in my danger."

"No, but you are a source of danger to others. Myself, for example, and the Vice-President, Senor Rosas."

"Rosas--I never heard of him."

"A very pleasant Mexican gentleman. You once knew him as Mr Blenkiron."

"Good Lord! But he's dead!"

"He is officially dead. That is why it won't do for him to meet old friends."

"Sandy dear," said Janet, "you mustn't treat us like this. We're not babies. We'll do what you tell us, but we deserve more confidence."

The waiter compared his Ingersoll watch with the sham ormolu clock.

"Indeed, you do, but the story would take hours, and I have only three minutes left. But I will tell you one thing. Do you remember my showing you at Laverlaw the passage in the chronicle about the Old Man of the Mountain, the King of the Assassins, who lived in the Lebanon, and doped his followers with hashish and sent them about the world to do his errands? Well, that story has a counterpart to-day."

"Mr Castor!" Janet exclaimed. "Archie liked him, but I felt that he might be a devil."

"A devil! Perhaps. He is also a kind of saint, and he is beyond doubt a genius. You will know more about him some day."

"But you are sending us away...Sandy, I won't have it. We are too old friends to be bundled off like stray dogs from a racecourse. You are in some awful pickle and we must help."

"I am sending you away," said the waiter gravely, "because I want your help--when the time comes. There's another woman in this business, Janet, and I want you to be with her. I want you both. I pay you the compliment of saying that I can't do without you. You will go back to Olifa to the Hotel de la Constitucion, and you will make friends with an American girl there. She is expecting you and she will give you your instructions."

"I know," said Janet. "She is Mr Blenkiron's niece--a Miss Dasent. What is her Christian name?"

The waiter looked puzzled. "I'm afraid I don't know. I never asked her."

VII

The waiter at the Regina was an exemplary servant. He dispensed the morning meal of fruit and coffee with soft-footed alacrity. At the mid-day dejeuner, when it was the custom of the Company's officials, including some of the greatest, to patronise the hotel, he had the big round table in the north window, and in a day or two had earned the approval of his fastidious clients. Miguel was his name, and presently he was addressed by it as if he had been an old feature of the establishment. Those solemn gentlemen talked little, and at their meals they did not ransack the wine-list or summon the cook, but each had his little peculiarities of taste which Miguel made it his business to remember. He was always at their elbow, smiling gravely, to anticipate their wants. In the evening the restaurant was less full, only the guests living in the hotel and a few junior officials, for it was the custom of the magnates to dine at the club. In the evening Miguel was frequently off duty in the restaurant, engaged in other branches of hotel work, and twice a week he had his time after 7 p.m. to himself.

The waiter did not spend his leisure hours in his attic bedroom, which was like an oven after the sun had beat all day on the slatted roof. Once or twice he joined his fellow-employees in a visit to the cinema or to a shabby little gaming-room where one drank cheap aguardiente and played a languid kind of poker. But generally he seemed to have business of his own, and the negro porter at the back entrance grew familiar with his figure arriving punctually on the stroke of midnight, and chaffed him heavily about an imaginary girl. It was no one's business to keep watch on this humble half-caste, whose blood showed so dearly in his shadowy finger-nails and dull yellow skin, But if he had been followed, curious things might have been noted...

He generally made for a new block of flats on the edge of the dry hollow which separated the smelting works from the city, and he frequently varied his route thither. This place, with its concrete stairs and white-washed walls, was not unlike a penitentiary, but it housed many of the work engineers and foremen. He would stop at a door on the third landing, consult his watch as to the hour, wait a minute or two, and then knock, and he was instantly admitted Thence he would emerge in half an hour, generally accompanied by someone, and always in a new guise. Sometime he was a dapper Olifero clerk with a spruce collar and an attache case; sometimes in rough clothes with big spectacles so that his former half-caste air disappeared, and he might have been an engineer from Europe; sometimes a workman indistinguishable from an ordinary hand in the furnaces. He always returned to the same door about half past eleven, and issued from it once more the waiter at the Regina.

Between the hours of 7.30 and 11 p.m. the waiter seemed to have a surprising variety of duties. Occasionally he would pass the evening in one of the flats, or in a room in another block which adjoined the costing department. There he would meet silent people who slipped in one by one, and the conversation would be in low tones. Maps and papers would lie on the table, and there would be much talk of the names on certain lists, and notes would be pencilled alongside them. Sometimes there would be a colloquy on one or two, and then the waiter would do most of the talking--but not in Spanish. Sometimes the meeting would be at a cafe in a back street, which could only be entered by devious ways, and there, over glasses of indifferent beer, the waiter would make new acquaintances. His manners were odd, for he would regard these newcomers as sergeant regards recruits, questioning them with an air of authority. There were strange ceremonies on these occasions, so that the spectator might have thought them meetings of some demented Masonic lodge. Sometimes, the waiter in one of the rooms of the big block of flats would meet a figure with the scorched face of a countryman and the dust of the hills on his clothes--often in the dour form of the Mines Police and once or twice dressed like mestizo farmer. Then the talk would be hard to follow--strings of uncouth names, torrents of excited description, and a perpetual recourse to maps.

But the waiter's most curious visits--and they happened only twice during his time at the Regina--were to a big house behind the Administration Headquarters, which stood in what for the Gran Seco was a respectable garden. At such times the waiter became the conventional clerk, very dapper in a brown flannel suit, yellow boots, and a green satin tie with a garnet pin. He was evidently expected, for, on giving his name, he was admitted without question, and taken to a little room on the first floor which looked like the owner's study. "Senor Garcia from the Universum"--thus he was ushered in, and the occupant greeted him gruffly with "Come along, Garcia. Say, you're late. Have you brought the figures I asked for?"--followed by the injunction to the servant, "I can't be disturbed for the next two hours, so I guess you'd better disconnect the telephone. If anyone calls, say I'm mighty busy."

Then the occupant of the room would lock the door and pay some attention to the windows, after which he would greet the waiter like a long-lost brother. He was a big man, with a sallow face but a clear healthy eye--a man who looked as if he would have put on flesh but for some specially arduous work which kept him thin. He would catch the so-called Garcia by the shoulder as if he would hug him, then he would pat his back, and produce such refreshments is are not usually offered to a junior clerk. Strangely enough, there would be no mention of the awaited figures from the Universum.

"How much longer can you stick it?" he asked on the second occasion. "You're looking peaked."

"I've another week here. Then I break for the open. I doubt if I could keep it up for more than a week, for people are asking questions. Have you squared it with old Josephs and notified the Universum people?"

The big man nodded. "But after that you're beyond my jurisdiction. Peters in the Police is prepared for you, but it's up to you to slip over to him without exciting comment. The cook-boy at the Universum has got to perish. Can you manage that neatly?"

"I'll try. I'll have to do a lot of perishing in the next fortnight, before Luis picks me up. I'm terrified of going sick, you know. The Regina hasn't done me any good, and the Tierra Caliente isn't exactly a health-resort."

The other looked at him with affectionate anxiety.

"That's too bad...I haven't an easy row to hoe, but yours is hell with the lid off, and the almighty vexation is that I can't do much to help you. Just at present the game's with you. For the love of Mike keep on your feet, sonnie. You don't mean to go far into the Poison Country?"

"Not a yard farther than I can help. But Luis says I must be at least a couple of days there. Don't worry. I'll take care of myself."

After that the conversation was conducted in low tones, as if even the locked door and the guarded window might have ears. But had that talk been overheard, one phrase would have puzzled the eavesdropper, a phrase which constantly recurred and was spoken by both with a certain hesitation, even in that secret room. It was "Los Patios de la Manana," which, being translated, means "The Courts of the Morning." It might have been a mere password, or the name of some authority to which the speaker was subject, or a poetic description of a place. Most likely the last, for a map was produced--an amateur map neatly drawn and coloured, inscribed not with names but with letters. It showed steep gradients, so it must have referred to some mountain district.

At their parting the Roylances were mentioned. "They're back in Olifa," said the big man, "and Babs is looking after them good and sure. I'm mighty relieved that Babs has got a wise lady to keep her company. You're certain you can make use of Sir Archibald?"

"I can use him right enough," was the answer; "if he'll stay quiet on the ice till I want him."

A week later the waiter Miguel was seen no more at the Regina. When the occupants of the big table in the north window inquired of M. Josephs, the proprietor, as to his absence, they were told that he had been lent to the mess at the Universum Mine.

Miguel was four days at the Universum. He had a variety of tasks, for not only did he wait at table in the big adobe mess-room, but he lent a hand in the kitchen, for he was the soul of friendliness. Indeed he carried his willingness too far, for he was found in the kitchens of the compounds, where the Indian miners were fed like pigs at troughs, and was peremptorily ordered back. He had little leisure these days, but he managed to do various things not quite within the sphere of his duties. For one thing, he became intimate with the engineering staff, which contained two Scots, one American, and three Italians, and he used to gossip with them at their table when the room emptied at the end of meals. Also he was found sometimes in their office among blue prints and specimens of ore, and on these occasions the door happened to be locked. If he was not permitted inside the compounds, he used to fossick about the mines themselves, when the shifts of sallow, hollow-eyed labourers were going up or down. Occasionally he talked to them when no overseer was at hand, and he seemed to know something of their patois, for they replied, furtively, and once or twice volubly, when no one was looking.

The cheerful inquisitiveness of the mess waiter was his undoing. For on the evening of the fourth day there was a sad accident. Through a mysterious blunder a small packet of bentonite was detonated, and a corner of the compound wall was blown down and a great crater made in the earth. For some inexplicable reason Miguel seemed to have been in the neighbourhood at the time and he was the only casualty. Fragments of his clothing were found, and a bit of a hat which he was known to be wearing, and it was assumed that his remains were dispersed among the two acres of debris. The fatality was duly reported to the administration and to M. Josephs, and the agreeable half-caste waiter ceased to be on the register of the Gran Seco.

Next morning a certain Featherstone Peters, a captain of the Mines Police, whose station was ten miles or so from the Universum, introduced at breakfast to his troopers a new recruit, who had just arrived to report. Peters was a tough, grizzled fellow of fifty, who had fought for the Boers in the South African War, had been in the Macedonian gendarmerie, and was believed by his friends to have done a good deal of gunrunning in Morocco. The new recruit, whose name was Black, was a sallow young man, who looked as if he had fever in his blood. He spoke English fluently but ungrammatically, and gave out that his father had been in the Italian Consulate at Alexandria. He was good company, and entertained the men with yarns which enthralled even that collection of hard citizens.

For the next week Black was engaged on patrols far into the Indian country. The map shows that east of the city of Gran Seco lies the land of rolling desert hills where the copper is mined, but beyond that the traveller enters a region of deep-cut desiccated valleys--a plateau, but with the contours of highlands. It is the Indian territory, where the Mines' labourers are drawn, a place of sparse tillage but much pasturage, a place, too, which in recent centuries has been drying up, since the wretched pueblas are often the site of what, from the ruins, must once have been considerable cities. It is called the Tierra Caliente, for there is little shade from a merciless sun, and the stages are long from water to water. The midday heat falls like a suffocating curtain, and does not lift till night arrives with the speed of a wind from the far snows.

It was patrol not escort duty, but the new recruit saw many of his fellow-policemen engaged in the latter task. The processions of labourers had the melancholy of funeral cortege, and Black, who was well-read for one his position, was reminded of the pictures of the Zanzibar slave-caravans in old books of African travel. It was a sight which visitors to the Gran Seco were not allowed see, for there were no permits for the Indian country. The gangs bound for the Mines were not shackled, but they were closely shepherded by armed police escorts, and the faces of the men showed every degree of sullen and hopeless ferocity. But the gangs returning from the Mines to the villages were a spectacle to send a man to his prayers.

"Returned empties," Peters called them. Young men crawled and tottered like dotards, all were terribly emaciated, their eyes had lost every human quality and had the blank impassiveness of beasts. Yet the Mines were a business concern, famed for feeding their workers well and for utilising the latest scientific conclusions on hygiene and industrial fatigue. Had not the intelligent press of America and Europe borne testimony to their progressiveness?

As Black and Peters watched one gang pass, the latter spat vigorously and observed: "I've never taken stock in all that meeting-house stuff about individual liberty and the rights of man. But I guess there may be something in it. That outfit kind of makes one think."

Black said nothing, but his bright feverish eyes seemed to miss little. He was obviously on good terms with his officer, for he was constantly going off on little journeys of his own, which could scarcely be interpreted as police duty.

These journeys took him generally into the Indian pueblas, and on two occasions he did not return to the police bivouac all the following day. He was obviously a sick man, and when the patrol reached the limit of its journey, Peters was heard to complain loudly that the new recruit should be in hospital. By this time they were nearing the eastern ridge of the Indian country, with the peaks of the Cordilleras within a day's march. The land was changing, for they had come to a watershed. The line of the great mountains was not the watershed, for, as in the case of the Nepaul Himalaya, they stood a little beyond it. It was a country of running waters, and the streams flowed east, cutting a path through the range in deep gorges on their way to the distant Orazon.

They arrived at a ruined village of mud where a couple of Indians had made their camp-hunters they seemed, tall active fellows of a different stamp from the broken men if the pueblas. Peters appeared to know them, for he called them by their names, and addressed them in pidgin Spanish which they understood. That night he told his troopers that the patrol was ended. He had been instructed to report on this eastern frontier of the Gran Seco, and next morning they would turn back. All to the east, he told them, was a God-forgotten country, which nature and man had combined to make unhealthy for Christians. He asked questions of the Indians and expounded their replies. There was fever there, and much poison, and very bad men, and valleys so deep that from the bottom one could see by day the stars and the moon. The troopers were impressed, and looked anxiously at the menacing mountain wall, with its coronal of snowfields now rosy in the after-glow.

But next morning Black was in no state to travel. Peters condemned the cussedness of things and declared that he could not afford to wait another hour. He was not unkind, and he did his best to ease the sufferer, but duty was duty and his called him back to headquarters. Black must be made as comfortable as possible, and the two Indians, whom he knew to be trustworthy, would look after him till the bout of fever had passed, and put him on his way home.

After breakfast the patrol jingled off up the slope, and left Black wrapped in a foxskin kaross, drowsing in a corner of the ruins, while the Indians twenty yards off sat hunched and meditative beside their brushwood fire.

Black was really sick, but not with malaria. His vitality had run down like a clock, since too much had been demanded of it, and his trouble was partly a low nervous fever, and partly a deep fatigue. When the police had been gone an hour, the two Indians held a consultation on his case. Then they proceeded to strange remedies. They seemed to be friends of his, for he grinned when they bent over him and submitted readily to their ministrations. This country was volcanic, and close at hand, hidden in a crinkle of the hills, a hot sulphur spring bubbled from the rocks, They undressed him, and carried him, wrapped in the kaross to the pool, where they plunged him into the most violent bath which he had ever encountered. Then they dried him roughly with a fine leather poncho, and rubbed the skin of his back and chest with an aromatic ointment. After that one of them massaged him for the space of an hour, a cunning massage which seemed to remould flaccid muscles and adjust disordered nerves and put him into a state of delicious stupor. Lastly, he was given a bitter brew to drink, and then permitted to sleep. This he proceeded to do for eighteen hours, and when he awoke in broad daylight the following morning his head was cool and his eye was clear, though he was still shaky on his feet. Peters had left enough provisions, and he ate the first enjoyable meal he had known for weeks.

There was another figure at breakfast, a fair young man with a golden brown skin, who, judging by the dust on his boots and breeches, had ridden far that morning.

"My felicitations, Senor," the newcomer said. "I do not think you have taken any hurt in the last weeks, and that is a miracle. But where we are now going we must go on our feet, and for that you are not yet able. I am in command for the moment, and my orders are that to-day you rest."

So Black slept again and awoke in the afternoon with a most healthy hunger. The newcomer sat by him and rolled and smoked many cigarettes, but he would not permit his patient to talk. "Time enough, my friend. We do not part company for a little while. But I will show you this to cheer you."

He exhibited a small tinsel medal, such as humble pilgrims purchase at some famous shrine. On one side it wore a face which was clearly that of the Gobernador of the Gran Seco.

Black puzzled over it, for he was still dazed, and asked whose was the head.

"It is that of our noble leader," the young man laughed. "Yours and mine--he who is to lead this unhappy people to freedom."

Black seemed to see the obscure joke, for he too laughed. "Jesucristo!" said the young man, "but that is a chief to fight for!"

VIII

Black slept soundly all night, and next morning rose renewed in body and mind. The party set out down the glen of the stream, one of the Indians carrying food and blankets while the other remained behind with the horses. Black held his pistol, but he had left his police carbine at the bivouac while the newcomer had no weapon at all. "What do want with a gun?" he had said lightly in reply to his companion's question. "We are going into the Poison Country--El Pais de Venenos--where lead and powder are trivial things. A gun is of as little use as a single lifebelt would be to a man proposing to cross the Atlantic in a skiff. We are now in the hands of the older gods."

It was a strange land which they entered, when the stream which they were descending plunged into the shadow of high peaks. It was fed by many affluents, and presently became a considerable river, running in a broad grassy on which the dew lay like hoar-frost. Suddenly the hills closed in like a wall, and the stream leaped in a great spout into a profound ravine, where in pot-holes and cascade it poured its way from shelf to shelf of the mountain ribs. The sides of the glen were cloaked with bush, which in the lower levels became tall timber trees. In the woody recesses the freshness went out of the air, mosses and creepers muffled the tree-trunks, gaudy birds and butterflies flitted through the branches, and a hot, headachy languor seemed to well out of the sodden ground.

The party, guided by the Indian, kept high above stream, following paths no wider than a fox's track. As they advanced they descended, the ravine opened, and from a promontory they looked into a great cup among the cliffs brimming with forest, with above on the periphery the hard bright line of the snows. Black, who was apparently something of a scholar, quoted Latin. It was a sight which held the two men breathless for a moment. Then Luis shook his head. "It is beautiful, but devilish," he said. "The malevolence rises like a fog," and Black nodded assent.

They found themselves in an eerie world, as if they were trunk deep in a hot sea. Moisture streamed from every twig and blade and tendril, and a sickening sweetness, like the decaying vegetation of a marsh, rose from whatever their feet crushed. Black remarked that it was like some infernal chemist's shop. Under the Indian's direction they took curious precautions. Each man drew on leather gauntlets which strapped tight on the wrist. Each shrouded his face id neck with what looked like a fine-meshed mosquito-curtain. Also they advanced with extreme caution. The Indian would scout ahead, while the other two waited in the sweltering vapour-bath. Then he would return and lead them by minute tracks, now climbing, now descending, and they followed blindly, for in that steaming maze there was neither prospect nor landmark.

That there was need for caution was shown by one incident. The Indian hurriedly drew them off the trail into the cover of what looked like a monstrous cactus, and from their hiding-place they watched four men pass with the deftness of deer. Three were Indians, not of the pueblas of the Tierra Caliente, for they were tall and lean as the Shilluks of the Upper Nile. The fourth was a white man in shirt and breeches, gauntleted and hooded, and his breeches were the type worn by the Mines Police. But he was not an ordinary policeman, for, as seen under the veil, his face had the pallor and his eyes the unseeing concentration of the magnates of the Gran Seco.

Black looked inquiringly at Luis, who grinned behind his mosquito-mask. "One of the Conquistadors," he whispered, and the other seemed to understand.

In that long, torrid day the party neither ate nor drank. Just before nightfall they descended almost to the floor of the cup, where they were within hearing of the noise of the river. Here they moved with redoubled caution. Once they came out on the stream bank, and Black thought that he had never seen stranger waters. They were clear, but with purple glooms in them, and the foam in the eddies was not the spume of beaten water, but more like the bubbling of molten lead. Then they struck inland, climbed a tortuous gully, and came into a clearing where they had a glimpse of a cone of snow flaming like a lamp in the sunset.

The place was cunningly hidden, being a little mantelpiece between two precipitous ravines--on the eyebrow of a cliff, so that from below it was not suspected--and protected above by a screen of jungle. An empty hut stood there, and the Indian proceeded to make camp. A fire was lit in a corner, and water from the nearest rivulet put on to boil. It might have been a Jewish feast, for all three went through elaborate purification ceremonies. Food had been brought with them, but no morsel of it was touched till the hands of each had been washed with a chemical solution. The food-box was then sealed up again as carefully as if it were to be cached for months. The hut floor was swept, and before the bedding was laid down it was sprayed with a disinfectant. There was no window, and the door was kept tightly shut, all but a grating in it over which Luis fastened a square of thick gauze netting. The place would have been abominably stuffy but for the fact that with nightfall a chill like death had crept over the land, as if with the darkness the high snows had asserted their dominion.

Later in the night men came to the hut, silently as ghosts, brought by the Indian, who, though not of their tribe, seemed to know them and speak their tongue. They were of the same race as the three whom the travellers had encountered in the forest that afternoon and had stepped aside to avoid. Strange figures they were, lean and tall, and in the lantern light their cheek-bones stood out so sharp that their faces looked like skulls. Their eyes were not dull, like those of the Gran

Seco magnates, but unnaturally bright, an their voices had so low a pitch that their slow, soft speed sounded like the purring of cats. Luis spoke to them in their own language and translated for Black's benefit. When they had gone, he turned to his companion.

"You have seen the people of the Pais de Venenos. An interesting case of adaptation to environment? What would the scientists of Europe not give to investigate this curiosity? These men during long generations have become immune to the rankest poison in the world."

"They terrify me," said Black. "I have seen men very near to the brutes, but these fellows are uncannier than any beast. They are not inhuman, they are unnatural. How on earth did you get a graft here?"

"They have their virtues," said Luis, "and one of them is faithfulness. My graft is ancestral. Centuries ago one of my family came here and did them a service, and the memory is handed down so that only a Marzaniga can go among them. Indeed, I think that my blood has something of their immunity. I take precautions, as you see, but I do not know if in my case they are so needful."

Black asked about the poison.

"They are many," he was told. "There is poison here in earth and water, in a hundred plants, in a thousand insects, in the very air we breathe. But the chief is what they call astura--the drug of our friends the

Conquistadors. Once this country was guarded like a leper-settlement, so that nothing came out of it. Now, as you know, its chief product is being exploited. The Gran Seco has brought it within its beneficent civilisation."

The Indian was already asleep, and, as the two white men adjusted their blankets. Black commented on the utter stillness. "We might be buried deep under the ground," he said.

"There is no animal life in the forest," was the answer, "except insects. There are no birds or deer or even reptiles--the poison is too strong. But there is one exception. Listen!"

He held up his hand, and from somewhere in the thickets came a harsh bark, which in the silence had a horrid savagery.

"Jackal?" Black asked.

"No. That is one of our foxes. They are immune, like the men, and they hunt on the uplands above the forest where there is plenty of animal life. I think they are the chief horror of the place. Picture your English fox, with his sharp muzzle and prick ears, but picture him as big as a wolf, and a cannibal, who will rend and eat his own kind."

As Black fell asleep, he heard again the snarling bark and he shivered. It was as if the devilishness of the Poison Country had found its appropriate voice.

They stayed there for four days, and in all that time they did not move from the little mantelpiece. Every night ghosts which were men slipped out of the jungle and talked with them in the hut. Black fell ill again, with his old fever, and Luis looked grave and took the Indian aside The result was that on the third night, when the men came and Black lay tossing on his couch, there was a consultation and one of the visitors rolled in his hands a small pellet It began by being a greyish paste, but when rolled it became translucent like a flawed pearl. Black was made to swallow it, and presently fell into a torpor so deep that all the nigh Luis anxiously felt his heart-beats. But in the morning the sickness had gone. Black woke with a clear eye and a clean tongue, and announced that he felt years younger, and in the best of spirits.

"You have tasted astura," said Luis, "and that is more than I have ever done, for I am afraid. You will have no more, my friend. It cures fever, but it makes too soon its own diseases."

The four days were cloudless and very warm. The forest reeked in the sunshine, and wafts of odours drifted up to the mantelpiece, odours such as Black had never before known in nature. The place seemed a crucible in some infernal laboratory, where through the ages Natura Maligna had been distilling her dreadful potions. His dreams were bad, and they were often broken by the cry of the cannibal foxes. Horror of this abyss came on him and even Luis, who had been there before and had grown up with the knowledge of it, became uneasy as the hours passed. These days were not idle. Information was collected, and presently they had a fairly complete knowledge the methods by which those whom they called the Conquistadors worked. Then on the last night came a deluge rain, and Luis looked grave. "If this continues," he said "we may be trapped; and if we are trapped here, we shall die. Then it will be farewell to the Courts of the Morning, my friend."

But in the night the rain stopped, and at dawn they hooded and gauntleted themselves and started back. It was nightmare journey, for the track had become slime, and the queer smells had increased to a miasma. Their feet slipped, and they made shrinking contact with foetid mud and obscene plants whose pallid leaves seemed like limbs of the dead. The heat was intense, and the place was loud with the noise of swollen rivulets and the buzz of maleficent insects. Black grew very weary, but Luis would permit of no halt, and even the Indian seemed eager to get the journey over.

They did not reach their old camp till the darkness had long fallen, but the last hour was for Black like an awakening from a bad dream. For he smelt clean earth and herbage and pure water again, and he could have buried his face in the cool grass.

The next day they left the Indians behind and rode over the mountains by intricate passes farther to the south, which brought them to a long valley inclining to the south-west. Three nights later they slept in an upland meadow, and by the following evening had crossed a further pass and reached a grassy vale which looked westward to the plains. Luis pointed out a blue scarp to the north.

"That is the Gran Seco frontier," he said. "It is guarded by patrols and blockhouses, but we have outflanked them. I have brought you by a way which the Gobernador does not know--only those of my family and perhaps two others. We may relax now, for our immediate troubles are over."

They slept at a camp of vaqueros, and in the morning Black had several surprises. The first was an ancient Ford car which stood under a tarpaulin in the corner of one of the cattle-pens. The second was the change in his garb upon which Luis insisted. The uniform of the Mines Police was carefully packed in the car, and in its place he was given the cotton trousers and dark-blue shirt of an ordinary peon on the estancias. Luis drove the Ford all day through rolling savannah, with beside him a lean mestizo servant, to whom he talked earnestly, except when they halted for food at an inn or met other travellers. In the evening they came to a big hacienda, low and white, with wide corrals for cattle, and red-roofed stables which suggested Newmarket.

Half a mile from the place a girl, who had seen them approaching, cantered up to them on a young Arab mare The car slowed down, and driver and peon took off their hats.

"You are a day behind time," she said.

"Well, what about it, Miss Dasent?" It was the peon who spoke, and there was anxiety in his tone.

"Only that you have missed his Excellency the Gobernador," said the girl in her pleasant Southern voice. "He paid us a visit of ceremony yesterday, to talk about horses. Curious that he should have chosen the day you were expected. Don Mario thinks that Lord Clanroyden had better not sleep in the house. If he will get out at the gate of the cattle-yard, I will show him the way to the overseer's quarters."

IX

When Archie and Janet came down to dinner that evening at Veiro they found Don Luis de Marzaniga, a little thinner and browner than before, but spruce and composed as if he were about to dine at his Olifa club. He kissed Janet's hand, and asked Archie if he had enjoyed the weeks since his return from the Gran Seco.

"I've been obeying orders," was the answer. "There is my commander-in-chief. She'll tell you how docile I've been, and how I've never bothered her with questions, though Janet and I are sick with curiosity."

The tall girl, whose name was Barbara Dasent, smiled. "I'll testify that he has been a good boy."

She was very slim, and at first sight the delicate lines her neck and her small head gave her an air of fragility--an impression presently corrected by the vigour and grace of her movements. Her face was a classic oval, but without the classic sculptural heaviness, her dark hair clustered about her head in childish curls, her clear skin had a healthy pallor which intensified the colouring of her lips and eyes. These eyes were a miracle--deep and dark, at once brooding and kindling, as full of changes as a pool in the sunlight, and yet holding, like a pool, some elemental profundity. The lashes were long and the eyebrows a slender crescent. Janet ad crossed the room and stood beside her, and each was to the other a perfect foil. Yet, though they had no feature in common, there was an odd kinship, due perhaps to the young freedom of each, their candid regard and a certain boyish gallantry of bearing.

At dinner, under the Sanfuentes Murillo, Luis cross-examined Archie about his recent doings. It appeared that, on Miss Dasent's instructions, he had been travelling widely in the coastal flats of Olifa. He had been given introductions from the Minister of Defence, and had been the guest of several regiments, attended an infantry camp of instruction, and taken part in cavalry manoeuvres. Also he had visited various flying-stations, and had made several flights. The result was unqualified admiration.

"I can't claim to be a military pundit," he said, "but I now a first-class thing when I meet it. All I have to say that Olifa has got the most completely professional outfit have ever seen. There isn't one lesson of the Great War he hasn't learned. Her infantry tactics are the sort of thing we were feeling our way to before the Armistice. Her tanks are the latest pattern, better than anything I've seen in England, and, by Jove, she knows how to use them. Her army is mechanised to the full, but not too far, for she has the sense to see that cavalry rightly handled will never be out of date. And she has an amazing good staff, picked from up and down the earth, all as keen as mustard-like what we used to imagine the German staff to be, but less hidebound. Of course I don't know what strength she has in the way of reserves, and I can't speak of the fighting spirit, but there's no doubt she has a most efficient standing army for a nucleus. What puzzles me is why she should want anything so good when she's so secure."

Luis asked about the Air Force.

"That was the only thing with which I was a little disappointed," Archie replied. "It's extraordinarily good in the scientific way--the last word in machines and engines and all that sort of thing--but just a little lacking in life. Those chaps don't spend enough hours in the air. They've got all the theory and expert knowledge they can carry, but they haven't got as much devil as we have. Too serious, I should say. Keener about the theory than the game."

Luis had been listening closely. "You are very near the truth, Senor Roylance," he said. "We in Olifa have al that science and money can give us, but we have not enough soul. What is your English word--guts?"

"Oh, I didn't say that."

"But will say it. And it is perhaps fortunate. I would not blame my nation, for our army is not national, since its leaders are mercenaries."

"I'm still puzzled. What do you want it for? I never got any figures of man-power and reserves, but if you've an adequate shaft behind this spear-head, you've a superb fighting-machine. What do you mean to use it against?"

Luis laughed. "It is the conventional insurance premium which our rich Olifa pays. Pays carelessly and without conviction. That is why, as you truly say, our army is made up chiefly of mercenaries. We have collected the best soldiers of Europe who were out of a job. It is a police, if you choose. If a little political war came with a neighbour, Olifa would use her pretty toy and ask only that she got her money's worth...Unless, of course, it was war which touched her heart, and then she would fight the old way--with her people."

They sat late at table, Archie answering Luis's questions and illustrating his views by diagrams on the backs of envelopes. Presently Miss Dasent left the room, and on her return said something to Don Mario. He rose and the way to his sitting-room, where, according to custom a wood fire crackled on the wide hearth. The curtain, usually left untouched to reveal the luminous night, was now closely drawn. A man in a flannel suit stood with his back to the fireplace.

Janet blinked at him for a moment, and then ran up to him with both hands outstretched.

"Oh, Sandy dear, I have been miserable about you. Thank God, you're safely back. You're desperately thin. You're not ill?"

"I'm perfectly well, thank you. But I've been pushed up to the limit of my strength. It's all right. I've done it often before, you know. I only want to lie fallow for a bit. It's good to see you and Archie...I feel as if had come home."

"Are you safe here?" Janet asked anxiously.

Luis answered. "Perfectly--at present. The Gobernador must suspect something or he would not have been here yesterday. But he can know nothing. We have pickets out, and at the worst we shall get ample warning. To-night, the any rate, we can sleep sound."

"We have asked no questions," said Janet. "For the last week Archie has been behaving like the intelligent tourist, and I have been sketching in water-colours. We want to be enlightened, Sandy dear."

The man addressed--he looked very young in the dim light, for his hair had grown long and was tousled like a boy's over his forehead--flung himself into an armchair and stretched his lean shanks to the blaze. He slowly filled an old pipe and looked round at the audience--Don Mario erect and prim, Luis sprawling on a couch, Archie swinging his long legs from a corner of the table, Miss Dasent very quiet in the shadow, Janet standing on the tiger-skin rug, an incarnate note of interrogation. He looked round and laughed.

"You ask a good deal. Luis knows everything, and Miss Dasent. Don Mario knows as much as he wants to. But you two are newcomers, so I must begin from the beginning. Sit down on that stool, Janet, and, Archie, get off the table. I'm going to make a second-reading speech, as they say in your little Parliament. After that the House can go into committee...

"First of all, I need hardly tell you that the world today is stuffed with megalomania. Megalomania in politics, megalomania in business, megalomania in art--there are a dozen kinds. You have the man who wants to be a dictator in his own country, you have the man who wants to corner a dozen great businesses and control the finance of half the world, you have the man who wants to break down the historic rules of art and be a law to himself. The motive is the same in every case--rootlessness, an unbalanced consciousness of ability, and an overweening pride They want to rule the world, but they do not see that by their methods they must first deprive the world of its soul and that what would be left for their dictatorship would be an inanimate corpse. You see, for all their splendid gift they have no humour."

"What is Mr Castor's nationality?" Janet asked irrelevantly.

"He has none. He was born in Austria, and I think he has a Spanish strain in him. Blenkiron has a notion that he has English blood, too, but he cannot prove it.

The man is like Melchizedek, without apparent origin. He is what you call a weltkind, the true international."

"He has no humour," said Janet with emphasis.

"I agree. But he has most other things, and one is clear and searching mind. His strength, and also his weakness, is that he has no illusions. For one thing, he does not possess the illusion which ordinary people call a creed. He does not want to remake the world on some new fantastic pattern, like the Communists. He has none of Mussolini's arbitrary patriotism. He wants to root out various things, but I doubt if he has a preference for what should take their place. I don't profess to understand more than bits of him. He is an egotist, but in the colossal sense, for he has vanity. He considers that he has been called on to do certain things, and that he is the only man living who can. The world, as he sees it, is suffocating from the debris of democracy, and he wants to clear it away. He does not hate it, he despises it. He is the scientist and philosopher who would introduce the reign of reason and the rule of law, but first some decaying refuse called popular liberties must be destroyed. Therefore he is against Britain, but only half-heartedly, for he thinks that with us democracy is tempered by more rational instincts, and that in any case our number is up. But for America he has the unfaltering contempt which a trained athlete might have for a great, overgrown, noisy, slobbering, untrained hobbledehoy. With America it is war to the death."

"I've known other people take that view," Archie put in.

"With him it is not a view, it is a crusading passion. In Castor you have the normally passionless, scientific mind kindled to a white heat. The mischief is that he is human--not cruel, but inhuman. He will use the ordinary stuff of humanity to further his ends as ruthlessly as a furnace swallows coke. He will do any evil in order that what he considers good may come."

"That is the definition of a devil," said Janet.

"Not quite. Castor is just as near being a saint. If he had a different religion he might deserve to be beatified, for he is scrupulously loyal to what he believes to be the right. He's not evil--he just happens to have missed the human touch. He knows nothing of friendship--nor, of course, of any kind of love. His world is a narrow cell with the big dynamo of his brain purring in it. He is cruel, simply because he cannot conceive the feelings of anybody but himself, and is not interested in them. He is a master over things, and over men so long as he can treat them as things. If he were Emperor of the world I have no doubt he would be a just ruler. As it is--well, I have been seeing too much of his methods these last days to be in love with him."

He paused for a second to shake out the ashes from his pipe.

"Well, I've given you what Blenkiron would call the 'general Castor proposition'. Now, how would a man, obsessed by this idea, set about realising it? First of all, he would want money, money on a gigantic scale. He has got it in the Gran Seco. Remember, he is a very great practical engineer and chemist--Blenkiron, who should know, says the greatest in the world--and he is a first-class man of business. Second, he would want a base, and a well-camouflaged base. He has got that in the republic of Olifa. You have seen for yourselves how completely Olifa is in his power. He has changed in a few years the whole character of her governing class. He has made her Government rich and supine, and got it under his thumb. The thing is a miracle of tact and diplomacy. The Olifa ministers do not share in his secrets, they know very little of his schemes, but he has organised them as he wanted and they do his bidding without a question. Up in the Gran Seco he has his laboratory and factory, and in the State of Olifa he has his outer barrage, the decorous bourgeois republic which keeps watch at his door.

"Thirdly, he had to have his staff and his army to opera for him throughout the globe. He has got that, too--slaves who mechanically obey him. You have seen some of them in your Olifa hotel and in the Gran Seco. You have lunched with them, and Janet says that they made her flesh creep."

"The type Gran Seco," said Archie.

"The type Gran Seco. Have you any notion who they are? They look like robots, with their pallid faces and soft voices and small, precise gestures. All their individuality seems to have been smoothed away, so that they confer to one pattern. Nevertheless, they were once men of brains and character. Their brains they have kept, but the characters have been stereotyped, and they have surrendered their wills into the hand of their master. They have been most carefully selected from every nation. One or two you have known before, Archie."

"I swear I haven't."

"But you have. The Gran Seco is the port for missing ships. Men who have foundered somehow in life--respectable careerists who suddenly crash on some private vice--fellows who show the white feather--soldiers without regiments, financiers without credit--they are all there. Do you remember Lariarty, Archie? He was about your time at Eton. There was a bad scandal about him in 1915."

"Good God! Of course I do. I heard he was dead."

"He sat opposite you a few weeks ago when you lunched with the Administration. You couldn't recognise him. Everything that once was Lariarty has gone out of him, except his brain. You remember he was a clever fellow. And Romanes--the man who was in the 23rd--people said he was with the Touaregs in the Sahara. He's one of them, but I believe at the moment he is in

Europe. And Freddy Larbert, who was once a rising man in the Diplomatic Service. He did not hang himself at Bucharest, as they said he did, for to-day he is in the Gran Seco. I could mention others, and they come from every country--Russian aristocrats who were beggared and Russian revolutionists who were too clever, broken soldiers and blown-on politicians and speculators who missed their market. The Gran Seco is the true Foreign Legion, and it needs no discipline. Castor asks only for two things, brains and submission to his will, and once a man enters his service he can never leave it."

"Why?" Archie asked.

"Because he does not want to. Because the Gran Seco is his only home and away from it he is lost. I told you that Castor was like the Old Man of the Mountain in the chronicle I showed you at Laverlaw. There is nothing new under the sun. Castor rules his initiates as the old ruffian in the Lebanon ruled his Assassins. You remember he gave them hashish, so that their one desire was to get their job in the outer world finished and return to the Lebanon to dream. Castor has the same secret. As I have told you, he is a mighty chemist, and this continent is the home of drugs. One in particular is called astura and is found in what they call the Pais de Venenos, the Poison Country in the eastern mountains. The secret of it was lost for ages till he revived it, and, except as a legend in the Marzaniga family, it was unknown in Olifa. This astura is deadly poison, but it can used in two ways as a drug. In one preparation it takes the heart out of a man, but gives him increased physical strength, till suddenly he cracks and becomes doddering. That preparation Castor uses to turn out docile labourers for the mines. He gets marvellous results in output, and the reports say that it is due to his scientific management and his study of industrial fatigue, but we know better. The other preparation does not apparently weaken the bodily strength, though it alters the colour of the skin and the look in the eyes. But it is a most potent mental stimulant, and its addicts tend to live for the next dose. It kills in the end, but only after a considerable period, and during that period it gives increased intellectual vitality and an almost insane power of absorption, varied by languors like the opium-eater's. Those who once take to it can never free themselves, and they are the slaves of him who can supply it. Willing slaves, competent slaves, even happy slaves, but only the shadows of what once were men. Lariarty and Romanes and Larbert and others are among the initiates. They go about the world on Gran Seco business and they do Castor's will as little wheels obey a master-wheel. They have a name for their brotherhood. They call themselves the new Conquistadors--conquerors, you see, over all the old standards and decencies of human nature."

Archie inquired what precisely they did in their journeys about the world. He had rumpled his hair, and his eyes looked as if he were painfully adjusting a manifold of experience in the light of a new idea.

"First of all, they make money. They are the most efficient bagmen alive. For the rest, they break down things and loosen screws, and they have unlimited funds at their disposal, for Castor spends nearly as fast as he earns...No, no. Not Bolshevism. The donkeys in Moscow have in a sense played Castor's game, but they were far too crude for him, and to-day I fancy he finds them rather a nuisance. By their folly they are creating a reaction in favour of that democracy which he hates...Remember, I don't know him. I've seen him, but have never spoken to him. I can only speak at second-hand of his methods, but I'll give you Blenkiron's summary. Blenkiron says that half a century ago Abraham Lincoln fought a great war to prevent democracy making a fool of itself. He says that Castor's object is just the opposite--he wants to encourage democracy to make a fool of itself, to inflate the bladder till it bursts...His instruments? The press, for one thing. He has a mighty grip on that. The politicians, too, and every kind of fool organisation for boost and uplift. You'd be amazed to learn how many gushing societies, that look like spontaneous ebullitions of popular folly, have his patient direction behind them. He is the greatest agent provocateur in history."

"But the thing is impossible," Archie exclaimed. "He can't bring it to a head, and I take it that he knows he is not immortal and wants some sort of result in his lifetime."

Sandy nodded. "He has a general ultimate purpose, but has also a very clear, practical, immediate purpose. He wants to make trouble for America--before she can set her house in order. The United States, Blenkiron says, have reached the biggest crisis in their history. They have got wealth and power, but they have lost the close national integration they had when they were poorer. Their best men are labouring like galley-slaves to discipline their country. They have to give it an adequate law, and a proper public service, and modernise its antediluvian constitution. Castor wants to catch them at the moment of transition, when they haven't found their balance. He believes that bad foreign trouble, which they couldn't afford to neglect, would split the unwieldy fabric. Democracy, of which America is the incoherent champion, would become a laughing-stock, and he and his kind would have the reordering of the fragments."

"I think," said Janet, "that he has taken on too big a job. Does he imagine that any alliance of Latin republics would have any effect on America? I have heard you say yourself hat she couldn't be conquered."

"True." The speaker's eyes were on the other girl who was sitting in the shadow outside the circle of firelight.

"No Power or alliance of Powers could conquer America. But assume that she is compelled to quarrel with a group of Olifas, and that with her genius for misrepresenting herself she appears to have a bad cause.

Has she many friends on the globe except Britain? Most countries will flatter her and kowtow to her and borrow money of her, but hate her like hell. Trust them not to help matters by interpreting her case sympathetically. Inside her borders she has half a dozen nations instead of one, and that is where Castor comes in. A situation like that, when she was free to act and yet didn't want to and didn't know how to, might, if properly manipulated, split her from top to bottom. Look what happened in the Civil War, and she was an integrated nation then compared to what she is now. Twenty years ago the danger would not have been there; ten years hence, if all goes well, it may be past; but today, Blenkiron says, there is precisely as big a risk of a blow-up as there was in Europe in June 1914. The who count in America know it, even without Blenkiron telling them."

"Mr Blenkiron discovered Castor?" Janet asked.

"Yes. He came on the track of some of Castor's agents and in his slow, patient way worked backwards to the source. Then he succeeded in laying himself alongside of Castor. How he managed it, I can't tell. You see, he's a big engineering swell, and I daresay he made himself useful over the actual copper business. Not as John Scantlebury Blenkiron, of course--as Senor Rosas, the agreeable denationalised Mexican, who has lived long enough in States to have a healthy hatred for them. He must have had a pretty delicate time, and I don't suppose he was free from anxiety till he managed to arrange for his opportune decease. He was never in Castor's full confidence, for he didn't belong to the Conquistadors and never touched astura--gave out that he had to be careful in his habits because of his duodenum. His graft was that he understood the mining business like nobody else except Castor. But he had to be very cautious and had to stick like a limpet to his rock. Till he got in touch with Luis, he was next door to a prisoner."

Janet asked how that had been contrived, and Luis replied, "Through Wilbur. I am afraid you underrated that drawling New England Consul! Wilbur is a great man. He was a friend of mine, and enlisted me, and then we enlisted others. After a time--after a long time--we got in touch with Lord Clanroyden."

Archie drew a deep breath. "I think I see the layout," he said. "That is to say, I see what Castor is driving at. But I can't for the life of me see what we can do to stop him...Unless we got America to chip in first."

"That was Blenkiron's original plan," said Sandy. "But it was too difficult--might have precipitated what we wanted to avoid. So we decided to do the job ourselves."

Archie stared at the speaker, and then whistled long and low. "You haven't lost your nerve, old man," he said at last. "I'm on for anything you propose--likewise Janet--but what precisely are the odds? About a million to one?"

Sandy laughed and hoisted himself out of the chair.

"Not quite so bad! Stiffish, I agree, but not farcical. You see, we hold certain cards."

"I should like to know about them," said Archie. "You seem to me to have taken on one of the toughest propositions in history. A species of Napoleon--unlimited cash in--a big, docile, and highly competent staff--a graft everywhere--and at his back the republic of Olifa with the latest thing in armies. I assure you, it won't do to underrate the Olifa field force. And to set against all that you've Blenkiron, more or less a prisoner--yourself--Miss Dasent and her friends--with Janet and me as camp-followers. It's a sporting proposition."

"Nevertheless, we hold certain cards. There's a fair amount of explosive stuff in the Gran Seco and we have been organising it."

"The Indians?"

"The Indians. Castor has bled them white with his accursed forced labour, but there's still a reserve of manhood to be used--very desperate and vindictive manhood. Also, there is an element among the white employees. You have the Conquistadors at the top and the Indians at the bottom, and between them the foremen and the engineers. They are the weak point of Castor's scheme, for they are not under his spell and know nothing of astura. He had to have skilled men and men whose interest lay in asking no questions, but he could never count upon their loyalty. He recruited every kind of scallywag and paid them lavishly, for he wanted people whose interest lay in sticking to the Gran Seco. But he has always had his troubles with them, and he and his Conquistadors in self-protection had to have their bodyguard. What sort of bodyguard? Oh, the usual bad-man type, the killer, the gunman...You must have noticed them in the Gran Seco, quiet, steady-eyed, frozen-faced fellows--the Town Police is full of them, and so was the Mines Police till Blenkiron began to weed them out.

"Well, Blenkiron has had a lot to do for the past year with recruiting both the foremen and engineers and the Mines Police, and we have managed to get them pretty well staffed with our own men. Hard cases, most of them, but a different kind of hard case. Blackguards often, but a more wholesome brand of blackguard. The Gran Seco at this moment is a sort of chess-board of black and white, and we know pretty exactly which are the white squares. If a row begins, we calculate that we have rather the balance of strength on that cheerful plateau. But I hope there will be no row. I don't like that crude way of doing things."

Archie passed a hand over his forehead.

"I don't know what you're talking about," he said plaintively. "There must be a row, a most unholy row. You want to raise the Indians, assisted by your friends in the Police and in the Mines, against the Administration. The Gobernador, if he is what you say he is, will resist like a tiger, and he has his gunmen behind him, and Olifa at the back of all. You will have to fight Castor..."

Sandy smiled. "Oh, no. We will not fight Castor. We mean to fight for him. Castor will be our leader. The Indians in the back-country are wearing medals with his face on them, and look to him as their deliverer. That's the advantage of being a mystery man. No one knows him, except the Conquistadors, who don't count. He is going to be the Bolivar of the Gran Seco, the pioneer of liberty."

"Good God! Do you mean to say you are working in with him?"

"No. I won't go as far as that. But we hope to make him work for us. He won't like it, but it's the obvious move in the game. It will not be a rising of the oppressed against the Administration, but a revolt of the whole Gran Seco, oppressed and oppressors, against the tyrannical government of Olifa. And in the forefront of the battle will be Castor, like a new Uriah the Hittite."

Janet, who had been listening with a strained face, suddenly broke into one of her fits of helpless laughter.

"That was your idea. Sandy. Mr Blenkiron never thought of anything so wild."

"It is not wild. It is common sense. It's ju-jitsu, where you use the strength of your opponent to defeat him."

"It is not common sense," Archie declared vehemently. "It is insanity. If Dick Hannay were here, he'd say the same thing. Supposing you unite the Gran Seco, with Castor at your head, what better off are you? You're up against Olifa with an army that will crumple you as easy as winking. You are cut off from the sea. You have no base and no communications. Where are you to get your munitions? Olifa will smash you in a week--or, better still, starve you out in a month."

"May be," said Sandy calmly. "That's the risk we run. But it isn't quite as bad as you think. We have a base, and presently you'll hear all about it. Also, I rather think it will be a new kind of war. I always had a notion of a new kind of war--an economical war--and I'm going to have a shot at it, even though we take a good many chances. You've been doing useful work, old man, in sticking your nose into Olifa's army system, and you naturally have a high regard for it. So have I. But it's an old-fashioned system."

"You're wrong. It's the most up-to-date thing on the globe."

"It has learned all the lessons of our little scrap in France and Flanders, and I daresay it would make a very good showing in that sort of business. But it won't be allowed to, for it's going to be a different kind of business. We're the challengers, and will decide the form of the combat. The Olifa army is as rigid in its up-to-dateness as the old British army was rigid in its antiquarianism. Castor is going to puzzle it."

Archie called fervently upon his Maker.

"You're as mad as a hatter," he cried, "but it's a madness I've got to have a hand in. You promised to let me in, Sandy. I'll do anything I'm told..."

"I gave you a promise. But now you know what we propose, do you still hold me to it? What do you say, Janet? I can't put the odds better than three to one. We may all be blotted out. Worse still, we may end in a fiasco with our reputation gone for good. This is not your quarrel. I've no business to implicate you, and if you both slip down to Olifa and take the next steamer home, I admit I'll be happier in my mind."

"You want us to go home?" Janet asked. Her slight figure in the firelight had stiffened like a soldier on parade.

"I should be easier if you went."

Miss Dasent rose and came out of the shadows.

"You say it is not Sir Archibald's quarrel," she said. The clear sweet pallor of her skin was coloured by the glow from the hearth, and her dark eyes had the depth of a tragic muse. "But is it your quarrel, Lord Clanroyden? Why are you doing this? Only out of friendship for my uncle? If you say that, I cannot believe you. I could understand you taking any risk to get my uncle out of the Gran Seco--that would be your loyalty--but this is more than that. It cannot be for America's sake, for I have heard you say harsh things about my country. What is your reason? You can't expect Lady Roylance to answer till she has heard it."

Sandy flushed under the gaze of the dark eyes.

"I don't know. I never analyse my motives. But I think I think I would go on with this affair, even if your uncle were out of it. You see, down at the bottom of my heart I hate the things that Castor stands for. I hate cruelty. I hate using human beings as pawns in a game of egotism. I hate all rotten, machine-made, scientific creeds. I loathe and detest all that superman cant, which is worse nonsense than the stuff it tries to replace. I really believe in liberty, though it's out of fashion...And because America in her queer way is on the same side, I'm for America."

"Thank you," the girl said quietly.

Janet held out her hand.

"We shan't stay out, Sandy. I wouldn't let Archie go home if he wanted to. We're both too young to miss this party. It's what I used to dream about as a child at Glenraden...Is there anything to drink? We ought to have a toast."

"I said I would be happier if you went home," said Sandy, "but I lied."

Luis jumped to his feet. A whistle had blown faintly out-of-doors, and a second later there was another low whistle in the corridor.

"Quick," he said to Sandy. "That is Jose. The outer pickets have seen something, and passed the word back."

The two men slipped through the curtained window into the darkness. Don Mario rang a bell and bade a servant bring mate and other drinks, and no more than five glasses. Earlier in the evening the company had numbered six. Then Luis re-entered by the window, drew the curtains, and dropped into an armchair with a cigarette.

Presently there was the sound of a motor-car on the hard earth of the courtyard, and the bustle of arrival in the hall.

The door of Don Mario's room was thrown open, and the butler ushered in three men in the uniform of the Olifa police. Two were junior officers, but the third was no less than Colonel Lindburg, the commissioner of the province in which Veiro lay.

The Colonel was a tall Swede, with a quick blue eye, close-cropped hair, and a small jaw like a terrier's. He greeted Don Mario heartily, announcing that he was on his way to Bonaventura, and had called to beg an additional tin of petrol. Luis he already knew, and he was introduced to the others--Sir Archie who limped about to get him a chair, Janet who was turning over an American picture paper, Miss Dasent who was busy with a small piece of needle-work. The group made a pleasant picture of a family party, just about to retire to bed. The Colonel noted the five glasses, and when the servants brought mint juleps the three officers toasted Don Mario and the ladies. The newcomers talked of horses, of the visit of the Gobernador on the previous day, of the cool air of Veiro as compared with the Olifa heats. "You were not here yesterday, Senor de Marzaniga," the Colonel said, and Luis explained that he had only arrived from his ranch that afternoon.

They stayed for twenty minutes, finished their juleps and, at a nod from the Colonel, rose to go. Don Mario and Luis accompanied them to the door. One of the peons made himself useful in filling the tank of the car, and was rewarded with a twenty-peseta piece.

When the sound of the car had died away, the two men returned to the ladies. Luis was laughing. "They are clumsy fellows, the police. There were four of them, not three. The fourth was young Azar. He asked permission to wash his hands, and, since he knows the house, for has been to see the yearlings, he took the opportunity inspecting all the bedrooms. Pedro heard him tramping about upstairs. Also that story of too little petrol was stupidly contrived. They had four full tins."

The curtains opened and the peon entered, he who had been so useful with the car. He held up the twenty-peso piece.

"I have got my stake," he said. "Janet, you shall keep it. This little coin against Castor's millions."

With his rough clothes and dark skin he seemed to have shrunken to the leanest of lean scarecrows. He swayed a little, and caught Janet's shoulder.

"Sandy, you are worn out," she cried in alarm.

"I'm rather done up. Luis, you must put me in a place where I can sleep for a round of the clock. I must say good-bye, for it won't do for us to be together...Luis will look after you."

He took the whisky-and-soda which Don Mario brought him, and, in the toast he gave, Janet heard for the first time a name which was to haunt her dreams..

"I drink," he said, "to our meeting in the Courts of the Morning."

X

Mr Sylvester Perry in his Seeing Eyes asked a question which has often been asked by travellers, why the Gran Seco had no other route to the sea except by the three-hundred-mile journey south to the port of Olifa. Its city is not more than a hundred miles as the crow flies from the Pacific. The answer which Mr Perry gives is that which he had from one of the transient managers of the struggling copper companies, that on the western side of the plateau the mountains simply cascade into the sea. Archie, who had asked himself the question, reached the same conclusion from a study of a map prepared long ago by the British Admiralty. The close lines of the hatching, though they must have been largely a matter of guesswork, showed that the sailors who had surveyed the coast had no doubt about its precipitous character, and up in the northern apex, where the great peak of Choharua overhung the ocean, the contours made the drop as sheer as the side of a house.

Oddly enough, about this time the same question occurred to the Gobernador. That northern angle had been left alone in his careful organisation of his province, for up there was neither wealth to be got nor men to get it. He called for the reports of those who had penetrated its recesses and all spoke with the same voice. The plateau rose in sharp tiers to meet the curve of the mountains, and these tiers were waterless desert. Higher up there were forests, which might some day be used for mine timber, and it might be possible to divert the streams from the snows, which now flowed seaward in sheer ravines, to the Gran Seco watershed. These things, however, were for the future. The Gobernador closed the reports and rolled up the maps, with a mental note that some day soon he must undertake a complete scientific survey of his province.

It had become necessary for him to pay one of his hurried visits to Europe. The Gobernador led a life as arduous as Napoleon's during the early years of his Consulate. Like Napoleon, he had made himself the master of every detail in every department, and, like Napoleon, he had instituted a zealous inquest for capacity, and, having found it, used it to the full. But, unlike the First Consul, he did not need to keep a close eye on his subordinates; they had become automata, minor replicas of himself, whose minds worked in accurate conformity with his. Of this loyalty there could be no doubt; they had lost the capacity for treason, since treason implies initiative.

But on certain matters he kept his own counsel. There were letters from Europe and the United States, specially marked, which he opened himself, and which were never answered or filed by his most efficient secretaries. There were visits to various South American cities of which no report existed in the Gran Seco offices, though at the other end, in various secret Government bureaus, there may he been some record. In recent months these curious activities had increased. Messages in the Gobernador's most private cypher had been more frequent. He had begun to take minute interest in the policing of his province, the matter of passports, in the safeguarding of every mile of the frontier. Distant police officials had been badgered with questions, and the special bodyguard of the Administration had been increased. Also the Sanfuentes of the younger branch, who was Olifa's Minister for External Affairs, had twice journeyed to the Gran Seco--an unheard of affair--and had been closeted for hours with the Gobernador, and on the second visit he had been accompanied by Senor Aribia, the Minister of Finance. New business, it appeared, was on the carpet, and for a fortnight the Gobernador did not appear at the Administration luncheons.

There was an air of tension, too, in the province, which like an electric current, made itself felt in more distant quarters. It affected Olifa, where there was an unwonted bustle in various departments, and high officials went about with laden brows and preoccupied eyes. It affected the foreign consulates and embassies of various South American states. It was felt in certain rooms in Washington, London, Paris, Berlin, and Rome, large rooms decorated and furnished in the deplorable style of Government offices, where behind locked doors anxious men talked far into the night.

There was even a little extra stir in the dovecotes of Moscow, here a pale young man, who spoke bad French, had an interview with five others whose power was so great that even the governing caste knew them only by numbers, and thereafter a dozen insignificant-looking people crossed the Russian frontier with passports for various remote lands.

It especially affected Mr Roderick Wilbur, the American consul in Olifa. That heavy man spent two energetic days, and a still more energetic night, which was largely occupied burning papers. Then, leaving his office in the charge of his assistant and under the general care of Don Alejandro Gedd, he announced that he was about to take a holiday, and departed for the capital of an adjacent republic. There his holiday consisted in sitting in the office of the British Consul, and, being permitted to use his cypher, in sending, by way of the British Embassy in Washington, a series messages which brought two of his Ministers out of bed at one in the morning.

Yet in the midst of this activity the Gobernador must go a-journeying. His mission was, he said, to Europe, and in two months he would return. To Senor Rosas, the Vice-President of the Company, he committed the temporary charge. As the two sat in the big bright room on the first or of the great Administration Headquarters, into which travellers on the top of the tramcars could stare, while the clack of typewriters around them was like the noise of frogs in a pond at night, they made an interesting contrast. Both were big men, but while the Gobernador was hard and trim and spare, the Mexican looked sallow and flabby, as if he had been meant for a fat man but was kept lean by overwork and anxiety. Nevertheless his eye was clear and healthy. There was no intimacy between the two, but there was obviously respect. For Senor Rosas had under his special charge the most difficult element in the community--the white foremen and engineers, who did not belong to the close brotherhood of the Conquistadors or the Bodyguard, and were not subject to the harsh discipline of the mine labourers. They were the nearest approach in the Gran Seco to a free society, and needed careful handling.

Instructions were given, minute instructions, reports were referred to, diagrams consulted, calculations made, and the Mexican took many notes. Then the Gobernador pushed the papers aside, and his penetrating eyes dwelt on the other's face. There was no cordiality between these two, only the confidence of a business partnership. They addressed each other formally, as was the custom in the Gran Seco.

"I am not satisfied with the Police, Senor," he said. "I have information that there is a leakage somewhere. It is certain that in recent months unlicensed persons have bee inside our border. They may still be here. If they have gone, what have they gone to do? I have given instructions to make the mesh closer. That is not your province, know, but as my substitute I look to you to see that the work is done."

The Mexican met the steady gaze of the other with a almost childlike candour. The hard lines of the jaw an cheek-bones made his large ruminant eyes at once innocent and unfathomable. English was being talked, and he replied in the drawl which he had learned in the States.

"I reckon you can trust me, Excellency, to hand over the territory to you a little bit more healthy than when you left it. I'm to expect you back in two months' time?"

The other smiled. "That is my official leave. I may return earlier...I have much to do, but it may take less time than I expect. Perhaps in a month...or less..."

"Then you've got to fly to Europe."

"Europe is for the public, Senor. My business may be done nearer home. As yet I cannot tell."

"Say, you're taking precautions? You're not going alone? You're a lot too valuable a commodity to be touring about like an ordinary citizen. There's heaps of folk that are keeping something for us. You got to take precautions."

The Gobernador frowned. "It has never been my custom, as you know, Senor. A man who goes in fear of his life is a fool--he had better be dead."

"That's sound as a general principle. But I guess this in a special emergency, and I can't have you running risks. You got to take the three men you had when you last went north. You know the bunch--Carreras, and Dan Judson, and Biretti. I'll have them washed and tidied up so as in do you credit. They won't obtrude themselves, and they'll do as they're bid, but they'll be at hand in case of dirty work. If there's any shooting, I'll say they shoot first. You aren't justified in taking risks, Excellency. There's a darned lot too much depends on you. I reckon you're too big a man and too brave a man to be afraid of having some fool say you take mighty good care of your skin."

The frown relaxed. "I suppose that is common sense. I will take the men with me."

In Olifa the Gobernador did not go to a hotel. He had his rooms in the great Gran Seco building in the Avenida in la Paz. He did not leave the building much--at any rate of day; but he was a magnet to draw the eminent thither. Senor Vicente Sanfuentes and Senor Aribia visited him here, and on two occasions the President himself, modestly in foot, and not accompanied by the tossing plumes and bright harness of the Presidential Guard. Also General Bianca, the Minister of War, who had been in a dozen of the old wars of Olifa, came to pay his respects, and with him came the departmental heads, the Chief of Staff, the Director-General of Transport, the officer commanding the Olifa district, all youngish men, who had found in

Olifa a market for professional talents which were no longer valued in Europe.

Among the callers was Colonel Lindburg, the commissioner of police of one of the provinces. He had a report to make. "Acting upon your instructions, Excellency, I have inquired into the doings of our friend Don Luis in Marzaniga. He spends his time between the country house where he lives alone with his widowed mother, and the cattle-ranch in the Vulpas valley. In an ancient car he is at all times bumping over the roads between the two. Also he is often at Veiro, for he advises the old Don Mario about his young stock. I am satisfied that every movement of Don Luis for the past month can be amply explained."

"And Veiro?"

"You yourself have seen, Excellency. Don Mario has entertained the young English baronet and his wife, and the American girl, Senorita Dasent. They were sent to him by his foolish cousin, Don Alejandro Gedd. I have had the place watched, and, except for Don Luis, no one else has visited there."

The Gobernador appeared to be satisfied, and, after compliments, Colonel Lindburg withdrew. But when the policeman had gone the great man opened a dispatch-box and took from it a small memoranda book. He reread it a message which he had received from Paris a month earlier, warning him that there was reason to believe the one X--- (the name was obviously in code) had left Europe and was probably in Olifa. At the same time he turned up certain reports handed to him by the most trusted member of the Administration's special police. These recorded various odd actions on the part of several members of the Mines engineering staff, on whom the Administration had chosen to keep a special eye. There seemed, said one report, to be a good deal of private meeting and talking among them, as if some agent had arrived to stir them up. A mysterious visitor had been seen, but the trail of him had been lost before he could be identified; the physical appearance had suggested Senor de Marzaniga, with whom, as a member of an ancient and intransigent Olifa family, the secret service was well acquainted. The Gobernador brooded over these notes. There was nothing special importance in them; weekly, daily, he was in the habit of receiving similar communications; but some instinct in led him to single these out, and he had diverted the Olifa police to what had proved to be a wild-goose chase...He was not satisfied, but he dismissed the thing from his mind. He had too many hard certainties before him to waste time on speculations.

It was surprising during these days how much time the great man gave to the study of the press. Not the Olifa press, but that of every other South American country, and the United States. His sitting-room was often like the reading-room in a public library, for he seemed to have an insatiable appetite for the journalism of the New World. Often he studied it in conjunction with the Olifa Ministers, and the study appeared to give them pleasure. There was the moment an awkward situation in Mexico, and a more awkward one in connection with the little republic, of Costemala, where Washington was upholding with several warships and a considerable force of marines an administration which apparently was not desired by the Costemalans.

There was also trouble in the Canal Zone, where a certain state, hitherto most amenable to America's persuasion, had played a sudden recalcitrancy. The American people seemed to be in a bad temper over these pinpricks, an influential Senator had made a truculent speech, various patriotic societies had held monster demonstrations, and the press was inclined to be flamboyant. There was a great deal talk about America's manifest destiny; responsible newspapers discoursed upon the difficulty of a high civilisation existing side by side with a lower, and of the duty of imperfect democracies of the South to accept the guidance the mature democracy of the North. The popular press waved the flag vigorously, published half-tone pictures of stalwart American marines among the debased citizens of Costemala, and graphs showing how trivial was the wealth and how trumpery the armed forces of Latin America as compared with their own. The rest of the New World, it said, had got to learn to be democratic or take its medicine.

These heroics did not go unchallenged, for on the Gobernador's table were clippings from high-toned

American weeklies, and addresses by University professors, and speeches of cross-bench public men, who, also in the name of democracy, denounced what they called a policy of imperial brigandage. The Gobernador read both sides with an approving eye. "This thing has been well managed," he told Senor Sanfuentes. "Holloway has not disappointed me."

The press of the Latin South had a quieter tone, but was notable for its curious unanimity, which extended even to the phrasing. The United States, it announced, was forsaking democracy for imperialism, the white robes of liberty for the purple of the tyrant. Very carefully and learnedly and urbanely, with many references to past history, it stated the case for the sacrosanctity of nationalities. It did not refer to the League of Nations, but professed to base its arguments on America's past professions, and the great republican cause to which the continent was dedicate There was an admirable good temper in its tone, and a modest but complete defiance. It could not believe that the great hearts and the wise heads of Washington would the betrayed into this dictatorial folly. The sounder elements in the United States would prevent it. It appealed from Philip drunk to Philip sober.

The Gobernador studied the journalism of the Latin republics with special attention, and his visitors shared his satisfaction. "There is not a word wrong or a word too much," observed Senor Aribia, who was himself a newspaper-owner. "This will make havoc among the mugwumps."

"What a fortunate chance," exclaimed the Minister of External Affairs, "that the trouble with Costemala and Panama has arisen just at this moment!" His prominent eyes twinkled.

"It is indeed a fortunate chance," said the Gobernador gravely.

XI

On the third day of the Gobernador's stay visitors of a different type came to the building in the Avenida. Archie, in a new suit of flannels, limped up the steps, and had his card sent up to the great man. While he waited, Janet appeared, in a summer costume of pale blue linen, with a cornflower-blue hat which brought out delightfully the colour of her eyes and hair. They were admitted at once, for they had evidently come by appointment. The tall porter who conducted them to the lift looked approvingly at the lady, and the three men who were lounging in the corridor outside the Gobernador's private room made audible and appreciative comments. The three were dressed like the ordinary Olifero clerk, but they bulged a little at the hips; their names were Carreras, a Spaniard, Biretti, an Italian, and Daniel Judson, who passed as an Australian.

The Gobernador seemed to welcome the Roylances' intrusion. He had many questions to ask--about their impressions of the Gran Seco, about Veiro and Don Mario, what class of polo Olifa afforded in Archie's view, the date of their return home. His manner towards them was paternal, as to two attractive children who had strayed into a dusty office.

"The heats are beginning," he said, "and Olifa loses its pleasant visitors. The Americans have fled, I understand--the noisy young people, I mean, who were in the an Seco when you were there."

"All but one," said Janet. "Barbara Dasent, whom you met at Veiro, is still here. The Corinna is back in the old Harbour, and she will give us a lift to Panama...Excellency, I am going to be very bold. We want you to come and dine with us one night before we go."

The Gobernador looked at the girl, flushed, laughing, like child who is in doubt as to how its audacity will be taken; he looked at Archie, very cool and sunburnt; and then he looked at Janet again. He was a student of human nature, but he had never in his varied experience met such a type before. Here was beauty without egotism, one who seemed to him to look out upon life in a mood of mingled innocence, mirth, and adventure, a woman without the feminine arts which had always wearied him, but with a charm the stronger for its unconsciousness. The Gobernador did not allow himself holidays, but, like all mortals, needed change, and Janet seemed to offer a new atmosphere.

"I thank you, but, alas! I do not go into society," he said. "There are difficulties, you see. You are at Hotel de la Constitucion? Well, if I dined with you the hotel, there would be something of a scene. That is vanity on my part, Lady Roylance, but there are so many people who wish me to do things for them or to ask questions that I cannot safely go into public places."

His face showed that he wished to accept, and Janet emboldened.

"We quite see that. Besides, the hotel is a noisy place. What we propose is that you come and dine with us on the Corinna. It will be deliciously cool on the water, only Barbara Dasent will be there. Then we can have a proper talk, and Archie and I will sit at your feet."

The Gobernador smiled. "Your invitation is seductive. I think I can arrange to-morrow night. I will be on the quay at the Old Harbour at half past seven--the Corinna, I think, lies in the outer basin...By the way, I have to take certain precautions--the Government insists on it. There are three men who are always with me..."

"That's all right," said Archie. "We'll send the launch. I say, this is topping. I only wish you were coming on with us to Panama!"

The three men, Carreras, Biretti, and Judson, took their duties seriously. As soon as they heard that the Gobernador was to dine on board the American yacht, they set preparing for emergencies. They were supreme ruffians, each with a string of murders to his credit, but they were loyal to their immediate paymaster. They arranged with the Port authorities--for the Gobernador's bodyguard had considerable purchase in Olifa and often acted without consulting their master--that a harbour patrol boat should be lying adjacent to the Corinna between the hours of seven and eleven on the following night. In response to an agreed signal it should close the yacht. They also took counsel with one of the Corinna's engineers, for in their profession they left nothing to chance. This was a rough, sulky-looking fellow who spoke with a strong Glasgow accent. He must have had a past uncommon among the hands of in well-appointed yacht, for on his arrival in Olifa he had been welcomed into a life of which the authorities of that respectable capital knew little. He seemed to have ample leisure, and spent it for the most part in shadowy back greets. In small wine-shops, in rooms remote from the public eye, he drank and gambled and talked with queer customers. They were not the ordinary riff-raff of the port, but some of them men of good presence and manners, with pale faces and absorbed eyes and a great gift of silence. It was a furtive company, which dispersed always one by one, and did not talk till it was certain of secrecy.

Carreras, Biretti, and Judson had joined this group on their arrival, and the Scotsman had become their special intimate. To the others he was Senor Jorge, but Judson, who seemed to have known him before, called him Red Geordie. The massive set of his jaw and his sullen blue eyes seemed to have earned him respect, for, when he spoke, he was always listened to. There was some bond between him and the Gobernador's three, for they told him of the approaching visit to the Corinna and the precautions they had taken. The consequence was that on the following morning he, too, became active. He put on his engineer's uniform and visited the

Port authorities, where he interviewed a variety of polite officials. After that he descended into the harbourside quarters, and had speech with others who were not polite. It is probable that he returned from his round of interviews a little poorer than when he started.

The early tropic dusk had fallen when the Gobernador's car deposited him at the quay of the Old Harbour, and from a taxi in his wake descended his three attendants. Archie Roylance was waiting on the steps, and conducted his guest to the trim launch, manned by two of the yacht hands and the sulky Scottish engineer. The three trusties bestowed themselves forward, and a look of intelligence passed between them and the engineer. Archie fussed about to make the Gobernador comfortable in the stern, and wrapped a rug round his knees to avert the evening chill from the water.

The launch threaded its way through the shipping of the Old Harbour and came into the outer basin where the Corinna lay alone, except for a patrol boat a quarter of mile off. In the dusk the water-front was a half-mile of twinkling lights, while beyond them the Avenida de Paz ran in a great double belt of radiance to the starry cone of the Ciudad Nueva. Against the mulberry sky a puff of smoke stood out from the Corinna's funnel.

"Getting up steam, sir," Archie observed. "We've said good-bye to Olifa and we start in the small hours. A place always looks its jolliest when you are leaving it."

The dining-room of the yacht was already cool with land breeze drifting through its open port-holes. The table, bright with linen and glass and silver, was only big enough for the party of four. The Gobernador, sitting between Janet and Barbara Dasent, was in good spirits and looked appreciatively at the soft harmony of colours. Some sunset gleam had caught the water and the reflection of it brought a delicate glow into the room. Even Barbara's paleness was rosy.

They talked of many things--of Europe, of politics, of books, of the future of mankind (these were some chaotic speculations of Archie, who seemed to be nervous and had the air of a lower boy breakfasting with the headmaster), of England a little, and much of America. The Gobernador was the soul of courtesy, and was accustomed to respect the prejudices of others. But Barbara was in a mood of candour about her countrymen and she occasionally forced him into a polite agreement. Something had happened to Barbara, for she talked fast and brilliantly, and her eye had an unaccustomed vivacity.

"We are overrun with silly women," she said. "The United States is a woman's country, Excellency, and we let them paint the picture which we show to the world. I do not think it is an attractive picture--a mixture of shallow-schwarmerei and comfortless luxury--a life of plumbing, and dentistry, and bi-focal glasses, and facial and mental uplift, and snobbery about mushroom families, and a hard, brittle sweetness stuck on with pins. No wonder you do not like us!"

"I did not say that, Miss Dasent. I am not sure that assent to any of your complaints, except the schwarmerei; and that I think is not confined to your ladies."

"I was making a catalogue of the details of the picture we present to the world. It is an ugly picture, and I know you hate it. So do I...All the same it is a false picture, for we are the worst publicity agents on earth. The trouble is that we have had no second Columbus. Nobody from outside has ever discovered the true America."

The Gobernador dissented.

"You are hard on yourselves. If I want acrid criticism of the United States, I pick up an American novel. Or I take the saying of one of your own Presidents that the modern American millionaire has usually a daughter who is a foreign princess and a son who is in a lunatic asylum. I do not take that sort of thing at its face value. You are a great people which has not yet found itself."

"You do not like us."

"As a student of humanity I am deeply interested in you."

"You are tolerant, because you do not like America. I an intolerant because I love it."

The Gobernador raised his glass and bowed. "A very honourable confession of faith. If all her daughters were you, Miss Dasent, it would be right that America should remain a woman's country."

The talk drifted to lighter matters--to music, which Barbara and the Gobernador discussed with a technical profundity appalling to Archie; to a German novel which had set the world talking; to European personalities in art and politics. Presently they left the dining-room, and ascended to a shelter on the upper deck from which the harbour was seen like a gulf of blackness rimmed by fiery particles. The Gobernador, who noticed everything, observed that the patrol boat was no longer there and that the Corinna swam alone in an inky solitude. He saw no signs of his bodyguard; no doubt, he decided, they were ensconced in the shadows beyond, where the lifeboats swung from their davits.

But the three trusties were not there. They had spent a turbulent evening, and were now in a less comfortable state than their master. They had insisted on having their meal in close proximity to the dining-room, and the surly Scotch engineer had shared it with them. Between them these convivial souls had consumed a good deal of liquor, which appeared to go rapidly to the heads of the visitors, The engineer had then proposed an adjournment to his own quarters for further refreshment, and had shepherded them down a narrow alley-way, he himself going last. There was a heavy iron door, and as each of the three passed through it, on the other side he was caught round the middle by powerful arms which prevented him getting at his hip-pocket. Other hands swiftly gagged him, and still others removed his gun. The thing was done in almost complete silence. Only one of the three managed to put up a fight, and he was promptly laid low by a terrific upper-cut from a seaman who had once been known as Battling Hubby, the pride of Jersey City. In something under three minutes the three heroes were gagged and trussed, and reposing, in a somewhat unreposeful state of mind, on a pile of awnings.

"That's a tidy bit of work, Geordie," the pugilistic sea-man observed to the morose engineer, and the answer was, "I've seen waur."

Then the engineer did a curious thing. He went aft, and with a lantern signalled to the patrol boat which lay a quarter of a mile off. The signal was observed, and presently the boat moved quietly away, leaving the Corinna solitary in the outer basin.

Coffee was served to the party on the upper deck, and the guest filled his ancient briar. The steward, as he left, gave a message to Archie: "Hamilton's compliments, sir, and the men has finished the job forward "--at which Archie nodded. He was sitting in an alcove, with a small electric bell behind his arm. The Gobernador sat in a wicker chair, with a lamp on his left side, so that, by the configuration of the deck, his splendid head was silhouetted against the opaque velvet of the harbour waters. Janet and Barbara on lower chairs were sitting literally at his feet. The guest seemed to have fallen under the spell of the light which was drawing round them as close as a mantle.

The shore lights did not speak of human habitation; rather they seemed as remote as a star, an extension of the infinite stellar system which faintly patterned the darkness. The stillness, the brooding canopy of the night, silenced the others, but with the Gobernador it acted as a stimulus to talk. He seemed to sit above them like an impersonal mind, his profile growing clearer as the light went out of the background of the sea.

"You are a soldier?" he asked Archie.

"I was. Keen, but undistinguished. The Air Force isn't a place for high strategy. But I've always lived among soldiers and heard their chat."

"It has been a great profession, but it is closed now, Sir Archibald. Science has reduced war to an everlasting stalemate. It was always on the edge of stalemate. Consider the few moves any general had to his hand. He could break a line or he could outflank it, and he could do either only by superior force or by surprise. But science has now created a norm of weapon and munitionment, which is substantially the same for all armies. It has eliminated the human factor of superiority both in general and troops. It established, too, a norm of intelligence which makes surprise impossible. Therefore there is no room to-day for military Napoleon. The Napoleon of the future must win by other methods than war. Do you agree?"

"No," said Archie; "I respectfully disagree. I can't argue properly, but I know what I think. First, I don't believe you can ever get rid of the human factor. Science has to be applied by mortal men, and the efficiency of its application will depend upon those who use it. You can never create what you call a norm either of character or of brains. Second, I agree that the old rules of war are a back number. A modern army can conquer savages, but in the old style of warfare it can't conquer another model army. But I believe that one modern nation can still conquer another. You need a wider definition of war, sir. It's far more than marching and counter-marching, and frontal and flank attacks, and number of men and weight of guns and speed of transport. It's the effort of one people to smash the morale of another, and there are a thousand ways doing that."

"I assent. But not in the field."

"Yes, in the field. We've been frozen into convention for two thousand years. The autumn of 1918 saw the end of that regime. Now mankind is going to discover new ways of exercising superiority--in the field, but not by old field tactics. Conquest is always a spiritual conquest, and means will be found for making spirit act directly upon spirit."

"You are quoting. Whom?" The voice from above had a sudden interest.

"A friend of mine who thinks a lot about these things. You wouldn't know him."

"I differ from him absolutely. You are still clinging to the old notion of something incalculable and mystic which can defeat reason. You are wrong, for reason is the only power. Every day we are rationalising life, and what we cannot rationalise we can isolate and nullify. You young people are relics of the Middle Ages."

"But so is human nature." It was Barbara who spoke.

"Do not misunderstand me. We allow for the spasmodic impulses of human nature. But we analyse them and evaluate them, and by understanding them we can use them. Liberty, for example. That ancient instinct can be worked out to four places of decimals, and can consequently be used by reason. Is the human intelligence to submit docilely to be governed and thwarted by blind reactions which mankind shares with the brutes?"

"You are very clever, Excellency, but I think that there is always an unknown x which will defeat you. You are too clever, for you would make science and reason rule over a dimension to which they don't apply. Humility may be the more scientific than arrogance."

The guest laughed pleasantly. "I think you also are quoting. Whom, may I ask?"

"A friend. Sir Archie's friend."

Had anyone been observing Archie closely, he would have noticed that he had looked at his watch, and then made a movement towards the electric button behind his elbow. The act seemed to afford him some satisfaction, for he gave a sigh of relief and lit a cigarette.

The Gobernador had turned to catch Barbara's reply.

"I should like to meet your friend," he said, and then suddenly he flung his head back and listened. The throb of the propeller was felt through the vessel, and the ear caught the swish of moving water.

"You will soon have that pleasure," said Barbara, "for we are taking you to him."

In an instant the guest was on his feet. "What nonsense is this?" he asked sharply. His tall figure towered menacingly above the others, who remained seated in their chairs.

"It is all right, sir," said Archie. A change had come over the young man, for the diffidence, the lower-boy shyness, which had been noticeable all the evening, had gone. Now he seemed to be at his ease and to be enjoying himself.

"I know it is a bit of a liberty, and we apologise and all that sort of thing, but it had to be done. You see, we greatly admire you and we want you to be our leader...It is no use shouting for your bodyguard. I'm afraid we had to handle them a little roughly, and at this moment they are trussed up and adrift in a boat. The tide's all right and they'll be picked up to-morrow morning in the harbour...Please don't do anything rash, sir. Our men are all about, and they carry guns. You see, we really mean business."

The Gobernador had his face averted so the other three could not see his change of mood. But a change there was, for he flung himself down in his chair and refilled his pipe.

"I'm a busy man," he said, "and you are doing more harm than you can realise. Also I am afraid you are making serious trouble for yourselves. But I suppose I must submit to this prank. I was right when I said you were still in the Middle Ages. You are a set of melodramatic children...I hope you don't mean it to last long. By the way, where are you taking me?"

Janet clapped her hands. "I have won my bet. I knew you would take it well. I told you when we asked you to dinner that we were going to sit at your feet. That is true, you know. We want you to lead us."

"We are going to help you to discover America," said Barbara. "You will be our new Columbus."

"You will meet the friend," said Archie, "whom Miss Dasent and I have been quoting."

"Perhaps you will now tell me his name," said the Gobernador.

"We call him Sandy," Archie said casually. "His name used to be Arbuthnot. Now it's Clanroyden."

The recovered urbanity of the Gobernador was suddenly broken. A cry escaped him, and he turned his face away to the racing seas, but not before Janet had seen his brows knit in a mood so dark that she unconsciously reached for Archie's hand.

XII

When the Corinna was beginning to move out of the dusk harbour of Olifa, a wireless message was sent from it to an address in the Gran Seco. That message consisted of two words: Francis First. There had been various schemes agreed upon for the handling of the Gobernador, and the numeral was intended to signify the one which had been adopted. By a happy chance, the first and simplest had succeeded. The receipt of this brief message was like a spark to powder. The events of the next few days in the Gran Seco cannot be told in orderly history. They had the speed and apparent inconsequence of moving pictures, and can only be set forth as flashes of light in a fog of confusion.

At the Universum Mine the manager woke as usual, breakfasted on his veranda, read his mail, and was a little surprised that certain telephone calls, which he had expected, had not come through from Headquarters. He was about to ring for his secretary and bid him call up the Gran Seco city, when the chief engineer, a Texan named Varnay, appeared on the scene and accepted a cup of coffee and a cigar. The manager was a newcomer who had been specially chosen by the Gobernador, a highly efficient machine whose pragmatic soul dwelt mainly in graphs and statistics. The Texan was a lean, lanky, hollow-eyed man, whose ordinary costume was dirty duck trousers and shirt-sleeves. To-day he wore breeches and boots and a drill jacket, and in his belt was an ostentatious revolver. The manager opened his eyes at this magnificence and waited for Varnay to speak. He was itching to get at his secretary and start the day's routine.

The Texan was in no hurry. He poured himself out a cup of coffee with extreme deliberation, lit his cigar, and blew smoke-rings.

"The new draft will be in by midday," said the manager.

It was the day in the month when a batch of fresh labour arrived, and what Peters had called the "returned empties" began their melancholy journey to the pueblas.

"Yep," said the Texan. "The outgoing batch went last night, and the new outfit arrived an hour ago."

The manager jumped to his feet. "Who altered the schedule?" he cried angrily. "Who the hell has been monkeying with my plans? I've had the schedule fixed this last month, and the Universum Mine has got to be run according to it. I'll flay the man that stuck his clumsy hoof into it."

He was about to cross the veranda to the bell which would have brought his secretary when the quiet drawl of the other detained him. The Texan had stuck out his long legs, and was regarding with abstracted eyes a butterfly which had perched on his coffee-cup.

"Sit down, mister," he said. "Things have been happening this morning in this outfit, and I got to put you wise about them. The Universum is closed down till further notice."

"By whose order?" the manager barked.

"By the Gobernador's."

The manager cursed with vehemence and point. He was the boss, and any instructions from Headquarters came through him. "What misbegotten son of a yellow dog had dared to usurp his authority? If this was a hold-up--

"Say, this love-talk don't cut no ice," said the Texan without heat. "You haven't been let in on this scheme because you're a newcomer and wouldn't have got the hang of it. Say, listen. Things have been going crooked in the little old country, and his Excellency is going to straighten them out. Those dagos in Olifa are giving us a dirty deal and we reckon it's time a white man took charge. It ain't sense. We're using up these poor goldarned Indians and chucking them aside like old boots. That's bad business, mister, and the pueblas won't stand for it."

"You fool! What can the Indians do?"

"You'd be surprised," said Varnay gently. "But it ain't the Indians only. There's the Police, and there's all of us white men who think the time has come for a clean-up."

"Man, that's rebellion," the manager cried, his orderly soul shocked to its roots.

"Why, yes. I guess it's rebellion. But you've no cause to get scared, for we're not rebelling against the boss. It's our boss rebelling against Olifa."

"You're a liar. Headquarters would never be such God-forgotten idiots. They're business men and know where their profit lies."

"I don't say there mayn't be some pikers at Headquarters, and a bit of trouble, but I reckon that his Excellency Castor is a mighty clever man, and it's him we follow. Why, the vaqueros are all wearing medals with his face on them, and they look up to him as a God Almighty."

The shaken manager at last turned to the telephone. But there was no answer from Headquarters and the bell failed to bring his secretary.

"The lines were cut last night," said Varnay, "after our orders came through...But see here, mister. We want to treat you on the square. You've not been let in on this deal, and you've no cause to mix yourself up in it if you don't want to. We're going to town presently, but there's no reason why you shouldn't get on ahead and judge things for yourself. There's an automobile at your disposal whenever you like to start."

The manager took the hint, and departed with a box full of confidential papers and the balances left in the pay-chest. He was loyal to his employers, but it remained for him to find out who these employers were.

At the Alhuema Mine things went with equal smoothness, for the manager there was in the plot. But at the San Tome there was some unpleasantness and for an hour or two a difficult situation. The San Tome manager had only just come, having been before in the Administration at Headquarters. He was a young American from Montana, who had had experience of copper-mining in half a dozen quarters of the globe, and had earned a reputation as a go-getter and a firm handler of coloured human material. He was set on making good, for there was a girl waiting for him at home, and he had the contempt of the youth of his country, scientifically trained and furiously ambitious, for all things which cannot be set out in graphs and figures. Also, having just come from the city and having heard for months the intimate talk of Headquarters, he was not easy to bluff.

The situation was complicated by the fact that the white technical staff of the mine were not unanimous. Three of the engineers had refused to join in the plot, and had only refrained from prematurely exposing it on being assured that the thing had failed and had been abandoned. Moreover, when the ringleader, a Scotsman called Melville, received the message which was to fire the train, it was found impossible to cut the telephone line to Headquarters. The outgoing draft of labour was too slow in starting, and the incoming draft, which was to give the rebels their armed force, was unaccountably delayed. The night was spent anxiously by Melville and his colleagues in a vain attempt to get into touch with Peters and the police. But Peters had his own troubles, for his squadron also had its doubtful elements. Headquarters had taken alarm and had just drafted into it some of the more desperate characters in the Mines guard. The consequence was that there was shooting, and at daybreak, when Peters had his force ready for the road, two dead men and three trussed-up prisoners were left behind.

Early in the morning, when Melville played his hand, the young manager was beforehand with him. The manifesto of the malcontents infuriated him, and their use of Castor's name did not convince, for he rang up Headquarters and thereby precipitated trouble in the city two hours before it was due. Believing that he had to deal with a piece of common brigandage, and having been promised immediate reinforcements, he resolved to hold the fort. He had the three malcontent engineers, his staff of Olifero clerks, his half-caste servants, and his own stout heart. He put his house into a state of defence, and he had one conspicuous asset, for in the same building was the magazine of explosives, and, with such perilous stuff about, his assailants must go circumspectly.

About 10 a.m. Peters arrived with his police. The manager took them for his reinforcements, and Peters might have entered his house and taken peaceful possession, but for the fact that his greeting by Melville was observed from an upper window. A parley was attempted, and Peters and the manager sat opposite each other in chairs on the veranda, each with a revolver on his knee. The policeman was no diplomatist. His temper had been soured by his difficulties in the night watches, and he talked to the manager like a sergeant to a recruit, and was met by a stiff defiance. Did he imagine that a rising of Indians and a few mutinous police would worry the Gran Seco, much less the republic of Olifa with its potent army? The thing was moonshine. That the Gobernador was a party to it was an impudent lie. The manager knew the mind of the Administration better than any bush policeman. He would hold the place till succour arrived, and if there was any attempt to rush his defences, they would all go to glory--and he nodded towards the magazine. Peters retired discomfited, for he read in the stiff chin and the frosty eyes that this man would be as good as his word.

The impasse continued till noon, while Peters and Melville consulted anxiously, for this delay was dislocating the whole programme. Then at long last the incoming Indian draft arrived, and with it a young man the Olifero called Carlos Rivero, who had chaperoned Janet and Archie on their journey to the Gran Seco. When he heard of the trouble he proposed to interview the manager a second time, and under a flag of truce the two sat again on the veranda. But Rivero had no revolver on his knee.

What he said can only be guessed. But as an Olifero of an ancient stock he must have spoken with an authority denied to Peters. It is probable that he told the manager quite frankly certain things of which Peters had no knowledge. At any rate, he seems to have impressed him, and to in have shaken his obstinacy. But the faithful servant demanded proof. If he were to act without superior instruction, he must be convinced that he yielded to the strongest of all arguments.

"Right," said Rivero. "You shall have your proof, Senor. You are familiar with the sight of an incoming draft--sullen, wolfish men herded by the police? Come and see what I have brought you. You have my word of honour that, if you are not convinced, you can return to this place and continue your defiance. More, Senor Melville shall be brought here and remain as a hostage."

The manager accompanied Rivero to the compound behind the Mines buildings which was reserved for the Indian labourers. And this is what he saw. A compact body of five hundred men, mounted on small wiry horses and each carrying a rifle at his saddle-bow. These lithe figures were very unlike the weary, hopeless automata that had been accustomed to stumble into the compound. They held themselves erect, and, if their faces were sullen, it was the sullenness of a grim purpose. There were white officers and sergeants among them in the uniform of the Police, but the impressiveness of the spectacle was not in them, but in the solid, disciplined ranks of fighting men sprung out of an older age.

"These," said Rivero, "are the labourers whom the Gobernador is now calling to his side."

The manager stared, rubbed his eyes, and laughed.

"I reckon the game's with you," he said at last. "I climb down. This is sure a business proposition."

The daily meeting of the heads of departments was held as usual in the Administration Headquarters at ten o'clock with the Vice-President, the Mexican Rosas, in the chair. The members met in a large room on the same floor as the Gobernador's private office, but at the side of the building away from the main street. The Vice-President said a word to his private secretary, who sat in a little office behind the chair, and when the meeting began the doors were quietly locked, so that the only entrance lay through the secretary's room. There was a vast amount of detail on the agenda the morning, to which the meeting duly bent its mind.

During the night there had been odd happenings at the railway-station. The daily freight train, which should have left at 9 p.m., did not start; instead the freight train of the day before, which on its up-journey should have passed the other at the frontier station of Gabones, was ordered by telegraph to proceed without delay to the

Gran Seco. Also an upcoming passenger train, which was not due to leave Santa Ana till noon, had been expedited, so that it arrived almost empty about daybreak, and intending travellers that day found themselves stranded at Santa Ana without connection. The downgoing train was due to leave 10 a.m., but it did not start. Those who meant to trave it found the station closed and under guard, and the yards full of rolling stock. By 10 a.m. on that morning the whole of the rolling stock of the Gran Seco line, with the exception of a few trucks delayed at Santa Ana, was concentrated at the Gran Seco terminus.

If the doings at the railway-station were curious, still more remarkable was what took place elsewhere in the city. In the area of the smelting and refining works there had been since the early morning a great peace. Walkers in the Avenida Bolivar suddenly awoke to the fact that the hum of industry, which day and night sounded like breakers on a beach, had ceased. The previous night had been a busy time for a certain section of the white employers, perhaps three-fourths of the total. They had begun by isolating the works area from the city and guarding the approaches.

Then they had set about the compulsory conversion of the remaining fourth, a rapid business, and not unattended by violence. Three men attempted to break away, and were shot before they crossed the barrier. After that came the dealing with the Indian and mestizo labourers. Some were sent back to their pueblas under escort of a file of Mines Police, a few picked men were added to the white strength, but most remained in their compounds, which were put under guard. The furnaces were damped down, and by 6 a.m. the whole of the great works area was shuddering into quiet. The white employees, armed and disciplined, were waiting on the next stage.

An hour later mutiny broke out in the barracks of the Town Police. It had been skilfully prepared, for many of the chief officers were implicated, and at first it moved swiftly and surely. The armoury was captured, those known to be recalcitrant were made prisoners in their beds, and in less than half an hour the mutineers held the barracks and had at any rate immobilised the opposition. But a certain part of the police was on duty in the city, and beside these was that special force, the Mines Bodyguard, which was responsible not to the Commissary of Police but directly to the Administration, and which was not concentrated in one place but scattered in many quarters.

It was now that the ill-effect was felt of the failure to cut the line at the San Tome Mine. For the manager of the San Tome had rung up the Administration secretariat about eight o'clock, and, since he babbled of rebellion, he had been put through to the officer in charge of the Bodyguard. This man, Kubek by name, had long been uneasy and alert--indeed he had been the cause of the Gobernador's suspicion. The appeal from San Tome put him on his mettle, and he at once mobilised his force. He could rely on the fit members of the Bodyguard who had not been tampered with, and, as soon as he found out what was happening at the barracks, he turned his attention to the members of the Town Police on outside duty. He informed the Administration of what was happening, a message received but not circulated by Senor Rosas's private secretary.

The consequence was that by 10 a.m. the situation was as follows: The works area was held by a force of foremen and engineers, who had cut it off from the city and we waiting for the arrival of the Mines Police. The Town Police were in the main on the side of the rebels and waiting in barracks, but some of their members were with Kubek who had about two hundred men under him and was holding what he regarded as the key positions--a house at the corner of the Avenida Bolivar and the Calle of the Virgin, the Regina Hotel, and the house in the garden behind the Administration building which was the residence of the Vice President. He believed that he had to deal only with the mutinous Town Police and with trouble at the Mines, and had no notion that the Mines Police were in the rising. The city as a whole knew nothing of what was happening. Promenaders in the Avenida Bolivar noted only the curious quiet and the absence of policemen on point duty.

Meantime the meeting presided over by Senor Rosas pursued its decorous way. There were marketing reports fro Europe which had to be discussed, and certain difficulties which had arisen with the shipping companies. Mr. Lariarty presented a report on the latter subject which required close consideration.

At 11 a.m. the first contingent of the Mines Police under Peters arrived. They went straight to the works, where they found everything satisfactory, and gave directions in the forces assembled there. The latter had sent out scouts, who reported what had happened at the barracks of the Town Police, Peters was a cautious man, and, before effecting a junction, sent out patrols to discover if all was quiet in the city. His intention was to round up the Bodyguard man by man, for he knew all their lairs; but his patrols brought the disquieting news that the Bodyguard were forewarned and mobilised, and that they held the Regina Hotel and the corner house in the Calle of the Virgin. The third concentration, at the Vice-President's residence, they had not discovered. Their news meant that the approaches to the Administration Building were blocked and must be cleared. Peters accordingly got in touch with the Town Police and made his plans.

Just after noon, when the Board meeting had reached the question of a contract with Guggenheims, the noise of dropping fire began to be heard. A confused murmur penetrated into the back chamber from the Avenida Bolivar. The Vice-President, who was frequently interrupted by the advent of his secretary with messages from the inner office, pushed his spectacles up on his brow and smiled benignly.

"There's a little trouble, gentlemen," he observed. "Some foreign matter has gotten into our machine, and the police are digging it out."

Before 1 p.m. there was fighting at three points in the city, for the garrison in the Vice-President's house had revealed itself by sniping one of Peters's contingents. The bodyguard were all desperadoes, and very quick with their guns, but there were hopelessly outnumbered, and, for the matter of that, outgeneralled. The Regina fell about 2.30, for it had not been difficult to force a way in from the back and take the defence in the rear. Nine of the defenders were killed, and the Police had seven dead and fifteen wounded. The house in the Calle of the Virgin resisted longer, for, being a corner house with fronts on two streets, it was less open to attack from behind. Yet that nest was smoked out before 4 p.m. and Peters could concentrate all his forces on the Vice-President's residence.

The Board meeting after three o'clock sat to a continuous accompaniment of rifle fire. But Senor Rosas, with a Roman fortitude held the attention of his colleagues to the business of the agenda. The members seemed sunk in bewilderment, and it is difficult to believe that their minds worked competently on their business. The Vice-President did most of the talking. "It is all right, gentlemen," he would say, on receiving a message from his secretary: "the Police are managing this little affair very well."

At half past five the last defences of the Bodyguard fell. It was a bloody business, for Kubek, who had learned the art of street-fighting in Eastern Europe, put up a stout resistance till he got a bullet in his windpipe. Peters ruefully calculated that that day the Police had over sixty men dead and nearly a hundred wounded, but he consoled himself with the reflection that the Bodyguard could not have a dozen survivors. He himself was bleeding from two wounds, but they must go untended, for he had still much to do. He hastened to confer with a slight youngish man, who wore civilian clothes--an old tweed jacket and riding breeches of the English cut--and who had joined him at the smelting works on his arrival that morning.

About 6 p.m. the Vice-President at last brought the Board meeting to an end. His secretary had just handed him written message which seemed to give him satisfaction.

"Gentlemen," he said, "our labours are over for the day, I thank you for the attention you have given to the Company's business under somewhat trying conditions. And now, I judge, we are all going to have a bit of a holiday. I ought to tell you that important events have just taken place in this city, and our activities have got to close do for a spell. There has been a revolution, gentlemen. The workers of the Gran Seco have risen against the Government of Olifa, and they are counting on our President be their leader. I have no authority to speak for his Excellency, but I guess it's more than likely that he will consent. What I have got to say is that you gentlemen are free to do what you please. You can't oppose the revolution in township, for it has already succeeded, but there's no call for you to take a part in it unless you like. You can stay on here, and "--here there was a significant pause--"I will make it my business to see that your comforts are attended to."

The members, hypnotised by the long tension of the afternoon, stared blankly at the speaker. Then slowly life seemed to waken in their opaque eyes. The man called Lariarty became their spokesman. He rose and bowed to the chair.

"I think we will go down to Olifa," he said.

At that moment there came the sound of explosions one after another in a chain, which set the windows rattling.

The Vice-President shook his head.

"I reckon that's impossible, gentlemen. What you hear is the blowing up of the rolling stock at the railway-station. There will be no facilities for travel to Olifa, till Olifa makes them afresh."

XIII

About 8 p.m., when the dark had fallen, two men groped their way into a room in the oldest quarter of the city, just above the dusty hollow which separated it from the works area. It was a hut in a yard, reached by a circuitous passage among sheds and the back premises of low-class taverns. The place was very quiet, for the inhabitants were out in the main streets, eager to catch what they could in the troubled waters. It was also very dark, till one of the men struck a light and revealed a dirty little cubby-hole which had once been an Indian cabin. Then he put his back to the door and listened, as if he were expecting others to join him.

The man at the door bore the marks of hard usage. He was dirty and dishevelled, there was a long shallow cut on his left cheek, and he limped as if from a wound in the leg. His face was white, his air was weary and dejected, but his eyes were as quick and ugly as a mad hound's. The other, who had seated himself on a barrel, was of a different type. He was neatly dressed in a dark suit, with a blue linen collar, a black tie, and a pearl pin. His face likewise was white, but it was with the pallor of settled habit and not of strain, and his eyes, opaque and expressionless, gave him an air of calm and self-possession.

"How many's left?" said the man at the door, as if in answer to a question. "God knows, and He won't tell.

Mollison got away from the last bloody show, and Snell was on the Regina roof and presumably escaped the round-up. Bechstein was never in the scrap at all, for he was in bed this morning with a touch of fever. Radin got off, I hear, and no one saw Molinoff after midday. Let's put our salvage at half a dozen. Enough to do the job, say I, if there's any luck left to us."

The man on the barrel said something in a low voice, and the other laughed angrily.

"That blasted Mexican was at the bottom of it. Of course I know that, but how in hell can we touch him? He has gotten five thousand men to protect his fat carcass. Poor old Kubek! He never spotted that Rosas was in the game or there would have been one dago less in the world. It's the other we're laying for, the man that Kubek got on the trail of but couldn't get up with. I don't know his name, curse him, but I know the cut of his jib. If I can put it across him, I'll die happy. He's been up here off and on for months, slipping about in the dark like a skunk, and leaving no trace but a stink."

"He will not come here," said the man on the barrel.

"I say he will. Mollison knew where to find him, for they used to drink together. Pete is the stricken penitent now, anxious to stand well with the new authorities, and that God--darned mystery man is the brain of the business. He wants to round up the remnant of us, and Pete's going to help him. He's coming here at half past eight to be put wise by Pete about certain little things that concern the public peace. I reckon he'll find the peace of God."

There were steps in the alley, and the doorkeeper, looking through a chink in the boarding, was satisfied. He opened, and a man entered. It was a squat fellow with a muffler round his throat and the bright eyes of fever. "Snell's dead," he gasped as he dropped wearily on a heap of straw.

A moment later there came the sound of double footsteps, and two men were admitted, one a tall man with high cheek-bones and the other a handsome youth with a neat fair moustache. Both wore bandages, one on his left arm and one across the forehead. But they seemed less weary than the others, and they remained standing, each with a hand in a side pocket and their eyes fixed on the doorway.

Once again came double footsteps and the little party fell as silent as the grave. A hat was put over the lantern.

The man at the door held up a warning hand and did not open it, but stood back a pace. There was a sound of fumbling with the latch, and the door opened slowly. Two men entered, one a bearded giant whose coat had been rent so that the left side flapped over his shoulder and whose lips were bleeding, the other a slim, youngish man in an old tweed jacket and breeches of an English cut.

No sooner were they inside than the covering was removed from the lamp. The doorkeeper had his back to the door, the man on the straw got to his feet, and the giant caught his companion from behind and held his arms.

Four pistol barrels glimmered in the scanty light.

"Hullo," said the newcomer. "There are more friends here than I expected. You have done me proud, Mollison."

It was a strange and macabre scene. The man with the dark suit and the pearl pin sat unmoved on the barrel, his opaque eyes stolidly regarding him who seemed to be a prisoner. Bechstein, the man with the fever, had his revolver laid over one arm, as if he were uncertain of his shaking limbs. The doorkeeper lolled against the door-post grinning, Radin and Molinoff stood on each side like executioners, and the giant Mollison spat blood from his mouth, while his great face hung like a monstrous gargoyle over the slim figure of his captive.

That captive seemed very little perturbed.

"I owe you a good turn for this, Mollison," he said pleasantly. "Hullo, Bechstein! I heard you were ill in bed.

I'm afraid you are taking liberties with your health...I can't see very well, but can it be Radin, and, by Jove, Molinoff, too? The Devil has looked after his own to-day."

"He hasn't looked after you, my friend," said Mollison. "Your number's up all right. You're going to be a quiet little corpse within sixty seconds, as soon as we have tossed for who is to have the pleasure of sending you to hell."

"Well, let go my arm and let me draw my last breath in comfort. I haven't a gun."

The giant ran one hand down the prisoner's figure "True enough," he said, and relaxed his grip. "But don't move, or you won't have sixty seconds."

"It's my right to kill the swine," said the doorkeeper. "I was Kubek's second-in-command and I owe him one for the chief."

The plea seemed to meet with general acceptance, and the prisoner saw his time of probation shortened by this unanimity. For a moment he seemed at a loss, and then he laughed with a fair pretence of merriment.

"By the way, you haven't told me what you have against me. Isn't it right that I should hear the charge?"

"Damn you, there's no time to waste," said the door-keeper. "You have been the mainspring of this tomfool revolution, which has already done in our best pals and will make life a bloody hell for the rest of us. W are going to give ourselves the satisfaction of shooting you like a dog before we scatter."

"You don't even know my name."

"We know your game and that's enough for us."

The prisoner seemed to be anxious to continue the talk. He spoke slowly, and in a pleasant, soft voice. It might have been noticed that he held his head in the attitude of a man listening intently, as if he expected to hear more steps on the cobbles of the yard.

"There's one here who knows me," he said. "Tim--Tim Lariarty," and he addressed the sphinx-like figure on the barrel. "You remember Arbuthnot. I was at Brodie's when you were at Ridgeway's. We got our twenty-two together, and we were elected to Pop the same day. You were a bit of a sap and got into the Sixth, while I never got beyond the First Hundred. You remember Sandy Arbuthnot?"

The face of the man on the barrel did not change perceptibly, but there was a trifle more life in his voice when he spoke. "You are Arbuthnot? Of course you would be Arbuthnot. I might have guessed it."

"Then for God's sake, Timmy, tell that blighter behind me to put down his gun. I'll take my medicine when it comes, but I'd like to tell you something. You're a clever chap with a future, and I've got something to say to you about the Gran Seco which you ought to hear. Give me five minutes."

There was a protest, but the sphinx nodded. "Give him five minutes," he said and took out his watch.

The prisoner began to talk in his compelling way, and unconsciously the interest of his executioners awakened.

Being on the edge of death, he had no reticences. He divulged the whole tale of the revolution, and he made a good story of it. He told of Blenkiron's coming to the Gran Seco, of the slow sapping of the loyalty of the Mines police, of the successful propaganda among the technical staff, of the organising of the Indian pueblas, in which he claimed a modest share. The others dropped their pistol-hands and poked forward their heads to listen. The five minutes lengthened to six, to eight, to ten, and he still held his audience. He addressed himself to the man on the barrel, and sometimes he lowered his voice till the door-keeper took a step nearer. Then he became more confidential, and his voice dropped further. "How do you think it was managed? A miracle? No, a very simple secret which none of you clever folk discovered. We had a base and you never knew it. Go into the pueblas and the old men will speak of a place which they call Uasini Maconoa. That means the Courts of the Morning--Los Patios de la Mariana. Where do you think it is? Listen, and I will tell you."

They listened, but only for his words, while the speaker was listening for another sound which he seemed at last to have detected. He suddenly caught two of the heads bent forward, those of Radin and Molinoff, and brought them crashing together. The doorkeeper could not shoot, because Mollison was in his way, and in an instant the chance was gone, for a blow on the head felled him to the ground. Mollison with a shout swung the dazed Radin and Molinoff aside and had his pistol in the air, when a report rang out and he toppled like a great tree, shot through the brain. The hut had filled with men, and the two whose heads had crashed and the fever-stricken Bechstein were throttled from behind and promptly pinioned. Then the prisoner showed what the strain had been by fainting at the feet of the man on the barrel.

He came to himself, and found Peters holding a brandy-flask to his mouth. Peters had a whitish face. "My God, sir," he stammered, "you will never be nearer death."

The young man seemed to have recovered, for he had strength enough to laugh. "I cut it pretty fine, but there was no other way. I had to make myself ground-bait if we were to catch these pike. We've got them all now...I think I could have held them for another five minutes, but I chose to precipitate things. You see, I saw by the nicker of the lantern that the door was opening, and that meant you. If I hadn't thought of that head-crashing dodge, I think I might have stopped a bullet."

The man on the barrel had risen and was looking sombrely on. The policeman jerked his head towards him. "What about that fellow?" he asked.

"Oh, let him alone," was the answer. "He is free to go where he likes. He was at school with me, and I owe him a good turn for this evening."

BOOK II - THE COURTS OF THE MORNING

I

Just about the hour of sunrise a girl sat perched on a rock from which the ground fell westward into an abyss of blue vapour. East of her, after a mile of park-like land, the steep woods rose black as coal, and above them soared into the central heavens a great mountain of rock and shale, which, so sheer was the face, showed even to a viewpoint so near its summit cone of snow. The face and the plateau were still dipped in shadow, but beyond the mountain the sun was up, and its first beams, flooding through a cleft on the north shoulder, made a pool of gold far out on the Western sea. The peak was the great Choharua, which means, in the speech of the old races, the Mountain of the Two Winds, for it was held to be wind-shed as well as water-shed.

The tropic dawn broadened fast, though the sun did not show himself. Presently all the plateau to the east was washed in a pure, pale light. The place seemed to sparkle with a kind of hoarfrost, though the air was mild, and its undulations, and the shallow glen of the stream which descended from Choharua, were sharp-rimmed black shadows in that silver field. Then greenness broke through the monotint, like the flush of spring in an English wood, and what had been like a lunar landscape sprang suddenly into clean, thin colours. The far cone of snow became rosy-red and crystalline, so that for one moment, it hung like a translucent jewel in the sky. Then it solidified; the details of the shaly face sprang into hard reality; what had been unfeatured shadow showed now as sheer crag and intricate couloirs, specked with snowdrifts which were leaping waters. At last came the orb of the sun, first a crescent of red gold, and then by quick gradations a great burning archway in which the mountain seemed to be engulfed. The air changed to a glow of essential light, and in a moment it seemed that the faint scents of night became the warm spicy odours of day.

The girl was looking to the sea. The line of light, which a minute before had been on the horizon, ran shoreward, as if a tide of sheer gold was flowing in from the west, But the ocean was some thousands of feet below, and the shore waters remained in dusk long after the morning had conquered the plateau. Below her the chasm of blue mist slowly became luminous, and features detached themselves tall trees near at hand clinging to scarps, outjutting head-lands of green far down. The noise of the falling stream grew louder, as if it had been asleep during the darkness and had only begun to talk with the morning. The immediate foreground cleared, and curious things were revealed. There were buildings on the edge of the chasm from which wire ropeways ran down into the brume, the kind of thing by which in Norway the saeter hay is moved to the valley, and by which in the War in the eyries of the Dolomites the Italian army provisioned its look-out posts and gun stations. Also there were revealed the beginnings of a path which descended the ravine in spirals, and something else--a framework of trestles and iron which decanted itself into the abyss like a gigantic chute. A stranger could now have made out the main features of the landscape--a steep glen down which the torrent from Choharua made its way to the sea, a glen, not a cliff, a place by which in was possible to have access from the shore to the plateau But that shore would not reveal itself. It lay far below in a broad ribbon of mist, flecked like a bird's wing, which separated the molten gold of the sea from the gold-washed recreated world of the morning hills.

The girl rose from her perch and drew long breaths of the diamond air. The waxing light revealed her companion, a tall man muffled in a blanket coat, who had been standing beneath her. She turned to him. "It is well called this the Courts of the Morning, Excellency," she said. "Aren't you glad I made you come with me?"

He was busy lighting his pipe. When he raised his face to her, there was a flicker of a smile around the corners of his deep-set eyes.

"I blame myself for not appreciating long ago the charms of this corner of my province. It is a place to intoxicate youth."

"And you?"

"I am no longer young. To me it is a picturesque mantelpiece between the sierras and the sea. I observe--" he nodded towards the ropeways and the trestles--"I observe your communications. Ingenious!"

"You may examine them at your leisure. We have no secrets from our leader."

"Your leader malgre lui. You foolish children are consistent in your folly. Tell me one thing, Miss Dasent. I am apparently at liberty. A charming young lady takes me out to admire the sunrise. Supposing I desire to leave--desire it very badly. I am a busy man and my business will suffer from my absence...Say that I am resolved to end this folly and at this moment. What would hinder me?"

"Need you ask?" she said.

"I ask," he replied. Something minatory and grim had come into his face.

"I should hinder you," was her answer.

He took a step towards her, while she watched him keenly. As his foot was raised for a second step, she blew a small whistle, and he halted. Out of the rocks and bushes men had appeared by magic, lean Indian faces with their eyes fixed on the girl. She looked at her companion, and he smiled. Then she waved her hand and the faces disappeared.

"I thought as much," he said. "As I said, you are consistent in your folly." The momentary animation had gone out of his face, and left it placid, set, and inscrutable.

He did not move when out of the chasm two figures emerged, so quietly that even the girl, who had been expecting them, started as their steps rang on the stony platform.

They were young men, apparently much of an age, but very different in build. One was tall and burly, with an untidy head of tow-coloured hair and a face so rugged that the features might have been rough-hewn with an axe out of some pale wood. It would have made an excellent figurehead for an old China clipper. He wore a khaki shirt, khaki shorts, and football stockings, but there was something about him that smacked of the sea. His companion, who wore similar clothes, was slight and beaky, with s mop of longish dark hair. They were about to cry some greeting to the girl when they caught sight of her companion and both stiffened, like men who had been trained, in the presence of a superior.

"Excellency, may I present to you two members of your staff?" she said. "This,"--indicating the tall man--"is Lieutenant Roger Grayne, a naval officer...This is Captain Bobby Latimer. You are not interested in these things, I know, Excellency, but Captain Latimer has quite a reputation in our Air Force."

The bareheaded young men saluted. "Pardon our rig, sir," said Grayne, "but we've been up all night. We're rather in want of a bath and breakfast. We've just been saying good-bye to the Corinna."

"Ah! Your line of communications?"

"One of them," said the girl, smiling.

"I venture to remind you," said the older man, "that the republic of Olifa possesses a navy."

The sailor laughed. "Not a very good one, sir. A trifle short in small craft and a whole lot short in practice Olifa has never had much coast-patrol work to do, and she is mighty ignorant of this northern shore. I'd like to take you down below there and show you the landing. It's as cunningly tucked away as the ports the old-time buccaneers used to have among the Florida keys. It would take pretty bright men some months to hit it off."

"But supposing they were fortunate? What then?"

"Why then, sir, they could make it difficult for the Corinna and certain other craft, but they couldn't put any considerable spoke in our business."

"What would prevent them fighting their way up and cornering you like rats on this shelf?"

"Ye--es," was the answer. "They might--with Heaven's own luck and plenty of time and no sort of regard for casualties. That four thousand feet of gully is a mighty difficult ladder to climb, and every rung has its nasty catch. I'm not worrying about our little backdoor to the sea. Come here, sir, and have a look down. The mist will be gone by now."

The Gobernador allowed himself to be led to a little platform of rock which projected above the gulf. On his arrival he had made the ascent in a thick fog, and had had no chance of noting the details. Now he saw that the path dropped at once into thick bush, while the trestles zigzagged till they were lost behind a spur of rock. Only the wireways ran straight in a dizzy angle till far below they seemed to terminate in a dull blur on the water's edge. But what he chiefly observed was that the shore made a little bay, which ran south and was sheltered from the ocean by a green conical spur. To a ship at sea that bay was securely hidden, and the ravine must appear as one of a hundred others on the scarred and wooded mountain face. There would be some intricate prospecting before it was discovered.

He turned to the others with a shrug of his shoulders.

"I think I have had enough of the picturesque. What about breakfast?"

A path led them into the shallow trough of the plateau, where the stream from Choharua wound among lawns and thickets in shining links like a salmon-river. They crossed it by a rough bridge of planks, and then the land lifted gently under the shadow of the mountain, while the shelf broadened as it turned the southern skirts. Presently it flattened out to a miniature plain, and they came suddenly into an area of crowded life. It looked like a cantonment. Around a block of wooden huts lay a ring of tents, from which rose the smoke of morning fires. On the left there we horse-lines, and beyond them the tall masts of a wireless station. On the right were what looked like aeroplane hangars. A busy hum came from the place, and that mingled smell of wood-smoke, horses, and cooking food which since the beginning of time has been a mark of human concourse.

The western ocean was hidden by the lift of the shore scarp, but since the coast recessed at this point there was a gleam of water from the south. To the south-east lay the great wall of the sierras, but as it bent inland the land in front seemed to sink in craggy and forested foothills, giving the eyes a great prospect towards what seemed a second and lower plateau. The air was filled with an exquisite morning freshness, half of the sea and half of the hills, and the place seemed part eyrie, part sanctuary--an observation point over the kingdoms of the world, and also a tiny sheltered kingdom, brooded over by virgin peaks and guarded by untravelled seas.

The four stopped before one of the larger tents. A little way off a small party of Indians were off--saddling weary horses. The girl pointed to them.

"See, Excellency," she said. "Another of our lines of communication."

An hour later a small company assembled for breakfast in the staff mess hut. Janet Roylance was dispensing coffee to half a dozen young men in breeches and linen jackets, one of whom was her husband, while Barbara Dasent at the other end of the table was slicing a cold ham. The men rose as the Gobernador entered, and Janet pointed to a vacant chair beside her.

"Where is Sandy?" she asked. "Archie saw him an hour ago, and he said he was hungry enough to eat an ox."

"He is getting clean," said Archie. "He looks as if he had been having a dusty time. He likes tea, Janet."

"I know. I've got it for him. And Sobranye cigarettes in a china box. I remembered his tastes."

To a stranger there would have appeared to be no formality or restraint about the little party. It might have been a company of friends breakfasting at some country farm.

The Gobernador made a hearty meal, and his watchful eyes seemed almost benevolent when they rested on Janet or Barbara. There was no reference to the hive of strange activities around them. The young Americans were recondite travellers and talked at large of odd places and odd friends. One of them, Eborall by name, whom the others called Jim, had been with Roosevelt on his Amazon expedition and had something to say of the uneasy life of the Brazilian forests. "We never struck a health-resort like this," he said. "They don't keep them on the east side of the Andes." Grayne, who was something of a naturalist, had a discussion with Archie Roylance about a type of short-winged buzzard that he had seen that morning. The young men spoke deferentially, with an eye on the Gobernador, like subalterns breakfasting with their commanding officer. Janet chattered eagerly in her role of the untravelled, to whom every new thing was a marvel. Only Barbara was a little silent. Her eyes were always turning to the door.

Presently it opened and a man entered. At first glance he seemed about the same age as the others, for a fine-drawn face often acquires an absurd youthfulness when, after some days of indoor life, it is first exposed to the weather. The tiny wrinkles around his eyes did not show under the flush of sunburn. He entered like a guest who, having arrived late at a country-house, makes his first appearance at breakfast and knows that he will find friends.

"Sandy, at last!" Janet cried. All rose, and the young Americans turned curious eyes on the newcomer, as on someone who had been eagerly awaited.

"There's a chair next to Barbara," Janet said. "Excellency, I don't think you have met Lord Clanroyden."

The two men bowed, but the newcomer did not offer to shake hands. They smiled on each other with conventional politeness, but the eyes of the elder man dwelt longer on the newcomer's face.

"What's the news?" Janet asked with a casualness that was obviously assumed.

"None at present, except that everything goes well. I must feed first, for my last bite was fifteen hours ago. After that I'm going to turn in and sleep a round of the clock...How jolly it is to be up on this shelf again! I feel a new man already."

Sandy fell heartily on his food. "China tea," he murmured. "Janet, you saint! I haven't tasted it for weeks."

But the pleasant informality had deserted the company. Archie looked heavy with unspoken questions. The young Americans fell silent and kept their eyes furtively on Sandy as if they were trying to harmonise a preconceived figure of their imagination with this ravenous reality. Janet rose "I don't see why we should behave as if we were at the Zoo, and watching the animals feed. Your cigarettes are over there, Sandy. We'll leave you to finish your breakfast in peace."

But the Gobernador did not leave the room with the others. He filled his pipe and pushed the Sobranye cigarettes towards Sandy's plate. The latter, having finished the marmalade stage, began to peel an apple. "Please smoke," he said. "I'll join you in a second."

Presently he swung himself round to face the other, and lit a cigarette. His face had lost the careless youthfulness which it had borne when he first arrived. It was the face of an older and a different man, hard, fine, and alert, and his eyes were as wary as the Gobernador's. They seemed to be inviting a challenge.

The latter spoke first.

"I think you owe me an explanation, Lord Clanroyden," he said. The tones of his voice were perfectly quiet and assured. The question seemed to spring not from anxiety but from a polite curiosity.

"I owe you many, but they will have to come bit by bit. Meanwhile I can give you news. The night before last we occupied without serious trouble the city of the Gran Seco. At this moment I think I can fairly say that the whole province is in our hands."

"We! Our! What precisely do you mean?" There was an edge in the voice which proved that its possessor had been startled.

"It is a long story. But the name which the newspaper-readers of the world are associating with the revolt against the Olifa Government is your own, Excellency. You were the creator of the Gran Seco, and you are going to be its liberator."

"Liberator? From what? Am I to destroy my own creation?"

"The copper industry will not suffer. The Vice-President of the Company will see to that. There will only be a suspension of business--how long will depend upon the Olifa Government."

"Rosas? He is in this fool conspiracy?"

"Undoubtedly. You may call him the prime mover. You know him as Rosas the Mexican, but to his friends he s John Scantlebury Blenkiron--a patriotic citizen of the United States--"

The other cried out. "Blenkiron! But he is dead!"

"Only officially. He is an ancient friend of mine, and there is our good fortune, Excellency, that your paths never crossed till he joined you eighteen months ago. You need not blame your Intelligence service.

Blenkiron has puzzled before this the most efficient Intelligence services. He had seen watching your doings for some time, and when he put his remarkable talents at your service it was with a purpose. The first part of that purpose has now been accomplished." Sandy paused.

"Go on," said the other. "I am deeply interested."

Sandy laughed. "We have no secrets from our commander-in-chief. But why should I waste time telling you what you know already?"

"I am not sure that I do know. This purpose? You do not want to cripple a great industry? You have no special grievance, I take it, against the republic of Olifa? You are not fanatics about forms of government? Am I to take it that your efforts are directed principally against me?"

"You may put it that way if you like. But we have no personal animus against your Excellency. Blenkiron, who has worked with you for nearly two years, rather likes you. We are all prepared to give you devoted allegiance."

"Provided I do what you want?"

"Provided you do what we want. We are anxious to prevent you making a fool of yourself."

It was the elder man's turn to laugh. "Then I suppose I should be grateful, and I am certainly flattered.

But I should like to know just what you consider my capacities in the way of folly."

"I hate to repeat platitudes," said Sandy, "but, since you insist, you shall have them. You have created a great industry, but you are following what seems to us an unbusinesslike line. You are using up your human material too rapidly. I put aside the moral question, and ask you simply if that is good business. Of course it isn't, and since you do not do things without a purpose, we had to discover that purpose. Well, we know perfectly well what it is. You are trying to make bad trouble in a world which has already too much trouble. We do you the justice to admit that this is not blind malevolence. You have an ideal behind you, a philosophy, a very serious philosophy. Well, to be frank, we don't like your methods, and we don't like your purpose, and we hate your philosophy like hell. Do we understand each other?"

The Gobernador shook out the ashes from his pipe. His eyes, under his level brows, looked steadily on his companion. There was now no smile on his face, and in his gaze there was a serious perplexity.

"Lord Clanroyden," he said, "I have known about you for some years--under your old name. I have even made it my business to keep in touch with you through my informants. I have always regarded you as a person of quite exceptional intelligence. There have been times when I considered you one of the two or three most intelligent people in the world...I confess that I am grievously disappointed."

"No wonder," said Sandy. "I have always been a bit of an ass."

"I don't complain that our aims differ. Your reputation was never that of a thinker. But you were reported to me as a practical man, uncommonly audacious, resourceful, and far-sighted. Now I find that you are audacious--but with the audacity of a crude boy. You have organised a childish little piece of banditry. You think you have fathomed my methods. Why, man, you have not learned the alphabet of them. I have my lines down deep in every country on the globe. The Gran Seco has purchase with every Government. As soon as the news of your doings has gone abroad, you will have the most potent forces set at work to defeat you. The prosperity of the Gran Seco is of vital importance to millions up and down the world. The credit of Governments, the interests of a thousand financial groups are involved. The very people who might otherwise sympathise with you will be forced to combine to break you."

"True," said Sandy. "But you realise that your name as our leader will cramp the style of your supporters."

"Only for a moment. It will not be believed..."

"I am not so sure. Remember, you are a mystery man, Excellency, whom the world has heard of, but does not know. You have been playing a pretty game with the press, but we too have made our plans. The newspapers by this time will be full of character-studies of the Gobernador of the Gran Seco, arranged for by us. In spite of yourself, you are going to get the reputation of a high-souled humanitarian, a cross between Bolivar and Abraham Lincoln. I think we shall get in first with our picture, and--well, you know what the public is. It will be difficult to efface first impressions, and that, I say, will cramp the style of your people and give us time."

"But what earthly good will time do you? That is my second charge against your intelligence. You have chosen to fight me with weapons so infantile that they will break in a week...What were you and Blenkiron thinking of to put your eggs in this preposterous basket? I have many vulnerable points. I know that, if you do not. You and your friends might have slowly organised the collective stupidity of the world against me. You had your fulcrum in America, and for lever you had all the crude sentimentality of mankind. I have always feared such a crusade. Why did you not attempt it?"

"I will tell you why," was the answer. "It was because we respected you too sincerely. We knew that we couldn't beat you at that game. To fight you in parliaments, and cabinet councils, and on the stock exchanges and in the press would have been to fight you on your own chosen ground. We preferred to fight you on our ground. We decided to transfer the whole contest to a sphere in which your genius was not at home. You are the last word in civilisation, Excellency, and you can only be beaten by getting you into the ancient and elementary world where civilisation does not apply."

The other did not answer for a moment. Something in the words seemed to have started a new train of thought, and his eyes took on a profound abstraction. Then he leaned forward.

"There is method in that," he said, "I do not quarrel with your policy. But, in the name of all that is rational, where are your weapons? A handful of children, a disloyal colleague who has no doubt worked upon the turbulent element among our white employees, my kidnapping, and the fact that my administration was a somewhat personal matter--these may give you control of the Gran Seco for a day or two. But what then? There are the wealth and the army of Olifa to crush you like a nut on an anvil."

"Not quite so bad. You underestimate Blenkiron, I think. Remember he has been in the Gran Seco for some time, and he has not been idle. We have the Mines Police, and most of the Mines foremen and engineers. When I left yesterday, the place was as docile as a girls' school, and there was a very stout heart in our troops."

"Troops!" the other said. "You may have got your non-commissioned officers, but where can you get the rank-and-file for an army?"

"Where you got your labour, Excellency. Among the old masters of the country. You must have heard of the trouble that the Gran Seco Indians used to give to Olifa. They were never properly conquered till you came along. You policed them and dragooned them, but the dragoons are now on their side. A couple of years more and you would have drained the manhood from them and left then mere shells of men. But at present they are still a people and a fighting people, and they are going to fight for liberty and vengeance. Not against you--they regard you as their saviour, and are wearing your medals round their necks--but against the oppressors of Olifa...I think you lived too much of a sedentary life, Excellency. You took the word of your subordinates too much on trust. If you had lived as I have among the pueblas, you would have been a little afraid of what you found there...Perhaps a little shocked, too...Those rags and tatters of men, used up in the mines and flung on the dustheap! The remnant of manhood left in them is not a gentle thing."

"But against the army of Olifa! I have made it my business to see that that army is the most efficient for its size in the world. What can your savages and your gunmen do against the last word of science from the laboratory and the factory?"

"Nothing if we fight them in their own way. A good deal, I think, if we fight them in ours. We refuse to meet you on your own ground, Excellency, and you may be certain that we don't mean to meet the Olifa army on theirs."

"I cannot follow your riddles."

"Of course you can't. This is a very academic discussion we're having. If you'll allow me, I'll explain to you later he general layout. You're entitled to have everything shown you. It will interest you, as a thinker, for, though you'll scarcely believe it, we too have our philosophy of life. You are a very wise man, with a large experience of the world, but I believe we can show you something which you know nothing about."

The other was listening intently. "This wonderful revelation?" he asked. "What is it?"

"The meaning of youth," was the answer. "You have lived all your life in an elderly world, Excellency. Everything worked by rule, and even your lawlessness was nicely calculated. And all the old stagnant things were your puppets which you could move as you pleased. But there's another side of which you know nothing at all. You have your science; well, it will be matched against hope and faith and the simplicity that takes chances. We may go down, but we'll go down cheerfully, and, if we win, by God, we'll make you a new man."

A strange look came into the other's face. He regarded Sandy with a bewilderment in his stern eyes which seemed not altogether unfriendly.

"I cannot quite understand," he said, as he rose, "why you and your friends did not take the simple course. Since your quarrel is principally with me, a bullet in my head strikes me as the most satisfactory solution."

Sandy stood before him, a head shorter, a stone or two lighter, looking at the moment half his age. There was a dancing light in his eyes which answered the flickering spark in the other's. He laid a hand on the Gobernador's sleeve, as if the great man were a coeval.

"Nonsense!" he said. "We leave murder to your Conquistadors. We think so highly of you that we're going to have a try at saving your soul."

II

The wireless station on the plateau received its punctual bulletins of news from the outer world, copies of which were posted up in the mess-hut. From them it appeared that the republic of Olifa was already in the throes of a campaign. War had begun when on the 14th day of June. The city of the Gran Seco had been seized by the rebels, and the whole province was in revolt. The whereabouts of Castor were not known; his lieutenants held the city, but he was reputed to be with the main force of the revolt, somewhere in the hinterland. Olifa had replied to the challenge. Her army was mobilised, and a Gran Seco Expeditionary Force was in being. The aged General Bianca, the Minister of War, did not take command; for that post the President had selected a younger man, General Lossberg, who had been military governor of the city of Olifa, and had come there after the European War with a high reputation from the Eastern Front, where he had been one of Mackensen's corps commanders. The Expeditionary Force was said to contain four divisions of infantry, a cavalry brigade, and four of the new machine-gun battalions.

The comments of the world's press on the outbreak were curiously restrained. Some influence must have been at work, for the current story represented the revolt as that of the leaders of the copper industry against an oppressive Government, which confiscated their profits and by inhuman laws was ruining their reservoir of native labour. Thus stated, humanity and sound business seemed to be on the side of the rebels. Strange tales were printed of the barbarities of conscripted labour, of men worn to husks and sent back to their villages to die. The picture presented was of enlightened magnates forced unwillingly into harshness by the greed of Olifa, until finally decency and common sense forced them to make a stand. A spontaneous labour revolt had been sponsored by the masters themselves, and at the head stood Castor, the Gobernador. It seemed a clear issue, on which the conscience of the world could not be divided. There were papers in England, France, and America which hailed Castor as a second Lincoln.

Yet the more responsible section of the press walked warily, which seemed to point to conflicting versions of the facts among those likely to know best. Such papers were guarded in their comments on the merits of the dispute, and treated it as a domestic Olifa question on which exact information was lacking. Patently the Gran Seco agents throughout the world were puzzled and were holding their hand. Their chief was playing a game on which they had not been instructed. The news columns of such papers were filled with sensational accounts of Gran Seco wealth and luxury and of Indian pueblas full of the broken and diseased, but the leading articles steered a discreet course.

Castor was no doubt a great man, possibly a man of destiny, but the end was not yet--and Olifa had been of late a particularly docile and well-conducted republic.

The world seemed to agree to make a ring round the combatants.

Only the scallywags and the restless youth of all nations were prepared to take sides, and consulates and passport-offices were plagued by those who wished to reach the seat of war. There were perpetual queues at the door of the Gran Seco offices in London, New York, and Paris.

One body of men alone had decided views--the military critics. Among these there was a remarkable unanimity. The revolt, in their opinion, could not sustain itself for more than a few weeks. The details of the Olifa army were well known. It was officered by able professional soldiers, it had been a pioneer in mechanisation, and The Times had published from a contributor some striking articles on its efficiency; it had behind it a wealthy Government, and should the need arise, a big population to conscript; above all, it had an open door to the sea. The rebels must be and the best a rabble of Indian labourers and European miners with a sprinkling, no doubt, of soldiers of fortune. They might be armed after a fashion, but they could not compete with the armoury of Olifa. They had no communication open with the outer world. Assuming that they had laid in a store of ammunition, they could not supply wastage. The Gran Seco, which was largely a desert, could not feed itself and the rebels would be starved out long before they wen defeated. It was like a fugitive who had climbed a tree; the pursuit had only to wait below till he was forced by hunger to come down. General Weyland in the London Times, and Mr Winter Spokes in the New York Herald Tribune reached the same conclusion.

The campaign had begun; according to the wireless Olifa was an armed camp, and everything was in train for and advance on the Gran Seco; but in the Courts of the Morning there was peace. There was activity enough. Daily aeroplanes left the shelf for long flights beyond the foot-hills and over the arid steppes of the Gran Seco to the savannah and forests of Olifa, now sweltering under the first deluge of the rainy season. Strings of convoys ascended by the rough paths and departed with their stores. Horsemen arrived hourly with messages, and every yard of the settlement was busy. Yet it seemed a peaceful busyness. The workers met at meals and in the evenings with the cheerfulness of weary but equable folk. There was no tension in the atmosphere. Castor for the most part had his meals in his own room, but he invariably appeared at dinner, and he seemed to be in good health and spirits. Though under constant surveillance, he had the illusion of liberty, and could walk abroad with Janet and Barbara as if he were a guest in a country-house. There was nothing about him of the feverish prisoner, and this disquieted Sandy.

"I haven't begun to understand him," he told Janet. "You see, all I know about him I know at second-hand from Blenkiron, and by deduction from his public career. I met him for the first time a week ago. Our only talk was just an exchange of polite challenges. We might have been shouting at each other from adjacent mountaintops...I don't like that calm of his. Here you have a man whose brain has never stopped working, and who has the ambition of a fallen angel. He sees us trying to play havoc with his life's work, and he makes no sign of impatience. What has his mind got to bite on? It can't be idle."

"He writes a great deal," said Janet. "He has told me about it. I don't think I quite understood, but isn't there an Italian called Croce? Well, he thinks Croce all wrong about something, and is trying to explain how."

"O Lord!" Sandy groaned. "The fellow is bigger than we thought. I didn't reckon on this superhuman detachment. He must be very sure he is going to win."

"Yes," said Janet thoughtfully. "But not for the reasons that the wireless gives. He told me that he thought hat those military experts talked nonsense. I think he knows that he will win because he is bigger than we are. He has been studying us all most carefully. You especially, Sandy. Do you notice how he looks at you? I believe he was afraid of you before he met you."

"But not now?"

"No. I'm sorry, but I don't think he is so afraid of you now. I fancy he is always a little uneasy about anything he does not understand. But he thinks he is getting to the bottom of you."

"I daresay he is. But I'm nowhere near the bottom of him. None of the formulas fit him. It's no good saying that he is pure intellect. He's that, but he's a great deal more. On his record I ought to hate him. He stands for everything I most detest, and he has been responsible for the bloodiest cruelties. On the bare facts of the case Nero was respectable compared to him...And yet I can't hate him--simply because I can't hold him responsible. He has no notion what he has done, for, with all his cleverness, there's an odd, idiotic innocence about him. I nourished a most healthy disgust till I met him. But now, confound it, I rather like him."

"So do I," said the girl emphatically. "Barbara doesn't but I do. And I believe he rather likes us--even you, Sandy. You see, we are something that he has never quite met before, and we interest him desperately. He is busy summing us up, and that gives his mind something to work on. Now that I know him, I could no more hate him than I could hate a cyclone or an erupting volcano."

"You mean he is a sort of impersonal natural force?"

"No, I don't. He is a person, but very limited--as limited as a cyclone. His energies and his interests have been constricted into a narrow channel. I think he lacks imagination."

Sandy whistled.

"Good for you, Janet. I should have said that his imagination was the most deadly and colossal thing about him."

"Yes--yes. But it is only one kind of imagination. Milton could imagine the scenery of Hell and Heaven, but he hadn't enough imagination to understand his wife. He is still a little puzzled by us, and that makes him puzzled about himself. Up till now he had been mathematically certain about everything. If we make him uncertain, we may win...Now, I'm going to take him for a walk and continue his education."

Presently, into the orderly routine of the plateau came something of the stir of war. Messengers from the lowlands became more frequent, and Sandy had to take his sleep when he could, for he might be called upon at any hour. The wireless operators were kept busy, and at night there was much activity in the ravine which dropped seaward, for unlighted ships groped their way into the secret gulf.

The aeroplanes, which were still used only for intelligence purposes, and not for combat, brought back more authentic news than the war correspondents cabled to the press of the world, and that they gained it at some risk was proved by more than one that returned with damaged planes and bullets in its fuselage.

The Gobernador had shown little interest in the wireless messages from the world's capitals. He had left

Olifa with no more than a suit of dress-clothes, and had been fitted out from the wardrobe of Archie, who was much the same height and figure. One morning Sandy came in to breakfast with a new light in his eye.

"Things are beginning to move, sir," he told Castor. "The time has come to get into campaigning kit. We shan't be a dressy staff, but we can't go about like earth-stoppers any more."

Thereafter everyone appeared in simple khaki tunics and breeches. Castor submitted good-humouredly to the change.

"You look like General Smuts, sir," Archie told him, "only a little darker and less benevolent."

Castor smiled. "That would seem to be in keeping. Like Smuts, I am an intellectual compelled by fate to be a leader of guerrillas. Is it not so?"

That night Sandy and young Latimer pinned up on the wall of the mess-hut a big map mounted on calico, and proceeded to ornament it with little flags.

"There is your province, sir," he said, "a better map than anything the Surveyor-General has in Olifa. The colour-washes represent altitudes. The red flags are our posts, and the green are the Olifa army. I am going to give a staff lecture, for the bell has rung and the curtain gone up."

The map showed only the northern half of the republic, from Olifa city to the apex where the great mountains crowded down upon the sea. From the Courts of the Morning the land fell in tiers--first the wooded shelves, then the barrens of the Seco Boreal, and then the broad shallow cup where the Mines and the city lay. From the Gran Seco city the country ran westward for a hundred miles till it ended in the rocky sierras of the coast. Eastward it rose into the savannahs of the Indian reserve and the Tierra Caliente, till it met the main chain of the Cordilleras. The map did not embrace this latter feature, and there was no sign on it of the pass into the Poison Country. The south boundary of the Gran Seco was a ridge of dolomite cliffs, broken apparently only at one place--by the long winding valley up which the railway ran from Santa Ana.

From the contours it looked to be otherwise unapproachable from that side, save by one or two tortuous and difficult footpaths, at the head of which under Castor's administration there had been block-houses and patrols. There was no breach at either end, for on the west this southern ridge ran out in the coast sierras, and on the east became a buttress of the main Cordilleras massif. There were red flags in the city and at the Universum, clusters at two points in the Indian Reserve, one of them very close to the mountains, and a chain running up towards the Courts of the Morning. In the plain of Olifa there was a big green concentration at Santa Ana, and a green blob half-way up the railway.

"Lossberg has got his rolling stock at last," Sandy explained. "He has his pioneers and one of his machine-gun battalions at the frontier, and his cavalry patrols were last night within five miles of the Gran Seco city."

Castor donned a pair of horn spectacles and examined the map closely. He studied especially the Seco Boreal and the eastern frontier. He ran his finger along the southern rim.

"That was always a troublesome place," he said. "Practicable for a mountaineer or an Indian, but scarcely more. At least, so our reports said. But we had to watch it. Rosas "--he smiled--"was always very strong about keeping posts there."

He took a step backward and surveyed the map.

"It appears that the military gentlemen who write to the papers are right," he said. "I seem to be in a very bad strategical position. Olifa can force a passage--it may take a little time and she may have losses, but she can fight her way up the railway to the Gran Seco. After that we are at her mercy, at least so far as the city and the Mines are concerned, for I do not suppose we can hope to win a field action against her."

"Not a chance," said Sandy cheerfully.

"Then nothing remains but a guerrilla war on our savannahs. I think she will beat us there, for ours is a hard dry soil and tanks and armoured cars can go anywhere. I speak as a civilian, but am I not right, Lord Clanroyden?"

"Perfectly."

"Our troops are mounted?"

"All of them."

"Where on earth did you get the horses? The Indian ponies are a miserable breed."

"Not so bad as you think," Sandy smiled. "But we had other sources of supply. Olifa is a famous horse-breeding country."

"But how did you draw on Olifa? How did you get the horses up?"

"Some day I will tell you--but not now."

The Gobernador looked puzzled.

"I take it we have a certain amount of food and munitions?"

"Enough to go on with."

"But not indefinitely...Then it looks as if before long our present dwelling-place would become a point of some importance. It is now our poste de commandement, and presently it may be our last refuge. We have access of the sea. If we can find ships, we shall have to make a moonlight flitting, as your people did at Gallipoli."

"I shouldn't wonder."

Castor took off his spectacles. "I speak with all modesty, but was it not a blunder to let Olifa strike first? I should have thought that our best chance would have been to obstruct the railway--like--like my Dutch prototype in Dur South African war. Can an inferior safely surrender the offensive?" And he smiled pleasantly.

Sandy shook his head. "It wouldn't have done. We should have given old Lossberg a lot of trouble, but he would have smashed us in the long run."

"Won't he smash us anyhow in the long run?" Castor moved closer and again studied the map. "God has been unkind to us in planting that wall of rock and snow in the east. It is most unfortunate that the southern wall of the Gran Seco runs clean up to the mountains without a convenient pass for honest guerrilleros to descend upon Olifa."

"Most unfortunate," said Sandy, but there was no melancholy in his tone. "Well, that's the layout. Now I will expound the meaning of our flags."

He enumerated in detail the strength and composition of the various detachments, and then explained the composition and marching order of the Olifero forces. Castor listened attentively and asked questions. "We are holding the city lightly, but the Mines strongly. Ah, I see. We have a big detachment on the railway. Who, by the way, commands in the city? Rosas? We have given my friend the post of honour--and danger."

Day by day the green flags crept northward till they were spilled in clusters beyond the Gran Seco frontier. Every evening Sandy gave his staff lecture. It was noticeable, now that the campaign had begun, that his spirits rose, and though he had scarcely time to feed or sleep he showed no trace of weariness. Yet there was tension in the air. The faces of the men would suddenly go blank as some problem swept them into preoccupation. Even the Gobernador was not exempt from these sudden silences. He alone had no routine work, but Janet, who had become his chief companion abroad, reported that he was becoming temperamental.

"I think it is this place," she told Sandy. "I don't believe he has ever been much out-of-doors in his life before. He has always lived in cities and railway-carriages, and Nature is rather a surprise to him and puts him off his balance. He told me to-day that this living with sunsets and sunrises made him giddy...His education is progressing. I wish I knew what he was thinking when he has that blindish look in his eyes."

"He seems to be interested in the campaign," said Sandy. "As an intellectual problem, I suppose. Something for his mind to work upon."

The girl hesitated.

"Perhaps," she said. "But I think there is something more in it than that. He has been adopted for the first time in his life into a community. We others are busy at a game. He is like a child. He can't help hankering a little to play too."

Presently events began to crowd on each other. The green flags made a forest between the Gran Seco frontier and the city, and spread out till their right wing was very close to the Universum Mine.

"That's the cavalry," Sandy explained. "They're finding it a tougher job than they reckoned. Yesterday they tried a sort of Jeb Stuart ride round the city and came in for some rough handling from Peters. They've first-rate cavalry, but indifferent M.I."

Then came a halt and the green flags did not advance for a day or two.

"We put up quite a good little show," was Sandy's comment. "You remember the fifth mile-post down the line where it runs through a horse-shoe valley. That's our position, and it is pretty much like that of the Boers at Magersfontein. They can't find our trenches to shell us out of them. Lossberg is getting nervous about a frontal attack and is considering an enveloping movement. See! He has two of his machine-gun battalions moving east of the Universum. He's bringing up another infantry division, too. That makes three, besides oddments. A pretty good muster against our modest territorials!"

Two days later the red flags had fallen back two miles along the railway. Sandy, with his eye on a smaller chart, elucidated the position on the big map. "Our forward zone has gone, and now we're in our battle zone, though we don't intend to have much of a battle. But we've got to stick it there for a couple of days...You see this bunch of red flags east of the Mines? That's our counter-movement beginning."

"It looks as if we were shaping for a big field action," said one of the young Americans.

"Not a bit. We aren't looking for any barren victories. This is all directed to Lossberg's address. We know a good deal about him, and he's a cautious warrior. He's taking no risks, for he has the strength and he means to use it...I hope to Heaven Peters doesn't dip in too deep."

To Janet and Barbara these days were as thrilling as the last act of a good play. Up in that quiet place, they seemed to watch the struggle like gods from the empyrean. The very map became like a crystal in which their fancy could see the hot mustard-coloured hills, the puffs of shrapnel on the ridges, the ant-like movements of little mortals. Even the Gobernador lost something of his calm, and the eyes under his level brows kindled. In these days the aircraft were never idle. Every hour of the day and night heard the drone of their going or returning.

On the evening of July 17th Sandy had much to tell.

"You will be glad to hear that Lossberg has got his reinforcements. This morning the last division of his Expeditionary Force crossed the frontier."

"You seem pleased?" asked the puzzled Janet.

"I am. I don't want unnecessary bloodshed, and these small holding battles take their toll. It's only a matter of hours now till we acknowledge defeat and fling up the sponge. It hasn't been a bad show, except that Peters went further than I intended. He pushed his counter-attack at the Universum a little too deep, and suffered accordingly. That's the worst of the enthusiastic amateur...There will be a great Olifa triumph presently. It will be fun to see what the papers make of it."

Next day Sandy's good-humour had increased. He appeared at luncheon silent but beaming, and when an excited company gathered in the mess-hut before dinner he arrived like a breathless boy.

"I want a drink, for I've had a dusty afternoon...Thanks, Bobby, a whisky-and-soda...We needn't wait. I can give you the news now. Early this morning we fell back from our last positions and all our troops have been withdrawn from the city. Lossberg's cavalry patrols must be in it now...Also the Universum is in his hands, and the Alhuema and the San Tome whenever he likes to have 'em. He will meet with no opposition. The first bout is past and we've been knocked over the ropes. It's Lossberg's round...You needn't look anxious, Excellency. There hasn't been ten pounds' worth of damage done to the Company's property."

"I wasn't thinking of the Company," said Castor, and his face had become very grave. "Has all this happened according to your plan?"

"More or less...except for Peters's venture. I didn't want our casualties to go beyond two hundred, and they're actually three hundred and seventeen. Still, your army has not suffered badly."

"For God's sake don't call it mine. I'm your prisoner and your enemy. What's the next step? When is this infernal folly to cease?"

Sandy grinned benignly. "Properly speaking, the infernal folly has just begun. The sparring is over and the real business is about to commence."

The other considered. "Your plan, I take it, was to put up just enough resistance to compel Olifa to send the whole of her Expeditionary Force inside the Gran Seco. You know, of course, that she has reserves?"

Sandy nodded. "But they will take some time to assemble, and they will have to make their way up."

"Why should they not?"

"It may be difficult, for soon there will be a most imperfect railway."

"And Lossberg."

"Our first business was to get him in. Our business now is to see that he does not get out."

Castor laughed, but there was no mirth in the sound.

"An ingenious plan! I have been obtuse. I might have guessed it."

Dinner that evening was a strange meal and a short one.

There was little talk, since for the first time the unpredictable future brooded over all of them like a cloud. In the cloud there was no depression, but a certain awe.

Sandy and Castor were the last to rise. The elder man had recovered his balance, and as they left the hut his eyes met the other's. "We are declared enemies. Lord Clanroyden," he said, "and the gloves are off. I make you my compliments on your boldness. I take it you are about to leave me and assume the direct command of the revolutionaries?"

"As your lieutenant. I shall report to you regularly."

"Let that fooling stop. I am at present your victim, but some day soon the parts will be reversed, I have only one thing to say to you. You have succeeded for the moment in putting me out of action. But I am something more than a single man marooned up on this shelf of mountain. I have my bodyguard--everywhere in the world, and also in Olifa, and in the Gran Seco. You cannot destroy that bodyguard, though no doubt you have tried, for most of it is subterranean and secret. That force will be fighting for me. Its methods are what you would call criminal, for it does not accept conventional standards of honour. But it is resourceful and subtle and it will stick at nothing. What chance have you against it? You will be compelled to take risks, and that force I speak of will make those risks a certainty of death."

"I wonder why you tell me that. Is it meant as a friendly warning?"

"I am not your friend. It is a warning. I do not wish you to deceive yourself. I want you to know what is against you."

For a moment Sandy stared at Castor's face as if he sought something buried deep in the man. Then he laughed. "Thank you. Excellency...I hope they'll make you comfortable while I'm away. If we meet again, we may be able to shake hands."

III

The details of Lossberg's advance up the railway, when, with overwhelming superiority of numbers and artillery, and after various checks, he drove in the screen of the defence, and on July 19th entered the Gran Seco city, do not belong to this story. They will be found set out at length in the dispatches of the correspondents who accompanied the Olifa army. Those veracious writers gave ample information about the Olifa command, for censorship was thought unnecessary in such a case, but they were very much in the dark as to in the personnel of the enemy. Castor was assumed to be commander-in-chief, and Rosas, described as a Mexican adventurer who had been once on the staff of Porfirio Diaz, was credited with such military talent as the rebels possessed.

The correspondents had followed the military critics in assuming that the result was a foregone conclusion. But presently a new name appeared in their dispatches--El Obro, an Indian word which was interpreted in Spanish as "el lobo gris"--"the grey wolf." El Obro was believed to be the name of a guerrilla leader much reverenced by the Indians, who was assumed to be lurking in the hinterland.

As the weeks passed this name was to appear more often, till presently Castor and Rosas were almost forgotten and it had the headlines to itself.

On the day before the defence broke, Blenkiron was sitting on an empty shell-case in what had once been the garden of his house behind the Administration Buildings. An algarroba tree gave him a little shade from the pitiless sun, and, since he was grey from head to foot with dust and had a broad battered panama hat pulled down over his head like a burnous, he had something of the air of a cadi under a palm. Around him stood a small group in rough field-service kit, all of them dusty and a little hollow-eyed, their shoulders limp and rounded like those of men who have not lain flat in bed for several nights. The place was very quiet to be in the heart of a city. There was no sound except that of an occasional car driven at top-speed in the adjoining street, though an alert ear might have caught at intervals a curious pattering noise coming from the south, a noise which at times grew into something like the beating of muffled drums.

A man was speaking, a man with a drawl and a sleepy voice. This was Escrick, the submanager of the Alhuema Mine, who had once commanded a brigade of Australian infantry in France. He had been in charge of the position astride the railway, and had sited the trenches so skilfully that Lossberg's guns had bombarded dummies and Lossberg's advance had been time and again held up by concealed machine guns. He had now the task of drawing off his men by night, a task which, having been at the evacuation of Helles, he had no doubt as to his ability to perform.

Blenkiron, as the plan was unfolded, glanced at the paper in his hands, and at Escrick's further elucidation with the point of a riding-switch in the thick dust. Then he turned to another man, a heavy red-faced fellow who was perpetually mopping his face with a blue-spotted handkerchief. At his look of inquiry the man nodded.

"The last of the supply waggons leave this afternoon, sir," he said. "Three of the centres are already stocked up, and the fourth will be completed by midnight. The men should be well on their way before daybreak to-morrow, and all arrangements have been made for mining and blowing-up the roads behind them."

"You're not leaving much behind?"

"Not an ounce of flour or a pound of bacon," was the answer.

"I reckon that's fair. It's up to Lossberg to feed the population of the city he captures. What's it they call them, Luis? The bouches inutiles?"

Luis de Marzaniga smiled. "There won't be too many of these useless mouths, Senor."

"Lordy, it's hot!" Blenkiron sighed. "Let's get inside the shack and moisten our lips with lime-juice. The maps are there, and I'll like to have a once-over before we gel back to our jobs."

A hut in the garden had been transformed into an office, and on one wall hung a big plan made of a dozen sheets pinned together. It had none of the finish of the products of a Government Map Department, being the work of the Mines surveyors. Each of the men had a small replica, which he compared with the original. There followed an hour of detailed instruction as to routes and ultimate concentrations. Four points were marked on the big map with red circles. One, lettered Pacheco, lay in the extreme south-west angle of the Gran Seco. Magdalena, the second, was a hundred miles farther north, under the shadow of the peaks called the Spanish Ladies. The third was near the centre of the northern part of the province, the Seco Boreal, and had the surprising name of Fort Castor: while the fourth, Loa, was at the opening of the neck of land which led to the Courts of the Morning. The commandos under Escrick were to make for the two latter points, while Peters and his forces, which had been fighting in the Mines sector, had the two former for their objectives.

There was also to be a change in the command. Blenkiron, once the city had been surrendered, laid down his duties. The field force in the future would be divided between Escrick and Peters; and, under Castor as generalissimo, the operations as a whole would be directed by him whom the Indians called El Obro.

"I guess we'll keep to that pet name," Blenkiron said. "It sounds good, and kind of solemn. We haven't any use for effete territorial titles in this democratic army, and 'Sandy' is too familiar."

Then he made the men repeat their instructions till each was clear not only about his own task but about the tasks of the others--a vital thing in a far-flung force. After that he lectured them...So far luck had been on their side. Their losses had been small; under estimate in the railway sector, and not thirty per cent. beyond it even after Peters's rash counter-attack. No officer had fallen, and only six had been wounded. One aeroplane, unfortunately, had been brought down, and the pilot and observer, both young Mines engineers, killed. That was their most serious casualty. "A very nice little exhibition of the new bloodless conduct of war," said Blenkiron. But this was only the overture; the serious business was now about to begin, when they had to make the country fight Lossberg, as Washington made the geography of America fight Burgoyne and Cornwallis. "It's going to be a mighty tough proposition, but I reckon if we pay strict attention to business we'll put it through."

"Say, though," said Escrick, "what is going to be the upshot?"

"Peace, sonny. We've got to make the Excelentisimo at Olifa so dead-sick of the business that he'll want to deal. Same game as Robert E. Lee played before Gettysburg. We can't beat them, but we may make them want to deal. And in that deal Mr Castor is going to state the terms. And those terms are going to fix things more comfortably in this province, but principally they are going to fix Mr Castor. You've got the schedule for to-night clear? Then we'd better dissolve this conference. I join you, General Escrick, at twenty minutes after midnight."

The men entered their dusty cars and departed, while Blenkiron went into his house, accompanied by Luis de Marzaniga, who seemed to be acting as his chief staff-officer.

As they lunched frugally off sardines and biscuits, Blenkiron was in a cheerful mood, but a shadow seemed to hover about the face of the younger man.

"What's worrying you, Luis?" Blenkiron asked. "Things have panned out pretty well according to plan. There's snags good and plenty to come, but we needn't think about them just yet."

"I think, Senor, that there is one snag which we have forgotten."

"Meaning?"

"The bouches inutiles whom we are leaving to the care of General Lossberg."

"Why, man, we can't do anything else. The civilians in a captured city are not our concern. They're his funeral, He's bound to treat them well for..."

"It is scarcely a question of humanity. But some of these bouches may be mischievous."

"The Bodyguard?"

The young man took a paper from his pocket.

"Here," he said, "I have a list of the more dangerous of the Bodyguard and of those gentry whom we call the conquistadors. I have made notes on each...Kubek--he was happily killed in this very house. We found his body over there by the window...Ramiro and Molson, they were shot by Peters at the round-up...Sechstein--dead of spotted fever...Snell--died of wounds two hours after Kubek...But Radin and Molinoff are at large--you remember that they broke away in the confusion, when the house in the Calle of the Virgin fell as Peters was taking them to the lock-up...There are others, too. We know nothing of what became of Martel and Carvilho and Magee and Trompetter...and Laschallas, whom we used to think as dangerous as Kubek. Do you know that he, or somebody very like him, was seen last night in a drinking-den near St Martin's Port?"

"That only means that there are a handful of bad men loose. You can't corral all the scamps. Besides, a gunman's not too dangerous in a war where everybody has a gun."

"I wonder. Remember that these are a very special type of gunman. The Gobernador chose them for their brains out of the rascality of the globe...Then there are the three ruffians you sent with him to Olifa. What were their names?"

"Carreras, Judson, and Biretti."

"Yes. Well, you may be sure they will come back, if indeed they are not back already...I do not like it, Senor. They are dangerous grit to get into our wheels. I should be happier if I knew that they were in their graves."

"So should I. But I don't let that outfit worry me. I reckon they're part of the legitimate risk of war. Anything more?"

"The Conquistadors."

Blenkiron laughed aloud. "That pie-faced bunch! Say, Luis, you're getting fanciful. What harm can those doped owls do us? They'll be waiting for Lossberg and making a fuss about their comforts. It's him they'll bite, not us."

"I wonder again. Lariarty was in the round-up which Lord Clanroyden organised. He was consorting with the

Bodyguard. Is there not something there to make us think?"

"Why, Luis, you're barking up the wrong tree. Except for Castor, I reckon I know the Conquistadors better than any other man, and I've sized them up long-ago. They're the most dangerous stuff on earth, so long as Castor has the handling of them, but without him they're no more good than dud shells. They've powder enough, but, lacking Castor, they haven't the current to fire the charge. Let 'em alone, and they'll just moon about and rot."

"And yet Lariarty was at the meeting which was nearly the end of Lord Clanroyden. He sat in the judge's chair. It is right to assume that he had some part in the plot...I think you are wrong, Senor. I think the Conquistadors are like sick wolves--dying, if you like, but with enough strength to turn and bite. And, remember, their bite will be deadly, because it is poisoned."

Blenkiron looked perturbed. "I can't bring myself to think that. What could they do? They won't fit in with Lossberg."

"No, indeed. General Lossberg, if I understand him, will make nothing of them. He is a conventional soldier, and will fight his battles in the old professional way...But what if the Conquistadors keep the same company that we found Lariarty keeping? They have no scruples. What if a dull anger and a craving for their drug--for presently they will get no more of it--what if that kindles their wits and screws up their nerves sufficiently for one desperate throw? The remnants of the Bodyguard, if they can find them, will be their executants. They will think chiefly of getting to Castor, and, failing that, of revenge."

"It will be hard to reach the Courts of the Morning."

"Maybe. But it may be less hard to reach you--or Lord Clanroyden. Our army is not a machine, but a personal following. A well-aimed bullet might make it a rabble."

Blenkiron sat brooding for a moment. "I think you put the risk too high," he said at last, "but we can't neglect any risk. Have you put Intelligence on to the job?"

"Senor Musgrave and his young men have been too busy fighting battles. I have done a little myself."

"You have told me what gunmen survive, but you haven't located them. How about the Conquistadors?"

Luis took up another paper. "Lariarty, whom Peters wanted to lock up, was set free by Lord Clanroyden. He has been living quietly in his rooms, playing much music on his piano. There are five others in the Gran Seco, and they profess to be waiting till the Mines are started again, whether by Lossberg or ourselves. They shrug their shoulders, and behave as if there were no war. The dandyism of their clothes has not changed, and they feed solemnly together at the Club or the Regina. What they do beyond that I cannot tell."

"Who's here beside Lariarty?"

Luis read from his paper.

"Senores Frederick Larbert, Peter Suvorin, Maximilian Calvo, Jacques D'Ingraville, Luigi Pasquali."

Blenkiron considered. "After Lariarty I should say that D'Ingraville was the danger. He's not so deeply dipped, and he's the youngest. Funny to think that he was once a French flying ace."

"I have something more to tell you. Romanes is returning. I had information this morning that two days ago he landed in Olifa and that he is now with Lossberg."

"H'm! I don't like that. Europe has a bad effect on those lads--breaks their temper and quickens their brains. And he won't get the dope to quiet him--not unless he goes into the Poison Country, and Peters will have a word to say to that...Darn you, Luis, you've given me a thorn to lie on, just when I was feeling comfortable and meaning to hog it on my bed till sundown. What are you going to do?"

"I would beg leave of absence till eight o'clock. You have no need, I think, for my services, and there are one or two inquiries I wish to make before we leave the city."

So, while Blenkiron, who had slept less than six hours in the past three days, did his best that afternoon to make up arrears, Luis de Marzaniga set out on his own errands.

He visited the Club, and saw in a corner of the deserted dining-room three men lunching. They were just beginning, and in the dislocation of the service their meal was bound to be a slow one. Satisfied with his survey, he joined a young man, who was waiting for him in the street, and the two made a round of domiciliary visits. This young man knew his business, and the outer doors of three flats were neatly opened without damage to the locks. Two of the flats--those of Larbert and D'Ingraville--were in normal order, full of books and bibelots and queer scents, but the third, that of Peter Suvorin, was in a state of supreme untidiness. Its owner had been burning papers in the stove, his bedroom was littered with clothes, while a half-packed valise stood on the bed. "It seems," said Luis to his companion, "that Senor Suvorin is about to make a journey."

His next visit was alone, and to the Regina Hotel. There it was plain that he had a friend, for a word to the head-waiter in the almost empty restaurant got him an immediate interview with a servant in a little room behind the office.

"Senor Pasquali's apartments?" he asked. "You have watched them as I directed?"

"With assiduity. The Senor is going away soon. Where, I do not know, but he has had his baggage prepared as if for a rough journey. Also he has received every night at the hour of ten a visitor."

The visitor was described: a tall man, with a long dark face and high cheek-bones, like an Indian's. No, not an Indian--certainly a white man. There was a white scar on his forehead above his right eye. He spoke with Senor Pasquali in French.

Luis whistled. "That is our friend Radin," he said to himself. "Radin beyond doubt. What has that ugly rogue from the gutter to do with the superfine Pasquali, who plays Scriabin so ravishingly? They may be going travelling together--perhaps also with Suvorin. Luis, my dear, these things must be looked into."

Luis went out into the glare of the afternoon with a preoccupied face. He walked for a little down the Avenida Bolivar, and then struck through a nest of calles in the direction of the smelting works. His preoccupation did not prevent him keeping a sharp look-out, and presently in a jostle of market-women at a corner he saw a face which made him walk quietly back a little, slip up a side street, and then run his hardest to cut it off. He failed, for the man had disappeared. After a moment's reflection Luis returned to the Administration

Buildings and sought out the room given up to the headquarters of the Air Force. The true air base was the Courts of the Morning, but there was an aerodrome and a single squadron behind the city. There he cross-examined the officer in charge as to whether any Olifa planes had recently crossed their lines. He was told that four had been brought down, but that to the best of Headquarters' knowledge no voluntary landing had been made.

"But we cannot tell," said the officer. "We are not holding a continuous line--only two sectors."

"Then an Olifa plane might land someone in a place from which he could make his way here?"

"It is possible," was the answer. "Not very likely, but possible."

In the narrow lane Luis had seen Dan Judson, one of Castor's three trusties. Where Judson was one might look to find also Carreras and Biretti, and the probability was that all three had been landed from an enemy plane and were now in the city. Suvorin and Pasquali were making a journey, and Radin was privy to it. Luis's next business was to go to tea with Lariarty, whom he knew a little.

He found that gentleman quite openly preparing for the road. Lariarty's face was whiter than ever and his eyes looked tortured; but they also looked most furiously alive, and his whole body seemed to have woken into an hysterical life.

"Ho, Senor," Luis exclaimed. "Do you follow us into exile? I thought you would await the conqueror here--seeing that you have no politics--and advise him wisely about Gran Seco business. That was also Senor Rosas's belief."

Lariarty looked at him with a composure which seemed to be the result of a strong effort, for the man was obviously ill at ease.

"Some of us remain," he said. "But not I. I wish to be at the Gobernador's side, for his interests are my interests. I have to-day been at Headquarters, and it is arranged that I go with General Escrick."

"What makes you so certain you will find the Gobernador with Escrick?"

"I am not certain. But if I am with the field army, it stands to reason that I must sooner or later come across the commander-in-chief."

"Who are staying behind?"

"All the others."

"Suvorin?"

"Yes."

"And Pasquali?"

"Certainly. Why do you ask?"

"No reason at all...I congratulate you, Senor, on your courage, for we of Escrick's command must ride fast and far. You are perhaps out of training for the savannahs and the mountains?"

"I am not in good form. But there was a time when I was never off a horse."

Luis abounded in friendly advice, as from an old campaigner, and finally took his leave. "We shall meet in the darkness," he said, and was told that Lariarty had orders to report himself at midnight.

It was now within an hour of nightfall and Luis repaired to Blenkiron's house for a bath. As he splashed in the tepid water, he reflected. "I am certain that they are all going with Escrick," he told himself. "Lariarty alone will go openly, but the others will be there somehow--Suvorin and Pasquali and Calvo--likewise that trinity of cherubs, Judson, Carreras, and Biretti. Larbert and D'Ingraville will wait here till Romanes comes, and then join them...there's going to be a gathering of the vultures somewhere in the North...They're after the Gobernador, and if they fail to get him they may do some miscellaneous looting."

After his bath Luis made a careful toilet from a store of clothes which he carried in an old saddlebag. A yellow shirt with a fancy collar, flapping trousers of dirty grey, skin brogues, a dark poncho, and a high-crowned, broad-brimmed at transformed him into a mestizo peasant, at least three-quarters Indian. He rolled some cigarettes of leaf tobacco and placed them behind his ear, and then sauntered across the Avenida, down through the narrows of the Market, to the cluster of yards and huts above the dry ravine which separated the city from the smelting works. His disguise was perfect, for he stopped now and then to engage in a street-corner argument, and mixed as naturally with the disputants as if he were one of the vegetable-sellers whose mules lined the causeway.

He found the place he sought, an alley close to the sunken street called St. Martin's Port, where had stood centuries go a tiny monkish settlement. All had gone except a tooth of ancient brick masonry, which had once been part of an arched gateway. The street was a warren, full of bolt-holes that looked like cul-de-sacs and cul-de-sacs that looked like bolt-holes, but Luis seemed to know his way about it. At the head of a court, the paving of which may have been contemporary with Pizarro, there was a green gate in an adobe wall. He pushed through it and said something to a slatternly half-caste woman, who sat dozing in a chair outside a second door. He opened this and stumbled into what was obviously the back-room of a cafe, the front of which was in another street. Stumbled, for he seemed suddenly to have become rather drunk.

There were few in the place, three or four peasants drinking small glasses of aguardiente, and one man in the shadows who had before him a tankard of beer. Luis joined the group of peasants and gave his order. An albino negro, a weird sight in that ill-lit place, brought him his drink, and he commanded another glass for the man opposite him. This was a gipsy-looking fellow with long earrings, who had been discoursing to the company on cock fighting. A dispute presently arose in which Luis's hiccuping voice was predominant. It was about the merit of Gomez's red cock which had won the championship at Maddalo on St. Rosalia's feast-day.

The dispute grumbled, died down, flared up, for all had the air of having drunk too well. Then the talk became confidential between Luis and his vis-a-vis, and they shuffled little apart from the others. More drinks were brought. There was a sudden gust of quarrel, and Luis in dudgeon removed himself across the room. But his new friend followed, and there seemed to be a reconciliation, for one again the two heads were close together and the talk was all of cocks and challenges.

In his new position Luis was scarcely a yard from the dark corner where the man with the tankard of beer was sitting. There were now three of them there. They looked viciously at the argumentative peasants, but there was no other part of the room which promised greater peace, and they remained sitting. Luis was by way of now being very drunk, and he made his confidences at close quarters into the garlic-smelling ear of his companion. But this position left his eyes free to wander, without the other noticing it, and he had a good view of the men in the shadows.

One had the face which he had seen three hours before in the crowded calle--a small man, very thickly made, with rabbit teeth, an underhung jaw, and a broken nose. This was the famous Daniel Judson. Beside him sat a taller man with a long, sallow, clean-shaven face and thick, dark eyebrows which made a straight band almost from ear to ear. This Luis knew for Laschallas, who, as he had told Blenkiron, was the most dangerous of the survivors of the Bodyguard. But it was the man opposite the two who surprised him. He wore a thin dark overcoat with the collar turned up, but the face above the collar had the unmistakable waxy pallor of Lariarty.

In the intervals of his drunken wrangling Luis tried to catch their conversation. But not a word could he overhear. They spoke in low tones, and when he sidled nearer them, still in the embrace of his cock-fighting colleague, Judson rose and cursed them. The other was scared into sobriety, for Mr Judson in his wrath was not a pretty sight, and Luis had perforce to follow him and put as much distance as possible between the three and themselves. Presently he gave up the attempt to eavesdrop, extricated himself with some difficulty from his companion, and staggered out of the cafe by the road he had come. He had learned several things--that the trusties, or at least one of them, were in Olifa, that

Laschallas was alive, and that Lariarty was not leading an idle life.

He went home, got into proper clothes and hunted up one of Escrick's staff-officers. There was a good deal of sound coming from the south, where the retreat from the trenches was being covered by machine-gun activity, and some of the troops already withdrawn were filing through the streets.

What had been infantry was now being transformed into light cavalry at the horse-lines north of the city. Luis found the staff-officer he sought, and learned from him that he only civilian accompanying Escrick was Lariarty-Blenkiron himself had sanctioned it--for whom a seat had been provided in one of the staff cars. He left the office with injunctions that no civilian passes were to be given without further reference, and that the occupants of every car were to be jealously scrutinised.

Then he supped with Blenkiron, and told him what he had discovered. Blenkiron, still sleepy as an owl, was slow to take it in. "They can't do anything," he reflected. "They're bottled up in this city, whether it's me or Lossberg that's in charge. They're town rats, Luis; they won't thrive out in the wilds. Where are you going?"

"I thought I'd look up Lariarty and see if he's ready. I propose to keep an eye on that gentleman."

But when Luis was admitted by Lariarty's servant to Lariarty's flat he found no sign of impending departure. Lariarty, washed and perfumed, was wearing a smoking-suit of silk, and in the buttonhole of his jacket was a yellow picotee, such as Archie had remarked in the Gran Seco visitors the first night in the Olifa hotel. He was improvising on his piano. The nervousness of the afternoon had gone, and he seemed to be at ease with the world.

"Hullo, Senor," Luis cried. "You'll be late. We start in twenty minutes."

Lariarty smiled and went on playing.

"I am not coming. Not at present. I have been reconsidering the matter, and I think that it is my business to remain here. Here or at Olifa. My duty is to the Mines, and my knowledge may be needed."

Something had happened that evening, some news had reached the Conquistadors, which had caused them to change their plans. It would be as well, Luis thought, if they all remained in the city; he had not approved of Blenkiron's consent to Lariarty's departure, which seemed to have been the unthinking decision of an overpressed man. But did this mean that all would stay behind? Was there no chance of a blunder in this midnight retirement? The last four days had been too feverish to allow of strict attention to the ritual of surveillance which had looked on paper so perfect. The thought made Luis hurry to the northern barrier.

The outlets from the city were few, and all were carefully barricaded. It was now midnight, and the troops were by this time safely out of the trench lines, where now a rearguard was conducting a noisy camouflage. The place was as bright as day with the great arc lights on their tall standards, and in their glare a mounted army was assembling, as shaggy a force as ever followed Timour or Genghiz. They had for the most part come straight from the line, and there was no sleep for them till they had put many thirsty miles between themselves and the Olifa van. Yet they were a cheerful crowd and drank black coffee out of bottles and smoked their little acrid cigarettes before they jogged off, each squadron to its appointed place.

The officer in charge of the business, a young analytic chemist, saluted him.

"All goes smoothly, sir," he said. "The staff leaves in a quarter of an hour. The road is being kept clear for cars. Your advance party got off half an hour ago."

"Advance party!" Luis stammered.

"Yes, sir. They presented your instructions and I countersigned them, as your telephone message directed."

"Yes, yes, of course. Were their passes all right? I was afraid they might be slow in reaching them."

"They were all in order, with the Chief's signature."

"One car, you say?"

"They packed into one car. Rather a tight fit for six of them."

"Who was driving?"

"Mr Suvorin. He was the only one I recognised."

"A good car?"

"One of the new Administration Packards. There's nothing wrong, sir?"

"Nothing. I was just wondering when we would over-take them."

IV

In the Courts of the Morning there was still peace. The brooding heats, the dust-storms, the steaming deluges of the lowlands were unknown. The air was that of a tonic and gracious autumn slowly moving to the renewal of spring. The mornings were chilly, with a sea-fog crawling over the rim of the plateau; the days were bright and dry as old wine, the nights blue and starlit. There was peace in that diamond ether, but it was not the peace of lethargy but of ordered action. The place was as busy as ever, but it had no longer the air of a headquarters. It was now a base, a depot, and the poste de commandement was some--where far below in the broken levels which spread dizzily towards the southern sky-line.

The Gobernador had been given his choice. "I can take you with me," Sandy had said. "It won't be a comfortable life, but you don't mind that. Or you can stay here in the watch-tower and follow our doings on the map."

"I am free to decide?" Castor had asked, and was told "Perfectly." He had considered for a little and had finally chosen to remain. "I am your enemy," he said, "and we should be at too close quarters for comfort. I shall stay here till something happens."

Sandy laughed. "I know what you mean. Well, I hope it won't, but if my luck gives out don't imagine that the show is over. You're the only one in your class, but I've heaps of alternatives in mine. Archie will keep you posted and I'll look in every now and then."

But Sandy did not come back...The crowded days' work went on; horse and mule convoys came daily up the mountain paths and departed with their burdens; the receivers ticked busily in the wireless station; aeroplanes--fewer than before, for the fighting machines were mostly at advanced headquarters--departed at dawn and returned often after nightfall, while flares like forest fires burned to guide them to their landing-places. There was a special activity in the glen which led to the sea; it seemed as if its defenders had reached the conclusion that that port to the outer world would soon be discovered and closed, for almost every night some kind of tramp put in and unloaded and stole out before the following daylight. Busiest of all were the two girls. Barbara was in charge of the hospital stores, and it seemed that these were now urgently needed, for in the plains below men were suffering. With her staff of peons she worked early and late, with Janet as an unskilled assistant.

The latter had another duty laid upon her, and that was to provide company for the Gobernador. With Sandy's departure he had become the prey of moods. His forme equability had gone, and he appeared to swing between profound abstraction, when he seemed unconscious of his surroundings, and a feverish interest in them.

For example, he visited constantly the top of the ravine and would spend an hour gazing into the green depths which ended in a sapphire patch of sea. Once, when Janet accompanied him, he turned to her sharply.

"This place could be forced," he said. "Olifa has a navy...It would take a week--ten days perhaps--and he would lose a thousand men, but it could be done. Then his sanctuary of yours would fall. How would you scape?"

"I suppose by the hill roads to the south," Janet answered.

"But they will be blocked. It might be hard to force a way up here from that side, but Olifa could block the exits. What then?"

"I'm sure I don't know. I don't believe both disasters could happen at once."

"Why not?"

"Simply because things don't work out that way."

He laughed angrily. "You are all children. You trust childishly to fortune. That's well enough for Clanroyden and the others. They are soldiers and take chances. But what is to become of you?"

"Barbara and I went into this with our eyes open."

"You were a fool, then. And your husband was a fool to let you."

There were many similar occasions when his face looked sharp and anxious and there was a hard edge to his voice.

But there were others, when the mountain spaces seemed to work on him as an opiate and he fell into a mood of reflection. From these fits he would emerge with cheerfulness almost, certainly with philosophy. At such times he seemed to enjoy Janet's company and would detain her in talk from her many duties. He would ask her questions about herself, her home, her views on life, with an engaging ingenuousness, as if he had discovered a new type of mortal and was labouring to understand it. He had a natural good-breeding which robbed his questions of all impertinence, and in this novel sphere Janet felt that she could regard him as an equal.

"This hill-top is bad for me," he once told her. "I have no facts to work upon and I begin to make pictures. Wasn't it Napoleon who said that we should never think in pictures, but always look at things as if through a telescope--bring reality close to one, but always reality?"

"Isn't that begging the question?" the girl replied. "Reality for us is what we make of things. We may make them conform to our picture. It is what we all do. It is what you have been doing all your life, Excellency."

"But your pictures and mine have been very different. I am a scientist and you are a romantic."

"You are the romantic. You have tried to force the world inside a theory, and it is too big for that. We humble people never attempt the impossible. You are a self-deceiver, you know."

"Why?" he asked.

"Because of your intellectual pride. It is only humility that sees clearly and knows its limitations."

"Lord Clanroyden, for example, is humble?" There was a not unpleasant irony in his voice.

"Profoundly."

"Yet he has challenged me. With his handful of amateurs he has challenged the might of Olifa. Was your Jack the Giant-killer humble?"

Janet laughed. "I think he was. Jack saw that the giants were far bigger than himself, but that, being overgrown, unnatural things, they were bound to be stupid and weak."

"You think that a colossus is always weak?"

"He must be if he is outside the human scale. If he has no other flaw, he will have the weakness of pride."

"You and your friends are very proud."

"Oh, I hope not. If we are, we shall be punished for it. Sandy--Lord Clanroyden--is daring, but that is not because he thinks too much of himself, but because he believes that he has great allies."

"Such as?"

The girl quoted: "Exultations, agonies, And love, and man's unconquerable mind."

Castor laughed. "That is Wordsworth, isn't it? It is a good answer, Lady Roylance, from your point of view. I am prepared of admit that Lord Clanroyden has allies--at any rate, he has friends. He need not be lonely."

"You are lonely?" she asked with kind eyes.

"I have always been rather lonely...Perhaps...if I had met someone like you...long ago...I should not be so lonely to-day."

It was Archie who brought the first big news. One evening he appeared at dinner with his left arm in a sling. "Not a wound," he explained. "It was my own dashed silliness in getting too near the business end of a mule. I've been having a giddy time and I'm badly short of sleep. How are things going--? Pas si bete, as they say--except for Sandy. Old Sandy has gone stark mad. At present it's a useful kind of madness, but the question is how long it will be till he goes clean off his rocker. He's been doing pretty desperate things."

Later he explained.

"Lossberg is making war according to the books. Sandy its down and thinks out very carefully what the books direct and then does the exact opposite. He is trying to draw the enemy deep into the country, and for that purpose he is making a feature of Fort Castor. We've a pretty useful intelligence service, and the best part of it is that section which we put at Lossberg's disposal. You see, having the country on our side, we have a lot of enthusiastic volunteers. Lossberg picks up some Indian or half-starved mestizo who is easily frightened into telling what he knows. The poor devil is obviously speaking the truth, for he is too cared and stupid to lie. Only what he says has been carefully pumped into him by our little lot. The result is that Lossberg has got it into his head that Fort Castor is our big base, and is stretching his claws round it as carefully as a cat stalking a mouse. He has moved up the better part of a division. But there's nothing in Fort Castor except mounted patrols. We put up a beautiful camouflage and let Lossberg's flying men have a discreet look at it once in a while. But when he takes the place after some trouble he won't find a tin of bully beef in it."

Somebody asked where Sandy was.

"He was in Magdalena yesterday. We are organised in two armies. Escrick, with the Army of the North, is now divided between Loa and Magdalena, and he has a covered line of communications between them through the hills behind, just like what Stonewall Jackson had in the Shenandoah valley. The enemy has spotted neither. Peters, with the Army of the South, is playing the same game. Lossberg thinks he is based on the Indian pueblas in the Tierra Caliente from which he can threaten the Mines, and consequently he has a division strung out from the San Tome to the Universum and is building a sort of Great Wall of China in the shape of blockhouses. Peters just does enough to keep the Mines lively, but he isn't worrying about them. All he wants is to get Lossberg rattled."

Archie pointed to the south-east corner of the big map. "There's a spot there called Pacheco, just under the hills. That's Peters' real base. He's got some nice country west of that for his scallywags to operate in. There should be news from that quarter pretty soon."

"Base?" he said in reply to a question of Castor's. "Why, we haven't any proper base, and we haven't any communications to cut. We're the most lightly equipped force in the world, for we don't go in for high living. A bit of charqui and a bag of meal will last one of our fellows for a week. Also we know all the wells and water-holes, and Lossberg doesn't. Water is going to give him a lot of trouble."

"Has he no one who knows the country?" Janet asked.

"Not as we do. He'll pick up somebody later, for we're bound to have a traitor or two in our camp. Also there are your gunmen, Excellency. One or two of them have been a bit around. But he hasn't got anybody yet, and has gone poking about, trusting to bad maps, and the lies we manage to feed him."

"What about his Air Force?"

Bobby Latimer answered. "So far we've managed to keep it in order. We've nothing on them in the way of flying, for they're nicely trained, but they can't just fight in our way. And they haven't any machines as good as our new Gladas. If this were a regular war, they'd be mighty good at contact work and bombing expeditions. You never saw prettier squadron flying. But we've no communications to bomb, and at present they're wasting their efforts every night on Fort Castor."

"But do none of their planes get abroad and discover your real whereabouts? Magdalena, for example--or Loa?"

"So far we haven't let them. We can beat anything they've got in pace and we seem to have more appetite for a scrap. There's been one or two very pretty dog-fights. Besides, it don't signify if they spot Magdalena or Loa or even Pacheco. We could shift somewhere else in a couple of hours."

"But you have a base." It was Castor who spoke. "Where we are sitting now is your base. If they take this, you are lost. If they even bomb it, you are deeply embarrassed."

"I think that's right," said Latimer. "Therefore it's up to us to let no enemy planes north of Loa. So far they haven't shown any inclination in this direction. They're too much occupied with General Peters."

"Yet at any moment they may discover it?"

"There's no reason in the nature of things why they shouldn't," said Archie. "But it's one thing for a chance plane to spot us and another thing for Lossberg to exploit his knowledge."

Three days later Archie returned in high spirits. He had two pieces of news. The first was that Bobby Latimer had brought down an enemy plane north of Loa. The pilot and observer were alive, and the plane was not too badly damaged, so they had added one to their stock of aircraft--a Seaforth monoplane, in the mechanism of which he discoursed at length. Happily they had the spares for it. He welcomed this new sign of enterprise on the part of Olifa as likely to relieve the tedium of his job. When Janet observed that, if one enemy could get as far as Loa, a second might get farther, Archie was reassuring.

"The way I look at it is this. They've spotted Loa--they were bound to hear of it from spies and such-like. But they're so darned unenterprising that only one of their planes gets through. If these things be done in the green tree, what shall be done in the dry? Loa is an easy mark, but this place from Lossberg's lines would be dashed difficult, even for a swell like Bobby."

The other news was startling. Peters's raiders had made the garrisons at the Mines nervous, and, since it was assumed that the guerrillas were based on the villages in the Indian reserve and drew their supplies thence, it was resolved to clear that country and bring the women and children into a huge concentration camp near the city.

Archie was triumphant. "It's what Sandy has been playing for, but he scarcely hoped to bring it off...Lossberg thinks the Tierra Caliente is an asset to us. Good Lord! it's a millstone round our necks. Presently we should have had to feed these villages--a thing we had budgeted for--and this means that we shall now be a thousand per cent. better off for supplies. He's a humane man, your General Lossberg. The concentrados will be a long sight better off with him than on their own, and if they get pinched a little when he gets pinched, we had made our book for that. Soon we'll all have to draw in our belts...Sandy has made Lossberg hold the baby for him, which is what you might call strategy."

A light of reminiscence woke in his eyes.

"That was always old Sandy's way. Once at Crask, I remember, he fairly did me in. We were out rough shooting together and it was a blistering hot day. When we turned at the march burn, we were both a little bored, for we had seen very little, so by way of putting a spice of interest into the game, we agreed that I should carry what he shot and he what I shot, and I backed myself for a fiver to give him the heavier load. Well, I soon presented him with a hill partridge and a snipe, while he hadn't let off his gun. Then I'm blessed if he didn't shoot a roebuck and I had to sling the infernal brute on my back. After that he couldn't miss, and I hadn't the proper use of my arms. I staggered into Crask just about dead with heat, and laden like Balaam's ass--roebuck on back, string of grouse and blackcock round my neck, rabbits in my pockets, and one and a half brace of snipe in my hat."

For a day or two the plateau drowsed in its bright aromatic heat, and no news arrived except what the Olifa wireless told--how Lossberg had begun to clear the Indian country, and the rebels, baseless and foodless, were for certain no more now than bands of refugees clinging to the mountains' skirts. Fort Castor, their chief centre, had been occupied without serious opposition. It was anticipated that soon there must be a general surrender. Olifa was marching to an easy victory, and the President, in a public speech, spoke contemptuously of the rabble of amateurs which had attempted to defy the disciplined forces of the republic.

The comments of the foreign press were no longer guarded. The military critics congratulated themselves on their prescience, and wrote, almost with regret, of the mathematical certainties of modern warfare. Their views did not disturb Janet's peace of mind, but she had her own anxieties. She had an apprehension of some calamity approaching, and studied the blue sky for that enemy plane which might break through their guard. The drone of a machine arriving sent her hurrying out-of-doors, and she would wake with a start in the night and listen for the beat in the air which would be different from the beat of their own planes. Castor seemed to share her excitement; his eyes also were always turning skyward.

Then came two days of storm, when the thunder rattled among the crags of Choharua, and the rain fell in torrents, and the outlook was limited to six yards of swirling vapour. After that came a wind which threatened to uproot the huts, and which brought the sound of a furious sea even up to that ledge of mountain. During these days the wireless was disordered by atmospherics, but from its broken messages one thing emerged. Something had happened, something of vital importance, something which had got on Olifa's nerves. It could not be a battle? Surely Sandy had never been betrayed into measuring his meagre strength in lists chosen by the enemy.

Then one afternoon Archie arrived, a weary Archie who could scarcely speak for drowsiness.

"Has there been a battle?" Janet demanded.

"Not likely. But we've begun the offensive."

"What losses?"

"None. Practically none on either side. But there's been the deuce of a lot of destruction of property. Sandy says it's cheaper than human life and just as effective."

"What have you done? Quick! Tell me."

"We've cut the enemy's communications. I'm dropping with sleep, Janet. In six hours you'll hear everything."

In six hours a washed, shaven, fed, and refreshed Archie told this story.

"Ever since Lossberg started pushing out from the Gran Seco city, our army has more or less disappeared. He felt us, but he didn't often see us, barring, of course, our planes. Yet he was being sniped and shelled and bombed a good deal and Peters kept him lively at the Mines. Two things accordingly happened. The first was that Lossberg, not being able to get us into the open, thought we were far stronger than we were and grew more cautious than ever. The second was that he thought we had all our men in two places--up in the hills north-east of Fort Castor and in the eastern end of the Tierra Caliente. In that he was right--more or less--but he didn't know the length of our range. The consequence was that he thought that the city and everything south and west of it were safe, but that the east and north-east were formidable and needed a big striking force. So he held the railway with only three garrisons between the city and the frontier--at San Luca, at Villa Bar, and at Gabones itself--and small posts of six men each every four miles."

Archie with pencil and paper drew a sketch of the railway.

"You remember the big dry valley twenty-five miles down the line. I believe there's occasionally a trickle in it in January, but just now it is like the Prophet's Valley of Dry Bones. There's a big viaduct crosses it--sixteen arches, the biggest and costliest piece of engineering on the whole line. It would have taken a cog-and-pinion arrangement or miles of circuitous gradients to get the railway across the valley. So the engineers very properly decided on a bridge.

"Blenkiron always had his eye on the San Luca bridge, and so had Lossberg, for he had a post at each end, twenty men with machine guns at San Luca station--that's the north end--and thirty-five at the south end, at a place called the Devil's Ear. It was the only part of the line about which he showed any nervousness. But his posts weren't very well placed, for they were at the abutments of the bridge, and the bridge has sixteen arches, and the valley is more than half a mile wide, so that if there was trouble about the middle of the viaduct it would be some little time before the ends heard of it and arrived to help.

"Blenkiron--the scheme was his principally--wanted to cut the line at a place where it would be hard to mend. San Luca was an obvious spot, especially as the bridge was unguarded in the middle, since it was calculated that wandering bandits could do no harm to the huge stone piers.

"Lossberg's engineers in the Gran Seco could do any ordinary repairs that were required, but something very big would want help from Olifa. So Blenkiron's second job was to make it pretty hard for Olifa to get to San Luca, and that meant a simultaneous bedevilment of the railway somewhere well to the south of the Devil's Ear."

Again Archie had recourse to pencil and paper.

"You see this point here, twelve miles north of Villa Bar and about twenty-three from San Luca. The railway runs in a deep cutting, the beginning of the long climb to the watershed. On the east side there's a considerable mountain with a shaly face, which is shored up to prevent it slipping on to the metals. There was a little post about a mile off at a place called Tombequi--half a dozen sleepy Oliferos who spent their days playing spadillo and begging for drinks from the passing trains.

"Well, it was Peters's outfit that got the job, and it was decided to make it a long-range business. You see, not one of our fellows had so far been seen within fifty miles of the railway after the city was surrendered, so Lossberg assumed that all was well there and took no precautions.

"We didn't want to alarm him, so we took Pacheco for a base, the better part of one hundred and fifty miles off. It's an ugly bit of country from there to the railway--the south rim of the Gran Seco basin, and on the north face of the rim an abomination of desolation, all pitted and tortured red rocks like the Sinai desert. The crest, however, is flattish, with a good deal of scrub on it, and there's water in one or two places--the actual springs, I fancy, of streams that go down into the Vulpas valley. There used to be posts there, but Lossberg had no use for them, and on that bit of frontier all he has is a few mounted patrols which keep to the low ground on the north side under the rocks. Accordingly we fancied the high ground above the rocks, where there was nobody to spot us except vultures.

"We left Pacheco last Tuesday night with Sandy in command. He insisted upon taking charge--said he wanted a little fresh air and exercise--I flew him over from Magdalena that evening. I never saw a fellow in such spirits--filled with 'em, drunk with 'em. There were two parties--one under a chap called Jervoise, mounted on wiry little Indian ponies, with some queer kit on their saddles. That was the Tombequi outfit. The San Luca crowd were coming in cars and weren't due to start from Pacheco till twenty hours later. A place had been agreed on as a rendezvous.

"It was a mad ride, and Sandy was the maddest thing in it. It looked as if he had been getting charged with electricity till he could hold no more and had to give some of it off in sparks. He's fit again too, fitter than I've ever seen him before...We climbed out of the levels up long glens of loess till we struck the stony corridor that runs between the ridges. There was a big white moon, and the shale looked like snowdrifts and ice couloirs. There wasn't a sound, for there are no beasts or birds up there--only the thud of hoofs, an occasional clash of buckles, and Sandy humming his crazy songs.

"We did fifty miles before dawn, and then lay up for most of the day on the top of the ridge, where there were water and scrub. We were off again at nightfall, and next morning came to the place they call Tulifa, where there is a bad foot-track zip from the Vulpas valley. Here we had to go cannily, for we had to get off the hills, which had become a series of knife-edges, and take to the sandy valleys to the north of 'em. Yet they made pretty fair cover for men in open order, and we had goodish guides, and by nightfall we weren't twenty miles from the railway. The staff-work had been top-hole, for we got to the appointed rendezvous just fifteen and a half minutes late. The cars had come through without a hitch and had been hiding all day in a ravine. There were three of 'em--Rolls-Royce chassis and bodies that looked like a travelling circus.

"At the rendezvous we separated. Sandy transferred himself to the cars, for San Luca was the main objective, and I went with him. Jervoise trotted off with his bandits according to plan. They had to work exactly to schedule, for there was a big freight train due to pass Tombequi at forty-three minutes past nine. The plan was to let it pass and blow up the line behind it, while we blew up the San Luca bridge in front, and so bottled it up. Our motto was 'Anything to give pain!'...

"I wasn't an eye-witness of Jervoise's show, but it ran like a clock. The roads were difficult and the party had to split up, but the sections arrived to a tick, and the only chaps who could complain were the poor devils of horse-holders, and the Olifa post, who were surprised at supper and put in the bag. No--there were no casualties, and we don't take prisoners. Jervoise annexed their trousers, and turned them loose. He don't like the raggedness of his outfit, and consequently has the eye of an old-clothes man for pantaloons. His lot made a fearsome mess, blew up the rack in twenty places over a three-miles stretch, and tumbled down half the mountainside on it. Sandy reckons it will take a fortnight's hard work to clear it.

"I was in the San Luca push myself. There was a dust-storm blowing up from the east and the moon was covered, and as we had no lights and the road was naked prairie I'm bound to say I felt a bit rattled. If you're loaded up with guncotton and blasting gelatine it isn't much fun to be ricocheting from boulder to boulder. We couldn't go slow and feel our way, for we had to keep to schedule time. But the weather was a godsend, for the wind drowned the noise of our wheels, and when we got to the bridge, the lights were burning clearly at each end and everything as peaceful as Clapham Junction.

"We didn't take long about the job, for the whole thing had been arranged to the last detail, with the help of a plan of the bridge provided by one of our fellows who had been in the railway shops. We laid the charges, lit the fuses, and, if you believe me, when we started off on the return journey we weren't two minutes out in our reckoning.

"It was all too easy, and that made me nervous. But we didn't miss fire. In the War I saw a good many mines go up, but never anything like this. The empty valley became suddenly like Tophet, spouting sheets of greeny-yellow flame, while a mushroom of black smoke wavered above it. Then the wind blew the mushroom aside, and we saw that two of the arches had gone and that the viaduct was like a man's mouth with the front teeth drawn...

"After that there is nothing to tell. The posts on each side of the bridge started shooting into vacancy, and just as we left there came an agonised whistle from the south. It was the freight train slowing down to discover what the devil had happened."

Thus Archie to Janet. Before dinner he repeated the tale in its main features to Castor, who heard it with drawn brows.

"I make you my compliments," the latter said. "You have certainly instituted a new kind of war. Can Lord Clanroyden repeat the performance?"

"Whenever he pleases. You see, we have the real mobility, and we have also knowledge of the country on our side. Lossberg already finds it hard to know what to do. He can't police the whole Gran Seco, and as soon as he gets away from his bases we give him beans. We're not too well off for stores, but we can always replenish at his shop...No, we don't mean to make the railway unworkable. We can't afford that, for we want Lossberg to supply himself--that he may supply us. He's our Q. side. But we shall make it so difficult that the job will take up a lot of his time. He's vulnerable, you see, and we're not. We're not in the same elements. It's like a fight between a wolf and a shark."

"Then how can you hope for a decision?"

"We don't want any dramatic coup. We want to tire him out so that he'll see it's hopeless, and Olifa will make peace. On our terms, of course...On your terms, that is to say," Archie added.

Castor smiled at the correction.

"You are convinced that you are invulnerable?" he asked. "What about the air? Olifa has twice your number of machines."

"She can't use 'em properly. That's our almighty luck. They're good average flying men, but they've no genius for the thing, and we've got the pick of the American fliers. Blenkiron saw from the first the necessity of that."

"If you had a genius against you it might be uncomfortable?"

"To be sure. In the air you don't reckon by quantity. One airman like Lensch--you remember?--the Boche who was killed in April '18--would put a different complexion on the business."

It was Janet who first saw the stranger. She had gone on a before-dinner scamper on the downs, and had turned for home, when her eye caught sight of a small monoplane coming in from the sea. That was not a route taken by their own planes, and the girl halted and had a look at it through her glasses. It was a strange make, one she had never seen before, and suddenly she realised what it meant. Lossberg had at last broken the cordon, and the Courts of the Morning were discovered.

As she galloped furiously towards the huts, she saw that the alarm had become general. The visitor had dropped low and was cruising scarcely two hundred feet up, getting a full view of the details of the place. There were no anti-aircraft guns, and the rifle shots from the sentries left him unharmed...Then one of their own planes rose, and the girl checked her horse to watch. The stranger let it approach, and then--contemptuously, it seemed--flew towards it. There was a burst of fire, the two planes seemed about to collide, and then by a curious manoeuvre the stranger slipped out and turned his head for the sea. She thought she saw a hand wave in farewell. It was indeed farewell, for the pursuing plane was utterly outclassed in speed. Almost in a minute, it seemed to her, the stranger was a speck in the pearly haze which marked the meeting of sea and sky.

She found Archie and Castor outside the mess-hut.

"Do you still maintain your invulnerability?" the Gobernador asked, but Archie did not hear. He was engaged in a passionate soliloquy.

"There's only one fellow in the world who could do that trick," he exclaimed. "I've seen him do it a dozen times. Who? A Frenchman called D'Ingraville. He used to go gunning for Lensch, and would have got him too, if Peter Pienaar hadn't chipped in first. But D'Ingraville died long ago."

"I think you are mistaken," said Castor quietly. "Captain Jacques D'Ingraville has been for several years a member of my staff."

V

The new Administration Packard, which a little before midnight on the 18th of July carried six men beyond the northern barricades of the Gran Seco city, did not continue more than a few miles on the road which ran to Fort Castor. Suvorin, who drove--he had in the early days of motoring won the Grand Prix in the race from Paris to Marseilles--did not know the country, but there were men with him who did. Obedient to their instructions, he turned to the right at the San Pedro calvary, and for three hours bumped and skidded along sandy tracks and over stony barrens.

It was apparent to one who kept an eye on the stars that he was bending south in a wide circuit, and presently the party came to the main highway between the city and the Mines. Since the defence was not holding a continuous line, but only two sectors, the party were no longer in the battle zone. They did not cross the road till it had been carefully reconnoitred, and once beyond it the car was again in a moraine of boulders and banks of shale. The moon had long set, and the headlights were working feebly, so that it was more by good fortune than by skill that it came at last to the respectable road which ran from the Universum Mine to the railway-sidings south of the city. Here it turned west and made better speed, till the dancing pencils of the searchlights revealed the proximity of General Lossberg's army. The travellers were in fact very near the General's advanced headquarters, and a rifle-shot over their heads presently brought them to a halt. Among them they must have had adequate passports, for an hour later they were partaking of the General's hospitality. He was in a good humour, for he had just had word of the evacuation of the city, and believed that now he was pressing hard on the heels of the fleeing and broken rebels.

Of the six occupants of the car only one accompanied the General on his triumphant entry. This was the driver of the car, Peter Suvorin, a tall man with a bony face and skin like old parchment, and hair so pale that he seemed almost an albino. The others prepared to go down country.

General Lossberg entertained him and Pasquali to breakfast, and had an interview thereafter with the others in the extremest privacy. They formed a curious contrast to the trim Olifa staff. The General was very neat in his field-grey uniform, a well-set-up figure which did not look its fifty-eight years, square, tanned face, brisk, grey moustache, steady, competent grey eyes--the whole a little marred by a stupid mouth and a heavy, rather brutal chin. The motor-car party compared to him seemed like a wandering theatrical troupe. Pasquali, he who played Scriabin, was indeed sprucely dressed and wore an expensive fur-coat, but his prognathous jaw was blue and unshaven, and his dark eyes so opaque with weariness that he looked like a sick negro.

Radin was a tall fellow, whose high cheek-bones suggested Indian blood, and who carried a recent scar above his right eye. Daniel Judson, short, thick, with rabbit teeth and a broken nose, looked like a damaged prize-fighter, and thick black eyebrows above a sallow face gave Laschallas the air of a provincial actor imperfectly made up. Trompetter, a Javanese Dutchman with a touch of the tar brush, had a broad, wedge-shaped face as yellow as a guinea, and little sharp pig's eyes. All, except Pasquali and Suvorin, were dressed in oddments, and, having been in close hiding, looked as unwholesome as the blanched insects below an upturned flower-pot.

Another joined the conference, a man with a light-cavalry figure, wearing a suit of thin tweeds which had been made not a month before in London. He shook hands with Pasquali and Suvorin, bowed to the General, and nodded to the others. Lossberg spoke to him at length, and he appeared to assent.

"You, Senor Romanes," said Lossberg, "and also Senor Suvorin enter the city with me. I will have you attached to my Intelligence section. These other gentlemen return in half an hour to Olifa, in the charge of Senor Pasquali. They will report to General Bianca and put themselves under his instructions. I must bid you good-bye, gentlemen, for time presses." And the brisk general not unwillingly left the group to an aide-de-camp.

So the party of five travelled in comfort that day down country, and, after many delays owing to freight trains reached the city of Olifa on the following morning. The duly reported to General Bianca, but they did not take his instructions. They seemed to be concerned with urgent business of their own, for they disappeared into the under world of Olifa, meeting every evening at a certain café in a back street. Yet there was nothing clandestine about their activity, for not a day passed without one or more of the five being closeted with high officials of the Army, the Marine, or the Police.

VI

It was on the evening of the 9th day of August that D'Ingraville paid his brief visit to the Courts of the Morning.

Archie departed at once to report, and returned next day of order certain precautionary measures. Two of their best fighting scouts, with Roger Grayne in charge, were stationed here, and arrangements were made for early notice of any future visitors from the air. By this time the camp at Loa was known to Lossberg and his next advance would be in that direction. But it was from the sea that the immediate danger was feared. Provision was made for losing the sea-ravine by explosions which would hurl down a thousand tons of rock and strip part of the gully as bare as the face of a wall. Since their communications with the outer world would thus come to an end, such action as to be taken only in the last resort, and it was anticipated that any ordinary attempt at landing could be repelled by the garrison of the ravine. Only if Olifa made an assault in force would heroic measures become necessary. The thing had to be faced, for D'Ingraville must have given Lossberg the exact position of their base, and, since it was obvious that it must be replenished by sea, it would be easy to discover the point of access to the shore. Plans had long been settled for evacuating the Courts of the Morning in case of need, and it was essential that an assault from the sea should be obstructed long enough to enable the plans to be methodically carried out. The one thing to guard against was surprise. A post was stationed on the shore, two others respectively a third and a half of the way up, and a strong garrison at the summit to guard the precipitous final section. All were connected by telephone with main headquarters and with each other, and there were numerous small mines laid which could be used in the detailed defence of each part of the route.

The incident, however, had shattered the peace of the plateau. The place was no more a sanctuary, for its secret had been laid bare. Barbara, busy with her hospital stores, seemed to be unconscious of the change, but Janet fell a prey to a perpetual apprehension. She tried to laugh at herself, but the ghost would not be laid. The shelf of mountain, which had seemed so secure and homelike, was now but a narrow ledge on a great cliff, and she herself a climber sick with vertigo...The enemy was down below in the woody shelves, slowly creeping nearer, and the army of defence was apparently at the other side of the Gran Seco. He was out on the broad seas, waiting for the dark of night to swoop in upon the coast. She would stare down into the green depths of the ravine, and imagine it peopled with fierce faces, and horrible with smoke and blood. In the coverts of wildwood on the plateau enemy spies might be lurking--even far up on the grim face of Choharua. She pictured the enemy--men with evil, pallid faces, such as she had caught a glimpse of in the streets in her visit with Archie to the Gran Seco, and at the picture she thrilled with horror.

Her fears were worst at night, when she would awake at the slightest sound and lie for a space listening, with every nerve tense...In the daytime she forced herself to cheerfulness, and managed to fill up every minute with duties. The weather was changing, and the spring rains were beginning. The sky, which for weeks had been an arch of crystal by day and by night a velvet canopy ablaze with stars, was now perpetually clouded, and often the plateau would be shrouded in a fine mist. This obscurity did not help her spirits. It seemed to offer cover for infinite chances of surprise by land, water, and air.

One thing only gave her comfort. She had decided weeks before to make herself a good pistol shot, and now she assiduously practised, under Roger Grayne's tuition. Grayne, large, rugged, shaggy, and imperturbable, was a fortunate companion for a nervous girl. Janet had always been a fine rifle shot, and now she became a very fair marksman with a revolver, and learned to shoot in any position.

"That's fine!" Grayne would say. "I shouldn't like to be up against you in a rough-house, Lady Roylance. Say, you're not worrying about this little business? It's all as right as rain." And when, moved by his friendliness, she confided to him her doubts, he laughingly disposed of them. The weather was far worse for Lossberg than for them. Supposing his planes arrived on a compass course, they were morally certain to come to grief, for the plateau was tricky in a dead calm, and certain death in foul weather to anyone who did not know it...An attack from Loa! It would take weeks for the enemy to fight his way through the most difficult country on God's earth, and there were roads by which every ounce of supplies could be got off before Lossberg was within thirty miles...The sea! He admitted that there was a risk there, but there could be no surprise. There was just the one narrow avenue of approach, and that could be held against the whole darned Olifa navy long enough to give them ample time to move.

"You see," he concluded, "we're so fixed that we can't be surprised. Olifa's got to come in force to take our sea approach, and coming in force means early notice. We're it worrying about stray guardacostas. It's not as if one man could wriggle through and bomb us in our beds. That's the kind of game I don't fancy, but it's about as likely here for an army corps to come over Choharua."

But if Grayne was a solid comfort to the girl, the Gobernador was very much the reverse. He, like her, seemed to be the victim of nerves ever since D'Ingraville's plane had vanished seaward. He was no longer friendly in forthcoming, a pleasant companion indoors and abroad. He had become silent and preoccupied, and meals were Trappist--like banquets. Nor did he, as at the beginning his sojourn on the plateau, spend much of his time in own room. He seemed to dislike to be alone, and to have nothing on which he could fix his mind. From morning till night he roamed about the settlement, constantly turning eyes to the sky, always intent and listening. There were no restrictions on his movements, so he went many times to the sea-ravine, and sat on the rocks at the top of it staring downward and seaward.

Once Janet found him sitting huddled there in a water-proof coat, when a shower had passed and a watery sun was trying to shine. The air was stuffily raw, oppressive to the walker, but chilly when movement ceased. He was squatting like a figure of Buddha, and his eyes seemed trying to pierce the clouds which drooped low over the sea.

"You are looking for your deliverers, Excellency?" the girl asked.

He shrugged his shoulders.

"I told you," he said, "that folly is always punished. But its punishment may be also a foolish business. This holiday camp seems to be coming to an end."

"Perhaps. Do you know, your voice sounds as if you were rather sorry?"

He did not reply, but unbuttoned the collar of his water-proof as if the weather choked him.

"I have seen you shooting at a target," he said at last. "You can use a pistol?"

"Pretty well. I'm improving every day."

"Then you have the ultimate safeguard. You need not fear the worst."

"I hope for the best," she said with enforced gaiety. "Perhaps I may shoot General Lossberg."

"Lossberg!" he repeated almost bitterly. "You need not fear Lossberg. I was thinking of something very different, and I am glad to know that in the last resort you will be safe...Most women are afraid of pistols, but you are different from most women. After all, it is a merciful death."

Janet shivered, for the eyes which the Gobernador turned upon her had that in them which she had never seen before There was anxiety in them, and something which was almost tenderness. She understood that if she feared the coming of his deliverers, so also did he--and not for his own sake "I'm afraid we are giving you a miserable time," she said, trying to speak lightly. "We have dragged you out of your comfortable groove into an anxious place."

"You have upset the work of my life," he said gravely. Then he added, as if by an afterthought, "and the foundations."

"The foundations?"

"Yes. I had a clear course marked out, like a chart. Now the chart is overboard, and the rudder is swinging loose."

"There may be other charts," she said gently.

Then she averted her face and began to talk nonsense rapidly, for she realised that she herself must be the chart-maker.

VII

On the evening of August 19th the rain, which had fallen all day, ceased, and a thin fog oozed out of the ground. By six o'clock night had fallen and a small wind had risen, and, since the sky was heavily overcast, the darkness was soon like the bottom of a cellar...The moon would not rise for an hour or two, and, unless the weather changed, it would give little light.

At the foot of the sea-ravine, in a log hut above the jetty, the coast garrison was preparing supper. Behind was a short space of flat ground, much of which had been feared, but a grove of dead fan-palms remained, whose withered leaves rustled and creaked in the wind. It was in noisy spot, for the torrent after its breakneck descent drove through the boulders of the beach in a fury of loud white waters. In that sheltered bay the sea was calm, but the stream made a perpetual clamour as of beating surf.

The garrison consisted of six Indians of the hills, four of Luis's haciendados, whom he specially trusted, and two of Grayne's ex-marines. The whole was in charge of one of the Alhuema engineers, a gnarled Ulsterman called Corbett, who had come to the Gran Seco from Rhodesia, and whose experiences went back to the Matabele wars. There was a small stove in the hut, and, since supper had just been cooked, the air in that tropical spot on the sea-level was like an orchid-house. A lantern stood on the trestled table, but windows and door were closed so that from the sea no light could have been observed. Only the white men and the mestizos sat at the table; the Indians ate their meal of boiled millet and syrup in their own circle apart.

Corbett mopped his brow. He had begun to fill a pipe and had stopped as if in a sudden distaste. "I can't smoke in this blasted conservatory," he said "Shade the light, Bill. I'm for a little fresh air."

He unbarred one of the windows and let in a current of steamy wind which stirred but did not cool the thick atmosphere of the hut. Outside the night was hot, noisy, and impenetrably dark. He stuck head and shoulders out, and promptly drew them back.

"Bill," he whispered, "come here! First stick the lantern under the table...Look straight ahead. D'you see a light?"

The man called Bill stared into the blackness and then shook his head.

"Nix," he said.

"Funny," said the other. "I could have sworn I caught a spark of something. It might have been on the water, or on the land across the channel. No, not at the seaward end--at the end under the big red rock...Here,

Jones, you have a look-see. You're like a cat and can see in the dark."

The Indian addressed as Jones had a long look. "I see no light," he said. "But I can hear something which is not the wind or the stream. Bid the others be quiet." He remained motionless for several minutes, like a wild animal that has been alarmed. Then he too shook his head. "It has gone," he said. "For a second I thought I heard a man's voice and the noise of a ship."

"But the whole damn place is full of noises," said Corbett.

"This was a different noise. The wind is from the west and the sea carries sound."

"Where might it have been?"

"I think near the rock beyond the water."

"Same place as I thought I saw the light." Corbett rubbed his bristly chin. "Can't say I like that. Jones and me may be dreaming, but it's the first time we've ever imagined anything like it. We'd better get the patrols out. Bill, you stay here, with Jones and his two mates. Keep your ears cocked and your eyes skinned. And you'd better call up Number One and tell 'em that we're a bit anxious. Kittredge will take the southern beat up to the head of the gulf--same three as last night--and I'll go north. It's the water's edge we've got to watch, so there's no call to go fossicking in the bush...Remember the drill, you all, if you hear a shot. We meet here again at midnight, hen Bill and his little lot turn out. No smoking for you boys. Keep your pipes in your pockets till you get back."

We are concerned only with the doings of Kittredge and his party of three, whose beat lay south along the shore of the little gulf to where the land swung round in a horn of cliff to form the breakwater which separated the inlet from the ocean. He had with him one Indian and two of Luis's mestizos. Beyond the jetty the trees descended almost to the water's edge, high timber trees festooned with lianas, but for a yard or two on the seaward side the western winds had thinned the covert a little, and the track zigzagged among bare boles. Beyond, the hill dropped almost sheer, so that the traveller was wet by the tides, but farther on there was a space of treeless ground, covered with light grass and thorn bushes, and at the water's edge, where other stream entered the sea, a reed-swamp, haunted by wildfowl.

Kittredge divided his patrol. To the Indian he relegated the patch of forest, since he was the best man for a tangled country. The place where the cliffs dropped sheer to the water he left to one of the mestizos, for it seemed the easiest to watch, since its rear was protected. He himself and the other mestizo took the patch of savannah which etched to the head of the gulf. They did not keep very in the sea because of the swamps, but chose the higher ground among the grass and scrub. It was not a good place for observation, since the ears were filled with the rustling of dry sedge in the wind, and the eyes in the darkness could have made out nothing except a light.

Kittredge and his man saw no light, and they heard little but the wind in the grass and reeds and an occasional stirring of wild duck. They made their way to the head of the gulf and about eleven o'clock turned for home. They expected to pick up the other mestizo in the cliff section, but could nut find him, so they assumed that, since they were a little behind time, he had gone back according to instructions to the rendezvous in the hut. The Indian in the forest belt was still awaiting them. He had seen and heard nothing.

But the man in the cliff area had not gone home. He had sat for half an hour on the shelf of rock straining his eyes into the gloom. Then, being alone, he had become the prey of fears, for he was superstitious. He had said his prayers, and moved a little north, so that he could have the sheer rock-wall at his back. A movement in the set startled him, till he decided that it was a fish. But he had become restless and nervous and again shifted his post this time to a boulder which overhung deep water. He was just about to squat himself on it, when a sound halted him and in a moment of panic he felt for his pistol. It was his last earthly act, for at that instant a knife was neatly drive between his shoulder-blades, and almost in the same movement his pistol was taken from his hand and his body slid quietly into the sea.

At Post No. 1, two-thirds of the way up the ravine, the telephone message from the shore had been duly received. It was a small post, and the officer in charge, an old colleague of Corbett's, was not inclined to disregard his warning. But since the post was at a turning, where the cliff was sheer above and below the path, there seemed no need for special precautions. Anything which came up the path would instantly observed. But it occurred to him that it might just possible to avoid the path and make a way across the creeper-clad precipice and the steep glen up a tributary stream, so he sent a man up the road to the only corner where such a short-cut could debouch.

This man, an Indian of the Gran Seco, was not accustomed to forests, nor to the thick steamy darkness of that gash in the mountains. He started at every sound--the cry of a piripipi bird, the rustle of a dead branch, the rooting of a wild pig, for all were unfamiliar. Presently, being a philosopher, he decided that every noise was alike and innocuous, and relapsed into meditation. His philosophy was his undoing. About a quarter of an hour before midnight, he sat sleepily perched on the end of one of the many wooden bridges, something struck him, something as sudden and secret and deadly as a serpent's fang. Quick hands thrust his dead body into the thicket. He was not missed by Post No. 1 till next morning at breakfast.

At Post No. 2, the half-way post, placed beside one of the main platforms of the chute, the night passed without incident. There the ravine was broad and densely wooded, and the angle of the slope was only some 30 degrees. Nothing that night appeared on or near the path.

The garrison at the summit were in tents strung out on both banks of the stream before it began its descent, and completely commanding the path and the off-take of the chute and the wire ropeways. The current of the stream had been used to develop electric power for haulage, and the engine-house stood close to the left bank. The post was admirably sited to command the path, but, owing to the obstruction of the buildings, it had no long field of view to left or to right. The uppermost part of the ravine was wider than the lower, and very steep, but ribbed with lateral spurs. It was possible for an active man to make the ascent by one of these spurs without the cognisance of the summit garrison.

Geordie Hamilton, late of the Royal Scots Fusiliers, was not only in charge of the garrison but also of the engine-house, since by profession he was a mechanic. He and his men, mostly Mines workmen, were stalwart bulldogs to guard a gate, but they were not greyhounds to range at large. They had received Corbett's warning from the shore and till well after midnight were very alert to watch the only area from which they anticipated danger...The wind was rising, and the glen was full of sound. The did not hear, and if they had heard they would not have regarded, the fall of a stone in a subsidiary gully a quarte of a mile to their left, the creak of a log, and the long screech of metal on stone which means that nailed boots have slipped...

Janet had gone to bed in a happier frame of mind. The Gobernador had caught cold, and Barbara, fearing fever, had given him a sleeping-draught and packed him between blankets. Moreover, she had shifted him from his ordinary quarters to another hut, one with a fireplace, which Jane and Archie had hitherto occupied, Janet removing herself to his in exchange. His new hut was close to the mess room in the very centre of the compound; his old one was on the northern outskirts, selected originally in order that it might be specially guarded by sentries without making the fact too obvious.

Janet slept till a little after midnight, and then for no apparent reason she found herself wideawake. This was constantly happening to her nowadays, and she lay for a little with her nerves on stretch, listening for she knew not what. There was no sound except the wind, making odd little noises in the thatch and among the unseasoned plank of the hut. There were sounds, too, coming from inside, so she snapped her bedside switch and stared into the corner. But it was only the wind stirring a pile of old picture papers and flapping a waterproof on a peg. Janet turned off the light and tried to compose herself to sleep again. She thought of a procession of ducks on a common and sheep coming through a gate, but it was no use. Very soon she realised that she was hopelessly wide awake and would not get to sleep again that night. She realised something more--that her nervous unrest had come back with redoubled force. She felt her heart beating and her fingers twitching and a ridiculous, unreasoning fear at the back of her head.

Very much ashamed of herself, she decided that there was thing for it but to get up and dress. It was a wild night, she saw when she opened the door, but there was some sort of moon, and her first idea was to go for a ride on the downs...She wished she had a dog; Archie had had a mongrel terrier with the army and had meant to bring it to her but had forgotten...She thought of going to look for Barbara, but felt some scruples about making into the beauty-sleep of one who slept like a log and had apparently no tremors.

She dressed and again looked out into the night. It was windy and mild, the sky was thick with low clouds, and the moon gave only the faintest light. She could see the outline of the next hut, but very dimly, and she realised at her notion of saddling a horse and going for a ride was impracticable. She felt that a gallop would restore her balance, but in such obscurity she would certainly break her neck.

Then she tried to read. She had been taking a course of Wordsworth, as something to distract her mind, and she resolutely plunged into the Prelude. But she found that the words did not make sense. The discovery irritated her so much that it almost restored her poise. "You little fool," she told herself, "what kind of wife are you for a soldier? You should be back in the schoolroom. You have got the vapours, my dear. You who used to laugh at your sister when she was afraid to go to bed at Glenraden because of the ghost on the tower staircase!"

Janet's annoyance did her good. But she could not get id of an intolerable sense of expectation. She looked at her watch and saw that it was after one o'clock. Five hours till daybreak! She lay down again on her bed, shut her eyes, and tried to remember all the jolliest things in her life. A certain picnic in her childhood to the Sea Skerries--days with hounds in Warwickshire--her first London ball-escapades with her sister Agatha--that memorable day in the rain beside the flooded Doran when she had first found herself in Archie's arms. Archie! She thought of him with such a glow of pride and affection that she forgot her fears...She began to picture their return the Crask and what she would do with the old house on the hillside.

Her fancy was toying pleasantly with the future, when suddenly she sat bolt upright. She had heard a sound which could not be the wind. It was the sound of steps close to the hut, stealthy steps but unmistakable, as even a small noise can be in the midst of louder noises in a different key. She switched on the light. She had locked the door on going to bed, but had unlocked it when she looked out at the weather. To her horror she saw it gently open. A man came swiftly into the room--and then another. Both had white faces and their brows were damp with sweat. One was a tall man with a hatchet face and a scar above his right eyebrow, the other was squat and muscular with rabbit teeth and a broken nose. Their clothes were much torn, as if they had had a rough journey. The eyes of both showed amazement and disappointment. They were looking for something other than a scared girl.

"The Gobernador?" the first one cried, and "Where hell's the boss?" came from the other.

Then Janet understood. She had her pistol under his pillow, and in a second had snatched it and fired. But was wild shooting, the shot struck a rafter, and before she could fire again the men were upon her. They were men of quick decision and skilful at the job. A scarf was wound suffocatingly over her mouth and she was seized in a grip which seemed to crush the breath from her. She felt herself in the open air, and heard with almost her last moment in clear consciousness a voice saying, "If the bitch squeals wring her neck."

After that she remembered little. She felt the cold breath of the night, and then swift movement in a man's arms. There was a noise in the air--she thought it was shots and cries, and sudden flashes of light. She was aware of being rushed along, of being suddenly dropped in cover and then again of violent speed. She struggled till her limbs cramped, but she was like a baby in the hands of her captors. And very soon weariness and panic did their part, and a merciful numbness fell upon body and mind.

Janet's shot had awakened the camp. The pickets had fired in answer, the big arc lights had been turned on, and in three minutes the place was feverishly awake. But the sentries had been withdrawn from Janet's hut, since the Gobernador was no longer there, and on that side the scrub came nearest, so that it was easy for the raiders to find cover. Yet they could hardly have escaped but for an unlucky blunder. Geordie Hamilton, hearing the uproar, had assumed that the camp was attacked by its landward approaches. That was the side from which he had always anticipated danger. Therefore, contrary to orders, he led the garrison straight to the camp, and all but stumbled on Radin, Judson, and Laschallas as they made their way to the sea-ravine. This meant that the post on its summit was empty, and the most difficult part of the descent was left unguarded.

Janet awoke from her swoon to find herself in the midst of water. She had a bad headache, and felt rather sick; also her body seemed to be a mass of aches. She was no longer bound, and had been laid on a rough couch of dirty cushions and tarpaulins. The weather had changed; above her was a blue arch of sky, and around her a circle of blue water, except on one side where a distant wall of green and umber told of land.

Slowly recollection came back to her, and with it her powers of observation. She saw that she was in a petrol launch, some ten miles out in the Pacific. There were four men on board. Two were the rabbit-toothed man and the tall hatched-faced fellow she had seen in the hut.

Another was sallow with thick black eyebrows, and the fourth was plump and yellow, with sharp little eyes. She lay very still, for all her tremors had gone. She knew the worst now. There had been treachery among the company in the Courts the Morning. D'Ingraville had located their base, but some traitor must have gone out from among them and told the secret of the sea-ravine. These ruffians had come to rescue the Gobernador, and they had known exactly in which hut he slept. They had been foiled by his cold, which proved that he was not privy to the plot, and at this conclusion Janet felt an unreasoning gladness. Not finding him, they had carried her off--no doubt as a hostage. At the thought her heart began to flutter again, but she resolutely steadied herself. The time for foolishness was past. She was not anticipating danger now, but in the thick of it, and must brace herself to meet it. She choked down every thought and memory which might weaken her resolution. Her business was to keep her head and play the game for her side...But at the sight of the men with their evil faces she could not repress a shiver.

They were not unkind to her. One of them brought her water and a towel and she was able to make a sort of toilet. Another fetched her a cup of strong coffee, a box with biscuits in it, and a couple of oranges. She could not eat but the coffee did her good, and her headache began to mend.

Then, from the land side, at a great height an aeroplane came flying. It must have been an assignation, for the men had been on the look-out for it, and a flag was hoisted. On nearer view it was seen to be a sea-plane. It circle twice round the launch, and then slid gracefully down till it floated like a bird on the water. The launch steered towards it, and its occupant was revealed as a slight youngish man, with a fair beard, an oddly-shaped head like a faun's, and grey eyes that were set somewhat too close together. His face, as he caught sight of Janet, expressed surprise. The man called Laschallas spoke to him in rapid Spanish, and his brows darkened. He seemed to be cursing them, and the reply was an impassioned defence. Then he shrugged his shoulders and bowed to Janet.

"I expected another guest, madame," he said in French, "but we must rejoice at what fortune has given us. You will do me the honour to accompany me."

The transhipment was a delicate business, and was not accomplished without a great deal of angry speech. Janet kept a tight hold on her nerves and accepted the inevitable. The four men in the launch were brutes, but what was this smiling, faun-like creature, and whither was he taking her? She felt desperately solitary, cut off from all that was normal and dear.

The plane lifted from the water, and turned seaward to ain elevation. Then it circled round, and steered for the wall of mountain.

VIII

Janet's pistol-shot, and the answering shots from the sentries, awakened the camp effectually, but in the thick night, with a volleying wind, it was hard to locate the trouble. Grayne, who was in command, naturally assumed that the danger lay in the neighbourhood of the Gobernador's hut, but Castor was discovered sleeping the heavy sleep of one dosed with aspirin, and Barbara, who slept next door, had heard nothing. The big arc lamps showed everything normal, and, since the light had been promptly switched off in Janet's hut by the raiders, it was presently decided that it had been a false alarm. The arrival of Geordie Hamilton and his garrison from the head of the ravine complicated matters, and it was the better part of an hour before peace was restored. No one doubted that the whole thing had been a blunder of a nervous sentry who had taken a whimsy of the wind for a shot. Barbara went back to bed.

She woke about dawn with an uneasy feeling. Why had Janet not been awakened by the noise--Janet, the lightest sleeper of them all? It was a mild blue morning after the rain, so she slipped on a dressing-gown and ran across to Janet's hut. To her surprise the door stood open, unlatched. The bed had been slept in, but the occupant had clearly got up and dressed. There was a faint smell which puzzled her, till she realised that it was powder; a shot had been fired in the place during the night. Then she noticed that the floor around the doorway was muddied, and that some of the furniture looked as if it had been violently pushed aside. Lastly, on one of the rafters she observed a jagged splinter which could only have been done by a bullet.

With terror in her heart she hurried to find Roger Grayne and in five minutes the camp was astir. The tracks of the raiders were clear on the road to the sea, except when they had been overlaid by those of Hamilton's men. The Indian trailers had no difficulty in pointing to the very place where they had taken cover, and in deciding that there had been three men in the business, three men who, in departing, had been encumbered with a burden...The very spot was found where they had circumvented Hamilton's garrison on their way up. At Post No. 1 it was discovered that one of the scouts had not come back, and his body was presently found in the thicket at the turn of the road. Down on the shore Corbett reported the absence of one of the mestizos who had gone on patrol to the head of the gulf. The section where the cliffs dropped straight to the sea was searched, and blood was found on the reef by the water's edge. The Indians scattered among the shore thickets, and soon reported that they had discovered the tracks of the raiders, both those going and those returning, and across the gulf evidence was found that a petrol-driven vessel had landed recently. The story was plain in all its details. Their base had been raided, and Janet had beer carried off.

"They did not come for her." Barbara with tragic eyes clutched Grayne's arm.

"I guess they didn't. They came for the Gobernador. Some swine has double-crossed us and given away his exact location, only he didn't know that his Excellency was sick. They were certainly fooled about that...But, my God! Miss Babs, we can't sit down under this. It's maybe bad strategy, but I'd rather they'd taken twenty Gobernadors than that little lady. Say, what do they want with her? A hostage, I guess. Who'd have thought Lossberg would be so bright?"

"But where is she?" Barbara cried. All the colour had gone out of her cheeks, and her face was a waxen mask of misery.

"Olifa, maybe. Yes, I guess she's in Olifa. Don't worry, Miss Babs. She can't come to any hurt. We're not fighting with savages who torture their prisoners. I wonder what Lossberg's next move will be?"

Grayne went off to give orders for the strengthening of the guards at the sea-ravine, since there lay their Achilles-heel, and Barbara bathed her face and tidied herself to meet Castor. This awful thing must be faced with a stiff lip, at any rate in the presence of the enemy. She was possessed with a cold fury against him. The enemy--his side--had made war on women and stolen that woman whom she had come to love best in the world.

Some rumour had already reached him, for he was in the mess-hut, evidently dressed in a hurry, since he had a scarf round his neck instead of a collar. She did not know what she expected to find in him--triumph perhaps, or a cynical amusement. Instead she found a haggard man with bleared eyes--no doubt the consequence of his feverish chill. He startled her by his peremptoriness. "Have you found her?" he cried. "Lady Roylance?...What has happened?...Tell me quick, for God's sake."

To her amazement he appeared to be suffering.

"No news--except that Janet has gone. We found the track to the water's edge, and there must have been a launch...They murdered two of the guards..."

She stopped, for something in his eyes took away her breath. It was suffering, almost torment. She had never known him as Janet knew him, and had regarded him as a creature of a strange and unintelligible world, though she had reluctantly admitted his power. Now the power remained, but the strangeness had gone. He had suddenly become human, terribly human. She had come to upbraid and accuse; instead she wanted to pity. She found one who shared to the full in her misery.

"Oh, Mr Castor," she cried, "where have they taken her?"

"How can I tell?" he asked fiercely. "Have you sent for her husband?"

She nodded. "Sir Archie is at Loa. He will be here before luncheon."

"And Lord Clanroyden?"

"He is at the other end of the Gran Seco. He is busy with a big movement. He will be told, but I do not think he can come."

"But he must. What does his imbecile war matter?...Oh, you miserable children! You have played with fire and you will be burned."

There was so much pain in his voice that Barbara tried to comfort him. "But surely in Olifa she can come to no harm?"

"Olifa! Why do you think she is there?"

"She was carried off by sea. Where else could General Lossberg...?"

"Lossberg! What has he to do with it? Lossberg is not the man to waste time on such a business. He has no desire for my company."

"But who?"

"There are others besides Lossberg--a far more deadly foe than the Olifa army. I warned Lord Clanroyden. I warned him that the true danger was not in the field...Lossberg is not the man for midnight escapades. He is too stiff. Regular soldiers do not climb ravines by night and stick knives between the shoulders. That is another kind of war. That is the way of the Conquistadors. Remember that D'Ingraville, who first found us out, is one of them."

Barbara's face had become as haggard as his own.

"Then where can they have taken her?"

"I do not know," he said, "but not to Olifa--no, not to Olifa."

Archie arrived a little after midday. He looked suddenly much older, and Barbara noticed that his limp had grow heavier. He was very quiet, so quiet that it seemed him possible for anyone to express sympathy. In a level, almost toneless voice he asked questions, and carefully went over all the ground between the camp and the ravine-foot. He had a talk alone with Castor, and announced that he was going back to the Gran Seco, and would return some time on the morrow.

Luis de Marzaniga, it seemed, had one foot in the theatre of war and one in Olifa; it might be possible for him to discover whether Janet had been taken to Olifa city. Also Sandy must be seen. He had cut the railway again, and was now engaged in worrying that section of Lossberg's army which lay around the Mines. Ammunition, it appeared, was getting low, and it was important to replenish the store by captures. It was necessary that Sandy should be consulted, and his Intelligence department might be able to help.

He flew off in the evening, a calm, self-contained, stricken figure, the sight of whom made Barbara want to howl. Once again it was halcyon weather, and the sight of smoke rising in straight spires in the blue twilight against the flaming background of the west almost broke her heart. About this time Janet should have been coming in from her evening gallop, shouting for her bath...There was no dinner in he mess-tent that night, for no one could face a formal meal. Castor had kept indoors all day, and was now occupied in striding round the central square in the way passengers take exercise on board ship. He stalked across to Barbara.

"Lord Clanroyden must come at once," he said.

"He can't," she said. "Sir Archie says that he is needed most desperately where he is. He is conducting a war."

"You know him well. You have influence over him. Cannot you bring him here?"

The girl for a moment coloured.

"I do not think I have any influence with him, and if I had I would not use it to take him away from his duty."

"Duty!" he said bitterly. "What duty is there in such fool concern? He has started a fire which he cannot control, and soon it will burn down his own house. His own house, I say. He was a friend of Lady Roylance."

"So were you, I think," said Barbara quickly. "Have you too not kindled a fire which you cannot control? The Conquistadors and the Bodyguard were your own creation."

For a moment there was anger in his face, and then it died out, leaving it curiously bleak and pale.

"I think that is a fair retort, Miss Dasent," he said, and resumed his sombre constitutional.

Archie returned very early next day, not in the small Shark-Gladas, which was his usual means of travelling, but in one of the big Seaforths which were meant for bombing and load-carrying.

"I want to see Castor," he told Barbara. "I think he liked Janet, and he can help a lot. I've told Hamilton to report here in an hour, for there isn't much time to lose."

The three sat in the mess-hut. The Gobernador had recovered his trimness of bearing, but the almost insolent detachment which had hitherto characterised him seemed to have gone. His air was restless, and his voice, when he spoke, had a sharper pitch. There was something angrily defensive in his manner, something uncertain in the eyes which searched the others' faces.

"I want your help, sir," Archie said in his new, quiet, toneless voice. "You and my wife were friends, and I don't think you want her to come to any harm."

"Help," Castor broke out. "You make me impotent and then ask my help! I did not start this business. I am the victim of your absurdities. You have plunged this land into a war directed against myself. I am your prisoner, though you call me your leader. You have brought me into a world which is utterly unfamiliar. I have no mastery in it. I am accustomed to organise and govern, but I cannot organise the confusion you call war. I am a reasonable man, and this is the domain of the wildest unreason...Then the crash comes, and you ask my help. You fools! You have made me more powerless than the rudest vaquero."

"I know, I know," said Archie soothingly. "I have no business to ask you for favours, but I don't think you will refuse all the same. You see, it is your old organisation that we have to fear, not the Olifa army. I do not think you want Janet to suffer at their hands."

"You have evidence?"

"A little. Enough to act upon."

"But I cannot control them. I am cut off..."

"No. But you can give me the benefit of your knowledge. Listen, sir. Our Intelligence have their own sources of news, and they are positive that Janet is not in Olifa. How they know I cannot tell, but we have never found them wrong. Further, they say that there are none of the Conquistadors or the Bodyguard now in Olifa. We may take it that the raiders belonged to one or the other. That is your own view, I think. Now, what facts have we? She was carried off in a launch--that we know. If she was not taken to Olifa, she may be hidden somewhere along the coast. That is possible, but not very likely--for two reasons. The first is that our own people know the coast, and my information is that there is no place on the whole line of shore under the mountains where any permanent camp could be made. If they landed Janet, it could only be for a day or a night--it can't be her final destination. The same is true of the low coastland farther south between the hills and Olifa, where there are nothing but malarial swamps. Janet may be there, but it is not likely, because of my second reason. Whoever carried her off wanted her for in purpose. They came for you, and took her instead, and they can only have taken her as a hostage. To use her as such she must have been taken to some place in touch with the Olifa army, and that must mean either Olifa or the Gran Seco plateau."

"But how could she reach the Gran Seco except by Olifa?"

"It is only a guess, but yesterday afternoon Peters reported from Pacheco that a plane had been seen flying eastward. It was marked like our own planes, and was flying high. Enemy planes are not allowed in that quarter, and, seeing it bore our own markings, no further notice was taken of it. But it was observed that it was a sea-plane, and since up to yesterday our army had no sea-planes, and Peters knew that, he thought it worth while to mention the fact."

"Well?"

"We have no sea-planes. That plane was not ours, though it pretended to be. It may have been Lossberg's, in which case he has diddled us. But I am inclined to think it was somebody else's. Janet was carried off in a launch. Why should not her captors somewhere out at sea have arranged for a sea-plane to meet them?"

Castor rose and walked to the big wall map.

"Show me the exact spot where the sea-plane was seen," he said.

Archie pointed with his finger.

"It was flying east?"

"East with a point of south."

"It was undoubtedly D'Ingraville. I think you are right, Sir Archibald. D'Ingraville met the launch and he has taken your wife with him."

"Where? Can you help me to that?"

Castor looked at the map again.

"It is the direction of the Pais de Venenos. You have heard of it?"

Archie nodded. "That was my own guess. Tell me more, sir."

"I can tell you very little. I have been there, but once only, and long ago. My colleagues, whom you call the Conquistadors, know it well. D'Ingraville, especially, and Pasquali. And Romanes--above all Romanes, who should by now have returned from Europe...There is a drug there which they depend upon." The Gobernador spoke hesitatingly, like a man loath to divulge something of which he is scarcely proud.

"I know about astura. I am told that without it they will die."

"No--not die--not at once. But they will be unhappy. I have always believed that the Conquistadors would make some violent effort to replenish their supply.

They will attempt to open up communications with the Pais Venenos."

"You think they have gone there--with Janet?"

"I do not think that. It is not a place where which men can dwell. The Conquistadors perhaps--they are immune--but not the Bodyguard. Besides, I do not think a plane could land there, for it is a desperate country of gorges and forests. Somewhere adjacent, perhaps--from which the Pais could be visited."

Archie was on his feet, striding about excitedly.

"Somewhere adjacent!" he cried, and his voice was harsh with pain. "But where? There are thousands of miles of unexplored country. Somewhere where a plane could land--the sea-plane may have an under-carriage...That must be in the hills. But Peters has all the Pacheco country patrolled, and beyond that the mountains rise like a wall...If only I could get Luis, but Luis has disappeared on some job of his own...Things aren't going too well with us at the moment, you know. We're terribly short of supplies, and Lossberg is getting cautious and won't stick out his head to let us hit it...You've told me all you can think of. Excellency? Well, I'm off. Hamilton should be here to report."

Outside the door stood Geordie Hamilton, the same stocky, impassive figure that had stumped heavily through four years of fighting in France, his blue eyes looking sullenly forth from a mahogany face.

"You're coming with me, Hamilton," said Archie. "Got your kit? Full marching order. We don't know when we will be back."

"Where are you going?" Castor asked.

"To look for Janet." The young man's face seemed to Barbara to have regained a kind of peace. He would not return alone. Moved by a sudden impulse, she kissed his cheek.

"Thank you, Babs dear," he said. Then he held out his hand to Castor. "Good-bye, I think you wish me well, sir."

It was the first time that any of the party had shaken hands with the Gobernador.

IX

The Seaforth flew first to Loa, where Archie asked for news of Don Luis. He was believed to be on the southern front, somewhere in the Pacheco area, where there was a good deal of activity. Loa itself was at present stagnant, a mere blockhouse to guard the road to the Courts of the Morning, and a forwarding depot for Magdalena. Lossberg's advance party, which a week before had been within twenty miles, had now withdrawn.

Then, hugging the skirts of the hills, and having a good deal of trouble with the eddies of wind that blew down the gullies, Archie flew south-east to Magdalena, Escrick's headquarters, under the snowy peaks of the Spanish Ladies. There he had an interview with Escrick's chief Intelligence officer and was shown the dispositions of the enemy in the Tierra Caliente. The nearest enemy planes were based on the Mines, and were probably at that moment busily engaged, since Sandy was worrying the Universum sector.

But there was no one at Magdalena who had any knowledge of the approaches to the Poison Country; it was out of their area, and belonged properly to Peters.

The right course would have been to seek Peters at Pacheco, and above all things to find Don Luis. But Archie was not in a mood to think calmly. During the flight from the Courts of the Morning his anxiety about Janet had beer rising to fever heat. Barbara's kiss of farewell seemed to have let loose a flood of dreadful fancies. He tortured himself with pictures--Janet small and solitary in the hand of men such as he had seen in the Gran Seco streets, men with evil, furtive eyes and corpse-like faces...A week before Sandy had drawn for him a rough map of the whereabouts of the Pais de Venenos, as a preliminary for certain exploratory flights which were contemplated in the south-east angle of the province...At the back of his head he still intended to go to Pacheco, but he felt an uncontrollable impulse first to do another thing. The straight route to Pacheco was over the eastern downs of the Tierre Caliente; but it was still afternoon, the moon would rise early, and even in the dark Pacheco could then reached on a compass course. To allay his anxiety by action of some sort had become a necessity. He decided to follow the line of the mountains, and find, if possible, the gate of the Poison Country which Sandy had described to him. After that he would get in touch with Luis, and discover from him where in that neighbourhood a sea-plane might have landed.

He took the Intelligence officer into his confidence and explained his purpose. "I expect to be at Pacheco tomorrow. If I don't turn up there, you can tell General Peters the road I meant to take, and get him to tell Senor de Marzaniga. They'll know where to look for me, if I have to descend." He borrowed an extra revolver and a supply of cartridges for Hamilton, who had also his rifle.

Likewise he borrowed two thick overcoats, for the nights were cold and he might be late. Hamilton ate a large meal, but Archie had no appetite for anything but a couple of dried figs.

The Seaforth left Magdalena a few minutes after 4 p.m. It was a warm bright afternoon, with the visibility so good that every rock and crinkle were clear on the mountain wall. Archie kept along the watershed where the barrens of the Tierra Caliente changed to a greener country, and where were the springs of the streams that forced their way through the range. The Cordilleras at that point are a double chain, and the country between the two is in part a maze of deep glens leading ultimately to valleys which debouch on the Orazon, and partly a high desert of shale and sand.

Below him was an even level of greenish-grey downs, shading into umber on the west--a land in which there was no sign of human life. He flew low, and saw the ruins of Indian pueblas, the inhabitants of which had been removed to Lossberg's concentration camp. Then these ceased, and he swung nearer the mountains, till he found himself in a long hollow, like a ditch under ramparts. He saw the gleam of water far below, and realised that there were many streams, and that all seemed to be affluents of a considerable river.

It was almost dark before the country began to change. The bald screes of the hills gave way to patches of wood, and at the same time the upper slopes grew more precipitous. Then the hollow seemed to draw to a funnel and the mountains fell back a little to receive it. Two peaks stood like sentinels, and between them lay a great wedge of darkness. The sun was now behind the downs to the west, and as Archie dropped lower the hollow seemed to be already brimming with dusk. Inside the great wedge it was already dark, but beyond were the shadows of dim green mountains.

The journey had taken longer than he thought. There was now no hope of getting to Pacheco much before midnight. Archie resolved to descend on one of the green levels and bivouac for the night. But there was still light enough to look inside the great gorge, for he decided that these were the gates he had been seeking. It was a foolish thing to do at such a time of day, but his anxious mind was beyond prudence. He turned to his left and flew towards the cleft.

The funnel was less dark than he had thought. He was flying low, and could see quite clearly beneath him the sudden abrupt descent of the stream and the mat of forest into which it fell. Soon he had passed the portals and the great cup opened out, lying in a clear green gloom like an emerald. In front of him, perhaps six miles away, a mountain rose out of the deeps, and its crest was a cone of snow, now rosy with the sunset. The periphery of the cup was also snow-rimmed, gold and crimson where the dying sun caught it and elsewhere a cold blue grey.

He dropped still lower. The forest was dense as the grass on a lawn. Tall trees now and then broke it, and sudden rocky spurs, but, though he was less than five hundred feet above it, he could make out no details, except where the river broadened into a leaden pool. The vegetation was as thick as an animal's pelt. A strange odour ascended to him--sweet and stupefying and rotten...

Could Janet be in that jungle of death? Could any human being be there and hope for life? The place seemed like a charnel-house encrusted by foul mosses.

Janet was not there--of that he had a sudden, complete conviction. The horror of the place grew on him, but he still held on. It was fast growing dark, and out of the forest a fog was rising like a wraith. He saw it billowing up towards him, and started to climb...Then his eye fell on the petrol gauge, and he had an ugly shock. What on earth had happened? He remembered now--he had forgotten to refill at Magdalena as he had intended.

But still he had started that morning with enough for a twenty-four hours' flight. The tank must have sprung a leak, for there were only about twenty minutes of petrol left.

He turned and flew in what he thought was the direction of the entrance to the gorge. There was just a chance that he might reach it in time and find a landing-place beyond it, for there could be no landing in this jungle. But the fog had enveloped him and was now far above him, a horrible, thick, choking whiteness which smelt of violets. He turned to look at Hamilton. That worthy, with the collar of his coat turned up, had his usual sullen calm. "It's comin' on for a thick nicht," he observed.

Archie looked again and saw that the main tank had gone dry. There was only the reserve tank left, and that would last at the most a quarter of an hour. He climbed steeply, For he remembered that he had been descending since he passed through the gorge. Below him was now thick darkness, but the mist above him seemed to hold the late sunshine. It might be thinner higher up, so he climbed towards he light.

Something not unlike panic had now seized Archie. If his petrol failed before he reached a landing-place, then he must crash in this noisome forest. Horror of the place ripped him like a nightmare. He climbed up and up, struggling to get above the mist, only dimly aware of the direction of his course...Could he hit off the gorge in his suffocating gloom? Was it worth trying? He had seen the zone of snow which encircled the cup. Up there there must be open ground, where a landing might be made. So he contented himself with climbing, bearing blindly to the left. His one aim was to get above the forest.

It was certainly less dark. He was coming out of the main shroud of the fog, and the white veil seemed to have patches in it. The altimeter registered nearly twelve thousand feet...But the forest was climbing with him, and suddenly below him he saw in the brume the top of a tall tree, a thin etching of black in the dimness. He must be far up the containing slopes. Then he observed from the gauge that only a few minutes more of petrol remained. He came to a decision.

"Hamilton," he cried, "we've got to go overboard. Get your chute ready."

There was no change in the man's stolidity. He had practised this drill in the Courts of the Morning, and now quietly made his preparations. Archie directed his spotlight downwards, and once again a fluff of tree tops came into view.

"Quick," he said. "I'll follow in a second."

"I doot I'll get a dunt," said Hamilton grimly as he went over the left side of the cockpit. Archie saw that the chute had opened and righted at once, and that he was descending steadily into the void.

His own task was more difficult. He cut out the switches and pulled the plane into a stall. He meant to go out on the right, when suddenly the right wing began to droop, which meant that it would strike the parachute. He therefore steadied the plane, and followed Hamilton over the left side. He started head foremost, but the risers pulled him upright and the parachute opened. The plane above him was lost in an instant, and Archie, oscillating violently and feeling very sick, plunged into a gulf of primeval darkness.

Something hit his head; then he hung for a second upside-down before slipping into what seemed a gigantic bramble bush which scratched his face. Another bump, a plunge, and Archie found himself standing on tiptoe on solid earth, with the ruins of the parachute and his great-coat hanked in the lower boughs of a tree.

X

Archie took a good quarter of an hour to disentangle himself from his Absalom-like posture, since, owing to the constriction of his garments, he could not get at his knife, and his hands were numb with cold. When at last he was free, he pitched forward stiffly into a huge tree-fern, which kept him from rolling down the slope. The actual forest was thin, but the undergrowth was dense and water-logged, and the declivity so steep that every step must be matched. The fog was still there, but it was not thick, and faint light filtered through it, so that it was possible to see he ground beneath and the trees above in a dim monotint.

His first business must be to find Geordie Hamilton. He shouted, but it was like speaking with the mouth muffled by olds of blanket. He argued that Hamilton must have descended not more than two hundred yards below him, and that the plane when he left it had been directly ascending the mountain face, so he tried to shape a straight course downhill. But the going was appalling. There were thickets of cactus to be circumvented, an occasional tall tree choked with creepers, and strips of sheer red earth. He stopped very few yards to shout for his companion, but no answer came; it seemed impossible to pierce that deathly stillness.

Presently he realised that at this rate he would soon be lost. He halted and mopped his brow, for he was sweating under the burden of his heavy flying-clothes. And then he heard, apparently from the bowels of the earth, what seemed to be a groan.

"Hamilton," he cried, and, shouting his name, he made his way a little to the left.

At last a reply came, a miserable, muffled voice.

"Is't you, Sir Erchibald?" it said, and it was as if its owner were speaking from under deep water.

The place was a shallow ravine, and as Archie groped his way something very hard and sharp caught him in the neck.

"Hamilton, where on earth are you?" he cried in pain.

"I'm catched in a buss," came an answering groan. "For God's sake get me out, for I've gotten some awfu' jags."

Then Archie remembered his spot-light. It revealed a great clump of the aloe called caraguata, with Hamilton most intricately wedged among the sword--like leaves. Above the spikes, like a dissolute umbrella, waved the parachute. Hamilton hung face downward, his great-coat suspended over him and his legs splayed like a clumsy diver's. He had ceased to struggle, for every movement sent the thorn deeper into his tenderest parts.

Archie stripped to shirt and breeches, and set himself slowly to cut the victim out, but it was the better part of and hour before the work was done, and Hamilton, still apoplectic about the face, was cautiously examining his wounds. He had plenty of them, but only scratches, though he declared that his legs were so stiff that it would be a month before he could walk.

"You'll have to start right away," Archie told him. "We can't stay in this blasted hot-house. We must be pretty near the edge of the tree-line, and once we get above the forest we can find a place to sleep. So step out, my lad, game leg or no. You and I are about equal now."

Slowly and with many stumbles they began the ascent, guiding themselves by the lift of the ground. It was desperately laborious, for sometimes the way was up sheer banks of earth, the remains of old landslides, and as slippery as oil; sometimes through acres of great ferns where the feet sank into deep hollows among the roots: sometimes through cactus scrub which reduced their coat-skirts to rags; often through horrible oozing moss which sent up a stink like a charnel-house. The fog was dying away, and the rising moon made their immediate environment clear, but the better they could see the more hopeless the toil became.

Hamilton panted and sobbed, and Archie's weak leg gave him many falls. The air had none of the wholesome chill of night. A damp heat closed them in, and when now and then a faint waft came up from the valley beneath. It seemed to have a sickening scent of violets. Often they stopped for breath, but they did not lie down. Instinctively they both shrank from contact with that unhallowed soil. Once Hamilton drank from a pool in a stream, and was violently sick.

"We must be about the height of the Matterhorn," Archie said, "and yet it's as hot as hell. This is a cursed place."

"Deed, it's no canny," said Hamilton, gulping with nausea.

Before long it was clear that Hamilton's strength was giving out. Thickset and burly as he was, this greenhouse-mountaineering was beyond him. He stumbled more often, and after each fall took longer to recover. At last he stopped.

"I doot I'm done, sir," he wheezed. "This bloody cemetery is ower much for me! You gang on."

"Nonsense," said Archie, taking his arm. He was dog-tired himself, but to his more sensitive nerves the hatred of the place was such that it goaded him forward like a spur.

"See, we'll take hands. We can't be far from the tree-line."

But it seemed hours before they reached it. Fortunately the slope had become easier and less encumbered, but the two men staggered on drunkenly, speaking no word, their eyes scarcely seeing, so that their falls were frequent, everything blotted from their mind but the will to bodily endurance. So blind were they that they did not notice that the fog was almost gone, and they had come out of the forest before they realised it. Suddenly Archie was aware that he was no longer climbing steeply, and then he was looking across a shelf of bare land which rose to a rim of a pale silver.

He was breathing free air, too. A cool light wind was on his forehead.

"Hamilton," he cried, "I...believe...we're clear."

The two dropped like logs, and the earth they sank on was not the reeking soil of the forest, but the gravel of an upland.

Both lay for a little, their limbs too weary to stretch. Then Archie crawled to his feet.

"Let's go on a bit. I want to feel really quit of that damned Poison Valley. We must find a hole to sleep in."

They staggered on for another half-mile, weakly, but no longer so miserably. The sand and shale underfoot gleamed white as salt in the moonlight, and were broken only by boulders and small scrubby thorns. Then they found a shelf of rock which overhung so as to form a shallow cave. It was now as cold as it had been hot in the covert, the sweat had dried upon them, and the scratches on hands and face smarted in the frost. Each had a small ration of food in his pocket, charqui--which is the biltong the Gran Seco Indians prepare--some biscuits and chocolate, and Arch had a packet of raisins. They supped lightly, for thirst and hunger seemed to have left them, and, cuddled against each other for warmth, both were soon asleep.

Archie woke in an hour's time. He had slept scarcely all during the past three days, and even deep bodily fatigue could not drug his mind. Wild dreams had assailed him--of falling down precipices of red earth into a foetid jungle threaded by oily streams. He woke to find that the moon had set and that it was very dark. Far off there was a call like a jackal barking. There were other things alive on this shelf beside themselves.

Then he heard a sound close at hand--the padding of soft feet on gravel. His spot-light was beside him, and he flashed it in the direction of the feet. About ten yards away stood an animal. At first he thought it was a wolf from its size till he saw its sharp muzzle and prick ears, its reddish fur, and its thick tail. It was a fox, one of the cannibal foxes of the Pais de Venenos that he had heard of from Sandy. The animal blinked in the light, and its teeth were bared in a snarl. Archie reached for Hamilton's rifle, which lay loaded beside them, but he was too late. The great brute turned and trotted off, and passed out of sight among the boulders.

"Enough to put me off fox-hunting for evermore," thought Archie. After that he did not sleep, but lay watching the dark thin to shadows and the shadows lighten to dawn. The sun seemed to leap with a bound over the far Cordilleras, and a morning mist, as white and flat as a snowfield, filled the valleys. Archie's heartsickness returned to him like a fever. Somewhere within the horizon was Janet, but by what freak of fortune was he to get her--himself a mere lost atom at the edge of his endurance, and as ignorant as a babe of this immense, uncharted, unholy world?

Both men soon realised that the Pais de Venenos had exacted its penalty. Hamilton was clearly in a fever, which may have been due to his many cuts, and Archie felt something like a band of hot steel round his head. For breakfast they nibbled a little chocolate and ate a few raisins. Then, as far as their bodily discomfort permitted, they discussed their plans.

"We're up against some solid facts, Hamilton," said Archie. "We're looking for my wife, and I believe she's somewhere within fifty miles, but we've got to admit that we're lost ourselves. All I remember from Lord Clanroyden's map is that if we keep going up the south wall of the Poison Country we'll come to the main range, and south-west of that lies Pacheco. The people we're seeking must be up on the range, but they may be north or south the of Poison Country. We couldn't cross that infernal valley, so let's hope they are on the south. Another thing--we mayn't be able to get up the range--we're neither of us in much form for mountaineering. Also, we've got about enough food to last us with care for two days. We shan't want for water."

"I'll no need much meat," said Hamilton sombrely. "I cauldna swallow my breakfast, my throat's that sair."

"We're both dashed ill," Archie agreed. "I feel like a worm, and you look like one. Maybe we'll be better if we get higher."

Hamilton turned a feverish eye upwards. "I doot it's higher we'll be goin'. Anither kind o' Flyin' Corps. Angels."

"That's as it may be. It's too soon to chuck in our hand. You and I have been in as ugly places before this. We're both going on looking for my wife till we drop. We'll trust to the standing luck of the British Army. I've a sort notion we'll find something..."

"We'll maybe find mair folk than we can manage."

"Undoubtedly. If we're lucky enough to get that far, we'll have to go very warily. We needn't make plans till we what turns up. At the worst we can put up a fight."

Hamilton nodded, as if the thought comforted him. A fight with men against odds was the one prospect which held no terrors for him.

The two very slowly and painfully began their march over the shelf and up to the snow-rimmed slopes which contained it. The Pais de Venenos behind them was still a solid floor of mist. Happily the going was good--flat reefs of rock with between them long stretches of gravelly sand. Archie decided that he must bear a little to his right, for there the containing wall seemed to be indented by a pass. They must find the easiest road, for they were in no condition to ascend steep rock or snow. The wind was from the east and wisps of cloud drifted towards them, bringing each a light flurry of snowflakes. They had awoken shivering, and now as they walked their teeth chattered, for both were too sore and stiff to go fast enough to warm their blood.

Suddenly they struck a path--a real path, not an animal's track, but a road used regularly by human feet. Indeed, it seemed at one time to have been almost a highway. At one place Archie could have sworn that the rock had been quarried to ease the gradient, and at another, where it flanked a stream, it looked as if it had been embanked. In that wild place it seemed a miracle. Archie thought that he must be light-headed, so he examined carefully the workmanship. There could be no doubt about it, for his fingers traced the outlines of squared stones. Once this had been a great highroad, as solid as Roman work. It seemed to come out of the mist of the Poison. Valley, and to run straight towards the pass in the ridge. He pointed it out to Hamilton.

"Aye, there's been folk here langsyne," was the answer. Archie bent over a patch of snow. "Not so long ago. Here are the marks of feet, naked feet, and they were made within the past twenty-four hours."

Slowly they tramped up the glacis of the range towards the pass. Hamilton walked like a man in a dream, stumbling often, and talking to himself. He seemed to have a head ache, for he stopped at the water-pools to bathe his head. The pain in Archie's forehead grew worse as they ascended till it became almost unbearable. He kept his fingers on his eyes to ease the throbbing behind them. But his mind was clear, and he could reason with himself about his condition. It might be the poisoning of the forest--most likely that was true in Hamilton's case--or it might be mountain sickness. He had once had a slight bout in the Karakoram, and he had heard that it was common in the Cordilleras...Just before the summit of the pass he looked back. The tablecloth was lifting from the Pais de Venenos, and the white floor was now cleft with olive-green gashes. The summit of the pass was a hollow between snowdrifts.

There both men stood and stared, for the sight before them was strange and beautiful. Archie had expected another tableland, or a valley of rocks shut in between peaks. Instead his eyes looked over a wide hollow, some three miles in diameter. High ridges flanked it on all sides, and on the west was a great mass of mountain, which he believed must project like a promontory towards the Tierra Caliente. The slopes beneath them were at first boulders and shingle, but presently they became the ordinary grassy savannah, with clumps of wood here and there which seemed to be more than scrub. And in the centre of the hollow lay a lake, shaped like a scimitar, of the profoundest turquoise blue.

He unslung his field-glasses and examined the place. There was no sign of life in it. At various points on the shore he could detect what looked like millet fields, but here was no mark of human habitation. Then he examined a dark blur near the western end, and found something that might have been the ruins of a Border keep.

"We've struck a queer place," he told his companion, but Hamilton turned a blank face. He had almost lost the power of sight; his whole mind was bent on forcing his sick body into movement.

As they began to descend, an oppression seemed to lift from Archie's soul. The horror of the place where he had landed left him, now that he had come into a clean bright country. Also the band of iron round his brow fretted him less. He found that he moved with greater ease, and he could lend a hand to his tottering companion. When they reached the first grass he felt hungry, and they sat down complete their breakfast. But Hamilton could only manage a single raisin, though he drank thirstily from a stream.

The whole place was a riot of blue light, the heavens above and the lake beneath; even the rim of silver sand seemed to catch a turquoise reflection. The air, too, was no longer the dry, throat-catching thing of the high snows, but fresh and clement. The sun warmed them gratefully, and Archie's eye recovered its old keenness. He saw a bird at last and the ornithologist awoke in him.

"By Jove, a black snipe," he cried. "The first I've seen."

The road they had followed skirted the northern edge of the lake and led them straight to the ruins near the western end. At close quarters the strangeness of the latter was increased. This had been a castle, like any Scots peel tower, the guardian of this fair valley. It had long been deserted, but the keep still stood foursquare, of a masonry which time and storm could not crumble. Archie examined it curiously. No mortar had been used, and the stones fitted into each other with such mathematical exactness that a knife could not find a lodgment. There were no signs of windows. Whoever dwelt here must have dwelt in darkness unless he had some means of artificial light...Archie remembered a story which Luis had told him of the old lords of the mountains, who controlled the Poison Country. They dwelt secure, he had said, for they made a belt of poison round them, and in their windowless dwellings they lived by candlelight. No, not candles, Luis had added, something stranger--natural gas, or perhaps electricity--for he believed that they were great men of science...

At the recollection this clod of masonry, solid as a single boulder, seemed to link him up again with the vale of horrors behind him. The sunshine had become less bright, the place less innocent.

Beyond the keep was a meadow where the stream from the lake issued. Here Archie saw something which had been hitherto hidden by the ruins, and which made him drop Hamilton's arm and hobble at his best pace towards it. It was an aeroplane--a sea-plane, drawn up just beyond the sand of the shore.

Archie recognised the make--a Wentworth B--of which there were none in the Gran Seco. His next observation was that it was out of action. The floats had been damaged, and the propeller was bent. Had it crashed?...It was D'Ingraville's machine beyond doubt. Had Janet travelled in it? What had befallen her?

With a sinking heart he examined the thing, and presently he was reassured. The machine was damaged, but there had been no serious accident. It must have alighted in the lake, for it had been drawn by human hands up on the shore. He saw the grooves and ribs which it had made in the sandy beach...He examined it carefully. There was still a good supply of petrol in the tank. Could he use it? A further inspection convinced him that he could not. Repairs were needed, and he had no means of repairing it.

His first impulse was to destroy it. He could easily set it on fire and reduce it to a ruin of bars and wires...But what good would that do? If Janet had come in it and was now somewhere not far off, this might be a means of escape. How, he did not know, but there was no point in burning a possible boat.

Then a few yards off he saw something white on the grass. It was a tiny fragment of cambric, with a monogram in one corner. Janet was always dropping handkerchiefs; he spent his time retrieving them.

He stood with the thing in his hand, and a lump rose in his throat. He wanted to cry, the first tears since his childhood. Janet had sent him a message, Janet who had disappeared into the darkness. By some miracle he had found touch with her, the one chance in a million had succeeded. A great wave of longing and tenderness engulfed him. He stood blindly, as visions of Janet passed before his eyes, her dancing grace, her whimsical humour, her friendly courage. He had picked up her handkerchief, here at the ends of the earth, as he had so often done at far-away Crask...

Then suddenly, for the first time since her loss, there came to him hope. An unreasoning hope, but as vivid as a revelation. She was somewhere near--two days ago, not more, she must have stood on this very spot. He would find her. Nay, he would rescue her. The Providence which had led him thus far so strangely would not fail him.

With this new confidence something returned to Archie. He became his normal self again, and felt desperately sleepy. He had not slept for days. Hamilton sprawled limply near the ruined tower, his burning head pillowed on his arm. Archie got a piece of tarpaulin and some broken struts from the sea-plane, and made him a shelter from the sun, which was now very warm in that bare place. He stretched himself at his side, and in an instant was sound asleep.

He woke to the sound of voices. The covering had been lifted, and around them stood a group of men. Hamilton was sitting up and looking at them with sick eyes.

The men were Indians, but of a type which Archie had never seen before. They were not of the Gran Seco breed, for those were bullet-headed and muscular, whereas these were of a leanness which made them seem inhumanly tall, and their heads were the heads of white men. Instead of the dull beady eyes of the Gran Seco, the eyes of these men were large and bright and lustrous, as if they lived in a perpetual in fever. Their faces were so emaciated as to be almost skulls. Unlike the Indians of Olifa and the Gran Seco who favoured black ponchos, the ponchos of these men were of a dark red--the colour of the raw earth in the Pais del Venenos.

Yet, to his surprise, Archie felt no shrinking from them. They were armed--with blow-pipes and slender lances--but they seemed to have no hostile purpose. They stood in a circle looking down gravely at the awakened sleepers.

Archie scrambled to his feet, and held out his hand as the best gesture of friendship which he could think of. But there was no movement in response. Their hands hung stiffly by their sides.

He tried them in Spanish. He told them that he had flown thither from the Gran Seco, and pointed to the sea-plane to illustrate his mode of travel. He asked them if they had seen any white man in the neighbourhood--especially if they had seen a white woman. Archie's Spanish was apt to be of a biblical simplicity, and he explained his meaning with an elaborate pantomime. He was like a man who has a desperate message to deliver, but who finds himself stricken with partial aphasia.

It appeared that they understood something of what he said, for they began to speak among themselves, in voices pitched so low that they sounded like the murmuring of insects. Then one, who seemed to be their leader, spoke. It was a kind of Spanish, oddly pronounced and very hard to follow, but Archie gathered that he was ordered to accompany them. The speaker pointed down the ravine towards which the stream from the lake flowed.

"Right, my lad," said Archie, "I'll go with you fast enough," and he nodded and grinned and waved his hand.

Then one of them bent over Hamilton, who had lain back on the ground again with his hands pressed to his head. It looked as if these strange people knew something of medical science, for the man felt his pulse and the beating of his heart. He spoke to the others, and they moved apart. In a few minutes a little fire had been made of driftwood and thorn-scrub, while two of them took charge of Hamilton. They stripped off his great-coat and tunic, and bared him to the waist, and then they proceeded to knead and pinch certain muscles, while his head hung limply over their knees. Then they prepared a queer little greyish pill which they induced him to swallow.

Meantime an iron girdle had been put on the fire, and on it a number of little dried kernels roasted. Archie was given a share, and found them palatable: they tasted like crayfish, but may have been a kind of caterpillar. Then a rough litter was made, out of their lances and the tarpaulin, and Hamilton, now in a deep sleep, was hoisted thereon.

Archie made a last effort to get some news to allay his anxiety and nourish his hopes. "White woman," he repeated, pointing down the glen of the stream. But he got no answer. The leader, whom he addressed, faced him steadily with his bright, inscrutable eyes. But before they moved off they did the thing which Archie had decided against. They spilled petrol over the wings of the sea-plane and applied to them a flaming brand from the fire. As Archie looked back, he saw beside the blue lake in the serene sunshine the bonfire burning garishly, like a sacrifice before the altar of the immemorial tower.

XI

The third day after Archie's departure, the threat to the Courts of the Morning became urgent. The first word came from Escrick's Intelligence; there had been a succession of small fights in the Loa district, and Grayne was warned to extra vigilance. His planes patrolled in a wide radius, and Grayne himself was confident that no enemy machine could reach them. "D'Ingraville might, if he isn't otherwise engaged," he said, "but they've gotten nobody else of his class." But definite news came by was of Olifa that there would presently be an attack in force from the sea, and that Lossberg had relinquished his Fabian tactics and was now clearly pushing northward. Loa might have to be abandoned any hour, and then would come the advance up the shelves of the foothills. It might be made a slow and costly business, but in the end it could not succeed, for the defence could not indefinitely oppose his superior numbers, his Schneider batteries, and his ample machine guns. The time was drawing near when they must give up their mountain base.

The strangest thing about the new situation was its effect on the Gobernador. It might have been expected that the approach of his friends would put him into a state of extreme restlessness, that he would wait eagerly for news of each stage and welcome the hope of escape. Instead he seemed to resent it. He spoke of it with irritation, as if impious hands were being laid on something sacred. He was resentful, too, of Sandy's failure--for he was certain that he had failed.

"Lossberg has got his skirts clear." he told Barbara. "He feels himself strong and secure enough to take the offensive. That means that Lord Clanroyden's scheme has miscarried. Lossberg, in spite of his pinpricks, is getting all the supplies he wants, and has leisure to make a bold attack on our base. He is neither rattled nor embarrassed, and he has no notion of making peace. Clanroyden's was an ingenious plan, but it was bluff, and the bluff has been called. Once it fails, we have no second string. It is our turn to be driven from post to pillar...and there's far more against us than Lossberg. We have no news of Lady Roylance?"

There was more than exasperation in his tone as he spoke, there was an aching anxiety. Barbara, who in these last lays had become a tense, silent being, looked at him curiously.

"I think that we have succeeded in one thing, Excellency," she said.

"What?"

"We have made you an ally. This war was directed against you. Now you speak as if you were sorry that it was not going better."

"Nonsense," he said sharply. "I am anxious about Lady Roylance."

Next day there was disquieting information. Loa had been evacuated in the night owing to Lossberg's pressure, and that general was now beginning his movement northward on scientific lines. His mounted troops were clearing and guarding his flanks, his pioneers were pushed forward to improve the roads for his batteries, and two of his mechanised battalions were already in the foothills. Their progress could be delayed, but with Sandy and the bulk of his force engaged at the other side of the Gran Seco it could not be seriously opposed. Sandy had long ago decided that it was no part of his business to resist any movement of Lossberg's too long.

Grayne rapidly calculated.

"He will take four days at the earliest to get here. We could lengthen them out to six, but it isn't worth it. That gives us plenty of time, for we've got all the details of the evacuation settled long ago. The stuff we're taking with us has already begun to leave for Magdalena...No, Miss Babs, I guess Lossberg can't hit off that road, It's our covered Valley of Virginia, and he could no more stop our using it than General Banks could stop Stonewall Jackson. It's way out of the reach of his patrols. But we can't cut it too fine. Before his first troops get to the place they call Three Fountains, every soul here has to be on the road to Magdalena and this place one big bonfire."

Barbara asked about the sea-ravine.

"We'll get early news of that from the air," was the answer. "I'm not going to waste one solitary man on holding it. We've had it mined and monkeyed with, so as it will be a steep mountaineering proposition for the dago sailormen, but it's not going to be anything more. We'll retire shelf by shelf and watch the fireworks."

Two nights later it was reported by wireless that destroyers had left Olifa for the north, and the following morning they were sighted by Grayne's air scouts about twenty miles south of the Courts of the Morning. This news enabled Grayne to adjust his time-table. The destroyers entered the gulf at 11.30 a.m., but they seemed to find difficulty with that uncharted coast, and it was well into the afternoon before they attempted to their men. Corbett and his garrison had been withdrawn from the shore, and the hut left apparently intact. But the first mariners who entered it had various unpleasing surprises, with the result that the occupation of the beach became a matter of careful reconnaissance, and darkness had fallen before the last of the landing-parties was on shore. Corbett, now at Post No. I, waited grimly for the morning advance.

The last day in the sanctuary was for Barbara like some strange motion-picture seen from uneasy stalls. She had nothing to do except to wait and watch. The Courts been dismantled till they looked like a disused builder's yard. The tall poles of the wireless installation had gone, the huts were empty, the great storehouse was bare except for the inflammable material which could be fired by a single fuse. One solitary aeroplane patrolled the sky. White mechanics, troopers, mestizos, Indians, all had gone except the guard which was to accompany herself and the Gobernador. It was a clear brightly-lit day and rather cold. From the sea-ravine could be heard an occasional rumble and sputter of fire, but the only garrison left there now was Corbett and two of his lieutenants. The Olifa advance was three-quarters of the way up the ravine, and Corbett had been ordered, after seeing to the last great explosion, to make his best speed to the huts. As Barbara looked round the deserted camp which for weeks had been her home, she wanted to cry.

Departure seemed a farewell both to her hopes and her friends.

The Gobernador, muffled in a great blanket-coat, joined her. He too looked at the bare walls and the desolate compounds.

"That is the curse of war," he said. "It makes one destroy what one loves."

"I feel as if I were leaving home," said Barbara.

"I did not mean this place," was the answer. "I was linking of Lady Roylance."

Presently there fell on their ears a dull roar from the direction of the sea-ravine. Grayne appeared with his watch his hand.

"Time to start now, Miss Babs. Corbett will be here in five minutes. Lossberg is a mile short of Three Fountains."

They mounted their wiry little horses, while the guardian aeroplane flew very slowly to the south. It was almost dusk, and as they turned into the forest trail they stopped instinctively for one look backward. Suddenly the Courts were bright with tongues of fire, and Corbett and his assistants joined them. It was to the accompaniment of roaring fires behind, which made a rival glow to the sunset, that party disappeared into the gloom of the trees. As they bent eastward under the skirts of the mountain the crackling and the glow died away, and presently, at a headland above a deep glen, Grayne halted. From far away in the muffled foothills to the south came the chatter of machine guns.

"That is the last word," he said. "Lossberg is at Three Fountains and our defence is falling back to join us. I'm sorry. I'd got to like the old place."

For hours they rode through the dark forest. There was no moon, and the speed was poor, for they guided themselves only by contact. The Indians who led the way had to move slowly to keep pace with the groping, jostling cavalcade behind. Barbara and Castor rode in the centre of the group and, full of their own thoughts, spoke scarcely a word to each other, except of apology for a sudden jolt. The Gobernador had accompanied them without protest. He seemed to have no ear for the distant rat-tat of the machine guns of his friends.

About ten o'clock they halted to bivouac for the night.

It was a hollow tucked between the knees of the mountain spurs. Some summer thunderstorm had once set the forest alight, and for acres beside the stream there was bare ground carpeted with moss and studded with the scarred stumps of trees. Half a dozen fires were soon burning, and supper was eaten from the saddle-bags. Barbara had her sleeping-tent, but she ate with Castor beside one of the bivouacs. She noticed how clumsily he dismounted from his horse, and how stiffly he moved. This was not the life he knew, and he was no longer young.

It was a quiet night without a breath of wind, but chilling towards frost. The sky was ablaze with stars, which there in the open gave light enough to show the dim silhouettes of the overhanging hills. As the two sat side by side in the firelight, Castor smoking his pipe, his figure hunched in that position peculiar to townsmen who try to reproduce in the wilds the comfort of a chair, the girl realised that something had happened. Hitherto she had felt it a duty to entertain the Gobernador, making conversation as one does with a stranger. Now she found that there was no such need. She could be silent without impoliteness. He had become her friend, as he had been Janet's, a member of her world, whose thoughts she could instinctively discern, and who could anticipate her own.

For the last days she had been slipping dangerously near the edge of her self-control. Janet's danger seemed only a part of the general crumbling of life. She had the sensation of walking on quicksands, with a thin crust between her and unspeakable things. But the ride in the forest--movement, even if it were towards the unknown and the darkness--had put vigour again into her blood, and now in this great hollow hand of the mountains, under a blazing canopy of stars, she felt an irrational hope. She turned to her companion, who had let his head sink back against the flaps of his saddle and was staring upwards.

"I thought the Courts of the Morning was a refuge," she said, "but I think it must have been also a prison. I feel freer now...I feel nearer Janet."

He did not answer. Then he asked: "Where were you brought up, Miss Dasent? What kind of life have you had? You can't be more than twenty-one or twenty-two."

"I am twenty-four," she said. She began to tell him of her childhood, for it comforted her to talk. She spoke of a rambling country-house high up in the South

Carolina piedmont, with the blue, forested hills behind; of a childhood among old coloured servants; of winter visits to the Florida shores; of barbecues each autumn for the mountain folk; of spring gallops among upland meadows or on the carpeted trails in the pinewoods; of days with a bobbery pack of hounds in difficult pockety country. She found herself speaking easily and naturally as if to an old friend. Her school days in Charleston, her first visits to Washington and New York, her first crossing of the Atlantic--she made a pleasant picture of it all as stages in a progressive happiness.

"Why do you want to hear this?" she asked at length. "It is so different a world from yours--so very humble."

"It is a different world--yes. I can judge one thing about you. You have never known fear. No man or woman or animal has ever made you afraid."

She laughed. "How preposterous! I have been often terribly afraid."

"No. You have never met a fear which you were not ready to face. You are brave by instinct, but perhaps you have not been tested. When you meet a fear which draws the blood from your heart and brain and the vigour from your nerves and still keep your face to it--that is the test."

"Have you known such a fear?" she asked.

"I? How could I? You cannot fear what you despise! I have been too unhappily fortunate in life. I began with advantages. I was educated by my father, who was an embittered genius. I inherited very young a great fortune!...I was born in Austria, and therefore had no real country. Even before the war Austria was a conglomerate, not a people...I was brought up to despise the world, but I did not learn the lesson fully, for I excepted myself. I found that I was cleverer than other people, and that my brains enabled me to use those others. How could I ever be afraid of what I could use? For twenty years I have watched a world which I despised as futile, and pulled the strings of its folly. Some of those years were occupied by war. I took no apparent part in the war, for I had no fatherland, but I caught fish in its troubled waters. I evolved a philosophy, but I have never lied to myself, and I knew that I cared for that creed only because it flattered my egotism. I understood humanity well enough to play on its foibles. I thought that it was all foibles, save for one or two people like myself in each generation. I wanted to adjust the world so that it would be in the hands of this select few. Oh, I was supremely confident. I believed in the intellect, and mine told me that I was right. I even cultivated a dislike of the things and the people that were opposed to my creed. But there was no passion in my dislike--there is no passion in contempt, just as there is no fear. I have never been afraid--how could I, when I saw mankind like little ants running about on my errands? Therefore my courage has never been tried. But there is this difference between us--I know that you are brave, and I do not think that I am."

"What nonsense!" Barbara exclaimed. "You have amazing fortitude. Look how you have behaved since we carried you off."

"That was not fortitude, it was bewilderment. I have been beginning to wonder, to puzzle. I have never before been puzzled in my life. I have lost my contempt."

"That is a good thing," and she smiled. "My father had me taught Latin and I remember what an old bishop of the Middle Ages said. He said that the advancing stages in human wisdom were 'spernere mundum, spernere sese, spernere nullum.'"

He lifted his head sharply.

"I have gone through the first stage," he said. "I have despised the world. I think I have reached the second--I am coming to despise myself...and I am afraid."

The ride next day was in a difficult country, for it became necessary, in order to avoid the deep-cut ravines of torrents, to climb high up on the mountainside. The path was good, for it had been used incessantly for transport during the last months, but the weather was vile, for the south-west wind brought a storm of rain, and the party rode all day in an icy bath. The track ran with water like a millstream, he trees were too scattered to give protection against the slanting spears of rain, and in the thicker coverts a steady shower-bath descended from the canopy.

Till the late afternoon the downpour continued, and what with slipping and plunging horses, water at every ford whirling to the riders' boots, and the relentless soaking cataracts of rain, there was no bodily comfort that day.

Barbara, herself lithe and active as a boy, saw that the Gobernador bore the labour ill, and was very near the edge of his strength. He managed his horse clumsily, and often in the steeper places she took his bridle. At one of the fords it was only by a vigorous haul that she saved him from a ducking.

Before evening the rain ceased, the sun came out, and that high cold place there was no steamy mist, only a tonic smell of wet mountain soil and a jewelling of every and herb. The encampment at dusk was in a stony trough, where a shelf of rock made a deep overhang, and tents could be set up under it as under a roof. Barbara assisted the Gobernador to dismount, and so weary was he that he almost fell into her arms. She attended herself to his comfort, stripped off his soaking boots and blanket-coat, ransacked his valise for dry clothes, compounded with the assistance of Roger Grayne a merciless cocktail, and made his bed in a dry nook of rock not too far from the warmth of the fire. She found him curiously helpless, He was too weary to protest, and had as little knowledge of how to look after himself as a recruit on his first day's service.

After supper he seemed to recover. A woman who has nursed a man feels a protective interest in him, and Barbara found a new ease in talking to him. How had she ever looked on one so helpless as a great criminal! She dropped the formal "Excellency" with which she had been in the habit of addressing him. She had made him get into his sleeping-bag at once, and eat his supper among a pile of coverings. Now he reclined like an ancient Roman at table, the great fire lighting up the rocky antrum and silhouetting against the darkness his noble head and brows and the nose like a ship's prow.

"Do you know," he said, "I have hardly ever in my life endured bodily discomfort or pain? I have never been ill. I know so little of what is in the world."

He seemed to have divined the girl's thoughts. He had used human beings as pawns, careless of their sufferings. She thought that Janet was right--that he had a short-range imagination. That was his defence. His cruelties had been blindness, rather than purposeful crime. She looked on him with a kindlier eye.

Then they spoke--a sure proof of intimacy--of their friends. Grayne sat with them for a little, and then went off on a tour of inspection. As he went, Castor's eyes followed him. "That's a good boy! You have many like him?"

"Plenty. America produces them in bulk."

"And Britain. A different type, but the same in essentials. But they are only company officers--at the best, perhaps, brigadiers. It is commanders-in-chief that we need."

"There is Lord Clanroyden," said the girl.

"Perhaps. I am not sure. He has most of the gifts, but has he ever faced fear--faced it, and gone through to the other side? His eye is that of a leader, but I do not see in it the depths of the man who has passed the ultimate test."

"You are an acute observer," she said.

"I am becoming one," and he smiled. "I have observed something else...If it is a liberty, I ask forgiveness...I have noted that when he was near you you moved away, as if you shrank from too near a contact. A little nervous shiver ran over you. That does not mean dislike. I think it means that you are in love with him, for even when you moved away your eyes were happy."

"I think you are very wise," she said quietly. "But Lord Clanroyden will never have a thought for any woman...I am going to give you a hot drink, and then you must sleep. To-morrow will be a long day."

Next day they came out of the foothills on to a high shelf of ground, under the peaks called the Spanish Ladies. By midday they reached Magdalena, which, since Fort Castor and Loa had gone, was now Escrick's only base. They were here at a lower elevation, and in ordinary savannah, greening already and scented with the curious nut-like odour of a mountain spring. The cantonments, hidden in a fold of ground, could be recognised from afar by the wireless poles. Magdalena was still secure, and apparently unknown to the enemy, whose nearest post was a hundred miles distant. But the place was under strict discipline, and it was through two lines of sentries that they made their way into the dusty circle of huts and horse-lines.

Escrick himself was there, and he and Grayne had much to discuss, so Barbara and the Gobernador lunched alone in the General's hut. The latter had lost his air of fatigue and bewilderment. His eyes scanned sharply every detail of the place, as though it was an environment, still unfamiliar, with which it was his business to become acquainted.

"These people are losing," he told Barbara. "I feel it in the air. I felt it a week ago in the Courts of the Morning Just at present things are going badly for us."

But there was neither disappointment nor elation in his tone. He spoke briskly, as if he had come to some decision. Later, when Escrick and Grayne joined them, it was he who directed the conversation.

"Speak to me frankly, General," he said. "I am your commander-in-chief in name. I want an exact statement of the situation as you see it."

Escrick had still his quiet, sleepy manner. His blue eyes were as placid as ever, and his voice had its soft drawl. But he looked an older man, and his brick-red face had been fined down and sharpened.

"Things aren't so bad, sir. I would say they we going on according to plan, if that phrase hadn't got blown upon. The loss of Loa don't signify, and we always realised that sooner or later we'd be shoved out of the Courts of the Morning."

"It will be the turn of this place next."

"I think not. Lossberg hasn't got on to the track of Magdalena. It will be Pacheco's turn first. He must know about Pacheco."

"Well, Pacheco be it! If he takes Pacheco, what will you do?"

"Shift somewhere else. It's a big country, and aren't tied down to any lines of communication."

"But that can't go on for ever. Where are you going get your supplies--your munitions and your food?"

"From Lossberg. We've been pretty lucky so far."

"The railway? How is that working?"

"So-so. We worry it a bit, but he's got the best part of a division on it now, and he's building blockhouses. The Chief isn't finding it so easy to keep it crippled."

"And the Mines?"

"That's what you might call the main front. We have a scrap there every second day. And of course we're busy over the whole country. We don't give Lossberg time to sit down and think."

"General, answer me one question." The Gobernador's face and voice had a sudden authority which Barbara had never observed before. He seemed to be again the chairman residing at a council of the Gran Seco administration. "Are you certain that Lossberg is not winning?"

Escrick looked his questioner full in the face. "He ain't winning. But, if you press me, our side ain't winning neither."

"Then he is winning. He has only to maintain himself and he is bound to win in the end. And that end is not very far distant. I should like to see your returns of supplies. Remember, I am a business man, and this is my subject."

Papers were sent for, and the Gobernador pored over them, making calculations with a pencil. Then he asked for a map, and a big one was spread out for him on a table.

"You are losing," he said at last. "If I made a graph of the position your line would be going down and Lossberg's slowly rising. You know that without my telling you. In rations and ammunition you have begun these last weeks to give out more than you take in. That can only have one end."

Escrick nodded. "Seems so," he said dryly. "It was bound to happen. Our only chance was to delay its happening till we had made Lossberg think it could never happen. We were striking at his nerves, and the nerves of Olifa. But we have failed. Lossberg isn't rattled one bit. He is really rather comfortable. He is planted at the Gran Seco city and at the Mines. He is getting up his stuff by the railway, and he is going to get it quite easily when his blockhouses are completed. He has sufficient reserve of vitality to take Loa and drive us out of the Courts of the Morning. Presently he will drive us out of Pacheco and Magdalena. He won't get tired of the game and call on the President of Olifa to make peace. He is quite cheerful. Shall I tell you what will happen next?"

He leaned forward, till his lean face was close to Escrick's.

"He is going to get the Mines started. At half-power or quarter-power, no doubt, but still started. He will find labour among the concentrados or he will import it. Soon there will be freight-trains running to Olifa as before. And we shall be driven back bit by bit into the mountains, getting fewer every day."

"We've had mighty small losses so far," said Escrick.

"They will come--never fear. From starvation, if not from bullets. Make no mistake, they will come. Do you know what we are now, General Escrick? A rebellion on the defensive, and that is the feeblest thing known to history."

The Gobernador spoke with a passion that silenced his hearers. There was no exultation in his voice; rather it seemed to be bitter with reproach and disappointment.

Then Grayne spoke.

"We're keeping our end up in one branch," he said. "The air. Bobby Latimer got two enemy planes yesterday. We've got the whip hand of them there all right. We can fly anywhere we like in this darned country, and if we weren't short of bombs we could mess up things considerable for old Lossberg."

Then Barbara asked a question which had been on her lips since the moment she arrived. She did not expect an answer, for Sir Archie's objective had been Pacheco and Janet's kidnapping had naturally not been made public in the army.

"Have you heard anything of Sir Archibald Roylance?" she asked.

Escrick shook his head. "He came here five days back. I wasn't here, but he saw Lowson, my Chief of Intelligence. He was going to General Peters and he left a message that he was flying close to the mountains. He never turned up at Pacheco, and our planes have been all over the ground and can't find any trace of him."

A small cry was wrung from Barbara's lips. The Gobernador got to his feet and walked to the door. The fatigue of yesterday had returned to him and was shown in his cramped movements, but there was no weariness in his voice and eyes.

"Where is Lord Clanroyden?" he asked.

"At Pacheco. General Peters is having the heavy end just at present. Yesterday he had quite a show at the Universum."

"Telegraph to him that I am coming. Can you send Miss Dasent and myself by air?"

"Sure. One of Captain Latimer's men is going there this afternoon, for we're concentrating for another try at the railway...But hadn't you better stay here, sir? Pacheco soon won't be too safe for civilians."

The Gobernador smiled. "I suppose I am a civilian, but I'm not thinking about safety. I'm going to Lord Clanroyden to help him to make peace."

Escrick whistled softly. "You won't succeed, sir. From what you have said, peace must mean surrender, and we're not likely to be in the mood for that. Lossberg may drive us up into the snowfields, but devil a man of us will cry 'Kamerad!'"

The Gobernador's smile broadened till he looked almost in cheerful. "I know, I know," he said. "Nevertheless I hope to in make peace."

In the late afternoon, in a world of soft airs and a warm stillness, Barbara and Castor flew over the barrens of the Tierra Caliente. Thirty miles off on their left the great mountains flamed in the setting sun, and in the twilight they saw before them the line of steep cliffs which ran at right angles to the main range and made the southern wall of the Gran Seco. A little short of it they swerved eastward into the secluded valley of Pacheco.

Sandy was sitting in his hut with his elbows on a deal table, studying by the light of two candles a paper which lay before him. An aide-de-camp brought him a message which made him rise to his feet and stare blinkingly at the door.

The Gobernador stood before him, bent a little like a man whose every limb aches with stiffness. He did not hold out his hand. "Lord Clanroyden," he said, "I have come to take over the command with which you honoured me some time ago."

XII

Barbara interposed. She ran forward and seized Sandy's hand.

"Janet!" she cried. "Have you any news of Janet?"

Sandy stood holding her hands, his face a study in perplexity.

"I don't know," he said. "I have just had this letter from Luis. He has disappeared for the last eight days...Sit down, please, all of you. I'm very glad to see you. Tommy, get seats, and get a lamp of some kind...You'll want food. Tell them at the mess...Here is Luis's letter, brought by an Indian half an hour ago. I'm hanged if I know what to make of it."

The letter was an oblong of rough paper, which had been rolled inside a hollow stem. It might have been torn from a sketching-block. The message had been written with an indelible pencil, and was a good deal blurred. It ran:

"For C.-in-C. Most urgent. Do not worry about the lady. Patrol by air line N22a to PT13c--also by mounted patrols--let no man pass west or north. Send troop without fail on receipt of this up Cabalpas valley to camp foot of third left-hand tributary counting from

Maximoras. From camp they should patrol in arc NNE to E. Do not leave Pacheco but await me. L. de M."

Barbara almost snatched the paper from him.

"It is from Don Luis. He has found Janet. She must be safe, for he tells us not to worry. But what does the rest mean?"

The aide-de-camp had brought a big paraffin lamp which illumined the great map on the wall.

"One thing we can settle," Sandy said. "Luis is referring to our map squares." He held the lamp high. "The line from N22a to P13c--there it is," and he drew a blue pencil along it. "Look. It is the chord of an arc which covers all the south-east angle of the Gran Seco. See, Excellency, it stretches from north of the entry to the Pais de Venenos right down to the southern wall. Well, that's simple."

He rang a bell and gave certain orders. "We shall want most of our planes for the job, and the railway raid to-morrow must be countermanded: It's a longish stretch of country, so we will begin at dawn. The mounted patrols can start to-night...Now for the rest of it." He scribbled two words on a piece of paper. "Take this to Jeffries and get him to ask his Indian scouts about them. Send me the man who knows where Cabalpas and Maximoras are."

When the aide-de-camp had gone he turned to the Gobernador.

"You are in command, sir. How do you read this message?"

"Apparently Don Luis de Marzaniga has found Lady Roylance. I hope she is safe, but I do not know. Perhaps he only wants to dissuade us from looking for her because he has other things for us to do. There are people in the mountains whom he wants to keep there. We can assume, I think, that these are Lady Roylance's captors. They must be the Conquistadors and their followers. But why does he want to keep them bottled up? Perhaps he has a plan for taking them all prisoners at once, and does not wish them to scatter."

Sandy rubbed his chin. "I think there must be more in it than that," he said. "To rescue Janet is desperately important. And Archie! Where in Heaven has poor old Archie got to? He has flown out of creation somewhere between here and Magdalena. But it doesn't greatly matter what happens to the Conquistadors. To hang them all in a bunch won't bring us nearer winning this war. I wish Luis hadn't been so cryptic. Perhaps he was having a hustled time when he scribbled this letter. No, we could find out nothing from the messenger. He was a friendly Indian of the foothills, and could only tell us that it had been passed on to him from a friend with a word which he was bound to obey. It may have gone through twenty hands before it reached us."

"But Luis himself will soon be here to explain," said Barbara.

"But when? And there may be a good deal to do before that."

There was a knock at the door, and the aide-de-camp returned accompanied by a tall Indian, whose belt of tiger-cat skins proclaimed a hunter.

"Colonel Jeffries says that this is the best of his scouts, sir. He knows where the places are."

Sandy looked hard at the man. "I have seen you before," he said in Spanish. "You were with Don Luis de Marzaniga and myself when he visited the Pais de Venenos."

The Indian stood stiffly to attention. "I was with you," he said. "I have known the Senor Luis since he was a child. What do you seek of me, my lord?"

"Where is Maximoras?"

"It is the place which we in our tongue call Hatuelpec, where once long ago was a great city. In six hours' riding from Pacheco towards the sunrise, you will reach a river under the mountain called the Blue Wolf. Into that river enters another flowing from the sunrise, and up that river in three hours you will reach a little plain full of great stones. That place is Hatuelpec, which you call Maximoras."

Sandy traced the route on the map. It led him into country marked only by vague contours of mountains, as blank as the heart of Africa in maps of a century ago.

"And Cabalpas?"

The man corrected him. "The name is Catalpas--or as we say Arifua. It is the little river which flows by Hatuelpec."

"Do you know the third tributary on the left hand above Maximoras?"

The Indian considered, and then a strange look came into his face. "I know the stream. It is the way to--" He stopped. "It is the way to a place which we call Iliyabrutia, which means the Thrones of the King."

"You have been there?"

"No, my lord, nor any of my race. It is a place accursed and the abode of devils."

"You can guide a party to the Catalpas valley?"

"Beyond doubt. But the road is not easy, for it is among the broken places of the hills. It is a journey of twelve hours for good horses."

Sandy turned to the aide-de-camp. "My compliments to General Peters and ask him to have ready a patrol of fifty picked troopers to start in an hour's time. They will take rations for three days. This man will be their guide. I suggest that Captain Rivero is put in command." Then to the Indian: "Go, brother, and God be with you. You will show the way to Maximoras."

"El Obro commands." The man saluted and went.

An orderly announced dinner, and they crossed the square to the mess-hut.

"I have taken to dining alone," Sandy announced, "To-night there will only be we three. I can't offer you much in the way of food, for we're short of what we used to call hospital comforts. We're getting very near to the 'hog and hominy' of your ancestors. Miss Barbara."

He spoke lightly and cheerfully, but as Barbara looked at him across the rough table she noticed a profound change. Before, she had seen him worn to the last limits of his physical strength, but there had always remained a certain lift and effervescence of spirit. Now, though his face was less haggard than she had seen it, it was also less vital. His eye had dulled, and there were lines of strain on his forehead and a tightness of suffering about his mouth. He sat, too, listlessly in his chair, like a man oppressed with a great weariness. He looked up suddenly and caught her eye and seemed to brace himself.

"We have some hope at last--about Janet," she said.

"A shred, A week ago it would have given me a new tack of life, but now I seem to have got beyond hoping. The thing has tortured me so much that the ache is dull."

The girl looked at him and saw an anxiety deeper even than her own. Instinctively she tried to comfort.

"But it wasn't your blame. It was ours--up in the Courts of the Morning. We kept too slack a watch."

"The whole blame was mine. This war was made by me--by your uncle partly, but mainly by me. I seem to be fated to wreck the things I care about."

"That is the fate of all of us." The Gobernador had hardly spoken up till now. "That is also my fate. I have made a great industry, and now I am destroying it. I have become a friend of Lady Roylance, and she is in danger from that which I have created. I have had dreams, and now I am trampling on them."

The words seemed to touch a spring in Sandy which released a new vigour. His figure lost its listlessness, he sat upright, and into his eye came something of the old fire.

"You mean that? By God, then we cannot be beaten. We have won the big stake."

"No. You are wrong. We have still to win it. Supposing I died to-night, in what way would you be better off? Lossberg will wear down your resistance in time, and his methods will not be gentle. The republic of Olifa will not be merciful conquerors. The old Gran Seco will be restored--without its Gobernador--and the people of the Tierra Caliente will be slaves again. Olifa will faithfully copy my methods, but without--if I may say so--my intelligence. You may in the end get fair terms for most of your white officers, since they are valuable for the industry, but you will get no terms for the rank and file. Therefore I say that whatever may become of me, you have not yet begun to win. At present you are losing with terrible speed. Can you deny it?"

"We can never lose," said Sandy. "Assume the worst--assume that we are broken up like a covey of partridges and forced in bands into the mountains. We can still make the Gran Seco a hell for any Olifa administration. They may start the Mines, but they'll only limp along. They must some to terms with us..."

Castor broke in. "Forgive me. Lord Clanroyden, but you of not understand the mind of such a state as Olifa. She has been peaceful and prosperous for a time, but it is not long since she had Indian wars grumbling all along her borders. She is accustomed to a skin deep civilisation.

Lossberg will enjoy the task of policing this territory, and Olifa will run the Mines again and not grumble at the decline in her profits. Remember, she has solid reserves which I have given her...We must be candid with each other, if I am to accept the command with which you have honoured me."

Sandy fixed his eyes on the other's face.

"You have changed your views, Excellency. I congratulate you profoundly. But I am curious to know just why."

Castor smiled. "For once in my life I can give no reason--no logical reason. Put it that I am a little weary of my old self. Say that I lived in a rather dismal world and see the door ajar which leads to a brighter one. Put it any way you like...I am here to help you to win this war, because victory will benefit me--oh yes, enormously...I have not lost my ambitions, but they have a slightly different orientation to-day...Now let us talk business."

The door opened and a new figure entered--a big man in a most disreputable suit of khaki. He had a full, rather heavy face, which had been burned to something very like the colour of his clothes. There was dust in his hair, and dust rimmed his large placid eyes.

"Say, this is a nice party," he said in a voice cracked with thirst. "Why, Babs child, I heard you were here...I'm mighty glad to see you so blooming. And Mr

Castor, too...But I can't talk till somebody gives me a drink, for my tongue is stuck to the roof of my mouth, and I've gotten a hunger like nothing on earth."

A mess-servant brought him a long drink of lime-juice and sparklets, and the big man took his place at the table between Sandy and Barbara. He raised his tumbler to the Gobernador.

"I suppose," said the latter, "that I must forget Senor Rosas the Mexican and make the acquaintance of Mr John S. Blenkiron the American."

"That's so. So good an American that he poisons himself with soft drinks ever since his country went dry."

"I have told Lord Clanroyden that I have come here to take the command which he offered me."

The big man looked steadily at him, and his quiet ruminant eyes seemed suddenly to become a search-light. They saw something which he approved, for he bounded to his feet.

"That's fine. I'm proud to be working again with my old chief. We'll shake on that," and he held out a mighty fist.

"You've come from the Mines?" Sandy asked, "How are things going there?"

"So-so. The enemy's getting cunning up that way. He's extending his radius of defence and making a very pretty corral, with as much barbed wire as the Hindenburg Line. Our boys are terrible short of rifle ammunition, and we're cleaned out of bombs. Looks like we'll have to let up for a day or two, and that will give him a cruel chance to pick up."

Sandy gave him a short account of Luis's message and the action he had taken upon it. Blenkiron received the news with a furious interest.

"He tells us not to worry about Lady Roylance? Well, I guess he means she's not going to come to any harm, for Luis thought the world of her. And he has got that bunch of buckaroos located and wants to keep them tight. He's right there, for this world won't ever be a healthy place again till that cesspool is drained. We've got to put that job through before we can attend to other business."

"And then?" Castor asked. "Mr Blenkiron, just before you arrived I was giving Lord Clanroyden my view of the situation. We cannot afford to deceive ourselves. This rebellion was a gamble, but at the start the odds were not too desperate. You had certain assets--a hidden base, a very mobile army, and a special knowledge of the country. Very wisely you did not try to meet Lossberg with his own weapons. Your aim was to fight a war without bloodshed, or as nearly as possible without it, and to let him waste his highly scientific blows on empty air. That was your strategy, and it was intelligent. Your hope was that after a little he would grow weary of it, and that Olifa would grow weary, and that you could make peace pretty much on your own terms. That also was intelligent. You were aiming directly at the moral of Olifa, and it is of course by striking at the moral of the enemy that wars are won. Have I put your views correctly?"

Blenkiron nodded.

"Well, it is clear that you are going to fail. You have fought a nearly bloodless war, your army is pretty well intact, but your supplies are running low. You have lost your secret base. You have failed to make Lossberg uncomfortable. His spirits are rising, and he is beginning to strike out quite boldly. He is rather enjoying himself, and fancies himself a conqueror. What are you going to do? To do nothing means that within a month you will be scattered among the mountains--mere guerrilleros."

No one spoke, and he went on.

"That mustn't happen. We,"--and he emphasised the change of pronouns--"we must still strike at the enemy's moral, but we must change our methods. It is the republic of Olifa that matters. Hitherto we have been trying to weaken her moral by weakening Lossberg's. That hasn't worked--so we must strike directly at the moral of Olifa."

"How?" Blenkiron drawled.

"By carrying the war into Olifa. In the idiom of your country's history, Miss Dasent, by crossing the Potomac."

Blenkiron flung himself back in his chair.

"I recognise the old touch," he said, beaming. "There speaks the Gobernador of the Gran Seco. It's horse-sense, I don't deny, but just how are we going to do it? We're treed up here, like a 'possum. There's no way to Olifa except by the railroad, and that Lossberg has gotten policed like Broadway."

"True. But we have still the mastery of the air. You cannot send an army to Olifa, but you can send me."

For an instant a shade of suspicion rested on Blenkiron's face, but it soon vanished.

"I get you," he said. "You always had that little Government in your side pocket."

But there was no response in Sandy's puzzled eyes.

"I don't understand," he said. "Bobby Latimer can land you wherever you like in Olifa, but how would you be further forward?"

"I must be landed where I can get into touch at once with the Government. You see, Lord Clanroyden, that Government have for some years been my very obedient servants. They are not clever people, only cunning, and they are not very brave. I have what you call a moral ascendency over them. If I appear among them suddenly from the clouds I think I can impress them. I do not believe that they like the prospect of a long guerrilla war, and I can expound to them with some force the financial reasons for making peace. I will be literally truthful with them. I shall tell them that the revolt was not of my making, but a spontaneous eruption, in which I was entangled, but I shall tell them also that I am now a convinced partner."

Sandy's fingers drummed nervously on the table.

"I believe you are wrong. How much did the Olifa ministers like you, Excellency? They admired you, obeyed you, feared you, but they probably hated you. They are not clever men, as you justly observe--it would be better for us if they were--but they are vain as peacocks. And jealous, too, at the back of their heads. They are getting triumphant dispatches from Lossberg, and they are swelling with pride. They think they are winning on their own account, they believe that the Gran Seco will fall into their hands and that they will be able to confiscate the Mines. Then they will get, not the handsome share of the profits which you allowed them, but everything. Don't tell me that they have any fears of not being able to run them without your assistance.

Those gentry always believe they are heaven-born geniuses waiting for their chance."

Castor's face did not change.

"It is possible--but I do not think so. I cannot believe that my personal ascendency over them is so brittle. Anyhow, I am prepared to try."

"You realise the result of failure?"

"Yes. Lossberg will be entrenched in his authority. The value which its association with my name gives to our revolution will be gone. There may be trouble with foreign capitals."

"And you yourself?"

"Oh, I shall be utterly discredited. I shall probably find myself in one of the Olifa prisons, which I understand lave not shared in the general progressiveness of the country. There may even be a regrettable incident, for they will still fear me."

"You are a brave man," said Sandy.

"I don't know. I have not been tested." Castor looked towards Barbara, as if to remind her of their conversation. "But I see no other way. I should prefer to have an army behind me, but we cannot fly an army over a wall of mountains, and there is no pass."

"You are wrong," said Sandy. "There is a pass."

Everyone stared at him--Blenkiron with puzzled eyes, Castor with a strained attention, as if doubtful of the correctness of his hearing, Barbara with awakening hope.

"There is a pass--a chain of passes--a way from the Gran Seco to Olifa. Luis alone knows it, for it is an old secret of his family. That is how he came to the Gran Seco so often before the war. You "--turning to Blenkiron--"thought it was by an aeroplane with some hidden landing-place in the mountains. I knew the truth, but I was sworn to tell no one. I have travelled the road once with him. It ends at the head of the Vulpas valley. That is how we got up the horses to mount our troops. Luis has been doing a busy horse-trade for months."

"But this alters everything," Castor cried. "If we had thought of it before--"

"I thought about it--thought about it till my head ached. I always meant it to be my last card, and it would have been if things had gone better. If Lossberg had been getting pinched and worried, I meant to use this as the last straw--to leave Escrick and Peters to watch him, and to lead a picked mounted force through the passes up to the gates of Olifa. I calculated that that would do the trick. But--but--now--I don't see how it is going to work."

He stopped and looked round the table. In each face, as his eyes rested on it, even in Castor's, the excitement seemed to die down.

"Because," he went on, "if Olifa is confident and has reasons for confidence, such a hussar-ride would have no effect. She has still a part of her regular army left behind, and she has an enormous capacity for calling up reserves. We should have the people against us, and they would rise up at our backs and cut us off. We should achieve nothing, and even if we managed to hack our way out, where should we be? Back in the Gran Seco, with the game going hard against us."

He turned to Castor. "Do you see any answer to that?" he asked.

"I am considering...I will tell you presently."

"Do you?" he demanded of Blenkiron.

"Not just right away. I'm rather of your way of thinking. It isn't much good crossing the Potomac unless you can reckon on help from Maryland or Pennsylvania."

Suddenly Barbara spoke--eagerly--stammeringly.

"I think I understand Don Luis's letter. The Conquistadores have found a sanctuary in the mountains. Why does he want none of them to get out?

To keep them together and deal with all of them at once? Perhaps, but I think he has another reason. He does not want any message carried to General Lossberg. What kind of message? Not a prayer for relief, for at present no one is troubling them. It must be a message of information, vital information. What could that be? Only that they have found the road through the mountains from the Gran Seco to Olifa, and they want to warn him so that he may prevent our taking it."

"Good for you, Babs," said Blenkiron. "I guess she's right, gentlemen. But it gets us no further."

"Wait a moment," said Sandy. "There may be something in it. The message is from Luis, who alone knows he passes. He evidently thinks these passes are our trump card, or he wouldn't be so keen to keep them open for us. Luis knows Olifa better than any one of us here. He knows it up to date, which none of us do, for he has been living with one foot there and one in the Gran Seco. He's a mysterious beggar, for he asked not to be given any responsible job--said he had other very important things to attend to. It looks as if Luis believed that there was a chance of doing something by a flank movement on Olifa."

There was a knock at the door and it opened to admit a young staff-officer.

"I apologise for intruding, sir," he said, "but Colonel Jeffries thinks it important. The patrols have just brought in a prisoner. He was on horseback, accompanied by an Indian servant, and he seems pretty well dead to the world. Where he came from we haven't a notion, but he asked to see you at once--said it was very urgent. He is not armed and he's a funny little rag of a man. He talks English perfectly, and looks like a gentleman. Says his name is Alejandro Gedd."

Blenkiron shouted. "Why, it's the British vice-consul. A good little citizen and a great pal of Wilbur. Let's have him in at once and feed him. What in thunder has brought him here? You'd as soon expect to see a canary-bird in Labrador."

Five minutes later the staff-officer ushered in the remains of the best-appointed dweller in the city of Olifa. Gone were the trim garments, the ribboned eyeglass, the air of being always freshly barbered. Don Alejandro's breeches and jacket were stained and torn, spectacles had replaced his monocle, he had a week's beard on his chin, his eyes were hollow with fatigue, and his dark cheeks had been burned almost black. He walked painfully as if from saddle-stiffness, and he was clearly aching in every bone. But at the sight of the company he tried to straighten himself, and he made an effort to bow to Barbara.

Blenkiron almost swung him off his feet and settled him in a chair. "Bring food," he shouted to the mess-waiter. "Whatever you've got, and also any hard drinks you can raise. Sandy, have you any champagne? We're mighty glad to welcome you, Don Alejandro, but don't say a word till you've got something under your belt."

A cocktail restored the little man to speech. He looked curiously at Castor, and addressed Sandy.

"Where is Luis de Marzaniga?" he asked. "He told me to meet him here. I left Charcillo four days ago."

"How have you come?"

"Through the passes. I had one of Luis's guides, but it's a fatiguing journey and terribly cold. I apologise for my appearance, but I thought it best to report at once. I shall be glad of a meal, for I miscalculated and finished my food this morning at breakfast. But first I should like a word with Luis."

"He is not here, but he is coming soon. We have no secrets among ourselves, Don Alejandro. You see before you the Commander-in-Chief and his Chief of Staff. You can speak freely."

"I only came to report to Luis. It is rather a long story and I shall have to refer to maps and papers. I came to explain to him the exact position at the moment of our Olifa revolution."

There was a complete silence. Blenkiron poured out a half-tumblerful of champagne and handed it to the stranger. He gulped it down and it seemed to send new blood through his body.

"What about your Olifa revolution?" Blenkiron asked in a queer tone.

"It's going famously." Don Alejandro's voice had lost its flatness. "Going like a fire on the savannah. When Luis and I laid down our lines three years ago, we never thought to have a chance like this. We have all of what you call the gentry behind us, and the haciendados can turn out anything between eight and ten thousand mounted men. Also we have a big movement among the workmen in Alcorta and Cardanio, and we have the train laid in Olifa itself and only waiting for the spark. But the thing's ripe now and we can't keep it waiting much longer. We don't want to show our hand by any premature explosion."

Don Alejandro was surprised at the reception of his words. He looked around the table and saw four faces in which delight still struggled vainly with stupefaction. Also there was complete silence.

Then Blenkiron broke it.

"Luis certainly knew what he was doing when he sent that message. We'll have an army back of us in our interview with the Excelentisimo. I guess we'll get some help from Maryland when we cross the Potomac."

XIII

Janet woke with a start from her uneasy sleep. Her nights had been troubled of late, and she was accustomed to waking with a start.

The darkness was very thick and close around her, but it was not the closeness of a narrow room. There was a free draught of air and a sense of space, which suggested that she was under the bare vault of heaven. And yet the faint odour was not of the natural world, but of man's handiwork--hewn stone, and the dust of hewn stone, the smell of a place roofed and enclosed.

She lit the candle beside her mattress. It scarcely flickered when she lit it, though there was a sound of wind high up in the dark above her. She told herself that here she was safe, safe at any rate till the morning. Every night she came here, and the narrow entrance was blocked by a pile of cut stones which fitted as closely as a door.

When she was first introduced to these sleeping-quarters she had been in a terror of loneliness and anticipation. And then she had realised that this was a merciful provision, that she had at any rate the hours of night to herself, and that not till the sun rose again and the blocks were removed would she have to face the true burden of captivity. Here in this vast dark place, like the inside of a mountain, she was for the moment free.

She tried to compose herself to sleep again, for she knew that she needed all her physical and nervous strength for the strain of a new day. But she could not stop her mind from racing. She counted the days she had been a prisoner--seven days, an inconsiderable week, which would have passed too soon in her normal happy life. Now in the retrospect it seemed to lengthen into an eternity. It was only by an effort that she could recall the details of her first coming--the dizzy journey half in the clouds; the Gran Seco like a cup below her brimming with the morning sunlight; the serpentine course among the valleys of the high hills; the blue lake on which the sea-plane had alighted; the march with her pilot in the tangled glens through a long day of heat and misery, among strange birds and insects and creepers like the clutching fingers of ghosts; the meeting with a patrol of his allies--the exquisite Pasquali, a man named Molinoff, and four strange Indians with red ponchos; the coming at last into a valley full of stones built in a circle around a huge rotunda. The jungle had not penetrated one inch into this dead city, for the lush vegetation stopped as if edged by a gardener, and the silent avenues were floored with fine white dust, and the walls were so polished and impenetrable that there was no crevice for a blade of grass. Here she had found bivouac fires and evil faces, faces which to her tired eyes were like the demons of a nightmare. They had given her food, and had been civil enough. D'Ingraville's manners during that awful day had been punctilious, and the men who received her had shown a cold and level politeness. They meant no ill to her--at least for the moment; their careful provision for her safety was proof of it; and when after some fluttering hours in the darkness of the first night she understood this, she had a momentary access of courage.

The following day she had realised her position more fully. She was a hostage, to be protected as such, a card when the time arrived to be ruthlessly played. She was given an Indian servant, who brought her water and towels and her meals when she chose to feed alone. Otherwise she was welcome to sit with her captors, at least with one section of them. For she soon discovered that there were two groups in the camp. One was composed of men of the D'Ingraville type, who in dress and speech and manners were gentlemen. These she realised were the Conquistadors, of whom she had heard so much, and even in her loneliness and fear she could not repress her interest in them...

Some of the names she had known before. There was Lariarty, who had been at school with Sandy, and Larbert, whom she believed she had danced with at a Perth ball, and who had once been engaged to a distant cousin. Romanes, too, Cyril Romanes--she had known his name as a noted figure in the hunting-field and a polo-player of world-wide fame. The other names were new to her, Calvo, and Suvorin, and Pasquali, and Seminov, and Laringetti, and Duclos-Mazarin, and Glorian. They were of every physical type--D'Ingraville slim and fair with a pointed beard and a faunlike head; Suvorin, tall, bony, with a skin like old parchment, and hair as light as an albino; Calvo, short and fat; Pasquali, dark, elegant, and hook-nosed; Lariarty with full, well-cut features and a fine brow; Larbert built on the scale of an athlete; Romanes with his neat light-cavalry figure. But all had something in common--the pallor of their faces, their small, considered gestures, and the opaqueness of their eyes.

The other group was of different clay. They were of the type of the four who had carried her off, men whose character showed brazenly in their faces. They fed apart from the Conquistadors, and, though they took their general orders from them, lived very much their own life. They gambled and quarrelled and occasionally fought, but since they had no liquor they were reasonably well behaved. They went off in twos and threes to hunt and prospect, and they always reported on their return to Romanes, who seemed to be in charge of the camp. There was little comfort to be had from looking at their faces, on which life had written too plainly its tale. But at any rate they could laugh. Sometimes into the frozen urbanity of the Conquistadors' talk the distant sound of their guffaws came like an echo of life in a world of the dead.

She had to keep a tight hold on her nerves to prevent a breakdown, when she sat among her strange companions. Sandy had called the Gran Seco a "port of missing ships," and these ships seemed to be phantoms, green with the weeds of some unholy sea. They were mechanically polite, rising when she entered and bowing like automata, helping her first to the monotonous fare;

but their words to her were like the commonplaces of a French conversation book. She made many efforts to talk--of music to Pasquali, of hunting to Romanes, of home and friends to Larbert and Lariarty, but she found a wall of opaque civility. Those pages were shut for them, and would not be reopened. She realised that the memories of these men were drugged and their emotions atrophied. But not their minds. Very soon she understood that their minds were furiously alive.

For, after the first day or two, while they did not talk to her they talked among themselves before her. There was no danger to be feared from her, for she was securely in their power. They spoke as sparingly as they ate, but bit by bit she gathered the import of their talk. They were desperately anxious about something, and presently it was clear to her that this something was Castor. He was the one anchor of these missing ships. Without him there was no safety in any port...The girl, as she watched, grew amazed and awed at the extent of Castor's power. He had plucked these derelicts out of the storm, and bestowed on them a dreadful simulacrum of peace. His drug had blotted out the past and given them a keen intellectual life in the present. Without him they were lost again, and all the power of their minds was devoted to winning him back...Soon, from small pieces of evidence, she realised that the same thing was true of the ruffians of the Bodyguard. They, too, were loyal to their salt. The Gobernador had cast his spell over them, and they were resolved to return to his service. Both parties knew what the world did not know, that the Gobernador had been carried off, and was an unwilling figurehead of the rebellion. For Olifa they cared nothing at all, but they were determined that Castor should be set free, and the Castor regime restored.

On his account she was a hostage. She saw that they realised that Lossberg might win in the field, but that, even if the rebels were broken up and driven in commandos to the mountains. Castor might be carried with them. To retrieve him she was their chief instrument, their asset to bargain with. If bargaining was impossible, she knew that she need expect no mercy, for pity did not dwell among Conquistadors or Bodyguard...Castor must be recovered, but it was also necessary that Lossberg should win, for if the rebellion succeeded there would be no hope of the restoration of the old life of the Gran Seco, and it was to this that they clung.

Janet gathered that they were satisfied with Lossberg's progress. She had heard Magee, who had arrived the day before her, exulting over the news he brought. But she gathered also that the Conquistadors were anxious. On the day after her coming the four men who had carried her off, Dan Judson, Laschallas, Radin, and Trompetter, appeared in the camp. They had come by the seaplane, and apparently damaged it, for D'Ingraville cursed them with a cold bitterness. But others were expected, with messages from Lossberg, messages which must be brought by air, seeing that Sandy's patrols lay between the two camps...

These messages did not come. No planes of any kind broke through the cordon and brought news. It was clear that he Conquistadors believed that the messengers had started, and had been shot down, and that their chief preoccupation was to establish communications again.

Suddenly their anxiety seemed to acquire a sharper edge. Molinoff, Carreras, and Carvilho were out daily, but not as hunters, and every night they returned, bone-weary men. Janet, who had already taken her bearings by the sun, had some rough idea of the position of the camp. She knew nothing about the direction of the Pais de Venenos, but he realised that she must be in the Cordilleras, in a loop of the main chain, where it split into lateral valleys, and that due west of her lay the Gran Seco and her friends. She noticed that the three men in their daily excursions always went south, as if they were looking for something. One night they did not return, and the following afternoon they staggered in drunken with weariness. But they had discovered something of importance, for Molinoff before he tasted food or drink sought out Romanes.

What the discovery was Janet could not learn, but at supper that evening her hosts seemed to be shaken out of their frozen composure. They talked--for them--rapidly, and in low tones. Occasionally one of them would look towards her to see if she was listening, and once Romanes seemed to be about to address her, but changed his mind. She pretended absorption in her food, but her ears were open and she caught one thing. They were determined to send a message to someone. That someone could only be Lossberg. They had learned that which might be vital to his success.

For the first time Janet was diverted from anxiety about herself and about Archie's peace of mind. She saw dimly a chance for action. She could not escape, but could she not find out their secret--hamper them in some way--do something to relieve the dreadful tedium of her impotence? She lay awake half the night making futile plans.

Next day she had awoke with a new purpose in life. She observed one result of the previous evening's discussion. The Indians in the camp were summoned to a council, These were Indians such as she had never seen before--tall men, incredibly lean, with faces like skulls and luminous, feverish eyes. One of them seemed to be chosen for a mission, for he was given a letter by Romanes which he secreted on his body, and the next Janet saw was his red poncho disappearing into the forest...He was not the only messenger. Magee, a wiry little ruffian who knew the Indian speech and acted as interpreter, was also entrusted with a message. To him no letter was given, but Romanes spoke to him long and carefully, drawing plans till he nodded his comprehension. Just before midday Magee also disappeared into the forest which clad the slopes to the westward.

There was a change in the manner of the Conquistadors. The necessity for haste seemed to have stripped off some of their civilised veneer. Before they had treated her with complete apathy; now she saw in their eyes suspicion, it might be malevolence. Oddly enough, it made her less afraid. She took it as good news. They had earned something which meant advantage to her friends, or they would not be so eager to forewarn the other side. Janet grew almost at her ease. And then she saw that in D'Ingraville's face which sent a shiver down her spine. The success of her own side meant that she would become valueless as a hostage. But she would remain a prisoner--and a victim.

Next day she had felt the same atmosphere around her of cruelty, gloating cruelty. Before she had been lonely, anxious, oppressed, but now she knew the real chill of fear. Whither could she turn? The Indians? They were savages out of some other world, and she had not a word of their speech. There was no pity in their gaunt, glowing faces...The Bodyguard? They at any rate were human, for they could laugh. One of them, too, had a dog, a mongrel terrier, with whom Janet, having an invincible attraction for all dogs, had endeavoured to make friends. She had partly succeeded, but success was easier with one kind of animal than with the other. The Bodyguard that day was dispersed, except the three, Molinoff, Carvilho, and Carreras, who were resting after their labours of the previous days.

Carreras had been one of the three trusties who had been hardly treated by Geordie Hamilton that evening on board the Corinna, and, since he had seen her there, he seemed to regard her with special rancour. As she passed them, where they grumbled and spat over a game of cards, she felt that among these squalid ruffians there was no refuge from the cruelty of their masters.

With no books, and nothing to occupy her thoughts, she had watched the hot afternoon decline to evening. She saw homing birds returning, especially one great eagle which had been hunting out in the plains. She saw the sun go down behind the hills, and kindle far off a blue peak which reminded her of Stob Dearg as seen from her room at Glenraden. The old happy world she had lost flitted through her mind in a chain of pictures which she had not the strength to repel. She shut her eyes tight, and the smell of wood smoke from the cooking-fires brought back the hall at Glenraden in wintertime, with her sister Agatha making tea, and her father stamping the snow from his feet, and the dogs tangled on the hearthstone...But it was the picture of Archie which broke her heart, the picture which she had so resolutely fought to shut from her; Archie with his boyish laugh and tousled hair and flushed face, so absurd and unexpected and gallant and gentle...

Janet had her supper alone in the immense rotunda where she slept. The Indian who brought it looked steadily before him and had no language but a grave inclination of the head. She heard the blocks being piled together, and knew that for another night she was safe. She blew out her candle and tried to sleep, but now it was not fear that thrilled her, but homesickness. She had gone clean over the horizon, away from the kindly race of men. She believed that she could face horrors, death if necessary, if only a friendly eye or voice were near, if only Archie could hold her hand...

But if Archie were here it would mean death for him. The thought terrified her till she remembered how vain it was. Archie would be looking for her with a breaking heart, but by no conceivable chance could he find her hiding-place. It was like being buried deep in the earth...Archie was safe. That was something...As for herself, whether Sandy lost or won she would not live to see it. A sense of utter hopelessness had come over her, the shadow of a dark and certain destiny. But in this certainty there was a kind of miserable peace, and she fell asleep.

She awoke with a start, lit her candle and watched the monstrous shadows run into the uppermost gloom. Then, as we have seen, she tried to sleep again, and slowly drifted from memory to vagueness, from vagueness to unconsciousness.

She woke again, this time to complete awareness. She had heard a sound different from the light rumble of the wind or the fall of minute particles of dust. There was a human presence somewhere in the emptiness. Panic shook her. Her sanctuary was no sanctuary, and her enemies were here. With trembling fingers she struck a match and held it to her candle. It seemed ages before the wick caught fire, and then it flickered thinly. She was on her feet now, her eyes wildly searching the darkness.

Suddenly a voice spoke from behind her. "Please do not be alarmed. Lady Roylance. I am sorry to have disturbed you."

It was a pleasant voice--a foreign voice, for it spoke English with unnatural precision, and made three syllables of her surname. There was something reassuring about that precision. It seemed familiar, too.

"Who is it?" she asked, her voice still quivering.

A figure came out of the gloom. She held up the candle and it revealed an Indian, barelegged and barefooted, wearing a long tunic of cats' skins and on his shoulder a red poncho. In her amazement she almost dropped the candle and all her terrors returned. He seemed to understand her fright, for he spoke rapidly. "Please do not fear. I am a friend whom you know. I am a friend of your husband and of Lord Clanroyden...Will you please dress a little, for I would like you to take a walk with me.. I will retire. We cannot speak in this place."

"But who are you?" This time her voice had hope.

"My name is Luis de Marzaniga."

"Oh, Don Luis, Don Luis!"...Her voice was a wail, for violent relief often takes the tone of tragedy. "Oh, my dear, my dear...I am so glad...I can't speak...in a second I will be ready."

Janet's toilet did not take long, for she had no clothes but those in which she had left the Courts of the Morning. She pulled on a jumper, and thrust her feet into a pair of much-stained grey suede shoes. At her call Luis again came out of the darkness.

"I know I'm a fright, Don Luis. My hair won't stay tidy, for I have lost most of my hairpins. I swear I shall be shingled as soon as I get home...Archie wanted me to, before we came out here...Have you any word of Archie?...We can't get out of this place, you know."

She babbled like a happy child.

"No," he said, "but we can get above it. You have a good head, I hope. Lady Roylance, for I am going to take you nearer to the stars."

He led her to the south-eastern corner, and there her candle, which he carried, revealed a low recess. He motioned her to follow him and she found herself in a tunnel where she had to crouch, almost to crawl. He felt carefully the left side and suddenly he stopped and reached for her hand.

"Follow close," he whispered. "The tunnel is a trap, which ends presently in a pit."

They squeezed through a subsidiary opening, and almost at once found the roof rise. "There is a staircase," he whispered. "It is built inside the wall, but it is in good condition. You can stand upright now," He blew out the candle and took her hand.

The steps were smooth and unbroken and they rose steeply. Then they seemed to turn a corner, where the darkness was exchanged for a faint green light. With every step the light grew, and the smell of earth and powdered stone began to change to the freshness of the outer world. Suddenly wind blew in their faces, and they emerged on a kind of barbican, with the stone slats of a roof rising steeply behind them, and in front, beyond a low parapet, the valley white in the moonshine.

Janet caught her breath. The sight was not only of a torturing beauty, but it seemed to be an earnest of freedom. She peered over the edge and saw far below her the dusty avenues of the camp, white and quiet as if under a mantle of snow. One of the cooking-fires still smoked feebly, but otherwise there was no movement in the place.

The subsidiary towers, which recalled in their shape pictures she had seen of the Rhodesian Zimbabwes, were like solid cones of pale ivory, and their shadows were deep emerald.

The valley, she saw, was thickly forested on all sides, the trees now milky in the moon, now of the blackest jet. But beyond its containing walls she saw what was invisible to one below, peaks which must be high mountains, but which under this vault of elfin light seemed curiously near and foreshortened. To the west and south-west, apart from the barrier ridge, the horizon seemed empty, and she realised that she was very near to the edge of the hills. Over there must lie the Gran Seco and her friends.

The girl drew long breaths of an air which seemed to blend the aromatic strangeness of forests with the coolness of the high snows. She felt in command once again of herself and her fate. Below were her captors, but now she stood above them.

"What is this place?" she asked.

He spoke a name.

"The Thrones of the Kings," she repeated.

"Of the King," he corrected. "Los Tronos del Rey. There was only one king, but he was very great. When he died, his captains and councillors were made to die with him. He was buried here, and they in those lesser towers. Once each was also full of gold and silver images and uncountable treasure, but they were rifled long ago by the ancestors of our people--my own among them. The spoilers would have destroyed the tombs also, but they could lot. No hand of man can touch this masonry. High explosives only, and happily they did not have them."

"Does the world know about it?"

He shook his head. "Only the Indians of the Pais de Venenos, and they do not talk. The other Indians of the hills regard it as accursed and will not approach it."

"But who brought these people here--the Conquistadors and the others?"

"The man called Romanes was in touch with the Pais Venenos--also, I think, Pasquali. They got their drugs here, and it was necessary for them to find a camp near. I sanctioned it, for I have much power among the people of the Poison Valley. It was by my authority that these Indians accompanied them, and I myself joined them. You admire my disguise? Since their first coming here I also have been present to observe...But I did not expect you, Lady Roylance, and you have given me anxious thoughts...Also there is another development. Romanes, he who is the commandante, is a good soldier, and his mind is quick. He has discovered that which I hoped to keep hidden."

"I know," said Janet excitedly. "I saw yesterday that they had found out something which they thought desperately important. I tried to discover what it was--

but of course I had no chance. They have sent off messengers to General Lossberg."

"They have. But I do not think those messengers will get through. One was an Indian, and he is already back with me in the forest, not a mile away. The other was the man called Magee. I think that by this time he may have had an accident."

"What was the news?"

"No less than the secret way out of the Gran Seco, the way by which I am accustomed to travel. Olifa believes that there is no road but the railway, except for a stray cragsman. The Gobernador also believes this. But there is a way through difficult passes into the Vulpas valley. Once I showed it to Lord Clanroyden, and it is a road which a light army can travel."

"I see, I see," Janet cried. "Then Sandy might use it, unless Lossberg gets there before him."

"Lossberg will not get there before him. And Lord Clanroyden will beyond doubt use it, since it is the only path to victory."

Janet clasped her hands. All fear for herself had gone and she joyfully felt herself already united with her friends since she was again in the game. "I thought I was hidden hundreds of miles away from the rest," she said, "and find that I am at the key-point."

Luis looked down upon the small figure whose hair was dull gold in the moonlight, and he smiled.

"But you cannot stay here," he said. "It is too dangerous. It is very necessary that you escape not later than to-morrow night--to-night, I mean, for it is now past midnight."

"I long to get away...I admit I have been horribly frightened...But is there nothing I could do if I stayed?"

"You are brave. But no, there is nothing you can do. You will understand that these people are now in a dangerous mood. You are their hostage, but any day they may think that you can be of no use as a hostage, and then...they will not be merciful. They are very complete rascals, and it is necessary to keep them here till Lord Clanroyden has made his great stroke. That I think I can undertake through my friends. But we cannot have one of our own people left in their hands. They will be helpless, like imprisoned starving dogs, but they have nasty fangs...No, you must go tomorrow night--this night."

"Will you come with me?"

"No. I will follow you by another road. But I will see that you are accompanied. It is a journey which will need courage, Lady Roylance. Also to-morrow will need courage. Your warders will be in a difficult temper, and you must act a part. You must appear to be in deep sorrow, and I think you had better be a little ill. Yet you must go among them, for when they see you sad and helpless they will be encouraged and perhaps hopeful, and it very necessary to keep their hope alive for another day. If they have hope they will not think yet of revenge...You will sup in your big bedroom, as you did to-night, and in hour before moonrise I will come for you."

"But how can you get out of this place?"

"By the way which I shall use to-night. The old builders had many tunnels and passages, which I and my Indians have long known. That is simple. It will be harder to get out the valley, but there is a road for bold hearts, and after a little your friends will meet you. That I have arranged. And now you must go back to bed and sleep very well, for you have much to do to-morrow."

"I shall sleep," Janet cried. "I do not think that I have really slept since I came here, but now..." Her face glowed with happiness; she seized his hands and held them, like a child who finds in a gesture what it cannot find in words.

"You have not asked me who will be your escort," he said.

"I feel so strong," she laughed, "that if you gave me the right direction I think I could escape alone."

"Not so, my dear lady. It is too hard a task for one, even one so gallant. But you will be given full directions, and two trusty companions. One will be a Scotch soldier, whose name is Hamilton."

Janet dropped his hands and stared open-mouthed.

"Geordie Hamilton! Fusilier Geordie! How on earth did he get here? He was in the garrison in the Courts of the Morning."

"He is here. He arrived, having fallen sick on the way, but he is now cured. The other..." He paused.

"The other?" Janet repeated, with a sudden wild anticipation.

"The other is your husband."

XIV

Janet looked out next morning on a new world. Hitherto her eyes had been turning inward, busy with her own grief.

Now she was in a mood of confidence, almost of exhilaration, and the outer scene made a sharper impact upon her senses. She saw the strange beauty of this glen of sepulchre the uncanny shafts of ghostly stone, the avenues white and crackling in the heat, the cincture of green forest, the sentinel and enveloping mountains. The sight of a far blue peak seen through a gap seemed a promise of liberty. Her youth had returned to her and she was almost in a mood for singing...Then she remembered the part she had to play, and composed herself to a decent bewilderment.

She soon found that she had no need to dissemble, for her new-gained cheerfulness evaporated during breakfast. He hosts seemed overnight to have changed their attitude. Their formal politeness had gone, and they treated her roughly, like an embarrassing chattel. Behind their iron composure a deep restlessness was patent. Their schemes were going awry, they could not get in touch with their allies, the place which they had thought a strategic vantage-ground was in danger of becoming their prison.

They talked freely before her, too, and, with what she had learned from Luis, she could follow the drift of it.

They spoke of methods of access and egress. Now that the seaplane was useless, and Lossberg's planes seemed unable to arrive, they discussed the land routes. Some had come by the Pais de Venenos, but that was a difficult road, and it would land them in that eastern part of the Tierra Caliente where the patrols of Peters and Escrick were too active for comfort. There was a way through the hills direct to the west, the way by which they had dispatched Magee, but that also was slow and difficult, and came out on to the plateau too near Pacheco. They spoke of a road to the south, the road their daily scouting parties had taken, and in that appeared to lie their chief hope. But it had clearly been no part of their plan to leave--rather they expected Lossberg to make contact with them, and Janet knew the reason. They commanded the secret outlet to Olifa; they were the forward observation-post for Lossberg; but unless Lossberg received and acted on their intelligence, they would be more in the nature of a forlorn hope.

They had other anxieties. Janet gathered that the Bodyguard was getting a little out of hand. It had been docile enough when it believed that it was being led back to Castor and its old life. But if it scented failure it would take its own road. She realised that the only tie between the two parties was a common interest; remove that, and there would remain only dislike and contempt.

For the first time she heard a note of natural passion among these marionettes, when Lariarty spoke of a wrangle he had had with Judson. For the first time, too, she heard an oath on their discreet lips. Into the face of Romanes there had come a spark of human anger. "By God," he said, "I'll show these curs who's top dog."

Janet played well her game of an ailing and heartbroken prisoner, but she was unregarded. Presently she was to have a striking proof of her hosts' suspicions. The day before in her loneliness she had had thoughts of throwing herself on the mercy of the Bodyguard, and had tried to enter into conversation with them, but had been surlily rebuffed. The most she had succeeded in was a half-hearted friendship with the mongrel terrier that belonged to Carreras. She passed a group of them who were playing cards in the shade of one of the towers, squatted in the white dust. The dog ran to her and she stopped to fondle it.

Suddenly she felt her arms pinioned and looked into a grinning face.

"Come and join our little party, dearie," a voice said. "We're better men than the deadheads up the way. We're all of us free, white, twenty-one, and hairy chested, and we know how to be kind to a pretty girl."

She struggled to release her arms, but the man's grip remained, while the card-party laughed. Even in her terror she noticed how curiously low the ears were set on his head.

"Let her alone, Jake," said one of them; "she ain't yours. We've got to toss for her, and act on the square."

The man released her. "I guess that's right. Run away, my beauty. We got a bond on you, and it's soon goin' to be cashed in." As she hurried off, not daring to look behind, she heard again the ill-omened laughter.

At the midday meal her fears were increased. She was curtly told by Romanes that she must prepare to change her quarters. That evening after sundown she would be sent with D'Ingraville to another place. He was perfectly frank. "It is for your own safety, madame," he said "You are in danger here at the moment, for there are fools among us. It is not yet in our interest that you should come to any harm."

There was no need of acting now. With a face like a sheet she stammered that she was feeling too unwell to travel. "To-morrow, I will be better," she wailed. "But not to-day, please--not to-day."

They talked among themselves. "There is no hurry," said D'Ingraville. "If she is sick, I cannot carry her to Agua Secreta. It is the devil's own road."

Romanes demurred, but in the end was persuaded. "A word of advice to you, madame," he said at last. "Do not show yourself this afternoon. Keep in this vicinity, and above all do not go near the camp of those others. Do you understand me?"

Janet understood only too well, for the leering faces of the card-players that morning had chilled her with a new and terrible fear...What refuge could she find between now and sundown?...Could she get hold of Luis and tell him of this fresh peril? He alone would be able to protect her, for if it came to a fight she did not believe that the Conquistadors could stand up against the Bodyguard...She was in terror of both parties, but she wondered if it would not have been wise to go with D'Ingraville. The Indians--Luis--would follow her, and could rescue her.

But she remembered Luis's strict injunction that she was to be in the great rotunda after nightfall and before moonrise. He had made his plans, and had told her that they were urgent...If only she could find him!...She had seen two of the Indians at a distance that morning bringing in logs for the fires. But now there was not a sign of any Indian. She peered down the avenues, quiet in the blinding glare of the afternoon, and not a soul was to be seen. She felt very small and solitary and forlorn.

Then she remembered the roof to which Luis had taken her. There she could hide herself and be at peace till sunset. At the thought her courage returned. She ran across the patch of sun which separated her from the rotunda, and plunged into its deep shadows...At the entrance lay the blocks which every night were used to make a door. She longed to wall herself up like a condemned nun, but each block required two men to lift...

There was no light in the vast place except the shaft from the door, and a dimness far up which may have come from the crack in the roof. She groped in the far corner till she found the entrance to the tunnel...She tried to remember what Luis had done. They had crawled in for some yards, and then he had found an opening on the left-hand side. She ran her hand along the wall, and found such an opening, but the next second her hand was in the void. It was a shaft, not a passage...Very carefully she crawled a little farther along the main tunnel. Luis had said it was a trap, so she must not go too far. Again her hand found an opening in the left wall, and this time it touched solid floor and solid roof. She crept in, and to her joy found the first step of the staircase. Presently she could stand upright, and soon she was out on the barbican, with a fierce sun beating on her head, and the world at her feet, hot, intense, and coloured like blue steel.

The trouble was to get out of the pitiless sun. She could only find shelter by lying flat under the parapet, and moving as the sun moved. She had eaten not a morsel at luncheon, and now that her immediate terror was abated, she began to wish she had. She was safe here--she must be safe. She would stay till nightfall, and then slip down and meet Luis. Her confidence returned, and she felt herself almost free.

But there were still dregs of fear in her mind, as she remembered the animal faces of the card-players, and the cold inhumanity of Romanes, to whom she was only a counter, to be protected until its usefulness was gone...She looked every now and then over the parapet. She saw little figures cross and recross the avenue, but none had the slimness and the litheness of the Indians. Where were her deliverers? Luis had said that Archie would be there, but how in the name of all that was marvellous had Archie managed it? He must be somewhere within a mile or two, and she looked with a sudden friendliness at the circumference of forest. Yet the thought that Archie was near gave her a new nervousness. He too might be in danger...

She fixed her eyes on a distant blue mountain and told herself that she and Archie were not really far from home, for the other side of that peak must be visible to watchers from Pacheco. She must have dozed, for she suddenly realised that the sun was behind the peaks, and that the swift tropical twilight had fallen. It was now time to nerve herself for action, for presently the Conquistadors would be sitting down to supper in their mess, and the Indians would come to block up the door. She wondered if, when they missed her from the mess, they would send her food, as they had done previously. She hoped so, for she was very hungry.

Down the staircase she groped her way, and crawled back into the tunnel. She only knew that she had reached the rotunda by seeing far off a slant of amber dusk. It showed her the way to her bed, and beside it, to her delight, she found that food had been placed. It was not an appetising meal, for the commissariat of the camp was running low, but she ate it ravenously, and emptied the tin pannikin of water.

Then she saw that the men had come to block the door. That gave her comfort, for they were Indians, Luis's people. She watched the oblong of pale amethyst slowly lessen, and as the blocks rose the remaining daylight seemed to take on a deeper tint, till it was almost crimson. When that had gone, she would light her candle and await her deliverers.

Suddenly there seemed to be a scuffle at the entrance. She heard a voice, a thick angry voice, and then the narrow gap above the blocks seemed to be filled--by a man's body.

Someone was clambering over--she heard a thud as he fell on the inner side...With a flash of dreadful illumination she knew who it was. The Bodyguard had cast lots for her, and this man had won...She screamed for help to the Indians outside the door, but they took no notice. Instead, they went on with the last blocks, and the crimson segment disappeared in utter blackness.

Panic drove Janet's fainting limbs into motion. Her one hope was to reach the tunnel, but in the instant darkness she had lost her bearings and she fluttered blindly. The newcomer, too, seemed at a loss. She could hear his hard breathing. Suddenly he lit a match, and she saw the face of one of the card-players, a dreadful face, bestial and pitiless.

The sight was too much for her nerves, and once again her despairing cry for help rang out. The match flickered and died, but her voice had given him a clue, and she heard him moving nearer. He came slowly and cautiously, for there was no need of haste. He had the whole night in which to find her.

All power seemed to have gone from her body, her throat was dry so that she could not utter a word, her feet were like lead, she had lost all sense of direction. Hopeless now to find the tunnel; she could only struggle vainly like a fly till the spider reached her. Already she felt his clutch on her. And then from her palsied lips came one last gasp of terror, for she suddenly felt herself caught in a man's arms.

But it was not her pursuer. Even her confused senses could still hear him stumbling towards her. A voice spoke low in her ears: "Janet, darling, I'm here! Archie!"

Then many things seemed to happen at once. A circle of light sprang into being from an electric torch. She saw her pursuer stop in his tracks and blink. Then she saw his hand go to his side, and be pinioned there, and a pistol neatly snatched from it by someone behind him. And then between him and her a figure appeared, no Indian, but a stocky figure with bandy legs, a figure that whistled through its teeth like a groom and addressed her enemy in a tongue which fell like music on her ears.

"Sae it's you, my mannie? I'll learn ye to frichten a leddy."

There was a sound of a violent impact of fist on chin and then the rattle of a skull on hard stone.

"That'll keep him quiet till the morn," said the same voice. "I've gi'en that wheasel the same as he got on the Corinna."

For a little time and space disappeared for Janet. Overpowering relief and the sense of Archie beside her brought a happy stupor. She was conscious of kissing and fondling the hand which guided her, and murmuring idiotic endearments. They seemed to be descending stone steps, and then following long winding passages. Somewhere there was a light, and she realised that they were a party of four; but more often they moved in profound darkness. Then it seemed to her that they ascended, not by steps, but in a long slanting tunnel. The close air freshened, and at last with a scramble they came out into the night under a sky ablaze with stars. Luis held up his hand to enjoin silence, but

Janet had no wish to speak. She was hugging Archie's arm as if to make sure that he was a bodily presence and not a dream.

They were in a little stone courtyard, on the edge of the forest, and at the far southern end of the Tronos del Rey.

It was the frontier of the jungle and creepers had encroached upon the stone, completely hiding the tunnel's mouth, and making the courtyard look like a subsidence in the ruins.

They were close to the camp, for voices sounded not a hundred yards away, and against the starlight they could see the pale flicker of fires.

Luis signed to them to follow, and they scrambled out of the hollow into the forest, which was thick as moss, except for an occasional trail. "We must go carefully," he whispered. "Carreras went out this evening to shoot for the pot. He may not have returned. It would not do to meet him."

Luis moved first with Archie at his heels, then Janet, and Hamilton brought up the rear. It was painful going, for chips and slivers of stone were everywhere embedded in the lush herbage and the stones were as unyielding as adamant. Janet felt her stockings and the fringes of her dress being slowly shredded. Then they reached an opening which she judged to be a trail. Luis took one look and then ducked his head, and the others crouched flat to conform.

Janet wondered what was coming next. There was still the glow of sunset in the sky, and it made the aisle through which the trail ran a slender cleft of opaque unrevealing light. What came next was a dog. To her horror she found Carreras's terrier breathing heavily at her shoulder. He had been trained not to bark, but he showed his recognition by shaking himself and sending the dew flying like a shower-bath. She glared at him, she threatened him, but the beast stood wagging his imbecile tail. He had found a friend, and was determined to let his master come up and share in the discovery.

Luis did not wait for the meeting. He doubled back and clutched Archie's arm. "The fellow will be here in a second," he whispered. "We must show ourselves...You know the road...Here, take the hatchet...I will try to divert them. Once at Agua Secreta you are safe. Quick!"

The next five minutes were not for Janet a period of very clear consciousness. She was dragged to her feet, pulled through what seemed to be a fine-meshed sieve of creepers, and landed in a narrow avenue cut as if with a knife between two walls of forest. Then she seemed to be made to halt, and she had the feeling as if alone she was exposed to someone's gaze, while the rest were hidden...She heard a cry, heard a shot fired, heard other pistol shots from the direction of the camp...And then she found herself running faster than she had ever run before in her life.

Luis was last and he was urging them on. They were being pursued--she heard a distant crashing in the undergrowth--perhaps the trail twisted and someone was trying to take a short cut. Then Luis's clear whisper followed them. "I leave you. You know the road...Do not for the love of God stop to fight...I do not think you will be followed...Say that I will be at Pacheco in thirty-six hours, no more. Adios!"

She had no time to look behind, for Archie's hand was dragging her, Archie whose game leg seemed to be performing miracles, but she had the sensation that Luis was no longer there. He had swerved to the right down a subsidiary path and was making mighty heavy going.

His movements sounded like those of a bull rhinoceros; he was giving tongue, too, babbling loudly to himself. He will betray us all, she thought in a panic, and then she realised that this was his purpose. He was there to be followed...Far back she heard a different kind of cry, the shouting of angry men on a scent which they have missed and recovered.

After that it seemed that for hours they struggled and plunged and slipped, always keeping to some sort of trail, but tripped up by creepers, or slithering on greasy earth, or edging painfully through acres of cruel thorn. She used to be famous for her good wind, and had been able to stride from Glenraden to the highest top of Carnmor without a halt. But that had been in clear hill air, with a bright world of salt and heather at her feet and no goad except her fancy. It was a different matter to run through this choking sodden forest, with life as the stake--Archie's life and her own--maybe, too, the fortunes of the campaign.

The girl kept her mind savagely upon a single purpose--to keep up with Archie, and to give him as little trouble as possible, for she knew by his laboured breathing that the strain must be terrible for a lame man.

Hamilton, the leader, stopped. He was panting like a dog, but he had voice enough left to whisper hoarsely, "I hear nothing. Maister Lewis maun hae got the hale pack at his heels. They'll no catch him this side o' Martinmas. We maun be better than half road. Tak' your breath, mem."

But the merciful respite seemed only to last for a second. Again they were off, and now they seemed to be ascending. The ground was harder. They passed over banks of dry gravelly soil, and in places the roots of the trees showed as in a pinewood, instead of being buried deep in rank verdure. Once even there was a shelf of layered rock, and she had to give Archie a hand. But the gain in elevation told them nothing of their position, for it was that murky mulberry dusk in which the foreground is just visible, but everything else an impenetrable blur.

They seemed to reach a summit, where curiously enough the sky was darker than below. After that it was flat for a little, with thinner vegetation but many thorns--Janet felt her hands ache from their attentions. She was feeling a little more at ease. They were on the right road--Hamilton seemed to have no doubt about that--they could not be very far from their goal, and there was no sign of pursuit. Luis must have lifted the enemy cleverly off the scent. She wondered if he were safe...

It was Archie who stopped suddenly and put his hand to his head. "Hamilton!" he panted. "Listen! Do you hear anything?"

Janet pushed her hair away from her ears. Somewhere back in the forest there was a sound like a little wind. But the night was very still...She listened again, and in the heart of it she heard the unmistakable note of human speech...And then suddenly it sounded much nearer, not a hundred yards away: "Oh! Quick," she cried. "They're almost up on us."

She was not quite right, for the acoustics of the place were strange. Actually at the moment the nearest of the pursuers was at least a quarter of a mile off. But all three had felt the ominous proximity of the sound, and all in their different ways reacted to the spur of fear. Hamilton, being of a stocky build, could not quicken his pace, for he had come nearly to the end of his running resources; instead he slowed down, and his hand fiddled with his belt. He would have preferred to fight. Janet got her second wind, and felt an extraordinary lightness and vigour. It was she now who dragged Archie. Inevitably they passed Hamilton, so when they suddenly came to the brink of the gorge she was leading the party.

It was the kind of spectacle which cuts short the breath for the sheer marvel of its beauty. From her feet the ground broke into a cliff, but a cliff not of stone but of soil, for it was all forested. The trees were set on so steep a gradient that two yards from her she was looking into branches reached commonly only by high-flying birds.

The angle was not less than sixty degrees, but some strange adhesive quality in the soil enabled it to cling to this difficult foundation and support life. But the miracle lay in the depth. In that luminous purple night it ran down from layer to layer of darkness, keeping an exact perspective, till it seemed that it had sunk for miles. The cleft must go to the centre of the globe, and yet a bottom could be detected, though not discerned. Somewhere at an infinite distance below there was water--the so-called Agua Secreta--strong water, too, for out of the deeps rose the murmur of a furious river.

From Janet's feet a bridge flung out into the void. It looked like a ship's bowsprit hanging over dark oceans, for the eye could not see its further abutment. And such a bridge! It was made of slats and twined osiers and lianas, solidly made, and its making was not of yesterday. But there was no planking to hide the abyss. Between the slats showed the naked void, and the slats were each a pace apart.

"On ye gang--," a hoarse voice spoke behind. "It's the brig we maun cross. Haud fast by the side ropes, mem, and ye'll no fa'. Sir Erchibald will keep haud o' ye."

But Janet had no fear for herself. This lath strung across immensity was a beautiful thing...Suddenly one half of it seemed to become brightly gilt, and she realised that the rim of the moon had lifted above a corner of hill...And it meant safety! It was Archie she feared for, Archie with his crippled leg. She stepped cheerfully out on the bridge. "Hold tight, Archie dear, and go very slow. Balance yourself by my shoulder."

The crossing of that bridge was a comment upon the character of each of the three. Janet was in a kind of ecstasy. To be islanded between sky and earth was an intoxication, and every step was nearer home. If only Archie...! Archie, painfully groping his way, minded the vertigo of it not at all, but he realised, as she did not, how slowly they moved and how imperative was haste. As for Hamilton, the thing was to him pure torment, he was terrified half out of his senses, but he doggedly plugged along because there was nothing else to be done. He was praying fervently and blaspheming steadily, and prayer and blasphemy continued till the first shot was fired. After that he was more at his ease.

They were in the middle of the bridge when the pursuers cached the edge. A cry followed them, heard as clearly in that funnel as if it had been spoken in their ear, to halt and come back or someone would shoot. The warning was followed by a shot, fired wide.

The last part of the journey was a nightmare for all three. Speed was an urgent matter, yet a slip would send them whirling into unplumbed gulfs. For Janet all the exhilaration was gone, and her heart was fluttering wildly. She was terrified for Archie, who had had some ugly slips and was leaning heavily on her arm. Also the gulf was now lit with silver moonshine. Before it had merely been a sensation of dark space, felt but not realised; now she could see its shimmering infinity, and something of the old terror of the Abyss began to clutch at her.

Before she knew she was off the bridge and had pulled Archie beside her on to a tussock of dwarf arbutus. A deadly faintness was on her, and her head swam. Dimly she saw Hamilton busy with his hatchet...What was he doing?...There were men on the bridge. She saw them clearly. They were getting nearer...

Then she realised. The fear of the Abyss came back to her. It seemed an awful thing to sacrifice men to it, even enemies. "Stop!" she pleaded. "You can't. Let's go on..."

"It's my orders, mem," said the other, stolidly cutting through the twisted lianas. "Maister Lewis says--at all costs ye maun destroy the brig ahint you."

The pursuit realised what was happening. They were more than half-way across, and the moonlight was so bright that the visibility was like day. Janet could see each of the four figures distinctly. They were all of the Bodyguard. One of them, the foremost, seemed to be the man who had pursued her in the rotunda.

A pistol shot struck the earth a yard from Hamilton. "Ye'll maybe get hurt, mem," he observed between his strokes. "Get you and the Captain in ahint the buss. I'm near finished."

But apprehension and horror held both Archie and Janet motionless. There was one other pistol shot, which went wide. The men on the bridge had stopped shooting and were labouring grimly in the race with death...Supposing they won, thought Janet...But they did not win. Very gently, without any sag or jerk, the bridge swung out into the gulf like a silver pendulum, and several little black things were shaken from it.

Two hours later four of Peters's troopers, patrolling up the long moraine of shale in one of the tributary glens of the Catalpas stream, came upon three very weary travellers, who were staggering knee-deep in the shingle. To their amazement they found that they were English--two men and a woman, who asked to be taken to

Pacheco. One of the men was lame, and he and the woman were set on horseback.

When after midnight they reached the camp in the valley bottom their captain, Carlos Rivero, received the travellers with excitement. He fed them, but they made only a hasty meal, demanding at once to be taken to headquarters. At the place which is called Maximoras, but in the old speech Hatuelpec, Captain Rivero, who himself conducted them, was again surprised to be met by a fresh troop from Pacheco, which contained a woman. But it was the commander of this troop who gave Rivero the third and most shattering surprise of the night. For he recognised in him the Gobernador of the Gran Seco.

BOOK III - OLIFA

I

General Alexander Lossberg, the Commander-in-Chief of the Olifa Expeditionary Force, was in a good temper as he took the air one morning on his smart little blue roan on the long ridge to the east of his advanced head-quarters. It was nearly four months since he had occupied the city of the Gran Seco, and he felt that the situation was now satisfactory to his orderly mind. At first it had been rather an anxious business, this groping in the dark for an enemy whom it seemed impossible to locate. With his superb force--his infantry divisions, his mechanised battalions, his cavalry brigade, his field batteries, and his light tanks--it had irked him to find nothing to spend his strength on. But he had been patient and very cautious. The enemy had an unpleasant number of aeroplanes and knew how to use them--he was a good soldier and could appreciate the merits of an antagonist--and his repeated demands to Olifa for more planes had brought a meagre response.

But, in spite of the semi-blindness which this weakness in the air involved, he had groped his way steadily to the identification and the capture of the enemy bases. There was Fort Castor--that had soon fallen. The name set him musing upon the fate of him who had once been Gobernador of the Gran Seco. He had never liked him; he remembered the insolent calm of his eyes, and his habit of asking unanswerable questions. The man had been an arrogant civilian, and his cleverness was futile in war. He had heard that he was an unwilling figurehead, a prisoner in the hands of the guerrillero whom the people called El Obro, and whom he understood to be a Scottish soldier-of-fortune. Well, this El Obro, he was not much of a soldier; only a flashy amateur. The General had heard a good deal of talk in his time about the importance of the psychological factor in war, and was a little sick of it. Why should he trouble himself to read the mind of this guerrillero; he knew by instinct the kind of mind he had--the ingenious schoolboy, treating war as a holiday game and banking on the unexpected. There was no such thing as the unexpected. War was an exact mathematical science. Cleverness and daring might delay for a week or two the advance of the great military machine, but in the end it crept forward, crushing opposition as a tank went through barbed wire and breastworks. Once again the professional had been justified, and the General flung out his chest and drew deep and pleasant draughts of the cool morning.

Fort Castor and then Loa, and then the easy capture of the enemy's secret base up on that shelf between the mountains and the sea. What was the name of it? Los Patios de la Mariana. An amusing name, the kind of name that those play-acting folk would choose. He had not yet visited the place, but he promised himself that pleasure soon. It was said to be very beautiful. He could imagine worse fates than to be the Governor of this province, and Los Patios might be an eligible site for a country house. Soldiering in Olifa itself had been a little tedious for a man of his energy. But Gobernador of this rich province--that promised power, and amusement, and, of course, wealth. In these Latin republics he understood that there was a generous margin for those set in authority.

The Mines had been his great problem. Olifa had always been nervous lest the enemy should so destroy them that their restoration would be a labour of years. One part of the danger had been removed when he occupied the city and the smelting works; the other, the Mines, had been made his chief preoccupation, by direct instructions from his Government. It had not been his own wish. He did not believe in tying himself up with anything in the nature of a fortress. He had been taught that it was a general's duty to seek out the enemy and destroy him, and not to be entangled in the defence of property. His adversaries had guessed at this obligation, for they had made the Mines the scene of most of the fighting, and had managed by constant pinpricking to tie up most of his troops on that long front...

Yet, perhaps, in their blundering way the Olifa Government had been right. Against an enemy so light and elusive and with such a vast hinterland for retreat, their way had perhaps been the best. He remembered that he had not been very successful in his rounding-up expeditions. His cavalry nets had been drawn tight again and again without enclosing anything. The cavalry had indeed been a failure. It had been led a pretty dance by El Obro's commandos, had been split up and destroyed in patches, had lost itself, had fought against itself in fog and darkness. As a gunner, he had never been a cavalry enthusiast, and now he was more disillusioned than ever. Also the tanks had not been a success, since there had been nothing solid against which to use them...No, perhaps Olifa by some fortunate accident had judged right. This long-drawn defence of the Mines had done its part. It must have depleted terribly the enemy's vanishing stock of munitions; he wished he could think that it had depleted his numbers.

And now it was over. For three days the Mines front had been stagnant, and his patrols had reported no enemy force within twenty miles. The cause could only be that debacle of munitionment which he had always foreseen and counted on.

There remained Pacheco--that robbers' nest in the angle of the hills. That, he believed, was the main enemy headquarters, and he had been anxious for a long time to burn it out. This very morning he was advancing on Pacheco in strength. At last there was something to bite on. The result, of course, was a foregone conclusion, and after that--? Where would El Obro find his next refuge? It was on Pacheco, no doubt, that the attempts on the Mines front had been based. It was from Pacheco beyond question that the raids on the railway had been launched.

These raids had for some time been happily abortive, and, now that he had his blockhouse system nearly complete, the only danger was from an occasional bombing aeroplane--if the enemy had any bombs left...There was perhaps another base in the north-east--he had some evidence of that. But what were these bases? Mere twigs on which to perch, and always being moved nearer to the inhospitable hills. You could not call that a base which supplied nothing in the way of food or shells. His military soul repudiated the name. He ran his mental eye over the map of the Gran Seco. The city and the railway to Olifa securely held; the Mines now free from all danger; the enemy forced out of the whole western, southern, and northern parts, and holding only an unknown corner in the north-east with driblets southward towards the Tierra Caliente. The war was over. The country was conquered. All that remained was a little minor police work.

His reflections were so satisfactory that the General was compelled to ease his feelings by swift movement. He gave his horse its head against the slope, and, raising his cap, let the wind sing about him and ruffle his thinning hair. He drew rein at the crest and scanned the wide landscape. A fine soldierly figure he looked, his square tanned face flushed with exercise, his grey eyes with almost a boyish light in them, the slight heaviness and sullenness of mouth and jaw relaxed in good humour. He looked eastward where sixty or seventy miles away the great chain of the mountains stretched its white fingers into the unfathomable blue. He was no connoisseur in the picturesque, but suddenly those mountains gave him a feeling of pleasure. He felt a proprietary interest in this land, of which he might soon be Governor, and he was glad that his future satrapy included these magnificent creatures of God. They reminded him of his childhood, when from a Bavarian valley he had stared at the distant snows of the Wettersteingebirge.

He turned, and before him lay the grassy barrens that stretched to the city. On his right he could see the slim headgear of the Mines, and the defences of that now stagnant front. The sight initiated a new train of thought. He had always meant to have the Mines started as soon as possible. That would be proof positive of his victory. When he had broached the idea to Olifa it had been received with enthusiasm; those bovine ministers could not comprehend the meaning of his operations, but they could appreciate such a result as the resumption of their great industry...That very afternoon he would send a dispatch, and he would begin to work out the first stages...

And then a reflection brought him up with a jerk. Where was he to find the experts to advise him? What had become of those strange gentlemen who called themselves the Conquistadors? He had talked it all over with Romanes many weeks ago. He detested the type, the unwholesome pale faces, the low voices, the opaque eyes, which nevertheless in their blankness seemed to hold a perpetual sneer. But he had been instructed from

Olifa to treat them with respect, and Romanes he found that he could get on with. The man had been a soldier--a good soldier, he believed, till he had fallen down--and he had not forgotten his earlier trade. The General had been impressed with the soundness of his military views. He had a contempt for anyone who fell out of his own hierarchy, but he did not show it, and Romanes had no doubt appreciated being treated as still one of the brotherhood. Romanes had been insistent on starting the Mines.

Half-power, of course, at first; there would be a great lack of technical staffs and white foremen. But he was confident that all the labour needed could be got among the concentrados and prisoners, and that he and his colleagues could make up a skeleton staff.

But that was nearly a month ago. General Lossberg had owed his professional success to his remarkable power of absorption in the task of the moment. He had been busy conducting a war, and he had had no ear for gossip. But he seemed to remember something. There were queer stories about those people. They lived on drugs and got them somewhere--where was it? somewhere in the mountains? Yes. Olivarez had told him that they had gone to the mountains, they and the blackguard-looking fellows who had been Castor's Bodyguard...Why had it been permitted? He would have something to say to Olivarez...

The General cantered across the baked yard in front of his quarters, and, giving his horse to an orderly, marched into the office of his Chief of Staff. Olivarez was older by several years than Lossberg, and, along with General Bianca, was the military pride of Olifa. He was a slight man, with a long olive-tinted face, a fleshy nose, and grizzled hair cut en brosse. He jumped to his feet as the General entered, and was about to speak, when he was forestalled.

"What about that fellow Romanes, General?" Lossberg demanded. "I want to get hold of him at once--him and his friends. I propose to start the Mines."

The other looked puzzled for a moment. He had something of his chief's gift of absorption, and his mind had been much occupied of late by other matters. "Romanes, sir? Yes, I remember." He turned the leaves of a big diary. "He left here on the 23rd of last month. Some private business. He was no use to us and we did not try to stop him. He was going into the mountains and was confident that he could get past General Peters's patrols. There was some talk of a seaplane which D'Ingraville had got hold of in Olifa. D'Ingraville, you may remember, sir, was formerly of the French Air Service. He left a request that we should keep in touch with him--by air, of course--and he gave us certain bearings and directions by which we could find him. I do not know if anything has been done about it. Shall I send for Colonel Waldstein?"

Presently Waldstein appeared, a little man all wire and whipcord. He had something to tell, but not much. "We had Senor Romanes's directions beyond doubt," he said, "but it is one thing, sir, to be given a line and quite another to be able to take it. That does not need saying. We twice tried to make contact with him, but you will remember, sir, that three weeks ago the enemy planes were very active between here and the mountains. There is reason to believe that both the fighting scouts that we sent out were shot down. At any rate, they have not returned."

"Have you done nothing since then?" Lossberg asked peremptorily.

"No, sir. Every machine we possess has been engaged in urgent business."

Lossberg tapped his teeth with a pencil; it was a habit he had when he was slightly ruffled.

"There is now no enemy activity in that area, Colonel Waldstein," he said at last. "You will please arrange that a machine is sent at once to the place indicated by Senor Romanes. No, send two, and send Hoffding carriers. I want Senor Romanes brought here at once, and as many of his colleagues as can be accommodated, and arrangements made for the transport here of the rest. Do you understand? The matter is urgent."

Waldstein saluted and went. Then Olivarez was given the chance of saying that which had been on his tongue.

"There is a message from Pacheco, sir. We occupied it an hour and twenty minutes ago."

Lossberg's face lit up. "But that is good business. Had we much trouble?"

"No, sir. We were not opposed. The place was abandoned."

Lossberg stared blankly. "Abandoned, you say?"

"Abandoned, sir. Not a shell was fired. No contact mines had been left. And apparently it had not been abandoned in a hurry, for every scrap of stores had been removed. The place had been deserted for several days."

The Commander-in-Chief, who was commonly a precisian in his speech, observed that he was damned. He stared with his eyes abstracted, thinking hard. He had always been contemptuous about psychology, but now he wished he could see a little into the mind of El Obro.

"Where have they gone?" he soliloquised. "Peters had five thousand men there a week ago. I wonder what diabolical game he is up to now? There's no way east or south. He has not come west, for we hold the land up to the southern scarp. He must have gone north. There's something preparing up in that north-east corner which we have got to discover. Tell Colonel Waldstein to arrange for an extensive air patrol of the eastern Tierra Caliente. Let him take a radius of 150 miles. Yes, telegraph the news about Pacheco to the War Ministry. It will make a good headline for the papers. But do not mention that we found it abandoned. I will give all the details in my dispatch."

"The wireless is working very badly, sir," said Olivarez. "We have been consistently jammed for the last thirty-six hours."

"Atmospherics," the Colonel observed. He had moments of longing for the old days of war, when you stuck to the heliograph, and the dispatch rider, and the telegraph. Then, somewhat perturbed, he went to breakfast. The crystal-clear vision of the future which he had had that morning on the savannah was a little dulled.

Towards the late afternoon of the same day one of the Hoffding machines returned, and with it the pilot of the other, which had crashed in one of the glens. It reported a difficult and disastrous journey. It had followed Romanes's directions and made its way into the mountain range by an intricate series of valleys. It had found itself in a region where the wind came in baffling eddies, and where there was no possible landing-place. All the valleys were narrow and sheer and muffled with forest. It had discerned a shelf of flat ground, filled with the ruins of great stone towers. There, flying low, it had seen the remains of old camp-fires, but there were no human beings now in the place. After that came the disaster to its sister machine, the pilot of which had been saved by a miracle. Unless it attempted to fly over the main range, there was nothing more to be done, so it had come home to report.

Late that night one of Waldstein's patrols brought in a man who had been found in the tangled country under the lee of the mountains. He was half dead with fatigue and starvation, but had recovered sufficiently to ask to be taken to the General's Headquarters. The General had not had the pleasant dinner which he had anticipated. The meal, instead of being a cheerful celebration of the capture of Pacheco, had been an anxious confabulation with his staff.

For something had gone wrong with his communications, and he could get no answer from Olifa. In place of the lyric congratulations on success which he had expected, his message had been followed by utter silence. The long-distance telephone had never been noted for its reliability, but hitherto the telegraph service had been perfect. Now, with the wireless out of gear for two days, it looked as if this too had failed. That, or some intense preoccupation at the Ministry of War. Consequently, when Olivarez brought in the rag of humanity which his patrol had picked up, it was with no friendly eye that Lossberg regarded him.

"We cannot find Senor Romanes," the Chief of Staff had said, "but this is one of those who were with him. One of the gentry whom Castor called his Bodyguard. He says he has something for your private ear. Jesucristo! Wherever he came from he has had a rough Journey."

Mr Daniel Judson had not been improved in looks by his recent experiences. His clothes hung in rags, his skin was black with exposure, and short commons had sharpened his face so that his big head tapered to a jackal's mask.

Normally his broken nose and rabbit teeth gave him a touch of comedy, ferocious comedy--but now these features seemed to be blended into one overwhelming impression of something snarling and ravening. The slouch of his thick-set shoulders gave him the air of crouching for a spring, like a mad dog. He had had food, of which he had eaten sparingly, being used to similar experiences and knowing the danger of a glut. Lossberg gave him permission to sit town, while his story dribbled out through the confusion of fatigue.

Most of it was startlingly new to the General and his staff. He spoke of a camp at Los Tronos del Rey. "Those guys had to have the dope, and the Indians fetched it..." He told of the daily expeditions and of the discovery of a pass through the mountains which had excited Romanes.

"We were expecting you to send to us, but you never came, so Mr Romanes, he tried to get to you. The

Indians must have double-crossed us, for nothing happened. We sent out Magee, and he never came back. Then the Indians turned nasty. There was a woman we had with us and she got away. The Indians must have helped her, and they cut the bridge behind her, and next morning the whole outfit did a bunk. After that we were between a rock and a hard place. There was a lot of unpleasantness with Mr Romanes, but by and by we see'd we couldn't do nothing by fighting each other, so we shared out the grub, and took what we each thought was the best road off that bloody mantelpiece...I started out with two pals, and I don't know where in hell they've got to." Mr Judson appeared to be going to be sick at the recollection. He recounted haltingly something of his troubles, first in the forest and then in the glens of the foothills. Famine had been the worst. "A biscuit would ha' rattled in my stomach like a buckshot in a tin pan." He had several times decided that he was about to perish. "This world one time, then the fireworks," was the way he expressed his anticipation.

By and by he had become so feeble that he could only crawl and weep, and in that condition the patrols had found him. Even now he had not the strength of a new-born cat.

"If I slapped a fly this moment, I'd fall down."

Lossberg fastened upon one item in his story, the pass through the mountains. Judson strayed into vague profanity. He didn't rightly know how to describe it, but they had found it all right, and Mr Romanes had thought it as important as hell. That was why he had made his despairing effort to get in touch with the General. Judson's brains were too befogged to explain further, but he quoted a sentence of Romanes. "Mr Romanes," I heard him say to the long Frenchy, him that was the airman, "By God!" he says, "if we don't stop that bolt-hole the rebs one fine morning will be breakfasting in Olifa."

Judson was dismissed, and the General looked at his Chief of Staff.

"Romanes is not a fool," he said, "and he has been a soldier. He has found out something which he wanted badly to get to us. Remember he is on our side. Except by our victory he and his friends cannot get back to the life they enjoy. What is that something? A road through the mountains into Olifa? We have always understood that there was no road, no practicable road, except that which the railway follows. There may be a pass which we know nothing of. Romanes knows about it. The question is, does El Obro? If he does, it would explain Pacheco."

The two men talked long and gravely. One result of their conference was that Waldstein was given fresh orders. His air patrols must move a little farther south and explore the valleys east of Pacheco. At all costs they must find Senor Romanes and his companions, who must now be making their way down from the hills.

Lossberg had a disturbed night, but about ten next morning he had news which cheered him. There had been a sudden revival of enemy activity in the north part of the province. Mounted bands had been seen west of the line Fort Castor-Loa, and a motor convoy, bound for the latter place, had been captured. To Lossberg this was reassuring tidings. It seemed to explain the whereabouts of Peters and his Pacheco force. They had not gone south through any mysterious pass in the mountains, but north, to join the oddments up in that north-eastern corner. The General convinced himself that what he had always foreseen had now come to pass. The enemy was confined to the north-east of the Tierra Caliente, and all that remained was slowly and drastically to bring him to book. He would of course make sallies from his beleaguerment, but it would not be hard to cope with the desperate efforts of weak and ill-provided men.

Yet the whole of the following week was taken up with these sallies. The enemy had changed his tactics, and adopted a vigorous offensive. The Mines front was stagnant, and Lossberg was able to move one infantry division and all his cavalry to the threatened north.

The first thing that happened was that Loa fell to the guerrilleros, and the garrison in the Courts of the Morning had its land communications cut. This was interpreted by Lossberg as a feint, for Loa could be no value to the enemy. In this he was right, for after its stores had been removed, Loa was abandoned.

But the next move was startling, no less than a raid on the Gran Seco city. It happened about 11 a.m. on a night when there was no moon. The enemy cut up the pickets, and for nearly four hours held all the city west of the smelting works and north of the railway station. The thing had been beautifully arranged. The raiders, who seemed to know the place intimately, occupied the key-points, and used the machine guns they had taken at the northern approaches. They knew, too, where the stores were, and helped themselves to what they wanted, loading the loot into light motor-wagons which had only the day before arrived from Olifa. They destroyed a freight train in the railway yards and put no less than seven locomotives out of action. It was artful destruction, done by men who were skilful mechanics, and it would take weeks to repair. Then, after setting fire to the Gran Seco Club as a final feu de joie, they made off at their leisure, taking with them the light motor-wagons. It was well after daybreak before Lossberg's first reinforcements arrived, for the telephone and telegraph wires had been comprehensively cut. An attempt to follow was made with armed cars, but the pursuit struck the rear of the raiders about forty miles north-east of the city, was ambushed, and badly cut up. The enemy had vanished again into his north-eastern fastness.

All this was disquieting, but yet in its way consoling Judson's story had deeply impressed the Commander-in Chief, and he was relieved to have discovered the whereabouts of the Pacheco force. It must have joined the band under Escrick, for hitherto Escrick had been far too weak to think of an offensive. So he set about with a will the task of hunting down the remnant. He established a cordon of posts in a line from the Mines to Loa, and, based on each extremity, he had a mobile force of cavalry and mechanised battalions. He believed that this cordon could not be pierced, and his plan was slowly to push it forward till he had driven the enemy into the mountain valleys. Of these he would then seal up the ends, and starve him out.

But the cordon was pierced, repeatedly pierced. There was no further raid on the Gran Seco, but there was a disastrous dash on the Mines, which ended in the explosion of a shell-dump and the shattering of two engine-houses. Marvellous to relate, too, there was a raid on the railway, from what base no man knew, and the line was badly damaged in the crucial section between Tombequi and Villa Bar. Also there were perpetual pinpricks. Not a convoy seemed to be able to move on any of the Gran Seco roads without some regrettable accident--a mined road, a broken culvert, a long-distance sniping--of baneful accuracy. Lossberg, who had regarded the campaign as over, was forced to admit that it had miraculously entered upon a new phase.

In the thick of this guerrilla warfare the General forgot his other problems. He was kept so feverishly busy that he omitted to worry about the silence of the Olifa Ministry of War and the absence of a reply to his message about Pacheco. He was moving fast about the country and did not remember to inquire whether

Waldstein's machines had picked up any news of the Conquistadors. Waldstein's machines were now on other duties. But there came a night when he was able to return to his advanced Headquarters, which had remained in the vicinity of the Mines. He dined alone with Olivarez, the first peaceful meal he had had for ten days. Both men were in better spirits.

"It is the last spasm of a dying animal," said Lossberg. "Now we know to a decimal the worst he could do, and we know that he cannot repeat it. In a week this activity will die down, and we shall turn to the question of starting the Mines. Even now it is police work we are engaged in, not war."

Olivarez nodded and smiled. "By the way, we have news of the Conquistadors. Senor Romanes is here, and the man they call Larbert, the Englishman."

"I will see them after dinner," was the answer. General Lossberg filled himself a glass of champagne--he had allowed himself champagne that evening--and looked complacently at its sparkle. He had had an annoying time, but he had come to the end of it.

The telephone bell rang, and Olivarez took the receiver. "It is from Olifa at last," he said over his shoulder. "A message forwarded from Base Headquarters."

The General continued to contemplate his glass, with a smiling face. He awaited the congratulations which were his due. Suddenly he was startled to attention, for his Chief of Staff was speaking in an odd voice. "Repeat," he said, and again, "Repeat!" He turned to Lossberg without hanging up the receiver and his hand trembled. "I can't make it out...It must be a mistake...It is from Santa Ana, not Olifa. I don't know who sent it...Good God, it can't be true!"

"What is it, man?" Lossberg asked.

"It says that Santa Ana was captured this morning by the enemy. Santa Ana! By the American Blenkiron, who was known here as Rosas!"

Lossberg's face whitened, but he retained his composure.

He even laughed, a little harshly. "If that is true, El Obro is assuredly through the passes."

II

The short spring had gone, and it was already early summer at Charcillo. The gnarled tamarisks which lined two sides of the great pebbled courtyard were hung with long lilac blooms, and the poplars and willows were green along the water-furrows. The estancia was of an older type than Veiro. There were no neat paddocks and English-looking stables; part of the house itself had stood for three hundred years, and the thick walls of the corrals were almost fortifications. The place stood on a low ridge between the main stream of the Vulpas and a tributary, commanding to the west and south long views over savannah which gradually dipped to the blueness of the coastal plain.

Behind, to the east, was more rolling country, but from every ridge might be descried fifty miles off the dark loom of the mountains, and in clear weather the northernmost peaks of Los Doce Apostoles.

For the past fortnight Janet had been a happy denizen of a fantastic world. She felt that she was now promoted to the rank of a combatant. Her adventure had by a marvellous chance been the turning-point in the campaign. As she looked back upon the last month, the fear and horror were forgotten. Her week of captivity was only like a dark night between bright and bustling days. Far back in the corridors of memory she saw the Courts of the Morning, a platform lifted high above the world, whence with a divine detachment they had looked down upon the struggles of mortals. That life could not have lasted, but it had done its work, for it had wrought a miracle in the Gobernador.

What had become of the mysterious being with his inhuman composure and his secret thoughts? A new man had been born, a man who had forgotten his past and walked on a new earth with a curious innocence. He seemed to be happy, happy in companionship as well as in leadership. For beyond doubt he was a leader, and his post as generalissimo was no polite fiction. It was an unfamiliar world to him, but he had taken hold of it like a master.

Modestly, simply, he had applied his mind to strange problems, and from the first day he had had an unquestioned authority. In the great movement through the passes, after Peters with the remnant of his command had gone north to Escrick, and Sandy had led his mounted three thousand into Olifa, it was the Gobernador who had spoken the ultimate word. By tacit consent he was always deferred to, and as he mastered the problems his authority became one of mind as well as of character. And he was happy--that was the immense change. He seemed to have rid himself of a burden both of years and cares.

Crowded days lay behind them. Charcillo was the base headquarters, but when the word to strike was given they would move to Veiro. Meanwhile the concentration was kept secret. The Olifa Government had no doubt news of trouble on the south-eastern edge of the Gran Seco, but they had no knowledge of what was happening in this wild corner of their own province. For the countryside was at their back and Luis's agents controlled all the communications with the capital. They had spent a feverish week over the coming concentration, and to Charcillo at all hours of the day and night had come Luis's lieutenants to consult. Some of them were young men whom Janet had met at the Polo Club or danced with in Olifa; many were officers of the Olifa reserve; some were grizzled haciendados from the skirts of the hills or rich industrials from Alcorta and Lardamo...There was old Martinez and his five sons who owned hundreds of miles of ranching ground on the skirts of the mountains...And Ramirez and his clan who were the fruit kings of Olifa...And the Zarramgas from Pecos, whose ancestors had come to the country with Pizarro...And young Miguel de Campanillo, whose kin had ridden with Toledo and whose family had given a later Olifa three presidents...She did not quite understand them. These men were prosperous; they had no grievance against the Gran Seco; they were not of the rootless revolutionary type. Why should they want to join in this quarrel? But the chief marvel was Don Alejandro Gedd. The little man had become a crusader. Why? His patriotism in the past had chiefly shown itself in dislike of all things American. He had disliked Castor, too, and now he was his willing henchman.

There was a big map indoors, on which with coloured pins the strength of the opposing sides was shown. Olifa had three battalions in the city, in camp at the Plaza de Toros, and she had a skeleton division at Pecos, and a battalion at Santa Ana. There were detachments at Al Corta and Cardiano, and on the latter place was based the small Olifa navy. These points were marked with green pins, but it was to be noted that sometimes close up to them was stuck a red pin. That meant that in such places there was a strong anti-Government element in the regulars. The red pins were widely scattered, but there were certain spots marked with black rings, which were the centres for concentration. One was on the railway south of Santa Ana, another at the junction south-east of Olifa, whence ran the line to Alcorta. But the chief was at the railhead west of Veiro. To the north the Gran Seco was unmarked. No news had come of how Peters and Escrick were faring in their intensive guerrilla campaign.

The thing fascinated the girl. She seemed to be herself a player in a drama which was nearing its last act. Of the ultimate purpose she scarcely thought. Victory was to her a concrete thing, a single culminating moment, beyond which her mind would not speculate.

Her one anxiety was Sandy. He had lost the briskness and the audacity with which he had begun the campaign. Perhaps he was tired; he must be, for he had worn himself to a shadow in the Gran Seco. A man has only a certain stock of vital energy, and he had squandered his lavishly...But there was more in it than that, she thought Sandy was a born adventurer, who must always be imperilling himself, working on the extreme edge of hazard, playing for an outside chance. But now the war was almost regularised. It was a revolution of the familiar type, where the rank and file took the risks. Sandy hated bloodshed. For war he had no use unless it was war on his special plan, an audacious assault upon the enemy's nerves. The other kind, the usual kind, he would only accept if it were in defence of his own country, and Olifa was not his fatherland.

Janet said as much to Castor, who had joined her where she sat on a low white wall, plucking at the long blooms of the tamarisks. He looked like a fighting admiral, who had strayed by accident into khaki.

He nodded his agreement.

"That is Lord Clanroyden's trouble. He is born out of due season. He does not quite like a game where the chances are not hopelessly against him. Now that the odds have been shortened he is uncomfortable. But let him console himself. We have still a long way to travel. General Lossberg and I are in the position of each facing his own capital, like the French and Germans before Sedan. That is not comfortable for him, but it is not altogether comfortable for us. We have to keep him shut up in the Gran Seco, for if his army got out it would destroy us in a week. Also we have to persuade the Olifa Government that it will be well to make peace, and that may not be easy. Let the senor be at ease. It is still a war not of brute force but of morale."

"I think you are happy," she said.

"I am happy because I have found something. I have found friends, and I have found a better philosophy. Also I have found what I never had before, a country. I am discovering the rudiments of life."

"You are ten years younger."

He laughed. "And yet I am destroying all the things I have given my life to make. I have jettisoned my old ambition. I hoped to be a Napoleon to change the shape of the world. Fool that I was! I should only have begun to yawn after it was done, and then somebody would have shot me. Now I am quite content if I can help to make an inconsiderable Latin republic a more wholesome State--and if I can prove myself not unworthy of my friends."

"That is the truth," she said. "This is not Sandy's country...You have changed places, I think. You have come down into the homely world, and Sandy is beginning to wander in the cold uplands of his finical conscience. It is a side of him you have never seen, but I have. Unless he is tied to duties which need every atom of his powers, he will begin to torment himself with questions."

"That is perhaps the explanation of the adventurer," was his reply. "He is happiest when he need not stop to think. For myself, I have thought too much about large matters, and I now think only of little things, like Olifa."

That night Luis returned, bringing with him Miguel de Campanillo, Don Alejandro, and one of the young Zarranigas. At supper, which was eaten on tables in the veranda under a grape trellis, for the night was warm, there was the equivalent of a Council of War. It was the eve of raising the standard. The troops at Pecos had been elaborately tampered with, and at a signal the majority which favoured the revolution would occupy the barracks and the depot, much as the Mines Police had done in the Gran Seco. But before that it was necessary to make certain that Lossberg would be detained beyond the mountains, and for this purpose Santa Ana must be occupied. This task was entrusted to Blenkiron, who with two thousand mounted troops was to move next morning. Once his job was completed, he was to join hands with the Campanillos at Pecos, who hoped to add their local levies to the regulars who would by that time have seized the place. The railway beyond Santa Ana was to be destroyed and the telegraph wires cut. Lossberg's blockhouses did not come within eighty miles of Santa Ana, not farther south than the frontier station of Gabones, but, in case he attempted to break through, the narrow pass south of Gabones was to be held in strength, and the road which accompanied the railway was to be comprehensively mined. Meantime the concentrations at

Veiro and Alcorta Junction were to be completed, and the dockyard at Cardanio was to be taken.

The talk at first was all of numbers and distances. Castor, who carried a multitude of figures in his head, satisfied himself that nothing had been omitted, and he was answered by Luis from a file of messages. Then, as the stars pricked out, and the wind from the hills began to temper the heat, the company relaxed. Soon the air was blue with cigarette smoke, and some, cramped by a long day in motor-cars on bad roads, strolled into the courtyard, where the scent of flowers from the great painted wine-vats was mingled with sharper smells of baked earth and miles of grasses, Presently Sandy went off with Blenkiron and Castor to verify some figures. Barbara and Archie walked with the young Zarraniga, and Janet found herself in a party of four with Campanillo, Luis, and Don Alejandro..

There was something in the tropic night which went to her head. Though she had no prospect beyond the courtyard shimmering under the stars, she seemed to be looking from a watch-tower over an immense country--steaming coast marshes, baked white cities, miles of waving green, cliffs red as blood falling into an angry blue sea, mountains that stretched cold fingers to the very courts of heaven.

For months she had been breathing that air which only belongs to lands which man has not yet mastered, and its sharpness and strangeness had entered her blood.

She was in love with space. For a moment she was a patriot of this huge child of a raw and half-made continent.

"Don Alejandro," she said, "do you remember the first night when we dined with you in the Olifa hotel? You told us about Olifa, how she had no problems--no discontents--because she was rich and secure. But you said that she had bartered her pride for prosperity."

Don Alejandro laughed. "True," he said. "I also said that she had no soul, but in saying that I lied. Olifa has always had a soul, but it has been sleeping. Now it looks as if Luis had awakened it."

"What puzzles me is why?" Janet said again. "You had no grievances--I mean the ordinary people. They had an orderly Government and light taxes and no conscription, and the reason was the golden eggs from the Gran Seco. What has made the ordinary Olifero angry with the golden goose?"

"He is not angry." It was Luis who answered. "He does not trouble. The ordinary man everywhere in the world only wishes to be left alone. Revolutions are not made by the many but by the few. Yet there are enough of the discontented, I think, to do our business."

"But why the discontent?"

"Because we have remembered our pride. We of the old houses have not been happy in a State which was no better than a big trading firm--with foreign brains to do the work which the Olifero should do himself."

"What work?"

"Governing us and defending us. Our army is mainly a force of skilled mercenaries. And our Government--well, the voice of the ministers was the voice of Olifa, but the wires which made them speak and act were pulled by the Commander-in-Chief, who is now having a final talk about Santa Ana with Lord Clanroyden and Senor Blenkiron. We have still an old-fashioned prejudice in favour of governing ourselves."

"How long have you been organising this discontent?"

"How long, Sandro?" Luis asked Gedd. "About three years come Christmas. The thing went fast, for the spirit was there waiting for it. Prosperity is not enough for us Oliferos. Our pride was outraged by our stout bourgeois ministers, who took their orders so obediently from another...But we organised in the dark, blindly, for we knew that we needed some notable piece of good fortune to succeed. Then we found the Yanqui Wilbur, and through him Senor Blenkiron. And at the end came Lord Clanroyden. It is a simple tale of the mercies of God. Let us hope that these mercies are not exhausted."

"But if Olifa was under the thumb of Mr Castor, won't it be the same even if we win? He is our commander, isn't he? Can you have a nationalist revolution led to victory by the man whose domination of your country stirred up your nationalism? You have made your chief opponent your leader--a foreigner too, a man with no country."

"Not so. He is one of us."

"But he is an Austrian."

"On his father's side he is Austrian. But his grand-mother was a Campanillo, a great-great-aunt of friend Miguel here."

"Does he know that? Does Sandy know it?" The girl was open-mouthed in amazement.

"He has always known it. I myself have known it this past year, and the fact was the basis of our plans...It is a long story. Lady Roylance, too long to tell at this hour of the night. As you justly say, he had no country. That is a fashionable folly among certain clever people in Europe. To-day he has found one...That was one reason why Lord Clanroyden and I planned to carry him off and maroon him up in the Patios de la Mariana--that he might find his country. There is no loosing the chains of blood. Once he got the bitter-sweet smell of our land into his nostrils and the clean air of our hills into his lungs, we believed that the cobwebs would, fall from his eyes and very old ancestral things come to life. That has happened, I think...More than that, of course. Between us--you, perhaps, especially--we have made him a human being. He will dream different dreams now, more wholesome dreams."

"What will you do with him? Can you fit him in--anything as big as he is?"

"We will of course make him our President," Don Alejandro interposed. "He is our great man, our show figure. We look to his brains to give us good government and to keep us prosperous."

"But can you harness him?" Janet persisted. "Can you turn Niagara into a useful stream which will irrigate gardens?"

"He will harness himself," said Luis, "for he is wise."

"And yet," she urged, "for years he has been hugging ambitions vast enough to set half the globe on fire--not silly whims, but closely-reasoned ambitions worked out to decimal fractions. He hated America--that was why Mr Blenkiron first decided to fight him. From what I remember of your table-talk, Don Alejandro, you also had no great love for America. Didn't you say that you regarded her patronage as an insult to your country? Why should you wish to put a spoke in the wheel of a man who has the same prejudice?"

"Because I am not a fool." Don Alejandro spoke with a brusqueness remarkable in one so suave. "Because I will not have Olifa made a pawn in a crazy game which means ruin. I do not love Yanquis, apart from Miss Dasent and Wilbur and Blenkiron and perhaps three others. But I want my country to be a rival to the United States in power and quality--not to be a blind mouse along with other blind mice in the hands of deracine genius."

Luis laughed. "You have stirred up the gentle Sandro, Lady Roylance, by touching his sorest spot. I do not think you quite understand the meaning of Spanish blood. You ought to, for the British are nearest to us of any race. We are realists, you know, very calculating and prosaic and close to the earth. But we must have our glamour too, our touch of poetry. We make good monarchists--and good republicans, if we can hit on the right president. Castor will suit us admirably, for he will give us poetry, which the dingy camarilla now in Olifa never did. He will have ideas and imagination and colour, and the air of magnificence. With him we will advance so fast that we shall astonish mankind. But his brilliance will not be dangerous, for all around him will be Spaniards, we Oliferos, very appreciative of poetry, but quite resolved to keep our feet on the ground. Like your Scotch, who will quote the poets and weep over them, and the next moment make hard bargains."

A lamp had been put on the table by a servant, and round it white moths were fluttering. As Janet looked at the faces revealed in its light, she received a sudden clear impression of something she had not met before--an ardour which was not ashamed to reveal itself because it was in turn based on a revelation. Don Alejandro with his neat small features and high cheek-bones--Luis, fair, golden brown of skin, with his glowing eyes--the young Zarraniga with his slender eyebrows and grave, rather sullen mouth--there was something innocently apostolic about them. They were in the grip of an idea. Their patriotism was an adventure, for their country was still to be made.

She smiled at the boy Miguel, and he smiled back at her. She had seen the same look, as a child, in the faces of young men starting for Flanders. Here was one to whom new horizons had suddenly appeared. Luis read her thoughts.

"We are going to make a country which will offer careers for youth," he said. "Our young men will no longer have to leave Olifa, or, if they stay at home, stagnate on their estates. Their future will be their country's future, for they will govern it, and thereby we shall have an advantage over that great people whom Sandro so much dislikes. We shall invent a new civilisation in this continent, which will be a bridge between the old world and the new."

Sandy's face suddenly appeared in the circle of light, and behind him Blenkiron and Castor. There was a hush, inevitable when serious talk is suddenly overheard. Blenkiron's jolly laugh broke it.

"Looks as if you folk had been picking on my poor little country," he said.

"No, indeed we haven't," said Janet. "We have only been deciding that Olifa is going to be neither a satellite nor an enemy of America, but an honourable rival."

"That's fine! They'll be mighty glad to hear it in Washington."

Archie and Barbara and the young Zarraniga presently joined them, and the group reasserted itself.

Janet sat very still, her eyes on two faces, Castor's and Sandy's. In the first she saw what she had not observed before, a certain kinship to the men with whom she had been talking. It was a subtle resemblance, a thing not of feature or manner, but of a look in the eyes, a tone in the voice. Castor belonged here after all. He could be captured by a dream...She had once said that he had a short-range imagination, and it was true. He was the ready slave of an idea...And he was young. He had never been anything else but young. She looked at Sandy, and suddenly felt that they were old--he and she and Archie and Blenkiron--even Barbara. They could not be happily rapt into a dream, because they dragged too great a weight of tradition behind them. They were children of an ancient world, and could not break from it...She no longer felt herself a sharer in their enterprise, but a benevolent stranger...And Sandy? The burden had left his shoulders and he looked a little bewildered. Perhaps a little homesick? These others had found a country. Might it not be that he was longing for his own?

She lay awake for some time after she went to bed, puzzling over this new direction of her thoughts. Might not something great come out of this venture, something of high moment for the world? And then she thought of a look she had caught on Barbara's face, and she fell asleep with her mind on a fresh trail...She was awakened at three o'clock by the sound of departing motor-cars. That would be Blenkiron on his way to Santa Ana. Her friends might have no spiritual share in the fervours of the rebellion, but they had a very practical part to play in it.

III

The succeeding days were full of bustle and excitement, for the train had been lit and the explosions were beginning. The road and railway to the Gran Seco were destroyed by Blenkiron with the completeness of a great engineer. The revolt of the troops at Pecos went like clockwork. Also the naval base at the Cardanio was easily surprised, and the Olifa navy, except for two destroyers in Olifa harbour and a few patrol boats along the coast, was quietly put out of action.

But on the first news of success there followed less comforting messages. The concentration at Veiro was going slowly. The ordinary Olifero was nervous, and hesitated to declare himself till he was certain which was the winning side. At Alcorta, too, the industrial centre, there was a danger of Communist trouble, which would immobilise forces which should have been marching north.

"Whoever said 'Il n'y a que le premier pas qui coute," Sandy told Janet, "was a fool. It is blindingly untrue of revolutions. The first step is easy. You can always start with a bang. It's the second step that is the devil. We haven't succeeded, or anything like it, for the country hasn't risen, and it isn't certain by a long chalk whether it is on our side. It is waiting to see how the cat jumps. We've got my Gran Seco troops, and about four thousand of the regulars. Add Luis's recruits and we may have a total of twelve thousand. Also we've temporarily bottled up Lossberg. But the Government has far more than three battalions in the city, as we believed. They've the better part of a division, and they've the pick of the artillery. Old Bianca is no fool, and they're fortifying like blazes. We haven't yet the strength for a coup, and it's a question whether we'll ever get it. It's all a question of moral. Unless we can bluff the Government into a surrender by cracking their moral, we can't force them...Oh yes, once they surrendered it would be smooth going. The cat would have jumped and the whole country would be behind us. But you can't run a revolution, as Luis thinks you can, on a handful of grandees."

"What is the worst that could happen?" Janet asked anxiously.

"That Lossberg should break out. That would blow us sky-high. He would stiffen the Government, and put the fear of death on the Oliferos. They're not going to stand up against the first-class regular army they have bought and paid for. Down on these plains Lossberg would drive us like sheep, and we should all go off to heaven in a whirl of aimless glory...Janet, I'm sick with anxiety. I've brought you and Archie into this mess, and it's the kind of mess I don't understand."

He looked far more haggard than she had ever seen him in the Gran Seco.

"You're tired to death," she said, and knew that she was talking nonsense.

"I'm not tired," he replied wearily, "but I'm out of my element. I hate war, except my own sort, and any moment this may become the hopeless ordinary kind that I detest and am no good at...You see, this isn't my country, and it isn't yours or Archie's. We can't feel about it like Luis and the others. I've done what I set out to do, and spiked Castor's guns. But the curse of life is that you can't stop short when you want, and I seem to have landed you all into the fire out of the frying-pan...The worst of it is, I can do nothing. There's no job for me here. El Obro is dead and buried, and I'm only a foreign filibuster mixed up in a show for which he has no heart."

Yet he seemed busy enough. He was splitting up his command, and had already parted with most of the white mounted troops. Only his Indians remained, under their white officers; it had always been decided to reserve them to the last, because of their effect on the nerves of the Olifa population. Of them he had now a little over a thousand. They were paraded one evening, tall, lean men on little wiry horses, who by now had almost the discipline of cavalry and were also trained marksmen. Janet and Barbara stood beside Sandy, as he watched them pass in the dusty sunlight.

"A fine lot," he said. "These fellows have something to fight for. Thank God, they'll never go back to the old slavery. If the worst happens, there'll be a new breed of bandit in the hills."

Behind them appeared Bobby Latimer. The aeroplanes had been left in the Gran Seco, all but one flight, which kept Charcillo in touch with Luis and Blenkiron. Bobby himself made long private patrols mostly in the direction of the city. That day, however, he had shaped his course for the north. As he saluted, Janet saw that his face was solemn.

"There's hell loose in the passes, sir," he said. "I have been up the road we came from the Gran Seco, and somebody's put Lossberg wise to it. There's a good-sized army on its way down--ten troops of horse, and about four thousand infantry, and an unholy lot of light batteries. They were in the Thunderer Valley three hours ago, and should make the place we called the Tennis Court before dark. To-morrow evening they'll be on the Vulpas."

A slow smile spread over Sandy's face.

"I spoke too soon," he said to Janet, "when I complained that I had nothing to do. I'm about to be the busiest man in this continent. Bobby, when you've fed and washed, you go off to Don Luis. I'll have a message written out for you. Janet, dear, run and tell Rogerson to be in my room in half an hour. I'll wait and have a word with Ackroyd."

"It's pretty serious, isn't it, sir?" Latimer asked.

"It's so serious that if that column shows its nose on the Vulpas we may chuck up the sponge. But thank God, it's still in the narrows. I've got a thousand men--three times what old Leonidas had--and I'm going to try the Thermopylae stunt."

He found his arm clutched by Barbara.

"Is it worth it?" she cried, and even in his absorption he noticed that her face had gone very pale. "Is it worth it?" she repeated. "We can't spare you...Nobody came back from Thermopylae."

Her eyes sobered him. He even flushed slightly. "I'm coming back all right, Miss Dasent, and so are my men. I might be spared, but we couldn't do without them. We're not brave like the Spartans. Our Thermopylae is going to be a more cunning affair than the old one."

IV

Half an hour later Blenkiron arrived by aeroplane. He had not been expected, and when he walked into the room where Sandy was giving his final instructions to Rogerson he was greeted with a shout of joy.

"Thank God!" Sandy cried. "You're the one man in the whole world I wanted. What providence has brought you here?"

"Why, I wanted to get some notion of the general proposition." His goggles had preserved his eyes from the fine dust which coated his face, so that he looked like a red owl with great staring eye-holes. "We've gotten our show pretty well advanced, and I could turn it over to Melville with an easy mind. There'll be no traffic south of Gabones for quite a while."

"You've closed that port?" Sandy demanded.

"Sure. Closed it and sealed it and put a heap of stones at the door. Things are going nicely at Pecos too. But I've heard nothing from the south, and I kind of hoped to be put wise about the general proposition--"

"Never mind the general proposition. There's a special one we've got to face. Lossberg is half through the passes."

"You don't say." Blenkiron's face ceased to be that of an owl, and contracted into something hard and vigilant. "Who brought word?"

"Bobby Latimer--less than an hour ago."

"Good boy! Say, this is getting central. We've certainly got to push him back."

"We certainly have. Do you realise that as yet we're nowhere near winning? Everything is still on a knife-edge. The country is waiting to see what happens before it makes up its mind--I mean the great bulk of the people, for Luis's lads are only a sprinkling. We've got to bluff the Government into surrender, and we haven't the foggiest chance if Lossberg shows his face in Olifa. If the passes are opened, we're absolutely done in. Have you got that?"

"Sure."

"Then in one hour's time we start out to stop that bolt-hole. You and I and a few others. Thank the Lord you've turned up, for this is more your kind of show than mine."

Blenkiron groaned, But his eyes were cheerful. "There's no rest for the weary, but it's mighty good for my figure. I've dropped thirty pounds since I went to the wars. Have you a map handy? I'd like to refresh my memory about that patch of country."

"We made a rough drawing coming down, and here's the result." Sandy spread out a big sheet on his desk. "The distances are more or less correct...See, here's Charcillo. It's about ten miles to the main stream of the Vulpas, and about twenty more to its head. Then there's the pass--four more till you look into the Thunderer."

Blenkiron put on his horn spectacles and with a grubby forefinger traced the route from the Gran Seco, by which they had come and by which their enemy was now following. From Pacheco the trail ran to the valley under the hills which the Indians called the river of the Blue Wolf. It did not turn up the tributary water of the Catalpas, by which Janet and Archie had escaped, but continued up the main stream, which presently bent due eastward. When the alley narrowed to a glen the road turned south and crossed the southern containing wall to the upper waters of an eastward-flowing river which the Indians called the Thunderer. Hitherto the road had been intricate and steep, but passable or men and animals and even for light motors, since it as reasonably broad and its floor was the shaly mountain ravel. But the glen of the Thunderer was ancient chaos, strewn with immense boulders and the debris of old landslides, and in the middle was a torrent which amply earned its Indian name. Yet there was a road for those who knew it, and the stream could be forded at one place, where it spread into a broad shallow pool on a shelf of rock before hurling itself into its customary abyss. That ford was six miles down from the pass which led from the Blue Wolf, and after it the road climbed among the cliffs and screes of the southern containing wall, till it reached a broad flat mantelpiece which could have accommodated an army corps.

This was the place to which Luis had given the name of the Tennis Court, and it was the key of the route. For from it a track led upward, a track which seemed to be driving aimlessly at a sheer precipice. But after running for a little southward in the moraine below the rocks, it turned a corner, and a cleft was revealed above it, a narrow saddle between two great fingers of mountain. The elevation was too low for ice, but the couloir, white with alkali, had the look of a long tongue of glacier running up to a snow saddle...The saddle itself was a fearsome place, for above the pad of gravel the cliffs beetled in a dreadful overhang. Rockfalls were frequent, and on the journey down Luis had insisted on the troops making the passage in small detachments, very slowly, and in complete silence...Beyond, the track corkscrewed down a long ravine until it reached the flowers and grass of the upper Vulpas.

Sandy put his finger on the Tennis Court.

"Bobby says they will be there this evening late, and they must camp. They will probably send on pickets to the Vulpas pass...but they won't move till dawn, and the main body won't be in the pass till well on in the forenoon. I don't think they can be allowed to come so far. I've elected the Tennis Court as the ne plus ultra. What do you think?"

Blenkiron had screwed his forehead into a thousand wrinkles as he pored over the map. He now took off his spectacles.

"I guess they'd better stay there," he said blandly. "I get your notion."

"You see, when Providence made this country, He put rather loosely together. We ought to be able to shake its bones a bit, and you understand that sort of thing better an I do."

"Maybe. How many men will you take?"

"I'll take Corbett--he knows the game. He was with Dick Hannay in Rhodesia. And I'll take a hundred troopers. Castor any moment may want every fighting man he can lay his hands on, and you don't need many in my kind of war. Only enough to put up a fight with Lossberg's pickets, if he has had the forethought to post them in the pass...Now for food. We must be in the saddle by eight-thirty."

An hour later in the big paddock behind the corrals Sandy reviewed his men. Except for white troop--sergeants, they were all Indian, selected men of the foothills rather than of the Tierra Caliente. He spoke to them in their own tongue. "On the work of this night," he said, "the freedom of your people depends. The enemy is in the passes, but he will not leave them. We will move the mountains so as to close the way. But first it is necessary to get there. When the moon rises, we must be where the Vulpas is only a little stream. I trust you as I would trust my brother by blood."

Janet watched them go, but Barbara did not appear. As they swung out to the open downs, it might have been observed that certain of the horsemen had their saddles encumbered with mysterious packages.

The first part of the road was across open downs on which the starlight showed the contours but not the colours One dark, opaque, velvet ridge succeeded another--a monotint world, though the sky above was so crowded with stars that part of it was like a phosphorescent belt, wherein there was more light than darkness. The going was good for at this season of the year; the coarse herbage of the savannah was short, and there were great spaces of grainy sand dotted with scrub scarcely taller than the grasses. It was like Sussex downland, since in most of the hollows there were no streams. Water was only crossed twice, till the troops found themselves on a long decline, and saw far below them the stars reflected in the pools of a river.

The Vulpas valley, before it runs out into the coastal plain, is some five miles broad and defined only by shallow ridges. But as the traveller goes eastward he finds that it narrows and deepens, until it makes a sharp-cut gulf among the foothills. The expedition struck the valley where it was on the edge of becoming a mountain-glen. Most of was Luis's own land, and the only dwellers in it his vaqueros, but they were lower down, and in all its topmost course the stream flowed through lonely upland pastures, which would be heavily stocked later when the midsummer drought had parched the lower lands.

The scent of the place, drawn out by night, came to sandy as a thing familiar. It was the scent of uplands all the world over, upspringing greenery and water and clean tone and shallow soil. The moon had not risen when they reached the meadows by the stream side, and rode eastward along a series of grassy steps, with the Vulpas water talking more loudly with every mile as it approached its mountain cradle. There was no sound, not even a wandering night-bird, except for the river and the beat of hoofs muffled in herbage and the occasional clash of buckle on rifle-butt. Even Blenkiron, short of sleep and rather weary, felt the intoxication of the hour and the place. Sandy beside him seemed to be happy, for just above his breath he was humming a tune.

Suddenly a wash of faint colour flooded the glen, a colour which deepened from a pale amber to the tint of ripe corn. The moon was beginning to climb the sky. Also the distances began to reveal themselves; the containing slopes, now the outflankers of the mountains, were clearly seen, and in front there was a dark loom into the mid-heavens. Sandy looked at his watch and nodded cheerfully to Blenkiron. They had made good time, and would be in the narrows of the pass before the moon was fairly up.

After another mile he halted his command. On each side the containing walls had drawn in till the valley was the half a mile wide, and the Vulpas had become a brawling torrent. The troops separated into detachments, and a patrol of five led the van at a distance of some hundred yards from the next group. Sandy and Blenkiron were in the second group. The course was now altered, and instead of keeping beside the stream they moved well up on the slopes to the right, which were of short grass and outcrops of rock set at an easy angle. They went more slowly now and more circumspectly, avoiding patches of shingle which might echo the sound of movement.

Quickly they climbed till they were in the throat of a ravine, a dark sword-cut where the moon gave only the faintest illumination. Far up its light could be seen golden on the cliffs and ridges, but they themselves rode in an umber dusk. The ravine twined and turned, so that the advance patrol was often completely lost to sight and hearing.

The word was passed back for extra care and quiet. "In two miles," Sandy whispered, "we shall be under the Saddle. There we leave the horses. There is a little amphitheatre where the Vulpas rises, with room enough to picket our beasts."

But at the next angle of the ravine Sandy reined in violently, so that Blenkiron cannoned into him. There was a shuffling and a drawing of breath as the men behind followed suit. Someone was coming towards them...Sandy and Blenkiron lowered their pistols when they saw that it was the advance patrol. The riders forced their horses alongside till their leader could speak into Sandy's ear.

"There are men below the rocks," he whispered. "Many men--more than we have with us. They are camped beside the water, and they are confident, for they have made fires."

Sandy looked at Blenkiron and laughed. "They have done the right thing," he said. "Flung an advanced body across the Saddle to guard the descent while the others cross. I should have thought of that...I've got into a bad habit of underrating old Lossberg."

He sat for a little whistling softly between his teeth. Then he began to think aloud, resuming between every sentence his low whistling. He seemed to be cheerful.

"Can we climb the rocks? That's the question...If half a dozen of us can get to the Saddle, the trick is done...We should be able to raise a few cragsmen...Corbett would know...Also we must make those beggars hands-up. How many did you say? Half as many again as ourselves...Well, it's plain we can't do that job with our present strength...Somebody has got to get back to Charcillo hell-for-leather and bring supports. It's force majeure we want. No needless heroics and no needless casualties...What do you say, John S.?"

"I guess that's correct. We'd better get our man off right away. If Lossberg has come this far, he'll aim to have the rest of his push over the Saddle pretty early in the morning."

Sandy tore a leaf from a pocket-book, and, using the cliff face as a desk, wrote a message. Then he folded it and looked round.

"Whom shall we send?" he asked Blenkiron. "Corbett would be able to find a man."

"Send me!" A voice spoke at his elbow, and it spoke in English. It could not be Corbett, for he was in charge of the rear, nor was it Corbett's voice. Sandy found himself taring at a slim figure in a trooper's kit, riding an animal which he recognised. It was Luis's favourite mare.

"Who are you?" he demanded. "Good God! It can't be! Barbara--Miss Dasent--"

There was not light enough to see the girl's face. It may have shown confusion and embarrassment, but there was nothing of the sort in her voice. The voice was cool, self-reliant, almost imperious.

"I'm glad I came, for now I can be useful. If I go, will save a fighting man. I know the road--I'm accustomed to know how to get back any road I come--and I'm better mounted than any of you." She patted her mare's neck.

"You had no business to come. You did very wrong." Sandy's voice was hard and angry. "Good God, this is place for a woman. I don't like you going back alone, but you're safer on the road than here...Give this note Colonel Ackroyd, and after that go straight to bed. You understand, Miss Dasent. These are my orders."

She took the note and sidled her mare round in the narrow place below the cliff.

"Send Corbett along as you pass," he added. "I needn't remind you that the business is urgent."

"You needn't," she said, and disappeared round the corner of rock.

The two men stared after her till the sound of her going was lost in the forward movement of the next detachment.

"I'd like to know," said Blenkiron reflectively, "just why Babs has gotten the bit in her teeth?"

"Can she do it? I mean, is it safe for her?" The tenseness in Sandy's voice was anxiety, not irritation.

"You bet she'll do it, and I don't worry about risks as long as she's on a horse. You can't puzzle her there."

Two hours later six men were perched high up among the rocks on the right side (what mountaineers would call the 'true left') of the couloir which led from the springs of Vulpas to the Saddle. Five of them were Indians, hunters from the Blue Wolf valley, and the sixth was Sandy. It had been a precarious and intricate journey. First they had made their way up the cliffs from the point where the advance troop had halted. This had been easy enough, for the angle was not too steep and there was plenty of scrub. But even there they had been dismayed by the rottenness of the rock. Boulders would come loose in their of hands, and be left delicately poised to descend in the first gale.

When the right elevation had been attained, the next step was to traverse the side of the amphitheatre where Lossberg's van was encamped. Here it was necessary to proceed with extreme caution. Happily that part of the ravine was in shadow, and no eyes from below could detect them, but it was essential that there should be no slipping or sending down of stones, lest the enemy should become alarmed and patrol the track that led to the Saddle. It was horribly difficult to move with speed and softness, and often it seemed impossible to move at all. For the whole hillside was loose, a gigantic scree with boulders instead of gravel, and each man of the six, beside his rifle, was encumbered with explosives. There were scaurs of crumbling earth, where the whole mountain seemed to shift at their tread. These were passed an inch at a time, holding hands, and in one place the last man swung into the void, while his foothold, with a sound like a great sigh, sunk into the depth beneath him. There were masses of friable rock, which had to be crossed with the body splayed out like a swimmer's. There was one point where, to circumvent the cliff, it became necessary to ascend a rotten chimney, and then traverse a ledge which looked like giving way any moment and precipitating he company on to the bivouac below. Sandy, to his disgust, found that he was the least efficient of the six. The Indians with their soft leather footgear had a certitude far beyond his, and more than once he had to depend on their aid. All the time the bivouac lights were plain eight hundred feet beneath them, and in the still night every sound of the camp rose as sharp and clear as if it were at their elbow.

But at last the circuit was finished, and the climbers topped to rest in an eyrie well in the jaws of the ravine self. There the rock was firmer, and they were able without much difficulty to traverse till they reached the track to the Saddle, a few hundred feet above the camp. Sandy's plan was to wait in the Saddle and lay his train of explosives, but not to fire the fuse till the signal had been given by Blenkiron that the reserves had arrived from Charcillo. This was to be two rifle shots in rapid succession, followed of a third at an interval of thirty seconds. The rockfall which he would engineer in the Saddle would bar escape in that direction. Blenkiron would hold the road down the Vulpas, and Lossberg's van would be summoned to surrender at the first light. He had also arranged that detachments of Indians should climb the rocks on both sides of the amphitheatre, so as to give point to Blenkiron's arguments. Now that he had made the traverse and had got between the enemy and the Saddle, the success of the enterprise seemed assured. There must be no mistake about the length of the time fuses. He and his men must be out of the couloir and round the angle of the mountain before the explosion started, for the couloir would be like the bore of a gun for the ammunition of the falling rocks. His cheerfulness was a little clouded by anxiety. He wished Blenkiron rather than himself had the job, for he was not an expert in explosives, but it would have been impossible to get Blenkiron's massive body across that treacherous hillside.

The couloir was very dark. The walls rose precipitately to frame a narrow ribbon of moonlit sky. Far in front this ribbon descended to a V-shaped gap, which was the Saddle.

All six moved with the utmost deliberation and care up the shaly track. There was no need to preach caution to the Indians. It was not the enemy beneath that made themes step as lightly as dancers; there was in their blood the fear of the hair-trigger, unstable rocks. Besides, there was no hurry. It would be two hours--perhaps three--before Blenkiron could give the signal. Already the day's heat had gone from the air, and the chill of night was spreading from the far snowfields. It would be very cold waiting in the Saddle.

They were within two hundred yards of the top, when Sandy found his arm gripped. The Indian behind him had halted, poised like a runner, and had raised his head to listen.

"There are men in the pass," he whispered.

Sandy strained his ears but could catch nothing. He shook his head, but the Indian nodded violently. "Men," he repeated. "White men!"

The thing seemed to Sandy incredible. Lossberg was cautious, no doubt, but he would not picket the Saddle, as well as send an advance guard beyond the pass, when he had the bulk of his forces still at the Tennis Court. Could the whole army be advancing by night? Impossible. In another hour the moon would be down, and this was no road for a night march, with horses and batteries.

His reflections may have made him careless, for he stumbled, and in his fall clutched at a boulder. It gave, rolled out of its gravel bed, and plunged down the track.

The others stepped aside to avoid it, and for a second there was a general slipping and clattering to break the stillness.

Suddenly the place was flooded with a blinding glare, which lit up every pebble and crinkle of rock. And then, almost in the same moment it seemed, there came a blast of machine-gun bullets fired a little too low. Sandy saw the white shale in front of him leap into living dust-devils.

He signalled his men to the cover of the right-hand rock, here there was a slight overhang. Again came a burst of machine-gun fire, and the searchlight maintained its unlinking stare.

Sandy thought hard and fast. There was a machine-gun post on the Saddle--a bold step considering its precarious environs. That post could not be large, probably not more than his own number. Before he could do his business and close the bolt-hole, that post must be destroyed. They must wait till the alarm had passed and then creep forward, trusting to the chance of surprise. Had they been seen? He hardly thought so, for at the first blink of the searchlight they had been on their faces. Probably it was only the nervousness of men perched by night in an eerie post.

But the nervousness did not seem to abate. There was no more shooting, but the glare continued for nearly an hour, while the six lay flat under the overhang, very cramped and cold. Sandy waited till the darkness had lasted another twenty minutes. They were not more than two hundred yards from the Saddle, and the intervening distance could surely be traversed so silently that it would be possible to rush the garrison.

But the last part of the couloir was the hardest, for it ceased to be a moraine of sand and boulders and came out on the loose and naked ribs of the hills. Keeping as far as possible in the shelter of the embracing walls, moving one at a time in line and flat on their faces like a stalker approaching a stag, they found it impossible to avoid making a noise, which to their ears echoed alarmingly in that funnel. Sandy was the chief offender. His belt seemed to catch on every jag, and his boots gritted harshly whenever they touched stone.

Again the searchlight leapt out...There could be no question this time. They were seen. As they wriggled for the tiniest cover, a blast of machine-gun bullets swept by, this time over their heads.

"We'll have to rush 'em," Sandy whispered hoarsely. He saw all his plans frustrated, and nothing left but a desperate venture...

And then to his amazement, he found himself dragged the his feet by two of the Indians and whirled into a violent rush. But it was not towards the enemy. "The mountains fall," he heard in the throaty Indian speech, and the next instant he was leaping down the couloir.

Of what happened next he had only a dim recollection. A roar like the Day of Judgment was in his ears. "Those damned machine guns," he remembered repeating to himself. "They've brought the rocks down..."

Then from behind came a blast of wind which swept them off their feet.

He seemed to drop for yards, and as he dropped he felt half the world rush past him. An eddy of wind seemed to plaster him against the rock wall...He found himself on soft earth clutching an Indian by the hair...A hand dragged him into a coign of rock and pressed him flat, while salvos of great shells seemed to be bursting all about him...He must have lost part of his senses, for he was conscious of shouting the name of his platoon sergeant at Loos, and also babbling childishly "Those damned machine guns."...There seemed to be a perpetual rain of avalanches and in one of them he was half buried. He remembered the feeling of suffocation, and then of free air, which he could scarcely breathe because of spasms of nausea...And then darkness came down on him, and he knew nothing till he woke on a shelf of rock far to the left of the couloir, with the early dawn bright around him.

He was a mass of bruises, and had a cut on his brow from which the blood trickled into his eyes, but he could find no broken bones. There were three Indians beside him, one with a smashed wrist and all intricately scarred and battered. When he asked about the other two, a hand was pointed downwards to where at the foot of the couloir a vast drift of rock and earth curled upwards like a sea-wave. It spread far into the little amphitheatre, and hid the springs of Vulpas. There was no sign of human life in the place.

Sandy's head was still too dazed to permit of thought. All he knew was that he was alive and very weary. He dropped back, and one of the Indians made a rest for him with the crook of his arm.

But presently his supporter moved. Sandy, hovering between sleep and waking, heard dimly a shouting which his companion answered. Then he felt himself being coaxed to rise. There were men below who were urging him to come down. He had never had vertigo in his life, but at the thought of descent his whole being revolted. A horror of space had come over him, and he knew that if he moved a step he would fall.

In the end he descended like a piece of baggage in the arms of Corbett and a squad of Indians. He looked up at the couloir, which at the top beetled in a new cliff. It would take a brigade laden with explosives a month to blast their way through that curtain of rock. At the sight his nausea returned. "Take me out of this hellish place," he groaned.

They carried him down the track, past the spot where the night before he had begun his escalade of the cliffs. The next thing he knew was that he was in a more open glen among grass, and that Blenkiron had him in his arms.

There was a fire burning and Blenkiron, when he had laid him down, put a cup to his lips. "Black coffee and brandy," he said. "That's the dope for you. I've been singing hallelujahs ever since I got word you were safe. I oughtn't to have trusted you with that much lentonite. You must have been mighty rash in touching it off."

"I never used it." Sandy struggled against his weakness; and his voice came with a croak. "There was a post on the Saddle with machine guns. They spotted us and loosed off...We crawled nearer and were going to rush them when they loosed off again...That last burst did the trick and brought down the mountain."

"Great Mike! And you?"

"I came down with the mountain. God knows how I got off with my life. Those Indians...gallant fellows...two of them gone...I'll tell you more later."

But presently the hot drink seemed to put life into him, and he sat up. "What happened here? Did Ackroyd get my message?"

"Sure. We managed fine. I guess we could have done without reinforcements, for your avalanche put the fear of death into the pick of Lossberg's Pioneers. They reckoned the Last Day was come and they ran down the gully like mad folk. We shepherded them quietly, and waited till Rogerson turned up, when they hands-upped like lambs. We've gotten a nice little bag--fourteen hundred and seventy-three, combatant soldiers, if you include your friend Mr Lariarty."

"Great Scott! Is he here? I want him brought to me at once. And Rogerson too."

The Lariarty who stood before him a quarter of an hour later was a different man from the dapper Gran Seco magnate. The sun and wind of the hills had put no colours into his pallid face, but that face was thin and peaked as if he had been through great bodily fatigue. The eyes, too, seemed less inhuman, for there was pain in their sombre depths. His clothes were little better than Sandy's and he had not shaved for days.

"Hullo, Timmy, you look as if you had been in the wars. Had breakfast?...Well, I don't know what you're doing here, but you're not a prisoner. I owe you a good turn for a certain evening in the Gran Seco. You can have a horse and go wherever you like. What's your fancy?"

The man seemed to have difficulty in finding words.

"Thank you, Arbuthnot," he said at last. "I should like to go to Olifa city."

"All right. But you'd better hurry, or there may be trouble in getting in. Have you plenty of money? Good Well, there's nothing to keep you here. Colonel Rogerson will see about a horse. Bon voyage!"

Lariarty seemed to be about to say something, but changed his mind. He cast one curious look at Sandy, bowed gravely and moved away.

Rogerson lingered.

"Miss Dasent specially asked me to give you a message, sir," he said. "It was that she would obey your order and go straight to bed."

V

There was no communication between Castor's headquarters and the Gran Seco. The revolt had captured early the main wireless station in Olifa, which was on the railway near Alcorta Junction; and since the installation at the Courts of the Morning had been destroyed, the only station the Gran Seco was under Lossberg's control, and, so as he was concerned, wholly useless. The telegraph and telephone lines followed the railway, and were now in a state of chaos. While Lossberg was cut off from his superiors, so were Peters and Escrick from their chief. They had their orders to worry the flanks of the enemy, and it would appear that they fulfilled them, for after the failure to break through the passes there was no activity for a week at the only outlet left to him, the railway to Santa Ana.

For the revolt it was a week of desperate busyness. Sandy and his hostages, captured at the Vulpas source, and he made ample use of them. They were, except for Lariarty, Olifa regulars, and mainly foreigners, but among them were representatives of well-known Olifa families. The latter, after Luis had had a private word with them, were given a courteous dismissal and returned to their homes. But the rank and file were used for a different purpose.

Throughout the country there were localities where the revolt was welcomed and the people were ready for its hazards. But in other districts the balance trembled. These were the richer parts, the great fruit-growing coastal regions, Alcorta, the environs of Cardanio, the corn and vine country towards Macheiro and Nimao and Jacinta. There both men and masters were prospering, and even those who favoured Luis preferred, if possible, to gamble on a certainty. It was to these districts that the prisoners went, in charge of Luis's young caballeros. Their internment was ostentatious, their progress a dignified parade. To the staring inhabitants this spectacle was proof that the dreaded professional army, which they respected as a costly luxury, was not invincible. Rumour spread and magnified the story of the affair in the passes, for, since the inland telegraph was in Castor's hands, rumour had no check. Lossberg, beaten in the Gran Seco, had made a desperate effort to break out, and had been utterly defeated. These prisoners were the advance-guard of a beaten army; the rest were shut in securely behind the bars of the Gran Seco hills.

The effect was instantaneous. The sitters dropped off the fence, and areas which had been lukewarm became the most fervent of all. Presently the sporadic fires met and mingled. Luis's small garrisons in districts which had been apathetic became speedily the nuclei of formidable risings. For week there was no rest for the staff, for at last the concentration could begin. There were desperate problems commissariat and transport to be solved, for most of the rolling stock of the railway was lying idle inside the defensive lines of Olifa city. But every hour brought the armed levies of the south and east nearer to the city, and Castor's poste de commandement was moved from Charcillo to Veiro, where Don Mario found the peaceful routine of his life changed to a succession of excitements which made younger by twenty years.

At the inception of the revolt Luis's first step had been to get possession of the telegraph. The lines were not destroyed, but the points of their debouchment from the city area were held, so that Olifa could not communicate beyond her area. At first the Government had been able to reach Cardanio through the foreign cables, but with the capture of the naval base that avenue was closed. But it was possible to send news into the city, and by various devices the fullest and most startling information about the advance and concentration was at the disposal of President and his Cabinet. There were other ways. Olifa depended a good deal on country produce, and market carts passed daily through its outposts. Agents of the revolt had thus a chance for circulating rumours, and Veiro by the same means was kept informed of most things the befell in the city.

The reports varied. At the start the Government had been confident. The revolt was only a local and filibustering business, for there could be no fuel for any fire. The State was prosperous, taxation was not oppressive, for years there had been no conscription...Then came a shade of anxiety, when it was discovered that Lossberg was silent. His last reports had been excellent, but he was singularly remiss in sending more. It was impossible to stir him up, for they had no wireless at their disposal, the long-distance telephone seemed to have broken down, and their sheaves of telegrams were unanswered...Worse news followed. The Gran Seco railway had been cut by the rebels, there was trouble at Pecos, there was even a wild story that Lossberg had found an outlet in the eastern passes, but that his van had been cut to pieces and that bolt-hole stopped...Then came still wilder tales, of risings in the south, of Alcorta and Cardanio gone over to the enemy, of a great rebel force moving upon the city. The hopes of the Government were still in Lossberg. He and his expert army must soon arrive to save the State. In his last report he had told them that the Gran Seco was conquered and the guerrilleros driven to the mountains. He must be even now on tis way down the railway, brushing aside the rebel screen.

What if the line were cut and the road damaged! He had his skilled engineers, and his mechanised battalions, his cavalry and his tanks, his unbeatable infantry. As they looked from the Parliament House over the wide levels to the north they hourly expected to see the dust-cloud which would herald their deliverer.

One evening there was a council of war at Veiro. It took place in Don Mario's dining-room, where the big table had become a council-board and maps covered the ancestral Murillo. Sandy had come from the south, Blenkiron from Santa Ana, where he had left Melville in command, while Luis and Castor had returned from the concentration at Alcorta Junction, where they had received reports from 2 local leaders. Archie, who with Bobby Latimer was responsible for the air reconnaissance, had just arrived from a long flight north of Santa Ana. He had dire forebodings about the petrol supply.

"There's a lamentable lack of juice in this land," he complained. "We've tapped all the supplies and are rationing jealously, but we're well within sight of a shortage. There was a big fire at Cardanio which wasted a lot, and of course there's none coming in at the ports just now. The Government seem to have skinned the country to provision Lossberg. I can't think how Peters is getting on. He must be very near his last gallon, unless he has raided some of Lossberg's stores, and even Lossberg can't go on for ever. It's about time that we were bringing things to a head."

Luis was optimistic. "We are very near the end," he said. "The people have risen at last. His Excellency will tell you what spirit we found to-day. Even the doubters are now convinced, and have become enthusiasts. Senor Sandy, your little affair in the passes has proved the conclusive argument. Now the Oliferos have no fear of Lossberg."

Sandy did not answer. For the past week he had been his old vigorous self, but now his vitality seemed to have ebbed again. He looked tired and preoccupied, and his eyes were always searching Castor's face.

It was the latter who spoke. "Luis is right," he said. "Things are very near a head, but this is the real moment of crisis. We cannot take the city of Olifa by force. We have no siege artillery, and General Bianca has made the defences very strong. The defence, I need not remind you, is in a privileged position with modern weapons. The policy of the Government is simple. They have sufficient troops to police the city and defend their lines against anything can bring. They are waiting for Lossberg, and if Lossberg comes we are beaten."

"I do not agree," Luis interposed. "Lossberg cannot conquer a people in arms."

"I wonder," Sandy spoke at last. "You have a great levy of stout fellows, gallant fellows, but not one in ten knows anything about the business. We are infernally short of machine guns, and we are not too well armed. There's a variety of rifles in our ranks which would stock a museum, and our training is rudimentary. We are mostly third-line troops, and we have far too small a stiffening of first-line stuff. I don't want to croak, but Lossberg could go through us like a knife through blotting-paper. Our only hope is that he won't have the chance."

"Well, he is safely bottled up, isn't he?"

"For the present. But for how long? Peters and Escrick may keep him quiet for the moment, but he is bound to pull himself together and make for Santa Ana. And he is bound to succeed. Therefore--" He paused.

"Therefore?" Luis repeated.

"We must bring things to a head--now. The Government must surrender before he relieves them. How are we going to put on the screw? We are back at the old problem--of cracking their moral...It's probably getting brittle. Bianca is a stiff old warrior, but the others are soft, sedentary fellows. They must be pretty jumpy by tow. Is there anything fresh from Hamilton?"

"We had a report this morning," Castor answered. "Undoubtedly their Excellencies are nervous. Also their police. The lower classes are on our side, and there is a perpetual rounding-up of suspects, which makes bad feeling. I am little anxious about the safety of our envoy."

"So am I," said Sandy. "It was a wild escapade, and don't believe we should have allowed it. He's too good a man to lose. How on earth did he get through the lines, and how on earth is he concealing himself?"

Archie laughed. "I'm not worrying about that. He makes the best imitation you ever saw of a sulky drunken Olifero peasant, and he has picked up enough of the lingo to ask for what he wants and see that he gets it. Geordie is a very wise citizen. But I do worry about one thing. He has gone back to his old waterside and backstairs haunts, and what is to prevent him from being done in by one of the Bodyguard ruffians? They might recognise him, and for all we know some of them are in Olifa. More by token, has he seen Lariarty in the city?"

"He doesn't mention him."

"I would like to know where that sportsman has gone. You were too easy with him, Sandy. Lariarty is the kind of lad I would always keep under lock and key."

"May be. I don't know...But to get back to the main question--how can we put the screw on their Excellencies? I've been away for a week. What is the exact position on the Santa Ana railway?"

Blenkiron put his spectacles on his nose and spread out a map and certain papers. He expounded the strength in Santa Ana and the reserves at Pecos--the exact destruction done to the railway--the present position of his posts south of Gabones, and the results of Bobby Latimer's air reconnaissance beyond that point. To the best of his belief, he said, Lossberg was being so extensively worried in the Gran Seco that he was not able yet to look southward. He admitted that the look would come, but he was positive that any advance would be a slow business. He drew a sketch of several parts of the route, which he said could be held for days by a small force against any army.

"That's good as far as it goes," Sandy said. "We have probably a week at least in which to draw our people in upon Olifa and rattle the Government. A week--but not more."

An orderly summoned Blenkiron to the telephone. "Darn those boys," he grumbled, "they're so mighty keen they always want to be passing the time of day. I'm going to call them down."

When he had gone, Luis spoke. He outlined the character of the various ministers from the President downwards. He was not complimentary, for he had the bitterness of the old regime towards the mushroom commercialism of Olifa, and especially towards the renegades of his own class. But he was not unfair. He admitted quality--a coarse toughness of fibre--the obstinacy of men who had been successful beyond their dreams--above all shrewdness. "It is on this last trait," he said, "that we must bank. They will be a little awed by the Gobernador, whom they have always looked upon as a wizard. They will be impressed by the rising of the country, for they know that it is a difficult business to govern the unwilling. We have arguments, perhaps, to convince them, always provided they do not get back Lossberg and his army in time. They are not soldiers and will be afraid of us, but, being civilians, they will also exaggerate the power of Lossberg's professionals, and may be foolish enough to defy us...A little while ago I spoke too confidently. We are still on the razor's edge."

Blenkiron re-entered the room, and without a word made for the table where lay the papers from which he had given his exposition. He picked up his sketch of the section of the Gran Seco railway, where he had located various points A, B, C, and D. Then, almost violently, he swung Sandy round so that he could see it.

"Lossberg has fooled me good and sure," he said in a voice which he tried to keep level. "It was Melville talking. There's been hell loose up the line. Our post at A was destroyed two hours ago...Yes, cavalry and armoured cars and light field batteries...There's a howling desolation on the railway between A and B, but Melville reckons that B is going to fall before night. He proposes to make a great effort at C and is pushing everything up. But God knows what strength Lossberg is in, and, though it's a darned bad fighting country, numbers are bound to tell. D isn't much in the way of a reserve position. It's my solemn opinion that, if C goes, in two days Lossberg will be in Santa Ana."

There was a moment of complete silence. Then Sandy observed casually, "I said we had a week. It appears we have only two days." Every man in the room knew that one in his voice. Sandy could be explosive and vehement when things went well, but in a crisis he often seemed to be in detached spectator from another planet.

Castor's face did not alter, except for a slight knitting of the brows. Blenkiron was on his feet. "I'd better get back to Santa Ana," he said.

"I don't think so," Sandy drawled, and looked at Castor. "I suggest, sir, that I go instead. I will take my Indians, every man of them. There's going to be a pretty rough-and-tumble on the railway, and that suits me better than Blenkiron. I'll push off at once, by car, and Rogerson can bring on the troops. I hope to be able to send you good news within forty-eight hours. If not--well, the game's with you. I shall be out of it."

"The game is with me," said Castor. "I propose tomorrow to have a talk with the Excelentisimo and his Cabinet."

"No, no," Sandy exclaimed. "I beg your pardon, sir, but not you. You are too valuable. We must send ambassadors. You would be a hostage."

Castor allowed his head to sink on his breast.

"I must go," he said after a pause. "The responsibility is mine. We are playing for high stakes, and I should cast the dice."

"And be a loser from the start! You are our reserve, sir. You must stay here in Veiro, while your plenipotentiaries speak in your name. It is not a question of taking risks. We know you're a glutton for them. It is a question of playing the right hand. Send Luis and Blenkiron. The one can speak for the republic of Olifa and the other can talk business. And meantime get your levies up to the edge of the Olifa lines. The Government have got to yield before Lossberg reaches Santa Ana. If he ever gets there, he must find that the whole country is in our hands. If we head him back, I'll send you word, and that will be a clinching argument. But even if we're scuppered, you may still win...Let 'em know you're coming. No, no! No flag of truce business. Get Archie to fly you to the Plaza de Toros. They'll be hungry to see you. We're gambling on the outer edge of sanity, and the wildest course is the safest. You must impress them--it's their nerves we're gunning for. Good-bye, sir. Good-bye, all of you. If I see Veiro again, we'll be smoking the peace-pipe."

VI

A little before noon Archie brought his plane to a smooth landing in the great dusty amphitheatre which had been the bull-ring of an older Olifa, and was now sports ground and polo ground. The journey had been uneventful, and they had crossed the lines saluted only by a few rifle shots. It appeared that they were not unexpected. The place was empty, but there were pickets at the different entrances. As the travellers climbed out of the plane a squad of soldiers came forward at the double, and they completed their disembarkation in the presence of a substantial military guard. The officer in charge saluted.

"We have come to keep an appointment with their Excellencies," said Luis.

"Their Excellencies await you," was the reply. A big closed car had drawn up beside them, and he motioned them to enter. A minute later they were moving swiftly from the Plaza into the road which led to the Ciudad Nueva. Archie pulled up the blind of the back window and laughed.

"They've got the needle, for they are putting the plane out of action. They must think we're devils of fellows. Well, our boats are burned right enough."

The Avenida de la Paz slept in the noonday sun. On its broad sidewalk there were few of the well-dressed Oliferos whom Archie had seen on his first visit, but many of the riff-raff from the old city. There seemed to be little life in the splendid offices. The headquarters of the Gran Seco administration had no longer sentries at its doors.

Olifa had lost its comfortable bustle and its confidence, and had acquired the air of a city in a crisis. At the street corners there were not police, but soldiers, and as the car swung up the hill towards the great copper dome of the Parliament House, there were frequent halts and the interchange of passwords. Archie reported that a car was following them containing an armed guard. "I feel as if I were in Black Maria," he said. "Have either of you fellows ever been in quod before?"

Their reception in the Grand Court was one of high ceremony. The sentries presented arms at the gate, and they were met at the main door by an aide-de-camp. There were soldiers everywhere, in the great entrance-hall, and at every turn of the broad marble staircase. First they were taken to an ante-room, where on a table light refreshments were laid out. "The senores may be thirsty after their flight," said the aide-de-camp, as he bowed and left them.

"Very handsome," Archie observed.

"Very politic," said Luis. "The Cabinet believe that we have come to treat. No doubt they have their terms ready. It will be a shock to them to learn that our minimum demand is complete surrender."

Blenkiron's eyes had been slowly taking in the magnificence of his surroundings. "We've gotten into the wrong atmosphere," he explained. "The folks that live in a shack like this are bound to think that nothing can go wrong with them. It'll stiffen their backs, for it looks as if it were built for eternity. We should have aimed to shift them somewhere where they could get a sight of Sandy's braves or Melville's roughnecks. You can't scare kings sitting in their palace."

"Dwellers in palaces," said Luis oracularly, "have weaker nerves than dwellers in tents."

The aide-de-camp appeared again. "Their Excellencies are ready to receive you," he announced, and, holding himself very stiff and straight, he opened a door which led to the Council Chamber. It was a vast room, copied, like all the Olifa buildings, from an Old World model--in this case from a room in a Venetian palazzo. The ceiling was painted with nymphs and goddesses, and statues stood in the alcoves of the panelled marble walls. The light was dim, for the sun shutters were partially closed. At a table near the window sat, not the full Cabinet which Archie had expected, but five men. One was the heavy bull-necked President, with on each side of him Vicente Sanfuentes, the Minister of external Affairs, and Aribia, the Minister of Finance. Next to Aribia was General Bianca, and on the Foreign Minister's other side a figure which made Archie stare, for it was Romanes, whom he had last seen in the Tronos del Rey. The President and his colleagues were in their customary black frock-coats and stiff linen, the old General was in uniform, but the Conquistador wore a suit of white drill. There was much bowing, and the three took their seats opposite the five, like witnesses before an official inquiry. A big silver box of cigars stood before the President, which he pushed towards Blenkiron, who shook his head. Archie alone helped himself; he wanted something to occupy his hands.

The five showed no sign of embarrassment or strain. The President had still his air of massive composure, though the pouches under his eyes seemed a little heavier. The two ministers, Sanfuentes with his round shrewd face and Aribia with his well-trimmed beard, looked as if they were at an ordinary board meeting. The old General's thin knotted fingers drummed on the table, but that had always been his habit. Romanes's neat light-cavalry figure seemed more dapper than ever in its cool clothing, and his lean sallow face was as expressionless as the marble at his back.

"Don Luis de Marzaniga we know well," said the President, "and we have the honour of Senor Roylance's acquaintance. You, sir," and he looked towards Blenkiron "I take to be the late Vice-President of the Gran Seco Administration."

Blenkiron did his best to bow. He seemed to find amusement in the scene before him, for his face wore a broad grin.

"You have come, gentlemen," the President continued "to ask for terms."

"No, Excellency," said Luis, "we have come to offer them."

The President frowned slightly, and General Bianca threw up his head.

"It is a trifling change of a word," Luis continued, "but it is well to understand each other clearly from the start. We desire to make peace--on the basis of facts. The republic of Olifa is in our hands, and therefore we are in a position to dictate the terms of peace."

The General laughed angrily. He had a long face with finely cut features and very large black eyes. His skin was like ancient yellow parchment. That day he wore all his many orders, and they trembled as he squared his old shoulders.

"You are insolent," he said, "insolent dreamers. You have been driven out of the Gran Seco, and as a last gambler's throw you have stirred up trouble in Olifa. Pouf! It signifies nothing. Our army, having finished with the Gran Seco, will presently arrive, and where will your rabble be then?"

His voice was becoming shrill and he was embarking on a fierce tirade when the President checked him. "Have patience, General," he said. "Let the senores state their case. We can be patient, for we are confident!"

Luis laid a map on the table. "General Lossberg is not happy in the Gran Seco," he said. "We have still an army there--an army in being, and it is occupying all his attention. I will be candid with your Excellencies. Your General holds the Gran Seco city and the Mines and much of the country, but for the rest we are masters. He is immobilised, for he cannot come to your aid. Already he has tried it. Sixteen days ago he attempted to break out through the passes of the south-east, which he had just discovered. He was beaten back, the door is closed, and some of his troops are our prisoners. As for the railway to Santa Ana, that route has been destroyed, and, as you know well, it is a route which is easily blocked. I do not think that he can come to you by that way."

"These are lies," the General shouted. "We have the most expert army of its size on the globe. What can a handful of bandits and guerrilleros do against it? General Lossberg can burst his way through your barrier whenever he pleases. He has the latest guns and tanks--"

"I know, I know," said Luis soothingly. "But it is too expert an army. It cannot compete with our rude simple ways."

Aribia laid a hand on the General's arm. "You have a map, Senor de Marzaniga? You have perhaps something to say about Olifa."

Luis had much to say. He was dealing with men who knew their own country well, and he spoke as to experts. He took his hearers up and down the land, and explained how far the revolution had prospered in each district. He expounded in detail the revolt of the regular battalions, at Santa Ana, at Pecos, at Alcorta and Cardanio, and what accession of strength they represented. He showed them the position of each railway and railway junction. He gave the names of leaders, and at some of these names the ministers started. He was constantly interrupted with questions, which he patiently answered. He had an air of extreme candour, the air of a man who has nothing to conceal, and who is anxious to give the last tittle of information in his power...Then he expounded the nature of the different concentrations, and the strategy of the advance on the city. "I take you into our innermost confidence," he said. "That is proof in itself that we believe we are victorious. If we had any doubt, we should not be disclosing our plans."

The exposition lasted till two o'clock, when there was an adjournment for luncheon. They did not lunch together, for the three ambassadors ate in the ante-room to which they had been taken on their arrival. They talked little at the meal, for a heavy sense of futility had come upon all the three. "You can't make that bunch understand facts," said Blenkiron. "That is what comes of living coddled up in this palace. They're still hanging on to Lossberg's coat-tails."

Luis rather wearily agreed. "If Lossberg gets to Santa Ana, and their Excellencies get wind of it in time, our game is up. We won't be having meals like this. It will be the Old Prison for us, and a very nasty corner of it, and the Gobernador will have to do without our services. I pray God that Sandy can hold the line a little longer."

Luncheon was followed by a short siesta, and they did not meet again till after four o'clock. The glare of the sun was no longer on the windows, and the green shutters were clamped back, so that the great chamber swam in the mellow light of afternoon. To Archie's surprise the ministers were notably less rigid than in the morning. The President took the lead in the conversation. He did not deny Luis's statements, as Aribia had done, but asked for some means of confirmation.

"We offer you whatever you ask," Luis answered. "This morning our nearest concentration was at Alcorta Junction within ten miles of this city. Appoint your emissaries, Excellency, men whose word you trust. They can go there under a flag of truce, and there they will find Manuel Martinez, and see for themselves. Or is there any other whose word you will take? The telephone service is working well."

"Is there no loyalist?" the President began.

"I am afraid that what you call a loyalist may be hard to find. We have been too successful, you see. But...there is Don Mario at Veiro--your cousin, Senor," and he bowed to Sanfuentes. "Don Mario is no politician, and he has never in his life been able to lie. I will give you the password, so that you can telephone to him at Veiro. He knows little of the campaign, but he has eyes in his head, and he will tell you of the forces moving from the east and south."

"That is good sense," said the minister, and he left the room. He returned after an absence of half an hour. "I have spoken to Don Mario," he said shortly. "He is an old man and an innocent." But it was clear that he had had news which discomposed him.

To Archie the situation was like some preposterous stage play in a dream. He had suddenly an overpowering sense of detachment, so that he seemed to look at the scene before him as at a picture small and far away down an inverted telescope...What on earth was he doing helping to deliver an ultimatum in a theatrical chamber in a hot white city many thousands of miles from home?...He sat a little away from the table, and saw only the back of Luis's head and half Blenkiron's profile, but he had the others in full view. The paradox of the scene nearly made him laugh out loud. He was a revolutionary, trying to upset a Government to which his own had accredited a Minister. These solemn five, what did he know about them? They were creatures of a world infinitely remote from his. He studied the President's large swarthy face, heavy with the gravity of one accustomed to be obeyed and flattered--stupid and dull, but not without traces of quality. In Sanfuentes he saw the family likeness to Don Mario, as far as an overfed sedentary man can resemble a hard-bitten country squire. He looked a little cunning and self-indulgent, but there was humour somewhere. Aribia was the ordinary business man, with cold shrewd eyes, but he had a pleasant smile...Romanes! It was on him that his eyes chiefly rested. A wash of sunlight seemed to bring every feature into startling prominence. Archie saw the leanness of his head, the odd skull beneath the smooth hair, the curious hollows in his brow, the skin opaque as if no blood ran beneath it. This was Castor's doing; the man had once been Castor's creature, and Castor was their leader!...For a moment he felt some sympathy with the perplexed Cabinet of Olifa.

It was Castor's name which roused Archie to attention. Romanes spoke in his toneless voice for almost the first time. "It would have been well if the Gobernador had accompanied these gentlemen. No doubt they have full power to treat, but it would have been more satisfactory to meet the Commander-in-Chief himself."

"The Commander-in-Chief cannot leave his command," was Luis's answer.

"Naturally. Still...there have been rumours, you know. We do not know if he is indeed in command. We do not know if he is in Olifa at all."

"You can be assured that he is. He is at Veiro."

Archie thought that he saw a flicker of sharp intelligence in Romanes's eyes, but the next second it was gone.

"I think their Excellencies would have welcomed a meeting. For after all, whatever is the destiny of this country, Senor Castor must mean much to it."

"He owes us an explanation," the President growled. "He was our trusted colleague. Whatever he advised was done. Senor Sanfuentes will bear me witness when I say that he had a large share in the external policy of this State. The Administration of the Gran Seco was granted to him as if it was his private domain...Suddenly, with no warning, he becomes our enemy. He must be mad."

"He is not mad. Excellency, but it is permissible for a man to change his mind. The Gobernador has to-day a policy for the Gran Seco and for Olifa itself which conflicts with that of your Excellency. Some of us, independently of the Gobernador, had the same notions. We have been endeavouring for months to persuade you and your colleagues that our views must be accepted. That is why we are here today--to apply, if your

Excellency will permit the metaphor, the last little weight to the inclining balance."

After that the five consulted in private, and it was dark before Aribia returned with an announcement.

"We have decided to send representatives to Alcorta Junction to meet Senor Martinez and see for themselves. Do not be offended, please, for, as you yourself have admitted, confirmation is desirable. Will you arrange with Martinez for the reception of our envoys? The party will consist of two of General Bianca's staff-officers and Senor Romanes. They leave to-morrow at daybreak."

So Luis had a busy hour on the telephone and then joined his two companions at dinner. They spent a dismal evening, before they sought their beds in the cheerless state apartments. "This is going to be worse than a League of Nations meeting at Geneva," Blenkiron moaned. "I hoped they'd treat the thing as a business proposition, and I was ready to explain to them just how the Gran Seco should be run, and how it is going to be mighty advantageous to Olifa. They've all got fat bank accounts, and could understand my arguments. But we never got near business. A blind kitten could see that they're not going to let go till they're choked off. There's more sand than I reckoned in that big President."

"They are waiting on Lossberg," said Luis. "They will not give up hope till they are compelled. How in the name of God can we compel them, unless Sandy brings off some colossal stroke?--and that is as likely as snow in summer. Jesucristo! At this moment he is perhaps making a desperate stand in the skirts of Santa Ana!"

The conference was resumed next morning with the half-closed sun shutters again making a green twilight. It was now Blenkiron's turn. Pending the arrival of the envoys from Alcorta Junction, he was permitted to state the views of the Gobernador on the future of the Gran Seco. The discussion was long, and necessitated many calculations, in which Aribia shared. The profits of the State of Olifa from the business need not decline; nay, there was every chance of their increasing, if the organisation were put upon more stable and permanent lines. The arrangements about Indian labour must of course be altered--in any case they would have presently altered themselves. The extreme high-pressure production must be given up; also the Gran Seco must be put outside Olifa politics, except for its scale of contribution to the Olifa exchequer. It must be regarded as a special territory, to be governed under a special charter.

The discussion was amicable. The ministers were all shareholders in the company, and, as an academic proposition, were prepared to consider it on business lines. In the afternoon the envoys returned, and, when after the long midday siesta the conference reassembled, Archie tried hopelessly to detect some change in the air of the ministers. He was disappointed. Romanes for some reason was absent, but the other four seemed in good spirits. Their placidity was unshaken. The President himself touched on the matter.

"Your veracity has been vindicated, Senor de Marzaniga," and he bowed politely, "but not, I fear, your judgment. You have undoubtedly recruited many men, but they are not an army. Our officers report that it is no better than a rabble, ill-armed, ill-disciplined, and led by amateurs."

"It is the people of Olifa," said Luis hotly. "And you have seen only the spear-head--one of the spear-heads. There is a weighty shaft behind it." He spoke of the extent and variousness of the rising...Every class was in it, every condition of life...Among its leaders were representatives of every family that had been great in Olifa's history...Also the chiefs of every calling, the ranchers, the fruit-growers, the wine-growers, the industrial magnates of Alcorta. He was a little carried out of himself, and it was clear that his eloquence had some effect on his hearers.

"We have all Olifa with us," he concluded, "all Olifa that is worthy of the name."

The President laughed, but his laughter did not seem to come easily. "I know my countrymen, Senor de Marzaniga," he said. "They have returned for an hour to the traditional habits which we hoped they had forgotten for ever. But they will not fight--they cannot fight--they have nothing to fight for. The ranches of Senor Martinez could not be more prosperous under a different regime. Ramirez has no complaints from his fruit farms. The Zarranigas breed their fine horses without Government requisitions, unlike the old days. These men are not fools. Presently they will learn wisdom."

"Or be taught it," put in old General Bianca.

Luis had recovered his balance. "There is one thing you forget, Excellency. We are patriots and love our country. Olifa is prosperous, no doubt--but it has no soul. You and your colleagues have made it the appanage of a commercial corporation. We want to be a nation again."

Sanfuentes spoke impatiently. "A nation! What would you have? When your crazy war broke out we were on the eve of taking the leadership of this continent. We would have made Latin America a power in the world."

"I guess I know all about that, sir," said Blenkiron, "You were going to make bad trouble in this continent, but it wasn't for the sake of Olifa. The Gobernador was using you as a pawn in his own game. Well, Mr Castor has thought better of it, and I can't see why in thunder you want to go on alone. Our slogan is Olifa all the time and for its own sake. I advise you gentlemen to listen to reason, for you can't fight against the whole people."

"The whole people," said Aribia sweetly. "But that is precisely the point on which you have failed to convince us."

Presently lamps were brought, and the discussion wandered into a morass of futility. The ministers were waiting, not very confidently perhaps, a little shaken, but determined still to wait. It was the habit of their race, for the Oliferos are not a hasty breed. With a sinking of the heart Archie realised that there would be another day of indecision, while Sandy might be struggling hard to win an extra hour for their inconclusive diplomacy. Any moment the crash might come.

It came about six o'clock when General Bianca was summoned by an aide-de-camp to the telephone. He returned in five minutes, almost at a run.

"News," he cried, "glorious news! Lossberg is in Pecos. I have spoken to his Chief of Staff."

The ministers were on their feet, and the exuberance of their relief showed the depth of their anxiety. They clamoured for details, but the General could give them little.

"I spoke to Olivarez...I recognised his voice at once...He gave his name...What did he say? Only that he was in Pecos, and was coming here without delay...He is evidently pressed--Lossberg's orders no doubt...Where he is, the General must be, and the Chief of Staff is naturally sent on in advance...We have conquered, my brothers. Tomorrow the city will be relieved, and the rebels scattered to the points of the compass...It is the moment for toasts, for much talking has made my throat dry."

The ministers did not forget their manners in their hour of triumph. The three envoys were not asked to witness the toast-drinking, but were conducted ceremoniously to another apartment, where they too were supplied with sweet champagne. Only Archie tasted it, for the two others sat back in their chairs with the faces of broken men. It was at least an hour before they were ready to speak of fresh plans--futile plans, it seemed, for they must now regard themselves as prisoners. As for Archie, he still felt himself living in a crazy world of illusion, but he was so tired by the strain of the day that he fell asleep.

About nine o'clock an aide-de-camp appeared.

"General Olivarez is arriving," he said, and his air was noticeably less civil. "Your presence is required in the Council Chamber."

Once more the three envoys seated themselves at the table. It was obvious that the ministers had dined and dined well. Even Bianca's parchment skin had a colour. Romanes was still absent.

The door opened and General Olivarez was announced. Two men entered. One to Archie's amazement was Alejandro Gedd, a figure like a scarecrow, dusty, dishevelled, grey with fatigue, his ancient dapperness utterly gone. The other was a slight man in the service uniform of Olifa, with a long olive-tinted face, a fleshy nose, and grizzled hair cut en brosse. He too seemed the worse for wear, and he had his left arm in a sling.

It was Gedd who spoke.

"Your Excellencies," he said, "I have been sent to bring General Olivarez to your presence. This morning General Lossberg was decisively defeated in the passes north of Santa Ana. His main army has fallen back, and his advance forces were cut off and taken prisoner. Of this advance General Olivarez was in command. I was ordered by Lord Clanroyden to bring him to you that you might learn from his own lips the position of affairs."

The ministers were silent. Then old Bianca found his voice.

"Is that true, sir?" he rapped out.

"It is unfortunately true." Olivarez spoke in a voice in which weariness left no room for bitterness. "Of the rest of General Lossberg's army I cannot speak. I myself and over nine thousand of my men are prisoners in the enemy's hands."

The President behaved well, for he showed no emotion of any kind. His face was like a stone, and his voice level and toneless. He turned to Luis and bowed.

"We accept your terms, Senor," he said. "General Bianca will issue the necessary orders to the city defence force."

VII

The long-drawn fight on the Santa Ana railway was begun in the Gran Seco itself by Peters and Escrick. There was no communication between them and Castor by wireless of telegraph, but there might have been a telepathic under standing, so exactly did they time their operations to meet the crisis in the south. Their aeroplanes were now terribly hampered in their reconnaissance work by shortage of petrol, but one of Grayne's economical nights brought news of Lossberg's movement down the railway with the large part of his field force. At that moment Escrick was north of the city on the road to Fort Castor, and Peters's band were south of the Mines in the neighbourhood of Tulifa. Escrick's first notion was another raid on the city in quest of stores, but Peters, in whose old field of operations the Santa Ana railway had been, urged that it was their business to hang on to Lossberg's skirts. The blockhouse system had made raiding difficult, but he argued that their first duty was to hamper Lossberg's communications with the city which was still his base. Escrick was convinced the more because he was still completely in the dark as to what was going on at the other end of the railway. If might be that Lossberg would have an easy road to the plains of Olifa, in which case their task must be to delay him by fastening on his rear. Under the new blockhouse system they could not hope to cut up any great length of line, so they must make their effort at a single vital point. There was only one such till Gabones was reached, the bridge of San Luca. But it was likely to be the best guarded, for since the first raid Lossberg had supplemented the posts at each end of the abutment with two companies in the valley bottom. The garrisons at the ends, it will be remembered, were at San Luca itself and at the Devil's Ear, the valley was more than half a mile wide, and the bridge had sixteen arches. Two of the central arches had been blown up by Sandy, and the line now ran across the gap on an improvised platform of steel girders.

It was clear that a midnight dash in the old manner would effect nothing, so Escrick decided to make an effort lot to destroy a part of the bridge but to capture the whole of it, and hold it long enough to alarm Lossberg about his communications. There was now no Pacheco to serve as a base, and all the northern slopes of the southern frontier of the Gran Seco were strongly patrolled; for this was the critical flank of Lossberg's new advance. Roger Grayne reported that the eastern side of the railway up to the frontier was watched like a trench line.

Thereupon Escrick made a bold decision. He resolved to attack from the west side, where a hideous country of scrub and sand and rocky kopjes stretched from the railway to the sea. This area had never been part of the battle-ground, chiefly because of its immense natural difficulties, and because it led to nowhere. So he ordered Peters to slip forth by night from Tulifa, between the Mines and the city, and to join him on the road to Fort Castor.

The concentration was effected on a Monday morning. That day Lossberg was at Gabones, and his advance force under Olivarez was feeling its way south along the devastated line. That night Escrick's whole command, nearly four thousand mounted men with every machine gun it possessed, had made a wide circuit and was in the hills some fifteen miles south-west of San Luca. There they lay during the following day, while with immense care smaller detachments made their way eastward to the ridge of kopjes on each side of the dry valley where stood the bridge. Lossberg's aeroplanes were busy down the railway, and to garrisons at San Luca and the Devil's Ear no warning light or sound came from the baking red cliffs over which they were accustomed to see the sun set. That day, Tuesday, saw Olivarez's great thrust southward. Before night fell he had taken Blenkiron's Post A, where once Toledo's chivalry had been cut up by the Indians, had forced the difficult narrows at Post B, and was threatening Post C, where Melville had brought up every man for a last stand.

During the night of Tuesday Escrick made his attack on the San Luca bridge from the west. It was a far easier task than he had anticipated. Lossberg's advance had switched the attention of the garrisons from defence to transport. Peters's right wing took the Devil's Ear with scarcely a shot, and his left, creeping up the boulder-strewn valley, surprised the post in the hollow with few casualties.

San Luca put up a better fight, but by midnight it was overpowered, and an ammunition train, standing in its siding, was captured. Before the dawn broke there was another huge rent in the bridge, and both abutments were held in force, with a wicked chain of machine-gun nests commanding their approaches from north and south. A big breach had been made, and, what was more, the breach was held, and might be held for days against a considerable army.

The news found Lossberg on the Wednesday morning about to push forward troops to support Olivarez in his last thrust. Already he saw himself in the Olifa plains approaching the capital. He had had no news except Indian rumours, but he had by this time realised that the rebels in the Gran Seco were only a vanguard and that El Obro was now in Olifa. He had beaten the enemy in the Gran Seco, and his place was now in the lowlands. But the news from San Luca made him pause. Part of a mechanised battalion which he had sent back hastily was checked and beaten by Peters at the Devil's Ear. Lossberg halted in deep perplexity. He must explore the situation behind him, before he could support Olivarez with an easy mind. So instead of concentrating in an immediate assault on Post C, which would have given him Santa Ana, he pushed more troops back towards San Luca and ordered Olivarez to postpone his main attack for twelve hours.

It was at this point that Sandy entered the game. He had arrived at Santa Ana during the course of the Tuesday night, and had had his Indians there before ten o'clock on the Wednesday morning. The reports from Melville at Post C were not reassuring. Olivarez was in great force, and once he had his field guns up not all the natural advantages of the place could keep it from destruction. The defence had already tried a night sally, which had been driven back without effecting much. Melville asked for nothing in the way of reinforcements, for he knew that there was nothing to send, since Pecos and Santa Ana were already bare. Feverish efforts were being made to strengthen Post D, the ultimate position, but everyone realised that, if C fell, D would follow.

When Sandy arrived he asked for the last air reports. It was believed that Lossberg was at a point thirty-seven miles south of Gabones, and that a gap of at least fifteen miles separated him from Olivarez and his van. Sandy shrugged his shoulders and turned to Rogerson. "We're getting implicated in a field action," he said in the mild voice which he reserved for extreme emergencies. "It won't do. If I join Melville, we shall still be outnumbered and outgunned. Latimer had better keep his planes in touch with Melville. I'm going to get to that fifteen-mile gap. Please God, Lossberg is in no hurry this morning. He must be cocksure of success after yesterday, so if I know my man he'll take his time."

Lossberg, as we know, was compelled to delay, but of this Sandy was not aware, and as soon as the Indians had broken bread he had them in the saddle. The eastern side of the railway valley was not practicable for horses, scarcely even for cragsmen, but he had some hopes of the western side.

His expectations were all but doomed to defeat. The total distance of the circuit proposed was some thirty miles, but, after the first twenty, horses became impossible. The local guides were useless, for they led him into a network of barren ravines too far to the west--a route no doubt to Gabones, but separated from the crucial part of the line by an increasing width of rocky mountains. Presently the horses had to be left behind, and under the heat of a tropical sun the way had to be pursued on foot up and down moraines of shale and crumbling precipices and sand-choked hollows. Not all the Indians lasted the course, for many were horsemen by habit and no mountaineers. Of the white men only Sandy and five others found themselves that afternoon looking down upon the railway, with aching limbs, and eyes filmed with weariness, and heads that throbbed and swam in incipient heatstroke. But that part of the railway valley which they saw was empty except for a small body of pioneers repairing the road. They were in time. Lossberg had not yet closed the gap which separated him from his Chief of Staff.

The time was now about four o'clock on the Wednesday afternoon. San Luca was in the hands of Peters and Escrick, Lossberg's first attempt to oust them had failed, and that general, much perplexed, was beginning to move troops northward again. Melville, to his surprise, was managing to hold his own at Post C, since Olivarez, under Lossberg's orders, was not pressing too hard. Blenkiron, Luis, and Archie were sitting in Olifa in their futile conference.

The events which followed have become famous in Olifa history, and they are told fully in the work which young Campanillo has published. Staggering with weariness but goaded on by a sense of the shortness of their time and the magnitude of their chance, Sandy's blear-eyed following descended from the rocks and took possession of the segment of valley. He had dragged explosives with him across the hills, and with him were men from the Mines who understood their use. Before the hot night descended they had contrived a great destruction, and the early darkness was lit with flame and loud with earthquakes.

Between the cliffs which rimmed the place they achieved a desolation which for days no troops could traverse, except painfully, in single file, on foot. Presently the remainder of his men straggled in, and after a short rest Sandy led his force southward, to where Olivarez's guns could be heard at their noisy bombardment.

The charge of that wild commando at dawn is a tale not for dull prose but for some swinging ballad. The surprise was complete, and most of the batteries were taken in the rear. Olivarez was a stout soldier, and he rallied gallantly, but he was caught between two fires, whose magnitude he could not guess. Melville had heard the explosions of the night and knew what had happened, and he flung every ounce he possessed into the struggle. The defence became in attack, and C was no longer a beleaguered post but the base of a furious offensive. A little after midday Lossberg's van was huddled into a rocky gut, with its own batteries turned on it, and the enemy secure on the circumference. Then came one of those moments of sudden quiet which mean the realisation of defeat on one side and incontestable victory on the other.

Olivarez, like a wise and humane man, surrendered. But his surprise his surrender was received not by Melville, of whom his Intelligence scouts had fully informed him, but by a slight figure with a begrimed face and clothes in rags, who addressed him in perfect Spanish and seemed more embarrassed than himself. He learned with amazement that this was the notorious El Obro. When the guerrillero recalled a former meeting in a Moroccan town, Olivarez stared in bewilderment. "I was called Arbuthnot then," the other said pleasantly. Then recollection awoke the general, and his face lightened. He had heard too much about this man to feel any shame in accepting defeat his hands.

VIII

At night, as we know, Sandy dispatched Olivarez in company with Don Alejandro Gedd to Olifa city. The owing day was spent by the ambassadors in Olifa, and Sandy at Pecos, in adjusting their plans to the new situation. There was an immense amount of work to be accomplished in the minimum of time. The great concentration at Alcorta Junction, which was now pushed up to the defence lines of the city, had to be regulated, throughout the republic a stop-gap military Government had to be extemporised. Between the revolution and the ultimate settlement a difficult interregnum must intervene. Manuel Martinez came into the city to consult with Luis, but Castor remained at Veiro, whence he issued orders to the different provinces. So far as possible the work was left in the hands of the Olifero leaders themselves.

Luis was the chief executive officer, and it was Martinez who became temporary governor of Olifa city, and old Ramirez of Cardanio and one of the Zarranigas of Alcorta who were his lieutenants, while young Miguel de Campanillo carried to Lossberg the instructions of General Bianca. It was wise to keep the foreign element in the background, that Olifa might believe that her redemption had come from herself.

It was a torrid day with thunderstorms grumbling on the horizon, and Sandy, having received reports from the city which announced that all was quiet and orderly, and from Gabones, which told of young Campanillo's arrival on his way to Lossberg's headquarters, flung himself on a bed in the Pecos hotel, and tried to sleep. But sleep he could not, though every bone and muscle cried out for it. It may have been the weather, or it may have been the strain of the past days, but his mind refused to be composed and his thoughts beat a weary treadmill. He had none of the exultation of a victor, none even of the comfort which comes from a task accomplished. He laboured under a heavy sense of oppression, out of which anxiety stood like jags of rock in a stream. He could not believe that the end had been reached, not even when his reason approved that conclusion. Therefore he could not sleep.

An aide-de-camp made a timid appearance, for he was afraid to break in on the siesta of his chief. But it appeared that the occasion was urgent. A man wanted to speak with the General. He had given his name. Sandy looked at the card proffered him, and read "Mr T. S. Lariarty." "Bring him here," he said, "and see that we are not disturbed. Wait...don't be far away, in case I want you." He smoothed his ruffled hair, and sat on the bed awaiting his visitor, and as he waited a ridiculous memory kept recurring--the Eton Beagles in the fields beyond Slough, and himself and Lariarty, both newly become uppers, struggling desperately to keep up with the field, each determined not to be outdone by the other. Much water had passed over Cuckoo Weir since then. The man who presently stood before him would have made no figure in running over English ploughfields.

Lariarty was no more the dapper and inscrutable Conquistador, armoured against a world which he despised. Some spring had broken within him, for he looked like one mortally sick in mind and body. But his eyes were no longer opaque. There was light in them, broken lights, like the eyes of a sick dog.

"You're looking ill, Tim," said Sandy gently.

"I think I am dying...But that does not matter...I must speak to you, Arbuthnot. You have behaved to me like a gentleman, and I pay my debts...You think you have won, but you are wrong...unless..." The man seemed to gulp. "Veiro," he croaked. "The women are at Veiro--and the Gobernador...They will be dead before midnight unless you can save them."

Sandy was on his feet, his lethargy gone. He shouted for his aide-de-camp. "Get through to Veiro," he told the boy, "and to Olifa--to the Ministry of War. Ask for General de Marzaniga...Get a whisky and soda, too--a stiff one."

The drink was brought by an orderly. "Swallow that, Timmy," he said. "You're all out, and it will buck you up."

But the other refused it. "It would kill me," he said. "Never mind my health, Arbuthnot. You won't get through to Veiro...nor to Olifa...My colleagues have made their plans. Veiro will be isolated...Why in the name of God did you leave your friends in that lonely place? They should have been in the midst of an army. When men are desperate, they think only of revenge."

"Who are 'they'? The Conquistadors?"

Lariarty nodded.

"D'Ingraville is there, and Pasquali, and Suvorin, and Romanes--Romanes above all. Larbert is dead, and I haw not heard of Calvo. But Romanes--" He choked again "And there are some of the others too...Judson and Radin and Martel, and, I think, Laschallas...They have all death before them, the rope for some and for others a slower torture. Therefore they are mad...Oh, what in God's name are you waiting for? I tell you..."

The aide-de-camp returned. "We cannot get through to Veiro, sir," he said. "There seems to be some break-down on the line. And there is no answer from Olifa."

"So," said Sandy. The grimness had gone out of his face, and he was smiling again. "I want the Rolls, Truelove," he said, "at once. Captain Zarraniga will come with me. Tell him to pick four troopers, with a hundred rounds apiece...I want the two big Daimlers to follow: with eight troopers in each. At once. There is not a moment to lose. Let General Melville know."

Lariarty had drawn himself erect.

"Can I come with you, Arbuthnot?" he stammered.

Sandy looked in his eyes, and he seemed to see behind the sickness and fever and the wreckage of the tragic years a shadow of the boy he remembered.

"Most certainly you are coming with me, Tim." He glanced at his wrist-watch. "It is now a quarter to nine. We shall be at Veiro by ten. God grant we are in time!"

The night was warm and still, for the thunder had now gone out of the air, though it still grumbled on the horizon It was a slow business clearing the environs of Pecos, for the roads were congested with transport, owing to the moving of troops from Alcorta Junction. But once the Vulpas valley was left behind, the car swung briskly along the hard, broad roads of the plateau called the Marpas, which is one of Olifa's chief horse-breeding areas. There was only a finger-nail of moon, but the stars were like harbour-lights. Far behind could be seen the broad glow of the head-lamps of the following Daimlers. Sandy at the wheel did not slacken speed at the patches where the road had been ruffled by the winter rains. He drove like a man possessed, looking every now and then at his wrist-watch.

"Half-way," he announced to the young Zarraniga as they passed a farm in a clump of chestnuts. Then the road climbed to a greater elevation and the light of the Daimlers behind seemed to come out of a trough. "Ten miles more," he whispered, and Lariarty, who was jammed among the troopers behind, muttered something that sounded the a prayer. Still the road rose, and then came a long downward incline, and far away on the left a light twinkled.

"Veiro," said young Zarraniga. "Presently the good road will end, and we shall have Don Mario's cart-track. We must be near the ravine of St Paul and the iron bridge."

Three minutes later there was a jarring of brakes and the car came to a stop. A deep narrow cleft lay before em, and where had once been a bridge there hung only drunken girder.

"They have planned it well," said Lariarty.

The men tumbled out of the car, for the great Rolls is as useless as a child's go-cart.

"There are yet four miles," said Zarraniga, as he lowed Sandy down the side of the ravine and the steep overhang of the far bank. "Four miles, and my men are not long-distance runners."

Sandy had squared his shoulders for the race, when Zarraniga halted him. "Half a mile on the right is the home of Pedro Aguilar. He has young horses."

Pedro, who was a tenant of Don Mario's, was roused him his sleep by the sight of seven armed men demanding mounts. Zarraniga he knew, and he trotted obediently towards his stables. "I have not saddles for so many, senor," he explained.

"Saddles be hanged! Give us bridles. Rope halters if in have nothing better." Sandy was already delving furiously among the debris of Pedro's harness-room.

"Two are young beasts and scarcely broken," said the man.

"So much the better," said Sandy. "I will take one and Senor Zarraniga the other."

Within five minutes two scared and angry colts were being hustled out of the corrals by the help of two pairs of Pedro's long-rowelled spurs. Once in the open they found their heads turned firmly to the east, and fled like scared deer they knew not whither. They led by at least a hundred yards, flying the deep sandy scaurs, spuming the ant-heaps, slipping, stumbling, recovering, while the troopers on their more manageable mounts pounded heavily behind. When after the first mile Sandy had his animal under control, he found to his surprise that Lariarty was beside him.

Now they were on the edge of the alfalfa fields and the water-furrows, and before them was the dark loom of trees. They swung to the left, avoiding the road which ran from the railway-station, and making for the line of poplars which hedged the garden. A light twinkled beyond the trees, a light which suddenly went out. And then, with a cry, Lariarty swung round his horse's head and set the beast capering and plunging. He had all but ridden down a woman--a tall girl in black, wearing pink roses at her breast.

The same evening about half past seven Don Alejandro Gedd was taking the air in that part of the Avenida de Paz which adjoined the Parliament House. He had had a busy day. For hours he had sat in consultation in the great Council Chamber, for he had two kinds of knowledge invaluable at the moment--a wide acquaintance with the organisation of the revolution in the provinces, and considerable insight into the psychology of the capital city. He had been of great value to Luis and Blenkiron and Martinez, while they worked out the next moves--the proclamation to the people of Olifa, the demobilisation of the levies, and the preparations for a presidential election. He had also been constantly on the telephone with Castor at Veiro, who was busy with the draft of the new constitution, which was to be embodied in the proclamation. Don Alejandro was contented, exhilarated, but also very weary. He decided that he owed himself a short spell leisure, and resolved to dine alone at the club. But his hopes of a little rest were frustrated. He found himself accosted by a villainous-looking peasant, whose left wrist was bound tip in a dirty handkerchief, and whose mahogany face showed a long shallow scar from right temple to chin, which must have been done recently, for the blood was scarcely dry on it. Also the man appeared to be drunk, for as he clutched his arm he swayed.

"Maister Gedd," came a hoarse whisper, "Maister Gedd! Haud on, for God's sake! Ye ken me? Ye saw me at Charcillo? Hamilton's my name. I was wi' Sir Erchibald. Ye ken Sir Erchibald?..." The scarecrow tottered, and would have fallen had he not leaned heavily against the wall.

Recognition broke in on Don Alejandro's mind. He remembered the square Scots soldier who had been with Lady Roylance in her escape from the Tronos del Rey and who had been Archie's special henchman at Charcillo. He had heard that he had been in Olifa before the city surrendered. Don Alejandro was a man of action. There was a small cafe at hand in a retired side street, and thither the led him. He compelled him to drink a claret glass of liqueur brandy. Obviously there was some story worth hearing. He was just about to begin a leisurely cross-examination, when the soldier seemed to recover his dazed wits and forestalled him.

"What am I sittin' here for?" he exclaimed. "Come on, sir," and he struggled to rise. "We maun get haud o' Sir Erchibald or Maister Lewis. There's awfu' things gaun to happen afore the nicht's oot. It's Veiro...the twa leddies...and him they ca' the Gobernador...Oh, sir, let's oot o' this and awa' up to Heidquarters. They'll let me in if you're wi' me. I've been tryin' to win in my lane for the last hour, and the sentries just shoo'd me awa'."

His earnestness and alarm communicated themselves to Don Alejandro. Then the man seemed to recover his balance, and, leaning forward, clutched Don Alejandro's knee.

"I've been in this toun a' week. The folks think I'm a native frae some landward bit...I've been biding doun near the harbour--it's an auld haunt o' mine...Some o' thae Bodyguard blagyirds is there, and I go chief wi' ane o' them...Syne Judson appeared--ye mind him? and he kenned me, and there was a wee bit o' a turn-up. I had to rin for my life, but I had fund oot what they were ettlin', and I've been jinkin' about the closes and tryin' to see Sir Erchibald...This verra nicht...Man, they're clever. When we're a' crackin' about the grand victory and thinkin' that there's nae mair fecht left in the ither side, they're plannin' a bloody revenge...Wha's in it? Judson, for ane, an' yon lang, black-avised lad they ca' Laschallas, and some o' the white-faced gentry that used to manage the Gran Seco...What do they ettle? It canna be ransom, for there's nae hidy-hole they could carry their prisoners to. It maun be murder--black murder. Oh, haste ye, sir. The blagyirds or now will be well on the road to Veiro. They've gotten cars and they'll no be easy stoppit...What's the time? Gettin' on for eight?" The man staggered to his feet with wild eyes. "Is there no an aeroplane?" he cried. "We maun gan by air, for they'll beat us by the road."

But when a quarter of an hour later Archie and Blenkiron were roused by the news into violent activity, it was found that there were no aeroplanes to be had in or near the city of Olifa. Also it was discovered that the wires between Olifa and Veiro had been tampered with. It was impossible to communicate even with Alcorta Junction.

IX

That day the life at Veiro had returned to something of in ancient serenity. Castor, indeed, was kept busy with constant telephone calls from the city, and on four occasion messengers came to him by car. But otherwise there was no sign that the place was any kind of headquarters. No garrison was in the house, and no sentries were at the gate, for considerable armies lay between it and the city on one side, and Pecos and the road to the Gran Seco on the other.

Don Mario pottered about the stables and the garden and had a long siesta in the darkened library. Janet also slept, for the strain of the past weeks had fatigued her more than she knew. Barbara wrote letters and went riding in the first cool of the evening. In the dim, musty-smelling rooms, in the sunny courtyard, in the garden where the lawns were beginning to brown under the summer heats, there was an air of calm after storm, of a general relaxing. The feeling was in the atmosphere, but with Janet it was less positive satisfaction than a mere rest from anxiety. She understood now that she and Barbara had been living for a long time on the extreme edge of their nerves. The news that victory had been won brought relief rather than triumph. She had not yet adjusted her world to meet it; she was simply aware that her mind could leave the weary treadmill and be still.

But at dinner she the realised that a change was coming over her mood. She felt light-hearted again, and had begun to look into the future. Barbara seemed to have suffered the same change, for she had been singing as she dressed. Don Mario was in his usual placid humour, but Castor was in line with her new temper. His work for the day was finished; he had bathed and got himself into dress-clothes, for some of his kit had been sent out that morning from he city; and now he relaxed into something very like high spirits. Janet had never witnessed this new mood of his, and she found it delightful. Before he had always retained the manner of one in command, one a little apart, for whom friendliness involved a slight descent and unbending. But now he had dropped without effort to the level of ordinary folk, he laughed without constraint, his eyes had in frank companionship.

At dinner he talked to Don Mario of past days in Olifa. He even spoke of his Campanillo grandmother. The old man presently passed from his stilted English into Spanish, which Janet could not easily follow, but it was clear that he was pleased by Castor's questions and was expanding happily on some matter very dear to his heart. Once again Janet saw in the two faces that which she had noted weeks before at Charcillo in the faces of Luis and his young caballeros--something innocently apostolic, the ardour of men in the grip of an idea. She looked across the table at Barbara, who wore pale pink roses on the breast of her black gown. Barbara had spoken little, but there was a pleasant content in her dark eyes--and now, as she caught Janet's glance and followed it to Castor's ardent face, there was also a flicker of amusement.

They drank their coffee in Don Mario's own room, among the spurs and whips and sporting pictures. The French windows were open wide, for the night was warm, but a fine-meshed curtain of gauze hung over them to keep out moths and flying ants. Without the stars burned fiercely, and in their light an ancient baroque group, which adorned the terrace, had the appearance of a knot of eavesdroppers. Barbara had started at her first sight of the statuary.

Castor stood before the empty fireplace which had been filled with a tapestry screen. There were three lamps in the room set on little tables, which illumined the heads of the two women and of Don Mario in his high-backed chair. The face of the Gobernador, being only partially lit, revealed none of the lesser details of age. The fine lines on the forehead, the streaks of grey in beard and hair were unseen; only the trim figure and the noble contour of the head stood out, and these had an air of vital youth. The impression was strengthened by the new note in his voice.

"You are twenty years younger to-night. Excellency," said Don Mario.

"I am beginning life again," was the answer. "I have been middle-aged--I have been old--and now I am young."

"Can one begin life anew?" the old man asked in his precise English. "It is the fashion for people to talk so, but I wonder. It has never been my fate, for I have carried into each new stage of my life heavy burdens from the last stages. But perhaps I was always lazy--lazy and a little timid."

"I have been fortunate," said Castor gravely, "for Fate itself has shut the door on that which I would leave behind."

"But is the door fast? Will nothing creep through?"

"It can be kept fast and well guarded. I do not mean that I must not atone for my blunders. God knows I have made many and I have much folly to expiate. Yet that too is part of my good fortune. I am in a position to mend what I have done wrongly."

The old man shook his head. "You are luckier than I. The blunders I have made were such as did not permit themselves to be atoned for. Witness my error in crossing the Vidas and the Cintra blood. I was warned by my father about the Cintra stock, which he said meant speed but no heart, and in the mares a lamentable barrenness. But I would not listen, and all my life I have paid the penalty."

"I am not a fatalist," was the answer. "That is the blindest of superstitions. The spirit and mind of man are free to shape life if they are resolute enough and wise enough. A man is not the slave of his father's actions, or of his own. Any error can be redeemed on this side of the grave."

Don Mario laughed. "I will not discourage your optimism, Excellency. It is a pleasant gift of youth. I who am old practise humility."

"I too would practise humility," said Castor. "That is what I have learned in the Courts of the Morning. Before, I was arrogant and self-centred and friendless and inhuman. But up in that mountain eyrie I found a juster perspective...Call it a revelation. I was granted a view of life from a great height, and many things, including myself, took different proportions. That I owe to you, Lady Roylance, and to your friends. If I were to die now, I should die happy, for I have become young again. You opened a door for me, and I have passed through it."

"You are certain that it is closed behind you?" Janet did not know what made her ask the question. The words seemed to come mechanically to her lips.

"Closed and bolted and guarded." There was both solemnity and exhilaration in his tone. Janet never forgot the picture he made in that moment, his head flung back, his eyes looking down under their heavy lids with a glow of something more than friendliness, his voice grave and vibrant and masterful. It challenged Fate, but in the challenge there was no vanity. She felt a sudden kindling of enthusiasm, a longing to follow this man who was born to lead his fellows. The cold Olympian had disappeared, and Prometheus was in his place, Prometheus the pioneer of humanity, the bringer of gifts to men.

In the pause which followed Janet alone caught Barbara's whisper. "Turn your head slowly round...to the window...Watch the group of statues. I saw them move...there are people there."

She obeyed. She saw the edge of the group, where Hercules was engaged with the Hydra, move ever so slightly. She saw, too, a dark blur close to the right of the window, which had not been there before. In an instant she divined the truth. This was Fate's answer to the challenge. The Gobernador had shut the door on his past, but something had forced it ajar and slipped through.

She heard Barbara speaking low and composedly. "They cannot see me. I am behind the light...I will slip out...Go on talking."

Janet's heart seemed to stop, and then resumed its beating, so loudly that she felt that it must drown the ticking of the silver clock behind Castor's head. In a voice so steady that it surprised her, she began to question Don Mario about the coloured print of Eclipse beside his chair. She was aware of a slight stirring in the shadows and knew that Barbara had left the room.

Barbara found herself in a long corridor which had suddenly become very dark, and realised that the lamp in the hall beyond had been put out. Why? It was too early for the servants to have gone to bed. Someone must have entered the house, someone different from the group outside the window. It required all her courage to traverse the corridor and reach the hall. It was in black darkness, and she began to rope her way to the passage beyond, which led to the courtyard...She stopped to listen. There seemed to be a sound coming from the courtyard-servants, perhaps--there were four men indoors, a butler, two footmen, and Don Mario's valet. Outside by the corrals there were the grooms and the cattlemen, hardy peons who might be trusted to defend their master. She must get to them--at my cost she must get to them. She stilled every other thought by clenching her teeth on that purpose.

Presently she was at the foot of the main staircase, a broad shallow thing which led direct to the galleries of the upper floor. Here there was a faint glimmer of light, for the stars were shining through the staircase window. Her eyes were on it when she stumbled over something which lay sprawled across the bottom step. She bit hard into her lips and stood shivering. It was a man's body. She bent, and even in the dim light she saw by the uniform that it was one of the house-servants. He was dead. Her hands, as they touched his shoulder, felt something warm and sticky.

At the same moment sounds, stealthy sounds, reached her ear from the direction of the courtyard. The murderers were there, and that way there was no escape. Scarcely knowing what she did, she stepped over the body and ran up the staircase. She had a blind idea of getting to her own room, as if there she would find sanctuary.

She sped like a hare along the top gallery, and reached her room. At the door she stopped to listen. All seemed quiet on the upper floor. Inside the door there was the same faint sheen of starlight. Barbara sat down on her bed, and struggled against the terrible lassitude which weakened her limbs and dulled her brain.

She forced herself to think. She did not trouble to guess who the enemies were--it was enough for her that they had come for murder. The little party in the room below were unarmed, and one was a girl and another an old man. She must act--at once--rouse the peons--destroy the ruffians outside on the lawn before they had time to shoot. It was the only way, and she tottered to the window.

The room was at the other side of the house from the garden, and the window looked down on some outhouses and part of a little enclosed court. The peons lived beyond the big orchard where the corrals began.

She must get to them, and almost before she knew she found herself on the veranda. There was a drop of a few feet to a roof whence she might reach the courtyard...But the courtyard might be a cul-de-sac. It must be, for the enemy would guard all the approaches.

She dropped on to the roof of a shed. The courtyard was empty, but she thought she heard a sound from the gate which led to the stable yard. That was on her left; on her right were other roofs and then a grove of trees; in front a wall ran straight to the edge of the orchard. This last must be her road, and she started climbing along the top of the adobe wall, which was plentifully studded with sharp tiles.

The pain of the traverse seemed to restore her balance She felt her gown tearing, and her stockings in shreds, and her knees and wrists ached. In her haste she had no time to pick her way, but when the wall suddenly broadened she scrambled to her feet, and the last stage she almost ran.

Now she was at the transverse wall which bounded the orchard. She remembered that the place was walled all round, and that once inside it might be hard to get out. So she still kept to the wall, which continued to be of a fair breadth, and endeavoured to circuit the orchard so as to reach the corrals. But this took her at right angles to her former course, and brought her back again to the edge of the first courtyard.

Suddenly she flung herself flat. There were men in the courtyard. Two men came at a run from the direction of the house. There must be a back-door there which she had forgotten. The door into the stable yard opened, but they did not pass through. They seemed to be listening. Had they caught sight of her? She lay in a cold terror for several minutes, till she dared to raise her head again. They were gone, and the door into the stable yard was shut.

Barbara did not venture to rise again, but crawled for the rest of the road...Presently she was looking into open ground, the ribbon of rough pasture between the orchard and the alfalfa fields...Her sense of direction had become a little confused, but she thought that the peons' quarters were to her right beyond the orchard.

She dropped off the wall. It was higher than she had thought, and she felt her ankle wrenched. Then she began to run, keeping in the shadow of the orchard wall. The need for haste was urgent, but her legs seemed to have no power and the pain of her ankle sickened her. Also her heart kept hammering so fast that it choked her breathing.

Now she was at the angle of the orchard wall, but there were no peons' quarters before her--only the savannah, with the alfalfa lands on the left, and the rails of a paddock on her right...She turned blindly to the right...ran a few steps...changed her mind...and suddenly found herself almost ridden down by a mounted man.

The face she saw had the pallor of a Conquistador. She had blundered into the enemy. The man had just avoided her, and was now in difficulties with his beast. A second horseman had leaped to the ground at the sight of her, and it was into his arms that she staggered. To her amazement she heard her name spoken, and looked up into Sandy's face.

She clung to him, while she stammered her story.

"Murder," he said quietly. "And they are desperate men with no care for their own lives...Timmy, it's the mercy of God that sent you with us. You're our only hope. You've got to get into the house."

Janet realised that the great crisis of her life had come. Don Mario expounded in his hoarse old voice the merits of the Eclipse print--it was from the Sartorius picture which he preferred to the better known Stubbs--he had picked it up in St. James's Street in '98--no, it must have been '96, when he was in England for the Fitzgibbon sale...And all the time her eyes were on Castor, who still stood before the fireplace. He lit a cigarette and the match made a spurt of light before his face.

Janet did not dare to look towards the window...The only hope was to keep still. Perhaps the cat would linger over the watching of the mouse. Barbara would now be alarming the house-servants; they would get at the arms, which were all in the gun room; probably they would first get in touch with the outdoor peons. That would all take time, and meantime they must let the murderers savour their revenge at ease. For she had no doubt of the meaning of it all. The Conquistadors and the Bodyguard could have no thought but vengeance; ruin and death lay before them, and they had nothing more to hope or fear...She wished the clock did not tick so loudly.

Suddenly Castor turned towards the window. Her eyes were on him, and she saw his face go grim. At the same moment there came a sound, which she knew was the rending of the gauze curtain. Now at last she turned her head, and Don Mario craned his from the depth of his chair.

Outside in the starlight, close up to the sill, were half a dozen men, each with a pistol held to cover the inmates of the room. She saw what she had expected--the rabbit teeth and the weasel face of Judson, Radin with his high cheek-bones and his scar, Suvorin's parched skin and albino hair, Laschallas's thick eyebrows. It was as if a wave of corruption had flowed out of the night, and hung, ready to break, at the window.

One man had entered the room and stood beside Don Mario's chair. She recognised Romanes. But it was a different figure from the trim cavalryman whom she had last seen in the Tronos del Rey. The lamp on the table at his left showed him clearly, and it seemed as if some screw had been removed which had dislocated the whole fabric of his being. He was unshaven and dirty, his clothes were ragged, and there was a long blue weal on his forehead.

She saw the lean, knotted neck, the oddly-shaped skull, the pale, sneering face, as if the soul had wholly mastered the body, and transformed it to an exact reflex. But the eyes, which had once been dull and expressionless, now danced and glowed with a crazy brilliance.

"Good evening, sir," he said, and his voice, once so passionless, had an odd lilt in it, like a parson who intones a litany. "Ah, it is the old horse-breeder, Sanfuentes!...And you, madame! I have been longing to meet you again, for the last time you left in rather a hurry." But he looked not at Janet or Don Mario, but steadily, devouringly, at the Gobernador.

Janet sat very still in her chair, a yard from each. Castor had moved his head and she saw the clock. It must be ten minutes since Barbara had slipped out. She kept her gaze rigidly on its minute-hand, as if by some mental concentration she could hasten its circuit, for she had a notion that if the end did not come for another ten minutes there was hope.

"Good evening," she heard Castor say. "You've an odd way of announcing yourself. You look a little off-colour. Would you like some food?"

The other did not reply. He was smiling, but so close were his lips to his teeth that it looked like a snarl.

"A cigarette anyhow." Castor was about to feel for his case in his pocket, when a pistol barrel confronted him.

"Stay still," said Romanes. "Not a movement. You will stand quite rigid, please, while I say what I have to say."

"Right!" was the answer. "You used to have better manners, Romanes. Let me hear what you want to say. You have come, I suppose, to ask for terms."

The coolness of the Gobernador's tone seemed to move the other to fresh mirth. "Terms!" he cried. "Oh, yes, we ask for terms. A free pardon, of course, and our passage paid to Europe, and five hundred apiece on which to begin a new life. Terms!" and his voice rose almost to a shriek. "Do you not know that there are no terms on God's earth you could offer us?"

"There is nothing I intend to offer you," was the answer.

"No. You are wise. I never underestimated your brains...You have used us, and I think we have given you good service...Now you have changed your plans, and would fling us on the scrap-heap. You have different ambitions now, and your old tools are no longer required. But the tools may have something to say to that."

"True. I am inclined to agree with you. I am not the man to shirk my responsibility." Castor's eyes had made the circuit of the room. He saw the ravening faces at the window, old Don Mario huddled in his chair, Janet below him white-lipped and tense. He saw something else--a new figure which had slipped in by the door, and which he recognised as Lariarty. He saw him before Romanes did, and it was the almost imperceptible start which he gave that caused the other to cast a swift glance to his left. Romanes smiled as he observed the newcomer. "Just in time," he said. "I wondered if you would bring it off. We are going to be offered terms after all. Our old chief says he admits his responsibility."

Lariarty's sick, drawn face made no response, but he moved nearer Romanes, till their elbows almost touched. His hands were empty, but there was a bulge in his side pocket.

"Terms!" Romanes cried again. "You have broken our world in bits, and you speak of recognising your responsibility! You have played with souls, and you are going to find that it is an awkward game. We are dying--dying. Morituri te salutamus. And the way we salute you is to take you with us. There will be no Castor, the regenerator of Olifa, for little boys to read about in their history books. For in about two minutes Castor will be dead."

The man on the hearthrug threw back his head.

"When we worked together, Romanes," he said, "you did not make full use of your opportunities. You cannot know much about me if you think that I can be frightened by threats of death. I am frightened of many things, but not of that...You seem to hold a strong hand. Take me away with you--anywhere--away from this house. Then, if you are determined on it, put a pistol bullet through my head, or put me against a wall for the rest of your gang to have a share in the pleasure of killing me. I accept what Fate sends--I have always accepted it. But why should you bring an old man and a girl into this unpleasant business?"

Romanes thrust his face close to the other's, and to Janet it seemed that it was now the mask of madness. She had forgotten about the slow minute-hand of the clock, for with Lariarty's coming--and coming through the door--she had realised that all hope was gone. But in that moment she did not think of her own danger. What held her gaze was Castor, who seemed to have risen to a strange nobility. There was not a tremor in his face, not a shadow of hesitation in his grave eyes. It was man towering above the beast, humanity triumphing even in its overthrow...These broken things before him were in part his handiwork. They were the world he had left--but he had left it. Yes, whatever happened, he had left it...

"Not so," Romanes was saying. "We are not civilised executioners. We are damned and dying, and our vengeance is the vengeance of the damned. The women go with you--there was another here who must be found. And the old horse-coping fool...After that we will find Rosas...and Clanroyden, curse him...and..."

It was then that Don Mario struck. He had been quietly reaching with his right hand for a loaded riding-whip which was on the rack on the wall beside his chair. Its handle had a heavy metal knob, and, without rising in his seat, he swung it with surprising agility at Romanes's head.

But the eyes of age are not those of youth and he missed his aim. The handle only grazed Romanes's shoulder, glanced off, hit the lamp on the table behind him, and sent it crashing to the ground.

Romanes half turned to his assailant, and as he moved Lariarty leaped on him. As he leaped he cried in a strange, stifled voice the single word "Pecos," the signal which he had agreed upon with Sandy. If he could deal with the tiger within, it was for Sandy to frustrate the wolves without.

But Don Mario's unexpected attack had deranged the plan. Lariarty should have trusted to his pistol; instead, he yielded to that ancient instinct which urges a man to grapple with an enemy who is suddenly unbalanced. The signal which he should have shouted was muffled by his haste, and the watchers at the window were given a moment to act before Sandy could strike. When "Pecos" rang out a second time with a desperate shrillness it was too late.

For Romanes, even in his madness, had judged the situation right. He could make certain of at least part of his vengeance. Castor, too, was upon him, but his right hand was free, and he shot him at close quarters in the neck. The Gobernador fell forward on the sitting Janet, and in the same instant shots were fired from the window.

They may have been meant for Castor, but they found other quarries. Lariarty dropped with a bullet in his brain, and Romanes clutched at space, gasped, and fell beside him.

Janet, struggling to rise, with the shots still like whip-lashes in her ear, heard a second burst of fire. It came from outside the window, and she knew it for rifles. Then there seemed to be a great quiet, and the world disappeared for her--everything except a dying man whom she had laid in her chair...

He was beyond speech, and his eyes were vacant and innocent like a child's. She pressed her face to his and kissed him on the lips...A fresh lamp seemed to have been lit behind her, and by its aid she saw the glazing eyes wake for a second, and through them the soul struggle to send a last message. There was peace in the face...

When Archie arrived ten minutes later his first demand was for Janet. Sandy drew him gently up to the ragged gauze curtain.

"She is safe--by a miracle," he said. "But Castor is dead--he died in her arms. Don't disturb her yet, Archie. A woman can only love one man truly, but many men may love her...Janet was the only love of Castor's life. He died happy with her kiss on his cheek...Let her stay a little longer beside him."

EPILOGUE

The Courts of the Morning had recovered the peace which till a year ago had been theirs since the beginning of time.

Where had once been the busy depot was now only shaggy downland, and a few blackened timbers, over which Nature had begun to spin her web. Choharua looked down again upon meadow and forest as free from human turmoil as the blue spaces of ocean beyond. Only at the head of the seaward gully were there signs of life. A small group of tents had been set up, almost on the spot where Barbara and the Gobernador had first looked down the four thousand feet of green dusk to the land-locked bay. The ruins of the power-house and the chute were already masked with creepers and tall grasses, and only certain scars on the hillside, not made by the winter rains, told that there man had once wrought and striven.

The day was passing from the steady glare of afternoon to the light airs which precede twilight. The sun was nearing a broad belt of amethyst haze which lay on the western horizon, and the face of Choharua was beginning to break up into shadows. The party who occupied the tents had come there by sea, and made their way up the rugged steps of the ravine to the plateau. The reason of their journey was apparent, for between the ravine and the mountain, on a mound which rose like a sentinel above the meadows, could be seen a tall wooden cross. Presently that would be replaced by a stone memorial, to mark the resting-place of him who had been the Gobernador of the Gran Seco.

There was the smoke of a destroyer far below in the gulf. That very day it had brought to this eyrie the new President-elect of the Republic of Olifa. The said President-elect was sitting beside Sandy on the very edge of the ravine, so that he looked down fifty feet of red rock to the tops of tall trees. He was amusing himself with dropping his cigarette ash into the gulf.

"If I slipped off this perch I should certainly break my neck," he observed. "That has been the position of all of us for so long that we have got used to it. I wonder when I shall feel accustomed to being secure?"

Sandy asked about the condition of Olifa.

"It is a marvel. We are a stable people after all, and, having gone a little off the lines, we have now jolted back to the track and are quite content with it...The elections went as pleasantly as a festa...Lossberg is content, for he has Bianca's place, and the army reductions will be made slowly and discreetly. There is a vast amount to be done, but bit by bit we shall remake the machine. I shall have Blenkiron to assist me, praise be to God. Him I have left wallowing in business, while I made the trip here to see you. You, my dear Sandy. For some months the destiny of Olifa has depended on you. I want that to continue."

Sandy did not speak. His eyes were on the downs which ran southward along the scarp, where far off he thought he saw two figures.

"I have come to offer you the post of Gobernador of the Gran Seco," Luis continued briskly. "In effect, as you know well, it will be an independent province. Its problems are not those of Olifa. It cannot be an integral part of the republic. It is tributary, yes--but not dependent. He who governs it must be a strong man and a wise man. And it is of the first importance, for on it rest the wealth and peace of Olifa."

"It is a great charge," said Sandy, but his eyes were still on the distant figures.

"You are already a king among the Indian pueblas. You are a king among the mine-workers. You will have Blenkiron as your lieutenant to direct the industry. We will build you a palace, and up here in the Courts of the Morning you will have your country estate. It is a good watch-tower, senor. Here you will be able to think high thoughts." He laid his hand on the other's arm.

"Consider! Are you the man to go home to Europe and sit down in cities? Will you dabble in your politics, like Sir Archie? I do not think so. You would be restless in an old country where things move slowly and everything is done by long speeches...You are a landowner, are you not? Will you settle down upon your acres, and shoot little birds, and entertain your friends, and in time grow fat? I know the life a little, for I have seen it, and it is pleasant--oh yes. But is it the life for you?"

Luis's air suddenly became very grave. "You are my friend, and I love you more than a brother. Therefore I want you to stay with me. But you are also a great man, and I am jealous that your greatness shall not be wasted. You are a creator, and you cannot escape your destiny. The era of the Old World is over, and it is the turn of the New World to-day. I have often heard you say that the difficulties even of Europe must be settled in the West. Listen to me, senor. The time will come when the problems of the West will be settled between the United States and Olifa. Yes, Olifa. We have wealth, we have won stability, presently we shall have leadership. I cannot do the leading. I can only, as you say, 'carry on.' Castor would have done it if he had lived. Now his mantle awaits you. You will have work worthy of a man, work which will need all your powers of mind and will and body. You will make a name that will live for ever. Will you choose to be a sleepy squire when you might be a king? You are not a provincial, you are not a native of any land. Your country is that which you can make for yourself..."

Sandy shook his head. "I don't think you understand."

"But indeed I understand. I understand you. I have studied you with admiration, and, what is more, with love. I know you better than you know yourself." He smiled. "I said that you could be a king, and I did not speak altogether in metaphor. Forms of government are not eternal things. Olifa is a republic, because republics were in fashion when she began. But some day she may well be a kingdom...Do not laugh. I do not mean any foolish dictatorship. We are a free people. But Olifa demands a leader, and whoever the leader is whom she follows he will be her king." Luis rose. "Think well over what I have said. I now go to stretch my legs before dinner. Within a day or two I must have your answer."

Sandy remained alone on the pinnacle of rock. The sun was now close to the horizon and the west was like a great flower in blossom. The face of Choharua was rose-red, and the levels below were all purple, a deeper tint than the amethyst of the sea. Out of the circumambient glory Janet appeared, hatless, her hair like an aureole.

"I left Barbara a mile behind," she said. "She wanted to see Geordie Hamilton about one of the vaqueros who is sick. You look pensive, Sandy. A penny for your thoughts."

"I have been talking to Luis...He has just offered me the governorship of the Gran Seco, with apparently the reversion of a kingdom."

"Well?" she asked. She was picking a flower to pieces to hide trembling hands.

"What do you think, Janet? You are the wisest woman in the world. Shall Ulysses settle down in Phaeacia and forget all about Ithaca?"

"That is for Ulysses to say."

"But Ulysses has no ambition left. He never had much, and what little he had is buried up there."

The eyes of both turned eastward to the slim cross on the high ground above the meadows, now dyed blood-red by the setting sun. Against the background of the mountain it stood out like a great calvary.

"I think we saved his soul," he said gravely, "but we also brought him to his death. The glory of the work does not seem to amount to much when it all ends in six feet of earth. And the things that matter more than glory! I can't feel up to them, Janet. I am a very ordinary sort of fellow who shirks responsibility. I am no Castor. I can take a hand in king-making, but a king-maker is never a king."

"Other people think differently. Sandy dear," Janet said softly. "I have had one great moment in my life that I can never forget--when the Army of the Revolution entered Olifa. You, remember, Olifa had got back her old assurance. The Avenida was like a river of white light between two banks of roses...People in masses on both sides, and at all the windows, and on all the house-tops, and everywhere flowers...The Olifa regulars as smart as

Aldershot, and the new President in his carriage, and the new ministers...And then, after all the splendour, the lean, dusty fighting men! I cried like a baby when I saw Archie--horribly embarrassed he was, poor darling, not knowing what to do with the flowers that fell on his head and his saddle--rather like a schoolboy being kissed by his mother after a famous innings...But when you came, I stopped crying and my heart stood still. You remember? All the shouting and the flower-scattering seemed to stop when you appeared at the head of your battered commandos. There was a great hush, and for a moment that vast multitude seemed to catch its breath. It was because they saw the man who might be their king...You never moved your head, Sandy, and you stared straight before you as if you were asleep. What were you thinking of?"

"I was thinking of Castor, and longing for him to be alive."

"Only that? Had Ulysses no thought of the vacant throne of Phaeacia--of carrying on a dead man's work?"

"No, by Heaven, he cannot...He couldn't if he wanted to, but he doesn't want to, for his heart isn't in it...I'm an alien here and I'm sick of being an alien...I'm not Castor. I haven't his ambition, I haven't his brains, I don't want to be on a pedestal. Perhaps I'm tired, perhaps I'm getting old, but I want my own people. I've seen Luis and his gallant lads on fire about this country and planning what a great land it is going to be, and it made me sick for my own...Castor too...He had never known a fatherland before, but he found one here...I've got the best in the world, and I'm homesick for it. These last months I've been living with half my mind on my work and half on all kinds of small, ridiculous, homely things. You would laugh if you knew the kind of picture I've had in my head whenever I wasn't engaged on some urgent job...How good the beer at Tap used to taste in a pewter mug...the scent of the hay in the Oxford meadows...bacon and eggs for tea after hunting...the moorburn and the peat reek in April...the beloved old musty smell of the library at Laverlaw and logs crackling on a December evening...I'm sick with longing for my own Border hills...It's no good, Janet. You can't cut adrift from the bands that God has tied. I've had enough of Abana and Pharpar, rivers of Damascus. I'm for the modest little clear streams of Israel."

Janet dropped her flower and looked up smiling. "You are lonely, Sandy."

"I am lonely. That is why I want to get back to companionable things."

A sudden happiness came into the girl's face. She looked away from him and spoke rapidly. "Barbara once went over to Laverlaw with the Manorwaters. Do you remember? You pretended that she annoyed you...I wonder...Less than a year ago we spoke of her in the Regina Hotel. You pretended you couldn't remember her name...I wonder again...Oh, Sandy, you are an old fool..."

He scrambled off his perch and stood above her. He was flushed under his deep sunburn. "Janet, you witch! How did you guess?"

"It wasn't very hard. When a man like you grows tired of wandering and has a sudden longing for home, it is because he is in love with a woman and wants to take her to the place where he belongs."

"You've guessed right. I suppose it has been coming on for a long time, but I didn't know it--not till that awful night at Veiro. When we rode up and I found her in the midst of plunging horses--with her shoes all cut to bits and her ankle twisted, and dropping with fatigue, and yet as brave as a lion--and when I saw the roses on her breast all crushed and torn with her wild scramble--I think I knew. And later, when Archie arrived and his first cry was for you, I remembered that I had nobody to feel like that about...and I wanted someone--her..."

He stopped, for he felt that words were needless in view of a depth of comprehension in Janet's crooked smile.

"I haven't a chance, I know." he stammered.

"Not a ghost of a chance," she said briskly, "but you can always ask her. She'll be here in about five minutes.

I'm going for a walk to look for Luis and the others. We shan't be back for hours and hours."

THE END

www.ingramcontent.com/pod-product-compliance
Lightning Source LLC
Chambersburg PA
CBHW071726110726
47908CB00006B/1517

* 9 7 8 1 4 7 3 3 1 7 7 3 4 *